TRUMP

TRUMP

THE GREATEST SHOW ON EARTH

THE DEALS, THE DOWNFALL, THE REINVENTION

WAYNE BARRETT

Regan Arts.
New York

Regan Arts.

65 Bleecker Street
New York, NY 10012

For Lawrence G. Barrett, Sr., a true American entrepreneur, and William C. McGettigan, Sr., who had the courage to climb back to the top after a long fall

CONTENTS

Frank Algernon Cowperwood does not believe in the people; he does not trust them. To him they constitute no more than a field upon which corn is to be sown, and from which it is to be reaped. They present but a mass of bent backs, their knees and faces in the mire, over which as over a floor he strides to superiority. His private and inmost faith is in himself alone.

Theodore Dreiser, THE TITAN, 1914

That's the way you do it—money for nothin' and your chicks for free.

Dire Straits

TRUMP

INTRODUCTION

By Wayne Barrett

In late 1978 my then colleague Jack Newfield, a senior editor at the *Village Voice* with a special feel for the ebb and flow of New York news, suggested I take a long, investigative look at the new kid on the block, a 32-year-old, little-known developer who had yet to build his first project: Donald Trump. Four months later, the *Voice* printed my three-part series of cover stories. Though the series would eventually prompt two criminal investigations and the impaneling of the only federal grand jury ever to target Trump, he was initially so excited by such extensive coverage in one of the nation's highest-circulation weekly newspapers that he called friends to boast about it. He also, however, had his lawyer and mentor, Roy Cohn, write a letter to the *Voice* threatening a suit that was never filed.

Though I ordinarily report for some time before trying to interview the subject of a story, I met Donald shortly after starting to work on this series, and I met him on his own terms. One of the first places I went in my investigation was to the offices of New York State's economic development agency, the Urban Development Corporation, to examine the mountains of files involving the tax abatement Trump had won for the Grand Hyatt Hotel, his only project then in construction. When the phone in the UDC conference room where I had been sequestered for several days suddenly began ringing, I was uncertain whether or not to pick it up, but finally did. The cheery voice on the other end greeted me as if I were an old friend: "Wayne, I hear you're going to do a story about me. This is Donald Trump. Why don't we get together and talk? This is a real opportunity for the *Voice* to do a positive story about a project that's good for New York." Obviously, someone at the agency that had awarded Donald the largest tax break in state history had also given him the phone number where I was reviewing the records of their deal. An awkward dance between us—far too early in the reporting process, as far as I was concerned—started that day.

I met with Trump several times over the next few months, taping fifteen hours of energetic monologue, riding with him in his limo, and relaxing through expansive interviews on his penthouse couch. One interview was cut short when Ivana insisted that a grumbling Donald go to the opera with her. There were long gaps between our meetings, and all the while I kept digging, so my interview questions grew tougher, and so did his mood. He must have done a little digging about me too, because at one point he raised a subject I'd certainly never mentioned—my somewhat-less-than-upscale apartment in the Brownsville section of Brooklyn—and said that I didn't "have to live there," adding that he had "plenty of apartments." When I didn't nibble at the carrot, he tried the stick, recounting the story of how a lawsuit he had filed had broken a reporter whose copy had irritated him.

After this series appeared, Donald refused to talk to me for eight years while I continued writing periodic articles about his New York projects. In his first memoir and handbook, *The Art of the Deal,* he made one indirect reference to my articles: He bragged about how brilliantly he had bamboozled the city and state into granting him the Hyatt abatement when he didn't even have an option on the property, noting that his submission of an option agreement signed only by him (with the space for the seller's signature left blank) had gone unnoticed until a nameless reporter discovered it almost a year after the deal closed. Donald was—as is his way—exalting over his own misleading filing with the city though he'd threatened to sue me when I first revealed it years earlier.

His second book, *Surviving at the Top,* published in 1990, when he was barely surviving and hardly at the top, named me in the first chapter and spent a number of pages turning upside down all the facts of our initial meetings. He claimed I called him and that he trustingly agreed to interviews. He said I had somehow managed to "record everything on tape," yet write "a vicious article in which virtually every quote had been changed or taken wildly out of context." He reported that federal prosecutors had begun "looking into Barrett's allegations about my business practices," revealing a probe of him that, until then, had remained a secret for a decade. Donald's passage on me was clearly a preemptive strike, anticipating this book.

The attack was somewhat surprising. In 1987, when I called his publicist, Howard Rubenstein, in the course of a *Voice* story Rubenstein said that Donald wanted to talk to me directly again, rather than through him, and Trump got on the phone, greeting me in the same friendly tone as he had years earlier. When a book I coauthored with Newfield about the corruption of the Koch administration in New York appeared in 1988, news accounts reported that Trump liked it so much he'd bought a hundred copies for his friends, even though he came in for a few unfavorable, though brief, references. In the spring of 1989, shortly after my contract with HarperCollins to do this book made news in New York, Trump and I chatted amiably at a Waldorf luncheon, where he said I was "the right person to write this book" since I was "there in the beginning." And when I took leave from the *Voice* that December and began intensively reporting the book, Trump used a mutual friend, attorney Tom Puccio, as an emissary between us, and it was Puccio who told me that Donald had indicated that he would be willing to meet and discuss some level of cooperation with the project.

But as Trump's problems surfaced at the beginning of 1990, he seemed to pull back and became more and more hostile. While I repeatedly sought clarification from Rubenstein about whether or not Trump was going to grant me an interview, I could not get an answer for months, and finally was told that my request had been denied. On Easter Sunday, Rubenstein called my home to read a statement from Donald, informing me that he had retained a well-known civil liberties lawyer to "monitor" my "activities."

In June, Trump's press office at one of his Atlantic City casinos said I could get press credentials to attend his birthday party there, but then reneged a day before the event, claiming it was "standing room only." I went to the casino anyway, said with a smile that I was certainly willing to stand, was scornfully rejected, and then watched the same press officers distribute large yellow press tags to dozens of other reporters. Uncertain whether I had been stigmatized by an overzealous aide or Donald himself, I planted myself among the gawkers waiting in the lobby along the path he would take to the party, determined to appeal to him directly, but Trump's burly bodyguards surrounded me and, when he approached, shoved me aside. I ducked into an empty stairwell, sidestepped Trump security, and slipped into the ballroom, where I was promptly arrested for "defiant trespass." Atlantic City cops who doubled as part-time Trump security even confiscated my pocket tape recorder. Handcuffed and hauled away, I kept insisting that the ballroom door to this supposedly private party was so wide open for everyone but me that, to pack it at the last minute, a large group of people with neither tickets nor credentials was allowed in. I did not mention that one of the people in the crowd was Tim O'Brien, my research assistant, who was apparently not recognized by the security army. When I was chained to the wall in an Atlantic City holding pen for hours that night—also by cops who were moonlighting for Donald—I finally began to get the point: Trump had decided not to cooperate with this book.

Despite everything I learned about Trump in thirteen years of covering him on my general *Voice* beat, and what I unearthed about him during the most recent year and a half of intense investigation, I must concede that his refusal to talk to me for this book has limited in some ways just how completely I can tell his story. I have never done a major article about anyone when a closing interview with the subject didn't cause me to revise my own thinking in some ways. Donald is a very persuasive force, and he, doubtless, would have done so, too.

In the absence of Donald's contribution, my book's accounts of him in action are, in most instances, versions of other people involved in his many deals. I only present the scenes and conversations I came to accept as credible—drawn from sources I found believable and corroborated by other research. However, since I wrote the book in narrative, rather than journalistic form, I have described the events unencumbered by the he-said-this and she-said-that news story formula. I have reported what happened based on all the available evidence. Donald may have a different version, but no writer can allow his subject's unwillingness to share it to become a bar to reporting the events at all. I have used court records wherever possible—for example, the account of tenant leader John Moore's give-and-take with Trump is drawn from sworn affidavits. But much of the direct quotation of Donald, as well as the description of his actions, comes from sources who witnessed the events. The limitation of a stonewalled biography like this one is that it is the story of Donald's life as seen through the eyes of hundreds of people who dealt with him, but almost certainly, not as he views it himself.

The associated limitation is that Donald saw to it that many people close to him refused to talk to me, again circumscribing my reporting. His investment banker, Ace Greenberg, for example, agreed to an appointment and then cancelled, explaining through an aide that Donald had asked him not to do the interview. When I complained to Rubenstein about this Trump-engineered cancellation, I noted that he was cutting off my access to friends of his who would have nothing but good to say about him. When Rubenstein said that Trump believed I did not want to hear anything good about him, I offered to instantly interview a list of ten sources Trump might provide through Rubenstein who would do nothing but speak well of him. Rubenstein said that sounded fair and promised to talk to Donald and get back to me. In the end, I was not given a single name. Since Greenberg and others persuaded by Donald not to talk to me may have seen the same events I describe with a different lens, my search for the total Trump story can be said to suffer from the shortcoming of their omitted recollections. I am certain, nonetheless, that I made a full-fledged effort to speak to everyone I could, and I believe that I was ultimately able to thoroughly explore the major episodes of his life described here.

Several hundred people did talk, and many had worked closely with him over long periods of time. I gathered fourteen file drawers of documents. I recruited two outstanding research assistants who worked with me for half a year apiece, Tim O'Brien and Jon Gill, as well as several who did spot work—Adam Cataldo, Joe Goldman, Susanah Doyle, Liz Garbus, Ed Borges, and Anne Watson. I relied on a career's worth of New York sources known to me as reliable from my *Voice* work, parlaying their information into the most detailed and disturbing account of his business practices ever uncovered. I spent five months in Atlantic City, where so much of Trump's rise and fall was staged. Recognizing how dependent Donald's early career was on his father's resources and guile, I rummaged through half a century of Fred Trump history, finding haunting parallels between the machinations of the father and son.

Even when the simultaneous explosions of Donald's personal and financial life became one of America's biggest stories in mid-1990, I resisted the temptation to rethink my reporting plan and produce a quicker, less thorough biography, capitalizing on what was unmistakably a flash flood of interest. For better or worse, I stuck with the demands of a serious and sweeping exploration of his life, hoping his significance would transcend the momentary peak of fascination prompted by his divorce and demise. One reason I stayed on course was that, from the beginning, I saw this book as not only Trump's story, but the exhumation of an era. That era ended as abruptly as the decade and, though it has only been over for two years, it seems already a faraway and blurred memory. I also wanted to explore the banking and political culture centered around Trump, extending from New York to New Jersey to Palm Beach, that in its heyday knew few ethical bounds.

The story of Trump is a saga of unseemly liaisons, but Marla Maples was the least of them. Uncovering and recounting each of these often intricate episodes in his business life was what kept me going on this long and difficult journey. While I have, to a degree, used Donald as a window to a decadent age, he has not been a mere symbol to me. In these pages he is a man of cunning and will and achievement, who lives with his own peculiar, self-inflicted pain. His rollercoaster ride from Coney Island to colossus to collapse is a tragedy that may yet require an epilogue. As Donald's new press agent called to warn me on the eve of publication, trying to persuade me to delete the use of the word "downfall" in the title of this book: Trump, he said, "will make a comeback."

1

UNRAVELING

Rushing like a great comet to the zenith, his path a blazing trail, Frank Cowperwood did for the hour illuminate the terrors and wonders of individuality. But for him also the eternal equation—the pathos of the discovery that even giants are but pygmies, and that an ultimate balance must be struck.

—*Theodore Dreiser*, THE TITAN

DONALD TRUMP had not granted an interview or smirked into a camera in nearly a month. It was his longest media dry spell since 1986—when he started taking reporters on grand tours aboard his black Puma helicopter, laying claim to the Manhattan to Atlantic City landscape with a lordly wave of his hand. At forty-four, despite almost daily, banner-headlined catastrophes since the beginning of 1990, he was still willing to play posterboy, and a birthday was a great photo opportunity. So, after weeks of hiding from a suddenly carnivorous press, he decided to surface at a birthday blast organized by his casino dependents. With his golden hair backing up beneath his starched collar, a wounded half smile on his silent lips, and perfectly protected by his ever-present blue pin-striped suit, the icon of the eighties—slowed in the first six months of the new decade to an uncertain pace—worked his way out onto a Boardwalk blanketed by a mid-June haze.

The gray clouds that clung to the spires and cupolas of the Taj Mahal—one of three casinos Trump owned in the seaside town—would not dampen his day. Neither would the newspapers, which had sunk to portraying him as a kind of pop prince of Ponzi, a colossal, one-man pyramid scheme. And neither would the dozens of bankers who were gathering back in New York even on this summer Saturday morning to pick apart the bones of his empire, to add secondary liens to nearly everything he owned. His organization—which he saw as a visionary amalgam of "artful deals"—had already suffered through three weeks of almost surgical exploration at the hands of chameleon moneymen who'd once thrown unsecured millions at him and were now barking at one another over how much life-support pocket change each would agree to offer him. It was just as well he'd gotten out of town, even if he had to leave aboard one of his overleveraged helicopters.

The thousands who were there to greet him—his Atlantic City army of dealers, maids, bellhops, cocktail waitresses, security guards, cooks, and half-dressed dancers—knew perfectly well what he meant to them. Anyone could hire them, but he was more than an employer. The Taj catering manager Barbara Epstein exhorted them from the stage set up in front of the casino's cement elephants. "Let's stand behind our Donald," she pleaded, "because he's the father of our babies." It was an image that troubled him, but he understood that they were reaching for words to define him. He was their life force.

Atlantic City mayors came and went, often departing for jail, but Donald Trump had just kept getting bigger and bigger—he now owned fully 40 percent of the city's casino hotel rooms and ruled it like a potentate. Hadn't he given wealth a populist glamour? Hadn't he lived his staff's fantasies, chasing the sky with flash and glitz, his towers rising from the sand like beacons? Hadn't he made their town his own, buying and building it felt table by felt table?

They were reaching out to touch him now as if he were still draped in dollars. They were saying they loved him. They were telling a nation it was lucky to have him. They were begging him to stay afloat.

Yet his gargantuan gaming empire had helped give the town its Third World economic flavor—its cash product siphoned out for use elsewhere, its casino enclave arrayed against a skyline of wilting poverty like desert mirages. Though the city's meager 37,000 population made it a small town, its stretches of decay interspersed with glitz gave it the look of a gutted big-city whore, cheaply overdressed and covered in splashy makeup. After a decade in New Jersey, and a symphony of promises, the Great Builder had yet to erect his first unit of housing on its downtown vacant plains, sidestepping obligations that were, at times, binding covenants that ran with the title to land he bought with city approval. The Taj itself sat on a seventeen-acre site, much of which was cleared with government funds earmarked for rebuilding the city. A side part of this parcel had long been designated for affordable, oceanfront housing, and while Donald had once agreed to build it, there was little doubt now but that it would never be completed.

Even as his subjects chanted for him that morning, the police were ripping up portions of the Boardwalk just a block or so away, scouring its underside for the decomposed body of a murdered homeless man who'd supposedly been buried inside the elaborate, garbage-strewn maze of tunnels dug by the city's legion of street people for shelter. Just as the rally ended, another homeless man, sleeping in four feet of grass and weeds on a lot near the Taj, was fatally chopped to pieces by a brush-hog mower attached to a tractor.

A screaming ambulance siren became background music for the birthday speeches. A roulette dealer took the mike to call Donald "a superhero" and repeat a homily she might have used on a loser or two at her table: "Success is getting up one more time when you fall down. He's a real success story." A professional motivator, Douglas Cox, hired to whip the crowd up, had them cheering frantically for Donald's brief thank-you statement. "This is unbelievable. You folks are fantastic," he said. "Over the years, I've surprised a lot of people. And the biggest surprise is yet to come." It was a word of encouragement wrapped in mystery, a tease designed to please the crowd while not offending the nervous bankers, who would not stand for another arrogant declaration of triumph. Donald posed for a photo with a vendor who presented him with an eight-foot-tall rug portrait of himself and prepared to leave. He disliked crowd scenes and was so formal and fastidious that he washed his hands after even boardroom handshakes, drank his diet soda through a straw, wore starch and a suit to tennis matches, demoted casino executives when he found as few as four cigarette butts in an out-of-the-way stairwell, and suggested AIDS tests to applicant bed partners. He knew he would have to go through one more of these flesh-pressing events that night, when a more intimate party of high rollers and hotel brass was planned at a ballroom in his marina casino off the Boardwalk, Trump Castle.

Even as he shuffled off—engulfed by the still cheering throng and bulky bodyguards in dark suits, armed with walkie-talkies—he was alone. He could not remember when he wasn't alone. Over the years, during his many media interviews and elsewhere, he loosely referred to mere acquaintances as "friends" if they were prominent enough. But those who knew him best said he had virtually no real friends—because, in his own view, no one was actually worthy of his trust. He'd watched his older brother, Fred Jr., die in 1981 and had diagnosed the cause as Fred's trusting nature. It had killed him at forty-three, when Donald's decade was just starting, and for Donald the tragedy had become a chilling message. Only a few months earlier, he'd confided to the million or so men who read *Playboy* that, while alcohol had technically killed his brother (the death certificate lists no cause), he had really died, swore Donald, of openness. "I saw people really taking advantage of Fred, and the lesson I learned was to always keep my guard up one hundred percent, whereas he didn't," he said. When he repeated the story on national television in an interview with Connie Chung, he said of Fred Jr.: "He totally gave of himself. And I tend to be just the opposite."

More than condos or casinos, he'd spent his life building defenses—walls to fend off the people around him. The tally for his three homes—including mansions in Palm Beach and Greenwich, Connecticut, as well as a double triplex in Trump Tower—was 250 rooms, enough to hide in forever. He'd bought a boat with another hundred rooms on six levels. He'd bought a plane large enough to seat 200, but had it redesigned to include a bedroom, full bath, and office. He had New York's largest living room in the Trump Tower complex. Even his grand and virtually sold-out condo project opposite Central Park, Trump Parc, was black at night because almost no one lived in its most expensive front apartments. The apartments were speculative investments or retreats for offshore corporate visitors. It was as if he could never have enough rooms, decorated in luxurious stillness. Each of the significant people in his life had also contributed, in his or her own way, to his loneliness. None had ever really got past his self-contained wariness.

He had turned his wife into a corporate officer and considered it a promotion. In the mid-eighties he'd given her a casino to run a hundred miles away from him and, week after week, their helicopters had passed each other in the early evening as she flew home and he flew to Atlantic City for the weekend. His top staffers had taken to calling it "the Asbury Park marriage" because that was just about the point in Northern Jersey where they calculated the choppers were close enough to almost touch. While he later shifted her to his landmark hotel in New York, the Plaza, she grew to like her Trump Organization job so much that she kept it when their marriage ended. The couple had not slept together for two and a half years when their peculiar partnership had finally been buried under an avalanche of jointly generated headlines four months before the birthday celebration.

Their life together had begun with an escape hatch—the first of four pre- and postnuptial bargains, the only love letters he'd ever written her. The architect who designed his signature building, Trump Tower, built early in their marriage, told friends that Donald had asked him to plan a second apartment in the building just for him, in case he and Ivana split. Donald would eventually admit that he might have had a "deep-seeded premonition" about life with Ivana, even at the very beginning. In news stories before their separation became public, he distilled their relationship to such a point of shallowness that he turned interview questions about her into opportunities to post notices of his own availability.

"How is your marriage?"

"Just fine. Ivana is a very kind and good woman. I also think she has the instincts and drive of a good manager. She's focused and she's a perfectionist."

"And as a wife, not as a manager?"

"I never comment on romance. She's a great mother, a good woman who does a good job."

Donald berated her scornfully in front of her staff—first at the Castle and later, at the Plaza. Though she had achieved revenue gains at her casino, inducing some of Donald's casino advisers to taunt him with the suggestion that it be renamed Ivana's Castle, he had decided abruptly in the spring of 1988 that she was through as president. Tales of her tearful departure—and scenes of his patronizing humiliation of her—were recounted by Ivana loyalists years later. "I don't need this, some woman crying," he reportedly said at her farewell ceremony. "I need somebody strong in here." After she'd left distraught, he'd reached her on a speakerphone while he met with her top executives in a Castle conference and insisted that she "say hello" to everyone, evoking another deluge.

Bringing her home to New York may also have doomed the marriage, for it put them in the same room—too often. His feelings about her were a mass of contradictions. He confessed to others "the guilt" he felt over having made her "totally subservient." She later acknowledged it herself, conceding in legal documents that she'd been persuaded throughout their life together that Donald "held all the cards," concluding: "This was apparently what he wanted me to think because it was important to him (although damaging to the children and me) for me to appear submissive." Ironically, the acquiescence on which he had insisted wound up crushing whatever interest he had in her. "She wasn't challenging," he confided. "I left essentially because I was bored."

He had had nothing but contempt for her social climbing—not recognizing her insistent pursuit of a role in New York society as a stubborn statement of her independence, a willful hunt to establish her own position in a wider circle. Gradually she must have become, in his mind, one of the stick women—bones tied together in $10,000 dresses—who haunted the dinner party circuit he abhorred. He freely castigated the very status she sought, telling reporters he couldn't stand 80 percent of her society friends.

But what really galled him was the part she'd come to play so eagerly in a scenario he'd written himself. He had created a fantasy life of personal excess as a commercial vehicle for the Trump Organization, all part of a sales strategy that magically merged his ego and business needs. But she had begun to love living the fantasy—she was enchanted by Mar-A-Lago, the Florida citadel he'd purchased for its aerial-shot impact, and she actually took South Pacific tours on the *Trump Princess,* the world's second-largest yacht he'd bought as a casino attraction, docked next to the Castle to lure big spenders. Didn't she realize this was just shtick? While he could step outside this charade, study it, tinker with it, smile at it, she had come to believe in it. Once she let herself become a beaming walk-on in the commercial life he'd scripted, she was as surreal to him as all the rest of it.

So he had started the new decade with a new declaration: He was leaving. But neither Ivana nor he was sure if he meant it. Ivana wanted to hang on, but almost as desperately, she wanted to win this new test of nerves between them. She'd heard him trumpet his conquest of Merv Griffin in the battle for the Taj at a New Year's party the year before, announcing "I wish I had another Merv to bat around." She was determined it wasn't going to be her. If the marriage ended, she would leave with the upper hand. She would also leave with a meaningful chunk of his net worth. And if they agreed to maintain the marriage, she was going to secure her future with a new nuptial agreement that gave her a fair share of his wealth.

Even before Donald took off for Tokyo for the Mike Tyson–Buster Douglas fight in early February, Ivana's lawyer and trusted friend, Michael Kennedy, was talking to Donald. Kennedy was making it clear that Ivana, wounded by a Christmas confrontation in Aspen with a brazen girlfriend of Donald's, did not want a divorce. But she was demanding a 20 to 25 percent slice of Donald's estimated half-billion dollars in assets, as published by *Forbes* magazine. She wanted this $125 million commitment in a new nuptial agreement, and the implication was that if she didn't get it, a public separation would ensue. In his softer moments with Kennedy, Donald said he was interested in an upward revision of the roughly $25 million agreement—$14 million in cash plus properties—that they'd signed a little more than two years earlier. But in the end, Donald brushed the suggestion aside and broke off the talks, insisting on adhering to the numbers in the 1987 postnuptial.

As soon as Donald was out of town, Kennedy, Ivana, and a hurriedly hired publicist named John Scanlon began planning a preemptive strike on Donald's iron bunker of a nuptial contract. Timed to appear while Donald was in the air on his way back from Japan to assure Ivana unanswered, first-day news dominance, the New York *Daily News'* front page was decorated by gossip columnist Liz Smith with Ivana's prepackaged version of the breakup, complete with vague allusions to Donald's "betrayal" and Ivana's role as his "full-time business partner." Donald's business trip had gone badly—Tyson, in whom he had invested millions, lost the heavyweight crown, and his hunt for deals and cash had produced neither. Then he got Ivana's bad news just as he landed and was enraged as much by the fact that someone else was manipulating his media as he was by its portrayal of him as a philanderer.

Hiding behind an imaginary spokesman, Donald began likening Ivana to hotel baroness Leona Helmsley, whom he'd just labeled in an interview "a truly evil human being" and a "vicious, horrible woman" who mistreated her employees "worse than anyone I've ever witnessed." This poisonous assault—and other leaks to gossip columnists so odious one described them as too offensive to print—boomeranged. He contemplated taking the Leona image a step further, branding Ivana as "the equivalent of Imelda Marcos and Leona Helmsley wrapped up in one," exposing parallels of Imelda's shoe glut in Ivana's own closet, while simultaneously circulating stories of her harsh management of the Plaza. "There are two Ivanas," he whispered, promising that the public would be "repulsed" by the truth about how she spent money. "If I wanted to, I could win the war of PR," he said, "but I don't want to." After his initial Helmsley potshot, even Donald may have sensed, as the suffering Ivana assumed heroic proportions in the media, that dumping on her was an image kamikaze mission.

He had tempted fate with the timing of the marital break. He, and only he, knew just how badly his empire was slipping. His advisers were warning him that his sudden and still secret problem in cajoling new financing out of the dry old holes was compounded by the spectacle he was becoming in the press. They told him that anything that made his financial statements take-home reading for the onetime trusting bankers was bad news. Even if the bankers had as strong a constitutional commitment to the sanctity of postnuptials as he, the advisers argued, they might unconsciously add up the unleveraged assets and divide them by two.

As the months wore on, Kennedy and Donald reopened their talks. They had known each other since Ivana and Donald got married in 1977, and though Donald had retained a battery of attorneys to handle his dispute with Ivana, he preferred to talk directly with Kennedy himself. At Kennedy's request, he got a letter from his lawyer permitting their continuing dialogue, without the presence of counsel. They talked numbers, and while they understood one another's math, they were at times talking past each other about the ultimate result. Kennedy was still in search of a new nuptial, with Ivana disdaining divorce, while most of the time at least, an undecided Donald seemed to be looking to set a new price for a final breakup.

The highest hard offer Donald made was $40 million, a $2 million-a-year allotment for twenty years plus the properties, bringing the total commitment to Ivana to well in excess of $50 million. When Kennedy balked, Donald hinted that he might raise it to $50 million in cash plus the properties. That convinced Kennedy he could get Trump as high as $75 million, and he told Ivana and her team that would be about as far as Donald would go, concluding that they were only a doable $25 million apart. Kennedy began telling people—and the newspapers reported—that Trump had made a $100 million offer. But that was just intended to give Donald face-saving room if they settled at $75 million.

Ivana and her lawyer decided to tough it out for this unattainable prize, rejecting the $50 million. Incredibly, the woman who had shared thirteen years of Trump's life and still bore the title of executive vice president in his compact organization knew so little about the true dimensions of his wealth that she and Kennedy had rejected an already impossible offer. An angry victim of his own hyped wealth, Donald cursed at Kennedy, "You will rue the day."

By then, the dispute between them had been in court for weeks, with Ivana having filed a civil suit. She was hardly in a position to file for divorce; she'd be left with the meager provisions of the latest nuptial contract. Instead, even though that agreement was the result of five months of intense bargaining and several drafts, she had challenged it as an illegal delusion, a product of her husband's misrepresentations to her about their marriage and his wealth. Once she'd rejected the sidebar offer Donald made to Kennedy, she had no choice but to push ahead in her effort to overturn the nuptial, even though she knew she was playing to his strong suit. In legal papers, she now demanded half his empire, valuing it at a ludicrous $5 billion, charging that the $1.1 billion estimate listed by him when they hammered out the agreement in 1987 was a hoax. She hired detectives—heavy hitters imported in cowboy hats from Texas—but she knew so little about him they had to work without leads.

She charged in court papers that "she believed" that Donald had engaged in extramarital relations for years, to which he replied that "continuing love and affection was not a material part of the 1987 agreement," as chilling a case-law suggestion as his lawyers could fashion. It turned out that the prescient Donald had removed the pledge, which had indeed been contained in the previous nuptials. In his mind, it may have been the price he exacted for increasing her booty so dramatically in the 1987 agreement. He had, according to Ivana, suggested as early as 1986 that an open marriage "might be interesting," but she had rejected the notion. The idea popped up right around the time that the *Village Voice* revealed that Donald had been buying jewelry at Bulgari's and using the old empty box trick to dodge the sales tax, but instead of sending the box to his home in Greenwich, he'd reportedly sent one package for a $15,000 purchase to the Greenwich home of his lawyer, Roy Cohn. The ruse address suggested it was a gift he didn't want Ivana to know about.

In any event, Donald seemed to regard her Christmas Eve execution of the new agreement as a form of release. Apparently believing that he no longer owed her a legal obligation of love, he withdrew it, as if that were the only reason he had ever offered a display of it. In the aftermath of this agreement, their marriage grew cold and Donald's onetime clandestine excursions became a bold and sustained high-risk adventure.

It was in the middle of this fierce exchange that another crisis hit, and Donald made a different kind of news. Hints of it had appeared since the beginning of the year. In January, a two-page ad for the *Trump Princess* in *Yachting* magazine had provoked speculation in the dailies as to why Donald was selling it. He tried to explain this sea-search for $115 million in cash by claiming he was replacing the 282-foot vessel with a bigger model. By early June, noting the drooping prices of Donald's casino bonds, Salomon Brothers publicly urged its customers to sell any holdings they might have. A noted casino analyst, Marvin Roffman, flatly predicted in one news story that the Taj wouldn't make it, and Donald's threats to sue pushed Roffman's investment firm to fire him. If that much-publicized "off-with-his-head" reaction hadn't sent shock waves to the financial community, the actual disastrous opening of the Taj certainly did. Gigantic crowds of customers, swamping horribly mismanaged accounting and coin-changing systems, forced the roping off of most of the slots for days. Even when the machines were finally opened, the waves of players were still not generating enough revenue to come near to covering the debt service.

On the heels of the Taj debacle, Neil Barsky, the *Wall Street Journal*'s crafty Trump watcher who'd broken the Roffman stories, cornered Donald for a wide-ranging interview. Feigning more knowledge of Donald's cash crush than he actually had, Barsky cajoled Donald into admitting in an April interview that he was trying to sell or refinance much of his empire. Barsky let Donald put the best face on the news, quoting him as saying he was on his way to becoming the "King of Cash," but the story was a warning disguised as a get-well card. Barsky's revelations were quickly followed by a *Forbes* downgrading of Donald's wealth, dropping him from the $1.7 billion that the magazine had pegged him at in 1989 to $500 million. *Forbes* and the *Philadelphia Inquirer*'s Dave Johnston, Atlantic

City's top casino reporter, simultaneously uncovered a confidential financial statement Donald had submitted to New Jersey regulators. Their analysis of its crystal-clear overstatement of the value of Donald's properties blew the lid off the business side of the Trump story.

With the grim bankers gathering around Donald's Trump Tower conference table like pallbearers, even Michael Kennedy was beginning to get the message. When the burrower Barsky exposed the hushed meetings in a June 4 front-page article, he cited unnamed banking sources who obviously thought, like Scanlon and Ivana had months earlier, that it was better if they shaped the news coverage of their ongoing combat rather than leave it to Donald. The "cash-shortage-has-become-critical" story was immediately picked up in papers across the country. The Trump debacle was almost as big a news event as his divorce, with imaginary "Best Banker I Ever Suckered" headlines hovering over the embarrassed table, recalling the *New York Post*'s ballyhooed quote from a Trump lover—"Best Sex I Ever Had."

The Barsky piece also linked the two cataclysms simultaneously shaking Donald's life. His "private life" had become "a liability," wrote Barsky, because the bankers were unsure "what portion of his empire could be claimed by his wife in any future divorce action." Barsky also quoted "people close to Trump" as saying that he intended, in view of his new situation, to seek a major reduction in the amount pledged to Ivana in the postnuptial agreement. While that was an obvious ploy, the damage the divorce mess had done to the image Donald had cultivated was unquestionably connected with his sudden financial distress.

A *New York Times* story noted "the erosion" of the value of the "tarnished" Trump name, quoting the chairman of a corporate identity firm as saying: "It's going to be hard to view Mr. Trump as a prudent individual. People may now think twice about flying on an airplane that bears his name." In fact, word was that an internal marketing survey done for the Trump Shuttle had revealed that caution wasn't the only motive for riding the competitor, Pan Am. Businesswomen were boycotting Donald's troubled airline in disturbing numbers—apparently out of anger at his perceived boorishness.

The dissolution of his marriage had also hurt him with a far more important group of potential customers—the Japanese. In the months since his return from Tokyo, nascent deals to sell the *Trump Princess;* blocks of apartments in his new condo building, the Palace; and a stake in the Plaza to Japanese buyers had fallen apart, as well as attempts to get a loan against his equity in the Grand Hyatt hotel.

The immediate cause of the bank meetings, which had been initiated by Donald in late May, was his inability to make a $43 million payment due on the bonds of Ivana's former casino, Trump Castle. He needed the bankers to loan him $20 million of that payment, and he had tried to convince them to contribute another $80 million for general operations. The consortium of his seven major New York and New Jersey banks started instead at $50 million, raising it by mid-June to $65 million but wanted to tie it to an overall restructuring of Trump's debts. Donald had personally injected himself into the bargaining—sitting with the major banks for twelve-hour stretches, calling foreign banks that were not at the table but had smaller stakes in his loans up to 1:00 A.M. and charming those reluctant about restructuring, even taking orders for fries, shakes, and burgers and making a run to McDonald's. As engaging as Trump was, the bankers also picked up another, less friendly message. They kept hearing that Trump was quietly negotiating a new loan with a major bank that had never lent him a nickel—Chemical was the rumor—and that he was ready to secure the loan with the last bit of real collateral he had. This was a fearsome prospect for the banks already up to their necks with Trump debt and looking to lay claim themselves, as part of any new loan and restructuring deal, to the equity he was supposedly marketing elsewhere. This mix of charm and, as it turned out, bluff about the new bank combined to push the bankers at the table toward the deal Donald wanted. The stage appeared set for a last-minute reprieve, with a bank agreement to be announced on the June 15 bond payment deadline, followed by a joyous birthday celebration the following day in Atlantic City. But, with the foreign banks particularly upset, the talks broke down that Friday over who would give how much and what they would take in return. When they did, Donald "turned white," in the words of a participant. While Donald did win a ten-day extension on the payment from the bond trustee, he had to attend his party without his prize.

Teams of bankers continued to scour his assets for any sign of value that wasn't already hocked, and found slim pickings. One of the few properties that at least momentarily seemed capable of attracting a price exceeding its debt was the Plaza. However, the bankers, the buyers, and Donald were all frustrated by the presence of Ivana. How would a new owner handle her? Throw her out? Be forced by public sentiment to keep her? It was just one more piece of a stymieing puzzle—as was the substantial, unleveraged equity in the Greenwich mansion and Trump Tower apartment, also protected from the bankers by Ivana's stake in them.

Ivana did not betray a hint of recognition of the gravity of Donald's crisis in her own daily life. On the day of his Atlantic City birthday bash, with the bank talks at a peak, she was off in London on what was reported as an extended shopping spree. On *The Tonight Show* Jay Leno said he'd seen a terrific photo opportunity outside the Plaza—Ivana tossing coins into the fountain and Donald diving in after them.

He was, of course, facing this humiliating comeuppance without her. The special distance between the two had become so familiar he actually seemed to miss it during these trying weeks. But she was only a part of his isolation. He wasn't seeing much of his three young children, either—none of whom made it to his birthday party. The eldest, twelve-year-old Donald Jr., whose self-absorbed poetic and artistic temperament had long distanced him from his father, refused to participate in any birthday activities (Donald was always saying that the more aggressive six-year-old Eric was "just like me" anyway). Donald Jr. had gotten into a fight at his exclusive Manhattan private school when another student had waved a cleavage-revealing newspaper photo of Donald's mistress in his face. Retreating into a shell, resentful, abandoned, and too old to be sheltered from the tabloid revelations about the tawdriness of his family life, the boy stopped talking to his father altogether for a while, a development that shook even Donald.

In happier times, he liked to tell reporters pressing him for domestic details that he always took his children's phone calls—as if it were a remarkable concession to them. When he was asked about whether he routinely made it up the Trump Tower elevator for family dinners, he'd respond by citing his warm availability on the other end of a receiver. Challenged about why he was seldom with the family on the frequent jaunts engineered by the peripatetic Ivana, he mastered the grinning explanation, often quoted: "There's only one reason. I love to work." As his wife had put it so memorably herself: "Donald has gone weeks on end without seeing the children at all."

While the frenzied demands of fame might have occasionally made it impossible to talk to his children, he often talked about them. In his view, granting them an appearance in the commentary on Trump life he conjured up for inquiring reporters was the next best thing to telling them a bedtime story. During these stream-of-consciousness sessions he did not hesitate to volunteer odds on the likelihood of the younger Trumps being as successful as he was. "Statistically, my children have a very bad shot," he liked to say. "Children of successful people are generally very, very troubled. They don't have the right shtick. I would love them to be in business with me, but ninety-five percent of those children fail in a sophisticated big business."

He was remote not because they didn't matter to him but because he had difficulty relating to them. They were abstractions, responsibilities. He had always prided himself on his incapacity for small talk, but it left him with nothing to say to eight-year-old Ivanka. With Ivana almost as absent a parent as he, the children were raised by nannies and security guards, their antiseptic bedrooms segregated off in a corner of the tower apartment. While Donald's office was decorated with a glorious array of his own magazine covers, it had no pictures of his children. He told prying guests that it was all a strategy to protect them from the potential kidnappers who visited him in his inner sanctum. No reason was offered for the absence of pictures of his wife, parents, or other members of his family.

His father, Fred Trump, was more than a friend to him, more than a parent. He was a mirror image, and that was about as much as another person could mean to him. He had grown up under Fred's stern watch and had always imagined himself in his father's shoes. In fact he'd already transcended his no-nonsense old man, but he liked to pretend he'd done it on his own, announcing that "the working man likes me because he knows I didn't inherit what I've built" and contemptuously deriding what he called the Lucky Sperm Club of heredi-tary, do-nothing wealth. "You know me pretty well," he told one reporter. "Do you think anybody helped me build this fortune?" He insisted there would have been no Plaza or Trump Tower if Fred called the shots. The Trump legend—invented by Donald himself—never acknowledged the defining imprint of Fred's money and hard-boiled business sense on the solid early deals that were the foundation of his success.

Donald told one of his closest confidants—Tony Schwartz, the journalist who coauthored his first book, *The Art of the Deal*—that his father had begun treating him "fundamentally as a business partner very, very early" in life. It was the same term Ivana's publicist, Liz Smith, had used in her column to plant Ivana's legal claim and trigger Donald's self-destructive public sniping at her. It was a particularly cold way to cast these central relationships in his life, espe-cially since one of Fred's and Donald's shared business goals was never to do a joint venture. Donald had tried to buy out every business partner that circum-stances had initially forced him to accept, as had Fred decades earlier. So Ivana's attempt to define herself as a partner, and Donald's upbringing as one by Fred, were a commentary on Donald's prolonged estrangement from both.

But now more than ever, Donald felt the ground shifting beneath his rela-tionship with his father. His financial trauma was allowing Fred to reemerge as the senior partner, his cautious and long-ignored advice now vindicated. The bankers sifting through Donald's assets had begun asking about Fred's; some were even busy calculating—away from the negotiating table—the life expec-tancy and legacy of the eighty-five-year-old patriarch. They sensed that his steady rental and co-op empire, thousands of middle-class apartments largely unencumbered by debt, might become Donald's, and thus their own, salvation.

They concluded that Fred had a minimum of $150 million "that could be drawn on," according to one involved banker.

Donald was reduced to courting Fred for a bailout without blame, but rigid Fred was unlikely to come to the rescue without rubbing it in, just as Donald had once waved his transcendent triumphs in his father's face. Fred came down to Atlantic City for the evening birthday celebration at the Castle, minus his wife, Mary, and sat at a V-shaped table in front of the stage. Standing to applause from the crowd of 300 or so when introduced by Donald, he was feted by the comics who performed and by master of ceremonies Robin Leach, the sycophantic purveyor of televised greed who'd featured Donald repeatedly on *Lifestyles of the Rich and Famous*. While Donald seemed, in these troubled days, to be drawing closer to his father, it was a manipulated, humbling intimacy that must have made him feel as if he were back in Coney Island, in a cubicle outside Fred's stark private office.

The friendships he'd formed with the handful of close colleagues he'd worked with for years had the same distilled and businesslike tone as his familial ties. There was humor and a certain comfort in these relationships, but always a forbidding distance. Even with his brother Robert, who was clearly the closest person to him on the Trump Organization staff. Though Robert was only two years younger, Donald treated him more like an underling than a peer. It was not that they didn't care for each other; it was that Robert had none of Donald's or Fred's rough edges. The quality Donald most admired in life was toughness—he brayed on and on about it whenever a ghostwriter or microphone was near. But Robert was a gentle mediator. Donald relished the animosity that he himself stirred up with his confrontational style; on the other hand, when Robert wasn't a victim of the bombast himself, he was desperately trying to make amends for it with those left in Donald's wounded wake.

When the Taj suffered its opening slot-machine catastrophe back in April, Donald had appeared on CNN to blast the Taj president as "a Type C, low-key personality," too contemplative to cope with the fiery demands of the mammoth casino. "I've never made money in my life with a Type C personality," he declared, describing such creatures as "people that fall asleep." The quickly sacked executive had been installed by Robert precisely because he was so comfortable with the man's waspish, banker air. Donald was the explosive antithesis of Robert, so despite all the obvious affection for him, Donald could never accord him the status of a real player or make him a true confidant. In fact, in the midst of the Taj crisis, he so assailed Robert at a session with other Taj executives that Robert packed up and walked out that day, flying to New York without notice. When the financial crisis hit and Donald was scurrying around looking for assets he could convert into income, he talked about evicting Robert from the apartment in a Trump building he'd given him. Robert was—despite all his skillful service—just another dependent and interchangeable part to Donald.

Robert was a guest at the birthday blast, too, sitting with his wife, Blaine, at Fred's family table. Blaine, an established queen of New York society, was virtually the only birthday reveler to attend both his and Ivana's 1990 parties. When Ivana had hosted a luncheon to mark her own birthday back in the middle of the February divorce battle—at a posh midtown restaurant surrounded by a jostling jam of madcap reporters—the Trump women had graciously attended, including the ones who would not be present at Donald's, namely Mary and federal judge Maryanne Trump Barry, the oldest of the children. Blaine, whose strained relationship with Ivana was described by Donald over the years as merely "civil," may have shown up at Ivana's party simply because she never missed a well-covered event. She was the perfect, tasteful complement to the perpetually pleasant Robert.

Other than Robert, few of the top executives who worked in Donald's New York headquarters made it to the Atlantic City festivities. His handful of long-term handlers had watched in anguish over the years as he encouraged one top aide after another to inch their way into his personal orbit, only to abruptly and inexplicably cut them out and shunt them aside. One aide who herself had ridden on this emotional roller coaster with Donald later came to understand it, after she anguished through a dinner party when dozens of hungry mouths pecked away at her with prying questions about him, consuming any tidbit. She called him that night because the experience had opened her eyes to what it was like to be him, what it was like to endure people clawing their way after him, grabbing for pieces of him. "Everyone was at him for something," she had come to understand. His response to the pressures his own pursuit of celebrity status had helped create was, even within his inner circle, to tease and retreat, invite and run, open up ever so briefly, then shut down.

And now, after years of infighting for favor, his key New York people were gradually leaving, many nudged by Donald. His staff counsel, Susan Heilbron, who had always displayed a maternal protectiveness toward him even though they were the same age, departed early in 1990. Tony Gliedman, the former New York City housing commissioner who joined Donald in 1986 and had personally engineered triumphs like his restoration of the Wollman Rink in Central Park, would quit before the end of the year, forced out by a storm of Trumpian abuse.

Also on their way out were Robert; Harvey Freeman, his top financial adviser;

Blanche Sprague, the scrappy chief of condo construction and sales; Barbara Res, Donald's hard-hat supervisor on a variety of jobs; Howard Rubenstein, the publicist who was dismissed after seventeen years and then blamed in a stinging, Trump-released letter that held him responsible for Donald's suddenly disastrous media coverage; and Jerry Schrager, the legal bludgeon he had kept on retainer for fifteen years to bang out the details of every one of his real estate deals. These cost-cutting departures would occur over the next year—culminating with Robert's and Freeman's—and would frequently be accompanied by Trump scapegoating. His rationale for his problems became the shortcomings of his staff—to whom he said he had granted too much managerial leeway. Even before this rash of farewells, however, Donald's small circle of advisers had lost other critical parts, like Der Scutt, the architect who designed Trump Tower, and Louise Sunshine, the lobbyist who had massaged state officials to gain approvals for Donald's first tax-abated project, the Grand Hyatt.

In Atlantic City, Donald was running through casino executives as if they were one-night stands. Willard "Bucky" Howard, the second Taj president in three months of operation, was at the time of the birthday celebration only weeks away from his own demotion. The sandy-haired, Alabama-bred magnet for high rollers had lasted longer with Donald than almost any other casino executive— but never before as a casino president. His only stretch off the Trump payroll since 1985 was the period surrounding his 1988 criminal trial, when he was acquitted of charges of extorting $100,000 in bribes from Trump Castle suppliers. Howard, who almost lost his gaming license when regulators pressed administrative charges against him after his acquittal, was singled out for praise from the birthday-party podium. But his weaknesses on the management side of the operation were already forcing Donald to hunt for a new president, reducing Howard to his previous title of vice president, with a salary that would soon reach a half million.

Howard's commanding position within the organization was a reflection of the disarray in Donald's casino ranks, much of which was, in fact, a consequence of catastrophe. Eight months earlier, three of Donald's top casino executives had perished in a freak helicopter accident, flying back to Atlantic City after a boxing-match press conference in New York. Donald seemed to be personally traumatized by the disaster—saying publicly that it "cheapened life" for him, showing him just how fragile everything was. His attitude toward the tragedy shifted, though, from moments when it seemed to move him deeply to times when he did not hesitate to use it for personal advantage. He planted stories suggesting that he had almost boarded the chartered copter himself, though he'd never ridden to Atlantic City on one, trusting only his Puma. When his separation from Ivana became public only a few months after the incident, he drew upon it as one of the causes of the split, claiming it had forced him to reevaluate his own life and place a premium on finding happiness while he could.

The deaths were a devastating blow to the organization, especially the loss of Steve Hyde, the Mormon father of seven who ran all of Donald's casino operations. A widely respected figure in the New Jersey gaming industry, Hyde was credited with making Trump Plaza the city's number one moneymaker in the late eighties. Donald publicly lavished praise on the dead men, naming the arena at the Taj after Mark Etess and the new marina facility at the Castle after Hyde. But at the same time, as if he were becoming concerned that they, rather than he, were being given credit for the organization's onetime casino success, he began sniping at them. His insistence on blaming them for organizational weaknesses even in conversations with one of Hyde's closest friends, Trump Plaza president Jack O'Donnell, helped push O'Donnell out the door in 1990, costing Trump his most experienced and successful casino executive.

In a June interview with the *New York Times* just a week before his birthday, Donald ascribed much of his troubles in Atlantic City—from lower profits at the end of 1989 to the Taj's opening problems—to the Hyde team. "After the crash, when I started getting involved and watching the operation in Atlantic City, I didn't like a lot of the things that I was seeing. Steve was my great friend, but I just saw things that I frankly wanted changed because I wasn't satisfied." He particularly assailed Hyde's executive appointments at the Taj, saying he had to remove several of them and "put the people I wanted in there." One of his selections, obviously, was the controversial Howard, whom Hyde had specifically decided not to rehire in any capacity immediately after his acquittal.*

But Howard was only one of many changes. Two days after the Taj's chief financial officer, Don Wood, was carried from the casino floor on a stretcher, suffering from preopening exhaustion and dehydration, Donald fired him. The Taj personnel director was not only terminated, but told his severance package would not be fully honored. Though Donald proclaimed that after these changes,

---

* One reason for Hyde's hostility might have been that the tapes at Howard's trial established that he had loaned another Castle supervisor $18,000 after the supervisor admitted to Howard that he'd taken kickbacks on the casino's contracts. The supervisor, who claimed he'd shared the bribes with Howard, used the money to pay his criminal attorney.

everything was "running flawlessly," his appointments were merely the first wave of personnel realignments. Over the next few months, Trump would name eight new presidents to the helm of his three Atlantic City casinos in a game of musical chairs unparalleled even in an industry known for its turnover. What he had once built in New York and Atlantic City as a close, private company—proud of its continuity and balance—had destabilized to the point of becoming as turbulent as his own life.

Adding to that turbulence was the ineffable Marla Maples, the portable, if temporary, remedy for loneliness whose notorious Aspen scene with Ivana had spurred the split. Donald's Puma, his plane, and his limos had been carting her from one end of his empire to the other for at least two and a half years, a dazzling display of the logistical abilities of Donald's vast private security army. Housed in New York in a St. Moritz hotel suite just three blocks from his Trump Tower apartment, her gal-about-town chauffeuring was carefully orchestrated by the security detail so that she and Ivana were never in the same place at the same time.

Once Donald pulled Ivana out of her casino job, just a few months after she signed the final nuptial agreement, Marla took up part-time residence with him in his various hotels away from home, usually ensconced in a suite on the same floor as he, accompanied in public by any one of a host of pliant beards. On occasion, she trailed unaccompanied twenty feet behind him as he strode through his casinos, insulated by her own bevy of bodyguards in a curiously obvious statement of their separate togetherness.

As she became more and more of a fixture, entranced by Donald's supposed promises of marriage, she began spending lavishly in the hotel shops, spas, and restaurants without paying a bill. Half proprietor already, she prevailed in a dispute with Plaza staff over whether an oyster bar or a boutique belonged in vacant Trump Plaza retail space. Donald had even assigned one of his top executives to draw up the blueprints and handpick the furniture for a year-round Marla supersuite in an out-of-the way noncasino hotel he owned off the Boardwalk. The plans were dropped when the executive, Jon Benanav, died in the copter crash. They were not revived when Donald moved to end his marriage barely two months later.

She was only twenty-two or twenty-three—a five-foot eight-inch, 125-pound model taking acting lessons and grabbing bit parts in B movies—when they met in late 1986 or early 1987. Her résumé consisted of movie roles like "the second woman, a tennis player, and a balloon pilot" and advertised her "special skills" as a "juggler, pool player, sharpshooter, and excellent driver." A long-legged, buxom winner of swimming suit pageants, gushing over with southern sweetness and sensuality, she was the ultimate trophy property, a purring metaphor for male acquisition. Trump reached a point, long before his own marriage ended, when he seemed to go out of his way to advertise their relationship to those around him—as much out of a need to stir the envy of the eyes drawn to her whenever she entered a room as out of any subconscious desire to be discovered. She was the opposite of Ivana in so many ways—girlish, all-American, naturally casual, unpretentious, and voluptuously fleshy. Reared by Baptist parents, she seemed capable of carrying a Bible to an illicit liaison, exuding an innocence as phony and adaptable as Donald's.

As comforting as he found her, Donald was not blind to the career uses she might have attached to their budding relationship. She had come to him in part through Tom Fitzsimmons, a former cop and current model who had dated her virtually from her arrival in New York in the mideighties. Fitzsimmons, a sometime bodyguard and driver for Trump, had known Donald since the early seventies, and when his two friends became lovers, he took on a peculiar facilitating role. Marla's constant companion, he began posing as her date, even on a helicopter ride with Donald and Ivana to an Atlantic City boxing match. Sometimes he wound up awkwardly sitting between Donald and her at concerts the three attended. Marla even registered in Atlantic City at times as Marla Fitzsimmons. Fitzsimmons's reward was that Donald would fulfill the dream Tom had had since he and his twin brother were savvy street cops. He would arrange financing for a movie project called *Blue Gemini*, starring the brothers and Marla—an actress whose biggest prior credit was as the victim of a watermelon avalanche in the otherwise forgettable *Maximum Overdrive*. Almost two decades earlier, young Donald had speculated about becoming a Hollywood producer. He now gladly fed Fitzsimmons's obsession, beginning with a token payment for a screenplay. (Tom told friends Trump advanced $15,000 on the screenplay.) Donald also insisted that the Trump Plaza Casino use Fitzsimmons as a model in its television commercial. The passing months never deflated Fitzsimmons, who bubbled over in conversations with friends about both the prospects for his movie and Donald's love for Marla, as if the two were part of the same plot in his mind.

Fitzsimmons had been developing grander plans as well. He believed that Donald could become President. It was a notion the golden boy himself had begun toying with at least as early as 1985, when New York state Republican chairman George Clark visited with him at Trump Tower to try to talk him into running for governor. "Have you ever thought about running for high public office?" Clark asked. Donald replied without a smile: "Yes. President of the United States." By the end of 1987, he'd advanced this almost eerie ambition with a well-timed appearance in New Hampshire and the formation of a nascent Trump-for-President committee. "This is a serious test of the political waters," his top casino executive, Steve Hyde, said at the time. "If things shake out, I wouldn't be the least bit surprised if he decided to do it." Donald continued conscientiously planting the seeds, talking about the presidency quite seriously in wide-ranging interviews and buying full-page ads on national political issues.

Fitzsimmons told friends that Donald believed Ivana was incompatible with such a campaign. Not only did her awkward English immediately convey her foreign roots, but she was raised in a Communist country. Marla, on the other hand, could be a key to his southern strategy; they would sweep the country with glamour.

The staff members who genuinely cared about Donald—who did not see him as merely their own ticket to success—adopted his secretary Norma Foederer's early and insistent demand that no one snicker at the relationship with Marla. "We don't know how he really feels," Norma had said. They knew his marriage had died years ago, and they agreed that he "was entitled" to reach out for love. They wanted him to find it, though even those who loved him did not really believe he had the capacity for it. To them, even with Marla, he would still be alone—"unaware," one said, "of his own tragedy." As they saw it, his deeply ingrained remoteness was so much a part of his unexamined life that he neither understood it nor regretted it.

From the moment the Liz Smith story of his breakup with Ivana hit, Marla became a hunted woman. For reasons never explained by either Donald or Marla, she hid out like an international fugitive for two months. Her disappearance, all carefully orchestrated by Donald's corporate police force, made no public relations sense, since it only fed the mystery. If she had parked herself at a desk in the city room of the *New York Post,* she could not have gotten more ink than she got on the lam. Sequestered in the Southampton beach home of a real estate broker friendly to Donald, she was whisked away at the last moment, just as *Daily News* reporters were closing in for the kill. Ivana's detectives, who were feeding the *News* tips on Marla's whereabouts, even came up with phone records from an apartment in Trump Tower a few floors below where Ivana and the children lived and across the hall from the apartment where Donald had retreated. The bills revealed calls to Marla's home, Dalton, Georgia—and were interpreted by Liz in one more spellbinding column as evidence that the cad had brought his wench right under his wife's nose. Ivana was said to be crying over the fact that the children might have bumped into Marla on trips downstairs to visit their father.

When Marla finally surfaced several weeks later, she appeared in a ratings-smashing interview on ABC's network newsmagazine, *Primetime Live,* questioned by her designee, Diane Sawyer. Conducted under the tightest of security, the interview occurred in the Atlantic City home of casino executives Jack and Caroline Davis, who told reporters that Marla had in fact been hiding there for a month, not in the Trump Tower apartment claimed in Liz Smith's columns. A few months after the interview, Donald named Jack Davis to succeed Bucky Howard as the new Taj president, and made Caroline the casino's special events coordinator (he also hired the broker who'd hidden her in the Hamptons).

The only memorable Maples remark during Sawyer's interview—described by PBS anchor Robert MacNeil as "one of the low points" in television journalism history—was that she loved Donald. "I can't lie about it," she said, though she seemed to have no problem vigorously denying that Donald was supporting her. "He's not the type of man that would choose to support someone else while he's married," she insisted, suggesting implicitly that she'd been paying for her St. Moritz and Waldorf suites, as well as a $2,700-a-month East Side apartment.

Questioned about whether Ivana's long-speculated plastic surgery change-over in 1989 was "an attempt to make herself look more like you," Marla confirmed what Ivana had long denied: "I think she's an absolutely beautiful woman. I think she was before surgery." Asked how she had met Donald, she replied: "I don't feel like, at this time, it's appropriate for me to say. There's pending litigation, Diane." Pressed about the then much-reported, jaw-to-jaw confrontation between her and Ivana in Aspen, the previous Christmas, she took the same position: "I just don't feel like I can talk about Aspen at this time."

While she refused to answer Sawyer's question about the Aspen flap, she confirmed the gist of the story a few months later in another carefully rationed series of public statements. According to Marla, Ivana had confronted her publicly, demanding to know if she was having an affair with her husband, apparently provoked by Marla's presence in Aspen while she, Donald, and the children were vacationing there. "I looked into her eyes and asked: 'Do you love him? Are you really happy? That's what's really important.' I wanted to strike something inside of her, make her think, and I needed to know if she really cared for him. She repeated over and over again the same warning: 'I have a happy marriage. I love him, stay away from him.' But I didn't believe her. The relationship was for the eye to see—but not the heart."*

Marla's account left no doubt that, in her own eyes, Ivana was no victim. In this confrontation with the woman whose husband she was stealing, there was not only an absence of shame, there was almost a missionary righteousness. Marla saw herself as the champion of unselfish love, cast in this scene against a picturesquely snowlit day, daring to challenge her loveless rival who wanted only the trappings that came with Donald.

In fact, he had placed her at a $10,000-a-week triplex penthouse for the second Christmas season in a row, more expensive lodgings than his own family had. The night of the snowy facedown he went with her, not Ivana, to a trendy New Year's Eve party. The host took a call that night from a broken wife asking if her husband was there with another woman. Though no one understood it at the time, the marriage was over.

Donald had orchestrated the *Primetime Live* and subsequent appearances as a substitute for the public debut he and Marla had planned but been forced to cancel. Trump had intended to unveil Marla at the grand opening of the Taj back in early April and had even told casino brass to print thousands of T-shirts announcing her presence. Extra security was planned to help handle what promised to be a massive media event, and a sequined designer dress was ordered. In March, Donald leaked the story to Liz Smith's counterpart at the *Post*, Cindy Adams, whose front-page celebration of this spectacular publicity stunt went so far as to suggest that Marla's Taj debut was the culmination of a conscious Trump media strategy that began with the split in February. Donald had a "no comment" response when Cindy asked whether he had actually bet someone, as she had heard, that he could make Marla "the world's hottest name in three months," in time for the Taj opening.

But pressure from Fred Trump and other members of the family had forced him to reconsider. It was just too tawdry and gigantic a display—her hanging

---

* When Ivana finally told her own version of these events on ABC's *20/20* almost a year later, she claimed that she'd accidentally overheard her husband on the phone talking about Marla while they were in Aspen and that she'd then seen someone identified to her as a friend of Marla's in a restaurant line and told the friend to tell Marla that she loved her husband very much, not realizing that Marla was standing right behind the friend. By Ivana's account, Marla then "charged right up behind me," announcing her own love for Donald in front of the children.

on his arm before the cameras of the world, with the children back in New York and no divorce action yet filed by either party. When Donald called off Maples' Taj appearance, he'd done it unilaterally, even catching Marla by surprise. Marla's press agent, whose consultant fee was paid by Trump, insisted at first she'd be there, claiming that "if they decided she shouldn't go, Marla and Donald [would] issue a joint statement." Subsequent news reports indicated a testiness between them that lasted weeks. But the opening had come and gone—with little pizzazz other than a laser light show and a genie—and Marla had remained in hiding. Instead, the Sawyer interview, and a curious late April appearance at the White House Correspondents Association dinner in Washington, were her coming-out parties, with Donald far away on both occasions.

Then, in late May, she and Donald finally made their first public appearance— at Elton John's concert at the Taj—but they sat with different people. She was still riding Trump limos and helicopters and showing up on the arm of a Trump stand-in, casino executive Ed Tracy. In early June, she and Donald went out to Las Vegas for a publishers' convention to peddle *Surviving at the Top*, his up-coming second book. It was the same day the *Wall Street Journal* ran the first Donald's-broke story, exposing the secret sessions with his bankers. A few days later, the *Post* reported that she was going to accompany Donald to the birthday celebration, even predicting a public kiss in a story just hours before the party.

But, in a repeat of the Taj turnaround, she was not present. Fred had again put a stop to her appearing. He reportedly said he would not be at the party if she was. Fred had not only directly urged Donald to patch his marriage up, he'd gone to business associates he believed Donald listened to and tried to convince them to do the same. They had, but there was no changing Donald's mind. At Ivana's birthday luncheon months earlier, Mary had pointedly laid claim to Ivana as a daughter—forget the in-law part, she said. The family pressure about Marla, as well as Ivana's lawsuit and other factors, were contributing to his growing isolation, cutting him off from her in the midst of the tensest days of his life.

Nonetheless, he was determined that night to show the crowd in the Crystal Ballroom, designed by Ivana and built during her reign at the Castle, that all the pressure wasn't getting to him. The payment he'd missed the day before was the first default in his life. As of that moment, he had nine days left of the grace period granted by the bondholder trustee before the casino could legally be taken away from him. It was a time for grit, and Donald had it.

Escorted onstage by a Buster Poindexter–led marimba band, showered by confetti dumped from a ceiling duct, surrounded by stars like Peter Allen and Joe Piscopo, Donald opened with some shots at the media, claiming he'd "gotten bad publicity" all his life "but it gets worse every year." He reminded the cheering crowd of his role in getting a site for the New York City Convention Center and rebuilding the Wollman Rink, expressing his certainty that the Taj would be a similar success. He even tried to make a joke out of the financial squeeze he was in, pointing to the Castle's new, thirty-two-year-old president, Tony Calandra, and quipping: "I hire Tony to run this place and a couple of days later I default on the bonds." (One of a rash of inexperienced new Trump executives, Calandra, who had suddenly been elevated from a junket sales supervisor to casino president, would be replaced in a matter of months.)

Donald thanked Robert, Blaine, and his sister, Elizabeth, and then praised "the world's best father," calling Fred to his feet for a spotlighted moment of appreciation. He tried the same upbeat tease he'd used that morning on the Boardwalk. "Some would say there's a method to my madness," he said with a smile. "Well, I have a few surprises ahead." The buzzword among those who heard that message and still believed in him was that he was deliberately causing the dramatic decline in the bond prices for all three of his casinos because he secretly planned to buy them cheap. The power of his hype was so strong that ordinarily savvy observers bought into these theories, including a prevailing hypothesis that he'd precipitated the entire crisis to mislead Ivana into a two-bit settlement.

Though a few dozen "entertainment reporters" were allowed to attend the festivities, straight news coverage was barred, and an army of twenty to thirty roving security agents enforced that edict. Most of the invited guests were the connoisseurs of risk Donald had come to admire. As he put it in *Surviving at the Top*, "I love the excitement of the scene, and I love hanging around with important casino customers. These are colorful, gutsy, unpretentious guys who usually come from modest backgrounds but who've managed to live by their wits and live rather lavishly." He'd compared this crowd with Ivana's "society people" and found them "far more attractive, and certainly more real."

One of the reasons for Donald's affinity for the high-roller crowd may have been that so many of them had other business interests that could be helpful to him. For example, one birthday party celebrant, Manny Ciminello, a frequent big spender at Trump casinos, was a construction contractor Donald used in New York whose ties with the racketeers dominating the city's concrete business had been spelled out by federal prosecutors in open court just a couple of years earlier. Donald knew that Ciminello's joint-venture partner in a project he had built for Trump was a company secretly owned by Paul Castellano, head of the Gambino crime family, and Fat Tony Salerno, boss of the Genovese family. In fact, the concrete contract Trump had awarded this partnership had become a count in the racketeering indictment of Salerno.

Ciminello—whose close friend and sometimes traveling companion city councilman Jerry Crispino was the chairman of the key committee that passed on all major development projects in New York—was a birthday symbol of the seedy characters who had often appeared in Donald's life, just like "good old boy" Bucky Howard.

The rest of the party show was a mix of the absurd and the jaded. A huge model of the Trump Shuttle, his hemorrhaging airline, was rolled onstage in front of replicas of the Taj, Castle, and Trump Plaza, all of which were in dire trouble. Out of the Shuttle stepped Robin Leach and a co-host, comic Freddie Roman. Leach blathered on about what a bad time it was to be doing a show on the rich, but urged the crowd not to count Donald out, insisting that he was the best there was and that he had made a career out of doing what others said couldn't be done. Leach was already filming his umpteenth *Lifestyles* show built around Trump—a feature on the Taj.

Dolly Parton and Elton John appeared on giant screens to wish Donald a happy birthday, with Parton asking to work the Taj instead of her regular Castle gig and promising to charge only $100,000 a show. Joe Piscopo did his Sinatra imitation on the birthday song, followed by a string of Jap gags—oblivious to the presence of several Japanese high rollers in the front rows—even cracking that Atlantic City would be owned by the Japanese if it weren't for Donald. A George Bush imitator declared Donald should be President. Donald introduced Edwin Edwards, the three-time former governor of Louisiana who had survived two federal felony trials, as "the past and future governor." A chorus line in skintight outfits gyrated around chairs singing longingly about Donald's dollars. Then Andrew Dice Clay appeared on another giant screen to thank Donald for the Taj hookers, saying they had stamps on their asses to show they'd had their shots. It had to be the high-water mark of Donald's day.

One more birthday surprise awaited Donald: a Monday morning Neil Barsky story, greeting Trump on his return to New York and announcing on the front page of the *Wall Street Journal* that Donald had personally guaranteed between $500 and $600 million in loans. The story—which, it turned out, understated the extraordinary level of Donald's personal exposure by $300 million—unveiled a recklessness not even Donald's longtime critics had imagined. It was one thing to saddle his properties with debt—if one of them couldn't carry the load, he could just walk away from it and leave it to the bank. Guarantees, on the other hand, were a chain around his own neck, leashing him to the banks. The only advantage to Donald of his $840 million in personal guarantees was that the sheer weight of his loans made it possible for him to pull some of his biggest lenders down with him, but most of the tug at the moment was coming from the other end.

After weathering Trump's libel threats, letters to his publisher, phone-call blasts berating him as "a disgrace," and attempts to get sources like Marvin Roffman to claim he had misquoted them, the thirty-two-year-old, painfully careful Barsky had managed, in the end, to publicly expose for the first time the true vulnerability of the Trump fortune. As Barsky explained it, in a story drawn from the accounts of "several bankers" anonymously cooperating exclusively with him, Donald's future choices had narrowed to bankruptcy or an "orderly liquidation of his assets under the watchful eye of his creditors." Barsky's story was the bankers' public warning that Donald's huge personal liability left him no choice but to turn over to them the authority to divide up and sell off much of his noncasino empire. Barsky reported that the banks had demanded that Donald hire a new CEO and CFO to run the Trump Organization, and while Donald eventually blocked the effort to replace him, a new top financial officer would soon be hired who would report directly to the banks.

At 5:30 P.M. on the tenth and last day of the grace period, the Castle bondholder trustee received his check from the banks. The payment was the first manifestation of a tentative agreement Donald and his banks had finally reached. The agreement suspended the annual $85 million in interest payments on a billion in Trump bank debt and deferred any action on Donald's personal guarantees for up to five years. The banks also agreed to extend a new $65 million loan to him—to be used to cover the $20 million shortfall on the Castle and to meet the operating expenses of an otherwise destitute organization. The reason the bailout had come so perilously down to the wire was that the major banks had had a hard time selling the agreement to the more than sixty other banks that had syndicated pieces of the Trump deals, particularly the French, German, and Japanese banks, whose initial reaction was to leave it to the American banks to bail out their national icon. Finally, all but one German bank came aboard, and that one agreed not to file suit in an attempt to overturn the new deal.

In return for this largess, Donald pledged as security virtually everything he owned, including the few properties with equity, like his remaining commercial and residential holdings at Trump Tower and his stake in Fred Trump's family businesses. Only his three personal residences and the dream site on the West Side were salvaged. The agreement permitted the banks to compel the sale of any

Trump asset after three years, and it put in place a sliding scale giving them from 50 percent to 90 percent of the profits on any sale. It also barred Trump from guaranteeing any further secured or unsecured debt, a bank demand that suggested that the bankers felt Donald had to be protected from shooting himself again. His real concession, though, was more metaphysical than financial: He agreed not to be Donald.

While the banks would no longer allow him to run his empire or make his deals, they decided to let him go on living as if he was still on top. The agreement restricted him, in a manner of speaking, to a monthly stipend of $450,000 for personal expenses, not including upkeep on his boat, jet, and helicopter, as well as the interest costs on his personal credit lines. The absurdity of his personal allotment—more than the salary of the chairman of the principal bank backing the deal, Citibank, and tallying $14,516 a day—baffled even real billionaires. "I have no idea how to spend $450,000 a month," said an anonymous one to the *Times*. "It's just phenomenal." As absurd as the expense allowance was, it was a new restraint on Donald, limiting his capacity to use his organization as a sinkhole, and stopping him from using it, as he had for years, to buy whatever he wanted. Since the allowance would in fact be reduced every year over the course of the multiyear agreement it was also a message about Donald's long-term personal condition. The excess that had once been part of his appeal had suddenly become a subject of widespread ridicule, particularly now that his mound of debt had made it clear that he had been paying for this lifestyle with the borrowed bank deposits of ordinary people.

But Donald was not defenseless in the face of this crisis. In his days on the top, he had often shared with interviewers his views of life, and while his imagination routinely ran away with him in these celebrity sessions, his oft-repeated philosophy had the ring of ingrained true belief to it. He told one reporter in the midst of the bank brouhaha: "I take things very much as they come. I deal with the cards that are dealt me. And I think I do it well. I'm very much a fatalist. I always have been but I'm more so now." In an interview a year before Donald's downfall, onetime Trump confidant Tony Schwartz said: "There's a part of Donald in the rare moments when he's not moving at about 140 miles an hour—and I have heard him articulate it in those moments—that he assumes on some level that this is a big bubble, and it's going to burst at some point. He is very fatalistic. He will say . . . as fast as you skyrocketed up is how fast you can plummet. He has told me he's looked at what happens to people who've been at the center of attention one day when their deals are working, or they've just accomplished something of moment. One of the people he looks at as a perfect example is Jimmy Carter. Here's a guy who was President and the day Ronald Reagan took over consigned him to a level of anonymity that you otherwise might associate with a traveling salesman."

Even though he blew his own horn until he was winded, when pressed about how he'd accomplished so much so quickly, as one member of a *Donahue* audience had, Donald conceded: "I don't know. It just all sort of happened." Of course, if his success was merely a consequence of fate, that same fate was also a ready explanation for failure.

To this fatalism was added a theory of genetic determinism, a set of principles that were as close as Donald ever got to grappling with the complexity of life. He had begun years earlier talking about the shaping power of heredity. "You're either born with it or you're not," he said. "Ability can be honed, perfected or neglected. But the day Jack Nicklaus came into this world, he had more innate ability to play golf than anybody else." Donald loved to tell the tale of a friend with an IQ of 190 whose nerves were shot worrying about a puny home mortgage. "Yet here I am," he concluded, "buying the shuttle, the Plaza, and I don't lose an ounce of sleep over any of it. That's lucky genes."

The irony was that this strange man who feverishly tried to control everything around him believed in a fundamental way that his own ultimate fate had been decided in his parents' bedroom. This faith never paralyzed him as he made his way to the top, but it comforted him on his way down.

Perhaps because of this credo, Donald never had any patience with the past or interest in the future. "He is the most present human being I ever met," said one intimate. "He lives entirely in the moment. He doesn't define himself through relationships or through some spiritual interests or concerns. He defines himself and redefines himself from day to day by what happens in his life." At the same time, those who have been close to him say he is "the most public person" they've known, inextricably intertwining the business and personal parts of his life so that "they almost can't be pulled apart."

Each of these elements of his character helped him face the simultaneous convulsions of divorce and financial demise with courage. His fatalism allowed him to hold himself blameless; his determinism convinced him he'd be a winner again; his fixation on the moment enabled him to accept his new status without nostalgia or foreboding. On the public stage where he'd played out every act of his life he was too much of a showman to be embarrassed by a single disastrous performance. The cumulative effect of this life view—so deep-seated it appeared to be instinctual—was the confidence that all of this would come and go.

"What are your goals?" he was once asked in a television interview when he was at the peak of his success. "Goals?" he repeated, apparently taken aback by this foreign concept, unable to imagine a sense of purpose grander than a scorecard. "You keep winning and you win and you win, and you win," he said in the midst of the crisis, reflecting on his better days. "You keep hitting and hitting and hitting. And then somehow it doesn't mean as much as it used to." Donald liked to recall his favorite *Twilight Zone* episode, which featured a venal man who died in an accident, was offered any wish he wanted, and declared: "I want to win, win, win. Everything I want, I want to get. I want to get the most beautiful women. I want to get the beautiful this and that. I want to never lose again." Then, as Donald recounted the story, the man was shown playing pool, winning every time. "Everything he did, he won," said Donald, until the godlike figure who'd granted his wish came back to the man. "And the man said, 'If this is Heaven, let me go to Hell.' And the person said, 'You are in Hell.'" Donald was intrigued by the notion that his own skyrocketing success, like his now departed wife, had come to bore him. He anticipated what he called his "resurrection" in conversations with associates, but sensed that "maybe new victories won't be the same as the first couple."

From the moment he signed off on the broad terms of the bank plan in late June, Donald knew it would be years before he could make another headline-grabbing acquisition—and perhaps he would never do so again. He knew he would lose large chunks of his once prized holdings and that the only deal making he would do in the coming years would be to try to protect what he could from the bondholders and banks—certainly not the makings of a glamorous new memoir. He had threatened the bank consortium to take himself out of play—to put himself in bankruptcy and tie up their assets in court for years—but at some point in the negotiations, they realized it was bluster. Bankruptcy closed the curtain. Anything short of it left him with room for maneuvering: His imagination could still soar, the play could still go on.

The bankers had, in fact, considered an extraordinary and tentative counteroffer—a buyout that would give him a lump sum of between $50 million and $100 million in exchange for all his equity and assets. The take-out price would have been enough for him to bide his time and start anew, but Trump saw it as a retreat. He still had the West Side to rebuild, a project that could again make him larger than life. The casinos could turn around in an up market. What would Trump Tower be without Trump? The Plaza would either remain his ultimate trophy, or be sold at a ransom price, rescuing him.

He would hang on. The world could gloat about which of his perilous fascinations had damaged him more—the $1.3 billion in casino junk bonds that he could not now repay or what some labeled "the junk blond" who had helped destroy the public image he'd so meticulously invented. He had already been exposed by the crisis as a modern Wizard of Oz—a booming voice box hiding behind a drawn curtain. He would not be burdened now by hindsight or self-doubt; he knew how to sidestep the bodies at his door. In addition to trusting no one else, was he now supposed to mistrust himself?

He did not expect happiness. Before the crash, he'd told his only real confidants, the incessant interviewers: "I don't consider myself happy or sad, I actually consider myself content. I love what I've achieved. I don't think of myself as being happy or sad. I don't have time enough to think about it. I must go on to other things." His life, he believed, had prepared him for just this moment.

With all the rooms he controlled, stretched across the Eastern Seaboard, he had frequently claimed that a studio was enough for him. And now, up in his Trump Tower exile apartment, he in effect lived in one. Armed with a channel changer, he had discovered that an empty apartment and season of gut-checking challenges was enough to keep him stirring restlessly until 4:00 A.M. most nights, when he finally got his three or four hours' sleep. He could be heard boasting to associates that the extra hours of loneliness gave him an edge over his sleeping competitors. That, finally, was his magic: He could find an upside anywhere.

2

ROOTS OF THE EMPIRE

Here hungry men, raw from the shops and fields, idylls and romances in their minds, builded them an empire, crying glory in the mud . . . earnest, patient, determined, unschooled in even the primer of refinement, hungry for something the significance of which, when they had it, they could not even guess.

—*Theodore Dreiser,* THE TITAN

FRED TRUMP was in trouble. But then, in March of 1934—almost six decades before his son's financial free-fall in a similarly swooning economy—who wasn't?

Trouble was a new experience for the twenty-nine-year-old, six-foot, blond and blue-eyed builder who claimed to have already finished 300 homes, starting in the working-class Woodhaven section of Queens seven years earlier and moving on to the elegance of that borough's upper-crust Jamaica Estates. But even self-promoter Trump conceded he hadn't built a home in two years, and it was more likely closer to three. What he didn't mention was that the Depression had reduced him to running a supermarket in Queens, forced out of the housing business he'd entered with such confidence only a few years earlier.

On March 9 Trump submitted a letter bid to buy out of bankruptcy the prime asset of a legendary mortgage servicing company that had long dominated the Brooklyn and Queens housing markets, the suddenly infamous House of

Lehrenkrauss. A network of Lehrenkrauss family companies had issued $26 million in mortgages over a period of fifty years for 40,000 homes, mostly to German Americans. But the companies had collapsed in late 1933, awash in fraud. The day before Fred Trump submitted his bid for the servicing piece of this once grand empire, sixty-seven-year-old patriarch Julius Lehrenkrauss stood somberly in court, dressed in a black sack coat, striped trousers, and wing collar, and listened to a state judge sentence him to a five-year prison term in Sing Sing on a larceny conviction. At the sentencing, Lehrenkrauss's attorney declared that Lehrenkrauss "pleaded no self-pity, and is willing to take his punishment like a man," announcing in a thunderous voice: "This day marks the termination of three generations of a proud family gone to destruction."

Like a number of other speculators Trump offered money up front to acquire the Lehrenkrauss list of serviceable mortgages. In addition to his $1,750 purchase price, Trump also offered to pay the bankrupt estate $500 for every $250,000 in mortgages he was actually able to service once he obtained the lists. The bankruptcy court estimated that whoever won the bid might be able to gain control of $6 million to $9 million in viable mortgages, drawing fees for collecting and distributing the monthly payments. Fred saw the lists as his way back into real estate.

In a succession of letters to the court, Trump tried to portray himself as the candidate best able to salvage Lehrenkrauss's shattered business, even though his only prior mortgage experience was the servicing of piecemeal mortgages he and his mother had sometimes granted to purchasers of the homes he'd built. The letters were a series of exaggerations, including the claim that he'd been in the building business for ten years, when public records established that he'd only been an active builder from 1927 to 1932.

These boasts were the public debut of hyperbole as a Trump trademark, beginning a seven-decade, father/son business career that would even distort the family's origins in the process. Trump mythology—promulgated first in Fred Trump interviews in the forties and fifties, and later embellished by Donald— would depict Fred as a struggling carpenter's helper who miraculously lifted himself by his teenaged bootstraps into a leading role in Queens home building. In fact, Fred's father, also named Fred, who had emigrated from Germany at the age of fifteen in 1885, already had substantial real estate holdings before he died of pneumonia in May of 1918, only forty-nine years old.

The senior Trump held fourteen mortgages at the time of his death, valued at over $20,000; owned outright six pieces of property, including several buildable lots; had deposits totaling over $3,500 in three different bank accounts;

and owned fifty shares of preferred stock valued at $3,662. With life insurance policies and loans due him, the total value of Trump's estate exceeded $36,000, a small fortune at the time. While Trump legend would describe him as the operator of "a moderately successful restaurant," his death certificate accurately listed his occupation as "the real estate business."

This was hardly the only misconception in the biography of Donald's father, Fred, sewn together over time by the family: He would be described in Donald's bestseller, *The Art of the Deal*, as born in New Jersey to Swedish parents, when in fact he was born in the Bronx to German parents (his mother, Elizabeth, was born in Germany in 1880). The Trumps would likewise claim that he had built his first house in 1922 or 1923, right after graduating from high school, when he actually built it in 1927—a fast enough jump-start for most titans, but insufficiently miraculous for Trump.

Trump's letters to the Lehrenkrauss bankruptcy court also debuted another family trademark that would later serve his son well. "During my building operations I spent thousands of dollars on advertising," Fred wrote. "The name Trump in connection with real estate is very well known throughout Queens County." Trump's letters to the court were written on F. C. Trump Construction Corporation stationery, with the logo "Permanence, Comfort" wrapped around a thumb-sized drawing of a chaletlike home.

Trump appeared alone at the first court date, a day when the city was blanketed with six inches of snow and when hundreds of unemployed men rioted after lining up outside sanitation department shops, trying unsuccessfully to get shoveling work. In the crowded hearing room on the seventh floor of the post office building in downtown Brooklyn, the young, mustachioed Trump was solicitous and self-assured. He had an erect, almost military bearing, musclebound and purposeful. The court stenographer mistakenly listed him as an attorney, since he was representing himself, and he made a brief oral statement to the court in a thick German accent. Every other bidder was represented by counsel, and most had substantial servicing experience. If Trump won the servicing business, he said, he promised to open a new mortgage company, relocating his base of business operations to Brooklyn, where Lehrenkrauss had been headquartered. He even had his site picked out—the same office building at 66 Court Street where the bankruptcy trustees had their own offices. The only other Queens-based bidder, insurance broker William Demm, presented an offer that clearly topped Trump's, and those of all the rest of the bidders, with a guaranteed $2,100 cash payment and the same pledge to pay $500 for each quarter of a million in mortgages actually serviced.

But in an apparent reference to both Trump and Demm, the lawyer for a third bidder complained about "two individuals who, there is no doubt in my mind, do not run a servicing company at all; and are trying to make a bid to buy something for nothing." The mystery to many in the court was how these two entrepreneurs had gotten on the short list invited to bid on this potentially lucrative franchise in the first place.

Hovering over the courtroom carcass of the House of Lehrenkrauss, predictably enough, was the all-powerful Brooklyn Democratic machine. Lawyers tied to it had already insinuated themselves in every aspect of the bankruptcy process, and none was more influential than thirty-three-year-old Charlie Kriger. Appointed by the creditors as a trustee of the estate to obtain the greatest value for the disposed assets of the failed firm, Kriger, like every good soldier reared in a Brooklyn clubhouse, heeded rather the beckoning command of an organization that made and broke men daily.

Kriger came from the Seneca Democratic Club, then ruled by a major power in Brooklyn politics, Frank V. Kelly. Kriger understood that Kelly, and the machine Kelly embodied, would shape the rest of his life. Lying ahead for young Kriger were machine-engineered appointments to several of the juiciest political posts controlled by the party—chairman of the city's Board of Assessors, which ruled on property tax assessments; state commissioner of purchase, which controlled millions in no-bid contracts; and federal area administrator of the Small Business Administration, the discretionary dispenser of low-interest loans. Kriger would prove in a few short days just what a hungry party player he was.

When the Lehrenkrauss bankruptcy hearings occurred, Kelly, himself a Lehrenkrauss shareholder, was in the midst of taking over the entire county party. Handpicked by John McCooey, the master of Brooklyn politics since 1909, who had died the previous January, Kelly was temporarily ruling the party as part of a triumvirate of leaders. By September of 1934, Kelly would shunt aside the other two and begin a ten-year reign as the ironfisted, solitary boss of Brooklyn. Though up to then just a small-time Queens builder, Fred Trump had already apparently managed to open lines of communication with Frank Kelly's Brooklyn boys. Old-timers believe he had somehow already gotten to know the late McCooey, and he was seen lunching with Kelly at the Montauk, a social club where the bachelor boss lived.

Fred Trump discovered that wintry day in 1934, however, that he was up against some formidable competition in the hunt to take over the right to service Lehrenkrauss mortgages. Henry Davenport, attorney for Home Title, a company with ties to McCooey's Madison Club, appeared personally and offered far less than Trump or Demm up front, but said he would pay $250 more than either for every million dollars in mortgages he actually serviced. Davenport could boast of $60 million in mortgages presently under contract, compared to Trump's meager claim of a half million. Kriger, who would formally recommend a bidder to the court-appointed referee in a couple of weeks, openly pronounced the Home bid "the best" as soon as Davenport finished presenting it.

The referee who would actually pick the winner, Theodore Stitt, had a reputation for being tough and independent. Unlike Kriger, who was handpicked by the creditors and shareholders of the Lehrenkrauss company, Stitt, a Republican, was the choice of a Republican federal judge. After Kriger finished his presentation of the bids, Stitt announced that bidders could improve their offers but that once the hearing closed all offers would be final. Trump's competitor from Queens, William Demm, immediately improved his bid to the same $750 per million in mortgages as Davenport, but Fred held firm. Demm was now $1,350 ahead of Davenport up front and bidding the same amount over the long term. Trump clearly appeared to be out of the running.

But when Stitt reconvened the hearing two weeks later, on March 26, Davenport did not reappear. Not only were Demm and Trump the only two of the half dozen original bidders who did actually show up, but they had since formed a partnership and were now submitting a joint bid, represented by the same lawyer, Bill Hyman. Hyman, Demm, and Trump had already trekked out to a Brooklyn high school to present their offer to the hundreds of outraged shareholders and mortgagees of Lehrenkrauss who had gathered there, negotiating a deal with them that would permit the shareholders to buy back the servicing franchise if a viable new company could be reorganized out of the bankruptcy within ninety days. Since the shareholders were concerned that a valuable asset of the bankrupt firm was being sold too cheaply, this plan seemed to offer some hope that it could be recouped. But the likelihood that a reorganization could be completed in only three months—if at all—was so dim that the offer was really nothing more than a skillful sham. It did mean, however, that the law firm representing the shareholders would be an advocate of the Trump bid in and out of court.

Kriger opened the hearing with the opinion that the combined Trump/Demm bid was the best; he barely mentioned the Davenport submission. He announced that the Trump bid was also favored by the equity receiver, John Curtin, a lawyer who was a personal adviser to boss Frank Kelly and had been chosen by the creditors to manage the few solvent wings of the Lehrenkrauss empire. Referee Stitt was faced with a thoroughly stacked deck of support for Trump—trustee Kriger, the receivers, and the shareholder group. But suddenly the lawyer for a new bidder from Manhattan appeared and announced a startling offer that was far better on its face (a $2,500 deposit and $850 long-term payment) than Trump's. When Kriger behaved as if he'd been ambushed, the lawyer claimed that he had approached Kriger about it before the hearing, but had been rebuffed. Kriger threw up a series of smoke-screen objections, supported by Hyman, who kept stressing the advantage of the side deal Trump and Demm had cut with the shareholders. In the face of this pressure, the new bidder agreed to double the window of opportunity for the shareholders to buy back the servicing unit, extending it to 180 days.

Referee Stitt was clearly tempted by the new offer and pressed Kriger, the only one of the three trustees present at this decisive hearing, about taking some time to review it. "I don't think that it would be necessary to make an inspection" of the bid, Kriger insisted, claiming to speak for the other trustees, to whom it had never been presented, and complaining that an adjournment would be "disadvantageous" because "the longer we wait the less we have to sell." Stitt observed that no one would "lose much ground between now and ten o'clock tomorrow morning," but he was met with a torrent of objections, including an attempt by a lawyer for the trustees to tally the votes of everyone present in the courtroom about whether or not the Trump bid should be accepted. "We are not going to decide this on any basis of vox populi," a pressured Stitt declared.

Not much changed overnight: The Trump group extended its window of opportunity for the shareholders to 180 days, and Kriger came back with some questions about the Manhattan bidder's finances, most of which were quickly dispensed with. Stitt finally relented nonetheless, and Fred Trump was back in the housing business. For the next thirty years, he would build principally in Brooklyn, attaching himself to a variety of powerful party leaders and only occasionally dabbling in his onetime Queens base. Just what strings Fred Trump pulled to win the Lehrenkrauss sweepstakes remains something of a mystery, and he may well have succeeded as much by his wits as by his connections. But the vigorous support he received from the Democratic Party players suggests that he was their designated winner, making Lehrenkrauss the introductory venture for an alliance between Trump and the Brooklyn organization that would last a lifetime.

After the deal was concluded, Fred's partner, William Demm, stepped out of the picture almost immediately and Trump became the sole stockholder of Metropolitan Investors, the company he formed to take over the Lehrenkrauss mortgage list. Bill Hyman became Fred's personal lawyer, representing him for the next fifteen years. Trump and Hyman soon began to use the Lehrenkrauss list as a kind of scouting system, buying out of foreclosure defaulting properties lost in the Lehrenkrauss disaster.

Within months of winning the bid, Trump would also form a partnership with Charles A. O'Malley, the appraiser selected by Frank Kelly's receiver friends to put a value on over a thousand Lehrenkrauss properties. In 1935 O'Malley and Fred Trump began to build what would eventually be hundreds of new houses in the Flatbush section of Brooklyn. Trump also wound up a regular customer of a company called Consolidated, the borough's preeminent politically connected insurance broker, which then employed a low-level functionary out of McCooey's old Madison Club, Abraham Lindenbaum, as its lawyer. "Bunny," as his wife, Belle, nicknamed him, would eventually become the most important clubhouse dealmaker in Fred Trump's career.

In Frank Kelly's universe of geographically distinct but intimately intertwined local political clubs, it didn't matter which constellation Fred attached himself to, as long as he became identified with one or more. His ties would, indeed, develop with the clubs where he did most of his Brooklyn building. These relationships—particularly with the Flatbush dynasty of the Steingut family and the Coney Island dominion of Kenny Sutherland—would prove to be the central determining factors in the evolution of his own empire in Brooklyn over the next three decades.

Fred laid the groundwork for this empire with a series of one- and two-family homes in the Crown Heights and Flatbush sections of central Brooklyn, the neighborhood where John McCooey's powerful Madison Club was based. McCooey had founded it in 1905, and it rapidly became the county's most powerful club, with over a thousand members. As county leader, McCooey had transformed Brooklyn by the 1920s into a solidly Democratic borough, with 125,000 more registered Democrats than old Tammany Hall in Manhattan, the legendary bulwark of the state Democratic Party.

A McCooey protégé, Irwin Steingut, had been elected the club's Democratic leader a few weeks after McCooey's death in 1934. Steingut had been the assemblyman from the district since McCooey handpicked him in 1921, and he became the assembly minority leader in 1930. When the Democrats won control of the assembly in 1934, Steingut became speaker. The balding, impeccably dressed Steingut, who wore tailored and monogrammed shirts with monogrammed pocket squares stuffed in his dark suits, had been introduced to McCooey by the leader of Tammany when Steingut moved to Brooklyn from the Lower East Side.

Irwin's father, Simon, had been such an important cog in the Tammany machine, a conduit between it and the teeming Jewish ghetto, that he had held the title "Mayor of Second Avenue" for almost thirty years.

Irwin had gone to law school, but never passed the bar. Instead he set up his own small insurance office at 66 Court, the same building where Fred Trump first opened Metropolitan Investors, the company that took over the Lehrenkrauss mortgage list. Steingut sold the insurance on the mob-run Brooklyn piers. He dabbled in state-regulated racetracks, buying stock that soared in value and putting it in a relative's married name and in the name of other fronts. He collected lucrative receivership appointments through the clubhouse-controlled courthouse, at one point even taking over the site where the Coliseum now stands in midtown Manhattan, a site he sold to his dear friend Joe Kennedy. With a cigar forever between his teeth and a barber shaving him every morning, he remained the undaunted caricature of an autocratic city boss, unapproachable on the street but warm and loyal at close quarters. So friendly with FDR that he regularly took his son Stanley to swim at the president's Hyde Park home, Irwin was a skillful champion of liberal Democratic legislation through years when the assembly was dominated by conservative upstate Republicans.

Steingut watched a tightly drawn network of social and political friendships begin to develop around the Madison Club. He was able to place his own brilliant young counsel, Nat Sobel, in the governor's office in the midthirties, and Sobel, in turn, brought an energetic young accountant named Abe Beame into the club. Sobel, Beame, and Bunny Lindenbaum, the lawyer from Consolidated, fast became an inseparable trio, in and out of the Madison orbit. Though he was a lawyer, Bunny functioned primarily as a public relations man for the politically wired Consolidated, and it was in that context that he met Fred Trump in the 1930s, when Trump began using and referring business to the company. It wasn't until the late forties that Trump went to Irwin Steingut needing help with a legal problem and, according to members of the Steingut and Lindenbaum families, the leader suggested he use Bunny as his lawyer. Bunny was busily setting up his own practice then, and in 1948 Fred became his new firm's first client.

Fred became part of the circle that included Sobel (who was elected a county judge in 1942 in a campaign managed by Bunny), Beame (who assumed the powerful post of deputy budget director for the city in the midforties), and Lindenbaum (who would ride his Madison connections to a $6 million personal fortune). Sobel remembers Trump picking the group up in his limo for dinners in Manhattan or Queens—at a time, he said, when limos were a rare sight. "He had an amazing knowledge of the tax laws," Sobel recalled. "It was the tax laws, he used to say, that compelled him to go from project to project."

Trump also became the single most important builder within the Madison Club district and a donor to the club. Club members and other neighbors began buying new Trump homes as early as November 1935, when he finished his first model in the Cortelyou Road area. In the next few years, he built at such a pace that he attracted newspaper coverage by setting up floodlights to enable his crews to continue working into the night. Trump claimed in news reports that, between 1936 and early 1939, he built 700 single-family homes on various nearby sites, most of them on an old Barnum & Bailey circus grounds within the Madison Club district. The same 1939 news stories described Trump as under thirty years old, however, when he was already thirty-four. His tendency to inflate the already grand also affected his housing production numbers—at one point he said he'd built 2,000 homes by 1935, when his Lehrenkrauss court submission had the number in 1934 at only 300. A flurry of stories through 1940 announced one new Trump project after another—hundreds of Flatbush units, again principally on circus land. The coverage was stirred by constant press releases and the stories continued to marvel at how Trump, described as "an example of the energetic American," could achieve so much at such a young age. But Fred's age was so consistently understated he seemed to be standing still against time.

The matchbox homes were affordable attached brick houses with six steps up to a brick porch and a garage beneath. They typically sold for about $6,000 and were as solid a buy as there was in the city. Trump was a driven man—building faster than anyone else, selling to working families and helping to make their lives whole, even converting his own industry into a kind of moral crusade. He became the statewide leader of a 1939 movement against what he regarded as the humbug adversary from another era—the apartment. Insisting that working families could own their own homes for monthly payments cheaper than their apartment rents, he tried to get the slogan "Own Your Own Home" printed on New York license plates. It was a doomed campaign, and indeed, within just a few years, Fred himself would begin a second career as a great apartment builder.

The financing for Trump's Depression-era housing came from the newly created Federal Housing Administration, and each dollar of it was approved by Tommy Grace, a bouncy little Irish politician who frequently visited the Madison Club and was enamored of Irwin Steingut. The product of the Democratic Club in Bay Ridge run by district leader Tommy Wogan, Grace was named the state's first FHA director in 1935, and among the first applications he approved for financing was Fred Trump's.

By the beginning of 1941, however, Fred Trump had pretty much exhausted the large tracts of available land in the Madison Club's Flatbush area and was beginning to move his base of operations out toward the eastern shore of Brooklyn, buying up valuable tracts in Brighton Beach and Bensonhurst. He announced the development of 200 homes a block from the beach in Brighton and the purchase of a pivotal fifty-five-acre tract near Bensonhurst Park right off the Belt Parkway, where he planned another 700 houses. While he continued to strengthen his Madison ties throughout the forties and fifties, he now also had to make his accommodations with the clubs that ruled the shore.

Trump's new base was the political turf of two neighboring clubs, Tommy Wogan's and Kenny Sutherland's. The Wogan club had long been a weak sister to that of Sutherland, who was the dominant Democratic boss along the eastern shore. Trump's Bensonhurst site was just three blocks from Sutherland's club, which was located in a three-story white shingle house near the bay. If Irwin Steingut was a polished rascal, Sutherland was a street rat. His United Democratic Club was run as a part-time casino, with an escape hatch hidden in the back so that gamblers (and Kenny himself) could escape to an upstairs apartment with the cash during a raid. Legend has it that he carried a pistol in one pocket and a blackjack in the other. A mere five-foot-four, Sutherland was called "The Little Giant of Coney Island" and reigned as the district's party leader from 1919 to his death in 1953.

In the 1920s Sutherland counted among his close friends Frankie Yale, the borough's leading mobster and mentor of young Al Capone, who'd come from Naples to work at Frankie's Coney Island cabaret, the Harvard Club (Yale changed his own name from Uale when he opened the club). Yale graduated from a hit man—who was said to have handled death "like a shopkeeper changing a five-dollar bill"—to the premier rumrunner on the East Coast. Much of his liquor landed in Seagate, where Sutherland lived and earned a rumrunner reputation of his own. Yale so controlled beer distribution throughout Brooklyn that Sutherland and other district leaders were known to arrange police escorts for Yale beer deliveries to parties hosted by the political clubs. Sutherland was the classic case of a politician who made his compromises with the mob in the Prohibition era and then found himself caught in a web of relationships that outlived it.

But Sutherland was also a veteran scrapper in state politics and had formed a lasting alliance with Irwin Steingut and the rest of the Jewish leaders in Brooklyn by rallying Christian leaders behind Herbert Lehman at the 1932 state convention, renominating Lehman for lieutenant governor and positioning him to replace FDR as governor. Sutherland was punished by Tammany for betraying their candidate against Lehman and lost his Tammany-controlled job. But Sutherland quickly found a new position in the Brooklyn courthouse and became a lasting favorite of the FDR/Lehman wing of the state party. Indeed, though Tommy Grace was from Wogan's club, it was Sutherland who cleared the FHA director's appointment through the Roosevelt patronage chiefs. And it was the lure of Grace's FHA financing that led Fred out to Sutherland turf, where he started his Brighton project immediately.

The war, however, brought a shutdown of FHA funding for housing in Brooklyn, forcing Trump to suspend his ambitious Bensonhurst project and sending him off to Norfolk, Virginia, and Chester, Pennsylvania, to build FHA-backed housing near shipyards for naval officers and related uses. It was Fred's experience in wartime housing that transformed him into a large-scale builder. He moved his base of operations to Virginia, leasing a Virginia Beach home for more than two years. Bill Hyman, whose Queens law firm had represented Trump since the Lehrenkrauss hearings, left the firm, became Trump's in-house counsel, and moved to Norfolk full-time with his wife and two sons. Fred himself commuted between his family in New York and Norfolk, sometimes by plane and sometimes in his torpedo-shaped Caddy with a three-note horn.

Married on January 11, 1936, to twenty-four-year-old, Scottish-born Mary MacLeod, Fred was already the father of four-year-old Maryanne and three-year-old Fred Jr. when the war broke out. A third child, Elizabeth, was born in 1942, shortly after her mother became a naturalized citizen. Most of the time, the children and Mary, who'd emigrated to New York at the age of eighteen from Stornaway, Scotland, stayed behind in the family's modest home at 175-24 Devonshire Road in Jamaica, Queens, though they sometimes accompanied Fred to the Virginia Beach house. The brown-haired and blue-eyed Mary, a lanky five foot eight inches, spoke with a heavier accent than Fred and played the role of a low-key, behind-the-scenes housewife.

As soon as he arrived in Virginia, Fred took on a partner, James Rosati, a plastering contractor from Queens. Rosati had beaten Trump and a host of other New York builders to Norfolk and bought up key tracts of land; he and Trump worked together on a day-to-day basis, first building an 864-unit FHA development. The garden apartments, called Oakdale Homes, were located in four-family houses built within a half mile of the Norfolk Navy Base. Not only did this represent almost three times as many units as Fred had ever attempted in a Brooklyn project, but he was, for the first time, leaving his proven formula for single-family housing behind.

Continuing to manufacture news stories about everything from his views on inflation to his housing achievements, Fred was quoted in one story proudly declaring that under the new FHA 608 program, "dividends or rates of return are not limited." The stories also suddenly stopped understating his age, thereby avoiding the question of why the thirty-six-year-old hadn't put on a uniform when war broke out. In late 1943 Trump spoke at a newspaper luncheon in Norfolk, railing against a "plot" by "big business" to steal the homebuilding market from rank and file homebuilders. The takeover, sponsored by "the promoters of prefabricated homes," was being "aided and abetted by amateur social planners, visionary industrial engineers, and revolutionary architects." While "none of us practical builders are afraid," he said, "it's a shame to see the public hoodwinked by the mass of hocus propaganda circulated from coast to coast for the past year."

"These drafting board dreams of prefabricated miracle homes that will be ordered through the mail, delivered and erected in 48 hours with the ultra modern electric equipment humming, the beds made and the dinner served by automatic gremlins are just like reading from Grimm's Fairy Tales," Trump warned. Alarmed by the government's preference for prefabricated wartime homes and fearful that this might carry over into the postwar era, Fred did not hesitate to use whatever press attention he could command to advance his own business interests.

Rosati and Trump tackled a second project in Norfolk, the 296-unit Talbot Gardens, and a 400-unit development in Chester near the Sun Shipbuilding Company. In addition to the projects Fred built with Rosati, he became an investor in other Norfolk ventures and bought some outright over the years. He would remain active in the Norfolk area into the seventies, accumulating an estimated 2,400 units at his peak, traveling back and forth from New York on a regular basis. With the same keen eye for key political relationships, he wove himself into the local old-boy network, using the vice mayor's management company to run one of his projects and cutting business deals with the area's most-connected FHA builder, W. Taylor Johnson, whose partner, "Piggy" Van Patten, had been the FHA's regional director in Norfolk.

Though Fred prospered in Virginia, he shifted his focus back to Brooklyn by late 1944. This time he moved into Sutherland turf with a bang. In October, with the war still on, he announced a number of large-scale one- and two-family developments, including 475 houses on his Bensonhurst site. Although he had an FHA commitment from Tommy Grace, the difficulty of obtaining building materials delayed the projects, and Trump was still in the throes of his Cropsy Avenue development two years later, selling houses that ranged from $9,500 to

$16,500. Grace approved a doubling of the units in Trump's Bensonhurst project, bringing the total to a thousand, a massive project even by Trump standards.

Fred had by then deepened his ties to both Grace and Grace's clubhouse mentor, Sutherland. He became a regular at Tommy Grace's new fish and steak house just off the Belt Parkway and ate there, and elsewhere, with Sutherland. When Sutherland hosted his annual captains' brunch, putting on an apron and serving the election district captains who pulled out the vote for the club, Fred and Tommy Grace joined the festivities. The club treasurer boasted that he had Fred Trump's unlisted phone number in Queens and that Trump, a loyal club donor, was available to help out in any emergency.

Quietly and methodically, Trump was also assembling virtually every major tract of land available in the Bensonhurst club's home base. But this time Fred was planning to build large-scale apartment buildings. Between late 1944 and January of 1945, he bought three vast plots of land, putting together a forty-acre site. He got one parcel directly from the city. The other two were in tax arrears, and he snatched them before the city could take them, getting them cheaply and assuming the tax bill. His political connections helped keep him one step ahead of the tax man. John Hyman, the oldest son of Trump attorney Bill Hyman, remembered that his father "typically bought land for Trump out of tax-lien sales," and that he had assembled the land for what turned out to be Trump's first two great apartment complexes just that way.

It was not until June of 1947 that Fred announced the first of these complexes, Shore Haven, to be built on a fourteen-acre slice of his Bensonhurst holdings adjacent to the hundreds of one- and two-family homes he'd just finished. Trump's plan called for 1,344 apartments, patterned after his four-story Norfolk buildings but two stories taller, right off the Belt Parkway and overlooking the bay. He promised "a procession of apartments such as one might expect from a belt line production," resulting in Brooklyn's "largest privately sponsored rental housing." The FHA commitment to the plan of $9.1 million was divided into three equal parts to avoid the $5 million legal limit on project financing. Tommy Grace, who announced the financing of the housing and inspected it while it was under construction in 1948, praised it as "one of the outstanding FHA projects in the East."

Shore Haven was a dramatic change for the two-story neighborhood, requiring all sorts of city zoning, sewer, and street support. The new administration of the brawny and blue-eyed mayor, Bill O'Dwyer, himself a product of Bay Ridge Democratic politics, was immediately supportive. The project was so popular that two months after it was announced, Trump announced he'd received over

8,000 applications and was taking no more. Though Trump has always promoted himself as a builder who finished projects on time and under budget, his first large-scale development was apparently neither. By the time Shore Haven was completed Trump's FHA mortgage was increased to $10.4 million, and his own claimed construction cost was raised to $9.5 million. The project wasn't finished until mid-1949, though Trump was quoted in news stories as predicting its completion months earlier.

Despite these problems, Shore Haven was a housing and financial triumph, and its apartments were tenanted, building by building, as soon as Trump could finish them. Trump let his old friend Sutherland refer tenants for apartments, extending the club's influence in the neighborhood where a Shore Haven apartment was a precious political plum. In addition to his fees as a builder, Fred managed to take a $1.6 million profit out of the mortgage proceeds. This kind of bonanza must have made the years of building and selling a block of one-family homes to finance the next block seem like lost seasons in his life.

It was in this immediate postwar period that Fred Trump became, for the first time, a truly wealthy man, and his personal life changed, accordingly. The family left its Devonshire Street house in the midforties for a brief stay just a few blocks away—at a small, Trump-built home at 85-15 Wareham Place in the exclusive Jamaica Estates neighborhood Fred had helped create twenty years earlier as a young homebuilder. Wareham was a two-block street just off the main, tree-lined entranceway into the Estates, called Midland Parkway. While the Trumps lived on Wareham, Fred began construction on a mansion on the large lot directly behind the house, fronting on Midland. The pillared Colonial Georgian home, built on the hill that dipped down toward the parkway, was a throwback to his Virginia days. The family moved into the nine-room mansion at 85-14 Midland Parkway in 1948. Pushing Fred in the direction of a larger home was the birth, in June of 1946, of his second son, Donald. Donald was born at the very moment that Fred was making his career change from homebuilder to big-time New York apartment developer, planning Shore Haven and Beach Haven. A third son, Robert, was born the year they moved into the Midland Parkway house.

At forty-three years of age in 1948—settling into the home he would live in for the rest of his life and expand to twenty-three rooms, celebrating the birth of his fifth and final child, developing two of the largest housing projects in the nation at the same time—Fred Trump had at last conquered his own restlessness. He began giving himself lessons in relaxation on golf courses and in a stream with a rod and reel in hand. But he was still relentless on the job site—tough on everyone around him, cruelly cost-conscious, a sun-bitten taskmaster with the weathered hands of a time-honed carpenter and the sharp tongue of a boot-camp sergeant.

It was during this period that he also tried, using a public relations firm, to turn himself into a celebrity. He began issuing public pronouncements on the state of the economy, getting himself into the papers with praise for Harry Truman's tightening of the mortgage credit market. His name was even mentioned in gossip columns as a possible candidate for Queens borough president, an idea he toyed with in conversations with influential friends. In 1950, he joined General Dwight Eisenhower, Guy Lombardo, Don Ameche, Winthrop Rockefeller, and Phil Rizzuto on the then coveted list of the ten best-dressed men in America. No one who knew Fred in those days could remember anything distinctive about his dress: gray suits around a still taut body, his hair slicked straight back, a penetrating, straight-ahead look in his blue eyes.

John Hyman recalled that his father brought the family on a dinner visit to the new Trump estate in the late forties: "It was raised up above the street with a grand front lawn, and on it were two iron figures of jockeys, freshly painted in bright jockey silks." Hyman's father, back now at his own law firm, wanted desperately to become a developer in his own right, but instead he worked six days a week at his small Queens law office, primarily servicing the day-to-day needs of his number one client, Trump. "It was a big bone of contention between my mother and my father that Dad should charge Fred Trump more, but he would just tell her that if he raised his price, Fred would take away the business," said Hyman. "Fred was so frugal."

Bill Hyman had once been an athlete, a left-handed pitcher on his City College team. But he was aging badly—skinny legs, a potbelly, and broad shoulders. He pushed his bulky body hard to meet the demands of a client who had a new, urgent need every day. Then, in February of 1949, fifteen years after their meeting in a Brooklyn post office hearing room, a still young Bill Hyman, climbing up steep subway stairs, collapsed from a heart attack and died. When his estate was filed years later, it revealed that the family had to repay Fred Trump $5,873 that Trump claimed Hyman owed him and that Trump had paid the estate $8,601 in fees and disbursements owed by several Trump corporations at the time of Hyman's death. The net payment to the Hyman estate was $2,738. Trump also sent Lillian Hyman a television set.

"If he was touched by my father's death, he didn't show it," said John Hyman. The other Hyman son, David, recalled: "He paid a condolence call; he didn't get carried away." Seven months later, Fred began construction on a project whose skillful land acquisitions Hyman had helped make possible. Young John Hyman was hired as a laborer on the job, and he watched Trump briskly stride about the site each day, conferring with his two top construction superintendents. Years later, when Hyman formed his own construction consulting outfit, now a successful business based in Chicago, he went to Fred Trump and asked him to buy stock in the fledgling company. Trump, by then a multimillionaire, said he was "overextended."

When construction on Shore Haven was barely under way, Trump moved on to an even grander project, with 2,000 units, just a short trip down the Belt Parkway, called Beach Haven. Fred knew from the beginning that his profits on Beach Heaven would dwarf those of its predecessor. Beach Haven was announced with great fanfare by Fred almost two years before he had any FHA commitment to finance it, so confident was he of his FHA hooks. He also knew from the beginning that the O'Dwyer administration would do all it could to expedite the project. The *Herald Tribune* had reported in 1947, long before Trump had any of the pieces together for the project other than the land, that "to facilitate prompt housing action in this strategic location, the laying of miles of city sewers throughout the tract is now being completed."

Since, like Shore Haven, this second great project was also located in the heartland of Kenny Sutherland territory, Trump's ties to Sutherland helped him with the FHA's Grace, as well as Mayor O'Dwyer, who had been associated with Tommy Wogan's old-time club before Kenny absorbed it into his own extended empire.

Beyond these carefully nurtured clubhouse ties Trump also took advantage of a very special connection that transcended machine politics: a path of access to the living legend of New York, Robert Moses. By the late forties Moses held nine state and city titles simultaneously, which effectively meant that no public improvement larger than a sidewalk shed could be built unless he approved it. When O'Dwyer was sworn in as mayor in 1946, his first appointment was a Moses man as his top deputy and his first executive order was the creation of the new position of construction czar, responsible for supervising all public improvements. The all-encompassing title was, of course, invented for Moses, who had bestowed his good-government imprimatur on the tainted O'Dwyer during the campaign. On his first day in office, Moses brought the new mayor a construction master plan that extended from one end of the city to the other.

For forty-four years, from the 1920s to the late 1960s, Robert Moses "shaped a city and its sprawling suburbs," as Robert Caro wrote in his classic biography *The Power Broker,* "[with] a power so substantial that in the fields in which he chose to exercise it, it was not challenged seriously by any governor or mayor." Moses first assumed imperial proportions during the seven years between 1946 and 1953, which were marked by the most intensive public construction in New York history. O'Dwyer, who would eventually be forced into a Mexican exile by the abject corruption of his own regime, facilitated Moses' ascension in this period of peak power. The marriage of a machine mayor and the embodiment of disinterested public service seemed surprising on its face, but beneath the surface Moses was as enmeshed in realpolitik as any longtime New York hack, distributing the insurance work controlled by his vast and unaccountable authorities to the plutocrats of both parties, including the tiny I. Steingut brokerage house.

Trump's route to Moses was a small Court Street law firm that began representing the two builders in the thirties. The firm was headed by Raymond R. McNulty, Moses' roommate at Yale and longtime counsel in various state capacities. One of Moses' most trusted confidants, singled out by the great builder in the preface of his own autobiography, McNulty acted as Moses' campaign manager in 1934 when Moses made the blunder of his career and agreed to become the Republican candidate for governor. (Moses suffered the largest loss in state history and thereafter was wise enough to stay behind the scenes, where his power would be subject to no democratic bounds.)

After McNulty's death in 1946, the firm, in the person of McNulty's protégé, Richard Charles, continued to represent Trump and many in the closest Moses circles. Charles's widow, Kathleen, recalled the byplay of her husband's intriguing client list: "I know he had a lot of meetings with Moses and, as McNulty got older, my husband picked up a lot of the Moses matters. We would go out together, Moses and his wife, McNulty and his, and us, and the men would go off together for long talks. I believe it was through his contacts with Moses that Dick met Fred Trump. He began to represent Fred in the late 1930s and into the 1940s.

"We would go to Fred's parties. He and Mary Trump began hosting the most marvelous parties for seventy-five or a hundred people at a club in Jamaica or a hotel in Manhattan. They were a wonderful, warm family. The grandmother would bring the kids to the parties. Dick and Fred got so that they had lunch every Friday at Lundy's, the Coney Island seafood restaurant." Charles represented Trump on both Beach Haven and Shore Haven and, among other things, won zoning changes at the City Planning Commission, an agency Moses, one of seven commissioners, dominated in the forties. William Lebwohl, who worked directly for Moses for over three decades, became a regular at intimate lunches arranged by Charles during the fifties at the Brooklyn Club. Fred Trump was frequently at the lunches, which would last for hours, and a rotating crew of Brooklyn politicians would join them, including Bunny Lindenbaum, Abe Beame, and Brooklyn Borough President John Cashmore. Lebwohl, who went as Moses' stand-in and reported on the meetings to Moses, recalled that the group discussed "the state of Brooklyn, what was happening and what projects were good for the city or state." Lebwohl lived in Queens, not far from Fred, and the two began to spend time together. Fred took him on driving tours of his projects, flashing a self-deprecating kind of humor as they rolled in his limo past Beach Haven and Shore Haven. "Maybe I'll make a dime," Fred would deadpan. Lebwohl, too, was invited to Fred's gala events at a club in Jamaica, and he and Fred began actively discussing Trump's possible selection as a developer by Moses' Slum Clearance Committee, the city's federally funded urban renewal program.

By the late 1950s and early 1960s, some of the aging Charles's Trump work was passed on to another partner in the firm. Bill Mattison, a onetime assembly candidate from Wogan's old-line club, and a new young associate named Mario Cuomo, a protégé of Charles's. Fabian Palamino, another associate in the firm, recalled that he, Cuomo, and other members of the firm would trek out for luncheon business meetings to Fred's Coney Island office, where Trump would serve them all cheese sandwiches.

In addition to the layers of political and governmental relationships aiding Trump, from Charles to Sutherland, there was one other engine driving at least his Beach Haven project forward. Fred Trump, who'd done Shore Haven and the bulk of his Brooklyn homebuilding projects on his own, suddenly took on a partner. Since Fred had publicly disdained the notion or need for joint ventures, even buying out his Norfolk partner Rosati, it was an intriguing development. His new partner, Willie Tomasello, a local brick contractor, became a 25 percent participant in the deal. Fred's decision to include Tomasello proved to be an uncharacteristically generous one—the two would combine to take as much as a $4 million profit out of the FHA mortgage before the job was completed, in addition to being paid as contractors and owning the project.

Trump would later claim that Tomasello advanced the project a half million dollars before the FHA mortgage funds were released. But, with the FHA commitment long guaranteed, Fred hardly needed an outside investor to finance the project. He could have taken the no-risk commitment to any bank and gotten a loan, or used his own funds. Trump had just sold some of his Norfolk projects, as well as earned a substantial profit on Shore Haven, making it doubly unlikely that Tomasello's small investment was all that made him an attractive partner.

What Tomasello did bring to the partnership, however, was a cloud. His tainted partners in virtually every other real estate deal in his life—including a series of multimillion-dollar development projects in Florida and upstate New York—were either individual members of the DiBono (also DeBono) family or that family's Long Island plastering company, Mario & DiBono. According to Organized Crime Task Force memos in the 1950s, Frank Scalise, the notorious drug courier for Lucky Luciano, was a silent partner in the DiBono company. Louis DiBono, a Gambino crime family soldier who was tied to Tomasello in four ventures, was killed years later in a mob hit. The DiBono company was eventually identified by law enforcement agencies as a joint-venture partner with Vinnie DiNapoli, a capo in the Genovese crime family, and their business was barred from doing any federal work. Other prominent New York developers, including Sam Lefrak, have said that it was known at the time that Tomasello was a Genovese associate.

John Hyman, who has since become a topflight construction manager,* recalled from his days on the Beach Haven job that "it was common knowledge on the job site that Tomasello was connected." Hyman said he could "always tell when a contractor was connected if he could hire guys right off the boat" without the unions, particularly the then notoriously mob-controlled bricklayers' union, "shutting the job down." Tomasello, he said, ran the enormous brick job at Beach Haven with boat labor. "I remember his son-in-law, fresh off the boat, standing on the bridge yelling, 'More mortar.' His job was to yell for mortar."

Tomasello also had the benefit of bringing along his own political allies, foremost among them East New York district leader Meade Esposito, a bail bondsman with a legion of mob associations who would eventually become Brooklyn Democratic boss. Esposito hosted his club parties in a Bensonhurst restaurant owned by Carlo Gambino, entered the pharmaceutical business with a close associate of Gambino's, met regularly on a bench in Brooklyn's Marine Park with capo Paul Vario, and was ultimately convicted in a federal conspiracy case triggered by wiretaps on another capo's home phone that picked up Esposito in almost daily conversations. Asked recently what he knew about Fred Trump, Esposito had a curt and unusual response: "He was my friend Willie Tomasello's partner."

Fred joined forces with Tomasello in the O'Dwyer era, when having a mob-connected partner was becoming a way of doing business in New York.

---

* For example, Hyman was retained in 1988 by the Bass family to estimate renovation costs at the Plaza prior to their sale of the hotel to Donald Trump.

This pattern of mob influence hardly changed in 1950, when the scandal-ridden O'Dwyer was suddenly forced from office and replaced by city council president Vincent Impellitteri. O'Dwyer had put the unknown Impellitteri, who was a secretary to a judge, on his ticket in 1949 as the designee of Tommy Lucchese, the city's rising new mob boss. Fred Trump had two dependable allies within Impellitteri's inner circle—Moses, who vacationed with the new mayor, and Kenny Sutherland, another Lucchese ally, who rose to county leader during the Impellitteri reign and ran the mayor's unsuccessful reelection campaign in Brooklyn in 1953. During the "Impy" years from 1950 to 1954, Trump completed Beach Haven, built several new luxury buildings in Queens after a twenty-year absence, and began accumulating land for a massive new beachfront housing complex in recreationally zoned Coney Island. His acquisition of key and expensive elements of the Coney Island site less than three months after Impy took office in August of 1950 suggested just how confident Trump was that he could obtain the zoning approvals necessary to build housing where no one else had ever been permitted.

The parcel Trump bought was the old Luna Park amusement site—eight acres right off the beach, gutted in a 1944 fire. Influential Coney Island business interests, committed to protecting it as an amusement mecca and interested in using the Luna site as a much-needed parking area, had publicly assailed any housing development there as part of "a Robert Moses plan to wipe out the Coney Island tradition of shooting galleries, roller coasters, sideshows and the other trappings of gaiety." Lebwohl in fact remembered many Trump meetings with Moses about the Luna Park site. Even with Impellitteri's defeat, Trump went right on assembling what became a twenty-nine-acre site, including the old Velodrome, where motorcycle races and prizefights had once been held. According to longtime Coney Island real estate observers, the Velodrome was partly owned by the husband of Kenny Sutherland's Democratic co-leader, Herman Rapps, a concessionaire believed by Sutherland's friends to be his secret partner. In a bizarre transaction that occurred shortly after Impy's 1953 loss, the city bought the property, supposedly to widen a street, and then, three weeks later, abandoned the widening and sold it to Trump.

Yet all these maneuvers proved to be dead ends when a sudden series of charges against Trump, emanating from Washington and tarnishing him for the first time in his life, doomed the Luna Park project. In the midst of Fred's sudden scandal, not even the Brooklyn gang could complete this deal.

• • •

Soon after taking office in 1953, Dwight Eisenhower, the first Republican President since the creation of the FHA twenty years earlier, ordered a massive probe of the abuses within it. When the counsel's office at FHA received an order from the White House to deliver key agency files to the Justice Department, the initial reaction of this agency, which had for so long called its own shots, was that the President did not have the legal authority to investigate it. By the time the tumultuous FHA scandal finally receded in 1956, the Senate Banking Committee had likened it to Teapot Dome, the agency's top rental official had been convicted, and the attorney general had wheeled out the old "riddled with corruption" cliché. The description proved apt when $51 million in mortgage gouging was identified during an FBI random survey of 285 projects.

Fred Trump was subpoenaed before the Banking Committee in July of 1954 and grilled about the millions in profit he had expropriated from Beach Haven, his barely two-year-old FHA masterpiece. Trump attended the hearings, called by the new Republican Senate leadership, accompanied by an influential Republican lawyer from New York, Orrin Judd. Close to Brooklyn Republican boss John Crews, Judd would soon be named by Governor Rockefeller to a top state post and, later, would become a federal judge. Crews, whose insurance outfit was also on the Moses dole, had a brother in the assembly leadership who'd worked closely with Irwin Steingut packaging bills for Moses. Despite his decades of Brooklyn Democratic coziness, Fred Trump was a registered Republican and frequently boasted of his close ties to Crews and other top Republicans. To him, bipartisan backslapping was merely a fact of business life.

Questioned by the committee's counsel, William Simon, Trump conceded he'd paid only $180,000 for the land underlying Beach Haven, but got the FHA to put an appraised value, without improvements, of $1.5 million on it. He then gave the land to a trust in his children's name and, using the inflated value, charged the Beach Haven project $60,000 a year rent for the land for ninety-nine years. Simon noted that Fred had to pay a gift tax when he gave the land to the children and asked what value he'd put on it for tax purposes. Trump conceded that he'd submitted it for the original $180,000. The taxing authorities rejected that figure, putting its value instead at $260,000—at precisely the same time Trump was getting his inflated FHA estimate.

Simon moved on to the windfall Trump took on the mortgage proceeds. The committee established that Fred had loaned $729,000 of the excess proceeds from the mortgage to affiliated corporations and kept another $3 million in the bank. This excess, which Trump acknowledged was actually over $4 million on a $16 million mortgage, was the difference between the amount he originally obtained through FHA, based on his preconstruction estimates, and the actual cost of construction. Trump conceded that he'd paid no taxes on the proceeds he was keeping and that he'd invested some of them already.

"Why don't you take that $3.5 million and reduce the mortgage, or at least take $2.5 million and reduce the mortgage by that amount so that the federal government won't have such a large liability?" asked Senator Homer Capehart.

"It wouldn't pay to do that, Senator," said Trump, as erect and formal as he'd been in his Lehrenkrauss court appearance twenty years earlier, still speaking in a clumsy German accent. One of the devices used by Trump, and other builders, to inflate their construction estimates was architectural fees. "In your application you filed with the FHA," Simon asked, "you listed architects' fees as exactly 5 percent, is that right?"

TRUMP: "I think so; yes."

SIMON: "How much were they paid for architectural services?"

TRUMP: "I would say a little under 1 percent."

SIMON: "When did you contract with them to furnish the architectural services?"

TRUMP: "Prior to the construction of the job."

SIMON: "They had to prepare the plans prior to the application, didn't they?"

TRUMP: "They prepared sketches, with the application."

SIMON: "When you filed this application did you contemplate that you would have to pay as much as 5 percent for architects' fees?"

TRUMP: "That was in 1949. I really don't know what I contemplated. I assume that is what FHA allowed by the regulations."

Asked if he would have built the project, which he conceded was charging the maximum rents permissible under the law, if he hadn't been able to take these mortgage proceeds out and instead had to make a 10 percent capital investment as required under the federal financing laws, Fred replied:

"No. Do you mean invest 10 percent? You couldn't do it."

CAPEHART: "You just wouldn't have built these buildings if you had to put any of your own money in them?"

TRUMP: "Well, I don't say any. All the money I can borrow."

Fred insisted on submitting a prepared statement to the committee, contending that he'd built 2,000 one- and two-family homes in his career—13,000 less than his press praise claimed half a decade earlier—and trumpeting once again the impact of his name. "An indication of the reputation for quality which I have earned," his statement read, "is the fact that when dwellings are offered for resale, they are sometimes advertised in the newspaper as having been 'Built by Trump,' which denotes in real estate a mark of quality." To justify his mortgage profits, he stressed his risk, noting that he'd given his personal guarantee on Beach Haven. "For almost 20 years in my previous experience I had avoided giving personal guarantees," he argued.

But the Banking Committee and internal FHA findings assailed the inflated cost estimates that had enriched Fred and dozens of other builders as "outright misrepresentation." The final report charged that the developers had "saddled tenants with the burden of meeting not only legitimate costs" but paying rents to cover the unexpended portion of the federal loans that the builders had pocketed. The investigators also condemned the "fictional division of single projects into two or more projects" to sidestep the $5 million limit on insurable mortgages, a tactic Fred employed at both Shore Haven and Beach Haven.

Beyond the specific scams, the stench of criminal abuse hung over the entire insider network around the FHA, including those closest to Fred. Tommy Grace, among others, came in for a public hearing. It turned out that throughout his FHA career, he'd retained his ties to a family law firm that listed his name, together with those of his three brothers, on its letterhead and Court Street door. The firm, which paid Tommy as a quarter partner, had done a box-office business processing FHA applications. Indeed, even as Tommy Grace took the stand to testify before the Banking Committee in the summer of 1954, the firm was drawing a $20,000 fee from an urban renewal project Fred partially owned. Tommy's brother George was counsel to the Development Builders of New York, an industry association chaired by Trump. George would eventually become a partner of Fred's in a major Brooklyn housing project, Starrett City.

The three-year statute of limitations on fraud cases prevented Tommy's indictment, as it did two other friends of Fred's—national FHA administrator

Clyde Powell and another Court Street lawyer, Abe Traub, senior partner in Dreyer & Traub, the firm that would become the Trump family's principal real estate advisers. However, both Powell, who was running the Virginia FHA office when Fred began building there in the forties, and Traub, who represented Fred on at least one matter, were convicted of contempt.* Traub could not explain millions in checks he'd written to cash and Powell could not explain hundreds of thousands in cash that he'd both secreted in safe-deposit boxes and gambled away. The committee openly suggested that Traub's cash had found its way into Powell's ever-open pocket. It established that two other Trump friends—W. Taylor Johnson, whose family business insured Fred's Virginia projects, and Piggy Van Patten—had covered Powell's losses at an illegal craps table in Virginia Beach while winning FHA designations from him.

But no one focused on the documentary evidence that Powell had personally interceded in 1951 to facilitate Fred's raid on the Shore Haven FHA mortgage. He pressured agency accountants to rush an approval of Trump financial statements for the project even though Fred had not reported the $1.6 million in improper dividends he'd exacted for himself from the government loan. When the FHA's comptroller found a laundry list of deficiencies in the Trump statements, Powell simply waived the requirement that Trump comply. The Banking Committee identified $100,000 in payoffs Powell had taken for precisely this sort of official favor.

Devastated by the media blast that accompanied the FHA hearings, Fred Trump retreated to New York, facing suits from his Shore Haven and Beach Haven tenants. His dream project at Luna Park was stillborn, and he was burdened with the mounting carrying costs for land he could not build on. It was time to assume a low profile. No more press releases or economic pronouncements. No more campaigns for celebrity status. No more FHA projects. In fact, blacklisted for years by the FHA, Fred was even threatened with a federal takeover of Shore Haven, where the Beach Haven mortgage scams exposed at the hearings had been tried first.

He had built an office for himself on Avenue Z, inside the Beach Haven project. It was his own boxlike hideaway with a parking lot that could accommodate no more than his limo and six cars. Ten gray cement stairs led into a tiny waiting room, separated from the half dozen bare cubicles by a glass wall. In his testimony before the committee, he had derided builders who erected "classy" offices

---

* Traub's conviction was later overturned on a technicality.

for themselves out of FHA loan proceeds. It was one of the only advantages he hadn't extracted from the agency's mortgages, and it would now become his isolated fortress. The unstoppable man who'd started at twenty-one, building his first house for a neighbor in Woodhaven, had discovered at forty-nine that even for him, there were limits.

In the aftermath of the FHA debacle, Fred's top priority was to find a profitable way to dump the Luna Park site he'd spent years assembling. He knew he could still count on his old-line Brooklyn connections to deliver a municipal buyer, even though the machine had backed the wrong horse, Impellitteri, in the 1953 race against the new mayor, Robert Wagner.

Wagner had already forced the resignation of Kenny Sutherland, installing Joe Sharkey as county leader, and Fred had wasted no time establishing a relationship with the new boss. "I heard there was a nice new young fellah over here," Fred told Sharkey when he dropped by party headquarters with a thousand-dollar check in 1954, making the first major contribution Sharkey received.

Fred hardly needed, however, to cement his ties with the other top Brooklyn politician, Borough President John Cashmore, a protégé of the deceased Frank Kelly. Fred was one of a select number of Cashmore friends to visit him periodically at his Park Slope home. When Wagner's Housing Authority chief, Warren Moscow, went to see Cashmore in 1955 to get him to support Authority projects on various Brooklyn sites, Cashmore had only one condition. "You've got to take care of my friend Fred Trump," the borough president said. "I want you to talk to Fred about his site in Luna Park."

In the end, the city paid Trump $1.7 million for the parcel, giving him a $300,000 profit. Then Trump bought back a commercially zoned slice of the site, paying the city almost precisely the profit he'd taken on the overall deal. Fred effectively got this prime property for nothing, and the nine-store shopping center he built there was an immediate gold mine, serving the 1,576-unit project that the Housing Authority soon opened next to it.

When the Authority approved the deal with Fred on February 2, 1956, the newest member of its five-member board, Bunny Lindenbaum, attending his first meeting, abstained. Tagged for the prestigious post by Sharkey and Tammany Hall boss Carmine DeSapio, Lindenbaum said he wasn't voting because he "represented Mr. Trump in other legal matters not connected with the Luna Park site." It was a ridiculous claim. As every insider in town knew, Bunny, who would reach new heights of power in the Wagner years, was involved in whatever Fred

Trump did. Bunny's own law partner, Sid Young, conceded as much years later, noting the firm's involvement in the Luna Park Shopping Mall.

Lindenbaum emerged in the fifties and early sixties as the embodiment of the Madison Club's new clout in city and state politics. When Irwin Steingut died in 1954, Bunny moved into his Eastern Parkway duplex, just a floor away from Irwin's thirty-two-year-old son, Stanley, who succeeded his father as the local assemblyman and Democratic district leader. The two were constantly in and out of each other's living room. Tying himself inextricably to Steingut and the club's other rising star, City Budget Director Abe Beame, Lindenbaum induced the two to become his secret partners in the acquisition of an Atlantic City hotel—the five-story, 315-room, wood plank Brighton, located just off the Boardwalk.

The beneficiaries of these compromising relationships were Bunny's clients— and none was more important to him than Fred Trump, who had signed on as Lindenbaum's first client even before Bunny left Consolidated Insurance and put up his shingle in 1948. For years Bunny advertised the closeness of this bond by including Fred, sometimes Fred Jr., Maryanne, and, by the sixties, young Donald as his guests at the annual dinner dance of the Brooklyn Democratic organization, the high-water mark on any local politician's social calendar.

It was this Madison Club influence that Bunny and Fred used, beginning in 1957 and ending in early 1960, to pave the way for the biggest project of their lives, a mammoth middle-income housing complex—dubbed Trump Village— in the heart of Coney Island. To get the city to condemn and sell him this desirable forty-acre site, Trump had to kill an already partially approved plan— championed by a powerful, nonprofit housing alliance connected to major labor unions and close to Mayor Wagner. Trump eventually succeeded in blocking the proposal of the United Housing Foundation even though it easily won approval from two of the three city agencies necessary—the planning commission and the comptroller. He launched his opposition two days before the UHF project was to be voted on at the planning commission, writing a letter that blasted the partial tax exemption UHF was seeking as "an outright giveaway."

Trump's complaint was that the minuscule $250,000 that UHF was offering to pay in annual property taxes gave its project an unfair advantage over his two nearby developments, Shore Haven and Beach Haven, where, he said, full taxes required him to charge high rentals. This argument ought to have been dismissed immediately, since it was clearly Fred's FHA windfalls that had jacked up the rents on his prized projects, but public memory being what it is in New York, no one made any reference to the three-year-old scandal.

"The taxpayers of the Borough of Brooklyn should not be asked to sub-sidize more luxurious housing than they themselves enjoy," Fred argued. The irony, of course, was that Trump's two rental projects had always been swamped with eager applicants, while the nonprofit UHF wanted to build co-ops and was seeking a maximum tax abatement to make the apartments more affordable for working families, not to fatten its own pockets.

Bunny went to Mayor Wagner with Fred's complaint, but the mayor had already committed himself to UHF. Wagner's planning commission approved UHF's Warbasse Houses, though the group was forced to increase its promised tax payments to the city and thus to raise its estimated per room charges for apartments. Undaunted, Bunny and Fred went to John Cashmore, took him on a trip out to the site as well as to Shore Haven and Beach Haven, and, as Bunny later claimed, convinced him of the righteousness of their cause.

UHF's tax abatement still had to win final approval at the Board of Estimate, where Cashmore was only one of eight members, but the unwritten law at the Board was that a borough president had veto power over a development project in his borough. So Cashmore, a red-faced dandy burned out at sixty-three years of age after almost two decades as borough president, became an unmovable traffic cop blocking the project for three long and frustrating years, killing it single-handedly at twelve different Board of Estimate public hearings.

Soon Trump—who claimed initially that he was opposed only to the abate-ment, not the project—submitted his own proposal for the same site, described by an independent citizen's group as an "echo" of the UHF plan. He even sought an abatement, but not as large as UHF's. Cashmore—who was nicknamed "Cashbox" and owned an office furniture store utterly dependent on business steered its way by Trump lawyer Richard Charles—introduced and supported the Trump alternative glowingly.

Faced with this new competitor, Al Kazan, the head of UHF, went to see Cashmore in his Brooklyn office several times, pleading with him to support Warbasse. UHF had already sold 2,500 apartments and had collected millions in down payments on them, he argued, as he hiked again and again the amount UHF was willing to pay in taxes. At hearings some years later, Kazan was asked if Cashmore stopped the project because he was opposed to the tax exemption. With nothing to gain or lose, Kazan, the grand old man of labor-backed housing, replied in an almost rambling, historical search for the truth: "I wonder whether the borough president was very much interested in the tax exemption or not. But he did not want to approve the job, that is all."

"Did it ever come to your attention that Fred Trump was friendly with the then borough president of Brooklyn?" Kazan was asked.

"Well, for that matter, I was friendly, too, with him, but it didn't help," Kazan said. "Friendliness didn't help in this case. All I know is that I did plead with the borough president to get approval, and we couldn't."

Finally, Kazan was forced to acknowledge his defeat. In late 1959, he was told privately by members of the Board that unless UHF surrendered part of its then sixty-five-acre site to Trump, the project would never be approved. The Brooklyn machine could, it seemed, stop a project as far into the future as any mortal could see. The settlement, rubber-stamped by the Wagner administration, was a total Trump triumph. Theoretically, it was supposed to provide for a fifty-fifty split of the original site, but Cashmore arranged to throw in an additional tract that hadn't even been part of the UHF site, so Trump wound up with forty acres and Kazan with twenty-nine. Trump was also granted the land nearest the water, while Kazan's buildings were pushed right up against the elevated subway tracks. Trump was allowed to build 3,800 apartments in eight buildings on his site, including a thousand rentals that would give him income in perpetuity, while UHF was given buildable space for six buildings and 2,400 co-op apartments. As Kazan would ultimately describe it: "Trump came in and took the entire job away from us."

Fred also scored a victory on the commercial strip, a repeat of the silver lining in his Luna Park deal. He was given nearly 75 percent of the allotted commercial area for a 3.5-acre shopping center, while UHF received only 1.3 acres. While UHF would use any earnings from the mall to reduce residential costs on the apartments, Trump's shopping center was a freestanding operation that enriched only him. When UHF tried later to increase the size of its allotted shopping area, Fred appeared at a public hearing to oppose it, and, as usual, he prevailed.

The terms of the compromise were hammered out by the man at the center of every development deal in New York for decades, Robert Moses. Bunny recalled, in a subsequent interview, that "Moses sat and listened to both sides" and then suggested the details of the deal. Kazan and the UHF may have believed that in Moses they had an unbiased arbiter, for little was known publicly about his, and Fred Trump's, long-standing connections with the same Court Street law firm. But Richard Charles was still lunching with Fred every Friday and submitting monthly bills to both Fred and Moses confidants like engineering consultant Earle Andrews. Lebwohl recalled Fred's repeated private visits to Moses about the site. The proof of Moses' bias, of course, was in the ultimate disposition of the property.

Before the deal could be voted on at the planning commission and the Board of Estimate, city comptroller Larry Gerosa, a Wagner antagonist who'd long championed the UHF project, had to be convinced to certify Fred's. Bunny and a mysterious Steingut emissary traveled together out to Arizona, where Gerosa was vacationing, and persuaded him to switch. Not only did Gerosa certify the Trump project, he voted for it as a Board of Estimate member and then negotiated and signed a detailed city contract with Trump funding the site clearance plan. While UHF did get a slightly better tax abatement than Trump did on their respective pieces of the original site, Trump was given a 72 percent tax write-off on the new parcel thrown in by Cashmore, more than UHF's. The campaign that had started as a Trump protest against abatements wound up winning one of the largest in city history.

Nine days after Trump Village won final city approval in the spring of 1960, Lindenbaum took office as the city's newest planning commissioner, replacing Moses on the powerful, part-time body. Blessed with the best of two worlds—public power in the same arena where he represented private interests—Bunny was perfectly positioned within the city's elite to deliver for Fred. The Lindenbaum appointment was just one indicator of Wagner's deepening commitment to Fred Trump's Madison Club allies. A few months later the mayor selected his budget director, Abe Beame, as his running mate for the 1961 election. With Gerosa's decision not to seek reelection as comptroller, Beame easily won the Democratic primary, giving the old Brooklyn gang their first citywide elected official.

A primary victor as well, Wagner, however, had one stiff challenge yet to meet—a general election race against a formidable Republican foe, State Attorney General Louis Lefkowitz. It didn't help that in the middle of the campaign, a major scandal erupted that damaged the administration. At the center of it was the irrepressible and ethically casual Bunny.

As Wagner later remembered it, Bunny hosted a Brooklyn luncheon for him in late September at Sakele's restaurant, right off Court Street. "We didn't know any of the details; it was just on the schedule. Bunny greeted us at the door and took us to a table. Frank Lynn from the *Times* was there. After a while, Bunny stood up and made a kind of introductory speech. He asked the people in the room to make pledges to the campaign. It began to look like a UJA fund-raiser, everyone standing and announcing a pledge. It got embarrassing, and I said I think we ought to leave. We did."

The problem, obviously, was that Bunny was a planning commissioner, and many of the forty-three businessmen in the room who pledged a total of $25,000 that day were in real estate and did business either directly before Bunny at the commission or with the Wagner administration generally. Fred Trump, for example, had risen to announce his $2,500 donation, the second highest pledge of the day and an extraordinarily large donation in those times.

Confronted by the press, the mayor contended that none of the luncheon contributors did business with the city, a claim that did not last a day before the newspapers discovered a half dozen who did. None were more prominent than Fred, who had a couple of Trump Village matters pending at that very moment before the planning commission, with Bunny, of course, as his lawyer. All the normally concealed contradictions and conflicts had dramatically surfaced in that scene at Sakele's; it was a bit too stark to pass unnoticed. Yet, to Bunny, it all seemed so harmless.

The voices of outrage were raised the same afternoon, and Bob Wagner instantly knew he had a problem. What made him angriest was that the City Hall reporters had been invited to the luncheon; this was no piece of investigative reporting. Lefkowitz and Larry Gerosa, who was opposing Wagner on a maverick third-party ticket, went predictably crazy in the ensuing days; but more disturbing were independent critics like Roger Starr, head of the respected Citizens Housing and Planning Council, and Milton Bergerman, head of the Citizens Union, both of whom demanded Lindenbaum's resignation. Starr called it "political payola" and said Bunny "should be fired" if he didn't resign, and Bergerman labeled Lindenbaum's actions "grossly improper."

"How can the mayor deny that he knew the identity of the builders doing business with the city," demanded an angry Gerosa, "when Fred Trump, one of the sponsors of a Coney Island project, appeared before the Board of Estimate in the Mayor's presence with Lindenbaum as his attorney? In fact there were several discussions in executive session in which both these men as well as the Mayor were present. Why does the Mayor try to pretend that he doesn't know these men?"

Bunny had to resign quietly, patted on the back as a sacrificial lamb by the established order, which sniffed at this brouhaha as much ado about nothing. Wagner, who won reelection handily, remained on friendly terms with Bunny, but the "overzealous" fund-raiser, as the *Times* called him, would never again hold a public post.

The Trump Village matters on the planning commission agenda when the luncheon occurred involved authorization for Fred to seek state mortgage subsidies, available under the new Mitchell-Lama program, to finance the project.

Fred had initially proposed it as a privately financed job, using city assistance just to acquire and clear the site. But Trump could not obtain his own financing, so he decided to try to seek funding for the $60 million project from the State Division of Housing—an agency dominated by Robert Moses throughout the Rockefeller years. The luncheon storm briefly stymied this switch, but the commission and the Board of Estimate approved it in early 1962, with new comptroller Beame actively supporting it.

Even though Trump Village became a state project, Beame remained the city official most responsible for its progress from 1962 to its completion in 1965—designated to receive monitoring reports every three months, to approve advances covering site clearance costs, and to sign off on any material changes in the project plan. During construction, the project mysteriously grew from 3,800 apartments to 4,600, with new floors quietly added in the night. It was just like the old days: Bunny, Abe, and Fred back together again.

When Trump applied for state financing, he retained the services of attorney MacNeil Mitchell, the Republican senator who'd sponsored the bill that created the new program, and architect Al Lama, the Brooklyn Democrat who'd sponsored it in the assembly. Mitchell actually submitted Trump's application to the state, while Lama served in less conspicuous ways. The Joint Legislative Committee on Housing, which Mitchell chaired, was located in the same midtown office as his law firm, and his law partner was counsel to the committee. It may well have been this enticing overlap of public and private roles, advertised on the front door, that attracted the interest of bargain hunter Fred. Leo Silverman, the senior auditor of the State Division of Housing who oversaw the Trump project, recalled years later that "anything Mitchell wanted in those days, he got up in Albany." Trump would eventually pay the senator $128,000 to get the Coney Island project funded.

Fred was so certain that his application for a Mitchell-Lama mortgage would be approved that he started the project, with city assistance on the land acquisition, long before it formally was. Indeed, half of Trump Village was completed before the state mortgage came through, and Fred was using the down payments made by thousands of families buying apartments to finance the construction, even though by law these funds were supposed to remain untouched in a trust fund. He couldn't obtain the mortgage more quickly because the allocation was so large the state finance agency had difficulty bonding it, especially with a builder who had never undertaken a comparable effort before. Trump Village cost three times as much as Beach Haven, Fred's largest prior project.

And Beach Haven was only six stories high, while Trump Village was twenty-three stories.

One of the ironies of the city's earlier willingness to dislodge UHF for Trump was that, while UHF had a track record as a large-scale builder, Trump was not in the same league. Fred himself discovered, in the middle of the construction of Trump Village, that he was still just a small-time builder. Unable to obtain bonding or complete the towers, Fred had to turn construction supervision over to a major builder, HRH. Trump had been using HRH in an advisory capacity since the project began. But as he later begrudgingly admitted: "We started the project. We had two buildings up to the 14th and 15th floor. The total on this was $19 million. We had the entire project, the piling was 75 percent driven. When we had most of the subcontracts negotiated, and I saw this was growing beyond a capacity which I wanted to undertake without assistance. So I called in HRH. I insisted that they put up the bond required by the state."

Fred's Trump Village Construction Corporation wound up with only watchmen, timekeepers, and cleaners on its own job site. Fred visited, but he became little more than a monitor at his own greatest project. He still huffed and puffed, rushing around the grounds with great purpose. But the builder—collecting a cool million-dollar fee from parsimonious Fred Trump—was HRH, and once HRH was in place, the state mortgage money finally started flowing.

Fred took a strong personal interest in the land-acquisition process. He had budgeted $7.2 million for it in his original contract with the city and in his state mortgage application. As he bought out or condemned each section of the project, the state advanced him monies to pay for the land needed for the next section. Auditor Silverman concluded that Trump's estimated land costs far exceeded the actual cost of acquisition based on an analysis of the first section's final prices. He tried to persuade state officials to cut back on payments to Trump for future sections, but he could get nowhere with his superiors. The city supervisor of the condemnation process, Abe Beame, raised no problems. Fred was systematically banking, and earning interest, on whatever he could save from the land acquisition advances. Likewise, since he'd started the job long before the mortgage closed, he'd also grossly overestimated interest costs and wound up banking his interest savings as well. The gimmicks had a familiar Beach Haven ring to them, as an unchastened Trump, a decade after his FHA blacklisting, was once again profiteering from a government mortgage.

One reason he was saving so much money at the acquisition end was that the condemnation prices he was paying for land were set in the Brooklyn courthouse, the province of the county Democratic Party. The new Brooklyn boss was none other than Stanley Steingut, elected by party leaders from assembly districts across the county in 1962. With Stanley as party leader and Beame as comptroller, Bunny was in his prime. His job for Fred on Trump Village was to convince the courts to approve the lowest possible condemnation awards, maneuvering among the Brooklyn judges he'd known for decades. Part of whatever Bunny saved on the awards would wind up in a spectacular legal fee for him, taken directly out of the mortgage excess. Since this wasn't Fred's own money, he was perfectly positioned to reward Lindenbaum without cost to himself—Fred could use state funds to pay Bunny whatever they could justify.

When Bunny presented a bill for the highest fee in state project history, $520,000, the state asked the city to review it. The state's reasoning was that Trump's contract on land acquisition was with the city, signed long before the state was even in the picture. Abe Beame, who had the power under the contract with Trump to audit the fee or any other project costs, demurred. The city implicitly endorsed the payment, accepting at face value all of Lindenbaum's stated work claims.

Bunny's red-flag fee was boldly submitted even though Fred had already been grilled in a private hearing by investigators from the State Investigations Commission about aspects of his profit-taking on Trump Village. With the project at last complete, and auditors suddenly all over his books, Fred must have been getting a déjà vu feeling, hearkening back to his experience with the FHA. Nearly a year would pass, however, before the public phase of this probe, which would once again place Fred before the cameras.

In the meantime, with Robert Wagner finally stepping down in 1965, the Madison crew prepared to make a run at the mayoralty. Abe Beame won the Democratic nomination in a tough primary, and Bunny was named in the newspapers as his principal fund-raiser. Fred Trump, openly speculating on a Beame win, bought a vast new tract of Coney Island oceanfront land, confident that a Beame administration would deliver the zoning change he'd need to build thousands of luxury units on the water.

Normally a primary win would have guaranteed final victory for Beame, but it was an unusual political year in New York, and the colorless clubhouse candidate lost to a glamorous East Side congressman on the Republican line, John Lindsay. During the campaign, Lindsay had announced his opposition to any zoning change for Trump's new property, siding with Coney Island business interests who regarded the Boardwalk strip as vital to the area's amusement development. For the first time in almost twenty years, a defeated Beame was out of public life. Simultaneously, Steingut had lost a bid for assembly speaker. It was a momentary low point in Madison fortunes, and Bunny and Fred were suddenly vulnerable.

In January of 1966, Fred Trump suffered the worst public humiliation of his career. Hauled again before the State Investigations Commission—this time at a public hearing—and hounded by television cameras, he testified for several hours about such an array of abuses on Trump Village that the commission chairman, Jacob Grumet, blasted him and Bunny as "grasping and greedy individuals" and asked state housing officials: "Is there any way of preventing a man who does business in that way from getting another contract with the state?" While state officials answered their own question with a no, the fact was Fred Trump was finished. After these hearings, he would never again build a publicly aided project—state, city, or federal.

He was grilled about an equipment-rental company he incorporated for this job, and the outlandish charges he was billing the state for secondhand trucks and backhoes. He charged $21,000 to lease a dump truck valued at $3,600. He billed $8,280 for two tile scrappers valued at $500 apiece, a ploy the commission cited as an example of Trump's "talent for getting every ounce of profit out of his housing project." Fred hid his ownership of the equipment company from the state, and state inspectors observed him using much of the equipment to build the adjacent shopping center, which certainly wasn't part of the state-subsidized project.

An irritated Fred exploded: "This is peanuts what you are talking about compared to $60 million," unconsciously making precisely the point about Fred's petty greed that the commission had set out to establish.

They moved on to the higher-ticket items. Only when faced with the threat of the hearings had Fred returned to the state the $1.2 million he'd kept by overestimating his land costs. He'd banked the first land advances for over two years. He also had used the state excess to pay for the land he needed for his own shopping center and two other parcels covered in the city's description of the total site, but unused in the Trump Village development. Silverman testified that Trump purchased these three large sections of the site for his own commercial development "without putting up a nickel of his own money"—in effect, duplicating his Luna Park triumph. Even though the state mortgage wasn't approved until he was almost halfway through the job, Trump had overestimated his construction costs by $6.6 million. Since his builder's fee was based on a percentage of the estimated, not actual costs, he took what the commission called a $600,000 "windfall," his additional fee based on the patently hyped cost predictions. When

Silverman testified about this padding, tacked on to a $3.2 million fee Trump had already collected as a percent of real costs, the commission was stunned.

In an interview years later, the auditor said that he and another audit chief had combined forces to "cut down on the requisitions of all the builders," but that they "couldn't do it with Trump." Every time they tried to lowball Trump's numbers, they were overruled by higher state officials. It was Silverman who had uncovered the equipment overcharges and the land scams, working, he said, "from the seat of my pants." Asked if he ever attempted to find out just why the state was looking the other way at these abuses, Silverman said: "I didn't want to know where the problem was in the state. I was ambitious, and I still thought I could go higher in the agency."

The commission closed on a high note—the Lindenbaum fee—and Bunny, too, was forced to face the cameras. State officials called the fee "unconscionable" and "outrageous." Bunny tried to defend it, filling the record with self-serving declarations:

"We devoted seven days a week to it."

"Not only myself, but my office, my staff. I would say there was steady work on it by two or three people."

"First we had a chart made of every piece of property. We appeared at the condemnation hearings. I certainly would. We saved over a million dollars. Now we saved that through the efforts of the judge presiding at that time, and also through the efforts of myself and my staff, getting up charts, showing the relative values of the properties."

The bills revealed that Bunny had charged for 4,500 hours of court appearances by himself, son Sandy (who was now a partner in the Court Street firm), and two others. But when pressed about just what his firm did, and what the city's corporation counsel did during the condemnation proceedings, he said only that the city attorneys had "full responsibility."

COMMISSIONER: "Just a moment. When you said you were engaged in
SARACHAN   the trial of a condemnation proceeding, it is my impression
           that you were trying the case."

BUNNY: "Oh, no. I am sorry. No. I was just an observer."

SARACHAN: "You sat there."

BUNNY: "I sat there."

An affidavit was read into the record from the city's principal attorney on the condemnations noting that Bunny never participated at trial and that the city never discussed appraisals or other related issues with his firm.

Then the commission moved on to Bunny's frequently invoked chart, establishing that the city and a relocation company, hired to move the 800 families who were on the site and separately paid almost $400,000 by the state, had actually prepared the sixty-page detailed chart Bunny had submitted with his bill. Bunny had also claimed extensive legal services in connection with the evictions of the on-site tenants, but the president of the relocation firm testified and flatly denied that Bunny's law firm had anything whatsoever to do with any part of the relocation process and claimed that there were only "one or two evictions" anyway.

The total of Lindenbaum's and Mitchell's legal fees on the project was almost $650,000, compared to $70,000 in legal fees on the UHF counterpart. The UHF construction fee from their state mortgage was a mere $350,000, compared with almost $5 million that Trump and HRH took out of Trump Village. The average monthly carrying charges in UHF's Warbasse Houses was twenty-three dollars a room, while Trump's went to twenty-six dollars. UHF built its own $6 million power plant and supplied free central air-conditioning to its apartments; Fred put a sleeve in the wall large enough for a small air conditioner and tried to have it considered comparable.

Joe Fisch, the staff attorney who handled the Trump investigation, referred the case formally to the Brooklyn District Attorney's office, a cemetery for public corruption probes of Brooklyn pols. The district attorney never questioned a witness or subpoenaed a document. When one of the commissioners encountered Lindenbaum at a dinner after the hearings, Bunny asked; "What's that Joe Fisch trying to do, get me indicted?"

Fisch, who moved on to become a judge years later, recalled: "Of course, that's precisely what I was trying to do. The Lindenbaum case was the type of case that today prosecutors would be fighting duels over. The climate in those days was that guys like Lindenbaum enjoyed psychological immunity. There was no concern that anything would happen. These people were untouchable."

Having survived the earlier FHA scandal, Fred Trump may not have realized just how much damage the state hearings had done to him. A highlight of the initial month of John Lindsay's first term as mayor, the news coverage established Fred, in the minds of this new reform administration, as a living symbol of the bad old days.

But it was not just the Trump Village revelations that were tarnishing Fred. Even while that massive complex was under construction, Fred had moved on to his next great project, and this time his scheme would raise the ire of citywide park and recreation interests.

In the middle of the 1965 mayoral campaign, he'd paid $2.25 million for the famed Steeplechase site at Coney Island, whose parachute jump and electric steeplechase course were legendary. The Wagner administration had ignored its own planning commission report, which urged the city to take the largely unused twelve-acre site for a state park, and the administration's unexplained reluctance became Fred's next opportunity. Fred, who intended to replace one of the city's prime amusement attractions with luxury apartments, was speculating on Beame's election, just as he had at Luna Park with Impellitteri almost a decade earlier. Candidate Lindsay made it abundantly clear during the campaign that he favored a park use for the site.

Trump acquired the site from the Tilyou family, whose decision not to open the thirty-two-ride park for the summer season in April of 1965 was an announcement that the attraction, first opened by George Cornelius Tilyou in 1897, was for sale. Marie Tilyou, who'd taken charge of a divided family's assets, seemed determined to sell the park to Trump, despite other offers and a Trump price that was barely its assessed value.

Immediately after Trump's purchase of the site, he began dismantling the Barrel of Fun, the Pantomime Theatre, and the wooden Steeplechase horses that caromed up and down a track that encircled the Pavilion of Fun. He hired Jimmy Onorato, who had run the park for decades for the Tilyous, and Milt Berger, the longtime Tilyou family publicist for his staff, and announced his intention of building "a modern Miami Beach type highrise apartment development" on the site. Onorato, who worked for Trump as a bookkeeper, recalled the reaction on Coney Island to Trump's acquisition and plans: "Anger! Shock! People couldn't believe it! I was hurt by the reaction. I wasn't glad to see the park fall into Trump's hands. I will never forget the party he held on September 21, 1966, to celebrate the demolition of the pavilion. He sent out invitations. He offered bricks to throw at the pavilion's windows."

Milt Berger, who has spent a lifetime representing a host of Coney Island interests, explained Trump's demolition party: "Fred moved fast to prevent the Pavilion of Fun from being declared a landmark. He tore down the magnificent Victorian structure, and it became a wasteland, a dead spot on the Island."

While feigning interest publicly in constructing a new amusement park, Trump began a behind-the-scenes campaign against the local businessmen opposing his high-rise project. Shortly after Trump hired him, Berger found himself in a meeting with Lindenbaum. "What have we got on the people down there?" Bunny pressed Berger, looking for building violations, or whatever he could find, as leverage against Trump's Coney Island opponents. "Let's put the squeeze on them." When Berger wouldn't cooperate, he was fired and had to sue to collect Trump's unpaid fees.

Much like Fred's prior Luna Park project, however, this new Coney Island venture was doomed. Just as the FHA hearings had killed the funding for the Luna project, the SIC expose had effectively blacklisted him again. Once Trump finished clearing Steeplechase of everything but the parachute jump, he submitted a 3,000-unit proposal to the city in 1967, but the plan for four thirty-story apartment towers, financed under a state Mitchell-Lama, won no support. With encouragement from Mayor Lindsay, the planning commission had already approved a 1966 proposal to buy the site for a park, and $3 million had been allocated for the purchase. "I'm fighting a lost cause," Fred conceded to the *Times* in a 1968 interview. "There isn't much hope in the atmosphere."

The city submitted a federal application for a $2 million grant to redevelop the site with trees, a swimming pool, and bathhouses, and it won approval in the spring of 1969. The Lindsay administration had dawdled for four years but seemed finally prepared to act, moving in Brooklyn courts to condemn the Steeplechase site. Fred was "heartbroken," his lawyer Sid Young recalls, but determined at least to make a profit on the sale. With Bunny back in his familiar condemnation role, Trump won a $3.7 million acquisition price, a tidy million-and-a-half-dollar gain. In Brooklyn courthouses, the old connections were still working. Even the Lindsay adminstration had changed its tune—approving the lucrative condemnation price tag. Lindenbaum had quietly led substantial segments of the Brooklyn machine into Lindsay's camp in the tough reelection race of 1969. It also didn't hurt that Abe Beame—out of public office altogether for the first Lindsay term—had reclaimed his comptroller spot, reviving the old Madison clout.

But the Steeplechase park was never built, and the city-owned site remains a vacant prairie today. The Lindsay administration was unable, over an eight-year period, to build anything there; all it could do was stop Trump. Nonetheless, Trump's removal of both Luna Park and Steeplechase from the Boardwalk amusement area is seen to this day by Coney Island promoters as the events most responsible for its demise. His two shopping malls at nearby Trump Village and Luna Park are similarly credited by local merchants with having gutted the market for the now depressed commercial strip right off the Boardwalk.

On the other hand, Fred is given credit for having built a solid housing project at Trump Village, with apartments that remain a good buy twenty-five years later and that have already housed a generation of middle-income New Yorkers, the lifeblood of the city. That contribution stands side by side, just off the ocean, with the wreckage he helped make of Coney Island's onetime amusement paradise. The juxtaposition—towering achievement scarred by boorish greed—left a legacy as contradictory as his turbulent life.

3

THE PASSAGE
OF POWER

*His thoughts as to life and control had given him a fixed policy. He could,
should, and would rule alone. No man must ever again have the least claim
on him save that of a supplicant. By right of financial intellect and courage
he was first, and would so prove it. Men must swing around him as planets
around the sun.*

—*Theodore Dreiser*, THE TITAN

TWO SCANDALS and two lost dreams on the Coney Island beachfront had finally taken a toll on the sixty-one-year-old Fred Trump. He retreated again from
public view after the state hearings, just as he had after the FHA investigation a
decade earlier. Though he would remain quietly active in his business for twenty-
five more years, Trump would never return to the public stage.

Stymied by the Steeplechase stonewall during the first Lindsay term, he concentrated instead on privately financed, 150-unit luxury apartment buildings,
which he built without any form of government assistance, both adjacent to his
major Brooklyn projects and spotted all over the hills around Jamaica Estates.
He became a recluse king in Coney Island, the most powerful man in a dying
stretch of town, lunching at Gergiulio's or Lundy's, driving around in his dark
blue stretch limo with the license plate FT-1. His grandest exile project became

his own Queens house, which he kept expanding, taking it from its original nine rooms to twenty-three.

The death of his mother in June of 1966, just a few months after his humiliation at the hearings, seemed to deepen Fred's need to recede. A woman of extraordinary determination, eighty-six-year-old Elizabeth Trump had pushed Fred into his initial homebuilding forty years earlier. The first Trump construction company was called Elizabeth Trump & Son, and it was no misnomer: She was intimately involved in the business. In addition to Fred, her other son, John, was an MIT professor and celebrated scientist who'd helped develop the first million-volt X-ray generator and chaired the famed Lahey Clinic in Boston. Before her death, John had won His Majesty's Medal, awarded by George VI in 1947; the President's Certificate of Merit, presented by President Truman in 1948; and the Lamme Medal, awarded in 1960 by the American Institute of Electrical Engineers. Her daughter Elizabeth's husband, William Walter, worked for Fred and owned a small piece of the Trump Village project. Ill for six years prior to her death, and living most of it just a few blocks down Midland Parkway from Fred, she left an estate of $456,925, most of which was a trust fund share of the Shore Haven project. Elizabeth was buried in a family plot in Lutheran Cemetery in Queens that she had bought when her husband died almost fifty years earlier.

In the aftermath of Elizabeth's death, Fred seemed to consciously move to do for his eldest son, Fred Jr., what she had done for him: establish the twenty-seven-year-old in the family business. Fred had been bringing the handsome, six-foot Fred Jr. to everything from property closings to newspaper interviews for years, but merely as an observer. Now the senior Trump was dispatching him as his representative at critical meetings, especially with community leaders in Coney Island. As grueling as the pressure from his father was, Fred Jr., a Lehigh University graduate with little drive or business ability, could barely feign interest in the family company's affairs. Those who met him at the Avenue Z office said he clearly preferred boating to managing a Trump building and, as engaging as he was, made no take-charge impression.

Other members of the family had long been involved in the business. Mary Trump, Fred's tough and practical wife, ran the laundry rooms in Fred's Brooklyn projects, collecting quarters out of the washing and drying machines. Always dressed very simply, Mary traveled her laundry room route in a Rolls-Royce with the license plate MMT. Brother-in-law William Walter actually owned a tiny share of Trump Village and was widely liked in Coney Island for his gentle and open way, getting himself in trouble with Fred once when he told a local

Lutheran minister about the family's Lutheran roots. Fred became annoyed when the minister—whose church had been torn down and shortchanged in condemnation court by Trump to make way for Trump Village—then tried repeatedly (and without success) to get Fred to make a donation to a church-run summer youth program. And finally, as the sixties wound down, the number two son appeared.

In the summer of 1968, Sam Horwitz, a friendly theater operator who rented a Trump Village site from Fred and had a zest for politics, visited Fred's office at Avenue Z and met his son Donald, already ensconced in a cubicle amid the cheap fifties furniture and plastic plants. Donald had just graduated from the Wharton School of Finance at the University of Pennsylvania, one of the premier undergraduate business programs in the country, and he wore the Ivy League degree like a badge. There was something about his resolute ambition that reminded Horwitz instantly of the old man. The theater he and Fred had operated for years had been a smash success, and though Fred's temporary office during the construction of Trump Village was literally next door to the movie house, Fred had never so much as stopped in for a peek at the frontline movies Sam showcased. He was just too driven, and Sam saw the same hunger in Donald.

Though he'd just started as a full-time Trump executive, Donald already seemed to have passed Fred Jr. by and moved into a commanding position, right beside his father in the tightly drawn organizational structure. He had been coming out to Fred's jobs for years, sometimes, according to the locals, putting on a chauffeur's cap and uniform and driving his father on his rounds, stopping for coffee and Danish at the local luncheonette, where Donald would try to hustle the young waitresses, making out with an English girl in the back kitchen. In his younger days, he'd been a carefree, friendly kid, awkwardly attached to his unsmiling father. But now, with a degree and a real job, he took on the older man's seriousness. Still, Horwitz found in him a congeniality and an open, searching mind, which he had never encountered in the reserved Fred. Donald loved to talk politics, for example, no matter how local, and Sam, a district leader in a county party dominated by Stanley Steingut and new boss Meade Esposito, could discuss Brooklyn politics forever.

There was no grand scheme afoot at Trump headquarters, with Steeplechase formally dying just before Donald arrived. The organization was just managing projects, mowing lawns, collecting rents. With Fred Jr. soon disappearing for a brief career as an airplane pilot, the most Donald and the senior Fred could do was engineer the purchase or sale of another defaulting FHA project or two. It was a peculiar hiatus—from the late sixties into the early seventies—with

Donald an apprentice and Fred a tired caretaker. But Sam Horwitz could sense it, as could many others who watched the two adjust to the transition that was quietly occurring. A new Trump era had begun.

Donald had grown up apart. His neighbors knew him by his papier-mâché Halloween mask and elaborate costume; otherwise they just watched him come and go by limo from his mansion on the long green hill. The family was very out of touch with the neighbors and grew more so as the years went on.

One of the few families in the neighborhood with a live-in maid (always white) and a chauffeur (usually black), the Trumps were "never really a part of the block," said one neighbor. While Fred Jr. had gone to public school, Maryanne, Donald, Elizabeth, and Robert went to Kew Forest, a small private Queens institution with a WASPy air about it, located just a few miles from the Trump home. The school's old black Chrysler with fold-down seats picked up a handful of kids from the neighborhood each day at 8:00 A.M. for the twenty-minute trip and returned them by four in the afternoon. Young Donald and the rest of the Trump children were also Sunday regulars at First Presbyterian Church in Jamaica, though Fred and Mary attended only sporadically. Six days a week, at school and at church, Donald was in coat and tie from a very early age, riding in his mother's rose-colored Rolls or his father's stretch Caddy when he wasn't in the school limo. Donald's earliest teachers described him as "a jolly little boy," in sharp contrast with the more introverted Robert. But as the years went by, his prankish, easygoing behavior got in the way of good grades at Kew Forest. He was the only Trump not to finish there, pulled out by Fred at the end of seventh grade and sent to far-off New York Military Academy for a little discipline. The school, stretched across 325 country acres overlooking the Hudson, was an attempt at a rich boys' haven.

If the Kew Forest experience had set him apart from the neighbors he grew up with in Queens, five years in uniform fifty-five miles upstate in Cornwall on the Hudson was as isolating as it was formative. Nicknamed "DT" by his friends at military school, Donald became an achiever, ultimately selected commander of the Honor Guard in his junior and senior years by the school's administration and designated to lead the school's brigade up Fifth Avenue in the Columbus Day Parade in 1963. He hit cleanup on the school's winning baseball team, batting .350 and playing a sweet first base in his senior year, with Fred standing up and screaming at every home game. A tall, slender, beaming, and talkative kid, he lettered in soccer, acted in the school play, and earned a B average. He lived alone his senior year by choice and kept a meticulously clean room, getting up every morning for 6:00 A.M. formation and drills. When he graduated, he had been on his own since he was thirteen years old, and he was ready to go home for a while.

He went to college at Fordham, a forty-minute trip to the North Bronx in his red Austin-Healey 3000. It was an unusual choice—a small Jesuit men's school whose Business Administration program was not highly regarded. But it was, in a sense, a continuation of the formula that Fred had discovered in the military academy: a structured and disciplined educational program that, combined with a steadying life at home, protected Donald from the sort of freewheeling campus life he might have found elsewhere.

Donald's two years at Fordham (1964 to 1966) were an uneventful mix of a light and undistinguished course load, combined with a sporting menu that ranged from squash to football. Recruited as the punter for the school's Division III football club because he had a fifty-yard kicking range, he hurt his ankle after three or four weeks and dropped off the team. Fred came to his squash matches, but he was a mediocre player on a less-than-mediocre team. Though his teammates thought he had the talent to be a ranked player, he "wouldn't practice hard," dogging it on the coach's mandatory five-mile runs.

His doubles partner on the Fordham tennis team said, "He had a big serve, but no ground game"—a lust for the spectacular but little steady court work. Another teammate recalled that his ground game consisted of "defensive lobs," waiting for the opponent to make a mistake. Beyond an aggressive serve, Donald played "a conservative game," with a "fierce" desire to win but "no killer instinct." When the team went on a trip, the players traveled in two or three cars, and once a group went to Maryland in Donald's sports car. Though the coach gave each driver cash to cover tolls and gas, Donald insisted on each passenger's chipping in, leaving one teammate resentful decades later.

Though he "got along pretty well" with everyone, he was "not one of the guys," said one of his closer friends. "You could see he was a cut different. He was a nondrinker, which was kind of rare. He never smoked. There was an air about him, not obnoxious or offensive, but distant. I recall going to parties with him, and he had a good line with the girls, but never had a girlfriend." It was back to a mandatory coat and tie, like in his grade school days, and Donald was always perfectly tailored—"not ostentatious, but everything matched, everything fitted." That, too, set him apart from the campus's convention of deliberate tie-askew dress.

After his sophomore year, he suddenly transferred to Wharton, without telling his friends or coach at Fordham. Everyone was surprised that he had been admitted since he was hardly a star student at Fordham and Wharton was a highly selective school. There he continued to coast in class and stayed far away from the antiwar tumult that hit Penn's campus in the late sixties. He graduated in 1968, though the campus newspaper did not contain a single reference to him, and not even a senior photo of him appeared in his graduating yearbook. He was not listed as a member of any sports team, club, or fraternity throughout his two years at Wharton, in sharp contrast to his NYMA and Fordham days. When Donald became a builder who preferred marble to his conservative father's familiar brick, Fred told friends like architect Philip Birnbaum that he "sent Donald to Wharton, and all they taught him to do was spend." Within days of finishing at Penn, he headed out to Avenue Z to start the career Fred had long been preparing for him.

Somehow, with five years of military training and a string of cadet honors at NYMA, the baseball-tennis-squash star qualified for a medical deferment, classified 1Y after a physical exam at the Armed Forces Center in New York on September 17, 1968. Neither the national anguish over Vietnam, nor the riots and racial conflict tearing apart Brooklyn at the time, distracted him. In fact, when he talked Brooklyn politics with Sam Horwitz, the borough's burgeoning reform movement was of no interest to him. Donald was already fixed on the world as it was, and all he wanted to know was who had power and which was the right button to push. Even as a young man out of college, in an era when his generation was marching for change, Donald saw politics as business, just another arena where connections could be converted to profits. In 1969, the same year Richard Nixon became President, Donald registered as a Republican.

His father's Trump Village scandal had hit the newspapers and television in the middle of his sophomore year at Fordham, but Donald was unfazed by the myriad allegations against Fred and Bunny Lindenbaum. He spent summers working out of his father's office and scoffed at the charges. When he started doing his own first Manhattan deals in the middle seventies, he chose Bunny as his lawyer.

Donald's Avenue Z years were anything but glamorous. He took on the title of president of an assortment of Trump entities. With Fred as chairman of the board, Donald lay claim to the management of forty-eight privately held corporations and fifteen family partnerships. Between his arrival in 1968 and 1974, when he first floated a Manhattan deal that looked as if it might go somewhere, his principal job was managing 10,000 to 22,000 apartments, depending on whose estimate of Fred's holdings one accepted. The dollar value of this empire—whose varying size reflected in part periodic sales and purchases—was said to be as little as $40 million and, in a 1975 *BusinessWeek* article, as much as $100 million. Running it, at least to Donald, was a grind.

The job was basically a matter of collecting rent and making repairs, hardly the sort of deal-making magic Donald had in mind. Years later, in *The Art of the Deal*, he would devote a chapter to a coup he claimed he engineered in these early years—namely, the company's acquisition of a troubled Cincinnati FHA project at a risk-free, bargain-basement price. But Fred had actually closed on the project in 1964, when Donald was far off in military school. The turnaround that Donald boasted about—transforming the half-vacant, 1,200-unit project into a fully tenanted and successful one—had also long been achieved by the time he came full-time to the company. Other than any work he may have done during his summer breaks, Donald's real role was limited to the 1972 sale of the project at a handsome profit.

A more typical deal he oversaw in this era was the two-year effort to lease storefront space in a Trump-owned Coney Island shopping center to the city's Off-Track Betting Corporation. The newly created OTB was busily setting up betting parlors all over the city, and the leases became a hotly pursued, clubhouse commodity. The Trumps were such a certainty for a lease that when community opposition killed a location in one of his shopping malls, the agency insisted on moving on to another Trump mall, as if the lease were the property of a particular landlord. "We made a commitment to Trump," one local leader remembers an OTB official saying.

Even with this all-but-guaranteed business, Donald had the audacity to demand that OTB pay him a $50,000 commission for renting the agency space at prime prices in one of his buildings. In a 1971 letter to OTB, twenty-five-year-old Donald wrote of his "tremendous respect for the off track betting concept" and justified his demand for the commission by promising to surreptitiously ease the current tenant, a men's store, out of the space. "It is imperative," Donald insisted, "that Atlantic Men's Store not find out that another tenant wants access to the store."

The initially planned site for the parlor at the Trump Village Shopping Center was so close to a school that outraged parents from the middle-class project ultimately killed it. Donald then got the agency to switch the lease to the Trumps' other shopping center—the Luna Park mall, which was also just a few steps from an elementary school, but one attended by poor and minority children who lived in the nearby public housing project. In a June 1972 letter to the agency, Donald said he'd been "recently informed that the Community Planning Board [would] not exert excessive pressure" against this second location, and, as promised, the local board—dominated by the neighborhood Democratic club housed virtually rent-free in a Trump storefront—quickly approved the site.

Trump constructed a tiny new brick store stall at the end of the mall, twenty-eight by ninety feet, and obtained a ten-year lease at $26,000 a year, with an annual escalation clause but no obligation to cover heat, electricity, or any other costs. The rent was $6,000 more than Donald had asked for in his June letter. The building did not even include a bathroom, and the daily crowd of bettors relieved themselves on the side of the building. Since Fred had acquired the land for the mall from the city at no expense years earlier, the parlor was virtually pure profit, Donald's first political booty.

There were other father-son Coney Island maneuvers. Donald and Fred plied their local and citywide political connections, including comptroller Abe Beame, to override neighborhood opposition and open a McDonald's franchise on the extra land the city had sold Fred for Trump Village. The theory had been, when Fred was awarded the extra site, that he would build a secondary parking lot for residents of the housing complex, but the Trumps came out on the winning side of a city ruling in the early seventies that said the additional parking was unnecessary. With Donald doing his first behind-the-scenes city lobbying, the Trumps were able to sign a lucrative lease with the fast-food chain, which was anxious to break into the massive middle-class market in the nearby Warbasse, Trump Village, and other apartment complexes.

Opposition was so strong that the planning commission, which feared that McDonald's would continue to pull customers away from the established Coney Island retail district, approved it by only a four to three vote, and City Council President Paul O'Dwyer denounced it as "a windfall" for the Trumps, atop everything else they had already taken out of the Trump Village project.

The Trumps also continued real estate acquisitions out on the old Brooklyn turf, but most were disappointing dead ends. They announced with great fanfare the purchase of a ten-year option on a hundred acres of Brooklyn waterfront land near Shore Haven, but federal housing subsidies were drying up, and they had no plans to build the anticipated 10,000 units without them. Fred went back to Marie Tilyou for one more purchase—the majestic Tilyou Theatre across the street from the old Steeplechase site. He tore it down, speculating on a new grand plan for Coney Island, but the city's and state's midseventies' fiscal problems stymied development, and he wound up renting the property for a parking lot.

A deal that did work out was the Trumps' purchase of a 25 percent stake in the state-subsidized, almost 6,000-unit Starrett City housing complex in Brooklyn. While the Trumps played no role in building the borough's biggest development,

Donald did join his Starrett Construction Company partners in discussions with state officials about the record $362 million mortgage that financed the project. He cited his role in the acquisition of the project in a successful 1975 application for a real estate broker's license, trying to use it to catapult himself past the ordinary one-year trial period as a licensed salesman. (In a January 1975 interview for the license, he told a state examiner that he received $50,000 in yearly income "from the properties owned and operated by him.")

The Trump companies were also still wheeling and dealing in FHA projects across the country. Sometimes, though, the Trump tactic wasn't a turnaround, like the Cincinnati job, which they bought cheap, rejuvenated, and sold at a profit. In Maryland, for example, Fred wound up handcuffed and arrested by Prince George County officials when he appeared at one FHA project that local officials said he was "bleeding" dry. The arrest came in 1976, but it was after at least four years of battling Trump to make repairs on the beleaguered 504-unit Gregory Estates, which county officials flatly called "a slum property."

With over a hundred vacancies, a series of disregarded code violations, a history of heat and hot water problems, defaulting payments to FHA, hundreds of thousands overdue to the gas and electric companies, and a minuscule local staff that "couldn't buy light bulbs without authorization for New York," the project was denied a license to operate. When repeated phone conversations with Fred proved fruitless, county officials surprised him on a visit to the project and charged him with noncompliance with a notice of violation. The housing inspection supervisor indicated that "as long as an effort was being made, we'd work with an owner," but said that no improvements were being made at the project.

The flabbergasted Fred was first taken to a local precinct and required to post $100 to secure a thousand-dollar bond, which he didn't have. The housing supervisor offered to loan it to him, and he sternly rebuffed the offer. He called an angry Donald in New York, an arrangement was made to get the bond, and Fred was released. When he reappeared in the district court, the judge levied a heavy fine on Fred's corporate entity. The repairs were rapidly made, but the Trumps soon sold the property—the only one they had in the Maryland suburbs outside Washington, D.C.

Things got almost as nasty in Norfolk, Virginia, where some of the FHA projects Fred had invested in years earlier turned sour in the seventies. Residents at two of his projects, the Hague and Pembroke Towers, staged what was called the city's first rent strike against Trump and filed a lawsuit charging "a lack of hot running water, sporadic or nonexistent air conditioning and elevator service, improper swimming facilities, and insect and rodent infestation." When Fred went to meet with the tenants they almost threw him in the top-floor pool.

Then young Donald appeared on the scene, called a press conference, and told reporters: "We want to make these the finest buildings in Virginia." The same day, a waterline burst in Hague Towers—at the time, the tallest residential building in downtown Norfolk—showering the lobby, a laundry room, a beauty shop, a maintenance room, and storage areas, causing one resident to declare: "We're going to have two swimming pools."

Donald arranged a meeting with tenant attorney O. L. "Buzz" Gilbert at the office of the Trumps' Norfolk attorney, Zeke Waters, a politically connected lawyer eventually appointed to the bench. "It was the strangest meeting," recalled Gilbert. "Zeke stood up and introduced himself and Donald, and Donald turned to him and said you sit down and shut up. He put his arm around my shoulder and said, 'Buzz and I are going to settle this thing.' I thought it was typical of a New York know-it-all. I said, first of all, 'My name is Mr. Gilbert, and I'm going to speak to your lawyer.'"

The suit was settled only when Trump attended to a long list of building violations, after which Donald tried what would become a trademark tactic: hiring the other side. "He called me up," Gilbert said, "and told me he liked the way I handled the tenant suit and asked if I'd be willing to represent them in Norfolk. I asked for a $500-a-month retainer and an hourly rate, and Donald at first said they weren't going to pay that much. He finally agreed. I represented them for a year and did nothing. I never got any calls. They paid promptly." The tenant war quieted down, with the newly retained Gilbert quoted in Norfolk newspapers praising the Trumps' compliance with the settlement. He and the Trumps parted ways after a year, and later the Trumps sold the properties.

But Norfolk and Prince George County were hardly where Donald planned to spend a career, and an OTB lease was apprentice work, no matter how lucrative the payoff. His first few years at Avenue Z he commuted with Fred from Queens, but in 1971, he moved to Manhattan, where he intended eventually to bring the family company. His first Manhattan apartment, a studio off Third Avenue at 196 East 75th Street, was on the seventeenth floor of an undistinguished, twenty-one-story, white brick building, with two windows that overlooked a water tank on the courtyard of the adjacent building. Though Donald would spend years railing against New York's rent regulation system, his first apartment was rent stabilized, meaning it was covered by a maze of state and city guidelines limiting rent increases and protecting tenant rights.

He tried partitioning the place to give it a larger feel, but then he jammed it with so much furniture that it shrunk visually. He met a young architectural associate named Der Scutt at an East Side bar and brought him home to get advice on how he should redesign the tiny space. He hired an Irish maid and quickly developed a reputation among the building's workers as a cheap tipper. Some of them remember one girlfriend who lasted a while and was frequently in the apartment—a very pretty stewardess. Apart from her, and the white Cadillac convertible he parked in the next-door garage, he was hardly a memorable presence.

He stayed on 75th Street for almost four years, through his late twenties, and when he moved out in late 1974, he turned the apartment over to his younger brother, Robert. One of the subterfuges that owners of rent-regulated buildings bemoaned was that tenants covertly transferred their apartments to friends and relatives—preventing the owners from getting large rent increases permitted when a new tenant signed a lease, or from decontrolling the apartments altogether, which was allowed under new statutes designed to return vacant units to the free market. Donald boasted to friends that he had done just that.

Yet, in January of 1975, he was pictured and extensively quoted in a full-page New York *Daily News* story assailing the "ridiculous" rent stabilization system and celebrating his recent court victory in a lawsuit against the meager rent increases authorized by the regulators. "Everybody in New York gets their increases but the landlords, and we are going to put an end to that practice," Donald promised the *News*.

He moved south, which was the right direction to go for an ambitious young man, though his new Third Avenue apartment was only on the fringes of the Upper East Side gold coast. The Phoenix, at 160 East 65th, was nonetheless a gigantic step up. Donald now had a one-bedroom penthouse with one and a half bathrooms on the northeast corner of the thirty-second floor, which he decorated in beiges and brown and lots of chrome, a style he would continue to favor through much of his life. A bank of living room windows that continued into the dining area offered views of the George Washington Bridge and New Jersey to the north and Great Neck, Long Island, and Brooklyn to the east. He brought along the Irish maid, but dropped the convertible for a new gray limo. On the verge of thirty, he was ready to shed the boyish lifestyle of his 75th Street studio.

He never wore casual clothes, even on weekends, and was always going in and out of the building in a suit or blazer, his initials sewn into his shirts and engraved on his gold cuff links. The garage bill for his company-owned car was sent out to Avenue Z, where he went most mornings as well, usually coming down from his apartment before 8:00 A.M. and getting home before eight at night. He drove the car himself until late 1976, when a newspaper profile published his address and a smiling photo of him in his apartment. Around the time of the profile interview, he hired an ex-cop chauffeur who doubled as an armed bodyguard, and became a bit more reclusive.

Living in Manhattan was, in Donald's view, an occupational necessity: He was studying the real estate around him. As early as 1972, shortly after Donald had first moved to Manhattan, a Trump entity made its first submission on a Manhattan project, bidding to get a piece of a huge Lindsay administration plan called East River Landing, a waterfront development planned below Wall Street that never came to fruition. He and Fred were also quoted in an early seventies' story as planning to build an East Side rental apartment building that never got off the drawing boards. Despite these aborted efforts, Donald remained on the lookout. Steve Weissman, who lived a floor below him at the Phoenix, remembers bumping into Donald on the street one day and Trump blurting out: "Steve, you're friendly with the owner of the building. Approach him with an offer of $10 or $12 million. There's a million in it for you."

At some point during his initial forays in Manhattan, he also met the man who, after Fred, would become the most important influence on his early career, Roy Cohn. Infamous for his 1950s role as chief counsel to Senator Joseph McCarthy, Cohn was by the 1970s a peculiarly New York institution, a lawyer who could simultaneously represent the Archdiocese and the bosses of several organized crime families. It is difficult to determine precisely when he and Donald first met. Trump testified years later that it was in 1970 at a Manhattan restaurant. Cindy Adams, one of the many New York gossip columnists once close to Cohn, said Cohn introduced her to Trump at a dinner party the same year. Yet Donald's account of their first encounter in *The Art of the Deal* dates it as 1973, when he claims they discussed a case that was filed against the Trump companies that fall.

Whenever Donald met him, Cohn was by the early seventies a walking advertisement for every form of graft, the best-known fixer in New York. In 1970, he was under indictment in both New York and Illinois. Already acquitted in two criminal trials in the sixties, he would survive these two as well. The Illinois banking indictment was dropped without a trial, while the New York bribery and conspiracy case ended with his third acquittal. Cohn was also in his second decade of annual IRS audits, occasioned by his refusal to pay any taxes at all. He lived like a millionaire, yet openly boasted that he had literally no income, drawing lavishly from his law firm's expense account and all the cash bribes he could collect. In his early forties, a balding, rail-thin five-foot eight-inch wraith whose bloodshot eyes, scarred nose, and surgically taut face gave him a demonic look, Cohn was senior partner in Saxe, Bacon, Bolan, a tiny firm headquartered in the East Side town house where he lived. His monied and mob clients gave him a Rolls, a three-and-a-half-acre Greenwich, Connecticut, summer house, a yacht, a Bentley, and a Cadillac convertible just like Donald's, all owned by the law firm.

The son of a Bronx judge, Cohn was reared in the clubhouse culture of the city, attending dinner parties as a teenager with Carmine DeSapio, Ed Flynn, and the other Democratic bosses who ruled New York. He had also met Abe Beame in his father's house, and over the years became an adviser to both Beame and new Brooklyn Democratic Chairman Meade Esposito. In fact, he played a pivotal role in 1973, when bridesmaid Beame, who was again city comptroller, finally won the mayoral election.

It was Cohn who privately convinced the *New York Times* that Beame's leading opponent, Bronx Congressman Mario Biaggi, had taken the Fifth Amendment before a federal grand jury the year before. Cohn happened to know this because Biaggi had come to him for legal advice and told him that he'd refused to testify. When the *Times* published the charge against Biaggi, with the source cited as anonymous, Biaggi denied it, the testimony was eventually released, and Biaggi's candidacy was destroyed. The gambit made Roy Cohn a fixture in Abe Beame's government and Beame a trophy at Cohn's frequent parties.

In the spring of 1974, soon after Beame's inaugural, both Cohn and the Trumps had tables at the Brooklyn Democratic Party's annual dinner at the Waldorf—a ballroom filled with a dozen indicted, soon-to-be-indicted, or convicted public and party officials. They listened as the new mayor told the crowd, including the two law secretaries to Supreme Court judges who would eventually plead guilty to stealing $100,000 in ticket receipts from this and three previous Brooklyn dinners, that "critics might call" the Brooklyn organization "a machine," but that he'd been proud of his membership in it for forty years and that "no one need apologize for being part of it." Brooklyn had proven, Abe Beame announced, that "effective party organization need not be synonymous with smoke-filled rooms." For Fred, a lifetime of binding friendships had culminated in Abe Beame's election. But for Donald and Cohn, it was just a new season of opportunity.

It was only a few months after Beame won the mayoral runoff that Donald first retained Cohn. The case in question had nothing to do with the city administration, but the timing of Cohn's retention had everything to do with the formal merger of these two disparate wings—one from Brooklyn, one from

Manhattan—of the loose amalgam that had helped make Beame king. To Donald, the case he put in Roy's hands was a mere nuisance. No money was at stake. The Justice Department had brought a major racial discrimination suit against the company, contending that the Trumps had systematically refused to rent to blacks. Four superintendents or rental agents working for Trump confirmed to federal authorities that applications for apartments were coded by race. Doormen were told to discourage applications from blacks by telling them that there were no vacancies or by jacking up the rents. One staffer said that his instructions came straight from Fred and the company went so far as to try to figure out how "to decrease the number of black tenants" already in one development "by encouraging them to locate housing elsewhere."

The government was willing from the start to sign a consent decree with the Trumps, compelling them to take certain affirmative steps to integrate their estimated 14,000 units in the New York area, but Donald and Cohn agreed that they'd much rather fight. Donald's public diatribe was that the Justice Department was trying to force them to take "welfare recipients." Cohn echoed him, declaring in a shrill affidavit that the government sought "the capitulation of the defendants and the substitution of the Welfare Department for the management corporation." Roy countersued the government for $100 million, but the judge called it a "waste of time and paper" and threw the suit out a month later.

Donald's deposition in the case in March of 1974 caught the essence of his social conscience. He didn't know what the Fair Housing Act of 1969 was and freely admitted that the company had done nothing to implement it. Asked when the first black had moved into one of his predominantly white projects, Donald replied: "I don't care and I don't know." In a color-blind pose, he repeatedly said he had no idea what the racial composition of his tenants or employees was even though he casually mentioned complexes the company owned that were 100 percent white and ones that were all black. He claimed that the company's only eligibility standard for tenants was the income of the man in the family, noting that "we don't generally include the wife's income; we like to see it for the male in the family."

Donald also debuted his talent for manipulating the truth, sworn or otherwise. In an attempt to put distance between himself and the discriminatory practices of the Trump companies, he repeatedly claimed he did not handle the rental of apartments. Asked if he "ever had anything to do with rental decisions in individual cases," he answered: "No, I really don't." Yet he told the state examiner for his brokerage license, according to written reports filed shortly after his deposition in the race case, that "he supervises and controls the renting of all apartments owned by the Trump organization." Indeed, he showed the examiner hundreds of files "containing leases and rental records for commercial and residential tenants, all of which contained applicant's signature and handwriting." Matthew Tosti, the longtime Trump attorney, also wrote state officials supporting Donald's license application and contended that Donald had "negotiated numerous leases for apartments."

Another example of this penchant for misstatement drew the attention of his federal interrogators. He had complained to reporters when the lawsuit was announced by the Justice Department that he'd first learned about it on his car radio riding to work, when in fact, according to the government attorneys, he and the organization had been notified both during the probe and at the time of the filing of the suit.

The litigation dragged on for a year and a half, with the federal investigation intensifying and Cohn deriding it as "a spit in the ocean." Finally, Donald signed the consent decree. The government called the decree—which required advertisements in minority papers, minority employment promotions, and a preferential vacancy listing with the Urban League—"one of the most far reaching ever negotiated." Donald sneered in news stories that the Trumps had won, since they still weren't required to take welfare recipients.

In any event, four years later, in the summer of 1978, the Justice Department found the Trumps in contempt of the decree and called them back into court. Cohn picked up his argument where he'd left off, branding the new case a "rehash" without "the slightest merit," attributable to "planted malcontents." It all remained irrelevant to Donald. The bottom line was that two government discrimination lawsuits had had no effect on the company's ability to make development deals, usually with the government's help. The charges were just not a part of the world in which he operated.

The decision to seek a settlement of the initial race suit in late 1974 came just as Donald was getting ready to put together the pieces of his first tangible Manhattan deals, just as he moved into the Phoenix, just as he put on the full-court press with state officials to qualify for a broker's license. He was positioning himself for the breakthrough deals that at last seemed right around the corner.

4

FIRST FORAY

He wanted fame and reputation, but he wanted money even more; he intended to get both. To one who had been working thus long in the minor realms of finance, as Cowperwood considered that he had so far been doing, this sudden upward step into the more conspicuous regions of high finance and control was an all-inspiring thing. So long had he been stirring about in a lesser region, paving the way by hours and hours of private thought and conference and scheming, that now when he actually had achieved his end he could scarcely believe for the time being that it was true.

—*Theodore Dreiser,* The Titan

EVEN IN THE hard times of the 1974 recession, the vast and largely vacant West Side rail yard, stretching from 59th Street to 72nd Street, had a sweet allure. A windswept prairie of plausible opportunity—just off the Hudson and directly below the green glory of Riverside Park—the ninety-three-acre yard emerged in the seventies as the largest slice of developable land in the heart of Manhattan. Streams of sun-glistened tracks still ran through this ghost town of abandoned loading platforms, but they carried fewer and fewer trains—barely half the number of carloads they had in 1970, the year the yard's owner, Penn Central, went bust.

With the nation's largest railroad disabled in a Philadelphia bankruptcy court, its onetime premier yard became both a relic of the manufacturing age it had dominated and an incalculable prize for new generations of designers and developers. It had once, through the cataclysm of the Second World War and its aftermath of boom, been a thriving commercial center. But with the demise of the produce and garment industries it had begun its decline by the start of the sixties, generating a series of railroad-encouraged housing, marinas, and park development plans for the increasingly underutilized property. The dream, which had already sustained fourteen years of costly and unproductive studies, was to transform the yard into a colossus New City within the City, the last frontier on an island of already redundant towers.

In 1974, with Abe Beame bringing the Madison Club from Eastern Parkway to Gracie Mansion, there seemed to be no limits to what the old Brooklyn gang, or its progeny, could do. Virtually from the day Beame won his primary victory in 1973, twenty-nine-year-old Donald Trump determinedly pressed his pioneer bid for the future of this dying yard, as if Brooklyn might at last stake its own gold coast claim.

With Stanley Steingut as assembly speaker and Beame as mayor, the ancient and insular wing of the Brooklyn party long identified with the Trump family was now the most powerful Democratic faction in state and city politics. There had not been such a concentration of power in a Democratic organization since the heyday of Tammany. In addition, as early as the final few weeks of 1973, the Trumps climbed aboard the then underestimated campaign of Congressman Hugh Carey, another son of the Brooklyn machine, who would in 1974 defeat Republican Governor Malcolm Wilson. Young Donald saw himself as uniquely positioned to be the golden-boy beneficiary of this combine's moment in the sun.

Trump coupled this political opportunity with a rational development agenda, whose first item was the bankrupt Penn Central's listing of Manhattan properties available for sale. Savoring this list as if it were a map of potential land deals, Donald started with the 60th Street yard, envisioning a 20,000-unit phalanx of waterfront towers that would transcend his father's Trump Village, Shore Haven, and Beach Haven in a single splashy stroke. He followed the tracks down to a second site at 34th Street, where the railroad owned another semi-abandoned yard, far busier than the 60th Street location.

While he was certain of the residential marketability of the uptown yard, which sat adjacent to existing luxury housing and Lincoln Center, he was not sure just what he would do with the smaller 34th Street site, which was wedged between the water and blocks of musty warehouses and factories. But he resolved to go after the forty-four-acre property without a clear idea of what he would actually build there (he initially said 10,000 units of housing, and later he would add attempts at a Penn Central hotel, a Lexington Avenue office building, and even the land the railroad owned under Madison Square Garden). Trump was trying to mesh the property assets of a gutted railroad with the political as-sets of a Brooklyn dynasty come to power.

The man at the other side of the table, who almost immediately grasped the genius of this plan, was Ned Eichler, the effusive and daring new manager of Penn Central's nonrail real estate assets in New York. A Californian with the scholarly confidence of a onetime Berkeley planning professor, the forty-four-year-old Eichler worked within the business world but never seemed to be of it—a perpetual observer, always standing outside the very events in which he was involved, studying them.

Like Donald, he was the son of a great builder. His father, Joseph Eichler, had created Eichler Homes in San Francisco in 1947, the same year that Fred Trump left homebuilding to start Shore Haven. The 10,000 redwood-paneled homes that Joe Eichler built made him the West Coast Bill Levitt, praised as a master builder in academic works his son began publishing in the sixties and would write into the eighties. But the same shift from homebuilding to high-rise apartment construction that had catapulted Fred Trump to great wealth bank-rupted Joe Eichler in the sixties. Ned, who was then in his thirties and a vice president of the company, split with his father over this diversification decision and left, never to return. By 1974, when Ned Eichler moved to New York to take over the management and sale of a withered railroad's assets, Joe Eichler was a small-time California builder of custom "Eichlers." In the middle of Ned's day-to-day negotiating sessions with Donald, Joe Eichler died of a heart attack. Ned's last letter to him, an invitation to play stickball in Joe's native New York, was found, unanswered, in his desk drawer.

Since his days with Eichler Homes, Ned had run a major garden apartment construction company in California and finally, in 1973, joined Victor Palm-ieri and Company, a California-based financial consulting firm. Palmieri had been appointed by the trustees of Penn Central to turn its real estate assets into cash and get the company reorganized out of bankruptcy. Assigned initially to the company's Washington, D.C., office, Eichler had stumbled across Trump's name in December 1973, when he read a letter written to the Palmieri company a month or so earlier inquiring about the two West Side yards. "Who the hell is Donald Trump?" he had blurted out to a receptionist.

Eichler checked with Palmieri and the Penn Central people in New York, but no one could answer his question. When he reached Trump on the phone, he understood why. He could tell from Donald's voice that he was too new to the scene to be familiar. All he could hear was a cocky kid telling him again and again that he was "the only appropriate candidate to act as a developer for this job." Trump was laying the family business history on the line and urging Eichler to visit their projects when he came to New York. "I'll send my limo to pick you up in midtown," Donald offered.

Penn Central had received inquiry letters from developers with bigger names, but Trump intrigued Eichler. Even in these first conversations, Ned Eichler felt the Trump energy climbing through the phone lines. He thought he heard the kind of maniacal drive he'd observed in many successful builders, including his own father.

From the moment Ned Eichler met Donald and Fred Trump in January of 1974, a few days after the inauguration of Abe Beame, thoughts of his own relationship with Joe Eichler dogged him. Ned discerned something in Fred Trump that was foreign, something far removed from what he had experienced during all of the years he and Joe Eichler had fenced with each other. He saw a rich and tough father, as he would put it years later, "proud of and even deferential toward a brash son seeking to climb into the big, glamorous and dangerous game of Manhattan real estate." A beaming Donald took him to see Beach Haven, Shore Haven, Trump Village, and even further down the road to Starrett City, a 5,000-unit job then in construction, and told him it was a joint venture involving Starrett and Trump. (In fact, the Trumps were merely passive equity investors in the project—billed as the largest subsidized development in America at the time.) The visit impressed him. The kid impressed him.

From the first phone conversation with Eichler, Donald had been boasting about his political connections, and Eichler knew well enough that the development of these yards was inextricably linked to politics. He would need political help to free the yards from the rail functions they still performed, since only federal, state, and city authorities could permit the closing of either yard and its sale for other uses. And, on another difficult front, only the city could lift the industrial zoning restraints that were attached to the land and rezone it for the sort of commercial and housing development that would give the site real value. Finally, only the state or federal government could create the subsidy package necessary to both pay the maximum premium for the land and finance the construction of the project.

The situation was further complicated by the fact that neither Donald, nor any other possible buyer, was prepared to pay cash for the sites commensurate with their rezoned future value. The only way to get real benefit out of the yards for the railroad (and Palmieri) was for Penn Central to effectively become a partner of the potential developer—to give him an option and to share in the sale price the developer ultimately won from whatever government entity agreed to subsidize a project there. An auction, Eichler knew, would produce a pittance. The larger the project a developer could get zoned and financed, the greater the land price would be and the grander the return for the railroad. It was also not an incidental fact that the Palmieri company's fees were pegged to a percentage of the gains they brought their bankrupt client.

Eichler understood that his own superiors at Palmieri, as well as the railroad trustees and a federal judge who had to approve every major transaction, would have doubts about conveying a hundred-million-dollar set of properties to an unknown young man. To reassure himself, he had to test the credibility of both the paternal and political commitments Donald boasted of so often. So during one early business meeting at Eichler's midtown office, he suddenly told Donald he needed proof of his clout.

"What kind of proof?" Donald asked.

"I guess I'll have to see the mayor," Eichler said.

Trump seemed irritated. "When do you want to see him?" he asked. Eichler already had a sense of Trump's gift for theater; he sensed a bit more of it was on its way.

"Tomorrow at two P.M.," Eichler said, playing along.

Trump did not hesitate. "Be outside your office at one-thirty," Donald demanded. "My limo will pick you up." Eichler was stunned. It was already late in the afternoon; how could Trump even know if Beame was in town? How could he be so confident of instant access?

The car arrived the next day without Donald. "Mr. Trump will join you at the mayor's office," the driver said and took him downtown to the steps of City Hall. When Eichler walked up to the main reception desk, he seemed expected. A secretary ushered him back to the mayor's private office, where Donald was waiting. Trump greeted him, introducing him to his father, City Planning Commission Chairman John Zuccotti, and the mayor. Abe Beame had been mayor for less than three weeks, and he had yet to be hit with the fiscal crisis that would soon level his government. For the moment, at least, the five-foot two-inch bookkeeper who'd entered politics as a Madison Club captain almost five decades earlier was riding high.

Donald made a brief statement about Eichler's role and his own hopes. The two made brief speeches about the threshold issue with the properties—the need to have the appropriate federal agencies define them as unnecessary for rail use, freeing them up for sale. Each noted how crucial the city would be in shaping federal policy. Beame asked a few innocuous questions. Then, somehow, the mayor got his arms around the respective shoulders of the two Trumps, even the taller and temporarily stooped Donald, looked directly at Eichler and Zuccotti, and announced: "Whatever Donald and Fred want, they have my complete backing."

Eichler had been around. He had met many politicians and was acquainted with their brand of casual hyperbole. He knew that relationships with them were often built on quicksand, but he sensed he'd encountered something very different here. There was nothing circumspect about Beame's performance, nor did it feel overblown or unreal. Ned Eichler believed in that instant that the mayor would do all he could for Fred Trump. Eichler had no doubt that it was Fred, not Donald, who'd arranged the overnight meeting and the oral commitment.

Zuccotti remained with Beame while the two Trumps and Eichler walked out into a sunny wintry afternoon. On the steps of City Hall, Eichler talked with Fred and Donald for twenty minutes or so about the building business and about Donald's grand move to Manhattan. Fred seemed to defer to Donald; at sixty-eight, he was willingly passing the family business on, energized by the visionary plans of his son.

Eichler discovered, however, that though Fred might have accepted a secondary role in public, he would serve as a necessary business partner for Donald and he was written into the body of the deal that Eichler and Donald soon began to structure. Fred Trump's name would appear a dozen times in the eventual agreement, and its final language would provide, buried in the fine print, an option that was as exercisable by Fred as it was by Donald. The option was in the name of the Trump Village Construction Corporation, the Fred Trump entity that had built his scandal-ridden project in the sixties.

Eichler and Donald cut the deal over the next six months, winding their way through a 65-page contract and working out a timetable for the first phase of the anticipated zoning changes and housing subsidies that reached thirteen years into the future. The long hours of negotiation cemented a relationship between the two, and Eichler could increasingly sense Donald's impatience with the unavoidably long-term and tentative nature of the project. Even before the West Side deal was done, he began hearing an anxious Donald, hunting for a quicker route to Manhattan stardom, talk about other Penn Central properties.

"I'll never marry and I'll die before I'm forty," he explained his rush to Eichler. "I haven't got much time."

Another time, during the months of talks, Donald and he took a rare walk in Central Park and Eichler discovered that for Donald, the park was merely the lawn in front of his future properties. He pointed to the buildings on Fifth Avenue and Central Park South and declared: "I'll be bigger than all of them. I'll be bigger than Helmsley in five years."

In addition to doses of Trump fatalism and optimism, Eichler also got a taste of a cynicism in Donald so ingrained it surprised Eichler, who, while fifteen years older, quickly came to recognize his own comparative naiveté and idealism. At one point Donald said to him that "someone in your position by now should have several million stashed away," suggesting that anyone with effective control over such a list of properties should have already used them to enrich himself. "I don't get you," Donald smirked. Trump sent Eichler a television set in the middle of their bargaining and expressed surprise when he returned it.

Another time, as they walked down Lexington Avenue together, Trump saw a newspaper headline announcing the arrest of a New Jersey mayor for allegedly taking an $800,000 bribe from a developer. "There is no goddamn mayor in America worth $800,000," Trump bellowed. "I can buy a U.S. senator for $200,000."

By July 1974, Eichler and Donald had at last reached agreement on an option. The Palmieri company then recommended approval of the agreement to the Penn Central trustees, and the trustees voted for it the same day. Before the contract could be legally executed, however, it had to be reviewed by U.S. District Court Judge John Fullam and the company's creditors and shareholders. That would prove to be a process that would test the will of the city's newest developer.

Just before Eichler went forward with the formal submission of the long-awaited Trump contract, he began to hear rumblings of other bids. The first came from Starrett, a surprising source, especially in view of the earlier tour Donald had given Eichler. The bid came in through the back door and at the last moment, catching Eichler off guard and making him uncharacteristically defensive. He would behave in the weeks of battle that followed as if any threat to Trump's bid was a challenge to the financial advisers who had recommended it. "It was my deal and I wanted it to work," Eichler said years later, conceding that he might have been a little too single-minded about getting the contract nailed down.

The Starrett bid originated in the old Penn Central real estate division, which continued to exist after Palmieri was retained in 1973 but lost much of its in-house clout. Herman Getzoff, a little-known Manhattan broker with longtime ties to the division's chief, had learned of the imminent sale to Trump and began hunting for a competitive bid, encouraged by assurances from his friends at the real estate division that he would be paid a brokerage commission if a bidder he produced could top the Trump price. A white-haired, courtly man with a theatrical air, the seventy-three-year-old Getzoff would prove an energetic and resourceful rival to Trump in the coming months.

Getzoff arranged a meeting with Eichler in mid-July, shortly before the formal petition to the court to approve the Trump deal was submitted. While the contingencies in the Trump contract made comparisons between the monetary values of the offers impossible, there was little question but that Starrett's bid was roughly as good, and very possibly better, than Trump's. The issue at hand was that Starrett claimed its maximum payment under a long-term, complicated formula would be $160 million for the two sites, while Eichler's own calculations for the maximum payment under the Trump deal was $123 million. Both sides had arguments about the reasonableness of the other's estimates, but no one ever heard the arguments. (In *The Art of the Deal,* Trump would peg his purchase price at $62 million and concede that Starrett's, which he inaccurately claimed came in after his contract was sent to the court, was "a lot higher than mine.")

When Getzoff volunteered to put in writing on the same day as the initial meeting a detailed description of the Starrett offer, Eichler asked instead for a letter from Starrett's chairman, Robert Olnick. Getzoff supplied the letter a few days later, but it was never presented to the trustees, and six days afterward the trustees formally petitioned the court to approve the Trump deal. Only the Trump proposal would be submitted to the court.

Eichler began aggressively fending off the persistent Getzoff, suggesting in a letter to Olnick that Getzoff had misrepresented himself as a broker selected to find buyers by Penn Central. This charge, vigorously contested by Getzoff, was in sharp contrast with the Palmieri company's indifference to Trump's hyping of his own role with Palmieri, including his repeated suggestions that he was the exclusive broker or optionee of Penn Central properties he did not in fact control—a Trump gambit that would continue for years. In the same letter to Olnick, Eichler rejected the offer on the grounds of tardiness and urged Olnick to seek "other parcels."

Eichler's spurning of a potentially superior bid made the Trump deal vulnerable to a court challenge from creditors, but Donald, apparently informed of the Starrett offer, acted quickly to end that threat. He paid a visit to Olnick on August 7, and as Getzoff eventually testified: "Trump and Olnick met. Trump is an investor with Olnick in Starrett projects. After that meeting, Olnick called me and told me he was withdrawing his offer. Nothing we could do about it. But Starrett advised me that if Trump lost this deal for any reason, he would still be interested as per his original offer now rescinded."

Asked to explain Starrett's withdrawal, which came so abruptly and long before the court could compare the offers, Trump said simply: "Starrett and Trump are partners in Starrett City, of which we own 25 percent and they own 5 percent. Frankly, if we hadn't put in the $7 million equity, the project wouldn't have been built. We have a big relationship with Starrett." With Olnick's withdrawal, Donald had met his first challenge head-on, but Herman Getzoff was not about to concede. He soon found an ally in a slight, balding Philadelphia lawyer named David Berger. Berger had once been the city solicitor, but he had since built a lucrative private practice, principally around an aggressive pursuit of class-action lawsuits.

Early in the bankruptcy proceedings, Berger had been selected to represent the shareholders of the publicly traded Penn Central holding company. Any shareholder claims stood far behind those of the banks and other secured creditors, making it Berger's job to create as much fuss as possible in the drawn-out proceedings so that his unsecured clients might get a few cents on a dollar if the company ever reorganized itself out of bankruptcy. The Palmieri group was already on Berger's enemies list; he had questioned its consulting contract, just as he had opposed many of the major expenditures or asset sales proposed so far during the bankruptcy. The Trump sale would be no exception.

But this time Getzoff would give him some ammunition—as would Eichler and the appraisal company selected by Eichler. Getzoff briefed a young associate in Berger's firm, Ed Rubenstone, and a well-armed Rubenstone began taking key witnesses apart in depositions. The twenty-eight-year-old Rubenstone started with Eichler himself and got him to admit that he had bypassed an entire list of interested brokers, developers, and attorneys to deal solely and secretly with Trump over many months.

"It seemed self-evident" that other developers would be interested, testified Eichler. "We proceeded to make a judgment as to which one we thought would be best and we judged that Trump would be. This developer had to be very, very high in his political position." Penn Central, said Eichler, was looking for the developer "who seemed best positioned in the New York market to get rezoning and government financing," and Trump was picked "to do what in our judgment if anybody can do, he can do."

Eight days before a November 11, 1974, scheduled hearing in front of Judge Fullam on the Trump sale, Rubenstone also challenged Bidder's appraiser in a 235-page deposition. The appraiser had understated the current, industrially zoned value of the two yards, comparing one of them exclusively to parcels in Brooklyn, Queens, and the Bronx, assigning no value to the structures still on the yards, and then discounting even his own estimate by 50 percent. He had assigned the 30th Street yards a four-dollar-per-square-foot value, when Penn Central had just sold a similarly zoned adjacent parcel for almost seven times that. Rubenstone openly declared that he thought they "had the deal broken," that the appraiser's deposition "was devastating in terms of the fair market value of the property."

When the deposition was completed, Rubenstone asked Getzoff to testify as a witness for the shareholders about the squelching of the Starrett offer. By now Getzoff had also been working on a new counteroffer from another major New York builder very familiar to the Trumps—HRH—and he told Rubenstone that its offer would be ready before the hearing. Rubenstone also asked Getzoff to bring a consultant he'd retained to analyze the Trump, Starrett, and HRH offers, Herbert Chason, an expert on subsidy programs. Chason, too, would testify, particularly about Mitchell-Lama, which both Trump and HRH planned to use to finance the land purchase and subsequent development.

The HRH bid was submitted to Palmieri, Penn Central, and the court on November 7, only four days before the showdown hearing. "We've been interested in developing the yards over a period of almost a decade," HRH president Richard Ravitch, one of the city's biggest builders, wrote the court. "However, we were not advised that the trustees were considering selling the yards until after a petition was filed with the bankruptcy court for approval of such a transaction."

Like the Starrett offer, HRH's looked better on its face than Trump's. The two key advantages of the HRH submission, from the railroad's standpoint, would occur at the beginning and very end of the project. Trump had won an extraordinary concession from Eichler: Penn Central would provide $750,000 in start-up funds, paying for much of the early design, title, survey, and other costs on its own. HRH, in contrast, agreed to do what developers in these circumstances routinely do: risk their own up-front money. Second, if the project was ever approved, the Trump proposal let him walk away with 15 percent of any profit the railroad made on the sale of the land to a government agency. Not only did HRH seek no such profit-sharing plan, but it also pointed out that Mitchell-Lama regulations specifically barred such schemes. On the other hand, the Trump plan did have a feature favorable to the railroad that HRH's did not have—an option for the company to own a piece of the projects eventually built—but this option had only very long-term speculative tax-loss value to the cash-starved company.

The HRH offer, the faulty appraisal, the damaging depositions, and the Starrett rejection gave Berger, Rubenstone, and Getzoff confidence that they had a genuine chance at blocking Trump. Berger was so certain of their position that he called Eichler in New York and summoned him and two Penn Central attorneys to Philadelphia for a Sunday night emergency meeting. He assailed them about the contract, denouncing it as "a disaster" and vowing "to move heaven and earth to stop it."

When the HRH offer was filed, Eichler took it far more seriously than he had the Starrett bid and prepared an immediate affidavit for the court analyzing it. While his affidavit sidestepped the two obvious HRH advantages and the contention that the Trump profit-sharing plan violated state regulations, it made telling points about HRH's deep, ongoing involvement in two troubled Manhattan rental projects. Eichler argued that these problems on sites so close to the West Side yards would be a distraction for HRH, if not an outright conflict of interest.

The Palmieri people had grown accustomed to Berger's histrionics, but to Donald he seemed a considerable adversary. Eichler watched as Donald became "a bundle of nerves," fearful that Berger might be able to stymie court approval. Donald was so anxious he began speaking with Berger on the phone, telling Eichler he had opened a dialogue with Berger but not revealing the subject of their conversations.

Only a few days before the hearing Trump paid a visit to Berger's Philadelphia town-house office. When Trump arrived, Berger, Rubenstone, and a few associates were meeting in the upstairs conference room, discussing the upcoming Penn Central hearings. Trump swooped into the room with a long, dark green cape wrapped around his shoulders, jittery and flushed. After quick introductions around the room, Berger and Trump adjourned to Berger's private office. The meeting continued, and Rubenstone eventually drifted back to his own office, where he worked until Berger summoned him. Trump had left, but Berger announced that he and Donald had reached an agreement. Berger told Rubenstone to cancel Getzoff's testimony; the firm would support the Trump contract.

Trump had agreed in his discussions with Berger to a couple of changes in the agreement, though the most significant of them seemed calculated to benefit him, not the shareholders. He had won the right to withdraw from the deal without penalty if the profit-sharing plan was barred by a government financing agency. That meant Penn Central could advance him $750,000 of its money to underwrite a project from which he could walk away without cost. While the new terms gave Penn Central a greater cut of the eventual project profits, these were fractional boosts in the most speculative aspects of the deal. When Trump and Berger brought the language they'd worked out to Eichler, the Palmieri group readily assented, though Eichler would say later that they all smelled a rat.

Berger was proud of the supposed concessions he'd won, but Eichler and crew were openly contemptuous of the real value of the seemingly minor changes. They were also intrigued by Berger's sudden turnabout. Rubenstone, who left the Berger firm in the months following this hearing, was devastated. "I thought we had a pretty solid case, and suddenly it was decided not to pursue it. That troubles me," he later said.

When the hearing before Fullam finally took place, Getzoff and his consultant Chason showed up anyway, determined to get their bid before the court. They watched Donald arrive, accompanied by the sixty-six-year-old Bunny Lindenbaum, the embodiment of Trump power in the Beame era. Getzoff and Chason were greeted that morning outside the courtroom by a solicitous Berger. "Berger took us aside and suggested that 'instead of fighting' wouldn't I withdraw the HRH proposal so the whole matter could be settled at the hearing," wrote Getzoff in a memo the same day. "Berger stated that he was sure that if we played ball, he could work out a very satisfactory brokerage commission for us. We informed Mr. Berger that 'we don't play that kind of game.'" Rubenstone, who was standing silently next to Berger during this exchange, became visibly agitated. Getzoff posed the obvious question that Berger's offer raised in the same memo: "From what source did Berger expect to get 'the very satisfactory commission'? From the court? From the trustees? Or the stockholders? Or a source whom neither Mr. Chason nor I represented?"

The "source" as Getzoff saw it, nominee Donald Trump, made his own approach to the broker later that day, aware that Getzoff was the final obstacle to the first big deal of his life. "This arrogant young man patted me on the back in a most patronizing manner and asked if I might be his broker," Getzoff recalled. "I assured him that I was not in need of having a patron builder. He said it's rare that you people—meaning brokers—are honest."

Berger's change of heart, though, meant that Getzoff could no longer appear as a witness, at least one called by the shareholders. When he attempted to testify anyway, Penn Central attorneys tried to block him, arguing that he had no legal standing in the case. But Judge Fullam wanted to hear the testimony: "I am not at all satisfied from what I have heard so far that there has been adequate consideration given to the competing offers. I would not like to create the impression that whichever offer was first seriously considered by the trustees is exclusive of all other possibilities." When Getzoff left the stand, Fullam reserved decision on the petition for the Trump contract, advised opponents of the Trump deal to "get in the posture of litigating," and ended the hearing. The litigation advice was in effect Fullam's expression of concern about HRH's failure to appear at the hearing, leaving two brokers, Getzoff and Chason, to make their case. The judge wanted to see a stronger sign of genuine HRH interest.

Instead of filing legal papers with the court, however, HRH's Ravitch submitted more letters, seeking a meeting with the trustees and making persuasive arguments to the court and to the trustees about his own preferable bid. The trustees, bound to the Palmieri firm they'd selected, declined to meet with Ravitch.

Finally, after waiting four months, Judge Fullam ruled in Trump's favor, faulting HRH for never having retained counsel and concluding that the company decided not to make a real fight of it.* He also made clear in this March 1975 decision just how crucial a role Berger had played. In an obvious reference to Berger, Fullam noted that creditors had undertaken discovery and retained experts to scrutinize the merits of Trump's and HRH's proposals and that these creditors had not previously hesitated to challenge recommendations of the trustees. But "no party to the reorganization proceeding has expressed objections to the present proposal," and none had "expressed a preference for the HRH proposal." Noting that he generally left the business judgments to the trustees, he said that his own comparison of the two bids left him "no basis for interfering with the trustees' choice." †

What Judge Fullam did not know was that David Berger and Donald Trump were quietly establishing a relationship with one another in an arena far away from the Penn Central proceedings. A few months before Berger's sudden switch at the November hearing, he and Donald had attended a meeting together in the offices of a Manhattan realtor named George Mehlman. The purpose of the meeting was to discuss an antitrust lawsuit that Berger was filing in federal court

---

* Ravitch had, in the midst of this conflict, been asked by the new governor, Hugh Carey, to take over the state's near bankrupt Urban Development Corporation. His preoccupation with UDC, and the hemorrhaging projects HRH was already building on the West Side, may have reduced Ravitch's challenge to the Trump deal to a halfhearted effort.

† What no one, including Donald, was aware of was the stark similarity between the maneuverings in this bankruptcy buyout and one that had taken place almost precisely forty years earlier in Brooklyn in 1934, when Fred Trump look control of the Lehrenkrauss mortgage servicing company. Like Donald at the Penn Central hearing, Fred won a bid battle without submitting the best bid, aided by the very attorneys whose job it was to maximize revenue to the bankrupt shell.

in Brooklyn on behalf of a loosely organized group of major New York apartment owners who wanted to challenge the oil companies for fixing the price of heating oil.

While Trump was not listed as a plaintiff in the initial papers filed in the case—which sought damages for oil company overcharges—he and several other large landlords were waiting in the wings, ready to join the litigation. Berger had a powerful financial stake in Trump's signing on for the lawsuit: His firm would get a third of any settlement, and the size of the award would be determined by the number of apartment units owned by landlords who became plaintiffs. Moreover, to cover the costs of litigation, each plaintiff paid a one-dollar-per-apartment advance to Berger. The oil companies actually charged in court papers that Berger had violated the canons of ethics by improperly soliciting clients, an indication of just how much this was a Berger-generated, as opposed to client-generated, lawsuit.*

When Trump ultimately became a plaintiff, he brought more apartments into the case than any of the other eight plaintiff groups. While Donald would later make much of the fact that he did not formally join the case until two years after Berger's switch on the Penn Central option, he agreed to sign on at the same time that the option was before the court. Eichler and Rubenstone did not hesitate to connect the two in later interviews: Trump's decision to join the oil suit, in their view, was a factor in Berger's turnabout on the option. Their conclusion is supported by the pattern of Donald's business life before and since: The repeated wooing or retention of critical public or legal opponents would become a lifelong hallmark of the Trump style.

In the end, of course, Donald had his yards, as well as a war chest to develop them that was funded by a failed railroad. But circumstances outside the bankruptcy courtroom, and well beyond his or anyone's ability to control them, were already undermining the prospects for developing his new prize properties. Warning clouds had begun to gather over New York City's economy even before Trump's deal for the yards had been submitted to the court. The city had lost a quarter of a million jobs in the early seventies, eroding the tax base at the same time that the costs of city services were exploding. Then, in early 1975, the state's

---

* This allegation was rejected by the judge, who did find, however, that blank forms retaining Berger's firm were being circulated among city landlords. The judge said, nonetheless, that there was no way of determining if Berger's firm was responsible for this "regrettable" mass distribution of retainer agreements.

Urban Development Corporation defaulted on millions in bonds. The term *fiscal crisis* came into daily use in every newspaper after the banks refused to renew the city's short-term notes that April, and a reeling Beame administration simply ran out of money. By the early fall of 1975, as part of a broad-based campaign of cutbacks, the city and state suspended construction of all new subsidized housing. Trump now held an option on the yards without a hope of exercising it.

But Donald was already changing direction, just slightly ahead of the fiscal storm. In late 1974, he had begun taking a look at Penn Central's four midtown hotels, and had cleverly fixed on the least attractive of them, the decrepit Commodore, which stood next to Grand Central Terminal. He and Eichler began talking about a deal for the property and had a draft purchase agreement by the following year. Trump sensed that, while hard times might freeze housing expenditures, they might also make a tax-abated hotel renovation in midtown more feasible. An impoverished government would have nothing to spend, but it might be quite willing to forgive a future generation of taxes for the right project and right developer.

Trump also decided to focus on the virtually unnoticed section of rail yard at 34th Street that was part of his option agreement with the railroad. Even before the option had been approved by Fullam, Donald had begun to explore his own, still secret concept for the site, which stretched from 30th to 39th Streets. While the petition before Fullam proposed the same sort of housing on this property as on the uptown yard, the truth was that the Palmieri group and Donald had long been wondering out loud about its appropriateness for a new city-sponsored convention center.

The only problem was that the old Brooklyn clubhouse gang had already laid claim to another convention center site, a few blocks up the West Side which they planned to build out over the water at 44th Street. Robert Tisch, whom John Lindsay had named to chair the city's Convention Center Development Corporation, had put his old friend and longtime lawyer, Bunny Lindenbaum, on retainer at the corporation planning the 44th Street site, an appointment that was enthusiastically supported by the then comptroller Abe Beame.

Also on the Tisch team was Howard Rubenstein, the public relations consultant who had moved from the Brooklyn clubhouse to his own booming Manhattan business on the strength of his widely perceived influence with Beame's City Hall. Tisch was himself so close to the Madison Club crew that he'd taken over the failing Atlantic City hotel that Bunny, Beame, and Steingut had owned in the 1950s. Not surprisingly, the presence of so many Beame cohorts on the 44th Street project was widely seen as an indication of the mayor's commitment to it.

The city had already spent at least $13 million developing and promoting the site, though the project was far from a groundbreaking. Nonetheless, Donald believed that the costs and impracticality of the construction would eventually doom the property—it was inherently more expensive to build on than other sites because of the piles required for the platform that would extend over the Hudson River. Ned Eichler had suggested that Donald promote 34th Street for the convention center during a bargaining session with Trump in mid-1974, before the contract for the yards was sent to the court. "This platform thing is the stupidest deal I ever heard of," Eichler told Donald. "The right place for the convention center is 34th Street. Suppose we walk into Beame's office and propose it. It's a chance for him to be a big hero, get a cheaper site and a much cheaper project. Plus we get paid." Donald resisted. "The deal at 44th Street," he replied, "is locked politically." He mentioned Tisch and mumbled that switching the site "would never happen." Eichler mentioned his idea to other Palmieri officials, but no one took him seriously, and it seemed to die there.

A few days before the November hearing in Judge Fullam's courtroom, the Beame administration had steered a special zoning district for the 44th Street site through a raucous Board of Estimate meeting. Residents of the Clinton neighborhood bordering on the site had pointed in the direction of 34th Street, but Beame's then planning commissioner, John Zuccotti, had opposed moving the center to this alternative site at a public meeting, saying the city was "not prepared to suggest that rail use at the site be terminated" because the yard is "an important element in goods distribution."

However, almost as soon as Trump got approval from Fullam for his option on 34th Street, Abe Beame's romance with the 44th Street site waned perceptibly and Donald began to openly discuss the advantages of 34th. Two months later, Tom Galvin, the Tisch center's executive vice president and a wary political insider, quit. "With Beame as mayor," he later explained, "I could see the death knell of the project coming, f-le put it in a state of limbo. He didn't throw a dagger or a life support at it." A few months later, Tisch quit as well. Bunny, his son Sandy (who had done most of the zoning for the site), and Rubenstein stayed on the center's payroll, but the project was politically finished. Rubenstein and Sandy, who had left Bunny to join a Manhattan firm by then, were also already on Trump's payroll as well, but listed as consultants only on the 60th Street projects.

In the fall of 1975, the mayor announced that he was suspending all city payments to the corporation planning the 44th Street center. It was a budgetary, not a site, decision, he explained, leaving open the technical possibility that the plan might be revived when the budgetary conditions changed. But Donald Trump got the message, and immediately he put Sandy Lindenbaum and Rubenstein on the tab of his 34th Street project and began building a head of steam behind it. Trump even sent an emissary to offer a job to John McGarrahan, the influential in-house counsel to the 44th Street development corporation—another example of his fondness for buying off key players on the other side of the table.

By the beginning of 1976 Trump was so certain that he would win the convention center war that he went back to another Palmieri executive, John Koskinen, to get approval from the bankruptcy court for a new Trump contract on the 34th Street yard. Koskinen, who had first discussed the idea with Eichler in 1974, was eager to pursue the plan and immediately filed a new petition with the court, switching from Trump's earlier housing plan for the site to a new package that anticipated a $12 million sales price for convention center use. The new proposal awarded Trump a minimum $500,000 commission for selling the site to the city, picked up $75,000 in up-front expenses Trump was incurring to market the site, and laid out a formula for Trump to receive a percentage of any land price paid by the city or state above $12 million.

Even though the deal was a dramatic reversal of the barely year-old option approved for Trump after so much controversy, it sailed through court approvals without an objection. Much more so than the contingent-laden housing deal, the land price for any convention center sale was fixed directly by the appraisal that Rubenstone had assailed in the 1974 deposition he'd taken of the appraisal company. Yet the Berger firm, minus the departed Rubenstone, silently assented to the new proposal.

While a public Beame endorsement of Donald's parcel proved elusive until the final months of his administration in 1977, the mayor continued quietly setting the stage for its inevitable selection. He rebuffed an offer by the Port Authority to finance the construction of the center at Battery Park in Lower Manhattan, privately railing against the site. And while Beame had no money to put into the project at the time, he reiterated the city's commitment to the center, describing it as the administration's top economic development priority

Preventing Beame from making a wholesale endorsement of 34th Street was his own top deputy, John Zuccotti, who had been promoted from planning commissioner at the peak of the fiscal crisis in 1975. Zuccotti had an independent power base as the unofficial designee of the banks, the newspapers, the bond raters, and a panicked but amorphous establishment—a competent manager at the highest levels of the distrusted Beame administration. He had long taken the public position that the 60th Street rail yards could close for nonrail development purposes, freeing up the land for Donald's housing project, but the

34th Street yard *had* to remain and even be expanded to compensate the loss of the 60th Street freight facilities. So Zuccotti was quoted when Beame stopped 44th Street as saying the decision was merely "a holding action." He promised to resume the development "at a later date," and he remained Trump's principal opponent in the site battle until he resigned in mid-1977.

With Zuccotti's departure Beame finally did publicly recommend the 34th Street site. It would take Trump nine more months, after Zuccotti's June departure, to finally kill 44th Street and get his own site designated. No one by then seemed to notice that the Trump-abetted removal of the 34th Street yard from rail freight classification meant the end of meaningful rail freight service to Manhattan. The issue would reemerge every few years thereafter, but in a period of almost surreal real estate development in Manhattan, talk of preserving precious blocks of land for the engines of another era could attract neither interest nor concern.

The truth was that the city was losing manufacturing jobs at a pace five times worse than the national average, and one of the reasons for its loss of 800,000 industrial jobs since 1962 was, expert after expert concluded, the decline of rail freight service. Several government studies had to concede, despite the bias toward the more glamorous and profit-intensive Trump-like development of these yards, that "a substantial market demand" existed for a real rail terminal at either 60th or 34th Streets.

In fact, the ailing railroad industry was beginning to make a strong comeback outside of New York by the end of the seventies, aided by escalating fuel costs, which were putting truckers at a sudden disadvantage. A West Side terminal at either of the Trump yards would not only have positioned the city to take advantage of this economic shift, it would also have dramatically reduced truckload traffic through clogged Manhattan streets.

Trump's simultaneous hold on both of the potential terminal sites for almost half a decade may have been a fatal blow to a manufacturing revival in New York. But this was the sort of substantive issue likely to be overlooked by Donald just as his father's schemes for Coney Island had indifferently deprecated its value as a recreation center. Once Donald prevailed at 34th, and that site was lost for freight service, the only logical remaining rail site was 60th Street, where the collapse of the housing subsidy market seemed like a permanent bar to the development he had planned. But Donald vowed that no freight train was going to roll over his dream project. He was not about to give up on the fantasy site that had drawn him to Manhattan in the first place.

•   •   •

Sally Goodgold will never forget the first time she saw Donald Trump. It was on her turf, in a place where he would remain a befuddled foreigner for a decade and a half: a West Side living room. Worse still, at least from Donald's perspective, it was in Sally's own home. Longer than a bowling alley, the living room looked out on the street through four large, uncurtained windows, with the morning sun pouring in, inviting Donald to enjoy precisely the sort of West Side view his planned mega-story waterfront towers would destroy.

Trump had suggested, shortly after he won his West Side option in early 1975, that Sally, her friend Doris Freedman, and other members of the community's Penn Yards Committee lunch with him at "21." But Sally liked to think she'd invented the power breakfast, and she held it weekly at 8:00 A.M. in her own apartment with Zabar's bagels. The famous deli's owner had once told her: "I know the state of the city by the size of your bill." The outgoing chairman of the city's Landmarks Commission had once threatened to designate her dining room table as a city landmark. So many politicians, contractors, and developers had assembled there for a stint of bagel diplomacy that a *Daily News* reporter had once appeared uninvited at a Goodgold gathering, insisting that the state's sunshine law—requiring open public meetings—had to apply to such high-level confabs. At forty-one, the schoolmarmish Sally was already a West Side institution, one of the forces on the community board who could make or break a project. At one forum of citywide officials and activists at which each, participant stood up and introduced himself with a lengthy résumé, Sally barely rose, announced tersely, "I fill the potholes in government," and sat down. It was not only her definition of herself; it was her idea of what it meant to be a citizen of New York.

She'd lived as a teenager with her parents on 72nd Street overlooking the northern tip of the rail yard; and now, with her doctor husband and two children, she lived seven blocks uptown in West Side elegance at 79th and Amsterdam. The moment the first report of Trump's attempt to obtain his 60th Street yard option had appeared in July of 1974, Sally and her fellow activists had trooped down to John Zuccotti's office and gotten assurances that the planning commission would listen carefully to the views of a special community board committee formed to consider Trump's plans.

While community boards only had advisory powers, the West Side board had come to possess a level of clout that transcended the law and was rooted in the advocacy and influence of its sophisticated leaders. Bordered by Columbia University on the north and Lincoln Center on the south, the Upper West Side was perhaps the city's most diverse neighborhood, an ethnic polyglot of rich and poor, an intellectual and cultural cauldron. It was, at least in 1974, as stridently different from the land of business suits on the East Side of Central Park as another proud and combative nation. The Penn Yards Committee had begun holding brown-bag meetings at the 63rd Street Y months before Donald's first visit to Sally's apartment, intending to be ready with its own plan for the yard when Donald announced his. During these open and robust sessions, Sally noticed a bent old man sitting alone in the back taking notes, never saying a word to anyone. No one realized until months later that it was eighty-five-year-old Robert Moses, forced from power after five decades, but still determinedly scratching out a role for himself in the development politics of the city.

Moses sensed that Sally's committee was the epicenter of political debate on West Side development. He would publish his own monogram in 1975 warning that the neighborhood "now faces the threat of overbuilding, overpopulation and overcrowding by ambitious realtors," concluding that "1,300 apartments housing 5,000 people on 11 acres would not be fatal" to the rail yard. As it turned out, even the great builder himself believed that the site could accommodate only a small fraction of what Donald planned for it. Moses was beginning to sound like a West Sider.

Trump arrived at Sally's home that spring morning dressed in a maroon silk suit with patent leather maroon shoes. He stopped at the entranceway and gazed around the apartment.

"Sally, your living room is bigger than mine," he said.

"Well, Donald," replied Sally, "build yourself a bigger living room."

Walking into the room, Donald picked up a museum piece from a tabletop. "You even have taste," he said. He wandered out of the living room and into the adjoining library. "You have your own library?"

"You know, we read." Sally would match him line for line.

"I can't believe this is on the West Side," said Trump, moving next into the dining area. "You also have a separate dining room?"

"You know, we eat," she deadpanned.

Tugging on his tie, he said: "I'm usually so uncomfortable on the West Side."

By now, recalled Sally, her politeness abandoned her. "Why, because you come from Queens?"

"I come from the *Upper East Side*," Trump emphasized, apparently oblivious to the geography of Manhattan taunts. Oh, the roots we leave behind, mused Sally to herself, madder about Queens than the other half of her own island.

"I understand," said Sally. "New money. Let's get something straight. I know you've had money for one generation. When you've had it for three, four, or five generations, you'll be comfortable anywhere. Even on the West Side."

Trump grabbed her by the shoulders and looked her straight in the eye. "You and I will get along just fine," he said. "You don't get intimidated."

It was the start of a long, curious, and frequently combative relationship. Over the years Donald would at times become solicitous, introducing her once to Malcolm Forbes with this description: "Whether you want it or not, you will get her advice, so you might as well seek it. A good part of the time, she's right."

Sally had decided that morning of his first visit to make it clear that mega-millionaires did not impress her. She had come from comfortable wealth, the daughter of the first Jewish president of the New York Stockyards. In the thirties, her accountant father had run the yards, just below the 60th Street rail terminal, and had been told to leave the day he refused to bring illegal liquor in under the cattle feed. He'd wound up the head of a hotel chain, and Sally had grown up as a pampered child resident of the Times Square Hotel. Shaken by her father's heart attack and early death, she did her first volunteer work with heart patients, and that was how she met the successful doctor who became her husband.

She knew Donald was considering 20,000 units of housing on the site, though he had no concrete plan yet. Sally and her activist group would not even react to such a preposterous proposal. The committee was discussing a low-rise plan of about 4,000 units. "We're not going to play some whittle-down game," Sally told Trump. "We won't even bring any 20,000-unit plan to the community." Trump would not highball them, she declared, into a compromise that left them with a 10,000-unit or otherwise intolerably cosmic project. The first breakfast, and other meetings that followed, ended in a stalemate.

The community stonewall, and the drying up of subsidies, soon forced Trump back to the drawing board. Finally, in May 1976, a year after the initial meeting, Trump formally submitted a 14,500-unit plan to the community board. It was the first concrete expression of a Trump vision for the site.

Beyond the massive density of the plan, Trump addressed the major development issue at the site with characteristic flair. He recommended lowering the elevated West Side Highway to grade and extending Riverside Park to 59th Street, situating the new parkland near the realigned highway.

The highway loomed over the site like an albatross. It would cost a fortune to get it out of the way of any housing development's view of the water or, if left in place, to build a project on a platform raised above the highway's ten-story height. Trump proposed carrying the cost of his proposed lowered highway on the tab of the subsidized project, just one more unrealistic element of a plan that no one on the West Side was taking seriously.

Within a few months, however, a scurrying Trump had shifted to a similarly sized housing project built on a platform with the highway left in place and a shopping center beneath the platform. In the new scheme, the parkland, rather than a lowered highway, would run along the water. He began to make stern 10,000-units-and-that's-my-final-offer speeches, but the West Siders were about as impressed as Sally had been that first morning. No one in the community flinched.

The Goodgold forces insisted on lower density and a variety of uses, until Trump suggested in a December 1976 letter that he would drastically revise the proposal to include commercial and recreational uses and less housing. By then, Jimmy Carter had been elected President, and Trump, who had publicly mused about how important a Democratic President might be for his West Side plans, was optimistic that new federal subsidies might bail out his stymied project.

In May of 1977, two years after the breakfast meeting in Sally's living room, Trump was down to 8,000 units, a marina, a specialty shopping center on the waterfront, and a commercial sports center. But he still had forty-four-story towers, 4,000 units too many, no specific plan that went beyond broad concepts, and only platitudes about the amount and location of open space. Most important, he still had no financing plan for the project, and the fresh new Georgia faces at the White House weren't proposing one into which he could tap.

Donald was still appearing at occasional bagel briefings at Sally's, and sometimes the meetings shuttled to Doris Freedman's even grander apartment at 25 Central Park West. Doris was the daughter of a successful Art Deco architect and the city's first cultural affairs commissioner. A petite, forty-five-year-old brunette wired into West Side and national Democratic politics, she had convinced a foundation to give the Penn Yards Committee enough money to hire its own consultants to evaluate Trump's proposals. Her family owned the luxurious building facing the park in which she had her apartment. It was just the setting for a humility lesson, and Freedman gave one, tweaking Trump for everything from parking his polluting limo outside during their talks to serious legal questions about whether Penn Central actually had the right to deliver title to him free and clear.

When Freedman pressed him once about the rail use covenants that did in fact cloud the title of the West Side property, he insisted angrily: "I own it all." And when his careful attorney, Sandy Lindenbaum, interrupted the byplay with Freedman to qualify Trump's assertion—delicately suggesting "Why not say that to the best of our knowledge we are in control of the site?"—Donald exploded. "I'm telling you it's all mine," he declared, chastising Lindenbaum with the direction: "I'll do the talking here." The reprimand drove Lindenbaum to the door, where he calmly told Freedman and Goodgold: "I expect to be around for a long time on matters like this, and I expect to deal with you on many of them. I am never going to lie to you. Goodnight." Goodgold in fact never dealt with Lindenbaum again on Trump's project, and the experience taught her an important lesson about the contrasting styles of Donald and his lawyer—Lindenbaum had a sense of the long-term and was not about to burn his bridges, while his client was a child of the moment, with neither a respect for the past nor an instinct for the future. All he knew was what he needed right then.

By the time of the fracas with Lindenbaum, however, the many pressures of the project had finally worn even Trump down. His grandiose dream city was turning into a nightmare that could not win hard financing. Penn Central's expense advances were all but exhausted, and the community was as relentlessly resistant as on the first day.

Nonetheless, in late 1977, he girded himself for one final rush at the zoning prize before the Beame era ended. Even if he couldn't build at that time, the value of the land would be greatly enhanced if he could get the variance. Within days of Beame's defeat in the Democratic primary that September, Donald submitted another proposal to the community board. The number of units did not change, but the generous open space was finally defined in a series of drawings, two stories were taken off the tallest tower, and for the first time a financing program with tax abatement and limited subsidies was suggested, but only vaguely. The bottom line was that Trump was now pressuring the city, and the community, to approve a special zoning district for the area immediately, insisting that they could work out the details of the actual project later. Trump now hoped he could push Beame officials to authorize the new zoning without his producing any commitment on financing, and the city's planning commissioner eventually capitulated, directing staff to prepare a zoning district resolution based on Trump's planned density.

One problem remained, however. Trump had overlooked a pivotal requirement for the site: an expensive and time-consuming environmental impact study. A new state law that had just gone into effect in September made an EIS essential, and Trump's failure to complete one killed his last-minute push for new zoning. But even this defeat didn't stop him.

He resumed his efforts in 1978 with the new Koch administration, though with little success. He began meeting with the new City Planning Commission chairman, Robert Wagner, Jr., telling the son of the former mayor that they should "build the city of the future together." But Wagner and the new mayor, Ed Koch, had never had an uncomfortable moment on the West Side themselves, were both seasoned Manhattan pols, and were not about to take on the city's most vociferous neighborhood on behalf of an overly ambitious and unfinanced project. Trump's option expired in October 1978, but Palmieri officials conceded him continuing site control and began negotiating a new deal with him. Palmieri had helped Penn Central reorganize itself out of bankruptcy, and was still on retainer to sell assets of the new corporate entity. This time, no court approvals would be necessary, and there was almost a casualness about nailing down the new agreement.

By May of 1979, Trump and Palmieri officials had agreed on the broad terms of a second, eighteen-month, option, with a right to extend for another twelve months. This time Donald was to put up a $300,000 deposit and commit to spending $700,000 of his own money to push the project through the rezoning process. As paltry as this million-dollar commitment was, it did reverse the terms of the original Eichler deal, which obligated only Penn Central to cover development costs and required no Trump deposit. But since Palmieri was letting Donald operate as if he had an option, there was no pressure on him to sign the new deal, so he dawdled.

Another reason not to sign was that by the summer of 1979, his West Side yard dealings had attracted a new kind of troubling attention. Federal prosecutors in Brooklyn had opened a criminal investigation into how Donald had obtained the option in the first place. U.S. Attorney Ed Korman was examining allegations that Trump's retention of Berger was a payoff for Berger's sudden switch on the rail-yard sale. Donald sent Roy Cohn to meet with Korman, who made it clear that Trump and Berger were the subjects of the inquiry and promised it would be a short and quiet one. Cohn dismissed the payoff allegation scornfully and offered an interview with Trump, unencumbered by a lawyer.

So a federal investigator went out to Avenue Z to interview Donald. It was Trump who picked the location—a barren cubicle in the back of Fred Trump's end-of-the-earth office. The same investigator had delivered a subpoena to Donald's elegant new office in The Crown Building on Fifth Avenue, where he'd been greeted by giant Trump Organization lettering when he walked off the elevator. The Avenue Z hideaway was a sharp contrast—one that the agent felt had been deliberately selected by Trump to try to strike the pose of an ordinary guy. To complete the homey scene, Ivana and two-year-old Donald Jr. played around the office throughout the hour-and-a-half interview.

The investigator ran through his traditional speech: "You're a target of a grand jury. We have information that may be criminal in nature and may not be. That's what I'm here to determine." Donald took off his jacket and rolled up his sleeves. He was at ease and talkative. He claimed that he'd agreed to pay too much for the properties. He talked about the difficulty of the zoning change approval process. He denied any quid pro quo with Berger.*

The investigation was a case of inference that never got past the inference. Though prosecutors rushed witnesses through a hasty grand jury, the probe had not begun until mid-1979, with the five-year statute of limitations just about exhausted. It died without an indictment and without ever hitting newsprint. Cohn would later compliment Korman about how carefully he'd kept the probe under wraps, adding that "now Donald's going around talking about it." When Korman, who subsequently became a federal judge, bumped into Trump at a dinner a few years later, Trump thanked him "for the professional way the investigation was handled," praising him for "no leaks." In fact, the probe remained a secret for a decade until Donald revealed it in his second book, *Surviving at the Top*.

Just as mysteriously as he had arrived on the West Side five years earlier, Trump finally, quietly slipped away in December 1979. He never told the architect who'd worked with him for years, Jordan Gruzen, why he was quitting. He never came up with a farewell plan, as he had promised. He never explained his departure. Everyone from Gruzen to Goodgold believed he had just grown tired of it all and moved on to other projects, especially Trump Tower, the monumental structure he planned for Fifth Avenue.

On the deadline day set by Palmieri for signing the new option, December 29, 1979, Donald came to Palmieri's Third Avenue offices and held out a bank check for $300,000, the deposit he was obliged to make. "I left this morning to come here thinking we'd close," he said. "I've been bouncing back and forth on it. But I've got Trump Tower going, got Atlantic City going. I'm getting out."

Ironically, the only issues that remained in dispute between Trump and Palmieri were questions that hung over the title—the very problems Sandy Lindenbaum and Donald had differed over in Doris Freedman's apartment years earlier. Palmieri was unable to secure a "clean release," from Conrail, which refused to state exactly what railroad utilities and equipment might exist under the surface of the yard. Donald seized on the problem as fundamental, as well as on another technical question affecting the air rights.

The Palmieri staffers were stunned. They were convinced that the legal

---

* Berger was represented in the probe by Fred Trump and Bunny Lindenbaum's old friend, ex-judge Nat Sobel.

loopholes were alibis. At first they suspected Trump might be trying to lower the ultimate purchase price to avoid paying the deposit. Palmieri had already obtained approval from the reorganized company's board of directors, which had budgeted the revenue in the business plan, including an agreed-upon $28 million purchase price at the end of the option, with a 2 percent price increase per month beyond the set deadline.

In Trump's stead, instantly and curiously, was Abe Hirschfeld, the city's parking garage king who'd never built a major project. Palmieri officials contacted him a few days after Trump departed and, without entertaining any other offers, promised him the same deal Trump was about to sign. They did not want to redraw the agreement with another possible developer and then resubmit it to their new, and highly skeptical, clients at the suddenly solvent Penn Central.

Hirschfeld was an old friend of Fred Trump's, a golfing partner from the Breakers in Palm Beach. He was also the joke of New York politics, an unsuccessful candidate for just about every major public office who'd often been backed by Fred. Bunny Lindenbaum had represented him for years, and he, Fred, Donald, and Bunny had sometimes shared the same table at dinners of the Brooklyn Democratic organization. A short, heavy, sixty-year-old Israeli with reddish hair and an awkward Polish accent, Hirschfeld was a millionaire who looked and sounded like the neighborhood Jewish tailor.

Hirschfeld was a bizarre selection for this option—the opposite of the ultimate insider depicted by Eichler when Trump got it. A few weeks after Hirschfeld was contacted, he and his wife, without a lawyer, arrived at Penn Central, paid the deposit, and signed the documents. Hirschfeld claims he neither read, nor negotiated, a word of the agreement. Instead, he just took on the obligations Trump had agreed to—he would forfeit the $1 million he advanced by deposit or expenses if he was unable to obtain the zoning change necessary for a buildable project.

Hirschfeld kept all of Donald's consultants, including Gruzen, though he had never used the architect before. Hirschfeld and an unknown Argentine builder and auto dealer named Francisco Macri soon began talks about a partnership on the yards.

Penn Central immediately notified the State Department of Transportation that it intended to abandon and dispose of the site, a formal warning it had never issued through all the Trump years. This notice, an attempt to at last clear the title of at least one crucial claim, opened the door for the city or state to exercise its right of first refusal and buy the yard itself for rail uses. The Koch administration acted quickly to put a legally permissible hold on the property until June 1980 while it considered taking the yard by condemnation.

Although a 1980 city report concluded that it should acquire the site for new freight facilities, it never acted on the recommendation. The deadline quietly passed without any city or state attempt to move to take the site. If the alternative had been a Trump superproject, rather than the prospective sale of the property to dubious Abe Hirschfeld, an aroused West Side might have forced consideration of the rail plan. Instead, the brief period of public preferential rights passed without commotion.

"The difference would've been night and day," recalled Goodgold. "No one took Abe seriously. If Donald had the option during that period, we wouldn't have been running around spinning wheels. Something would've happened."

Even before the site cleared the rail use obstacle, Hirschfeld had sold his option to the Argentine for $6.5 million, become a 35 percent limited partner for next to nothing, and been retained as a $6,250-a-month consultant by the new partnership. He was even reimbursed for the deposit and expenses he'd paid.

Several years would pass before Hirschfeld and his partner, Macri, could finally obtain a zoning change. Throughout that period, Donald carefully watched what was happening with the prized site he had inexplicably forfeited. He would later write in his first autobiography that the "toughest business decision" he ever made was "giving up my option on the West Side yards." As soon as the new owners won their elusive zoning change, however, Donald would leap back into the fray, negotiating with the Argentine to retake control of a site that had become an obsession. His day at 60th Street, he had determined, would come again.

5

TAX BREAK HOTEL

"Well," said the magnate, "I see our friend Mr. Cowperwood has managed to get his own way with the council. I am morally certain he uses money to get what he is after as freely as a fireman uses water. He's as slippery as an eel. I should be glad if we would establish that there is a community of interest between him and these politicians around City Hall. I believe he has set out to dominate this city politically as well as financially, and he'll need constant watching."

—*Theodore Dreiser*, THE TITAN

If I hadn't finally convinced the city to choose my West 34th Street site for its convention center and then gone on to develop the Grand Hyatt, I'd probably be back in Brooklyn today, collecting rents.

—*Donald Trump*, THE ART OF THE DEAL

MICHAEL BAILKIN has the throaty, soothing timbre of a psychiatrist and, when thinking out loud about the structure of a real estate deal, the creative dexterity of a jazz pianist.

When Donald Trump met him in 1975, Bailkin was a midlevel bureaucrat in a busted city, with more ambition than purpose, hidden away in the tiny offices of the Beame administration's Lower Manhattan Development Corporation. Trump had come to him seeking city assistance to redevelop a small downtown property, and Bailkin had rejected the idea over a lunch in the nearby Woolworth Building. But Trump must have liked something about the five-foot-six, bulldog-shaped Bailkin. A few weeks later, on a sunny early fall day, Trump returned, without an appointment, looking for advice about a giant midtown project far beyond the reach of Bailkin's neighborhood office. The project would change both Bailkin's and Trump's lives.

Though only thirty-five years old, Bailkin had already been chasing dreams for a lifetime, running away from his pharmacist father's Philadelphia home at the age of fourteen to join a motorcycle gang taking a run through the Deep South. His Harley, an equalizer for a puny Jewish kid from a tough Italian slice of Germantown, also attracted the interest of redneck cops and earned him a stint in a North Carolina jail. Then, at sixteen, Bailkin falsified his age to get into the army early, did a tour in a Panama jungle warfare training center, and wound up court-martialed. Next he became a roustabout in a traveling circus, putting up the big top and sweeping elephant droppings. Bailkin crammed a college and law school education in between escapades in the Danish merchant marine, the Peace Corps in India, and a martial arts academy in Japan.

When he met Trump he had been a lawyer for a mere five years, only one of those years on the private side of the negotiating table, mostly shuttling from one government job to another. Marriage and a five-year-old daughter had settled him, but it did not take Bailkin long to see in Trump the promise of a bold new adventure, a deal that could catapult two careers.

"I've got to show you this," Trump exclaimed, and pulled out primitive drawings of his redesign of the Commodore, the decaying East 42nd Street hotel that he and Ned Eichler had been talking about for months. The sixty-year-old hotel was a tired, brick 1,600-room relic on the Lexington Avenue side of Grand Central Terminal. In the 1920s the crowded hotel's slogan was "Always a room and a bath for two and a half." But now its rooms were empty 60 percent of the time and its lobby storefronts were taking on a pornographic West 42nd Street look, home to establishments like Relaxation Plus, a second-floor massage parlor whose additional services were neither difficult to imagine nor expensive to buy.

Bailkin listened to him argue that a glitzy new façade tacked to the old brick, and some refurbishing inside, would transform not just a never-grand hotel, but also a prime and troubled avenue in the heart of a crisis city. Bailkin was both annoyed and amused, as so many were and would be, by the shameless shilling of the kid.

The names rushed out of Trump's mouth: Hyatt would manage it. Equitable

Life would finance it. Abe Beame, his father's friend, would support it. His Palmieri allies at Penn Central—who'd just granted him the West Side option—had agreed to sell him the hotel as well. But he had a problem.

There would be no deal without a tax abatement. No one would finance what he said would be an $80 million renovation without assurances that the rebuilt hotel could save enough on property taxes to reliably make its mortgage payments. Trump told Bailkin that he had already tried to wrest an abatement out of the state legislature, with the city's support. Two of his dad's old Madison Club friends, Beame and Assembly Speaker Stanley Steingut, had combined to push a bill in Albany for a twenty-year partial tax reduction on all commercial development projects like this one. The Commodore deal had been one inspiration for the legislation, and Donald said he had worked directly with Beame's economic development commissioner, Alfred Eisenpreiss, designing the city-backed bill. Donald had lobbied through the 1975 session, but the bill was lost in the fiscal crisis panic, and Donald was too impatient to wait for the next January-to-July legislative session. Could Bailkin, Donald wanted to know, come up with an alternative abatement mechanism, preferably one that allowed for an even bigger tax break? Bailkin was puzzled as to why Trump was asking him this question. It was common knowledge in government circles that Fred Trump and Abe Beame went way back, and there was no doubt in Bailkin's mind that Donald could get the highest-level administration audience to entertain this proposition.

Although Bailkin may have seemed an almost obscure figure in a vast bureaucracy, he just happened to keep a desk at the Lower Manhattan local office as a matter of convenience and was actually counsel to all the city's neighborhood development corporations—a status, however, that he had not mentioned to Trump at their first meeting. He believed Donald didn't know what his broader title was, nor that he had privileged access to First Deputy Mayor John Zuccotti. Zuccotti used him as a semisecret sounding board, and sometimes executioner, for complex development matters. But Bailkin knew that Zuccotti would have told him if he was delivering Trump to his door. No, Bailkin suspected, Trump had dropped in because he happened to be in the building, which was right behind City Hall and filled with various city offices. In Bailkin's mind even years later, this historic meeting had a classically accidental quality to it.

Putting a development question to Bailkin, though, is like pulling the cord on a brand-new Chatty Kathy doll. A plan came to him in an instant. Trump would buy the property from Penn Central and donate it to the city. Then the city would lease it back to Trump for ninety-nine years. While the city would nominally pay full taxes on the property to itself, Trump, as a mere tenant, would pay none. Instead, the city would charge him a rent that was the equivalent of some negotiated portion of his prospective tax bill. Donald liked the sound of it. It was a potentially more lucrative abatement than the Steingut-Padavan bill, because it could continue as long as Abe Beame, and the seven other politically interdependent members of the Board of Estimate, were willing to authorize it to run. Donald immediately decided he couldn't get along with a day less than half a century. Theoretically, the abatement could also be for as tiny a fraction of the normal tax bill as the same board, or the bureaucrats who drafted the lease's fine print, were willing to impose. Donald knew he'd prosper with such wide-open discretion built into the plan.

He quickly contacted Sandy Lindenbaum at his Manhattan law firm. Lindenbaum, who was just beginning to establish his own credentials as a powerbroker at the Board of Estimate, called Bailkin to discuss the leaseback idea. Lindenbaum liked it, too.

Bailkin would get his own reward rather quickly. Soon after their lunch Donald went to Commissioner Eisenpreiss and suggested he pull Bailkin in from his neighborhood outpost to do the deal. Eisenpreiss did not know who Bailkin was, but he called him anyway. He told Bailkin that the city was already committed to the Commodore renovation, had pushed the Steingut-Padavan bill to implement it, and was intrigued about the new mechanism. He asked Bailkin to work on turning the broad concept into a practical plan. Zuccotti called, too, and gave Bailkin a mandate to proceed.

The onetime behind-the-scenes Bailkin suddenly became a familiar face at City Hall, talking with Eisenpreiss and the two deputy mayors who had become counterpoints within the Beame administration—Zuccotti and Stanley Friedman, longtime secretary of the Bronx Democratic Party and the cigar-chomping symbol of the Beame team's hack underside. Suddenly the central player in the city's only major ongoing economic development deal, Bailkin also began meeting with Charles Goldstein, a jowled, prematurely middle-aged lawyer close to city comptroller Jay Goldin.

Goldin was the only member of the Board of Estimate who worried Trump. His office had both the capacity and the responsibility to do a hard numbers-crunching review of the abatement. Having just taken office in 1974, Goldin, a maverick former state senator nicknamed the Young Dynamo, needed to be leashed to the deal. Trump and Lindenbaum had already met with Goldin to discuss it, and Goldin had asked his long-standing friend Goldstein to act as a kind of unofficial, pro bono, counsel for him, analyzing the terms. Goldstein had been the treasurer of Goldin's last state senate race in 1973; he and four of his partners were also the treasurers of fifteen different fund-raising committees for Goldin's 1973 race for comptroller. Putting him into the mix may have been Goldin's way of dangling an invitation before the ever politically generous Donald.

In his meetings with Bailkin, Goldstein kept raising problems in the deal. He was concerned that once the city owned the property, it would have to put it up for public bidding, rather than simply lease it back to Trump. More important, he questioned whether the city had the statutory authority to pass the property back to Trump under a long-term lease without passing the tax burden as well. Bailkin was convinced he was right on both counts, but couldn't satisfy the adamant Goldstein. Finally, Bailkin suggested a dramatically revised new mechanism: "Why not use the state's Urban Development Corporation?" Goldstein seemed stunned, and pleased. "The only thing wrong with that idea," he declared, "is that you thought of it."

The UDC option, indeed, had a number of advantages over the city concept. This state super authority had been created by Nelson Rockefeller in 1968 as a housing agency, empowered to override all local ordinances and build integrated housing throughout the state. It tried, and in 1975, it collapsed. Its near bankruptcy had helped trigger the ongoing city fiscal crisis.

Though moribund, the agency still possessed great powers: It could, among other things, condemn the commercial tenants in the Commodore, bypass building code requirements, and grant automatic and full tax exemptions to projects without public bidding. These extraordinary weapons had ostensibly become part of UDC's arsenal to pursue the grand integration objectives invoked by Rockefeller while he marched in Martin Luther King's funeral—on the day the UDC bill passed the state legislature. Bailkin, Goldstein, and Trump—an unelected triumvirate of ambitious men—would now move to put this arsenal at the service of Trump profits.

Goldstein had another reason for being interested in Bailkin's suggestion: He was already on retainer to UDC. Neither he nor the agency had ever done an economic development project together. But Trump's Commodore, the first of what would prove to be a string of joint city-UDC economic development projects, would lead to millions for Goldstein in legal fees over a period of years.

"I suggested that UDC retain Goldstein for the Commodore," matchmaker Bailkin would later say. "I thought it would secure Goldin's vote for the project." Bailkin even arranged it so that Trump, and each of the subsequent developers at UDC, paid Goldstein's bills even though Goldstein was UDC's lawyer. While this sort of financial arrangement would hardly put Goldstein at the service of any developer paying his tab, he did become, over the long haul, an advocate of Trump interests on several aspects of the Commodore deal. In any event, just as Bailkin anticipated, Jay Goldin routinely supported the Goldstein-vetted UDC projects, beginning with Trump's, though he audited and berated other tax abatement programs. Goldstein's firm continued to play its fund-raising role for Goldin, contributing $16,000 to him during the years it would take to finish the Commodore project and acting as treasurer of Goldin committees. Donald Trump donated $2,000 to one of those Goldin committees.

The other reason it made exquisite political sense to involve UDC was that Hugh Carey had just become governor at the beginning of 1975, and though he may have shed fifty pounds during the 1974 gubernatorial campaign, he hadn't lost his old-time Brooklyn machine allies. Bunny, Fred, and Donald Trump had been among his biggest and earliest backers in the 1974 race. Bunny loaned Carey $40,000, and the Trumps had put up $1,200 to get the first phone lines into Carey's headquarters, cosigned a $23,000 start-up loan, and contributed outright another $35,000. Early in the Carey campaign, Ned Eichler, Trump's friendly benefactor at Penn Central, had scheduled a lunch with Trump at the Four Seasons, and when a late Donald finally appeared, he was bursting with excitement about Carey, explaining that he had been held up at a campaign function. "Carey's a wonderful guy," Donald announced in a booming voice that could be heard six tables away. "He can be trusted. He'll do anything for a developer who gives him a campaign contribution."

Once Bailkin, Goldstein, and Trump had agreed on the use of UDC, the project took on new momentum. For the first time, the mayor himself was called to a City Hall meeting on the plan, as was the secret force front Avenue Z, Fred Trump. Fred's presence had been explicitly requested by Zuccotti to make sure that an experienced real estate person was behind the deal. Asked directly what his role would be, Fred replied: "I'm going to watch the construction and provide financial credibility." Whatever this declaration actually meant, the mere appearance of the wily and wealthy patriarch seemed to deflect questions about the financing for the project. There certainly wasn't much other evidence that the deal was fundable.

Handwritten notes of a city official, for example, scrawled at an early 1976 meeting that included UDC, Bailkin, Trump, and others, reveal that Donald's much ballyhooed "commitment" from Equitable Life to provide the long-term financing for the project was only "oral." When pressed for assurances about this loan, Donald would claim that "the lenders don't want to meet with officials," though he did offer confirmation of the commitment from broker Henry Pearce, who he said "could meet on behalf of the lenders."

But Pearce was working for Donald, not the lenders, and the sixty-seven-year-old financial adviser had, in fact, spent months touring the boardrooms of the city without picking up a committed dollar. Equitable had actually delivered what Pearce would later call a "knockout blow," rejecting Donald's $75 million request, saying that the most they would lend was $25 million and insisting that Pearce find a lead bank to act as a joint venture partner.

Much later, Donald would confide in his own book, *The Art of the Deal,* that he'd been so frustrated by banker resistance to the project that Pearce had to talk him out of abandoning it. Instead of giving up, Donald concluded that "the only way to get financing was if the city gave me a tax abatement." And the only way to get the abatement was to mislead the city into believing that he already had the elusive financing.

But Donald had not only made misrepresentations about the certainty of his financing, he'd also created the illusion that he controlled the Commodore site. As early as May of 1975 the *Daily News* quoted him as claiming that he had a "purchase contract" with Penn Central to buy the Commodore. In 1976, while the Board of Estimate was considering the abatement, the *Times* quoted him as saying that he had "an option—with no particular time limit—to buy the Commodore for $10 million from the railroad trustees." Bailkin and Zuccotti certainly knew that Trump was overstating his claim to the property. As early as December 1975 the Palmieri company had written Zuccotti a letter specifically stating that they were "negotiating with Donald Trump to sell the Commodore to a corporation controlled by Mr. Trump," with no mention of an existing option or a purchase agreement. When the city did ask Trump for a copy of the option he periodically claimed to have, he sent them one. No one paid much attention to the fact that the option bore only Trump's signature. While Trump's friends at Palmieri did meet with Bailkin and left the impression that they planned to sell the hotel to Donald, it wasn't until almost a full year after the abatement was granted that they signed an option.

The third critical element—a first-class hotel operator—was also uncertain. At first Donald had brought in the Westin Corporation, but they'd dropped out abruptly. He then moved on to Hyatt, which had agreed to join him at a 1975 press conference announcing, with great fanfare, the chain's nonbinding intent to manage the hotel if it was ever built. The tentativeness of this commitment was so apparent to the city and state, however, that every formal agreement with Trump up to the closing left open the question of what company would actually manage the hotel.

With all the uncertainty at the very heart of Trump's deal, it nonetheless moved forward with its own peculiar magic and logic. While it was true, Bailkin would concede, that no other party had been given an opportunity to submit a bid on the project—one that might have inflicted less of a tax loss on the city—he believed he had to cut the deal with Donald. He thought Donald had earned an exclusive right to do the deal since it was Trump's entrepreneurial impulse in the first place. He also contended that Donald was the only feasible developer because he had Palmieri's implicit support. And he was convinced that in the final analysis the project would pay long-term dividends for both Trump and the city. So, when pressed by reporters about a potential Trump windfall built into the abatement, Bailkin acknowledged that it was "possible for Trump to make high profits" and added, "I think that's excellent." Instead of acting as the city's final assessor on the merits of the deal, Bailkin had become in effect its in-house advocate.

Bailkin was also given the job of camouflaging this tailor-made Trump giveaway as some sort of broad, new administration approach to development. Zuccotti urged him to figure out a way "to make [the Commodore] a program or a new development policy, not just a one-shot Trump project." The hand-written instructions in one city memo said simply: "Rather than announce the project, announce the program with this as the first project." Bailkin therefore dutifully put together an ex post facto plan to cover the Trump largess with a good-government veneer, and Beame announced it as the Business Incentive Program in February of 1976, getting front-page *Times* attention. Zuccotti sent a formal letter to UDC inviting its participation in this grand, new, amorphous scheme and two days later sent another letter asking the agency to do the Commodore project as the prototype of the program.

As wired as the deal was on the city side, however, there was a roadblock awaiting it at UDC. While the governor might have been an old Trump hand, his designee in charge of UDC was nobody's pushover. When the authority hit rock bottom in 1975, Hugh Carey had installed the skillful and independent Richard Ravitch as its unpaid chairman. The millionaire builder had already decided to spend much of his life in public service, and his appointment was Carey's attempt at a reassuring brahmin message to the banks. Ravitch's third-generation family business (HRH) and scholarly demeanor—he saw himself as a gray eminence before he was either gray or eminent—positioned him, he believed, above the fixes and fray in the trenches. This did not mean, however, that he was above politics—he indeed saw himself as a possible candidate to succeed Beame as mayor in 1977. So the Trump project posed a complex set of problems for Ravitch.

He certainly was aware that Carey was beholden to the Trumps; indeed the governor had named Donald to his housing advisory group as soon as he took office. And then there was his own and HRH's history with the Trumps: He respected Fred, but did not like the brash, overreaching style of the younger Trump. Their sparring match over the West Side yards had left a bad taste in Ravitch's mouth. While he remembered Fred's appetite for private profit in public projects as a bit excessive, he sensed that Fred's son knew no limits. The terms of the Commodore deal struck Ravitch as just too rich an abatement for Donald.

When Trump first went to meet with the wary Ravitch, he overplayed his hand by bringing along his new employee, Louise Sunshine, the governor's chief political fund-raiser. The daughter of a New Jersey real estate family, Sunshine was at that very moment in charge of raising several million dollars to pay off the governor's 1974 debt and to prepare for a 1978 reelection campaign. In addition to her volunteer role as director of the Friends of Hugh Carey committee, she was the Carey-installed treasurer of the state Democratic Party, a national Democratic committeewoman, and a board member of the state Job Development Authority. Just four months after Carey took office, Donald had begun talking to her about coming to work for him. But since he was still just an employee of his father's without a staff of his own, a charmed Sunshine began in the latter half of 1975 to lobby for his convention center site without getting paid. Married to a wealthy doctor, the heavyset Sunshine undertook her early lobbying for Donald as a form of pre-employment work, getting a large foot in promising doors.

Her efforts for the Trump site were widely interpreted as a signal of the governor's support, but site selection was a city, not a state decision. So all Sunshine's state contacts could produce were influential endorsements of Trump's controversial site. She could be a far more decisive factor on the Commodore, however, since it was now being proposed as a state project. So two days after the city's first meeting with UDC brass about the agency's possible participation in the Commodore project, Trump actually hired her. The press announcement suggested that her only role with Donald was to coordinate the convention center effort, but her appearance at the Ravitch meeting suggested another agenda.

Ravitch was aghast when Sunshine arrived and became even angrier when Trump "hinted that they'd go over my head," as he recalled it, if there were problems at the agency. "Don't raise money for Carey and go around representing people here," bellowed Ravitch. The city-toughened Sunshine's capacity to shift from sweet solicitation to brusque aversion had set speed records in the highly competitive circles of hard-nosed New York politics. But Ravitch's directness proved too much for her, and she broke down in tears.

Trump tried to salvage the situation with a hurried letter to Ravitch, claiming that he'd been working on the Commodore for a year and that Sunshine "has not been involved." He insisted that Sunshine had become "aware of those activities only last week" and promised that she would "work exclusively on the Convention Center and have no involvement with any aspects of the Commodore project, either on the staff or decision-making level." Ravitch nevertheless called Carey and told him he "thought the whole thing with Sunshine was tasteless." He described the Trump proposal to the governor and, conceding that the project had no financial implications for UDC, said he was concerned about whether or not it was "prudent public policy." Carey told him to do what he thought was right.

Ravitch pressed the city to obtain a better deal, warning in writing of a Trump windfall. He insisted that Equitable come forward and commit on the financing, offering to subordinate the property taxes to the mortgage, which would've meant that any financial institution backing the project would be assured of getting its regular payments before taxes were paid. And finally, he warned that the city had to see to it that Trump didn't just mortgage out, using the generosity of the abatement to get financing that exceeded the total project costs. Ravitch wanted a mechanism to assure that Trump put real equity into the Commodore project. When each of his suggestions was rejected by the city, it became clear that he could not fundamentally change the elements of the deal.

The pressure on Ravitch was tremendous. The two top Democratic legislative leaders in Albany—Steingut and Senate Minority Leader Manfred Ohrenstein—called to push him to do the deal quickly. A prominent West Side liberal, Ohrenstein had been pulled into the Trump camp on the convention center and the Commodore by Sunshine, who was also fund-raising for his Senate Democratic committee. He had reversed himself on the convention center site, after having opposed the 34th Street location when others suggested it years earlier. Ten thousand Trump dollars found their way into his campaign coffers at the same time as his switch.

Ravitch also felt the heat of personal calls from Abe Beame and John Zuccotti. A massive city-assisted housing project on the far West Side on 42nd Street called Manhattan Plaza, under construction by HRH, Ravitch's family company, was in dire trouble. The fiscal crisis had forced the city to suspend making mortgage advances on the project, and Ravitch was now looking for a joint city-federal bailout. The Commodore controversy was putting him at war with the very officials who held the fate of his own business in their hands—just one more complication for a man struggling with many.

Undaunted, Ravitch began working behind the scenes, feeding information on the deal to several aggressive Manhattan city councilmen, including Henry Stern, who began pushing the city to better its terms. This guerrilla warfare led to yet another Bailkin idea, geared to counter the objections of the Stern group and Ravitch. This one, finally, pushed the deal over the top.

Bailkin had by then become a social friend of Donald Trump's. Donald liked to frequent a Third Avenue bar called Harper's, which was often filled with gorgeous models. Trump and Bailkin sometimes talked well into the night there, and the subject was usually business. Donald never really relaxed at the bar and rarely started a conversation with a woman. When he did make a move and pick up a phone number, his selections seemed to Bailkin to be triggered by the impact the woman might make on a room, never his ease with her.

But through it all, Bailkin saw past the blowhard in Donald and decided he liked him. While the older, more experienced government people who met Donald during the Commodore discussions dismissed him as shallow and offensive, Bailkin prided himself on being one of the first to see the substance behind the show. He realized that Donald was trying to co-opt and seduce him, but he also believed they had developed a genuine friendship. In the middle of the negotiations of the final terms of the deal, the two grew closer still, with Donald even occasionally touching on his personal troubles in their private talks—including the alcoholism of his older brother, Fred Jr., who was nearing forty years old and doing little with his life.

Bailkin's final Commodore proposal, first broached in one of these bar conversations, was a percentage rent on Donald's profits. The initial deal had required Donald to make only a flat rental payment, increasing every few years at first, then easing upward annually over the life of the abatement until it reached full taxes forty years into the future. The stretching out of the abatement over four decades was the special grease Donald had brought to the deal; Bailkin's new scheme would limit the grease.

Bailkin raised the subject of a city slice of Donald's profits deceptively. He told Donald that City Hall and the Board of Estimate would not go along with the deal without a sliding scale of secondary rents pegged to his revenue. In fact, Bailkin had been meeting only with the city council critics, and no administration official had forced him to seek this concession. Trump at first adamantly resisted, but eventually assented to the terms. Once they had an agreement on the concept, they began to hammer out the specifics, until Donald came to one of the numbers sessions with a look of angry recognition on his face.

"This is all *you!*" he blew up at Bailkin. "Nobody in City Hall is demanding these things, nobody gives a shit."

"No," Bailkin insisted, "this comes from the highest levels."

"Bullshit!" Trump screamed. "No one cares but you." Bailkin smiled an acknowledgment, but said Trump had already agreed to the concept, and was now committed to it.

When the deal was finally submitted to both the UDC board and the Board of Estimate, the percentage rent was included, but only vaguely described. Bailkin had won on the concept, but he had agreed to put a cap on the percent of profit the city could take so that Trump would never pay more than full taxes, and he had left the definition of profits to the framers of the actual lease, which wouldn't be drafted until after the authorizing resolutions passed both boards.

The UDC vote came first. To allow it to qualify as a UDC project, the board had to stretch its statutory authority in new directions—defining a hotel renovation as an industrial project and finding East 42nd Street a "substandard area." Four of the board's six members had to support the project if it was to pass, and only four did, with the other two votes abstentions—an almost unprecedented occurrence for the usually unanimous group.

One of the favorable votes was cast by the Bowery Savings Bank's vice president Pazel Jackson. The Bowery's main branch was located right across the street from the hotel, and the bank had written the city a strong letter of support for the project, warning that the Commodore was "a major blighting influence in midtown Manhattan." The bank was ultimately so moved by the need to dress up its own neighborhood it became the lead bank on a $45 million syndication to finance the project. But the decisive vote in favor was cast by the man of two minds, Richard Ravitch. He would later publicly declare it "a mistake."

The UDC vote left one more hurdle: the Board of Estimate. Opposition to the project was, however, beginning to coalesce. The Hotel Association and individual hotel operators like Harry Helmsley were criticizing the deal as overly generous. They wanted to know how they were supposed to compete at full taxes with the newest hotel in town paying virtually none. Henry Stern now had all but one of the Manhattan city council delegation vociferously opposed to the giveaway terms, but the council did not have the power to vote on land use issues. When the council members held a press conference in front of the hotel to question the deal, Trump suddenly appeared and warmly greeted his critics. It was one of his favorite ploys—a measure of his disarming confidence. He even offered Stern a political contribution.

The city board's vote was postponed three more times, but not because any one member was ready to oppose it. A few were just not certain they wanted to approve it and were looking for some improvement in the terms. A dramatic act was needed to finally get it to a vote, and Victor Palmieri provided it: The day before the scheduled board vote, he closed the hotel. While the company had indicated a possible September closing, the suddenness of the action was a shrill demand for passage, at last, of the abatement plan.

The closing had all but been dictated by the city and state. As UDC's executive director expressed it in a series of March internal memos: "The closing of the hotel must be imminent and definite to provide a basis for a blight finding required for an industrial project under the UDC Act," meaning that UDC could only use its extraordinary powers to revive the hotel if it was shut. "When the hotel is closed and boarded up," the UDC executive noted, "the property WILL BECOME a major blighting influence," suggesting that the state was now in the business of encouraging blight to justify the use of its power to combat it.

On May 20, 1976, the board, which met in the upper floor of City Hall, unanimously passed the Commodore deal, amid proclamations about how the project demonstrated the confidence private investors still had in the struggling city. In fact, Donald still had no option on the hotel, and had stalled obtaining it, thereby saving the $250,000 deposit he would have had to put down. Equitable had dodged any financing commitment as well. The private parties hadn't put a dime on the table, while the public sector had delivered a gigantic and exclusive tax break. The debut project of this bold entrepreneur was, in truth, a breakthrough example of the new state capitalism—public risk for private profit. Trump had been handpicked by bureaucrats and politicians to become the solitary recipient of an unprecedented giveaway, stretched so far into the future that it was statistically likely to outlive even its thirty-year-old beneficiary. Though other projects were later funded under the incentive program created to justify Trump's abatement, no other Manhattan hotel would ever receive so selective and grand a subsidy.

Mike Bailkin and UDC's economic development director, Dave Stadtmauer, who had steered the deal through the state process, sat that night on the steps of City Hall savoring their triumph and sensing that the business incentive plan that had grown out of the Commodore deal might have also created an opportunity for them. Bailkin had recently asked Zuccotti for a City Hall position as a kind of development commissar, but with Eisenpreiss still in place the promotion just wasn't feasible.

He had also talked to his friend Donald about his desire to move up or out of government. "I'd love to have you with me," Donald had offered. "I'm going to be going places."

"I think that might taint our deal," Bailkin said. "I don't think it'd be good for either of us."

Donald agreed, but then suggested that Bailkin ought to "go to work for Roy Cohn, the greatest lawyer in the world." Bailkin had taken this suggestion seriously and, at Donald's invitation, met Cohn. But he was put off by the Cohn ego.

So that spring night, on a high over their triumph, Mike Bailkin and Dave Stadtmauer decided to open a law firm together. Bailkin would leave the city the next day, and Stadtmauer would stay on at UDC for a few months, to steer the Trump deal through a public hearing and the necessary second vote confirming a final project and plan. The new firm, Stadtmauer & Bailkin, would highlight their own specialty: economic development deals with the city and state. Bailkin had already lined up a major client—a nonprofit theater group—that would redevelop most of a block on the far West Side on 42nd Street, using the same new abatement program he'd designed for the Commodore. As a paid consultant to the city, he would also come up with the financing device that would soon make Trump's convention center at 34th Street buildable—suggesting that the center use the state bridge authority to float hundreds of millions in bonds.

Ironically enough—perhaps because they'd decided to do it their own way—Stadtmauer & Bailkin would become one of the only major development firms in New York that Donald Trump would never retain.

Even though both UDC and the city formally approved the Commodore abatement by the spring of 1976, it would still take two long years before final closing papers were signed by all the parties and construction could start. Part of the delay was attributable to the mirage the project was when the resolutions authorizing it were approved, with title to the land, financing, and a hotel operator up in the air. But many practical public obstacles remained—a legally mandated UDC public hearing, a second vote of the state agency, and the negotiation of a detailed lease. The continued uncertainty of all the private pieces to the deal, particularly the bank loans, made it all the more difficult to nail down the state and city commitments. But Donald, with the withdrawal of Mike Bailkin, had a new ace in the hole.

If Bailkin had been the architect of the deal, Stanley Friedman was to become the mechanical engineer who would finally make it happen. "Bugsy" Friedman, who'd worked his way up the patronage career ladder from a Bronx clubhouse grunt to deputy mayor, was to the fix what Bailkin was to the structural concept.

Indeed it was the master fixer, Roy Cohn, who had arranged Friedman's and Donald's first meeting, and as surely as the historical ties between Abe Beame and Fred Trump had made the abatement bonanza politically plausible in the early stages, the bond between Cohn and Friedman would guide it to conclusion.

Though Cohn had ostensibly been retained by Donald to handle a single piece of litigation, the Trumps' racial discrimination case, he began in the mid-seventies to assume a role in Donald's life far transcending that of a lawyer. He became Donald's mentor, his constant adviser on every significant aspect of his business and personal life. Like Friedman, many of those with public and private power who met young Donald in those days were introduced to him by Cohn, whose Rolodex knew no bounds. The unmarried and childless Cohn, who concealed his frantic gay nightlife behind a façade of daytime homophobic toughness, literally adopted Donald. He began to see Trump as potentially his most successful protégé and instrument. While Cohn would ultimately be disbarred for stealing from other clients, he did not bill Donald for his on-call attentiveness, seeking occasional payments only when the firm was short of cash. There was no way to reduce what Cohn was getting from Trump—whom he saw as an extension of himself—to billable hours.

Cohn's exploitation of Friedman to secure the Commodore booty was an unforgettable lesson for Donald, exposing him to the full reach of his mentor's influence and introducing him to the netherworld of sordid quid pro quos that Cohn ruled. This almost ritualistic initiation not only inducted Donald into the circle of sleaze that engulfed Cohn, the bountiful success of it transferred the predatory values and habits Cohn embodied to his yearning understudy.

Cohn's hold on Friedman was simultaneously rooted in the past and framed by future promise. In addition to his City Hall title, Friedman was also secretary of the Bronx party, which made him county leader Pat Cunningham's right hand as well as his top city jobholder. Cunningham—whose three eventual indictments would exceed Friedman's tally by one—was a confidant of Cohn's. His father had been a Bronx judge and behind-the-scenes prince of the Bronx machine. To Friedman, a county leader like Cunningham was a near deity, all he had ever wanted to be.

In the middle of all the maneuvering around the Commodore deal, Friedman had actually been summoned to a grand jury probing Cunningham shenanigans. He hardly blinked. He would no sooner rat on the party's leader than he would drop one of the boss's contracts, and Friedman understood that the Commodore was a deal Cunningham wanted done. Cunningham backed it not just because of Cohn. Carey had made Cunningham chairman of the state party, and that meant Louise Sunshine was his treasurer. When she wasn't over at Donald's new two-room office at 466 Lexington Avenue—in Penn Central space offered Trump by the Palmieri group—she was in Cunningham's party headquarters. In fact, Cunningham, Sunshine, Friedman, and a young Republican named Trump worked together in 1976 to bring the Democratic National Convention to Madison Square Garden.

But this sort of intertwine could not explain just how far Friedman was willing to go to seal the Commodore deal. It surprised no one who knew the deputy mayor that he would join Roy Cohn's law firm the day after Abe Beame left office. He had, in effect, been working for the firm while he was running the government. Nothing more clearly expressed that premature private service than Friedman's many efforts to protect the secret treasure trove that sustained Cohn's millionaire lifestyle—namely, the cash hoards Cohn extracted from a half dozen city-owned parking lots leased to shell corporations headquartered at his midtown town house. As signed statements from the bagman who ran the lots for him later proved, Cohn's principal source of cash was the thousands delivered to him weekly from these lots. Since the lots were supposed to pay a percent of their gross to the city, the siphoning of this cash to Cohn was indirectly depleting an already impoverished city treasury. Yet Friedman spearheaded the most lucrative leases through city processes to deliver them to Cohn, and he installed Cohn operatives at the leasing agency who looked the other way when the gross revenues at the lots came in at laughable levels. Friedman was designated to do much the same for the Commodore boondoggle. Even before Bailkin's departure, it was Friedman who cast the mayor's vote at the 1976 Board of Estimate meeting and helped steer the deal through the board's political morass. And when Bailkin left, Friedman was the city's chief defender of the project at the July 1976 public hearing hosted by UDC, calling the closed Commodore "a disease" that would "spread" unless it was renovated. He also coordinated the city's successful legal defense in a lawsuit brought to challenge the abatement as an unconstitutional "surrender, suspension or contracting away of the power of taxation." Friedman's affidavit in the case falsely argued that the city had neither "initiated" nor "empowered UDC to proceed" with the project, but that it had merely been consulted by UDC before the agency decided to use its exemption powers.

And it was Friedman who pushed UDC for its final approval—a formal vote of its board in September 1976. A second vote was needed because the first had only authorized the agency to submit the proposal to a public hearing. This time the Bowery's Jackson excused himself as soon as the Commodore item was called, apparently now wary of the bank's conflict of interest. The state's banking superintendent, John Heimann, a critic of the deal, abstained, as he had on the first vote. Without Jackson, the project needed a decisive fourth vote from insurance commissioner Tom Harnett, who had also abstained the first time. Harnett had already communicated his opposition to the deal to Ravitch, saying he had a "visceral" reaction to its "sweetheart" terms. But with the chips down, Harnett walked out of the meeting, too, leaving a half hour ahead of Jackson. Harnett's special assistant, Murray Lewinter, thus held the fate of the project in his hands, and he cast the decisive vote for it.

Lewinter was a longtime Bronx district leader, had just succeeded Friedman as secretary to the Bronx organization, and was working in a patronage post as Harnett's special assistant. Harnett himself had been appointed commissioner on Cunningham's recommendation. Lewinter would say years later that he "only voted at Harnett's direction," and Harnett would express astonishment that his surrogate was recorded as casting the vote that made the Commodore deal possible. This manipulated UDC vote—engineered by Cunningham/Friedman operatives—was a precursor of the still-to-come sordid maneuvers that would finally lead to the execution of documents binding the city and state to the project.

But in the months between the UDC vote and the closing that Friedman would force before the Beame administration left office at the end of 1977, Donald agreed to terms on another deal that, like the Commodore, would shape his life. Though a bit more personal than the Commodore, this fateful transaction would also be framed in Roy Cohn's law office. In the spring of 1977—while Donald busily hammered out the details of a comprehensive lease for the Commodore with state officials—he also quietly married Ivana Zelnickova Winklmayr.

In early 1977, Donald still had a business reason to go out for drinks with Michael Bailkin. When Bailkin left the city for private practice, he was retained by the administration as a consultant to advise it on two matters—the Commodore and the convention center. The only thing the two projects had in common was Donald Trump, obviously Bailkin's area of expertise as far as the Beame administration was concerned. When he and Donald got together again at their old haunts, Bailkin noticed that Trump actually seemed interested, for the first time, in someone other than himself. He could not stop talking about a new woman in his life named Ivana. He told Bailkin that she had been on the 1972 Czech Olympic ski team and was now one of the top models in Canada.

Both boasts would become part of the Trump legend, and both were as true as his earlier attempts to convince Bailkin that he had an option and financing for the Commodore. In fact, Ivana was an unnoticed runway model for Montreal department stores, and the closest she'd ever gotten to the Olympics was public relations modeling she'd done for the 1976 Montreal Summer Olympics.

Two of the half dozen versions of how she and Donald met that they would eventually share with the media involved the Montreal Olympics. Their initial meeting was either at the games in 1976, or at a public relations event in New York to promote the games, or, as Ivana even told one magazine, when she was "competing" in the games. Another version had them meeting at Maxwell's Plum, a chic midtown Manhattan watering hole, either when Ivana came to New York for a Canadian fur fashion show or during an Olympics promotion. They also may have met at someone's house in New York, at a party in Montreal when Donald was on a skiing vacation, or at a fashion show there.

Several of Ivana's model friends definitely recall having seen Donald at a Montreal show, where he seemed so smitten he "never took his eyes off her." But these women thought the two had met fleetingly elsewhere and that Donald had come to the show expressly to watch her model. A tall, svelte, very poised model with "white-white teeth," bared by a full-lipped and shy smile, Ivana's accent and bearing set her apart from the New York women Donald was used to and vowed he wouldn't marry.

However they met, the twenty-seven-year-old Ivana, born to a Czech father and an Austrian mother, had a classy, European manner that instantly had Donald in pursuit. She had, in fact, had a modest downhill racing career as a member of a Czech national team. But years later she was forced to concede in a sworn deposition that she had tried out for the Olympic team and been passed by, insisting that *she'd* never claimed otherwise. Asked to explain the origin of the legend, an exasperated Ivana sputtered: "I have brown eyes and they are saying in articles for 15 years I have green eyes." Like so much else in the life Ivana would discover as a Trump, her own history had a way of magically reinventing itself, rewritten by the mythmaker she'd married. In late 1971, George Syrovatka, the boyfriend who'd coaxed her out of her rural Czech hometown to attend Charles University in Prague, arranged for her to marry an Austrian friend, Alfred Winklmayr, so that she could obtain a Western passport. Syrovatka, who'd met both Ivana and Winklmayr on the skiing circuit and was a leading Czech skier, had already defected to Canada. Even after her "Cold War marriage" to Winklmayr, Ivana remained in Prague until she finished school, graduating with a master's in physical education in 1972. In the middle of these fundamental changes in her life, she fell in love with an Austrian poet who was killed in a car crash. It was only after his death that she followed Syrovatka to Montreal.

In 1973, while living with Syrovatka in Canada, her marriage to Winklmayr was dissolved in a Los Angeles court. Though she was pictured in the Montreal *Gazette* in 1975 sharing an intimate moment with Syrovatka in their Montreal apartment, and quoted as calling him her "husband," there is no record of a marriage. When asked by one reporter if he'd been married to her, Syrovatka said, "Not exactly." Ivana met Trump a few months after the cozy *Gazette* photo, and the persistent Donald quickly became a source of tension in her eight-year relationship with Syrovatka, who was by then a minor celebrity in Canada and its premier speed racer.

"I always considered George and Ivana as married," Syrovatka's brother Michael said later. "In my family, marriage is just a formality. My parents treated Ivana as if she was their daughter-in-law. That's how George saw it, too." Donald, as usual, seemed to relish the competition. Ivana began taking weekend trips to New York to visit him, and after they spent a few days together in Aspen, he first raised the subject of marriage, but only very tentatively. He brought her to the house in Jamaica Estates to meet an approving Fred and Mary. After only six or seven months of long-distance dating, she decided to leave Syrovatka and marry Donald.

As intrigued as Donald was by Ivana's distinctive style, his attraction to her had the familiar trophy quality to it that Mike Bailkin recalled from their earlier conversations about women. This didn't surprise Bailkin, who believed Donald could not talk about anything with genuine emotional depth. In fact, at the same time that Donald first told Bailkin of his plans to marry Ivana, Bailkin was going through marriage difficulties that would lead to a divorce and, even though Donald was a good listener when it came to business, Bailkin decided not to tell him about his own problems because he was convinced Donald was constitutionally incapable of responding. To Bailkin, Donald's emotional range did not extend beyond a sensitivity to slights and profane outrage if he thought someone had tried to sucker him. Otherwise, Bailkin had concluded, Donald just coasted on a detached, emotionless plane, energized by his own compulsive ambition and oblivious to anyone else's feelings. Bailkin would never forget one brief exchange he had had with Donald in what were clearly Trump's halcyon days. Irritated by yet another Donald affront, Bailkin said to him: "You're a very shallow person. . . ."

"Of course," Donald replied, interrupting Bailkin in midsentence. "That's one of my strengths. I never pretend to be anything else." Watching Donald prepare for marriage reminded Bailkin of this proud declaration of uncomplicated superficiality.

Trump went about the marriage in his usual businesslike fashion. In March of 1977, he leased a two-bedroom apartment in Olympic Tower, an elegant new building on Fifth Avenue. The two-bedroom foresight was apparently as deliberate as it was fortuitous; eight and a half months after the two were married, Donald Jr. was born.

On March 22, Donald and Ivana signed a carefully drawn and detailed prenuptial agreement. The agreement was Roy Cohn's idea. "You're better off not married," Roy had bellowed when Donald came to him to discuss the marriage. "It'll just lead to trouble. I don't know why you want to do this." If Donald insisted, then he had to get her to sign an agreement that "would protect" the family's assets, Cohn argued.

The two drafted the agreement at Cohn's office, and one early version included a provision requiring Ivana to return any gifts Donald might give her during the marriage should they divorce. The demand provoked such protest from Ivana that it was replaced with language that explicitly authorized her to keep "her own personal clothing and express gifts from Donald or others." To entice an angry Ivana back to the table, Donald threw in a $100,000 "rainy day" certificate of deposit only she could draw on that would be given to her within thirty days of the wedding.

Another draft offered Ivana lump sum bonus payments for each child, according to the aide who typed it. Donald's attempt to include this provision, which also vanished in the final agreement, confirmed Ivana's belief that Donald saw her as little more than a well-tuned baby machine, healthy enough to produce a brood of attractive and healthy children. "I want five children, like in my own family," Donald told a close friend, "because with five, then I know that one will be guaranteed to turn out like me." Ivana was well aware of this Trump child quota and mentioned it to a reporter early in their marriage. "He'll get," she calculated, "maybe two or three," noting that she would love to work full-time, "but Donald's afraid I'll get so involved that I won't have another child." In the end, Donald would get the three children Ivana predicted, and Ivana would wind up with new nuptial agreements after the first and third child that would dramatically increase her scheduled alimony payments, just as the discarded bonus payment draft had anticipated.

The final terms of this first nuptial contained puny allotments for Ivana, giving her only $20,000 a year if their marriage split up immediately. If they remained married for nine years and then separated or divorced, she would still get a paltry $30,000 annually until she moved in with another man. Had the agreement still been in effect when the marriage actually did end—thirteen years later—Ivana would've had to make it on $45,000 a year. And if they had remained married for twenty-nine years under this agreement and Donald had died, Ivana would have been entitled to nothing more than a single half-million-dollar payment. These limited benefits were provided even though the agreement flatly asserted that Donald was "a multimillionaire," and claimed that "the exact amount of Donald Trump's net worth is impossible to accurately determine due to the illiquid nature of his holdings, which are worth millions of dollars."

Donald also wanted to make it clear that she shouldn't expect to live too well if they stayed together either. "Donald has explained to Ivana," read the agreement, "and Ivana warrants that she is aware that Donald's standard of living and lifestyle are neither opulent nor extravagant in that neither he nor the companies in which he has an interest own yachts, planes, or the usual appurtenances generally connected with large and substantial businesses . . . Ivana acknowledges that she is familiar with the fact that Donald's standard of living is basically simple and will continue to be so after the marriage herein contemplated." This gold-digger warning did not deter Ivana, though her transparent hunger for precisely the sort of extravagance depicted in the agreement may have been the reason Donald inserted it. Of course, this poor-boy passage was a doomed admonition, since even its author had no intention of living by it. Indeed, Donald's catalogue of forbidden acquisitions would later look like his personal shopping list.

Ivana signed the agreement, acknowledging that she did it "having been fully advised by counsel of her own choosing." Her lawyer, however, was Larry Levner, who was so close to Cohn he'd actually represented Cohn in at least one civil suit. When the divorce came years later, Ivana would claim that Levner had been handpicked by Cohn. Donald also pressured her to sign, pointing out that it was "much better for both sides to work out the details of a possible breakup while they are friends rather than after they have become enemies." In *Surviving at the Top* he concluded that his arguments were "so reasonable that I would question the motives of a prospective mate who heard them and didn't agree to go along." Ivana—who'd already ended her relationship with Syrovatka and announced the marriage to her family and friends—acquiesced.

On April 9, 1977, Norman Vincent Peale married Donald and Ivana at his Marble Collegiate Church on Fifth Avenue. Ivana wore a two-piece chiffon full-skirted off-the-shoulder dress, with a long veil but no train. Everyone else was in black tie and long gowns. Donald's sisters, Maryanne and Elizabeth, were bridesmaids, while Fred Jr. was the best man. Ivana's parents came, as did many of her Canadian friends.

Mike Bailkin, who was part of the wedding party, thought Donald looked almost as happy at the reception at "21" as he had the day the Commodore passed the Board of Estimate. While the late afternoon ceremony seemed to Bailkin almost perfunctory and devoid of grace or joy, the evening party had a lively, ebullient air to it. Comedian Joey Adams, a lifelong Cohn hanger-on whose gossip-columnist wife Cindy would become Donald's media confidant during the stormy divorce days in 1990, was the toastmaster, and the dinner party took on the tone of a combined power wedding and family affair, running until midnight.

Many of the 150 or so wedding guests were involved in the Commodore deal, including Bailkin, Beame, Sandy Lindenbaum, Roy Cohn, Henry Pearce, architect Der Scutt, and politicians like Queens Borough President Donald Manes, who had voted for the abatement as a member of the Board of Estimate.

With Sandy Lindenbaum's work at the Board of Estimate largely completed, Jerry Schrager, a senior partner at Dreyer & Traub (the same firm whose name partner had been helpful to Fred in the early FHA days), was also there. Schrager had become Donald's lead attorney on the unfinished aspects of the Commodore deal, particularly the lease itself.

Of course the old gang came, too, including Bunny, and a collection of Steinguts. Almost precisely forty years earlier, Fred Trump, also just thirty years old, had taken an immigrant wife, who would bear him a child as soon as practically possible and become a citizen years later. There were countless differences but, as with so much else about Fred and Donald, the commonalities were more than coincidence. Their lives had the feel of puzzle pieces, shaped to fit together in an unbroken interlock of mutual promise. With the Hyatt hovering over the wedding, the Trump breakthrough into Manhattan was finally visible on the horizon. It was a moment of great anticipation. The wedding became the setting for the family's celebration, but not just because Donald had found a wife. The marriage of Fred's and Donald's grand expansionist vision was about to be achieved.

In the weeks after the wedding, Donald and his lawyers finally concluded lease negotiations for the Commodore with the city and state, building into the fine print bonuses for Donald never discussed when the Board of Estimate and UDC passed their resolutions approving the project months earlier. The principal public negotiator opposite the skillful Jerry Schrager was Charles Goldstein, who had become a major force at UDC. Mark Levine, an assistant corporation counsel, was the city's main participant, with Friedman in the background.

The major issue to be resolved was the definition of profits, which would determine Donald's fluctuating payments to the city over time. The way that profit was calculated in the lease was so explicitly written to fatten Trump's pockets that even Bailkin would subsequently admit it was a giveaway. Trump's profit, a percentage of which he was to share with the city, was defined as the difference between his gross income and his expenses. But income, in this document, was described as only the "aggregate amount of monies *actually received* [author's italics]," while his expenses were all the costs he "incurred," whether he paid them during that year or not.

If, for example, a corporation leased the hotel's ballroom and several suites for a weeklong conference and made a down payment, but still owed thousands at the end of the year, the receivable wasn't counted as income. But all the hotel's expenses associated with the conference, paid or unpaid, were deductible from the income, a formula that lowered the profit unrealistically, and, hence, the percentage rent payment to the city. While this would at least theoretically even out over several consecutive years, the flexibility of this peculiar bookkeeping gimmick allowed Trump accountants wide latitude in computing payments due in lieu of taxes—latitude that would according to a city audit and lawsuit lead to shortchanging it by millions. Anyone negotiating a lease for the city would have wanted to maximize the income Trump had to report and minimize the expenses; this formula did the opposite.

In addition, the lease permitted Donald to partially deduct as an expense the costs of physical improvements and much of the tax depreciation he claimed on aging fixtures, furnishings, and other capital items. During Bailkin's early negotiations with Trump over the profit-sharing plan, Donald had raised these capital expense issues and Trump's insistence on winning these concessions had persuaded Bailkin that he shouldn't give in on them. The initial package presented to Beame in the form of Bailkin and Eisenpreiss memos specifically stated that these items were "excluded" as expenses. The UDC board submission contained a similar prohibition. Somehow, though, the language that Bailkin had drafted barring this write-off was mysteriously deleted from the actual resolution Friedman steered through the Board of Estimate. The absence of Bailkin's exclusion left the issue to the lease writers to determine, enabling Donald to cash in on this loophole once Bailkin was gone.*

---

* The lease's tolerance of deductions for capital expenses was so costly to the city that when Bailkin and Donald appeared years later at a joint forum discussing the deal,

The unusual concessions Trump won were in part made possible by a leadership vacuum at UDC. Ravitch had left at the end of March 1977, and UDC's president resigned a few months afterward, leaving the corporation without a chief executive officer. Governor Carey didn't name a new president for eight months, installing in the meantime an acting president, Robert Dormer, who was one of a few insiders angling for the full appointment. A conflict-inviting vacuum was clearly forming at·the top of what was becoming a powerful development entity, and the UDC bureaucrats competing for its presidency sensed, unsurprisingly, that the key to achieving it was through the political emissaries who had the ear of the governor—Trump, Sunshine, and, increasingly, Charles Goldstein.

Sunshine, who was now in full gear putting the financing together for the governor's 1978 reelection campaign, had also come back to UDC as an advocate of the Commodore deal. Two months before Ravitch departed, Sunshine and he discussed her possible return to active lobbying at the agency, and Ravitch, who was preparing to announce his own candidacy for mayor, consented. A few weeks before he finally left, Sunshine received a written dispensation from the corporation's president. She had reassured everyone that since the UDC board had already approved the project, her work on it there would be harmless technical housekeeping. It was, in fact, an absurd premise, because a pioneering project of this complexity required virtually daily discretionary decisions at the agency, and she was now free to influence each and every one of them.

Sunshine immediately attached herself to David Stadtmauer's successor as city development chief, the young and dashing Richard Kahan, as did her new-found friend and ally, Charles Goldstein. Goldstein was the sort of man who'd never laughed at a joke about himself. When he was fresh out of law school and clerking for federal judge Irving Kaufman, the judge came into his office one day, greeted him as "Charlie," and asked him to join him for a meeting. A stern Goldstein rose, inhaled deeply, and in front of the assembled staff announced: "Please, Your Honor, it's Charles." Remote, brilliant, and ruthless, he was also beginning to branch out politically, and would eventually become the personal attorney to both the governor and Carey's top aide. Goldstein clearly liked what he saw in Kahan's darting eyes; they understood each other's hunger.

Trump corrected Bailkin's assumption that the percentage rent due under the agreement must by then have been paying huge dividends for the city. Trump informed Bailkin for the first time that the depreciation deduction had been added to the lease and announced that because of it he was still making limited payments to the city.

Goldstein and Sunshine chose the thirty-one-year-old Kahan—who was dutifully processing the Commodore deal—as their candidate for the UDC presidency. It was Kahan, for example, who approved the Trump lease, writing a letter to Trump in September 1977 officially agreeing to the terms. The letter, which Donald used with financial institutions to verify the state's commitment to the deal, was written within days of Beame's loss in the Democratic primary. Kahan's rushed commitment was the opening salvo in a campaign to finally get the project nailed down before the new mayor, a maverick congressman named Ed Koch, could take office in January 1978. While Kahan strongly believed that the Commodore deal had intrinsic merit, he also knew his facilitation of it would earn him Sunshine's and Goldstein's decisive support for the UDC presidency.

Of course Kahan's partner on the city side in this push for a December 1977 closing was Stanley Friedman, and their next three months of panicked collaboration would constitute a tribute to the ability of government officials to perform at their self-serving best, delivering in record time on the one contract that would, in the end, make both of their careers. A suddenly anxious Trump—convinced he had to erect a wall of binding legal commitments around the Commodore abatement that Koch could not dismantle—was determined to get the city and state to close the deal even though his construction and permanent loans were still not in place.

Ever since his first meetings with Ned Eichler about the project in mid-1974, Trump had been touting the supposed $70 million permanent loan commitment of Equitable. But in truth all Equitable was willing to invest was what it had secretly committed two years earlier: $25 million. Even after Bowery signed on for a $10 million portion of the permanent loan, Donald still only had half a bank deal. The Bowery was ready to serve as the lead participant, promising to try to raise the other $35 million, but it was "under no obligation," according to the letter agreement, to bring in the rest of the financing. Until the rest of the permanent loan was in place, Donald could not obtain any of his $70 million construction loan. (Upon completion, the construction lender is repaid by the permanent mortgage.)

In addition to being forced to seek a city and state closing without fixed financing, Trump was also trying to rush approval of a last-minute addition to the planned new hotel, a glass-enclosed Garden Room restaurant that would hang over the sidewalk in front of it. It was an unprecedented attraction, never before permitted under the intricate system of laws designed to protect city pavements from commercial intrusions.

Trump would have to clear the overall project, and the Garden Room extension, through nine bureaucracies in the space of weeks, including a community board; the City Planning Commission; the fire, transportation, and buildings departments; the Bureau of Gas & Electric; UDC; the Board of Estimate; and, most difficult, an intransigent fiefdom peculiar even in New York politics known as the Bureau of Franchises.

With these herculean tasks before him, Trump's agent, Friedman, became a driven man. The inducement was the job Roy Cohn had already promised him. Friedman was even to get Roy's fifth-floor office in Cohn's town house, complete with a cathedral ceiling, bar, outdoor patio, a greenhouse where Friedman's secretary would work, and an adjoining apartment with kitchen, living room, fireplace, and loft bedroom. Friedman was guaranteed a six-figure salary for the first time in his life and, unless he stumbled, the rest of it.

And one further goal—the ultimate goal—was also coming into sight. Pat Cunningham was now in the most serious trouble of his life, with federal authorities about to close in. The word on the street was that he would be forced to step down and that he was headed for a cell. Friedman didn't know how soon all of this would happen, but he knew he had positioned himself to claim the leadership. With Roy's connections, cash, and clout, he'd have the perfect ally.

Friedman understood all too clearly that the Commodore was an assignment straight from his benefactor. Cohn was, in fact, already handling an assortment of Commodore legal matters, especially the unpleasant little business of forcing out the dozen or so commercial tenants on the first few floors. For Friedman, the Commodore rush was a Cohn test of his ability to push the buttons of a government where he had spent twelve years as an attorney in the city council and a top mayoral aide.

Given the time constraints, the only option left to Trump was an escrow closing. Hadley Gold, the chief assistant in the city's corporation counsel, had spent a lifetime processing major city real estate deals and he had never heard of the city doing an escrow closing. Almost by definition, it made no sense for a municipality or a state agency to allow one. Why would two governments sign binding contracts for a deal that wasn't ready to close and put those documents in escrow? Why would these governments sign a lease, a project agreement, a three-party agreement, and a purchase agreement that committed them irrevocably, while the private parties to the deal were not required to commit any money and could step aside at will?

Despite the apparent boondoggle air of the escrow plan, Friedman stormed ahead with it, confident of his ability to cajole city bureaucracies. He was assisted in his drive by a sullen Abe Beame, who during the final three months of his public life, let his administration become a free-for-all for insiders, unchecked by concerns about bad press or history. It was in this atmosphere that Friedman rewarded himself with a lifetime appointment as the $25,000-a-year chairman of the city's Water Board, a part-time post with a full-time limousine and driver. With Friedman's old nemesis, John Zuccotti, long gone, he was in effect the government of the City of New York for a few months—as frightening a thought as that was.

So Friedman put together all of the Commodore parties—Trump, the various city bureaucrats, UDC, and the Palmieri group—for what one participant called "a marathon session that went on for days." He barked at recalcitrant, or just time-consumingly careful, city lawyers, telling them to "move it." He personally signed each and every document as the designee of the by then semiretired Beame, including the mayor's formal letter giving notice of his approval of the lease to UDC.

All Donald produced was a queasy commitment from Equitable and Bowery that said on the cover page that they were "willing to participate in a loan," not that they were actually making one. Even this qualified commitment was legally defective, since the financial institutions conditioned it upon receipt of a letter from the corporation counsel that sweepingly overstated the generous abatement granted Trump. The final escrow agreement signed by Friedman, Kahan, Trump, Hadley Gold, and the agent in whose custody all the escrow documents were placed, Charles Goldstein, explicitly rejected the legal condition in the bank letter.

The Palmieri participants deeded over the property to UDC, which in turn leased it to Trump's entity, even though Donald didn't have the $10 million to pay for it. Of course, without UDC's control of the hotel, none of the other agreements could be executed. Like every other piece of this implausible puzzle, the transfer of title would be negated if the $10 million wasn't paid by September 1, 1978. That was the date written into all the agreements, the deadline for a final closing.

The Palmieri firm effectively declared itself willing to tie up the title to its hotel for eight further months, at the same sales price agreed to three and a half years earlier. Palmieri allowed this, even though the value of Penn Central's other Manhattan hotels was shooting through the ceiling in a suddenly upswing market (a package of three went for $10 million more than the agreed-upon price because Palmieri agreed to entertain belated bids). The company certainly had the right to take new bids on Commodore as well, since Trump's option had already expired and been extended several times.

On December 20 and into the morning hours of December 21, with just a week to go in the Beame administration, the city, state, and Trump lawyers and aides met all day and all night at the offices of Dreyer & Traub. The smooth, always dapper Kahan moved from starched shirt to starched shirt and dark suit to dark suit. Sunshine, who had begun championing him for UDC president a month earlier, never left the discussions, sitting on the floor, giggling over the banter. She and Kahan had become so friendly that they had spent weekends together—accompanied by other friends—at a friend's country home. Friedman didn't stay at the closing but Sunshine and the city lawyers had his phone numbers, and he was on call all night. Trump himself had been dragged by Ivana to a concert at Lincoln Center, and when a snag developed in the early evening, Sunshine called his driver and asked that Donald be pulled out to the phone to resolve the problem. Goldstein checked in periodically, too, but at this point the detail work involved didn't require his personal attention. At last the contract that would launch several careers was firmly in place.

With the escrow deal approved, Friedman and Kahan still had a few days to tie together the loose ends of the complicated consent needed for the Garden Room restaurant. This cantilevered bar and lounge would be described a month later by *New York Times* architectural critic Paul Goldberger as "the most controversial element" and "most exciting aspect" of the Hyatt plan. "The room looks as though it will be one of the city's most appealing public gathering places," Goldberger wrote, "a sidewalk cafe in the air, offering views up and down 42nd Street."

Friedman delivered the final authorization and signed a twenty-five-year consent for the restaurant on December 29, literally the last business day of the Beame years. He not only produced a consent in three months that, for the ordinary sidewalk café, would require half a year or more, but structured the deal so that Trump paid only a fraction of the regular franchise fees due the city for commercial use of public space. What Kahan's help, the consent was rewritten to make UDC its recipient, and any governmental user of a street or sidewalk routinely paid discounted fees to the city. Trump was probably charged less per year for the first ten years of operation—$24,000—than the restaurant was grossing a day. More important, Friedman switched the approval from a franchise agreement, which could not run any longer than ten years and would cost Trump much more, to a consent, which could last a quarter of a century.

Armed with the escrow documents and the Garden Room permit, Trump did finally put his financing together and close the deal on May 20, 1978, shortly after Ed Koch took office. For one last time Kahan, Sunshine, Donald, and the gang of thirty or so lawyers and title company representatives assembled. This second closing dragged on for two or three days, with Donald periodically making his rounds like a glad-handing politician at a fund-raiser. He learned everyone's name and said how "pleased" he was that each of them was there. He told a key city lawyer that he was doing such a good job that he wanted him "on the city team when I close on the 60th Street yards," perhaps hearkening back to the Beame days, when he had the power to name the city negotiator who would deal with him, as he had Bailkin.

This time, appropriately enough, Fred made an appearance as well. He had to come—his signature was needed on a crucial document. Fred must have wondered what would have happened if he, rather than Donald, had been the up-front Trump on this project from the beginning. The newspapers would have been filled with stories about the old-time ties with Bunny and Beame, and even the sixties' SIC scandal. The deal might never have survived the uproar. Only Donald could have taken on the Commodore without that stigma; his charisma was the distraction that displaced the otherwise inevitable old-boy network controversy.

But in the end Fred was once again quietly at center stage. In 1954, when he had been called before the Senate Banking Committee and questioned about abuses in his FHA projects, Fred had made much of the fact that he had personally guaranteed the Beach Haven mortgage, citing it as a measure of his own commitment to the project. He testified that he had never before guaranteed anything else he had borrowed. As it happened, however, without the guarantee Fred wound up giving his son, Donald would have had no Commodore mortgage. Fred came to the closing to sign the guaranty.

It was Fred and the Hyatt chain who jointly guaranteed the $70 million construction loan from Manufacturers Hanover, each assuming a 50 percent share of the obligation and each committing itself to complete the project should Donald be unable to finish it. Hyatt and Donald agreed that the chain would become a 50 percent partner in the venture with Donald's company. The price of Hyatt's guarantee was its promotion from operator to partner.

No document in the long paper trail attached to the Commodore deal better demonstrated the lack of bank confidence in Donald or the project, and none made clearer the limits of his promoter role. As indispensable as Donald was to the initial concept and political marketing of the hotel, he could not have made it happen without Fred's—and Hyatt's—signatures. Hyatt chairman Jay Pritzker said later that Donald simply "couldn't get the financing" and "we were able to help," with both Equitable and Manufacturers Hanover. When it came to the financial bottom line of the deal, Donald was barely a factor.

Concealed beneath all of Donald's public pizzazz, the fact was that Fred was his silent partner in the Commodore project, just as he had been hidden in the language of the option agreement for the West Side yards. In addition to Fred's guaranty, his Trump Village Construction Corporation loaned Donald nearly a million dollars during construction to repay draws on a Chase credit line for Donald that Fred had helped arrange. And it was Fred's two-decade-old relationship with a top Equitable officer, Ben Holloway, that had helped entice them to do the project.

Contrary to all the hype of his sales pitch with Eichler and Bailkin, as well as the asset description in his prenuptial agreement, Donald was, on his own, hardly creditworthy enough to get financing for any major project in the late seventies, much less one of these dimensions. His 1977 agreement with Ivana, for example, listed "his interests" as the 34th and 60th Streets yards—which consisted of a purely speculative option at the time—and stakes in six Fred projects. But even these vague holdings were more wish list than reality. In a sworn statement three years later, Donald claimed ownership of a 25 percent piece of only one of Fred's thirty or so operating entities.

His only salaried income at the time of the Commodore closing—less than $100,000 a year—was as an officer of his father's company, Trump Management. He paid $10,832 in taxes on $24,594 in income in 1976 and $42,386 in taxes on $118,530 in income in 1977. In addition to his salary, he'd begun collecting payments under a trust set up by his father in 1976, but he received only $19,000 in 1977 and $47,200 in 1978, the year the Commodore deal closed. Another trust established by his father in 1949 paid him $11,000 a year, and his grandmother's trust paid him $1,699 in 1977. In addition to the trusts, Fred regularly gave each of his children $6,000 a year at Christmas as a kind of family bonus.

He did draw a management fee out of one New Jersey housing project his father turned over to him, and he did occasionally collect brokerage commissions, the largest being the $262,500 staggered over three years for the sale of part of his father's interest in Starrett City. Since that sale was concluded in late 1977, it was hardly a significant number on his balance sheet when the Commodore closed.

Though Donald owned no publicly traded stock, he was already claiming that he'd made a fortune in gold and that he'd been involved in several successful California real estate deals; but his tax returns suggested otherwise—as did his lifestyle and the tiny office Palmieri was letting him use. Penn Central was still picking up most of his 60th Street expenses, and when Hyatt joined the Commodore project as a partner, it advanced him a million in start-up funds. At the time of the 1978 closing, these two subsidies were keeping Donald's struggling operation afloat.

Despite all that each had done to make the Hyatt happen, neither Fred, Bailkin, Kahan, Friedman, Cohn, Zuccotti, Beame, Stadtmauer, Sunshine, Ravitch, Carey, nor Goldstein drew a mention in Trump's autobiographical account of the deal that invented him. In *The Art of the Deal,* it was as if Donald walked out onstage alone. There were, however, other rewards for these key players.

- One month after the May Commodore closing, *Richard Kahan,* who'd held exactly three jobs in his life, became UDC president, the most powerful public development position in the state.

- *Charles Goldstein* cohosted a party at the Plaza celebrating Kahan's appointment, unfazed by the awkward fact that he had helped engineer the appointment of a man who would then authorize millions in public legal fees for him over the next few years. Goldstein would develop a host of private client relationships as a result of his work for UDC on development deals patterned after the Commodore. When he left, he would collect fees on one future Trump transaction, and regularly represent Trump's financing friends from Equitable.

- *Stanley Friedman* would not only join Roy Cohn's firm but would become Cohn's first Democratic county leader, a dream come true for both. Cunningham resigned abruptly in early 1978, and Friedman took control of the Bronx party days before the Commodore deal closed in May. One of Friedman's best paying clients over the years was Donald Trump, who also became the largest contributor to his Bronx party committee.

- *Hugh Carey* received $65,000 in contributions for his successful reelection campaign from the Trumps. Starrett and its principals, whose $40 million construction contract to build the Hyatt was its largest domestic award in 1978, also donated $27,000 to Carey. Trump retained the finance chairman of Carey's reelection effort, Arthur Emil, as a condemnation attorney for the Hyatt. Carey had fiercely opposed Beame's reelection attempt in 1977, and following that lead, Trump had not made a single contribution to the campaign of the doomed old man. Donald had actually claimed that it would have been a conflict to give to Beame because of the Commodore deal, an assertion he made with a

straight face, even as he prepared to dump donations on his gubernatorial benefactor. After Beame's defeat, the Trumps did give $5,000 to help
pay off Beame's campaign debt.

- *Louise Sunshine* became Donald's first partner. Five months after the
  new Hyatt opened in 1980, Donald invited her to purchase a 5 percent
  interest in the corporation that would, a couple of years later, build and
  own Trump Plaza, a co-op project on Third Avenue in Manhattan. His
  inclusion of Sunshine was some measure of the value he placed on her
  role in the convention center and the Commodore.

- Shortly after *John Zuccotti* went into private practice in June 1977, Donald tried to retain him on the West Side yards, where Zuccotti's community ties might have been particularly helpful. Zuccotti told Trump
  he thought it would create the appearance of a conflict and declined.
  Though Zuccotti soon became the top zoning attorney in the city,
  Trump never tried to hire him again.

- *Stadtmauer Bailkin* earned modest fees processing other projects under
  the incentive program they created. At the entrance of their East Side
  law firm they hung a wall-length poster of the Hyatt that described
  their role simply as "legal counsel" and "project manager," leaving to the
  imagination whether they'd worked on the public or private side of the
  deal.

- *Mark Levine,* the nuts-and-bolts man as corporation counsel who succeeded Bailkin as a key city bureaucrat on the deal, left in 1977 to join
  Goldstein's firm first and shortly thereafter Sandy Lindenbaum's. He
  filed Donald Trump's next application for a city tax abatement—a 1981
  request for an estimated $50 million write-off for Trump Tower.

- *Richard Ravitch,* who dropped out of the mayoral race, sold his family-
  owned business, HRH, two weeks after leaving UDC in early 1977. He
  had been talking with the purchaser, Trump's partners at Starrett, since
  1975 about the possible sale. Trump had begun negotiating a contract
  with HRH to build the Hyatt at the very time that Ravitch was closing
  his deal to sell the company to Starrett. Trump's selection of HRH as
  his Commodore builder may well have enhanced the value of the company to Starrett. Ravitch, though he cut his financial ties to HRH at the
  time of the sale, would actually move into Starrett offices, work with the

company on a number of projects, and retain his partnership interests in several HRH ventures. Starrett eventually became the contractor on five major projects connected to Ravitch's reign at UDC. Ravitch says he made no money on any of these deals, and almost six months after he left the agency he requested an opinion from the state's ethics board on the propriety of this complex intertwine, In less than twenty-four hours, the board's secretary wrote a letter identifying no conflict.

- *Victor Palmieri* was the only key Commodore player to be introduced for a bow in *The Art of the Deal.* No mention was made of Ned Eichler or John Koskinen, the two Palmieri executives who'd actually negotiated and executed the various Commodore options, and the agreements on the two West Side yards. In fact, in his book, Donald attributed conversations that had taken place with them to the much better known Palmieri and asserted that he'd "built a close relationship with Victor from the start," when he'd met Palmieri only a handful of times.

Manhattan United States Attorney John Martin initiated a brief inquiry of the Commodore sale to Trump. He personally interrogated high Penn Central officials, focusing on the company's willingness to stick with the hotel's $10 million purchase price. In the same period in early 1978, when Palmieri went ahead with the sale to Trump, the company had been involved in a separate deal that ostensibly included Trump. In that unrelated transaction, Palmieri collected a $2.5 million fee for arranging the purchase of a troubled home-building company, Levitt. The buyer was the ever-present Starrett and Donald, who also collected a $152,000 brokerage commission on the deal, claimed he'd gotten the parties together. This sidebar transaction cast a collusive cloud over the Commodore, but Palmieri brass insisted that Trump really had nothing to do with the Levitt acquisition. Martin closed the case as quietly as he'd opened it, but combined with the Brooklyn investigation of the West Side yards, Donald's dealings with Palmieri had twice become the subject of federal inquiries.

With all the career successes the Commodore deal generated, none received a bigger boost than Donald's. By the time the project, the first of his life, was in construction, he had ridden it to the top of his profession. Magically, he was dubbed the new Zeckendorf, the best-known developer of his era, though he was only now putting his first shovel to the ground.

In the mythmaking years that followed, Donald freely credited himself for the turnaround impact the Hyatt project supposedly had on the Grand Central area. No doubt the hotel's resurrection did help anchor a slipping section of prime New York real estate. But, while Donald depicted his project as both a jolt to a dead city economy and the savior of a slumping community, the fact was that it took so long for the Commodore job to get off the drawing boards that by the time it did, the city and the neighborhood had already begun to come back on their own. When Donald announced the renovation way back in 1975, the area near the Commodore was in such disarray that the owners of the landmark seventy-seven-story Chrysler Building across the street had defaulted on their mortgage. But when Donald was finally ready to start construction in 1978, Mass Mutual had already come to the Chrysler Building's rescue, buying out $34 million in mortgages and committing $23 million to restoration. What had begun as a vanguard project became just one of several simultaneous attempts to revive the 42nd Street strip.

The groundbreaking itself took place on a glorious New York day, June 28, 1978. Hugh Carey had appointed Richard Kahan UDC president the day before. Carey himself was in the middle of his triumphant reelection campaign, and that morning he would turn the Commodore event into a campaign stop: 1,400 new hotel rooms to celebrate, a three-story hotel with 19,000 square feet of ballrooms and thirty-seven meeting rooms, a solar-cooled glass exterior that would reflect the adjacent Grand Central Terminal and the Chrysler and Bowery buildings. It made for much better press than the fiscal crisis announcements of closed hospitals.

His blond hair dancing in the sun, Donald greeted Carey at the site. The hotel workers were picketing the celebration, and Carey introduced Donald to their new chief, Vito Pitta, a union leader who would be dogged for years by law enforcement and newspaper allegations of his mob associations.* A few months earlier Pitta had appeared from nowhere to take the leadership from Jay Rubin, the venerable president who had been trying unsuccessfully for a number of years to establish a relationship with Trump. Rubin had testified twice at the Board of Estimate in favor of the Commodore tax abatement; his insistent enforcement of costly provisions of the city-wide contract at the Commodore had helped force Penn Central to close it, adding to the momentum for Trump's

---

* Pitta was identified as an associate of the Colombo crime family and indicted in a major racketeering case in 1984. The charges against him, however, were dismissed a couple of years later.

project. Rubin had repeatedly attempted to get a commitment from Donald that the new Hyatt would sign the union contract, but all Trump had said was "We'll see what happens." Donald dispersed the protest that morning, though, with a simple promise to Pitta: "This will be a union shop."

In addition to the demonstration, the groundbreaking, which occurred at the hotel's elevated side entrance, was briefly disrupted. Demolition had already started inside, and a trash fire suddenly exploded, summoning a horde of fire trucks.

Carey would inflate every impressive number in his prepared text. He called the Commodore a $140 million project, adding the construction and permanent financing sums together, when one actually replaced the other. He said the hotel would generate 2,000 permanent jobs, when Trump's accompanying release boasted only of 1,300. "New York in the past had failed to give business the kind of incentive and support it needed to flourish," he said, "but that day is past."

In the years that followed, Donald would be unable to face the cameras without a peculiar, furtive twist to his public smile. It was the look of a man who could not conceal his contempt. When he looked into cameras it was as if he was eyeing himself in a mirror, admiring the triumph he'd become and, at the same time, laughing haughtily at the world. But this day, cynicism had not yet overtaken him. He had seen the amoral hunger of more men during this breakthrough deal than most people saw in a lifetime. In this triumphant moment, though, the tortuous process was a forgotten memory. He let himself be the boy he was, and shone with uncompromised joy.

6

THE PRICE
OF PETTINESS

Cowperwood was now entering upon a great public career. . . . Raw, glittering force, however, compounded of the cruel Machiavellianism of nature, if it is to be but Machiavellian, seems to exercise a profound attraction for the conventionally rooted. Your cautious citizen of average means, looking out through the eye of his dull world of seeming fact, is often the first to forgive or condone the grim butcheries of theory by which the strong rise.

—*Theodore Dreiser,* The Titan

GETTING THE SPADE into the ground for the Hyatt project had been a formidable test of Donald Trump's political and financial savvy. But now, for the first time, he found himself in charge of an even more exacting enterprise: the largest construction job under way in New York at that time.

Though Donald was theoretically running the project, he was in reality a man without an organization or even an office. Shortly after work started at the Commodore in the summer of 1978, the Trump Organization, such as it was, had to move out of its office next to the Palmieri suite at 466 Lexington Avenue. The staff consisted of Louise Sunshine and Philip Wolfe, the construction manager Trump had just hired to supervise the Hyatt. Wolfe moved over to the top floor of the Commodore, where he sat during the winter wearing a parka all day in a makeshift, windswept, on-site office with sample furniture. He soon took in a number two man, Jeff Walker, an old Trump buddy from the New York Military Academy. Sunshine operated mostly from her home.

Donald's office was his car, a silver Caddy with DJT license plates leased by one of Fred Trump's companies, driven by an armed ex-cop, and equipped with an early car phone. When the Commodore project started, he was still making frequent morning trips out to Fred's office at Avenue Z, then typically returning to Manhattan for the afternoon. But as the two-and-a-half-year project dragged on, and as he moved on to deals like Trump Tower, Donald drove out to Brooklyn less and less often. By late 1979, he was almost never there.

At the onset of the Commodore job, Donald, Ivana, and the newborn Donald Jr. were still living in their small, starkly modern apartment at Olympic Tower, with a living room, dining room–kitchenette, and two bedrooms. Donald used the 1,800-square-foot apartment in the showcase building at 51st Street and Fifth Avenue owned by Aristotle Onassis as a business address for the Trump Organization, the corporate name that Donald adopted and Fred did not use. Donald frequently held business meetings in the apartment—one, for example, with Hyatt executives visiting from Los Angeles in 1978. Ivana hovered around these gatherings with coffee, and also began to visit the job site a few blocks away.

A few months after work started on the hotel, the couple moved to a $3,000-a-month apartment on the top floor of a new rental building at 800 Fifth Avenue, precisely ten blocks up the avenue from Olympic Tower. The eight-room apartment symbolized their dramatically changing life—with a sweeping living room view of the park, platforms, mirrors, chrome wall sculptures, a bar, beige velvet sectional sofas, and two dining room tables made of goatskin hardened to a marblelike surface. The Trumps had a collection of Steuben glass animals which they displayed in the front hall on glass shelves outlined with a string of twinkling white lights.

Ivana hired an interior decorator named Barbara Greene of G. K. R. Associates, and together they designed the apartment, which Donald found so attractive he decided his wife had a decorating flair. As the Commodore renovation moved along, he asked her and Greene to oversee the hotel's interior work. Since he was so pleased by the apartment, and was still operating without a real office, he began holding business meetings and media interviews there, just as he had at Olympic Tower. Ivana described the sessions in their home as Donald "scheming and beaming." The Trumps also rented a summer house in Wainscott in the Hamptons and a ski chalet in Aspen. Ivana took on what one writer called a Hollywood style—"with helmeted hairdos and bouffant satin dresses," visiting beauticians several times a week. At Ivana's suggestion, Donald would match his tie color to the dress she was wearing on their nights out.

Donald was financing this upswing in their personal life with the millions of dollars in commissions and fees he'd begun to collect by 1979 and 1980, ranging from his convention center payment from Penn Central to a convoluted million-dollar brokerage fee on the acquisition of the Trump Tower site.

The best indication of his suddenly booming financial status was that he went from paying $42,386 in taxes in 1977 to paying none in 1978 and 1979. He escaped tax liability in 1979 on at least $3.4 million in earnings with a carefully structured package of real estate losses and interest payments. Judging from his tax returns, Donald became a millionaire in his own right in 1979, earning a Trump Organization salary atop his commission income.

Ivana and Donald rarely visited the Commodore site together, but they came separately often, conducting their own high-pitched inspections, shouting at just about anyone they could find. Donald had a strong sense of the image he wanted for the building and how to achieve it, but he was preoccupied with the visible. He wanted the richest and shiniest surfaces and was uninterested in the nuts and bolts of the job. Since Fred had essentially stopped active building when Donald joined the company in 1968, the Hyatt was Donald's first real construction experience, and he was wise enough, by and large, to leave it to HRH. While he was present regularly at the start and end of the project, he came infrequently midway through, when the job seemed to take on a momentum of its own.

This led to something of a logistical problem, for Donald had to sign every check for the project under a special cost control system set up with Manufacturers Hanover, the construction lender. All checks were issued individually by an outside check-paying consultant, rather than having the bank issue the builder a large check at intervals during the job, as was the usual practice. This way the bank and Donald jointly controlled construction expenditures. It also meant, however, that the consultant, an elderly accountant, had to track Donald down to obtain his signature almost every day. He would try the car phone or the Brooklyn office, where a secretary would occasionally have a sense of Donald's schedule. The accountant knew that even though he rarely ate anything, Donald would stop almost every afternoon at "21," the favorite lunch spot, for aspiring power-brokers. It was a ritual so regular—for Donald and his attorney Roy Cohn—that the consultant discovered he could predictably be found there to sign a check.

Ivana became a frequent presence at the site when the outer shell and inner structure of the building were essentially completed. She examined every inch of the acres of paradisio marble, the bronze columns, spirals, sheaths, the burgundy vinyls, the walnut paneling. Accompanied at times by interior decorator Barbara Greene, she almost inevitably issued edicts, and when construction supervisors would point out that her recommendations would require expensive change orders, she would shrug her shoulders and say not to "bother" her with money.

Donald had told the on-site staff that he wanted her involved, so they listened to her and, where possible, acted on her instructions. As often as she came—and her appearances got to be an almost daily occurrence—she could never remember anyone's name, and she addressed even Donald's top supervisors at the job without the slightest idea of who they were, certain only of her own desires. Social graces aside, Ivana was credited by Der Scutt, the architect who designed the Hyatt, with salvaging much of the interior design. In an interview several years after his last architectural work for Trump, when he alternated between praising and criticizing Donald in roughly equal proportions, he unreservedly cited Ivana as "very instrumental in making many, many changes at the Hyatt which, had she not intervened, it would have been very, very detrimental." Scutt said that Ivana reversed the decisions of interior designers who he referred to as "inferior desecrators" and "was astute enough to support us as architects." The Hyatt, he said, "is a much better design because of Ivana's input."

Since her father was an electrical engineer in Prague and Vienna, Ivana had grown up with blueprints and thought she could read one. She would haul the building plans and work schedules around the job site with her in high heels, infuriating the foremen and architects, demanding complicated changes in her insistent accent. Ivana always dressed dramatically beneath her hard hat, but she would repeat the same outfit every few days, to the point that the staff could confidently predict when she'd arrive in her black-and-white-check ensemble.

Though neither she nor Donald discussed their baby with the construction staff, they both, oddly enough, mentioned their prenuptial agreement in chats around the tiny Trump Organization office, with Ivana claiming that "they made me sign it." Her complaints—at the office and home—were apparently persistent enough that Donald, afraid she would leave him, had Cohn redraw the agreement in July of 1979, dramatically boosting her benefits and setting a $30,000 minimum in child support payments for Donald Jr. Referring for the first time to the "great love and affection" binding the two together, the new agreement guaranteed Ivana $100,000 a year for the rest of her single life if Donald died, as well as the right to live rent-free in their apartment. This contrasted with the niggardly one-shot payments of the voided first agreement. In the new agreement, her payments were no longer pegged to a sliding scale, depending upon how many years of marital bliss she'd given him. The alimony was also hiked to a base of $75,000 a year for the first ten years and $100,000 a year after that, with the apartment thrown in. These guarantees replaced the conditional schedule of the first agreement, under which she would have had to put in three decades of devotion to win a $90,000-a-year payout.

Still, language added to the new agreement that acknowledged that Ivana had been "working jointly with Donald since their marriage" was expressly scratched out and initialed by both, suggesting that Ivana had begun to think ahead well enough to try to put the claim in and Donald was sufficiently prophetic to make sure he got it out. By 1980, her rainy day certificate of deposit had grown to $145,000, including her earnings on the $100,000 payment under the first nuptial agreement (she would use this war chest to protect herself when the seemingly inevitable split came years later, paying lawyer Michael Kennedy's fees with it).

In addition to Ivana's and Donald's visit to the Commodore site, Fred Trump also was a frequent visitor. Low-key and friendly, he helped solve isolated problems, like the antenna system for the TV sets in each room. He knew little about a rehab job, never having done one, and nothing about hotels, but he was clearly comfortable on a construction site. He questioned on-site staffers about what Ivana was doing at a critical meeting, and she grilled the same staffers about why they were talking to Fred.

Toward the end of the project, Donald finally found a new office for his organization, and once again Fred was involved. In the summer of 1980, the Trump Village Construction Corporation subleased a 25,000-square-foot office for Donald on the second floor of the Crown Building on Fifth Avenue and 56th Street, just four blocks down the avenue from Donald's penthouse apartment at 800 Fifth and directly across the street from the Trump Tower site he had just acquired.

Using contractors from the Hyatt job, Donald designed a modern, sparse, and tasteful workspace, with provision for Sunshine again, as well as space for his first full contingent of record-keeping staff. With red carpet and gold fabric walls, Trump's own office centered around Donald's new burgundy desk, made from an Italian wood. The Trump Village entity paid architectural, legal, and rental costs connected with the Crown Building quarters, as well as loaning Donald $4.6 million during 1980, at least a million of which was an interest-free loan for working capital purposes. Though he set his son up at the center of every

New Yorker's universe, Fred Trump, at seventy-five, was content to stay on in his building on Avenue Z, nestled in his box office with the cigar-store Indian collection and collages of clippings.

The actual gutting and rehabilitation work at the Commodore was extraordinarily complex, requiring, for example, the drilling of 9,000 holes through the hotel's old brick front to the structural steel behind it in an effort to secure the aluminum and glass wall that was draped over the outside of the brick. Railroad tracks ran through the bottom of the building in a loop tunnel leading right into Grand Central, complicating the laying of the hot water piping, since there was in effect no real basement. The absence of a basement forced HRH to do the piping, and consequently the total job, from top to bottom, making it a construction nightmare.

The complications led to increased costs and delays. While Donald would later market himself as a masterful on-budget, on-time builder based on the Hyatt experience, the job was, in fact, disappointing on both counts. Jay Pritzker, in a 1990 interview, said that "the total project cost was $120 million; it was $50 million over budget." Pritzker had always thought that Donald's preconstruction cost estimates were "optimistic" and said that "Donald and I always disagreed about what the budget should be."

"The overruns were pervasive," continued Pritzker, specifically citing the unanticipated expense of the glass curtain wall. One of the ways the preconstruction estimates were artificially lowered was by excluding from HRH's contract a long list of items, enabling Trump to hire a general contractor for as little as $38 million—a misleading indicator of the final scope of the job. Construction executives involved in the Hyatt recall that an earlier $56 million HRH contract, with a much shorter list of excludables, had been rejected.

Trump came up with his half of the financing for the Hyatt overruns principally through a line of credit that Fred's old bank, Chase Manhattan, granted him in May of 1980, when the Manufacturers Hanover loan had just about been exhausted. Trump ran up a $28,500,000 debt on the Chase line that was specifically assigned to Hyatt costs. This was on top of the near million he borrowed from one of Fred's companies. These loans suggest that the overruns even exceeded Pritzker's memory and were closer to $60 million, almost doubling Trump's original budget. Despite his public bluster, Donald himself quietly put the final cost at $130 million, minus the $10 million for the land, in an unnoticed sworn submission for a 1981 corporate tax deduction.

The Hyatt's grand opening took place in September of 1980, a month and a half late. Though Trump had initially predicted completion by "winter 1980," he changed the schedule when it was announced that the Democratic National Convention would be held in New York beginning on August 11, and he began pledging he would finish by then. But construction delays cost him an opportunity to showcase the Hyatt during a nationally televised convention, an opening that would've been particularly appropriate for a tax-break hotel built one political pane of glass at a time.

When the hotel did open, a thousand guests led by the governor and a resplendent Roy Cohn attended the gala dinner party, eating filet de veau aux trois champignons on gold tablecloths in the Grand Ballroom. In the last-minute rush to get the mezzanine ready for the opening, Ivana created quite a union stir when she ordered electricians downstairs off the higher floors, where they were finishing the wiring of suites. She was so involved she personally planned the plant arrangement in the Garden Room, the cafe that quickly became the signature attraction of the hotel.

In truth, when it opened, the Hyatt was still months from completion. Trumpet's, its other restaurant, wasn't ready until the end of the year. The hotel suites opened a few floors at a time over a period of months, dragging on well into the spring of 1981. Hyatt officials were so concerned about the delays they sent a consultant to the site to write a report, and the analyst concluded that the job should have been completed six months earlier.

There was one paradoxical side effect of the Hyatt cost overruns: By hiding the true cost of the project, Trump may have been able to scrimp on payments due the state that were pegged to the cost of construction materials. Trump had been granted a sales-tax exemption on all materials used at the Hyatt, but he was supposed to collect the tax savings from the contractors and place them in a trust fund. The fund, set up as part of Donald's agreement with UDC, was to be used to finance a series of improvements on the adjacent Grand Central Terminal. Obviously, the more expensive the job, the greater the contributions to the trust fund should theoretically have been. But Trump's contributions were astonishingly small.

In his final memo on the project in late 1977, Michael Bailkin, acting as a consultant to the city, estimated the anticipated sales tax savings to Trump, and consequently Trump's expected contributions to the fund, at $2.25 million. As late as December of 1979, with the project under construction for a year and a half, the savings were still expected by state officials to reach $1.5 million. At that point John Simpson, the head of the Metropolitan Transportation Authority (MTA), which operates the terminal, and was thus the ultimate beneficiary of the trust fund plan, wrote Trump a letter announcing that his agency was planning to use the fund as a local matching grant in an attempt to qualify for federal financing of even more improvements at the terminal.

Unbeknownst to the MTA, the UDC had already received the bad news that Trump had only "identified about $600,000 in sales tax monies" so far, leading to a new final estimate of $800,000 in the trust fund contributions. The UDC memo concluded that "this is less than anticipated and may barely cover the work" already planned—the cleaning of the façade of the terminal. The memo simply took for granted the accuracy of Trump's submissions and concluded that it was "doubtful" that the five other promised terminal improvements listed in the lease would be undertaken.

The fact was, however, that the construction costs at the hotel were mushrooming. The overruns were attributable in large measure to costs other than materials but the $900,000 that was ultimately collected still seemed far less than what Trump should have paid. Kahan would say later that he was unaware of any Hyatt overruns, conceding, in effect, that his agency simply did not monitor real construction costs.

Trump, in the meantime, was hyping his trust fund donations in the media. Under the headline "Grand Central to Be as Good as Old," he was quoted in the New York *Post* as promising to restore the landmark terminal with a $3 million majestic plan—three times his real contribution. "It'll glimmer and sparkle," he predicted, adding that he would install a half-million-dollar illuminated fountain in front of the terminal. The exterior cleaning was done with such fanfare, highlighted by a banner emblazoned with Trump's name and stretched across the top of the terminal, that the city and MTA had to calm public fears that Trump had actually purchased the structure. "That's the ultimate ego trip, isn't it?" he proudly proclaimed.

Donald wound up paying himself supervisory and other fees of $137,000 out of the $830,000 spent on terminal improvements. In meetings with city officials, he quietly admitted that the trust fund offered "an insignificant amount of money." Though the lease and trust fund agreement bound Trump to "expend the total amount determined by an independent certified public accountant as being the actual amount of sales taxes which would have been payable," no Trump CPA statement was ever filed with UDC.

At the request of Koch administration officials in 1982, the city comptroller, Jay Goldin, conducted an audit of Hyatt payments under the lease. The audit, which took almost a year and a half to complete, concluded that the Grand Central improvements "have been delayed because of inadequate reporting and collection of sales tax savings." But the findings were uncharacteristically vague, never pinpointing an estimate of the amount in question or identifying the delinquent party. The audit also ignored the unfiled CPA statement and apparently overlooked the huge cost overruns as well. Trump was concerned enough about the investigation that he personally called the staff auditor, Frank Cannistra, to get oral assurances before it was completed that the findings would not be damaging.

The usually publicity-hungry Goldin did not issue a press release on the completion of the audit nor did he send a copy of it to the MTA, the only public party with a monetary stake in the collection of the millions that seemed to have gone unpaid. Low-level UDC staffers did receive a copy, and though it urged the agency to examine the books of several subcontractors whose payments were regarded as "questionable," word of its recommendations did not reach the top levels of the agency. Goldin's office never followed up to see whether UDC audited the subcontractors or whether collections were ever made. Donald, of course, was a Goldin contributor, and in the years after this audit his donations grew larger.

Eight years after the payments were supposed to have been made, the MTA was still writing UDC asking about them. A Koch administration official concluded in a 1988 memo that the issues surrounding Trump's tax savings and public improvements "remain unresolved to this date." The best indicator of where the missing funds may have gone was contained in a 1981 letter written by one of the Hyatt's subcontractors, Flour City Architectural Metals Corporation, which claimed it owed no sales taxes on a $7 million contract. The company president explained this in a letter to UDC by revealing that Trump's general contractor told him when he made his bid not to include any estimate for sales taxes because the Hyatt was "an exempt project." That direction permitted him to come in with a lower bid. When the contractor was asked later to pay what he'd saved in taxes to the trust fund, he said he'd already deducted them from his bid and would not pay them after the fact. Trump subsequently used Roy Cohn to sue this subcontractor to try to get him to pay the equivalent of his sales tax savings, but other contractors may have been in the same boat, leaving Trump the beneficiary of cheaper subcontracts. Even though Donald had won the largest abatement in state history, he was apparently quite willing to shortchange his public partners on the trust fund.

Tax issues aside, many of the subcontractors on the Hyatt job had curriculum vitas that had long interested law enforcement. The concrete contractor, North Berry, and supplier, Transit-Mix, were named in court cases as part of mob-dominated cartels. The demolition company, a Pennsylvania firm called

Cleveland Wrecking, whose contract was the first awarded by Donald on the job, was identified in FBI memos as secretly owned in part by a close associate of the Scarfo crime family, which dominated Atlantic City and Philadelphia. Wachtel Plumbing was involved in an attempted mob-backed shakedown in Atlantic City at the same time that it was doing the Hyatt job, according to law enforcement documents. A federal wiretap picked up the mob head of the carpenters' union, Teddy Maritas, citing the award of the Commodore's drywall contract to Circle Industries as an example of a fix by the racketeer-run club that dominated the business. "You think," Maritas deadpanned, "these things just happened out of the sky?"

While it was difficult to build an untainted job in New York at the time, the Hyatt team exceeded the normal tawdriness quotient. The sleaze extended even to the seemingly trivial—the newsstand in the hotel lobby was leased to Ancorp, a Cohn-represented operator whose top two officers were convicted in a video-taped payoff of Amtrak's real estate chief. Cohn, who feasted off Ancorp concessions much like he milked the cash cow parking lots, got Trump so entangled with the outfit that it listed him as one of three business references in a proposal for a city lease and described him as a "secured party" backing the company in a Dun & Bradstreet report. While the company at its peak controlled a couple of hundred subway and railroad newsstands, the Hyatt was its only hotel, a measure of the debt of gratitude Donald felt he owed its special counsel.

In fact, by the time Cohn did his triumphant table-hopping at the Hyatt's gala dinner party in the fall of 1980, he was as much a fixture in Donald's life as Fred. Trump repeatedly called him his "best friend"—even in conversations with reporters. He served as master of ceremonies at a birthday party for a hundred or so of Trump's friends at "Le Club," and Donald was a prominent regular at Cohn's Studio 54 birthday affairs, as well as many smaller parties at his town house and his estate in Greenwich, Connecticut. When *New York* magazine's Marie Brenner set up a luncheon interview with Trump that year, Donald came to "21" with Stanley Friedman, and the two spent much of the meeting swapping Cohn stories. "Roy could fix anyone in the city," bragged his law partner Friedman. "He's a lousy lawyer, but a genius," said Donald. The compliments were a measure of the cynicism Cohn had passed on to both of his jaded protégés.

But the construction of the Hyatt was not just a matter of unseemly subcontractors and scam newsstand operators or of bricks and marble. Searing yet hidden Trump abuses scarred the project from the outset—none more brutal than the handling of the tenants in the Commodore's ground-floor commercial space.

• • •

Donald proved quite willing to exploit every power of the public authority attached to his project, cavalierly calling upon the awesome threat of state condemnation. But Trump's war against the stores at the Commodore revealed a side of him that transcended mere questions of greed. For a relatively young man, he exhibited a cruel streak that disturbed even his allies at UDC and could not be explained by the meager monetary gain involved in some of the condemnation matters. As Daniel Levitt, a lawyer who opposed Trump in a condemnation case and was later asked to represent him on an unrelated matter, put it: "Donald just seemed to enjoy the cat and mouse game."

UDC could by law condemn any of the old Commodore's retail tenants, even the respectable ones. If it decided to use this power, it would pay a court-set fee to acquire the store's leasehold interests in the space and could then put the tenants in the street. Its agreement with Trump provided that he would reimburse the agency for all of its condemnation expenses, including outside legal fees. While UDC officials had expressly refused to sign a proposed 1977 agreement binding them to exercise their condemnation powers whenever called upon by Trump, they nonetheless allowed him to use the threat of those powers in that manner a mere year later. An aggressive Charles Goldstein and a passive Richard Kahan were responsible for allowing this excess. As he saw Trump shake the state's fist in the face of legitimate businessmen, a sympathetic Kahan did at least recoil, summoning Trump to meetings at UDC and trying to leash him in. But, in the end, only the courts were able to stop him.

The defensible theory for condemning some of the dozen or more stores was that Trump might need to force out recalcitrant tenants whose space needs were incompatible with the new hotel design. But Trump made it clear to Kahan in late 1977, with a carbon to kingmaker Louise Sunshine, that "even if it were physically possible to keep" the tenants, "their operations are generally of such a low caliber that they would seriously impede the image and success of a new Hyatt." A few months later, UDC supported Trump when he went after every commercial leaseholder in the hotel, including Strawberry, the large and successful women's apparel store at the corner of Lexington and 42nd. Strawberry received a condemnation notice even though Trump had singled out the store as just the sort he wanted to keep during his first meeting with most of the commercial tenants at UDC in 1976.

After this initial discussion, Strawberry's owner, Alan Ades, had tried for more than a year to set up another meeting with Trump. In December 1977 Ades and his partner finally did get an appointment and rode out to Avenue Z to spend a day with Donald. Ades was struck, during this and subsequent encounters, by Trump's combination of bravado and charm, his ability to soften a threat with a friendly smile. Yet much of his performance was transparently false, Ades thought, especially his peculiar claim that Ivana bought her shoes in his very middle-class store.

In the end, Ades and Trump shook hands and signed a letter agreement they had mutually drafted allowing Strawberry to remain but obliging it to pay a 50 percent rent increase for substantially the same space. Ades was relieved. The Commodore store employed thirty-five people and was the flagship of a small but growing chain that employed 300.

Months passed, however, and Ades was unable to get the formal lease Trump was supposed to prepare implementing the signed agreement. Then in April, Trump sent him a sixty-day notice to vacate. Since it would be another forty-five days before Trump actually closed the deal with the city and state and obtained the hotel, he was removing his best tenant before he even had title. There was a provision in the letter agreement with Trump requiring Ades to temporarily vacate on sixty days' notice, but only if and when it became unavoidably clear that the store's presence was slowing construction. Construction wouldn't start until June. And, most important, Ades was supposed to receive the lease before he closed the store so he could be confident of being able to return when construction activities permitted it.

Ades refused to move and sought another conference with Trump, and on June 1, 1978, he and his partner drove out to Avenue Z again. This time Trump opened the meeting with what Ades would later call a "bombshell." Donald simply announced, "I have changed my mind," and refused to fulfill the December agreement, explaining that Ades's failure to leave within sixty days had voided that document. When Ades pointed out that he still had six days to go to abide by the terms of the vacate notice and promised he'd leave the next day, Trump told him to stay and pay his rent until formally condemned. "I'll get the UDC to condemn you," he stated matter-of-factly, and added that he might negotiate a new lease permitting Strawberry to return when the hotel was built.

A few days later Trump spelled out just what he wanted from Ades. He demanded $100,000 up front—almost a full year's rent under the terms of the existing lease—a sum Ades considered "ransom." Trump also wanted to add $100,000 a year to the rent already agreed to, making it almost a 150 percent hike. Ades refused these terms, and three days later UDC served a notice to purchase. The agency offered $25,000 for Strawberry's entire twenty-one-year leasehold, including what Ades estimated as $600,000 in fixtures. The notice gave Ades seven days to respond, but even before that period had passed UDC filed a condemnation petition. The rush to judgment was apparently prompted by the fact that a new condemnation statute, just passed by the legislature and much stricter about the procedures imposed on a condemning authority, would go into effect on July 1.

Ades's description in the court papers of Trump's negotiating tactics surprised Trump's friends at UDC. And Ades was hardly alone. Legal papers were coming in from several tenants with all sorts of chilling stories—Trump had needlessly boarded up the windows of the stores along 42nd Street, cut off the hot water to a pizza parlor, and withdrawn a lease he proffered to another tenant. Concerned by these reports, Kahan summoned Trump to his office on June 22, five days before Hugh Carey would officially name him UDC president.

Trump was accompanied by his attorney Arthur Emil, who was then co-chairing the finance committee of Carey's reelection campaign. When Kahan sought an explanation for the action against Strawberry, Emil replied that the company had failed to vacate "in accordance with the requirements of an agreement." No one mentioned the absurdity of serving a sixty-day notice before the hotel deal had even closed.

Charles Goldstein then took over the direction of the meeting. He told Trump that he was "carrying UDC with him" in his dealings with the lease-holders and warned him to "limit his oral dealings with tenants" in the future. Emil should "supervise all contacts with store tenants," he advised, and Donald agreed. Goldstein then talked about the need for UDC to retain additional condemnation counsel to handle all the litigation. Everyone, including Kahan, agreed that "the litigation would be under the supervision of Arthur Emil"—a paradox, since UDC was agreeing to allow Trump's attorney, who was not on retainer to the agency, to supervise a small army of attorneys who did work for it.

Goldstein went so far as to say that "UDC would abide by Emil's judgment that further negotiation with an individual client is futile," but insisted that Emil meet personally with each tenant at least once. Goldstein had essentially delivered an extraordinary state power to one of the governor's principal fund-raisers to exercise in the interests of a private client.

Ades could not tell if Trump's intent was to use the condemnation threat to jack up the rent or if he was really trying to force his store out. Trump's purpose seemed to shift over time depending upon circumstances unrelated to the terms of their own discussions. One of the reasons for Donald's ambiguity was apparently the uncertain prospects for casino gambling in New York. Donald had talked openly in meetings with Ades about wanting part of Strawberry's space for gambling if it was legalized. The store's space included a massive old ballroom attached on the ground floor to the hotel lobby—a parcel that Ades knew would be ideal for a casino. Indeed, early in the reconstruction of the hotel, Donald had brought a local news television crew into the hotel shell to discuss on camera his casino plans for it. Even though Donald told Ades he was pressuring state officials to win approval of casino gambling, everyone knew it was a long shot. But the maneuverings with Ades indicated that Trump wanted to keep his Strawberry's space option open.

In a search for allies to counter Trump's heavy-handed use of UDC, Ades wound up at the city's Office of Economic Development, the agency that had spawned the Commodore project so many years earlier. Hank Gavan, counsel to the agency, filed a memo the same June day he met with Ades and his partner. If their allegations were correct, Gavan believed, "it is almost beyond belief that governmental powers could be used for such a purpose." Gavan also immediately wrote UDC, saying that the Strawberry allegations were "of great concern" to the city and asking that UDC take no further action against the store while the city investigated the complaint.

Gavan had Trump come to his office for a meeting with Ades to put both sides of the issue on the table. After listening to the two, Gavan, a tall and imposing man, rose and folded his arms. With an authoritative stare at Trump, he said, "This is not going to happen. You are not going to do this." Gavan wrote in a subsequent memo: "I concluded that the story previously presented by Strawberry was accurate, and that Mr. Trump had indeed decided that he could derive more income from these premises and therefore had sought to renege upon the prior agreement." But when Gavan later learned that Ades had brought suit to try to block the condemnation, he became wary about getting involved in a situation that was already in court and suddenly dropped out of the dispute, refusing even to return Ades's phone messages.

By now, in fact, the Strawberry matter was in two courts. UDC had brought its condemnation case before a judge who regularly handled such matters, Supreme Court Judge Margaret Mangin. Daniel Levitt, the attorney representing Strawberry, was one of a group of lawyers for various tenants fighting Commodore condemnations who went to a conference with Mangin shortly after UDC served its notices. Mangin had clearly indicated, as far as Levitt was concerned, that she was going to approve the condemnations by the end of June, only a few weeks away. To get away from Mangin and keep his client's case alive, Levitt filed a separate lawsuit contending that UDC's action constituted a breach of Strawberry's letter agreement with Trump. Levitt's suit wound up assigned to Supreme Court Judge Alvin Klein.

Even though UDC was the respondent in the case before Klein, Donald himself showed up at the hearings, in the company of Roy Cohn. The pair sat in the back of the courtroom as spectators. In an interview years later, Arthur Emil, who was supposed to be Donald's condemnation counsel, had a hard time explaining just where his role ended and Roy's began in these cases. The best he could offer was that Cohn was Donald's "general counsel" on all matters, "very, very close to Donald," and that Trump selectively brought him into cases where special circumstances existed.

The Cohn appearance in Klein's courtroom, and subsequent letters from Cohn to the judge, had clear political implications. Klein was a Bronx judge who had for fourteen years served as secretary of the county's Democratic organization until a Bronx boss ignored an American Bar Association finding that Klein was unqualified and elevated him to the bench. Klein's fourteen-year term was scheduled to expire in two years, and Cohn's partner, new Bronx boss Stanley Friedman, would determine whether Klein got another.

Klein rejected Strawberry's request to enjoin UDC from pursuing the condemnation, a decision that Levitt fully anticipated. What Levitt did not expect was that Klein also dismissed Ades's complaint, killing the case. No one had even filed a motion to dismiss it; Cohn had, however, written Klein a letter suggesting that if he denied the injunction that Levitt sought, he ought also to dismiss the case.

In open court the enraged Levitt attributed the bizarre decision to the judge's relationship with Cohn, who was so close to Klein that Cohn had invited the judge to join his table at Cardinal John O'Connor's annual Alfred E. Smith dinner. Levitt's brief criticized the way "the court conducts its business," arguing that dismissals of multimillion-dollar claims shouldn't be granted on so shabby a basis, "hopefully not even when Roy Cohn has a finger in the pie." Klein took the parties back to his robing room and offered to "undo" the dismissal, which he subsequently did. Cohn then wrote the judge another letter, but by that time the case before Klein had become almost irrelevant. The real action had shifted to the condemnation proceeding, where Judge Mangin, as it turned out, also had a Cohn problem. A gossip item (planted, no doubt, by Cohn himself) on the *New York Post*'s "Page Six" just a few days before a crucial hearing scheduled before her on all the Trump condemnations celebrated Cohn's latest bash at his Greenwich estate and listed all the prominent attendees, which included both Donald and Mangin.

Mangin opened the hearing with a little speech about the news item, saying that she would recuse herself from the case if any of the defendants thought her appearance at the party would affect her fairness. Levitt regarded it as an empty offer, since all the other lawyers were condemnation attorneys who would have to appear before Mangin on many matters and would thus be unlikely to object. When no one else raised a question, Levitt said he "accepted" her "invitation" and asked her to withdraw. Later, Mangin's clerk called Levitt to ask if he was serious, and when Levitt said he was, she had to get off the case. With Mangin's departure, the matter was reassigned to Judge Martin Stecher, an above-politics judge with a reputation for thoughtfulness.

After months of argument and depositions Stecher granted Strawberry and other complaining tenants a full trial, effectively blocking the condemnation. Stecher found that "the private profit" of Trump in the taking of these stores "seems to be at least as significant as the public purpose of halting blight." Stecher questioned whether Trump or UDC had ever established a need to condemn Strawberry. Within days of Stecher's ruling, Cohn signed a stipulation settling the Strawberry case. Dreyer & Traub then negotiated a new lease with Ades, but the bargaining went on for several months more. Trump did not sign a lease until the lobbying efforts on casino gambling failed in the Albany legislature in 1979. Having won his twenty-one-year lease at last, Ades remains in the hotel today.

The Strawberry condemnation was hardly the only example of Trumpian pettiness. Another episode during the construction of the Hyatt—an extraordinary saga of duplicity and miscalculation that fundamentally shaped Ed Koch's view of Trump for years to come—demonstrated just how self-destructive and stubborn young Donald could be.

The battle was over two easements, or permits, that Donald had promised to deliver to city officials. The one that would prove most problematic was a tiny 740-square-foot easement that would have given the city's subway system a 1.5 percent sliver of the Hyatt's retail area. The MTA desperately needed that space in order to expand a vital passageway and build an escalator between Grand Central Terminal and the Hyatt. More than 220,000 people traveled daily up and down the existing narrow stairwell to reach one of the busiest subway stations in the city. The other easement, for 3,600 square feet, was to build a connection in the mezzanine between the terminal and hotel retail areas. Joining the two separate mezzanines and creating new exits would reduce congestion throughout the terminal area—a goal both the city and the MTA wanted to achieve.

The Koch administration inherited Trump's vague Beame-era promise to permit these improvements and in June 1978 moved to guarantee them. Trump began meeting with top MTA officials, and the head of the city's midtown de-velopment office, Ken Halpern. A personal friend of Koch's, Halpern was his driver in the 1977 mayoral campaign, and his involvement in the easement is-sues helped raise what might otherwise have remained an obscure issue to one that persistently attracted the attention of the mayor himself.

Donald began the negotiations demanding a trade-off. He had committed himself, as part of the public improvement agreement for the tax abatement, to build at his own expense another entirely separate stairwell to the subway. While the one involved in the easement controversy was on the western side of the hotel, next to the terminal, the stairwell Trump was supposed to build was on the opposite, eastern end near Lexington Avenue. Trump said he would grant the western easement and allow the city and MTA to build its stairwell if they would waive the requirement that he build the other 500-square-foot eastern stairwell. On October 6, Ed Koch himself wrote a letter to Trump formally terminating Trump's obligation to build the stairwell and thanking him for the easement. This waiver saved Trump the expense of actually building the eastern stairwell in exchange for simply granting the city the right to erect—at its own expense—the western one.

Donald also tried to exploit the public interest in the easements to help him leverage a lucrative lease out of the MTA. At the same time that he was negotiat-ing with the MTA about the stairwell and mezzanine issues, he was also engaged in detailed bargaining with the MTA over a twenty-year lease to operate the old Vanderbilt Athletic Club, a tennis facility located on the far western side of the terminal.

Donald's principal negotiator on these matters during the summer and early fall of 1978—when his bid was selected and the terms were hammered out—was Louise Sunshine, who was simultaneously helping run the finance committee for the governor's reelection. All the conflicts that had compelled UDC's Rich-ard Ravitch to force Sunshine out of the Commodore discussions in 1976 still existed, magnified by the fact that the tennis court contract was awarded in the middle of the Carey campaign she was financing. But Harold Fisher, a mainstay of the Brooklyn Democratic organization who had been installed by Carey as MTA chairman, was hardly one to worry about appearances. To strengthen his case, Trump sent in the Carey-connected Arthur Emil to represent him and life-long friend Bunny Lindenbaum, who was also a Court Street crony of Fisher's. (Fisher's family law firm in Brooklyn would wind up representing Trump in-terests on a variety of matters over the years.) In addition to all this intrigue, Trump hired a man introduced to him by the MTA's real estate director during the lease negotiations. When Donald was awarded the lease, this newly hired acquaintance of the real estate director's became general manager of the tennis court complex.

That lease was granted to Trump, though he had offered to pay the MTA less than Hamilton Richardson, the country's top-ranked tennis player in the 1950s and a financially sound operator. The twenty-year, astonishingly favorable deal was four times the five-year maximum term set in MTA guidelines, and the rent increased less than 1 percent per year, even though the guidelines recommended a minimum escalation of 3 percent. Located in midtown, and right next to Donald's new hotel, the courts were a veritable gold mine.

The lease was approved by the MTA real estate committee on November 2, 1978, the day after Trump made an oral commitment to the MTA to deliver the two easements. City and MTA staffers then began working with Trump's architects to plan the new mezzanine and 42nd Street passageways. They reached a technical agreement in January 1979—the same month Harold Fisher signed the tennis court lease. Soon thereafter, Ivana began steering some of the Hyatt subcontractors over to the tennis facility to redo it and Trump moved to lease the 500-square-foot eastern stairwell space that Koch had just granted him, increasing the floor area of a retail tenant. Donald had managed to secure both of the prizes he had sought in the bargaining, while only giving the city and the MTA oral assurances about the items they wanted.

A few months later, the MTA submitted an application for $11 million in federal funds for the passageways and other elements of the Grand Central renovation. Trump reviewed the application before it was submitted and raised no objection. No money was budgeted in this application to acquire the easements from Trump by condemnation because the city and the MTA believed that Trump had agreed to provide them gratis. It was the city and MTA's understanding that in addition to agreeing to the stairwell easement in exchange for the Koch waiver, Donald had also made a commitment to provide the mezzanine space for the passageway.

But in April of 1979 Donald dropped his first bomb on both the MTA and the city by entering into an out-of-court settlement with Modell's, a sporting goods chain that had occupied a street-level store with substantial mezzanine space in the Commodore for decades. The new lease Trump offered Modell's created a problem because the store was in the middle of the mezzanine easement space that the city had been promised. Donald had been under tremendous pressure to settle the Modell's case—and most of it was sentimental. Pushing him behind the scenes was Bunny Lindenbaum, who had even cornered Donald at a seventy-first birthday party thrown for him at "21," hosted by Fred and attended by Modell's attorney Jerry Tarnoff, who was married to Bunny's niece and was Stanley Steingut's law partner.

"I'm building a first-class hotel," Trump told Tarnoff. "I want high-quality stores. It troubles me that I'm pushing Modell's out; it has a long history in New York. I'd like to work something out. But I can't have jockstraps hanging in the window." When Bunny arranged a settlement meeting, however, Donald finally agreed to let Modell's remain if the store would allow him to approve its window displays. But Donald's acquiescence left the city without the mezzanine space it needed for its new corridor.

When city officials came up with an alternate plan that would have permitted Trump to accommodate Modell's yet still provide the easement, Trump replied that he had already signed a bookstore lease that blocked that rerouting. As far as Ken Halpern was concerned, Trump was violating his promise not to enter into any leases affecting the easements without the city's prior approval. He also felt that Donald's new leases had given the city only two options—either abandon the retail mezzanine part of the project or use the city's condemnation powers to take the easement space from Donald and his tenants.

While UDC's sweeping condemnation of all the Commodore retailers including Modell's had been temporarily blocked in court, it was clear that a similar, city-engineered effort to obtain space for specific MTA improvements would prevail. But if the city moved to do that, Trump would collect a rather sizable condemnation award for his interests in the Modell's space, as well as for the easement space needed for the stairwell.

Doggedly the city kept trying to work out an arrangement that would satisfy Modell's and Trump as well as avoid a costly condemnation, but one or the other would invariably object. When the conflict dragged on throughout much of 1979, Trump finally blew up at the young City Hall lawyer assigned to shuttle back and forth between Modell's and him: "Don't you get it? I want to get rid of Modell's. I don't want discount sweat socks in my hotel, even in my basement. I'll gladly give up my space. Why don't you go ahead and condemn it?" He was thus submarining the agreement he'd worked out with Tarnoff within months of signing it—released in his own mind apparently by Bunny's sudden death in between.

Believing that this new condemnation demand from Trump violated the understanding that had led to the waiver on the eastern stairwell a year earlier, Koch wrote a memo in October 1979 to key staff making it clear that he would "be very opposed to paying a condemnation bill simply because of Trump's refusals." The mayor insisted that the city find a way to force Donald "to honor what I thought had been his commitment to provide both easements to the MTA without cost."

What followed was a frustrating City Hall showdown between Trump and Deputy Mayor Ronay Menschel. After the meeting, Menschel wrote the recalcitrant Trump a letter accusing him of "breaking a pledge" and reminding him that the city had "granted significant tax advantages to the hotel project" but not "to bring a new standard of luxury to the relatively small number of people who patronize it." Rather, she argued, the purpose of the project was "to bring the benefits of redevelopment to the entire population that works or passes through the area each day," a reference to the subway access improvements Donald was blocking.

Trump called Menschel to challenge her letter—particularly her assertion that the mayor was "concerned that the city has been misled by your organization"—and Koch responded with his own note to Donald supporting Menschel. Koch asked Trump for an unusual, face-to-face meeting. When Trump returned to City Hall for this second easement meeting, a horde of UDC, MTA, corporation counsel, and city planning officials had gathered in the Blue Room—all to discuss the fate of a few hundred square feet of retail space. Before joining the assemblage, Trump ducked into Koch's private office with the mayor and two top aides.

"Donald, you've got to do it," Koch said.

When Trump launched into a long sob story about all his problems with Modell's, Koch just sat there, unimpressed, barely listening. Koch repeated himself: "Donald you must do this." The one thing the mayor and his two aides would later insist that they clearly heard Donald declare was that he was not in this dispute to make a dime. "I will not profit from this transaction," he vowed, which they read as an explicit waiver of any condemnation award.

In the weeks after this meeting, Donald did attempt to make a new arrangement with Modell's and had his lawyers draft a stairwell easement as well, but the efforts evaporated into more meetings and correspondence. The city finally decided to proceed with a condemnation of both easements, relying on what they regarded as Trump's commitment to waive any award. The MTA approved the condemnation in June of 1980, but when Trump was notified, he refused to say he'd return any award, offering legal reasons that were seen as gibberish at City Hall. It was the second time in this now two-year conflict that Donald had, in the mayor's view, broken a promise made personally to him. Without a Trump waiver, the city was back to Koch's original position: unwilling to pay Trump and thus unable to proceed. By the spring of 1981, a top MTA official concluded the obvious in an internal memo: "Trump has no desire to cooperate with the MTA in completing this project."

The mayor decided to go to court, but just on the stairwell easement. The two-pronged strategy was for the MTA to go ahead with the Modell's condemnation on the theory that any award would have to be split between the store and Donald, minimizing any Trump gain.* The stairwell lawsuit, however, was designed, if successful, to avoid any condemnation payment to Trump. It sought to compel Donald to deliver the easement or, failing that, to build the eastern stairwell he'd originally promised. The city didn't really want the eastern stairwell; the one near the terminal was a far more heavily traveled subway entrance and desperately needed the escalator expansion that had long been planned. Since Trump had already rented the space that the eastern stairwell would have occupied, a legal victory for the city, even one mandating the unwanted stairwell, would give the city the bargaining leverage it needed to force Donald finally to grant the long-awaited easement on the Grand Central side of the hotel.

The city suit went out of its way to finger Trump—naming him personally as a defendant and calling him "the principal wrongdoer in the transaction" who had "fraudulently induced" the city and MTA "into relying on his promise when he did not intend to keep it." Charging that Trump's delays had already cost the MTA $600,000 in increased construction costs, the city said its "main goal" in bringing the suit was "to enforce Mr. Trump's personal promise," an argument that read as if written by Koch himself.

Once again Roy Cohn represented Trump, and the case wound up before another Cohn friend, Supreme Court Judge Andrew Tyler, the only sitting judge in the state who'd been convicted of a felony. Tyler, whose perjury conviction about his meetings with major mob figures was overturned on a technicality, was so tied to Cohn partner Stanley Friedman that he was known to ask Friedman to secretly supply him with the names of candidates for lucrative appointments as receivers. Unsurprisingly, Tyler ruled in Trump's favor, relying on two letters Cohn gave him at the last possible moment in the proceedings, with no time for the city to respond. The eventual, five-to-nothing appeals court's reversal of Tyler blasted Cohn and Tyler's conduct as "impermissible," but Tyler's long delay

---

* Modell's and Donald finally did work out a space accommodation, but not until 1985 and not until the ubiquitous fixer Stanley Friedman, who also represented the sporting goods chain, got Trump and Bill Modell to agree.

before his initial ruling and the time-consuming appeal had finally exhausted even Ed Koch's stubborn will.

By the time Tyler's decision was overturned, it was late 1982, and the easement war was entering its fifth year. No one was willing to start from scratch in the lower courts with the lawsuit again. Even with a win, any resumption of the litigation could prevent construction of the stairwell for a few more years, in view of the likelihood of Trump appeals. The city surrendered, and the MTA moved to condemn the western stairwell space, knowing Donald would get a sizable profit. Donald did eventually collect a $575,846 condemnation award, and the subway stairwell was at last expanded, completed almost a decade after Trump first agreed to it in the seventies. Ironically, for the average New Yorker, the new escalators leading into the subway station were a more important public improvement than the Hyatt itself.

Incredibly, an audit in 1989 revealed that Trump had somehow converted this condemnation award into a hotel expense and claimed it as a charge against income in the Hyatt's percentage rent calculations, using it as a reason to lower his payments to the city. The accounting maneuver—which tried to deduct the award because of the lost potential rent on the space—was disallowed, but Trump went to court contesting the audit and refusing to increase his city payments. The continuing litigation means, in a sense, that the two-bit easement war is now in its third decade.

Donald's half-million-dollar award, as he apparently looked at it, gave him a TKO over Koch in their first test of wills, but what Donald did not seem to understand was that the man lying on the canvas was a mayor with the clout to cost him a fortune. One of the city's most popular mayors when Trump took him on, Koch would remain in office for a dozen years, as long as any man in the history of the city. Even Donald had expressed doubts about the wisdom of facing off with him in a meandering conversation at his office with one city attorney involved in the easement negotiations, Phil Hess. In between free associations like "I admire your sense of leverage, Phil, you have to come to work for me" and "Do you think I should invest in Atlantic City?" Trump asked: "Do you think Koch likes me? I think he thinks I'm a bad guy."

What everyone who knew anything about Koch learned early on was that no one won a grudge match with him. He had a penchant for the trivial and eagerly transformed the most abstract disputes into personal vendettas. He methodically fixed on the incidents, and individuals, that he decided had offended him in a fundamental way, and he never failed to even the score. Even with advisers like Friedman, who had flattered his way into the mayor's inner circle. Trump had inexplicably flown in the face of conventional wisdom about the handling of this peculiar, and selectively vindictive, man. Prodded by his own Koch-like arrogance, Donald had consciously run the risk of poisoning his relationship with the mayor.

The relationship had, in fact, started on shaky ground, even before Koch was elected mayor. An underdog candidate in desperate need of contributions, Koch had called Trump from his campaign treasurer Bernie Rome's office and Donald had whined: "I'm tired of all you guys calling me." Months later, Koch told Rome he "could still hear Trump yelling in my ear." When Koch won the primary, Sandy Lindenbaum came calling, offering Rome $50,000 in contributions from his real estate clients for Koch's runoff race, and saying: "All I want is access." Though Rome told him he didn't "do business that way," Lindenbaum kicked in $30,000, and on victory night Donald and Ivana celebrated at Koch headquarters as if full-fledged members of the winner's team.

Before the easement dispute hardened, early in Koch's first year, the new administration had delivered for Trump on the Hyatt—going ahead with the escrowed deal, executing the closing papers, and even approving a last-minute Trump request to extend the glass curtain wall in the front of the renovated hotel eight inches beyond the property line, out over city sidewalk. Similarly, though Beame had paved the way for the designation of 34th Street as the convention center site, it was Koch who approved it. The $833,000 payday Donald had as Penn Central's broker on the city's acquisition of the 34th Street site was the biggest of his career at the time—ordinarily reason enough to convince a person with a long-range view not to take on the administration whose site selection had generated the check. As Donald certainly knew, these were hardly the last of the big-ticket items he would be bringing to Koch's City Hall.

Indeed, in the middle of the easement controversy, Donald was seeking city approval on multimillion-dollar zoning and tax abatement applications for his signature project on Fifth Avenue, initially dubbed Tiffany Tower, but eventually renamed Trump Tower. He was also assembling the site on Third Avenue where he would build Trump Plaza, a co-op with abatement and zoning implications as well. It was hardly a smart time to be making enemies at the top of a heretofore friendly administration over a tiny slice of retail space. There is little doubt, in fact, that the varying responses of city officials to his Trump Tower and Trump Plaza applications were linked at some level to the City Hall attitude about Donald that evolved over the tortured years of the easement war.

The miscalculation would prove costly enough in the short run, since both the Trump Tower abatement and the Trump Plaza zoning change ran into stonewalls with the city administration. But, far more important, before Ed Koch was through as mayor, the assessment he made about Donald Trump's character during this petty battle would help shape a policy judgment on Donald's grandest West Side scheme that, several years up the road, would fundamentally damage Donald, costing him hundreds of millions of dollars and setting the stage for his downfall.

7

A TOWERING TRIUMPH

To this throng Cowperwood has become an astounding figure: his wealth fabulous, his heart iron, his intentions sinister—the acme of cruel, plotting deviltry. Only this day the Chronicle, *calculating well the hour and the occasion, has completely covered one of its pages with an intimate, though exaggerated, description of Cowperwood's house in New York: his court of orchids, his sunrise room, the baths of pink and blue alabaster, the furnishings of marble and intaglio. Here Cowperwood was represented as seated in a swinging divan, his comforts piled about him. The idea was vaguely suggested that in his sybaritic hours odalisques danced before him and unnamable indulgences and excesses were perpetrated.*

—*Theodore Dreiser,* The Titan

ALMOST AS if he knew from the beginning that it would be his consummate project, Donald assembled the site for Trump Tower in 1978 and 1979 with a patience and brilliance he would never again equal.

He started with a location that was so rich everyone else assumed it could not be bought—Fifth Avenue and 56th Street, just off Central Park, catty-corner to the Plaza. Exploiting one more Louise Sunshine connection—a friendship within the struggling department store company that owned Bonwit Teller and had a twenty-nine-year lease on the building that occupied much of the block—

171

Donald pursued the Bonwit brass until he got a deal to acquire its lease for $25 million. This was merely the first step, however, on the long road to site control, but the Bonwit lease opened the door at Equitable, the financiers from the Hyatt deal who happened to own the land beneath the store.

Equitable was its somber and hesitant self. It told Donald it might be interested in becoming his partner in the construction of a massive new residential tower on the site, contributing the land and helping with the financing. But, just as it had demanded with the Hyatt, Equitable wanted Donald to deliver the government bonanza of zoning variances and special permits that would make the planned gigantic tower buildable before it would commit on the land or the partnership. That meant that to get Equitable Donald had to convince the City Planning Commission and the Board of Estimate to allow him to merge the Bonwit lot with the air rights over Tiffany's and a small third parcel, both of which he was carefully maneuvering to acquire. The theory was that if he owned the air rights on the other properties he could add whatever square footage it was legally possible to build over those properties to the permissible floor area on the Bonwit site. The combination of the three would let him build the city's tallest residential building at perhaps its most attractive location. The key to this "can't miss" proposition was that Donald had to win the extraordinary city approvals for this project without actually owning the Bonwit site. It was, once again, a Trump attempt to get government to spearhead a private project, bestowing the benefits that made it plausible before the other parties took a risk.

The Board of Estimate had so many Trump allies on it that the rezoning looked like a political cinch. Manhattan Borough President Andrew Stein had become a social friend—a relationship encouraged by Stein confidant Roy Cohn. Bronx Borough President Stanley Simon had been designated by Stanley Friedman to fill a vacancy at the beginning of 1979. While the Trump Tower matter was pending, Donald gave Simon's campaign committee $10,000, and the Cohn firm kicked in $50,000, helping Simon win the seat outright. The Queens and Brooklyn representatives on the board were old family friends and recipients of Trump contributions.

But before the variances could even make it to the Board of Estimate, the tower had to win the support of City Planning Commission Chairman Robert F. Wagner, Jr., son of the former mayor and designee of the current one. Just as the application for these bonuses came before Wagner's commission for a formal vote in October of 1979, Ed Koch's problems with Trump over the Commodore easements hit a high-water mark. Two weeks ahead of the commission's vote, Koch wrote a memo to aide Ken Halpern that rejected Donald's new request for a condemnation award on the retail space, concluded that "there must be leverage that we have against Trump" to compel him to live up to his easement commitments, and directed Halpern to discuss the issue with Wagner, who had, up to then, been uninvolved in the easement controversy.

If the implication was that the pending Trump Tower application might offer an opportunity for "leverage," it never happened. Halpern didn't tell Wagner about the proposed tactical linkage of the easement and zoning matters, perhaps because it was already too late to stall the tower application. Once the item had been calendared for a vote by the commission, it would've been almost impossible for Wagner to kill it. At this early point in the easement dispute, the city officials deciding the fate of Donald's rezoning were unaffected by the other increasingly bitter issue. But the potential interdependence of these matters had apparently surfaced—at least in the mind of the man who mattered most, Ed Koch.

Wagner had indicated from the outset that he had problems with projects like Trump Tower, issuing a statement condemning plans that tried "shoehorning large projects into confined space" and "piggybacking one building on another." Directing a major commission review of "overconcentration, congestion, and excessive building bulk" in midtown, Wagner seemed to be targeting the Trump proposal without specifying it. No other proposal put such a bulky building on that small a lot.

Trump countered these concerns with a last-minute pressure tactic, granting Bonwit Teller's a conditional lease for a new store in Trump Tower. The lease was expressly linked to Trump's receiving the maximum zoning bonuses. If he did, Bonwit, whose store had already closed in anticipation of the demolition, would have a new location for its flagship store. If Donald did not get his zoning breaks, the city would lose a prime retailer it wanted to keep. It was a revival of the old Commodore tactics—a once celebrated landmark vacated on the eve of a crucial public vote, with a promise to salvage it if the city would only give Donald what he wanted.

The Bonwit shutdown was just one of the factors pushing Wagner toward approval. While he could not be compromised, he had inherited his father's fondness for a consensus governance style and members of his commission, including one who was an associate in the Cohn firm, were certainly well disposed toward the project. Wagner was also susceptible to a semifavorable architectural review of the design in the *New York Times*. And it didn't hurt that the son of his father's old friend, Sandy Lindenbaum, was peddling the project (indeed Wagner's top aide, Jolie Hammer, wound up working as an associate under Lindenbaum a year or two later). On October 19, Wagner's commission approved the crucial zoning changes, allowing Donald to replace the twelve-story Bonwit building with a glass-sheathed fifty-eight-story tower. Within weeks of the Board of Estimate's rapid rubber stamp of this decision, Equitable became Donald's fifty-fifty partner in the construction of the tower and sold the land to the partnership for a nominal sum.

While the zoning changes were approved before the easement war had effectively poisoned Donald's relationship with City Hall, the tower's tax abatement application wasn't even submitted until January of 1981, when the mayor's bitterness over the easements was so deep it might easily have spilled over onto other matters. Halpern, already a recipient of two Koch memos stressing the need to find "leverage" to use against Trump in the easement exchange, wrote a memo of his own in 1980 to City Hall aide Ronay Menschel outlining a continuing tough city posture on the issue and making a clear connection between it and future favors Trump might seek from the city. Halpern just had the wrong favor and wrong project. His memo pointed to the likelihood that Trump would soon announce "a major residential development on Third Avenue"—the Trump Plaza co-op project—and noted that it was "quite possible that he will require the city's cooperation" on this project, as he had in the past. Halpern was right in that Trump would come to the city for a zoning variance on Trump Plaza, but he didn't until late 1981, and at that time Wagner's successor at the Planning Commission dismissed it out of hand. But long before that, Donald filed his Trump Tower request with the city housing agency for what he thought would be a routine ten-year abatement usually granted residential buildings. It was the first new Trump matter since the easement rupture with Koch. Donald was so sure he'd get the abatement that he actually began construction before he filed for it, even though the $50 million subsidy was supposed to be an incentive spurring the development. The late timing of the application underlined what Donald would later boast in an interview in the *Times*. "I don't need this one," he said when the tax break was denied. However, the fact was—evidenced by the half decade in court Trump subsequently spent fighting to get it—that he had risked millions by badly misjudging Ed Koch.

While the application was still pending before Housing Commissioner Tony Gliedman, Donald made a $9,000 contribution in early February to the Koch campaign committee, which was then gearing up for the mayor's 1981 reelection. It was the largest donation Donald had ever made to Koch. But by early March, Donald learned that the application had been removed from the bureau that ordinarily handled abatements for special review by Gliedman's counsel—a signal of coming trouble. The state law establishing the abatement program limited it to housing developments built on sites that were "underutilized" when the statute passed in 1971; Gliedman was examining the Bonwit Teller site to see if it met that standard.

Donald decided to try a political approach to Gliedman, a familiar Brooklyn clubhouse operative. Andrew Stein, the Manhattan borough president who was fast becoming a Trump lobbyist, called Gliedman and invited him to an early morning meeting with Trump in Stein's Park Avenue apartment. As Koch himself would later put it: "Trump and Stein were what I would describe as utilizers of the 'Old School Tie network.' They were accustomed to deals cut with public officials over drinks."

Gliedman told Trump to submit additional documentation to qualify for the abatement. Stein urged Donald to do the same, but stated flatly that he believed Donald should get the tax break. Trump and Louise Sunshine, who was also present, stated in sworn affidavits that were filed a few weeks later that Gliedman also said he "would probably not be able to rule positively because he was under political pressure," even though "the evidence was strongly" in Trump's favor. "Donald, I feel you are right," Gliedman said, according to Trump, "but with all the heat I'm getting on this, I would rather you won your case in court, and I feel you will win your case in court." Though Gliedman filed his own affidavit in the subsequent lawsuit, he never directly denied the Trump version of this conversation.

The pressure on Gliedman was coming from the mayor himself. According to top City Hall sources involved in the discussions, it was Koch who wanted the abatement denied: He didn't believe that this kind of luxury housing should be entitled to a gigantic tax break. And while his administration had generously granted hundreds of millions in tax write-offs to encourage other commercial, office, and residential developments—creating a potential political problem for the mayor in the upcoming Democratic primary—the mayor sensed that rejecting Trump would have a greater media impact than all the tax breaks he'd approved, perhaps even turning the tax-break issue in his favor. Donald's prolonged evasions on the easement issue had helped make him, in Koch's mind, a logical nominee for such selective posturing.

The day Gliedman rejected the application—March 20, 1981—Trump made another grotesque gaffe that would leave a lasting impression on Koch. Gliedman had called Donald at four-thirty that Friday and informed him that he was denying the abatement. An hour and a half later Donald telephoned Gliedman. Since the decision had already been made, the second call surprised Gliedman, as did Trump's angry comments. In a subsequent memo to Koch, Gliedman reported that Trump had repeatedly told him that his decision was "dishonest" and that Donald had closed the conversation with what Gliedman called "a threat."

"I don't know whether it's still possible for you to change your decision or not," Trump said. "But I want you to know that I am a very rich and powerful person in this town and there is a reason I got that way. I will never forget what you did."

Trump also phoned the mayor, claiming that he wanted to call to his attention "a miscarriage of justice being done by one of your commissioners." Koch simply urged him to sue if he thought he'd been treated unfairly and then wrote to Gliedman that he was "shocked" at Trump's threat and "delighted" with Gliedman's decision. In the words of Donald Trump, wrote the mayor, "I will never forget what you did," adding his hope that "my comment carries more weight than his in this town."

Trump did go into court immediately to try to overturn Gliedman's decision, with the help of two political allies—Andrew Stein and Stanley Friedman. Stein filed an extraordinary affidavit contending that he and other city officials had persuaded Trump not to erect the commercial office building on the site, that he could have built without a zoning change as he had intended. Convinced that Donald's planned hotel/office tower would contribute to congestion "at one of the most congested sections of Manhattan," Stein intimated that he'd used the tax abatement promise to lure Donald to build a residential tower instead.

Donald had contributed $2,500 to Stein's tough 1981 reelection campaign three days before Stein signed this affidavit and $25,000 more during the campaign. Trump also recounted in an affidavit his supposedly serious onetime intention to build a hotel/office building on the site. (This bogus contention was later contradicted by Donald himself in *The Art of the Deal* when he wrote that he'd always planned a residential tower for the site and had said so in his earliest meetings with Tiffany's and Equitable.)

Friedman came in handy on two fronts. Manhattan and Bronx judges were part of the same judicial district, and as the Bronx County leader he exercised real clout in Manhattan State Supreme Court, where the case was filed before an old-line clubhouse judge. The fact that the judge was only temporarily sitting in the Supreme Court section and was subject to reassignment to a lower court made him even more vulnerable to political pressure. When city attorneys asked for an adjournment that would have taken the case away from him, Trump's lawyers objected and put before the judge a three-page affidavit from Friedman. The affidavit contended that Friedman had talked with Gliedman before the application was denied and that Gliedman had "graciously" pledged that the city would seek no delays or adjournments but would "cooperate" in a swift trial of the merits of the case. Neither the city nor Gliedman ever contested this promise, and the judge remained on the case. By July he had awarded Trump the abatement. This decision led to a series of appeals that would continue for three years—with appellate courts split in contrary directions—and eventually result in a victory for Trump.

The cold war between Trump and City Hall—prompted by the abatement and easement disputes—dragged on until the summer of 1982. Koch was then in the middle of his second campaign in two years—an ultimately unsuccessful race against Lieutenant Governor Mario Cuomo for the Democratic gubernatorial nomination. Donald, who had stopped making contributions to Koch, suddenly donated $16,000. The contribution came as the city decided not to pursue the easement litigation and as Donald was quietly winning, without any publicity, the same sort of tax abatement he'd been denied at Trump Tower for his new thirty-seven-story luxury co-op on Third Avenue, Trump Plaza. Two weeks after the donation was made, Koch attended the July 26 topping-off celebration at Trump Tower, held to publicize the completion of the superstructure. The mayor's unusual appearance at a promotional event for a building ten months away from opening helped beat the sales drum for Donald, as did that of lame duck Hugh Carey, who'd announced months earlier he was not seeking reelection.

On the just-finished roof, a panoramic view of Central Park at his feet, the mayor read "an ancient Irish toast to the lord of a newly built castle" and went on to introduce Fred Trump, who, he said, "has done a remarkable job in his own right, and in particular in raising a son." Donald responded with a comment "from his heart," saluting Koch for "creating such a tremendous atmosphere that New York's become the number-one city in the world."

The rapprochement was arranged by brokers like Stanley Friedman, who was playing a pivotal role in the Koch campaign and was slated to become the state's Democratic boss if Koch won. The mayor was ahead by as much as eighteen points in the polls—plenty of incentive for Donald to bury the hatchet. Though the lawsuit over the tower abatement was on a track neither party could stop, Koch had apparently been convinced that it would be helpful in a statewide race to be identified with the flashy builder and his spectacular project. But the rhetorical flourish on the roof that day marked more of a cease-fire than an armistice. Hostilities between these mirror image egos would inevitably resume.

• • •

When Trump Tower opened in 1983, its golden entrance, eighty-foot waterfall, and rose-peach-and-orange-colored marble Atrium quickly established themselves as the most photogenic symbols of Trump glamour, repeatedly featured in the splashy media tributes to Donald that became commonplace in the eighties.

In the *New York Times* Paul Goldberger praised the six-story Atrium as "the most pleasant interior space to be completed in New York in some years" and found that the combination of the marble floors and walls with the polished brass "gives off a glow of happy, if self-satisfied, affluence." Goldberger, whose critiques of later Trump projects would draw Donald's ire, also saluted the "interesting and appealing apartment layouts," which he said were "as good, if not better than most of what is available in the new superluxury category." The intriguing apartment designs were made possible by the zigzags of the building's sawtooth exterior shape, with its twenty-eight different surfaces cascading in a dark glass sheath toward the street. Donald's brilliant piecing together of the air rights had made possible a building so large on so squat a site that it was likened to docking the *QE2* in a sailboat slip. But even his harshest critics conceded that, despite a footprint that is only 115 feet wide by 175 feet long, the design made this awkward site work.

Donald and Ivana personally earned the credit for some of the structure's successful flourishes—architect Der Scutt attributes "the use of the European mirrors and brass" to them and says it was Ivana who insisted on the waterfall, even when Scutt advocated Art Deco panels, sculptures, or tapestries. It was the City Planning Commission, however, that forced Trump and Scutt to double the width of the entrance, avoiding what commission architects feared would be the tunnel effect of the fifteen-foot doorway Donald planned. "Trump went crazy," recalls Scutt, "because that meant he'd have fifteen feet less for valuable retail space." But, in the end, Donald complied and, years later, he acknowledged the commission's better judgment.

It was Scutt who had to convince Donald and Ivana about the Italian marble that became the building's interior trademark. The Trumps, according to Scutt, wanted to use the same brown paradisio marble they'd selected for the Hyatt, but Scutt argued that it would be too dark. "At one point," he remembered in an interview, "to get them off the brown marble adventure, I suggested white tile. White tile would've been awful. Ivana, for a while, liked the idea of white tile. Finally, I got them to consider this rosy beige marble which I think is fun to be around, the kind of marble that's conducive to shopping." Ivana became such a champion of the rare Breccia Perniche marble that she went to Italy and trekked from one end of the quarry from which it was being taken to the other, picking the finest stones.

Scutt had to apply the same powers of persuasion on the applauded exterior: "For a long time, Trump in the early designs had us make a simple box . . . a plain base so that a tower was sitting on a box. . . . It was a feeble attempt to relate to the Tiffany structure. And I kept pointing out that this was really very boring. What we needed was a building that had a lot of action visually. For about five or six months I began to sketch alternative forms that were eventually englassed and fragmented with the cascading terraces . . . that give the base of the tower a rather interesting geometry." Ivana joined Scutt in this campaign until finally Donald, who Scutt says was "always doodling" with his own hand-drawn amateur sketches, agreed.

Scutt was less successful with the size of the Trump Tower lettering on the front entrance: "I argued that the height of the Trump Tower letters would be far more elegant if they were only eighteen inches high." "If you've ever noticed the lettering on the front of Tiffany's, it's very discrete and very small, and very elegant and very distinguished. Trump intercepted the shop drawings for the height of these letters and changed the design from eighteen-inch-high letters to thirty-six-inch. I guess he just wanted the name to be that much more prominent. Obviously, an eighteen-inch-high letter is still very visible from way down Fifth Avenue."

The architect said that the altering of the entrance lettering—and Donald's simultaneous heightening of the brass portal above the nameplate—was the only time Donald "simply bypassed me and got ahold of the shop drawings and made the change himself." He didn't even discuss the matter with Scutt, though on a typical day during the peak of their Trump Tower planning, Donald would start phoning him at 7:00 A.M. and call fifteen or twenty times before 9:00 P.M. "The height of the Trump Tower letters is very typical, I believe, of Trump's desire to be known, to be superior. It's a typical act by Trump to get his own way and to announce his presence. Bigness is not always greatness."

The building cost $201 million to build, including $44 million in interest payments on the construction loan, but it was an instant moneymaker. A 1986 *Times* story reported that the sale of 251 of the tower's 268 apartments had brought in $277 million, according to a financial statement from an outside accountant. The sale or lease of the remaining apartments was expected to add millions to that total, and Equitable and Trump shared the $17 million a year in earnings on the commercial and retail space. Trump also collected $11 million in commissions on apartment sales and was regularly paid an undisclosed fee for managing the building (listed as well over a million dollars a year on property tax expense reports).

Donald was, from the beginning, concerned about competition from a building going up just a few blocks down Fifth Avenue on 53rd Street, Museum Tower. Built on the air rights above the Museum of Modern Art and designed by internationally famed Cesar Pelli, Museum Tower hit the superluxury market at the same time as Trump Tower. Donald had tried to launch a covert campaign to block the project, contacting Dan Levitt, the lawyer for the Strawberry chain who had successfully blocked the condemnation of its Commodore store.

"He wanted me to challenge the air rights sale in court. He wanted to stop Museum Tower from going forward," said Levitt. "But he didn't want his name associated with the lawsuit I filed. He wanted me to represent a neighbor or someone to oppose it. I told him there was no way I could do it without using his name." Trump later successfully used this sort of substitute plaintiff gambit to force drastic alteration of the planned construction of a forty-four-story tower at 712 Fifth Avenue, directly across the street from Trump Tower—a project he feared would threaten the Atrium's chic European retailers.

No one ever did file the third-party lawsuit Donald wanted, but his subterranean efforts to kill Museum Tower proved wholly unnecessary. He outmarketed its owners in every way; his $2 million promotional campaign made Trump Tower the place to buy. A key to that campaign was a masterstroke of media deception. Trump called *New York* magazine's "Intelligencer," one of the city's hottest gossip pages, and on a confidential basis told a reporter that the Crown Estates, a holding company for the British royal family, had expressed interest in acquiring several apartments—totaling twenty-one rooms—for the use of Prince Charles and other members of the family. Somehow, according to a source at the magazine familiar with the episode, he even managed to produce a letter on Crown Estates letterhead. When the British family would not confirm or deny this supposed interest, the magazine attracted worldwide attention with a short and splashy item. In fact, as Donald would write in *The Art of the Deal*, the Prince never had the slightest interest in a tower apartment.

The advertising brochure expanded on the hype of the media campaign. It described the tower's ambience in terms that Donald, and many of his buyers, would have found irresistible:

> It's been fifty years at least since people could actually live at this address. They were the Astors. And the Whitneys lived just around the corner. And the Vanderbilts across the street.

You approach the residential entrance—an entrance totally inaccessible to the public—and your staff awaits your arrival. Your concierge gives you your messages. Quickly, quietly, the elevator takes you to your floor and your elevator man sees you home. You turn the key and wait a moment before turning on the light. A quiet moment to take in the view—wall-to-wall, floor-to-ceiling—New York at dusk. Your diamond in the sky. It seems a fantasy. And you are home.

Maid service, valet, laundering and dry cleaning, stenographers, interpreters, multilingual secretaries, Telex and other communications equipment, hairdressers, masseuses, limousines, helicopters, conference rooms—all at your service with a phone call to your concierge.

There was, however, another side to the grandeur of the tower, for not only did its opulence quickly outpace that of the Hyatt, Donald's only other project at the time, but so did the dubiousness of its origins.

The scandals associated with the project started with the demolition of the old Bonwit building, which began in early 1980. While Donald's Commodore demolition contractor had its mob ties, it was at least a well-known and capable company. Though Trump Tower was to be Donald's most lavish project, he decided at the very outset to try to cut costs in clearing the site, selecting a demolition contractor with no heavy demolition experience simply because it had agreed to do the job at Trump's suggested $775,000 price.

The contractor, William Kaszycki, was able to submit so low a bid because most of his workers were illegal Polish aliens working at rates one-half to one-third those of union scale. Kaszycki's wife recruited the workers in Poland, promising housing as well as four-to-six-dollar-an-hour wages. On Trump's job 200 of them worked twelve-to-eighteen-hour shifts with no days off or overtime and slept in groups of eight in a slum apartment or motel room. When Kaszycki began using his payments from Trump to cover costs on other jobs, as well as to pay the few union workers on the site, he underpaid many of the Polish workers, who were hauling asbestos-covered piping and other materials out of the building virtually unprotected.

Though Donald's office throughout the demolition was in the Crown Building, directly across the street from the site, he claimed in subsequent sworn testimony that he did not "think" he knew anything about the Polish brigade "until probably sometime after the demolition." So fainthearted a claim of ignorance was transparently disingenuous, since it was Trump himself who discovered Kaszycki and invited him to bid on the job.

Kaszycki had been hired in late 1979 by the company that owned Bonwit to do light, interior demolition on a 57th Street store adjacent to the Trump Tower site that Donald had leased to it. While Donald insisted on the witness stand later that he had "nothing to do with the work" on this side street store, he not only owned it, but he had agreed to give Bonwit $1.2 million to pay for the renovation of it as part of his lease agreement with the company. It was separated by a wall from the other Bonwit building on Fifth Avenue that Donald would subsequently hire Kaszycki to demolish totally.

Zbigniew Goryn, a Kaszycki foreman on both jobs, said that Donald came to the 57th Street job once and said he "liked the way the men were working." Goryn recalled that Trump remarked that the "Polish guys" were "good, hard workers." In fact, Trump hired away from Bonwit a construction supervisor who'd overseen its 57th Street work, Tom Macari, and put him in charge of supervising the Fifth Avenue demolition. Macari, whose office was in Donald's suite, went to the Fifth Avenue site "twenty to thirty times" from March until the job was finally finished in late August. One of only a half dozen or so Trump Organization officers at the time, Macari knew, according to the eventual findings of a federal judge, "that the Polish workers were working 'off the books,' that they were non-union, that they were paid substandard wages, and that they were paid irregularly if at all."

Trump's ignorance was even more improbable in light of Kaszycki's testimony that "hundreds, thousands of workers from Poland and other countries" came to the Trump Tower site and "stood in lines down the street, waiting, begging" for jobs. "You could see that all the time," Kaszycki said, "five, six, ten, twenty times—all the time—come begging for jobs."

Despite his savings by underpaying the Polish workers, Kaszycki's financial problems on the job became so severe—because the costs far exceeded his bid price—that he began shortchanging the Housewrecker Union's welfare and pension fund. While the union was willing to overlook all the nonunion labor being used, it threatened to shut the job down if the welfare payments on the union workers weren't made. Though this was Kaszycki's obligation, Trump himself began to make the union payments in June, rolling up over $40,000 in contributions. Macari "carefully scrutinized" the fund payments, according to the later judicial opinion, and "knew that contributions were being sought and made on only union members' wages."

In addition to its labor problems, the Kaszycki crew destroyed two fifteen-foot-high bas-relief Art Deco sculptures, reportedly worth hundreds of thousands of dollars, unleashing a howl of editorial and cultural criticism. Trump, who apparently authorized the destruction of the pieces (in part because

Kaszycki couldn't remove them except at great cost), had promised to donate the sculptures to the Metropolitan Museum of Art. The union and sculpture crises, plus wildcat strikes by the unpaid Poles and the grindingly slow pace of demolition due to Kaszycki's inability to bring down the heavy concrete structure, finally forced Trump to focus on the disaster just a few yards away. He authorized Macari to take control over the Kaszycki bank account for the job and, according to Kaszycki, Macari began approving payments not only to the union but "sometimes [to] the Polish" workers as well. Macari also started getting calls from a lawyer, John Szabo, representing several of the unpaid Poles, who threatened a lien or a suit. By the summer, Szabo did file $100,000 in liens. Macari and a Trump attorney toyed with and then threatened Szabo, at one point suggesting they'd go to immigration and seek the deportation of the unpaid workers. In July, after months of abuse, the workers were apparently so disgruntled that a large group of them threatened to hang Macari, and Trump had to personally summon a labor mediator friend of his to try to settle the situation.

The scandal didn't end with the completion of the demolition. By late 1980, Szabo was taking his case through the federal bureaucracy, going from the Labor Department to the U.S. Attorney's office in New Jersey. The reason he went to New Jersey was that agents from that office had raided two motels near Atlantic City where a Kaszycki crew of illegal workers had been holed up doing a demolition job. Kaszycki was convicted of importing and exploiting Polish aliens and was sentenced to several months in jail and a $10,000 fine. The Labor Department also won a $575,000 judgment against him for the Trump Tower abuses. Szabo later testified that he believed the Labor Department suit should have been brought against Kaszycki and the Trump Organization as joint employers but that Labor officials asked him to remove Trump's name from the draft complaint he'd prepared. When Szabo went to federal prosecutors in Newark, where Donald's sister was the first assistant to the U.S. Attorney, he testified that he was told "not to mention Trump's name" unless he "walked outside into the hallway." While there was no evidence that Maryanne Trump had anything to do with her office's handling of the case, the government's refusal from the outset to consider any possibility that the Trump Organization might have knowingly participated in this off-the-books scheme was certainly strange.*

The Newark office's explanation was that it viewed Trump as a Kaszycki

---

* Donald testified in a subsequent civil suit that he did not know what "off-the-books" meant.

victim—a dubious proposition, since the litigious Trump expressly refused to join any Szabo suit against Kaszycki and decided not to pursue Kaszycki for the hundreds of thousands in demolition costs beyond the contract that Trump had to cover, starting with the welfare fund payments. Kaszycki and Trump were jointly sued, however, by labor lawyers seeking the welfare fund payments for the Polish workers that were never paid. A decade after this litany of abuse, U.S. District Court Judge Charles Stewart finally found that the Trump Organization and the president of the union, who actually worked on the tower site, had "a tacit agreement to employ the Polish workers and deprive them" of union benefits, concluding that "the Trump defendants knowingly participated in the fiduciary breach." Stewart determined that $325,000 in welfare payments had been improperly withheld—and fined the Trump Tower corporate entity over a million dollars. Of course by then the workers who were supposed to get those benefits, as well as the hundreds of thousands in wages they had missed, had long scattered to the wind.

The demolition controversy—which also involved convincing evidence that the Polish workers had been exposed to massive doses of asbestos—was hardly the only Trump Tower matter to invite the attention of investigators. Even before the Kaszycki probe was under way in New Jersey, and before construction began on the tower in the fall of 1980, Donald was subpoenaed by prosecutors in another jurisdiction about the most fundamental judgment he'd made in designing and planning the building. Donald had decided to build the nation's tallest reinforced concrete job at a point when the concrete industry in New York, at both the union and contractor levels, was wholly dominated by organized crime. In the end, the tower would become one of the most expensive private concrete jobs in history—running up a $22 million concrete bill, compared with only $300,000 worth of touch-up steelwork. Each of the fifty-eight stories rested entirely on reinforced concrete beams, not steel. The 45,000 cubic yards of concrete weighed 90,000 tons, one and a half times the weight of all the steel used in the Empire State Building. The only real steel used in the building was the 3,800 tons of reinforcing steel rods inside the concrete blocks.

The choice of concrete for Trump Tower was hardly automatic, even though it was frequently used in residential construction. The mixed uses planned for Donald's building—with the bottom third of the floors relegated to retail and office space—left Donald with options, since office buildings are rarely just concrete. While concrete gave Trump a more rigid and solid building, it was also more appropriate because the tower was being built on a fast track—meaning it was being designed a floor at a time and going up as fast as it could be designed.

"When you change concrete," architect Scutt explained, "all you have to do is change the form a little bit. When you change steel, you have to send it back to Bethlehem, Pennsylvania, and it comes back five weeks later. To do it in steel would have been prohibitively expensive."

Using concrete, however, put Donald at the mercy of a legion of concrete racketeers, none more powerful than union boss John Cody. The balding, bulky, sixty-year-old Cody had weathered eight arrests, including one for attempted rape, and three convictions. Before Trump Tower was finished, he would be indicted in an eight-count federal racketeering case, charged with taking $160,000 in kickbacks. His mob associations were so strong that the FBI claimed that Carlo Gambino, the most powerful mobster in America, came to his son's $51,000 wedding in Long Island in 1973. His bodyguard, indicted on a murder rap and bailed out by Cody's investment banker son, was later shot to death.

Cody was president of the leading building trades union in New York, Teamsters Local 282. His members drove the barrel-shaped cement mixer trucks that would feed the Trump Tower job its daily requirement of concrete. The severe access problems at the site—located at one of the busiest intersections in the world and reachable only from the narrow 56th Street side—made the job utterly dependent on Cody's cooperation. Concrete can harden if it isn't used quickly, and Cody's trucks had to make their deliveries at precise intervals throughout the day. A slowdown—anything from delaying the pours to a full-fledged work stoppage—would have caused costly overruns or possibly even shut the job down.

In the summer of 1980, FBI agents investigating Cody served Donald with a subpoena demanding that he appear for questioning at the Brooklyn office of the Organized Crime Strike Force. The Strike Force, which had been investigating Cody since he took over the union in 1970, had received information from a source close to Cody that the union leader had strong-armed Trump and won a commitment from him for an apartment in Trump Tower in exchange for labor peace during its construction. The investigators knew this was typical of Cody's modus operandi. His indictment would include a count alleging that he'd shaken down one developer for a rent-free, $1,000-a-month apartment at Northshore Towers, a luxury Queens complex where a Cody mistress, Marilyn Taggart, lived comfortably. Scheduled to testify for the government at Cody's 1982 trial, Taggart disappeared shortly before it began.

Just as he had in the 1979 probe of the Penn Central acquisitions, Trump appeared at the interview without an attorney and willingly answered questions. He emphatically denied having promised Cody an apartment. Because all the investigators had was a loose allegation, apparently from a real estate broker who'd paid kickbacks to Cody, and since the building was so far from completion that any deal could not have been consummated, the investigators were forced to abandon the Trump trail.

The tower went up without problems and with John Cody frequently on site. "I knew Trump quite well," Cody said in a later interview. "Donald liked to deal with me through Roy Cohn," he claimed, characterizing Cohn as "a pretty good friend" and occasional legal adviser. Donald was told months in advance that Cody was planning a summer citywide walkout in 1982 and got Cody's help in completing the final floors in a rush before the strike. Even when an indicted Cody took his union out on a two-month strike on July 1, the close-out work at the Trump Tower job was unaffected. The topping-off ceremony in late July—featuring Ed Koch's Irish toast, 10,000 hot air balloons, and Hugh Carey's "when-do-you-want-us-to-move-in-Donald?" speech—was an ironic moment, marking the completion of the concrete work in the middle of a concrete work-ers' strike. Even after the tower concrete job was done, and after Cody was con-victed of racketeering in late 1982, he remained a key to Trump construction activities, including the concrete work at Trump Plaza on Third Avenue, which had just started. Cody could also still wreak havoc at Trump Tower, where con-struction continued through 1983, because his union's jurisdiction extended to all deliveries at a job site, not just concrete. Since Cody remained in full control of the union while he appealed his conviction in 1983, Donald continued to need his cooperation.

In fact, while the feds had failed to find it, Cody did have a special interest in a Trump Tower suite of apartments—six units on two of the top floors, all owned by a mysterious friend of his named Verina Hixon. Though the building was really fifty-eight stories high, Donald had juggled the floor numbers, skip-ping ten flights and renumbering it as if it were a sixty-eight-story structure. Tri-plex penthouses, including one reserved for Donald and Ivana, dominated the top three floors, with duplexes planned for the sixty-fourth and sixty-fifth floors right beneath them. Beginning in the summer of 1981, when the tower was mid-way through construction, Hixon, a strikingly beautiful Austrian divorcee with no visible income (or alimony), began negotiating with Donald to buy some of the duplexes. By the end of 1982, she had signed contracts to purchase three of them at a total cost of around $10 million.

The fair and slender Hixon, at thirty-seven, had shoulder-length light blond hair, a melting smile, an air of helplessness, and an international jet-set lifestyle. In between horse shows and ski trips to Europe, she lived in New York—at

Olympic Tower, where she got to know Donald and Ivana, and, later, at Trump Tower. Though she never held a job in her life, she dined at La Cote Basque, La Grenouille, Le Cirque, and "21" ("I have rich friends; they love to invite me") and had enough French couturier clothes, in her own phrase, to last a lifetime (friends gave them to her, she explained). Pressed by lawyers in later civil suits to explain how she lived, Hixon replied: "That's a good question." Her lawyer said she lived "off the skin of the city," arguing that "like the great land barons of this country," she was "land rich and dollar poor."

Donald had signed an unusual separate agreement with her that required that he construct her sections of two floors—right beneath his own—in accordance with specifications and drawings prepared by an architect she had hired (she had to use Trump's architect, but the building's design—on the floors her units dominated—was uniquely bound by plans drawn at her request). Hixon didn't want duplexes, and Donald agreed to build simplexes on each floor, combining the apartments. The design shifted back and forth from one simplex on each floor to two, with Hixon planning to sell some of the units, apparently expecting to earn enough on the ones she sold to pay for the ones she kept and lived in. Donald also agreed to build the tower's only swimming pool in the Hixon complex, which required a special concrete bracing effort.

While Cody and Hixon would disagree in subsequent interviews about the timing of Cody's earliest involvement with these apartments, they agreed that by early 1983 he was intensely involved in Hixon's efforts to renovate the units and to complete the financing arrangements so she could actually close on them. "Verina called me about problems with the apartment," Cody explained, mentioning specifically his personal monitoring of the pool bracing job and his resolution of a touchy dispute about the electrical plan.

"I'd set up a meeting with Donald, his construction people and whatnot," Cody continued, citing as an example the session he arranged with Trump when the work crews refused to connect all of the wiring to a single, central switching station. Confronted by Cody, "Donald agreed to do the job as specified by her," the union boss recalled. "When I set up a meeting, he would make promises. He would say he would do the right thing. He would tend to me, he would cater to me." Hixon added that when the wiring problem occurred, Cody "put a man from the union in front of the door of my apartment," barring workmen from entering it, "and the next day" the unspecified wiring that Trump had already installed "was removed."

When Trump balked at redesigning the floor plan for one apartment so that it would include a section of the building corridor—a highly unusual request—

Cody and Hixon cornered him in a nearby bar and got his agreement. "Anything for you, John," was Hixon's recollection of Trump's comment. When Hixon's bank financing fell short by $3 million, Cody spoke directly to Donald and asked him to arrange a mortgage. Trump did, and, according to Hixon, she was not even asked by the bank to file a financial statement or fill out any forms—a fortunate oversight since she could not have met single-family FHA standards. "I don't think I could've moved in without Mr. Cody's help," said Hixon.

While Hixon and Cody insist that there was never an intimate relationship between them, they believe that Trump thought there was. "Donald made his crack remarks," Hixon said, adding that he had "a foul mouth and a dirty fantasy." The two traveled together—to Florida and elsewhere—and frequently lunched at "21," where Donald sometimes saw them together. Cody was convinced that Donald came to think of the Hixon apartments as if they were, at least in part, Cody's.*

Indeed, as the renovation costs on the apartments skyrocketed from $850,000 in 1982 to $2 million by 1984, Cody did directly invest in them. He loaned Hixon a half million dollars in 1983, drawn from a Swiss bank account, relayed through a Cody friend in London and never repaid. The cash went right into the apartment improvements. Hixon later described the loan as Cody's gentlemanly way of helping out a friend "in distress," but Cody said he had a much stronger personal connection to the apartments themselves, explaining that he thought it was possible that he "might have moved" permanently into some of the units if he won his appeal or after he did his time. Convicted of racketeering, sentenced to a five-year prison term, and falsely insisting in federal court that he was unable to pay the $70,000 fine levied on him, Cody managed to secretly invest $500,000 in the Hixon suite—some measure of the stake he believed he had in them.

A Cody colleague, Nick Auletta, the president of a concrete company actually owned by the heads of two crime families who was later also convicted in a racketeering case, "loaned" Hixon an additional $100,000 in 1983, also to help cover the rising construction costs on the apartments. While Auletta's company, S&A, was not building Trump Tower, it was doing the $9 million concrete job at Trump Plaza. Though Hixon says she gave Auletta a diamond worth more than $100,000 to cover the loan, Auletta disputes the contention that the loan was repaid.

---

* Cody goes so far as to contend, contrary to Hixon, that he was involved in the very beginning, telling Trump he was interested in an apartment and advising him that Hixon would be calling.

Until he went away to federal prison in 1984, Cody was a frequent visitor at Hixon's Trump Tower apartment, sometimes seeing Donald in the building. He says he and a girlfriend who was carrying his child slept there occasionally; Hixon says just the girlfriend did. Even after he was sent to Danbury Prison in Connecticut, Cody managed for months to hang on to his power in the union. Hixon, who visited him often in jail, kept him abreast of the continuing construction problems with the apartments. According to Cody, he even called Trump once from prison on behalf of Hixon, and Donald greeted him nervously on the phone. "Where are you," Trump asked. "Downstairs?"

But by mid-1984, Bobby Sasso, the new union president who had been secretary-treasurer under Cody for years, had consolidated his own power, ending Cody's influence at 282. Trump himself got a taste of this change when a loyal Cody business agent at the union threatened him with a wildcat work action, and he called Sasso. Sasso said he'd take care of it, fired the business agent, and told Donald to call him about any future problems directly. Sasso, whose son was the union foreman on Trump Plaza and later Trump jobs, later told one developer that Trump had called him during this transition period in 1984 and asked him what he should do "with the Cody apartment" at Trump Tower. Sasso claimed that he told Trump to forget it; he wanted nothing to do with the apartments. (Sasso denied that Donald had ever spoken to him about this matter.)

In any event, soon after Sasso severed the union's ties to Cody, Donald sued Hixon, charging in a 1984 lawsuit that she owed Trump $250,000 on the apartment alterations (she'd paid almost $1.9 million). The suit marked a fundamental shift in Trump's handling of the apartments, dovetailing with the demise of Cody. Hixon countersued for $20 million, citing defects in the work and charging that Trump forced her to hire his architect and his construction company. She submitted documentary evidence that the architect had given Trump roughly 10 percent of everything she had paid for his services, calling it a "sponsor's fee" on the billings.

Labeling these payments "kickbacks" in court papers, Hixon's lawyer contended in an affidavit that they "may prove to be the basis of a criminal proceeding requiring an attorney general's investigation." Though it was Donald who initially filed suit, he agreed in March of 1985 to pay Hixon a half million dollars, extracting a commitment from her to keep the settlement confidential. Trump personally negotiated the terms of the settlement with Hixon and her attorney.

The suit, however, launched seven years of litigation against Hixon—by Trump, by the banks that had inexplicably loaned her $8.2 million, by the architectural firm, and others. She did not make even a full year's payments on a $3 million mortgage from Manufacturers Hanover and defaulted on a First Fidelity mortgage as well after an Arab friend stopped making payments in 1987. She hung on to her apartments in part because of claims she had filed against Donald, contending that the constant jackhammering in his triplex above her—for renovations that took years—made it impossible to sell her units. Her belief was that he was trying to force her out because he wanted her pool and that he would lay claim himself to her apartments once she was gone. Finally, in the nineties, bankrupt and living in a barren and unfinished apartment, Hixon lost all her Trump Tower property to the banks.

In addition to his complicated ties to Cody, the construction of Trump Tower sealed Donald's relationship with two other major figures in the concrete industry. Bif Halloran, who'd supplied the concrete to the Hyatt, was also given the Trump Tower contract. Cody's drivers worked for Halloran's company, and the two were so closely linked that Halloran had reciprocated with complimentary services for Cody in a Manhattan hotel he owned. Halloran had in fact been questioned by federal prosecutors in Brooklyn about his hotel suite and other payoffs to Cody shortly before they spoke with Donald in 1980. Halloran was another one-time Cohn client who, according to the government, "obtained his monopoly over the supply of readi-mix concrete through the direct intervention" of the mob, and was convicted in the federal racketeering case with Nick Auletta. While Halloran did, during the construction of Trump Tower, buy out the only other Manhattan-based concrete suppliers and establish a virtual monopoly, he had at least one wholly independent competitor at the time he was awarded the Trump job.

Halloran's companies supplied the concrete to the site, but the contract to actually build the concrete superstructure went to Dic Underhill, a company that did about 60 percent of the city's superstructure work. Construction supervisors on the site from the beginning of the project recall that Dic president Joe DePaolo first appeared there with Fred Trump, who'd used Dic a couple of decades earlier to build Trump Village. DePaolo and Fred studied plans for the project together, and Dic was hired shortly afterward to build the superstructure. While the Trumps' general contractor, HRH, selected many subcontractors on its own, the company's agreement with Donald gave him approval on every contract over a minimal threshold.

Dic had its own alleged mob associations. For example, DePaolo's brother owned a carting company that did Dic's hauling and just as the Trump job started, the carting company and the Dic accounts were sold to the brother of Carmine Persico, head of the Colombo crime family. DePaolo and other Dic principals were ultimately named by federal prosecutors as unindicted co-conspirators when they testified against the concrete cartel as government witnesses in the 1987 prosecution of Genovese crime family boss Fat Tony Salerno, Auletta, Halloran, and several other mob defendants.*

While Dic had aggressively over the years sought to dominate the concrete industry, the one contractor it cooperated with was S&A, the Auletta company that Salerno and Gambino boss Paul Castellano secretly owned. In March of 1981, at the very moment that Dic signed its Trump Tower contract, the company and S&A combined to rig the bids on the city's convention center. Other contractors were warned not to bid, and Dic agreed to overbid deliberately, leaving the state's Convention Center Corporation no choice but to accept S&A's $30 million bid. The fixed bid cost the state $3 million more than the pre-bid estimated ceiling. In this way, Dic and S&A divided up the two biggest concrete contracts of the era, with Salerno's company getting the easier public work, while the experienced and effective Dic got the unprecedented tower job. The convention center and Trump Tower contracts became a focus of the federal criminal prosecutions, and the awarding of a nearly $8 million contract for Trump Plaza to S&A was even listed a count in the indictments of Salerno and his codefendants. Manny Ciminello, the Bronx contractor who became so friendly with Donald that he attended his 1990 birthday party, was S&A's joint venture partner in the Trump Plaza job.

Everyone in this incestuous intertwine—Cody, Halloran, Auletta, Salerno, and Castellano—was tied to the Cohn firm, and most had actually been represented by Cohn. Several of Dic's principals were clients of Cohn partner Stanley Friedman, who later represented a Dic venture that won a multimillion-dollar city contract to repair parking meters.

While dealing with the concrete cartel was inevitable for any developer in the period when Trump Tower was built, Donald took the relationship several steps further than he had to—making the initial decision for a totally concrete structure, ingratiating himself with Cody, using Halloran (and, to a lesser extent, Dic) when he had other choices. FBI sources who questioned high-level mob informants about how Trump was able to win labor peace on his big New York jobs were told that he "did it through Cohn," a mentor who could reach into the mob combines that controlled everything from the concrete to the drywall work.

---

* The convictions in this case were overturned in 1991, and the government is preparing to retry the case.

Cohn may have even arranged a meeting in the living room of his town house between Donald and Salerno at the very time S&A was doing the Trump Plaza concrete work, at least according to one Cohn staffer who says she was present.

Other developers did find ways to fight the cartel. In the spring of 1980, right around the time Donald made his Trump Tower decisions, builder Sam Lefrak told John Cody that he planned to use structural steel and prefabricated concrete—both of which would be trucked to his 1,642-unit Battery Park City site in Lower Manhattan by drivers who were not members of Cody's union. Though most of the drivers would still have been Teamsters, Cody emphatically objected, vowing to "challenge the trucks at the city line." Lefrak agreed to meet with Cody and Dic's top officials, and the group worked out a compromise.

Unlike Trump, Lefrak spoke out publicly against the cartel, telling the *New York Times* that concrete was "a monopoly," that the contracts were "assigned," and that the few operators were "working hand in glove with the union." Another developer, the Resnick family, filed a civil racketeering lawsuit against Cody's union and others in 1982, while the Trump Tower work was underway. At the peak of the cartel's power, Donald's identification with Cohn put him at the opposite end of the spectrum from vocal opponents like Lefrak and Resnick.

In addition to the taint that the concrete and Polish worker controversies brought to Trump Tower's construction, there was another, less conspicuous scandal hidden inside the awe-inspiring new tower. The most glamorous attraction in the building—the five-story waterfall in the Atrium—was illuminated by special lighting, purchased principally from a politically connected Manhattan company, Lighting Unlimited. The company was owned by Bill Warren, the brother-in-law of Queens Borough President Donald Manes, who voted for the project's zoning variances as a member of the Board of Estimate. Warren had also been given a small amount of lighting work in conference rooms at the Hyatt, another project that Manes had voted for.

Warren would later be awarded lighting work at both Trump Plazas as well—doing some of the lobby work at the Manhattan co-op development and supplying a California company with fixtures for Donald's first casino in Atlantic City. Both of these projects were built in 1983 and early 1984, when Manes and Trump—who called each other Donnie and had known each other since at least the early seventies—were at the peak of their political relationship, jointly pushing Koch officials about a hotel/housing plan for the Rockaways in Queens and beginning to plan a football stadium next to Shea Stadium in Flushing Meadow.

As Warren told the story: "I remember being with Donald [Manes] on occasions when he'd bump into Trump, and Donald would say to Trump: 'Are you taking care of Billy?' And Trump would say, 'Oh yeah.' Trump's architect would write us into the job. The lighting consultant would have to show a reason why he didn't want to use us. On the Atlantic City job, we bid but didn't get the big job. So Trump called me repeatedly. He would say, 'I'm reaching out to you, Bill.' He told me to supply the California guy who won the bid. I supplied him, but the California guy went bankrupt. That was why he could underbid me. That's why I only got partially paid."

Warren, who described himself on city forms as a "special adviser" to Manes, freely conceded that with Trump "it helped" that he was related to Manes. But he said that Donald only wanted to appear to Manes to be steering business to him, insisting that he never got the large contracts that were promised.

Donald's relationship with Manes was a by-product of familiar, historic ties. Manes' father had died when he was a young man, and his father's best friend, a Brooklyn judge who was very close to Bunny Lindenbaum, had practically adopted him, binding his Queens political career to the Madison Club crew from Brooklyn. Warren recalled that Bunny used to sit in the "21" Club with him during the Beame administration, introducing him as Manes' brother-in-law to developers and contractors, trying to drum up business. It was Beame who anointed Manes in the seventies as Queens Democratic leader, underlying Manes' ties to the same Brooklyn clubhouse nexus that had helped invent the Trumps.

The intertwine continued until a scandal involving Manes and his secret partner in a parking ticket collection company, Stanley Friedman, exploded in early 1986. With federal prosecutors closing in that March, Manes plunged a kitchen knife into his heart, avoiding a certain prison term (Friedman was convicted in the ticket scam). Though Warren went to the Trump Organization seeking new business after Manes' death, he never got another job.

A final sordid element in the saga of Trump Tower was the criminal class that seemed drawn to it, buying or renting many of the tower's most expensive apartments. In sharp contrast to the theme of Trump's planted news story suggesting that even Prince Charles might shortly be a tenant, the tower became a magnet for every conceivable form of huckster, each of them apparently sharing in Donald's speculative fantasies, feeding off the Trump frenzy of endlessly rising real estate values. Roberto Polo, an Italian financier subsequently jailed on embezzlement and other charges, bought six tower apartments in the names of offshore corporations when the building opened in 1983. Polo was accused of swindling $110 million and was facing charges, as one gossip columnist put it, "in more countries than most people have visited."

Sheldon and Jay Weinberg, a father and son team who were eventually convicted in the largest Medicaid fraud case in history, rented three apartments on the sixty-third floor that Trump had personally acquired himself and was leasing at astronomical prices. The Trump Organization was apparently unperplexed about how Sheldon Weinberg, who was not a doctor but ran a health clinic in the Bedford-Stuyvesant section of Brooklyn, could afford $180,000 a year in rent. Jay Weinberg's grand larceny conviction in 1986, insurance fraud conviction in 1983, and the SEC's permanent injunction against him acting as investment adviser in 1984 had apparently no bearing on the Trump Organization's willingness to rent him a $46,000-a-year apartment. The facts of the insurance fraud case might have been of some interest to Trump, since it involved burglaries that Weinberg staged in his Brooklyn apartment so he could collect thousands in insurance claims. He was caught when he used the same receipts—including one for a $5,500 Coyote coat—as proof of his losses for two different burglaries. It wasn't until the end of 1988, following the conviction of the two Weinbergs for stealing $16 million in Medicaid funds targeted for the poor, that they moved out of the tower. They never paid the moving company.

David Bogatin, a high-level member of a Russian emigré crime family, bought five tower apartments in 1984 for $6 million. Donald personally attended the Bogatin closing, meeting Bogatin and his lawyer. Working with Colombo capo Michael Franzese, Bogatin was part of a ring of oil entrepreneurs convicted in a record-setting gas tax evasion scam. After he pled guilty in 1987, agreeing to pay $5 million in back taxes, Bogatin fled to Vienna before he was sentenced and remains a fugitive today. The state seized Bogatin's tower apartments, and state prosecutors concluded that he'd purchased them "to launder money, to shelter and hide assets" and used them on weekends and "for parties."

While there is no evidence that Polo, the Weinbergs, or Bogatin was personally close to Trump, other felon residents were. Convicted cocaine dealer Joe Weichselbaum, whose helicopter company serviced the Trump casinos, didn't move into the two adjoining apartments his girlfriend bought for $2.4 million until he got out of federal prison in 1989. But before that, the mysterious Weichselbaum—who was so friendly with Donald he was gossiping with his parole officer about Marla Maples well before her association with Donald ever hit the newspapers—rented an apartment owned by Donald in Trump Plaza. The single apartment Donald owned in the co-op building that he did not turn over to a member of the family, Weichselbaum only paid half of its $7,000-a-month rent, compensating Trump for the other half with bartered copter service.* After Weichselbaum went off to jail, Trump actually discussed moving Maples into his apartment, until he was convinced that his visits to see her would inevitably attract embarrassing attention.

Weichselbaum initially took the Plaza apartment two months after he was indicted in 1985, then got a 1986 letter for his sentencing judge from Donald praising him as "conscientious, forthright, diligent and a credit to the community" and in 1989 told his parole hoard that when he got out of prison he was going to become a consultant to Trump. The strange purchase of the tower apartments—without any mortgage financing—was merely the latest episode in what even Trump friends have found to be one of Donald's most bizarre business relationships.

Rounding out this list of rogues was Robert Hopkins, a Lucchese crime family associate who was arrested in his Trump Tower suite of apartments for ordering a mob murder of a gambling competitor. While the murder count was dismissed, Hopkins was convicted of running one of the city's biggest illegal gambling operations—taking in a half million a week and running numbers out of as many as a hundred locations. State investigators maintained a tap on his Trump Tower phone for months, concluding that he "controlled the enterprise" from the tower apartments.

Donald was not as friendly with Hopkins as he was with Weichselbaum, but he did know him through Roy Cohn, whose firm handled both his criminal cases and those of the major mob figure behind him, "Joe Beck" DePalermo. Cohn had, in fact, put the deal together, recruiting Hopkins to sign up to buy the apartments in 1981 and to pay almost $2 million, helping to set a high market value on the building's units early in the sales campaign. It took Hopkins almost two years to put together the financing to close on the purchase, and Cohn asked the young associate in his firm who had been appointed to the City Planning Commission, Ted Teah, to do the closing.

A mob-tied mortgage broker, subsequently convicted in two federal fraud cases, Robert Lamagra, arranged the mortgages for Hopkins that totaled nearly $1.7 million. Since much of Hopkins's income was too fluid to be found in a bank statement, it is unclear how he convinced not only the Trump Organization

---

* Brother Robert and sister Elizabeth live in apartments owned by the Trump Organization and another unit was turned over by Donald to Ivana, with her rental income going into a trust fund for her and the kids.

but Midlantic Bank that he could make the common charge and mortgage payments. The mortgages went bad even before the gambling arrest, and the bank had to foreclose.

Donald personally visited the Hopkins closing, to which Hopkins brought a briefcase containing as much as $200,000 in cash and sat at the end of Trump's conference table counting it. What happened with the cash eventually became the subject of an informal but dead-end federal inquiry after Lamagra, seeking to cut a pretrial deal with the feds, offered investigators a version of events that suggested an illegal cash transfer by Hopkins and made allegations which vaguely involved Trump.

This motley crew of apartment buyers—which collectively owned over two dozen tower apartments, many on the top floors—was in part enticed by the belief that they could trade on the Trump name, buying and selling their units at great profits. But none of them made money on this speculation, and several, like Hopkins, overpaid. The banks that mortgaged these purchases were often unable to get the value of their own investments out of them. And the more legitimate residents of the building were increasingly distressed about the criminals they kept meeting on the elevator rides Donald had so grandly advertised.

Resting high above all these scandals, at the top of the lower, was, of course, the Trump triplex, valued, according to Donald, at $10 million. "The finest apartment in the top building in the best location in the hottest city in the world" was Donald's modest description of his home, which was featured in the July 1985 edition of *Architectural Digest*. The apartment's twenty-foot, gold-leafed living room ceilings were celebrated as among the highest in any building in New York. With peach-pink mirrors, peach suede walls, a brown marble fireplace, and a banquette covered with a fabric painted in 24K gold, the apartment was described by the *Digest* as having a soft, comfortable, modern, and very feminine look, orchestrated by Ivana. The designer was actually a well-known master of understatement, Angelo Donghia, and he and Ivana had clashed often in their approach to the apartment, producing what many said was a "muddled message," alternating between the subdued and the lavish. Nonetheless, Donald told the magazine that he wanted "an important apartment" and he believed, at least for a moment, that he had one.

The young man who had been inordinately proud of his modest $1,000-a-month penthouse on East 75th Street until his marriage in 1977 was, ever so suddenly, sitting on top of the world. Though one news story a few years earlier had reported that he owned a chalet in Aspen, he in fact only rented. He and

Ivana had purchased a $3 million Greenwich estate in 1982, but that just made them one more wealthy New York family with a Connecticut getaway. It was the extravagance of the tower apartment that really began to set them apart, to mark them as symbols of the legendary rich.

But by the time the *Digest* tribute to the apartment appeared, several months after the photo spread was shot, Donald was already ripping up the apartment again. Back in 1984, he'd decided he wanted a wholesale redesign of it and had recruited the staff to supervise it. This time the decor would be his, especially since the latest nuptial agreement had reduced Ivana to a subordinate role in the ownership of the tower apartment. Whereas the 1979 agreement had granted Ivana the right to continue living rent-free or maintenance cost-free in whatever apartment the family occupied if a separation or divorce occurred, the new contract emphatically declared that "in no event shall Ivana be entitled to" or "have any right to reside in" the tower triplex should they separate. Instead, the May 24, 1984, agreement, signed shortly after they moved into the triplex, described it as "the sole property of Donald free of any claim on the part of Ivana." Ivana's trade-off for this concession was a $2.5 million lump sum payment at the time of Donald's death or a divorce, plus the Greenwich house—dramatic improvements over the stretched-out alimony schedule of the earlier contract.

Since it was now Donald's apartment, Ivana rarely participated in the design meetings Donald called and when she did make a suggestion to the staff Donald told them to ignore her. Donald was not just sprucing up his residence—he was creating a grand investment. He decided to combine the triplex with another, add a duplex, and build essentially two apartments within the complex—all owned by him personally yet regally renovated at corporate expense. As Donald told the story, the inspiration for this project was a visit he and Ivana made to a party at Arab billionaire Adnan Khashoggi's apartment in Olympic Tower one night. Donald came away awed by the vastness of Khashoggi's living room and later even asked his decorator to try covertly to obtain its measurements so he could be certain his own would be longer. The end result—when the two years of work on the apartment had led to four more—was that Donald had his eighty-foot-long living room, with bronze-edged floor-to-ceiling windows.

But virtually everyone who saw both apartments doubted that the second was an improvement. In conversations that started shortly after Ivana signed the nuptial, Donald worked out the broad strokes of his new concept for the apartment with a prominent California architect who'd done some interior work on Donald's first casino in Atlantic City, Harrah's at Trump Plaza, which had opened early in 1984. As Russell MacTaggart, the interior designer who ultimately finished the apartment, tells the story, the architect was barely a year into the renovation when "a lot of people started criticizing the way it was looking." Once the dining room and master bedroom were finished and Donald started showing them off, "people, while complimenting the apartment to him, would burst out laughing the minute Donald would leave the room." MacTaggart says that Trump staffers who witnessed this mockery tried gently to tell Donald about it. "The quality was there," said MacTaggart. "It was built beautifully . . . but it looked like a casino. So some of the people in the Trump Organization came to him and said we just don't think this guy is right for you. He's really good at what he does in the casino, but it's not going to be right for you."

Eventually, Donald and the architect had a petty dispute and parted company. MacTaggart, who had worked for Trump in an earlier phase on a design for the first apartment, was rehired and asked to reexamine the plan for the apartment. But MacTaggart was repeatedly frustrated by Donald's stubborn insistence on critical issues of style. The former living room with its celebrated twenty-foot ceilings had been changed, in the new layout, to a dining area. While the initial plan had called for a thirteen-foot ceiling in the new, far longer living room, the California designer had actually recommended it be reduced to eight feet.

"You have a thirteen-foot ceiling height," said MacTaggart. "Who wants to give up five feet of space? I tried very hard showing Mr. Trump drawings. I mean, a whole bunch of people badgering Donald, going to him and saying you've got to change this. And for two weeks he vacillated back and forth and then finally left it at eight feet. It's now finished with a primary ceiling height of eight feet with a couple of domes scattered around here and there . . . to take advantage of at least some of this pocket of space that was being hidden. To this day, Donald still will ask people: 'Do you think I really should have put it to thirteen feet?'"

Then there was the matter of the gilded capitals—the curlicued golden details that were intended to top off beautifully carved marble columns that Donald had installed in the apartment. "The capitals were too wide," said MacTaggart. "They overhung the columns. They were supposed to sit in them. They looked absurd. I had a meeting with Mr. Trump, and I said, 'By the way, there's been some talk about the columns, and I think we should talk about them.' He said, 'Yes, you know, I'm not really happy with them.' He said, 'They're too tall.' And I, startled, said, 'Well, no, they're too wide.' And I immediately realized my mistake. I should have said, 'Yes, they're too tall,' and he would've gotten rid of them.

"He just looked at me and said, 'No, they're too tall.' And I thought, Well, I've gone this far . . . if I explain why they're too wide, he'll understand this. Didn't work. The more I tried to explain that they were too wide, the more he insisted they were too tall. Then he said, 'Because they're so big, they'll be more impressive and therefore more people will like them. Let's leave them.' And then he walked out of the meeting.

"He has these ludicrously overscaled gilded capitals that rather overwhelm the entire apartment. Of course, because the ceiling's so low, instead of being at ten feet, where the capitals might not be so overwhelming, they're sort of at eye level. These gigantic gilded capitals. And he's very pleased with them."

Six years after the building opened, work finally ceased on the Trump triplexes. The $10 million reconstruction of his own apartment had become the longest-lasting project of his life, literally without a budget or a schedule. It was as if the image he wanted was of the tough businessman who had no patience for delays or the excesses of change-order contractors when he built for others but knew no limits when he built for himself.

He had a twelve-foot waterfall set against a background of translucent onyx, walls lined in Italian gold onyx, and a bathtub made of lilac onyx. "Onyx is like a precious metal," was all Donald could say to explain this new fascination of his, "many grades above marble." The ceiling moldings were 24K gold, and the faucets were gold as well. "There has never been anything like this built in 400 years," Donald told *Time* magazine. Others who saw it said it had a "Louis-XIV-on-LSD" look and that the "ugly opulence" of it reminded them of "the pizza man from Queens's kitchen."

By the time the apartment was completed in 1989, Donald had already begun to slip down the dark hole his debt had dug for him, though few saw the signs of it. But in 1984, when he first settled in at Trump Tower with his family, he was at the peak of his career. The Hyatt and Trump Tower were lavish successes; the convention center was in construction on his 34th Street site. Trump Plaza on Third Avenue, a new frontier for million-dollar co-ops, had just been finished at a cost of $125 million and was selling, smartly, albeit slower than Trump Tower had. Martina Navratilova announced she was buying an apartment there when she won the U.S. Open. Former Kentucky governor John Y. Brown and his wife, Phyllis George, as well as Regis Philbin and Dick Clark, moved in.

Indeed, the Y-shaped Trump Plaza was such an architectural success that another builder hired Donald's architect to design what the *Times* called a "mirror image" of it just across the street. Trump wound up throwing attorney Scott Mollen at the architect and the developers, and Mollen won a settlement that forced a redesign of the imitation project, then in midconstruction. The well-publicized legal triumph was fresh evidence that Trump projects were so successful others were literally trying to copy them.

Another dispute over the project, however, prompted an explosive split between Donald and longtime aide Louise Sunshine, who owned a 5 percent piece of it. Donald had structured the profit-and-loss accounting for the building in a way that left her owing a million dollars in taxes on her tiny part of it, and when she objected he tried to buy her out cheap. She hired a lawyer, forced Donald to pay three times his initial offer, and quit, saying the man she'd helped invent had "used his money as a power tool over me." But this nasty fight did not go public, meaning Trump was hardly damaged by it.

Just two months after Trump Plaza opened in New York, Harrah's at Trump Plaza, Donald's first casino, opened in Atlantic City. It, too, after years on the drawing boards, looked like an unqualified hit. A decade after he first moved into Manhattan to seek an option on the West Side yards, Donald had put together a string of successes with barely an entrepreneurial misstep. The dark side of his projects—from the brutality of his Hyatt condemnation actions to the shadiness of his construction compromises—was scarcely perceived and had no effect on the image he was inventing for himself. The principal audiences that mattered to him—the banks and the development community—judged him by the bottom-line results of his top-line projects. And on that scale, encouraged by an enthralled media, he was a colossal new force, a phenomenon whose day had come.

8

CAPTURING THE BOARDWALK

To a man who has gone through a great life struggle in one metropolis and tested all the phases of human duplicity, decency, sympathy and chicanery in the controlling group of men that one invariably finds in every American city, the temperament and significance of another group in another city is not so much, and yet it is. Long since, Cowperwood had parted company with the idea that humanity at any angle or under any circumstances, climatic or otherwise, is in any way different. To him the most noteworthy characteristic of the human race was that it was strangely chemic, being anything or nothing, as the hour and the condition afforded.

—*Theodore Dreiser,* THE TITAN

"When you went to Atlantic City, were you aware of the possibility that individuals you would encounter might have a lack of good character, and that that reputation would affect you?"

—*Mary Jo Flaherty, Deputy Attorney General,*
New Jersey Division of Gaming Enforcement, deposition of October 6, 1981

"Well, if I thought it would, I wouldn't go into the whole business of Atlantic City or gaming. If I thought it would. I am still not convinced that it won't and, therefore, I still have a decision to make. I really have a decision to make."

—*Donald Trump, a few months before he was awarded his first casino license*

THERE WAS ALWAYS something about the prospect of owning a casino that intrigued Donald Trump. As far back as 1976, before he'd consummated a single real estate deal in New York, he was telling reporters he would build the world's largest casino in Las Vegas and name it Xanadu. By then Donald had already made the first of what would become repeated pilgrimages to Vegas, not to gamble, but to visit Caesars Palace and the other cash farms stretched out along the strip.

Even before a referendum legalizing casinos passed in New Jersey in 1976, Donald had driven down to Atlantic City for a casual look at prospective sites. Soon after the New Jersey legislature enacted the statutes in 1977 that implemented the referendum and created the Casino Control Commission, a Trump family friend named Richie Levy, whose prominent New York real estate firm was busily assembling a New Jersey site for Bally's, put Donald together with an Atlantic City broker. The broker, Paul Longo, was handling several pieces of a prime Boardwalk site that he thought might appeal to Trump. But Donald was still biding his time. His interest in Atlantic City did not peak until its first casino, Resorts, opened in the spring of 1978 to mobs of fastbuck gamblers. During a seaplane visit to the city that summer, a wide-eyed Donald met Longo and prowled the Boardwalk, eyeing the site that would become his fantasy location.

On that trip Donald met over ice cream with Levy, Longo, and a slippery Philadelphia investor named Gene Alten, one of the parcel's principal owners. Trump made a halfhearted but multimillion-dollar offer to lease Alten's property but was rejected, and he trekked back to New York, still uncertain about making a real move. His decision to seek a lease rather than try to buy the parcel was fast becoming the pattern of Boardwalk deals. The advantage to a developer was that he could lay claim to a key casino property with so little up-front expenditure that, if the casino experiment faltered, he could still walk away from the investment with ease. Preserving his options was precisely what Donald wanted.

As confident as Trump was that he would ultimately do a casino venture somewhere, he was wary of its prospects in what was, in fact, a dying resort town and was waiting to see what could be accomplished in New York. He had been nosily lobbying for the legalization of casinos in the state, where pari-mutuel racing, bingo, the lottery, and off track betting were already producing three times as much public revenue as all the casinos in Nevada combined. To place a referendum on the New York ballot, the state legislature had to approve it in two successive years. The passage of a bill in 1978 by the Republican senate and the Democratic assembly—pushed by old family friend Stanley Steingut—encouraged Donald to keep his New York options open.

In 1979, when the campaign for gambling heated up in New York, Donald became a prominent public spokesman for it. Declaring in a multipart *Daily News* series on gambling that the still-in-construction Hyatt was designed for casino use, Trump said: "We designed the building so it can easily be converted to one larger than the MGM Grand in Las Vegas. The shame is that Jersey beat us to it." In a *Times* feature that July Trump warned, "We are missing the boat every day casinos are not approved," and once again contended that his new Hyatt was being built to permit "relatively easy conversion of its 65,000 square feet of lobby and retail space" to gambling operations.

Governor Hugh Carey was a champion of legalization, but beyond Carey, the pro-casino forces faced serious opposition. Steingut surrendered his Brooklyn assembly seat in 1979 after a stunning upset loss, and the new speaker, Stanley Fink, was cool to gambling, though willing to leave the issue up to individual legislators. While statewide legalization was unlikely, several sectors of the state coveted gambling privileges—from the Rockaways in Queens to the Catskills and upstate Niagara Falls—and a contentiousness developed about which region would get them.

Outside New York City, it was feared that if casinos were permitted in Manhattan, the bulk of the business would go there. Ed Koch, who favored casinos elsewhere in the city, expressly announced that he opposed them in areas like 42nd Street, saying they were wrong for the tourist core—a targeted and singularly deflating critique as far as Trump was concerned. Then, a Carey-appointed commission reported in August of 1979 that a $3 billion industry could be built in four areas of the state, including Manhattan but excluding its East Side. A Hyatt casino seemed doomed.

Carey announced that he was considering calling the adjourned legislature back for a special September session to vote on a gambling proposition that would appear on the November ballot, but he suddenly changed his mind, stating that a casino referendum might damage the prospects for a crucial half-billion-dollar transportation bond issue already slated for the ballot. The Carey decision effectively put the casino issue on hold for a minimum of two years, though the *Daily News* had given the referendum two-to-one odds for passage just a couple of weeks earlier. The postponement took the steam out of the campaign and fed doubts that gambling would ever come to New York.

While Trump would subsequently portray his belated initial land deals in Atlantic City in 1980 as a matter of prudence, waiting out the first wave of speculation, it was in fact his own speculating on a New York alternative that had helped slow him down. He may also have been awaiting the outcome of Brooklyn U.S. Attorney Ed Korman's probe of the West Side yard transaction, hesitant to put himself through the excruciating public review process that New Jersey's new regulatory agencies—the Division of Gaming Enforcement and the Casino Control Commission—were giving casino applicants. Until the Korman investigation was concluded in November of 1979, Trump was hardly positioned for easy passage through DGE's and CCC's tortuous process. When the investigation ended without charges, leaks, or any form of public notice, Donald seemed at last ready to really test the New Jersey waters.

He knew he wanted the Longo site; it had virtually stood still for him since his initial visit, occupied only by warring groups of owners, several of whom, like Gene Alten, had imagined themselves as casino developers but had been unable to get a project off the ground. The two-and-a-half-acre, largely vacant property was, in Donald's view, Atlantic City's Tiffany location, situated precisely at the center of the Boardwalk casino strip. It stood next to Convention Hall, where Miss America was annually crowned, and half a block off Missouri Avenue, the street into which the Atlantic City Expressway emptied, meaning that most of the traffic entering the city arrived at its doorstep. But the parcel was also problematic. The block on which it was located was half the size of most on the Boardwalk, since a short, hideaway street midway between Missouri and Mississippi Avenues cut the ordinary blocklong lot into two narrow pieces. Bob Guccione, the *Penthouse* publisher, was already building a casino on the contiguous half-block. The site was so narrow that Alten and the others who owned large parts of it had been unable to obtain city approvals to build the towering hotel-casino they'd planned. In addition, the one-lane streets on either side of it were no more than forbidding alleys, making access to any casino by car a potential traffic horror show.

The final problem was that the city's master plan called for expansion of the convention center in two directions: first, to a block directly behind the Hall and then north for three blocks, including the one next to Trump's coveted site. That meant Trump would be unable to build a parking facility behind his casino that could be attached to it by a skyway as other casinos planned to do. Visitors would have to park an extra block away and walk in the open air to Trump's casino—a trip inconsistent with every planner's vision of the long-term Atlantic City success formula. The city was so barren and hostile, with its boarded-up shells and vacant lots, that the architects designing the casinos and accompanying garages tried to guarantee that middle-class gamblers could remain ensconced behind glass and concrete from the moment they stepped out of their cars, separated from the wrenching poverty outside.

Even from 125 miles away in Manhattan, Donald saw all these limitations of the site as obstacles with political solutions. He would find a way to build a casino that dwarfed the site as well as a garage adjacent to it, making auto access to the casino itself irrelevant since cars would flow right off the Expressway and into his planned multilevel garage. It was only a matter of finding the right buttons to push. His Hyatt experience had taught him that.

His experience with Alten in 1978, however, had taught him just how difficult assemblage might be. He approached Levy and Longo one more time to see if a package could be put together on the site. Telling Longo simply that he was "ready to deal," Donald drove a limo down to Atlantic City in early 1980 with Ivana beside him and Levy in the backseat. After a Sinatra concert at Resorts and dinner at Bally's, Donald took a rainy, midnight walk with Longo down the Boardwalk to look at the site, leaving Levy and Ivana playing the slots at Bally's. When he got back, all he said to Levy was: "I love that plot."

Aside from five private homes spotted around the block, the bulk of the site was owned by three major groups of speculators, tied together by a maze of complicated contracts and leases redrawn every time one more of the various owners tried without success to build a casino there. Longo had his hooks into two of the three groups, and the one he didn't represent was the site's most recent would-be developer, Plaza Hotel Management Group, which was led by two New York dealmakers with unusual credentials—Columbia and Yale law professor Robert Lifton and former national Democratic treasurer Howard Weingrow.

Lifton and Weingrow had driven down to the resort town hunting properties in 1978, pulled into a parking lot that occupied part of the block, and asked who owned it. "Howard Hughes," replied the attendant. And he wasn't far from wrong. Robert Maheu, the former top aide to the legendary billionaire who'd once owned half of Vegas, had indeed formed an entity that had a goodly chunk of the site. He was just one of the site's mysterious emissaries from Nevada. Also involved was flashy Grady Sanders, who was said to be accompanied on excursions to Atlantic City by union heavies from the desert strip. Prodded by the parking attendant's tip, Weingrow went to a pay phone on the Boardwalk and called Maheu in Vegas, urging him to fly out to Atlantic City the next day. Eventually the Weingrow group struck a deal to build a casino with the Maheu and Sanders entities. But a federal judge issued a permanent injunction against the two Maheu companies after they allegedly made false and misleading statements in an attempt to push up the value of their stock. So Lifton, Weingrow, and another partner they brought into the venture took over control of the project, with the Maheu and Sanders groups assigned a secondary role.

In addition to the Alten and Plaza Management sectors of the site, there was a third, very local, group of owners. The parcel bordering on the Boardwalk was controlled by a group called Magnum, formed by Mac Seelig, the six-foot, 270-pound, thirty-three-year-old karate-king son of a prizefighter. Working with Longo from the inception, the group had obtained its option the day before the gambling referendum passed for a scant $20,000. Magnum also included two law partners whose small firm had its share of mob clients, including Saul Kane, who would eventually be convicted of running a million-dollar-a-month amphetamine empire for Atlantic City crime boss Nicky Scarfo. Kane's bar—a Scarfo hangout—sat on the middle of the Boardwalk block.

Donald's decision to lease the property, rather than to buy it outright, had its potential pitfalls, since New Jersey casino regulations required the licensing of landowners as well as casino operators, unless an owner was expressly exempted by the Casino Control Commission. If the Maheu and Magnum groups posed possible licensing problems up the road, the changing cast of characters on the Alten parcel certainly should have sounded a regulatory alarm for Donald. Pursued by a multimillion-dollar judgment from a Philly bank, Alten was experiencing all sorts of money problems in late 1979, and he turned in several dark directions for help. Cleveland Wrecking, the Hyatt demolition contractor from Pennsylvania with a secret mob investor, tossed in $110,000 to keep a foreclosing bank off Alten's back. National Kinney, whose tarnished subcontracting subsidiaries were then handling the plumbing, electrical, and drywall work at the Hyatt, met with Alten, but took a pass on a partnership offer. Another investor was Alten friend Danny Sullivan, who claimed to have been a member of thirty-seven Teamster locals and had a long but petty arrest record, including one weapon felony conviction later reduced to a misdemeanor. The explosive and mammoth Sullivan had been characterized as everything from Jimmy Hoffa's mortal enemy to his close ally, and everything from a mob associate to a mob-busting FBI informant.

Sullivan put together a new entity, SSG Inc., including himself and two Philly scrap-metal dealers, Kenny Shapiro and Elliot Goldberg, described by associates as the short, dumpy guy with the open shirt and lots of gold (Shapiro) and the tall, dumpy guy with an open shirt and lots of gold (Goldberg). Even though SSG—half of which was owned by Sullivan and a quarter apiece by the Shapiro* and Goldberg interests—had not yet actually bought the site from Alten, they wound up negotiating directly with Trump as if they owned the site. Donald never even attempted to deal with Alten, though he was told of Alten's desperate financial condition, which, of course, made him a vulnerable seller. Instead, Trump negotiated exclusively over a period of months in 1980 with the shady Sullivan group, and they waited to close with Alten until a few days before Trump signed his lease with them.

While the flamboyant Sullivan cast a long shadow over SSG, the real power was its managing agent, the cigar-chomping Shapiro, who would later be identified in law enforcement reports as "the mob's main dealmaker" in Atlantic City in the eighties. It was Shapiro who controlled the secret interest in Cleveland Wrecking. His two-story office building just off the Boardwalk became a checkpoint for visiting racketeers who passed through town. Shapiro was busily funneling Philly mob money into dozens of Atlantic City real estate deals, and the broker on thirty of his transactions in and around Atlantic City was none other than the son of mob chieftain Nicky Scarfo.

Trump's decision to negotiate ninety-eight-year leases with this collection of tawdry owners, even giving one group long-term rent increases pegged to hikes in the appraised value of the casino property, was either a fearless declaration of his confidence that the regulatory process could be politically managed or a revelation of his ignorance of the Jersey/Philadelphia landscape. It might have been a combination of both.

In any event, his leases with these owners would become the gravest threat to Donald's project over the years, and eventually Donald would have to move to acquire the SSG and Magnum interests, while Lifton and Weingrow would buy out the Nevada gang. But it would take eight years, and a couple of devastating DGE probes, before Trump would finally clean out the toxins beneath his royal casino.

While Longo, an amiable, politically connected broker, was able to put Trump together with Magnum and the Sullivan group, Donald had to fend for himself with Lifton and Weingrow. In late 1979 Trump turned for assistance to

---

* Sullivan contends that Shapiro's interests were held by a family trust, not Shapiro personally, for tax reasons.

the Weingrow group's architect, Alan Lapidus, whose designs for the site had been conditionally approved by the city, but only after the casino had been reduced, because of the narrowness of the site, from 50,000 square feet to 30,000. Lapidus had known Donald since Trump was in his teens—one more connection inherited from Fred, who'd retained Lapidus's father, Morris, to design Beach Haven, Shore Haven, and Trump Village. Ten years older than Donald, Lapidus had met Donald on the Trump Village site, where Donald had a summer job. "The first question I asked Donald," recalled Lapidus, "was why he wanted to get involved in Jersey, and he said you've got to do something to make life interesting while you're waiting to die."

Lifton and Weingrow were happy to use Lapidus as a go-between because their project was hitting the financial hard wall that had already stopped a number of nascent projects on the site. When Weingrow's financing fell through in March of 1980, he and his attorney, Nick Ribis, met in New York with Donald and negotiated leasing terms. With a Weingrow agreement in place, Donald then went to Atlantic City to meet with Longo and bargain with Magnum and SSG. The meetings took place on a hot March day in an un-air-conditioned Resorts suite, and as the hard bargaining wore on, Longo, the Dreyer & Traub lawyers who'd come down from New York with Donald, and many of the rest of the group got down to their shirtsleeves. Donald's only concession to the heat, however, was his unbuttoned suitcoat. He chatted and sparred with Shapiro and Sullivan and, after threatening at various points to "just forget about it," he finally arrived at the basic terms of a deal.

Trump had already hired the politically connected Howard Goldberg, a savvy senior partner in the city's largest law firm, to negotiate the leases. Goldberg's firm had long represented Longo's Philadelphia-based brokerage house and had put Longo together with SSG. With ties to both the Sullivan group and Longo, Goldberg was a natural for Trump, obviously well-positioned at the very center of the deal. Trump also retained Weingrow's architect Lapidus and lawyer Ribis, as well as a new partner in the Magnum group who had become its lawyer and principal negotiator, Lee Levine. All were on the Trump payroll, working on this casino project soon after the leases were signed. Trump even hired the flamboyant Sullivan, persuading Hyatt to retain him as a labor consultant to negotiate the hotel's new contract with the local Hotel Workers union.*

---

* Even before Sullivan took on the Hyatt work, Trump asked him to mediate the dispute between his Trump Tower demolition contractor and the illegal Polish aliens

When the final leases were executed with Magnum and SSG after twenty-eight consecutive hours of negotiating in Goldberg's office on July 17 and 18, Donald had won what he wanted most—minimizing his up-front expenditures. (The same was true of the Weingrow lease, which had been signed separately in New York a week before.) Though SSG's principals were the newest partners in the deal, having just closed with Alten, they received the biggest signing bonus—$1.4 million—over a million of which was applied instantly to Alten's two outstanding bank loans. The rest was paid into an escrow account controlled by Trump's lawyers. All of Weingrow's $800,000 initial payment was escrowed, as was half of the $1 million due Magnum. The monthly rent payments due Magnum and Weingrow were also put in escrow for the first nine months. In effect, Donald had arranged it so that he only had to pay out an unescrowed $1.5 million, and both SSG and Magnum gave him promissory notes that would require the repayment of even these sums if certain conditions weren't met.

The principal condition was that the state had to settle all riparian rights issues by March of 1981, meaning that Trump and Magnum, which owned the parcel closest to the beach, had to work out an agreement with state environmental officials determining just where the beach began and Magnum's rights ended. When this line was drawn in the sand, the leases would formally close, the escrowed payments would be released, and the promissory notes would be canceled. Until such a riparian settlement was final Donald would be able to avoid spending a single irretrievable dollar. These terms permitted Donald to tie up a choice Boardwalk site while preserving an option to back out.

Donald also won a major concession from Magnum and the Weingrow group, in that they agreed to suspend more than half the rent payments due under the lease until after the casino was built. They would then collect the overdue rent in payments strung out over the first few years of operation. Magnum agreed to these terms in the belief that the other parties had made the same concession, but the tough guys from SSG had in fact given Donald a flat rejection. Donald's acquiescence to SSG's payment demands was a subtle tribute to Shapiro's and Sullivan's connections and muscle.

The July signing in Goldberg's office was pandemonium, with over a hundred participants streaming in and out of conference rooms—preparing,

---

working for him on Fifth Avenue. Sullivan spent the latter part of July and most of August on the site, pushing the demolition project to conclusion and getting rid of the illegals—work he did without charge.

reviewing, and executing dozens of documents. The two ownership groups were kept apart and negotiated with the Trump team separately. Donald visited, but left the details to the precise and icy Goldberg. When the final papers were nearing completion in the early hours of the morning, Donald arrived in a limo, accompanied by a man who'd never appeared before throughout the months of negotiations with SSG and Magnum. Fred Trump, weary and a little grim, came in to sign the leases as vice president of the Trump entities that had been created for each transaction. A week earlier, he had appeared just as briefly to sign the Weingrow lease.

No one explained why Fred's signature was required, but no one had to. With the Hyatt still months away from opening, Donald had yet to complete a single project. His payments on these leases would be drawn from the same Chase credit line that had bailed him out at the Hyatt, a credit line from Fred's old bankers that had been extended because of Fred's dependable history. Chase, which shunned casino investment, was even willing to bend a few self-imposed rules to finance Donald's entry into Atlantic City.

When Fred finished, he pressed a wad of hundreds into Goldberg's hand, asking him to share them with the staff who'd worked all night. The two Trumps left the offices together at four o'clock in the morning. Upstairs, someone had discovered that Fred had mistakenly failed to sign a single document. Mac Seelig, held by the seat of his pants by little Paul Longo, leaned out the window, bellowing for the Trumps to return. The gregarious Sullivan was already breaking out the champagne, toasting the roomful of new would-be millionaires.

Fred, of course, returned to sign the final lease document and went right on signing whenever major cost items on the project were involved—executing Lapidus's architectural contract, for example. He even brought his own Trump Village agreement with Morris Lapidus to the contract discussions with Alan and suggested that they "do it just like that." Few knew it, but Fred was quietly trying to dissuade Donald from the New Jersey move, arguing that casinos were not the family's familiar territory. But Donald had already carried the cautious old man, and his fortune, into Manhattan, and he would now bring him on a roll of the dice into Atlantic City.

Bob Guccione stopped construction on his Penthouse casino in July of 1980, at the same moment that Donald was signing the leases for the site next door. Guccione simply ran out of money, and a decade later his beams were still baking in the ocean sun. The first great surge of casino development had peaked, and while Resorts and Caesars and Bally's were doing well, the market seemed suspended in midair, unsure if it was strong enough to sustain anything grander than a seasonal trade. The modest size of the local airport had made Atlantic City a bus and car town, hardly the high-roller mode of transportation. Big-bank antipathy to casinos had undercut financing, and even Donald's mainstream financiers were hesitant to bankroll his green-felt fantasy.

Donald's securing of the leases was but the first step on the long road to owning and operating a casino. For starters, Trump still needed a green light from state officials on everything from riparian rights to Department of Environmental Protection approval of the general project plan to the sensitive DGE and CCC review processes. But he had an ace in the hole who could help steer him through the state maze, just as she had in New York—Louise Sunshine. Sunshine came from a prominent North Jersey family with extensive business and political ties. As Hugh Carey's fund-raiser, she'd also worked with New Jersey's Democratic governor, Brendan Byrne, since Byrne and Carey used the same political consultant, David Garth. The combination gave her the entry to set up Donald's first meeting with Byrne, over lunch at the brand-new Hyatt in October of 1980.

She, Donald, and the patrician Byrne, a lame duck in the final year and a half of his second term, had a friendly talk about Donald's casino project. While Byrne recalled no specific requests or promises, he could not have helped but realize, especially with Sunshine's cheery presence, that if Trump committed to New Jersey, it might dim Carey's enthusiasm for casinos in New York. Sunshine was on friendly enough terms with Byrne that she went shopping with him after lunch for a birthday present for his wife. The governor returned to New Jersey impressed, and while he later said he could not remember if he spoke with other state officials about Donald's upcoming project, several state agencies did rush to make Donald feel at home—within days of the Sunshine lunch.

The New Jersey DEP announced in a news story later that month that it liked the preliminary plans for the project. A few months after the Hyatt lunch, Byrne personally approved a riparian rights deal that was highly favorable to Donald, shortcircuiting what was ordinarily a cumbersome process. "We broke records, but it wasn't anything nefarious," explained Lapidus in an interview years later. "Donald was a New York developer. That was the message they wanted to send."

Donald's new attorney, thirty-six-year-old Nick Ribis, was also making early headway for him at the Casino Control Commission, where Ribis had his own connections. Joe Fusco, the head of the CCC's licensing division since the commission was established in 1977, had been a classmate of Ribis's at Seton Hall Prep in West Orange and a lifelong friend. In addition to running the licensing

section, Fusco was commission chairman Joe Lordi's protégé. When Trump
hired Ribis, he had just left a New Jersey law firm whose senior partner was
closely associated with Roy Cohn. He was starting his own practice, and even
though the small, new firm was located upstate and had no casino experience, it
instantly attracted casino clients. Fusco would eventually become Ribis's partner,
several years after he left his commission post.

Ribis's principal casino client prior to Donald was the company that owned
the Claridge, and the partner who brought him in was Joe Pennullo, a pinball
and jukebox vendor. The son-in-law of the once indicted president of a mob-
dominated Teamster local in Newark, Pennullo was a close friend of Joe Lordi's.
While Pennullo was forced in the end to sell his share in the Claridge by a DGE
report that cited his association with "undesirable individuals," the Claridge
ownership before and after him continued to have its murky ties with Meyer
Lansky, the mob monarch of the gaming industry. It also continued to be represented by Ribis, who got it licensed with the aid of a critical vote by Lordi—his
last on the Commission.

Ribis's first real achievement for Donald had all the earmarks of a Lordi-
Fusco favor. Shortly after Byrne's meeting with Trump and several months before
Donald even filed an application for a casino license, Ribis collected two unusual
letters from CCC attorneys tentatively approving the leases Donald had executed
with the potentially troublesome landowners. The letters indicated that the lease
provisions would make it unnecessary for SSG and the others to obtain a license,
convincing Trump he could move smoothly through the process.

With this go-ahead on the three large parcels on the site, Donald began to
acquire the small lots, in November 1980, closing on the purchase of four of the
private houses (he'd bought another one a couple of months earlier). The $1.2
million that he paid for the five homes was his first unconditional investment in
the site. At the same time, his still tiny organization grew by two in anticipation
of the Atlantic City project—Harvey Freeman, a veteran real estate attorney who
became Donald's in-house counsel, and brother Robert Trump, a thirty-two-
year-old vice president of real estate finance at Shearson Loeb Rhoades. Donald
had been talking with Robert since the spring about coming aboard to run the
Trump Organization's Atlantic City operation, and Robert had instead left a job
he'd held for five years with Eastdil Realty and gone to Shearson. But as soon
as the casino project began to look real, he joined the family company. Donald's selection of Robert was a leap of faith, since Robert had never worked in
construction, spending eight years with three investment banking companies on
real estate and corporate financing packages.

A Boston University graduate with a gentle, almost laid-back personal style, the still single Robert lived modestly in Donald's old East 65th Street apartment, amid the long shag rugs and other decor that had gone out of style years earlier. When he finally sold the apartment and furnishings to a young doctor after he married the fashionable Blaine in the mideighties, Robert left a cocktail glass behind that was etched with either his or Donald's onetime motto: "The 11th Commandment: Thou shalt not invade thy principal."

At the time he came to work with Donald, Robert played a lot of tennis and drove a 1972 Oldsmobile Cutlass owned by one of Fred Trump's companies, Beach Haven Apartments. He earned $159,460 the year before coming to Donald, invested extensively in the market, and put away up to $300,000 in various savings accounts. He sold the apartment for $270,000 just before the new tax laws on capital gains earnings kicked in at the end of 1986. Alan Lapidus said the Trump boys "either have a hunger for development or they emphatically don't"— contrasting Donald and older brother Fred Jr. "Robert is the middle ground."

Soon after Robert joined the Trump Organization, Lapidus completed the casino plans, and in January of 1981, Atlantic City officials approved them. The costly plans, together with Robert's six-figure salary, represented additional signs of Donald's commitment to the project, though he still believed he could abandon it with minimal exposure. The discouraging news was that by the end of 1980, all six of the city's casinos were reporting operating losses for the first time. The upside for Donald of this downturn, however, was that he was making a bold move at the same sort of economic low point that had helped propel him to Hyatt riches—he was knocking at the door in Atlantic City when a temporary tailspin there had made it so hungry for new development that even the toughest bureaucratic hurdles might be easily surmounted.

Still remaining for Donald was the usually punishing casino review process, beginning with the character and integrity investigation of the state's Division of Gaming Enforcement, which was under the control of Attorney General John Degnan. A Byrne appointee, Degnan had challenged Resorts and Caesars, two of the first license applicants. He had urged the Casino Control Commission to reject Resorts and lost unanimously, despite seventeen serious objections; DGE's subsequent year-and-a-half probe of Caesars resulted in a 121-page report that took a softer tack, merely listing objections without taking an adversary position. The commission granted the license, but forced several top executives to step down.

A conscientious prosecutor deeply troubled by the criminal crassness of the casino industry, Degnan was caught between his own ideals and the economic development goals of the state's gambling champion, Brendan Byrne. Byrne had reportedly complained to Degnan about the slowness—and thoroughness—of the Resorts probe, telling him: "The best thing you can do is recommend they get a license. The next best thing is recommend they don't. Either way, get the damned investigation over with." Degnan had worked his way up under Byrne, starting as an assistant counsel in the governor's office during Byrne's first term. By early 1981, he was already planning a run to succeed Byrne as governor, and he needed, and eventually obtained, Byrne's endorsement.

While neither Byrne nor Degnan could recall years later if they ever discussed Donald's pending application, there was no doubt that Degnan, from the beginning, understood the governor's predilection for a casino candidate like Trump. To Byrne and Degnan, Trump was a builder whose distance from the casino industry was seen as an asset. They had yet to find anyone from the industry who hadn't been at least somewhat tainted by it.

In early 1981 Degnan received a call from a former law school classmate of his, Hugh McCluskey, a partner in the new law firm he had started just a year or so earlier with Nick Ribis. McCluskey wanted to arrange a preapplication meeting with Degnan for Ribis's client, Donald Trump. Degnan agreed, and a meeting was set for February in Ribis's office. Degnan summoned DGE director Mickey Brown, the bulldog prosecutor who had tried the Resorts case, and Brown's deputy, Guy Michael, up from their downstate office. Brown, another former assistant prosecutor in Joe Lordi's office, would eventually be in charge of the Trump DGE review.

Donald, Robert Trump, and Ribis attended the meeting, held only a few weeks before Degnan stepped down to run for governor. Donald promised that it would be easy for DGE to review his application, which had yet to be filed, saying he was "clean as a whistle" and wasn't "old enough to have gotten into any trouble yet." He argued that since his company was "not publicly traded," but was a small, closely held entity, it should be possible to grant him a quick license. He said he was "reluctant to commit to any project expenditures unless he could obtain indications that a license would be granted swiftly." Degnan assured Donald that he'd "have to be investigated like anyone else," but that "it was possible that it could be done quicker" than previous reviews, assuring him that they would "try to expedite it."

Trump insisted on a license within three months of his application because he "didn't want to start construction on the casino" until DGE and the CCC had found him qualified. He was determined not to repeat the pattern of previous applicants—building first and then seeking a license. But, as DGE would learn during the subsequent investigation. Trump was hardly prepared to build. He had no financing, and in an era when lending rates were climbing to all-time highs, it was doubtful that he could find any. He hadn't even closed on the leases, still operating under the nine-month extension with its escape provisions. His attempt to rush the DGE review had little to do, in fact, with an urgent plan to plunge a shovel in the sand; he simply wanted assurances he could parlay the Atlantic City downturn and his supposed Mr. Clean assets into an instant license, without too many questions.

Brown finally told him a three-month review would be "impossible," but added that the Division's investigation "should take six to nine months," insisting that this was not a commitment, but a feasible goal. The estimated timetable, faster than any in the history of the agency, gave Donald what he wanted.

It wasn't until Donald had these assurances that he finally gave up on New York. Eight bills, authorizing gambling in various parts of the state, had passed the New York legislature in 1980, shortly before Donald executed his leases. If legislators approved any of the eight when they came up for a second vote in 1981, gambling would wind up on the November ballot. But the legalization opportunity that had once tantalized Donald now threatened his mounting New Jersey investment.

As soon as he closed on his Jersey leases and filed his May 1, 1981, application for a casino license there, Donald turned into a fierce opponent of New York gambling.* Top officials of the New York statewide coalition for casinos said that the new naysayer Trump quickly moved to divide the membership of the Hotel Association, pulling at least one major chain onto the opposition side and diluting this once powerful voice for a New York referendum. With the vote imminent in the legislature in May of 1981, Donald hosted a press conference with

---

* Fighting the legalization of gambling wherever it reared its head soon became a Trump preoccupation. He underscored its perils over the years in Indiana, New York, and Louisiana, using the criminal vice that gripped Atlantic City as an object lesson. He even opposed a New Jersey Casino Association national advertising campaign that would have documented the constructive contributions of the industry in Atlantic City, fearing that it might stimulate competition elsewhere and suggesting instead that the association get out the word of just how bad crime was in the resort town to persuade other states not to take the risk.

his old nemesis from the convention center war, Robert Tisch, the Monte Carlo casino owner and a onetime major hotel owner in Atlantic City, to announce the formation of a business alliance opposed to legalization.

The day after Trump's conference, New York Attorney General Robert Abrams, who'd campaigned in favor of gambling when he won election in 1978, released a devastating twenty-four-page report assailing the Atlantic City experience and concluding that New York had to reject it. News reports flatly described the Abrams report as "the death knell" of gambling in the state. A jubilant Atlantic City *Press* front-page story highlighted Abrams's declaration that New York had to reject it or face the threat of undermining government institutions "in a manner similar to New Jersey." Hugh Carey was quoted as saying he would now have to review his own position on the issue. Abrams had directed his staff to prepare the report six months earlier, and from the beginning he seemed determined to marshal facts to justify a shift in position. Uncharacteristically, he personally phoned some of the state's leading opponents, gathering information for the report.

Planning either to seek reelection in 1982 or run for governor if Carey dropped out, the liberal Abrams knew that a tough law enforcement position on gambling would be an asset among voters where he was weakest—the conservative, upstate section of the state. Since Abrams was also genuinely persuaded that the New Jersey experience was a warning signal to New York, it was the sort of circumstance every politician hungers for—a perfect congruence of belief and benefit. A campaigning Abrams sternly regaled voters with stories about his trip to Atlantic City, where he "saw slots as far as the eye could see," and expressed his dismay at every aspect of "the venality and corrosiveness" of the industry. He did not mention that his principal adviser on the damaging potential effects of legalization was none other than his fellow attorney general, John Degnan, who was simultaneously running for governor on his record of combating the very criminal enterprises in Atlantic City that Abrams said were exploding.

Though Abrams would deny it years later, others said that he met with Donald prior to the issuance of the report in his office at the World Trade Center and that Trump laid out his plans to go to New Jersey and build a casino. There is no doubt that Ethan Geto, the campaign fund-raiser and operative who was to Abrams what Sunshine was to Carey and more, talked with his counterpart, Louise, before the report was released. Geto called Sunshine looking for a contribution in early 1981. Fearing that she and Trump might be unhappy with the conclusions in the upcoming report, he told her what Abrams would be announcing. "We think it's terrific," Sunshine told him. "We don't want any competition. We'd love to see casino gambling not come to New York." Geto recalled that his conversation with Sunshine did result in a Trump contribution, though no records exist spelling out the date and amount.* Trump, who had contributed to Abrams's first campaign in 1978, attended a small, intimate fund-raiser for twenty or so large givers a few months after the casino report. According to one partygoer, the gambling report was briefly discussed with the donors at this party.

In the aftermath of the Abrams report, Carey halted any real efforts to push a casino bill through the legislature, and it died, with the governor ending up as a public opponent. The Atlantic City *Press* celebrated in an editorial, a symbol of the enormous stake New Jersey had in New York's decision. Though the piece advised eternal vigilance against the threat from the north, casinos would never again mount a serious campaign in New York.

The emerging philosophy in New Jersey of government and industry officials, articulated expressly by the Golden Nugget's Steve Wynn, was to lure casino developers who might otherwise be interested in New York, thereby not only adding influential advocates to the New Jersey side of the issue, but subtracting them from the New York side. The welcome given Donald was the embodiment of that philosophy, making him the prime beneficiary of this bistate competition. New Jersey officials believed that if Trump was expeditiously approved, other New York developers would follow him to Atlantic City.

Donald was the white knight from New York that New Jersey desperately needed to lend luster and credibility to its casino industry. But it was not just the seemingly unimpeachable credentials of a builder whose projects attracted a partner like Equitable that made him so attractive. It was Donald's perceived role in the crushing of the northern threat that helped put him on New Jersey's licensing fast track.

And rushed it was.

DGE's check of Donald's integrity and character did not involve even a conversation with U.S. Attorney Ed Korman, whose Brooklyn office had conducted

---

* A state investigations report in the late 1980s revealed that Abrams and Trump had a troubling history of large contributions, embarrassingly intertwined with Abrams's handling of Trump co-op and condo plans. When Trump pledged a $15,000 donation at a 1985 breakfast with Abrams, he had four plans pending approval before the attorney general's office, a violation of voluntary campaign rules Abrams had imposed on himself and his donors.

the quick and abbreviated probe of Donald's Penn Central machinations with David Berger. The October 1981 report, which DGE completed in a record-breaking five months, made no mention of the Korman probe, or of Manhattan U.S. Attorney John Martin's investigation of the Hyatt deal.

As part of his application for a license as a "key" casino employee in 1981, Trump had to fill out a confidential personal history disclosure, which was the equivalent of a sworn statement and included on its cover page a warning that any answer that was neither complete nor truthful would result in the denial of a license. Donald was asked on the form if, to the best of his knowledge, he had "ever been the subject of an investigation conducted by a governmental investigatory agency for any reason." Yet while the form has never been made public, every indication—from a variety of DGE and CCC sources—is that Donald did not reveal either probe in his response on the disclosure form.

Donald clearly misled DGE in other answers on the form. For example, asked in the same series of questions about whether he'd ever been a party to a civil suit or "ever been cited or charged or formally accused of any violation of a statute, regulation or code" by any governmental entity, Trump answered "no," omitting any reference to the racial discrimination charges filed a few years earlier. DGE turned these erroneous answers into a footnote in its final report, since Donald had "volunteered information" about the suit before he was asked during a DGE interview. The DGE report also made no mention of the subpoena served on Donald when he was questioned in the 1980–81 probe of the concrete workers union boss, John Cody, though Trump would have had to answer two questions on the disclosure form that sought information about any such interrogations.

Even without Trump's straightforward acknowledgment of his role in these investigations, DGE might have ordinarily learned about them since they took place in the very jurisdictions where Donald had spent his entire business career. Instead, DGE overlooked not only the probes, but also the underlying charges about Donald's questionable conduct that prompted the Hyatt and Penn Central investigations. The agency was clearly aware of the allegations raised in newspaper stories about Trump's conduct in these deals because its investigators questioned the reporter who first revealed them. While the allegations were credible enough to prompt two federal probes, DGE chose not to inform the CCC of them, ignoring everything from Donald's deception about his nonexistent Commodore option to his coincidental retention of Berger.

The biggest break for Trump in the DGE report, however, was what it did not say about his business dealings with the lessors, particularly Kenny Shapiro.

Shapiro's mob associations were so well known to authorities that two weeks *after* Trump won his casino license in 1982, the state police began a twenty-four-hour watch on his Atlantic City office, noting that Nicky Scarfo, as well as other mobsters from all across the state, visited him, as had Donald and Robert Trump. The relationship between Shapiro and Donald had already extended beyond the lease, with the Trumps actively negotiating with Shapiro about the acquisition of a parking site near the planned casino. This combination made their business relationship a clearly appropriate subject for DGE review when considering a license for Trump.

In fact, DGE used Donald's multiplicity of business dealings with Shapiro's partner, Dan Sullivan, as the rationale for a lengthy and damning section about Sullivan in its Trump report. The agency concluded that Donald's promise to sever his ties with Sullivan meant that the relationship wouldn't hurt his license application, but the DGE report never explored why Trump had gotten so close to him in the first place. DGE focused on Sullivan's ancient misdemeanors, rather than on the implications of Trump's selection of him to negotiate the Hyatt's first contract with the hotel workers. This lapse was especially curious since DGE was simultaneously preparing a report on the Atlantic City local of the same union and branding it mob-controlled. Yet it was Sullivan's relationship with the national president of the hotel workers—a reputed associate of the Chicago crime family—that helped secure Donald's first contracts with the union at the Hyatt and later at the Barbizon. These contracts were consciously crafted outside the bounds of the citywide Hotel Association agreement with the union, laying the foundation for the special relationship that developed over the years between Trump and the union in New York and Atlantic City.

Not only did DGE omit Shapiro and sidestep Trump's hotel worker ties with Sullivan in their licensing report on Donald, it also concluded that none of the landowners should have to face a separate licensing review of their own. The agency submitted a memo to the CCC on December 31, 1981, urging that the commission waive all qualifying requirements for Sullivan and the rest of the lessors. The timing of this second report fell into a familiar Trumpian pattern—it was delivered in the final days of the Byrne administration with the entire state bureaucracy in flux, anticipating the arrival of a new, Republican, governor. Though reports filed with the commission for a public hearing are routinely made public, this unusual one remains a secret a decade later. The CCC decided to take a long look at this distinct question of whether or not the lessors required a license even while it granted Donald, Robert, and the Trump Plaza Corporation their licenses at a March 1982 hearing.

As Degnan and the DGE had predicted at that initial meeting with Donald, the Trump licenses were obtained in record time. But the commission specifically found that there was "insufficient information" to evidence "the financial stability, business ability and casino experience" of the Trump entity, noting that it was only certifying the Trumps as having established the character and integrity to own a casino. In fact, DGE never delivered the follow-up report it had promised on Donald's finances, and Trump's claims to the regulators changed dramatically each time he was questioned about his uncertain bank commitments. Still, Donald was the first licensee qualified by the commission before he began building his casino and the first recommended by DGE without objection.

But the CCC's ultimate decision on the lessors put the project in jeopardy anyway. The DGE recommendation that the landowners not have to qualify for a key license like Trump—or either of the lesser licenses—flew in the face of prior rulings, one of which had even required a mortgage holder to be licensed. The Atlantic City *Press* was quick to point out this discrepancy, asking in a blistering editorial what DGE would say if Trump were leasing from Meyer Lansky himself.

DGE's rationale for its recommendation was that the landowners would exercise no control over the casino, and thus did not require licenses. The owners were, for the most part, being paid flat rates over the ninety-eight-year terms of the leases, meaning they were not partners who would share in the success of the casino. Ribis claimed at the March hearing that he and the Lordi-Fusco staff had reached a settlement on the licensing of the lessors in 1980, telling the CCC that the two staff letters he obtained then "indicate unequivocally that licensure or qualification of the landlords would not be required." He argued that Trump had "based his determination to go forward and invest millions of dollars in New Jersey upon the ability not to have the lessors licensed or qualified." Donald took the same tack in his own testimony, claiming "we asked quite a while ago for a ruling" on the licensing of the lessors, and "I was led to believe that we got it," adding that "we were informed" that because the lessors were out of the profit or control picture they did not have to qualify. Trump told the commission flatly that he would not build if the lessors were forced to meet a licensing or qualifying standard.

While the commission seemed predisposed toward not requiring full licenses, several members also leaned toward forcing the landowners to meet the lesser criteria of a "financial source" or investor, meaning that DGE would still examine them and issue a less probative report on them. "I don't think there's anything wrong with these people," Trump pleaded in response. "Most of them have been in Atlantic City for many, many years and I think they are well thought of." Trump pointed to the annual lease costs of $1.8 million, contrasted it with an estimated purchase cost of $25 million, and threatened that if he was forced to buy the land rather than face a difficulty in licensing its owners, he might reach the conclusion that the project was just not buildable. To add to the pressure, Ribis read into the CCC record SSG's written position that it would not seek commission clearance as a financial source and that it would sue to oppose any requirement that it do so. But the commission, unmoved by Trump's or SSG's threats, voted to mandate the financial source review anyway.

Incredibly, even after the CCC decision and the DGE report assailing Sullivan, Donald drew still closer to the controversial SSG principals, seeking DGE approval to hire Sullivan as a labor consultant on the casino construction site and revising his position on key terms of the lease in a series of technical ways so as to align himself with SSG while putting himself at loggerheads with the regulators.

This war of nerves over SSG's licensing dragged on for a year and a half—while construction of the casino proceeded—only to explode again in October 1983. Incensed by SSG's and Donald's recalcitrance, the commission decided to up the ante, declaring that its own 1982 demand that SSG meet only the financial source standard did not appear "to adequately serve the public interest." The CCC's reason for rethinking its position was that SSG had "exercised an unacceptable and unanticipated level of control" over the Trump project—a reference to Trump's switch on the technical terms of the lease in favor of SSG and an implicit condemnation of Donald, considering just who the principals behind SSG were. The CCC then voted to reopen the question of requiring full licenses for each property owner.

Donald had to move to break this deadlock, so he called Sullivan and negotiated a November buyout of the SSG lease for $8 million, $3 million more than he would have had to pay under the terms of the lease if he had simply waited for DGE to deny a license to the group. Three years after he cut his deal with SSG, he had finally come to grips with the fact that he would have to rid himself of Shapiro and Sullivan if his casino was ever to be fully licensed. His timing could not have been better—he disassociated himself from Shapiro on the eve of a storm of publicity about Shapiro's role as the mob's conduit to Atlantic City Mayor Mike Mathews.

The trip was just one more lark for carefree Mike Mathews: a limo ride up the Garden State Parkway to Fifth Avenue to meet a billionaire—at least he thought his host, Donald Trump, was a billionaire. He knew Trump was a celebrity, and Mathews, who would cover his City Hall office in Atlantic City with photos of himself and Joey Heatherton and Vic Damone, loved celebrities. The sandy-haired, slim, and piercingly handsome Mathews was anxious to meet the golden boy everyone expected to make a big splash off the Boardwalk.

It was December 4, 1981, and the forty-seven-year-old Mathews, one of the five elected commissioners who ran Atlantic City's government, was about to announce his candidacy to become its first real mayor. A new charter had been adopted just the month before, abolishing the old commissioner form of government and replacing it with a strong mayor–city council structure. The betting line in a betting town was on Mathews, the only candidate whose appeal was seen as broad enough to transcend the neighborhood-based politics of the commission system and build a citywide electoral base. Previous mayors had been chosen only by their four fellow commissioners. Mathews, who had been a leader of the charter reform movement and a maverick on the maligned board of commissioners, was poised to become the resort's Great White Hope—the only candidate in an increasingly black city who could beat black public school administrator James Usry. Mathews had moved back into Atlantic City from a nearby suburb only a few years earlier to establish a residency there so that if a 1980 charter change passed he could run for mayor. He was already a state assemblyman whose district ran from his suburban community into parts of the city, and when the charter proposal failed he ran successfully for city commission anyway, serving as both an assemblyman and city commissioner since his election that fall. An accountant with six children, Mathews was the son of a gruff Irish shipyard worker, but he'd always favored his Italian half, flaunting the little bit of the language that his mother had handed down to him and enticed by the fast-track lives of the mob princes he'd grown up around. As Mathews would later put it: "So I didn't see them as bad, good or indifferent, one way or the other. These guys should be able to make a buck, too."

When Mathews went to see Trump, Donald had just gotten the go-ahead from DGE and was waiting for his licensing hearing with the CCC. As important as the state casino review process was to him, it was only one of the public arenas in which the fate of his project would be decided. Trump's architects were about to submit a dramatically revised set of drawings to Mathews's board of commissioners, and unless Donald was able to snare a virtually unprecedented package of planning concessions from the city, his casino might never go forward.

Trump's premium on location had resulted in a choice site, but its size limitations were proving to be an even greater problem than anticipated. The only way a 60,000-square-foot casino could be built on this site without taking on a bowling alley look was to extend it out over Mississippi Avenue and right up against Convention Hall, effectively transforming the city's prime public asset into an annex for Donald's facility—which he had tentatively dubbed Trump Plaza. It was an audacious plan, even for Trump, and he decided to try to do it without paying the city for the air rights it owned over the street.

A reconfigured space was also vital to attracting financing for the project, as well as getting an experienced gaming company to operate it. Donald was already talking informally to Harrah's, a successful, publicly traded casino company and subsidiary of Holiday Inn with one Atlantic City casino far from the Boardwalk and an avid interest in developing a second Boardwalk property. Harrah's had reviewed the previous Trump plans—minus the air rights—and gone away unimpressed. Without a skillful operating partner, however, Donald was having no luck with the banks. His familiar friends at Chase and Equitable did not do gambling projects, and Manufacturers Hanover wanted the Hyatt, Trump Tower, and everything else the Trumps could put together as collateral for a casino loan that would only cover half the construction cost. It was becoming clear to Donald that to get an operating partner and financing, he'd have to first win city approval of the air rights extension over Mississippi Avenue.

When Mathews arrived at Donald's Crown Building office, Donald greeted him with the declaration: "I understand you're going to be the next mayor of Atlantic City." As Mathews recalled in an interview years later, Donald "wanted to know if he could donate to my campaign," and Mathews told him he couldn't "if you're going to operate a casino in Atlantic City." Mathews, who was already actively fund-raising for a May 1982 mayoral election, declined Donald's assistance because state casino law barred operators from contributing to political campaigns in New Jersey.

Mathews was, in fact, simultaneously meeting with Frank Lentino, Frank Gerace, and Al Daidone, all Scarfo crime family associates who were also officers of Local 54 of the Hotel Workers Union. During a December 1981 dinner at an Atlantic City restaurant, Mathews agreed to support mob-backed projects if elected in exchange for as much as $125,000 in campaign contributions. Daidone, who would subsequently be convicted of murder, set up a second session for the mayoral candidate with Kenny Shapiro, the principal financier for the Scarfo organization. Shapiro agreed to help bankroll Mathews's campaign, which in small-town Atlantic City would only require about $150,000. Shapiro would actually generate $35,000 in cash contributions to Mathews, most of which the candidate apparently pocketed, and $30,000 in checks. The noncash contributions came from a variety of Shapiro-connected sources—his brothers, Sullivan,

Cleveland Wrecking, Elliot Goldberg, and a contractor who was already working on the Trump Plaza site. And, according to Shapiro and Sullivan, some of the funds were provided at the behest of their then friend, Donald Trump.

Shapiro and Sullivan told reporters in separate interviews over a period of years that in early 1982 Trump met with them in his New York office at a time when they were in frequent touch with him on everything from the Plaza lease to Trump's continuing interest in the nearby parking site principally owned by Sullivan's and Shapiro's trust. The two agreed that Donald discussed the possibility of contributing several thousand dollars to Mathews by getting New York subcontractors to make the donations, an end-run around the law. Robert Trump supposedly even gathered together some checks from the contractors, but everyone ultimately agreed that contributions from a batch of New York plumbers and electrical contractors would look strange so they were not made.

According to Shapiro and Sullivan, Trump then suggested that Shapiro put up the $10,000 and indicated that he would eventually pay him back. Shapiro made the contribution, according to the two, but was never reimbursed. Beyond this alleged Trump-inspired contribution, the publicly reported contributions to Mathews from sources tied to the Trump project—the only casino built during the Mathews mayoralty—were legion. Howard Goldberg's firm and partners kicked in $5,000, architect Lapidus $1,000, Paul Longo $825, SSG's lawyers $5,000, the Magnum Group's Harry Goldenberg, Kenny Mackler and Lee Levine, $2,000, planner Peter Karabashian $1,000, surveyor Arthur Ponzio $500, subcontractors Calvi Electric, Thomas Roofing, and R. T. Winzinger, Inc., $5,750, and Donald's investment banker, Bear Stearns, $1,500. Added to the reported donations from Shapiro himself, the almost $53,000 in contributions connected to the Trump project accounted for almost half of Mathews's total campaign receipts.

In February of 1982, with Mathews in the throes of his campaign, the Trump Plaza air rights issue came before the five city commissioners. Mathews immediately championed it, announcing "there's no reason to procrastinate over this," though he had been an opponent of other casino variances encroaching on streets less centrally located than Mississippi Avenue. Joe Pasquale, another city commissioner, told Robert Trump and other Trump officials at one point: "Just tell us what you want us to do."

A third commissioner, Ed Colanzi, annoyed that city attorneys were warning that more time was needed to analyze such a major change in the plans, told the lawyers to "stop playing games," adding that there was no room for argument over a project so beneficial to the city. But the lawyers, and Mayor Joe Lazarow, the two-term incumbent still considering a run for reelection, prevailed and laid the matter over for further study, announcing that they'd seek an appraisal of the air rights to determine if the city should demand fair market value for them.

The decision to delay the matter threw Donald into a panic. He had been holding a secret Trump card for a number of years—a behind-the-scenes relationship with powerhouse Atlantic City attorney Paddy McGahn. The city had long been divided by a virulent feud between the McGahns and the Perskies, led by State Senator Steve Perskie. Mathews was deeply entrenched in the Perskie camp and was such a fierce opponent of the McGahns that when Mathews ran, early in his career, against Paddy's brother, State Senator Joseph McGahn, he was taped by an undercover agent trying to enlist the agent's help in a scheme to plant narcotics in McGahn's car. Donald had aligned himself publicly with the Perskie wing from the beginning, inviting Perskie up to his New York offices for "get-acquainted" talks, using Perskie's broker Paul Longo, and hiring Steve Perskie's onetime campaign manager, Howard Goldberg.

But while Donald came into town on the Perskie welcome wagon, he had also covertly opened up lines of communication to the tough ex-marine and crew-cut son of a saloonkeeper, Paddy McGahn. Described by one city official as a man "whose connections go to heaven," McGahn was reported to have boasted that he controlled the City Commission. Planning and zoning board officials also were known to be McGahn clients or to have obtained their positions on his recommendation. His longtime representation of Resorts—the town's first casino—had given him influence over its hiring and comps—patronage and clout unparalleled by any local elected official. As "smooth as a battering ram," McGahn had won three Purple Hearts and a Navy Cross in Korea and loved to heave his rather substantial weight gruffly around City Hall.

One McGahn ally, City Commissioner Ed Colanzi, had been meeting quietly with Donald since 1979, starting with a cozy get-together in Donald's apartment. The ostensible purpose of the session was to discuss the expansion of Convention Hall in Atlantic City—an active proposition then before a commission committee Colanzi chaired. Colanzi and Donald talked a bit about New York's convention center, but then Donald asked: "Do you mind answering a few questions for me about Atlantic City?" When Colanzi agreed, Donald opened with a peculiar and memorable line. "Atlantic City. What is it?" he asked. "My mom and dad tell me they used to stay there." Colanzi and he began a half-hour discussion about the resort, with Donald pressing the commissioner about the city's plans for the convention center adjacent to the site he was secretly moving to acquire. When Donald phoned him several months later, Colanzi was hardly surprised by the news. "I'm calling because we've acquired an option to develop a casino in Atlantic City, and I'd like to talk with you," Donald said. Colanzi replied: "I have to assume you have an option on land between Mississippi and Missouri Avenues because I know you like building near convention centers." Donald confirmed Colanzi's suspicion, and asked him to keep it quiet.

The two continued to meet, usually in New York, and Donald asked Colanzi to work with Robert Trump and Harvey Freeman on the casino's zoning issues. Colanzi helped steer the first plans through an expedited city approval process in 1981, insisting at one public meeting that the Trump name—though Donald was then an unknown—had to be on the casino "in prominence and perpetuity." Colanzi became an open Trump propagandist, boosting him in early meetings with CCC members and state DBP officials and changing his position on the convention center expansion to oppose the condemnation of the block that ran directly behind Donald's casino site and was Trump's preferred location for a vast parking garage. Colanzi was convinced that his mentor McGahn was behind the scenes working for Donald throughout this period, but it wasn't until February 1982—with the air rights approval in jeopardy—that McGahn suddenly stepped forward. Though McGahn and Robert Trump told an Atlantic City *Press* reporter that McGahn was definitely not representing the casino, Paddy weighed in at the first City Commission discussion of the air rights, joining the Colanzi and Pasquale chorus in support of the Mississippi Avenue extension. McGahn even suggested that "if the Trumps are doing all of that"—namely, building support beams on the far side of the street for a $4 to $5 million casino overhang—"the city ought to be paying THEM."

The reporter, Tom Turcol, discovered over the course of the next week that McGahn was indeed representing Trump and that McGahn's partner had begun secret meetings with the city attorney who'd delayed the initial vote on the air rights, as well as the city engineer and planning board officials. The city attorney's concern, raised because of a federal probe of a prior city land conveyance, was that they obtain an appraisal to justify the bargain price Trump was seeking. Colanzi quickly recommended the retention of a supposedly "independent" local appraiser. The appraiser, Colanzi acknowledged years later, "came to see me and asked what he should do about this." Replied Colanzi: "Give him the consideration for the air rights—$100." Though the outside appraiser charged the city $2,000 for the opinion, he recommended Colanzi's price, and the city refused to make public the appraisal report. Armed with this scandalously undervalued appraisal for the city's prime Boardwalk block, McGahn quickly produced a favorable planning board vote, leaving only the City Commission to approve it.

But McGahn's emergence on Trump's side also had its political downside.

According to Mike Mathews, Trump had asked him back in their December 1981 meeting what lawyers he should use in Atlantic City, and cold warrior Mathews had replied: "Anyone but McGahn." With McGahn now openly on the Trump tab, the once supportive Mathews temporarily demurred. When language changes in the proposed ordinance came before the commission on McGahn's stationery, Mathews announced that he had "serious problems with the whole way this thing is being handled" and insisted that he needed more time to study it.

But at the final session a few days later, with the Goldberg and McGahn firms in tow to lobby their respective wings of City Hall, the Trump plan passed unanimously. Citing the "exceptional narrowness" of the Trump site, the city resolution allowed Donald to abut Convention Hall for 520 of the east wall's 636 feet and to build a skywalk connection along the Boardwalk. When the city and CCC processes concluded at virtually the same moment in March, the dramatically redesigned and quickly licensed casino now had location, size, and legality, making it a magnet for precisely the kind of operator, like Harrah's, that was already roaming the Boardwalk for a site.

There are a variety of versions of the events that led to Donald's lucrative partnership with Harrah's. Trump's favorite is that he "had never thought of a partner in Atlantic City" until Holiday Inn's chairman Mike Rose told him their Harrah's subsidiary was interested in becoming one. Donald claims he told Rose that he had the site, the financing, the license, and the approvals—"what do I need you for?" But Phil Satre, Harrah's president, countered in an affidavit that it was Trump who first raised the possibility of a partnership with Rose, and even Trump staffers acknowledge that Harrah's examined Trump's early plans for the project and balked. Contrary to his claimed indifference to the need for a partner, Donald had asked Paul Longo as early as 1980 or 1981 to find him one, and Longo had approached Harrah's. In fact Donald had spoken so openly about a partner that he'd even told Ed Colanzi, hardly a confidant, that he was actively looking for one.

However they began, the talks with Harrah's ended successfully by June of 1982, three months after Trump Plaza was licensed. With the project barely under construction, Donald signed a contract with the gaming giant that may have been the single best deal of his life. Harrah's agreed to pay him $22 million up front to cover his supposed project expenses, including a $2.3 million supervisory and overhead fee for himself together with nearly a million in legal fees, mostly for Dreyer & Traub, who handled virtually all his varied real estate matters. The $22 million was part of a $50 million investment that Harrah's agreed to make from its own funds. Under the agreement, Trump would build the casino and collect a construction fee, while Harrah's would operate it and share half the profits with Donald. Harrah's was even willing to guarantee Donald against operating losses for five years.

Little did Harrah's realize that had they waited to sign the deal for a few weeks, Trump would have had to halt the limited construction activity then going on at the site, since he would have literally been out of money. Haunted by the rusting Guccione beams next door, a stalled Donald might have been forced to deal on Harrah's terms. What Harrah's didn't know was that Donald was fishing for financing everywhere, even traveling with Drexel Burnham Lambert's casino consultant Daniel Lee out to Los Angeles to meet junk bond king Mike Milken for the first time—a pilgrimage described in Drexel inner circles as "kissing the ring of the Pope." While willing to consider financing his casino, Milken advised him, without any prodding, on the inapplicability of Milken's junk bonds to Trump's main line of business—Manhattan real estate projects.*

That lesson behind them, Milken, Trump, and Lee continued detailed talks over the succeeding weeks. Milken wanted Donald to come up with a $30 million equity investment in the project and to sign a completion guarantee. Donald was resistant to both demands, seeking 100 percent financing. In the middle of these negotiations Donald suddenly announced to a surprised Milken the terms of Harrah's offer. "It's a great deal," Milken told Trump, not even attempting to compete.

Harrah's apparently thought Donald had his touted bank financing in place for the project, but the Milken hunt showed just how illusory that was. In any event, Trump's financing fell apart shortly after their deal was signed. Though Donald would claim in *The Art of the Deal* that Harrah's had agreed to take over responsibility for the financing as part of their agreement, he conceded in court papers that he was responsible for contributing bank financing but that it was

---

* Milken told Donald that "the Saudis and the Kuwaitis have an unthinkable amount of money, and yet they could not buy the real estate on Wilshire Boulevard," arguing that valuable property was just too expensive. "There is a great and growing junk bond market," said Milken, then only in the early stages of the bond boom, "but real estate scares me. There's not enough junk money to do Manhattan development deals."

"lost" once Harrah's entered the picture. With the project in a crisis, Harrah's had to use its own corporate guarantee to secure an entirely new bank package.

Again, the parallels with the Commodore and Trump Tower deals were striking—Trump had laid claim to a prime location with a minimal early investment, parlayed political advantages and a locally downturned economy into a series of government concessions, and then used both the location and the concessions as a lure for an institutional partner that could help deliver the financing he otherwise could not obtain. What had begun in the seventies as a fumbling search for a buildable project had become a proven formula for success.

Harrah's and Donald signed their contracts the day before Mike Mathews was sworn in as mayor in July of 1982. Mathews had defeated his black opponent, Jim Usry, by a scant 359 votes in an election marked by a strong black turnout. When Mathews was sworn in, the black council members, Usry, and their supporters held their own rump inaugural. Usry had already launched what would turn out to be a damaging series of legal challenges against Mathews, beginning with an unsuccessful attempt to overturn the election, including evidence that Mathews's campaign workers had enlisted mental patients from Ancora State Hospital to cast absentee ballots. He would soon be pushing the first of two recall petitions, trying to force Mathews from office. With six children, a wife, and a blond beauty-queen girlfriend in her twenties to support, Mathews was hard pressed to pay the anti-recall legal bills that were keeping him in office.

Kenny Shapiro was a frequent companion of the mayor's during this period, meeting him almost every week, dropping in at City Hall to take him to Philadelphia for dinner, entertaining him at a beach condo just out of the city, or sneaking over to Mathews's apartment, where the mayor's back problems frequently kept him in bed. The Trump brothers were also regular visitors, with Robert visiting him at City Hall to talk about Plaza site problems from a parking garage to a skyway over Pacific Avenue connecting the garage to the casino.

When Mathews wound up in the Pomona Medical Center because of his bad back shortly after taking office, Donald called and, according to Mathews, suggested he transfer to a special surgical hospital in New York. Mathews did, and the two Trumps visited him in his new hospital room.

Parking was clearly going to be the Plaza's biggest problem, even though Trump had managed to secure all his state and city approvals to build the casino-hotel, including environmental permits, without having any parking plan. When

Donald and Harrah's signed their partnership contract, Trump agreed in a side letter to find a solution to the parking dilemma. There were two sites nearby that had long interested Donald, and both required a push from City Hall to get approval for garage complexes. Donald's primary focus was on the block directly behind the Plaza site, located between Pacific and Atlantic Avenues, the two main thoroughfares in downtown Atlantic City. Ever since that block had been de-designated for possible convention center expansion in late 1981, Trump had been free to try to acquire it, uninhibited by any fear that the city might eventually condemn it. But he was also interested in the Shapiro-owned parking site behind that—two blocks from the Boardwalk, between Atlantic and Artie. While the first site was closer to the planned casino, the Shapiro lot was the first buildable block off the Atlantic City Expressway and thus more inviting to incoming traffic. By his own count, Trump made five separate attempts to buy the Shapiro site over the years, beginning with a September 1982 letter offer of $15 million, twice what the Shapiro interests, Sullivan, and his partners had paid for it. Donald's letter indicated that he and Harrah's intended to use the site "as a secondary parking facility, with our primary facility being located directly opposite our project." But Shapiro, who intended to build his own 3,800-space garage with an adjoining noncasino hotel on the site, rejected the bid and said he would only deal with Trump about leased spaces in a Shapiro facility.

Trump was simultaneously moving, fueled in part by Harrah's money, to acquire the nearer block for the Plaza's primary garage. One reason he did not even consider leasing the site was that a key corner parcel on it was owned by two men who, experience had taught him, could never meet a DGE standard—Salvy Testa and Frank Narducci, Jr., the sons of two Philadelphia mob bosses who had been murdered in the blood wars that had broken out in 1980. Narducci and Testa—who headed Nicky Scarfo's hit-man squad called the Young Executioners—had paid a scant $195,000 in the summer of 1977 for Le Bistro, a rundown, one-story, brick nightclub directly across Pacific Avenue from Donald's Plaza location. Predictably, they could never obtain a liquor license to run a club there; but they were only speculating anyway. Donald paid $1.1 million in late 1982 for the site, having the title transferred first from Testa and Narducci to Paddy McGahn's secretary and then to a Trump entity. The $220 per square foot that Trump paid for the Testa property was the second most expensive purchase he made on the block, even though it was one of the first parcels he bought. He paid twice as much for it as comparable parcels. While the routing of the purchase through McGahn's secretary may have been designed to put some distance between Donald and the acquisition, Trump would later boast in an affidavit in a court case with Harrah's that he had personally assembled the parcels for the garage, describing his involvement in the assemblage as the "unique contribution" and "critical skill" he brought to the joint venture with Harrah's.

In mid-1983, with the Trump site mostly acquired, his and the Shapiro garage proposals were ready to go before city planning and zoning authorities. The two proposals had become so intertwined that Mathews had at least one joint meeting in his office with Shapiro and Sullivan on one side and the Trump Organization on the other. Shapiro was reportedly urging him to approve the Trump garage as well as his own.

Both projects became major controversies, however. Strenuous opposition to the Shapiro site from neighborhood groups concerned about traffic and other impacts was rebuffed by Mathews, who personally appeared at a July public hearing to champion it. For its part, the proposed Trump project was inconsistent with a host of city planning edicts. Zoning regulations for the block prohibited a parking facility whose use was restricted to casino-hotel use on the theory that any parking so centrally located should be for the general public. The regulations also prohibited a structure whose total floor area exceeded a ratio of 4.0 when compared with the size of the lot, and Donald's eleven-story concrete coliseum for cars was a much larger 6.39. Trump also wanted a building that was at peak point thirty-four feet taller than the legal limit, yet had parking spaces smaller than city requirements—all intended to accommodate 3,300 cars. With City Hall supporting the project, every variance was granted.

But the toughest hurdle was the skywalk. While many casinos would eventually win approval for walkways over Pacific Avenue connecting parking facilities and the hotels, Donald's was the first.

There was substantial planning resistance to the notion of blocking the view along the avenue closest to the Boardwalk, as well as concern that once casinos used skyways, there wouldn't be enough street traffic to sustain noncasino businesses along Pacific Avenue. But again, with Mathews's encouragement, the September 1983 resolution approving the garage also permitted the unprecedented pedestrian skyway.

The only other major Plaza matter requiring city approval while Mathews was mayor was the exceptionally large signs Robert steered through the zoning agency that November—signs that were far in excess of the city's limits and dominated the skyline at the time. It was an issue Robert was so nervous about winning that he had a Harrah's executive contact Frank Gerace, the mob-tied head of Local 54 of the Hotel Workers, to make sure a union-connected member of the zoning board showed up to vote for it.

The Shapiro, Testa, and Gerace mob cloud that hung over these Plaza issues extended to its construction phase as well. Three Plaza subcontractors had disturbing affiliations with the Scarfo crime family—including one, Robert T. Winzinger, who was eventually indicted and was said to have been visited by Scarfo himself on the Plaza site. The president of Trump's concrete contractor, Joseph Feriozzi, was accused by the State Commission of Investigation of evading questions under oath about why he awarded this unbonded work to two shadowy and inexperienced firms.

Not all of the Plaza job's mob ties were homegrown, however. Trump brought the law firm of Dublirer, Haydon, Straci & Victor down from New York to handle negotiations with at least one building trades union. The partner who worked with Trump, Paul Victor Viggiano, was a relative of a Genovese capo and had a major mob clientele, handling everyone from reputed hit men to the biggest narcotics dealers in the Bronx. Viggiano, who changed his name to Victor, was also Stanley Friedman's right-hand man and the parliamentarian of the Bronx Democratic Party. His previous partner, Benny Caiola, was convicted in the seventies of trying to bribe *Prince of the City* cop Bob Leuci to change his testimony in a heroin case. Victor and two others in his law firm wound up partners with Kenny Shapiro in at least three Atlantic City area real estate deals.

With the Plaza a few months from opening, however, the mob mayor who had helped make it possible suddenly imploded. In December 1983 New Jersey headlines were dominated by revelations of Mathews's mob-nobbing and pending indictment. It was revealed that the mayor and one of his principal Scarfo conduits, Frank Lentino, had been taped talking to an FBI undercover agent for almost two years. The agent, posing as a mob-tied businessman seeking city land for casino development and city supply contracts, had paid Mathews thousands in hand-to-hand bribes. All the Shapiro cash donations to Mathews had also been described in these conversations.

In the frantic days after he was first picked up by FBI agents outside a restaurant on December 6, Mathews vacillated between cooperating, even agreeing to wear a wire, and running, at one point disappearing from the assembly floor with two agents waiting for him in a Trenton hotel. He wound up fleeing to Florida, putting his secretary in charge of the city, and calling reporters only to complain about how slow the golf courses were. In the end, he decided to stonewall and went back to City Hall for his final few months in office, waiting for an indictment and a recall vote. Both came in March of 1984.

While federal investigators put their case together, there were uneasy moments for many who'd spent too much time with Mathews. Shapiro, who had managed to elude the tape recorder though his actions were frequently described on it by Mathews and Lentino, was immunized and put before the grand jury. After his testimony, he was named as an unindicted coconspirator in the Mathews indictment and scheduled as a government witness.

Whatever Shapiro told the grand jury, it apparently involved the Trumps. Shortly after Shapiro's appearance, the FBI confronted Robert Trump in a restaurant and grilled him about Trump attempts to contribute to Mathews through New York subcontractors or Shapiro. The agents regarded his blanket denials as misleading. The agents returned for other sessions, including one at Trump Tower, with Robert, Donald, and John Barry, the former Assistant U.S. Attorney who'd married Maryanne Trump and become one of Donald's prime attorneys in New Jersey. Barry attributed Robert's initial evasiveness to surprise. The various discussions with Shapiro and Sullivan about contributions to the mayoral candidate were confirmed at these meetings, but specific comments attributed to the Trump brothers drew muted denials mixed with memory lapses. There was little question but that the Trumps had contemplated donations to Mathews and had even sought a legal opinion from Nick Ribis about going forward with them.

Donald's name had even popped up in a taped April 1982 conversation involving Mathews and Lentino. In the middle of a Mathews boast about his ability to raise thousand-dollar campaign contributions, he revealed that he'd "met with the Trump brothers last December 4 up in New York and spent about three hours with Donald." After bragging about how "a billionaire wanted to talk to me for three hours," Mathews said: "I gotta be careful, you know, dealing with casino people." Mathews went on to claim that Trump had told him he would build a new casino if a bill authorizing funding for convention hall improvements passed the state legislature, and Mathews, who was then still in the assembly, assured him it would. The conversation was inconclusive, but combined with the Shapiro testimony, it was enough to attract FBI interest.

While federal agents decided quickly that they had no provable criminal allegation against the Trumps, it was also apparent to them that there might be a basis for a DGE probe, since any attempt to circumvent contribution restrictions might affect Trump's license. Though DGE was notified by the feds when the Trumps were questioned in February of 1984, the agency never reported the contribution allegations to the CCC. Initially, there may have been some federal concern that a DGE probe, which would require deposing the Trumps, could compromise their own case against Mathews. But that concern ended when Mathews suddenly interrupted his November trial and pled guilty. Mathews's plea also prevented Shapiro from taking the witness stand and kept under wraps the Shapiro grand jury minutes, which would have been released in discovery. Sentenced to fifteen years in jail, remanded immediately to a maximum security prison, and held in solitary for long stretches of time, the once effervescent Mathews retreated into a shell, an aging, broken man. He was brought to New Jersey in 1987 for a further barrage of federal questions about the supposed Trump contributions and other matters, but refused again to cooperate, at least in any way that the government viewed as helpful.

With the Mathews and Shapiro issues hovering over Trump, DGE sent its second report on him to the CCC in April 1984. This time their findings focused on Harrah's Associates, the Trump-Holiday partnership formed to run what would be called Harrah's at Trump Plaza, a name whose awkwardness graphically revealed the divisions that were already damaging the business relationship between the two. Though an uncritical evaluation generally, the report did contain two references to a lawsuit filed by the heretofore-unmentioned-by-DGE Paul Longo, who was suing SSG for the brokerage fees he'd yet to collect on the 1983 buyout of the SSG parcel. But DGE remained strangely silent on the implications of the suit, even when Longo ultimately won it. Longo was offering in sworn statements an entirely different version of how Trump had come to Atlantic City than the one Donald had testified about before the CCC and in his DGE deposition. The regulators ignored this conflicting testimony even when Longo's version went uncontradicted in the lawsuit by Donald, who was a witness in the case, and when the state judges who heard the case adopted it as fact.

In sharp contrast to Longo's testimony, Donald had repeatedly sworn that his initial contacts on the site were with the architect Lapidus, and he had specifically denied DGE suggestions in 1982 that a broker and attorney had been involved. Nonetheless, DGE never told the commission anything more than that a suit had been filed, ignoring the discrepancies in Trump's testimony. It remains unclear why Trump omitted any reference to Longo or family friend Richie Levy from his account, but Longo told DGE investigators who interviewed him that Donald was—at least initially—cooperating with the Shapiro and Sullivan efforts to deny him a fee. It was just as annoying to Longo that Donald told reporters over the years, and suggested in *The Art of the Deal*, that he'd hired a multiethnic army of salesmen to swarm over the site negotiating with immigrant owners who spoke several different languages. "It was all just me," insists Paul.

Under a new attorney general, Irving Kimmelman, and new DGE director, Tom O'Brien, the agency remained as supportive of Donald as it had been in the early days. Mickey Brown had announced his resignation the day after Donald obtained his license in 1982 and, when he and his deputy Guy Michael formed their own law firm, one of their first clients was Donald's new partner, Harrah's. Harrah's retention of Brown only nine months after he left DGE, when state law barred him from working for a New Jersey casino for two years, set off a storm of protest. But Brown got an ethics ruling allowing his work for Harrah's since it was the Nevada, not the New Jersey, subsidiary that had retained him.*

Kimmelman came to the attorney general's office from Kimmelman, Wolf & Samson, where Donald's brother-in-law John Barry was a partner. Barry was recruited by Kimmelman's firm in 1984, while Kimmelman was AG, and he brought to it much of Trump's New Jersey litigation work, a sizable piece of business for a small firm Kimmelman had founded and would return to, as senior partner, in 1986. Another, less direct, connection between Trump and the Kimmelman firm was its retention by Nick Ribis's only other casino client—the Claridge—in January 1982, one day before the new attorney general–designee appeared before the Senate Judiciary Committee for confirmation. DGE director O'Brien, the Kimmelman appointee who worked so closely with him, wound up a partner in Kimmelman's law firm as well, leaving the agency later in 1986.

Even before the DGE report or the swift CCC approval, however, a confident Trump had held a peculiar press conference at Trump Tower back in March. The ostensible purpose was to announce Harrah's at Trump Plaza's May opening date. But no one from Harrah's was present and the conference instead became a platform for Trump and the new mayor of Atlantic City, James Usry, who had just won a recall election. The same day his old ally Mathews was indicted, Trump praised Usry effusively, saying how "lucky" Atlantic City was to have him "as its new leader," and declaring: "We feel very strongly about that." Trump's embrace of Usry would last more than five years, until in 1989 he became the fourth of the last six Atlantic City mayors to be indicted. In the intervening years, the Usry administration delivered on everything from a waiver on housing construction commitments assumed by Trump to permitting the Trump Plaza signs on the Transportation Center to dominate the expressway exit. Everything got so cozy that just weeks before Usry's arrest, McGahn threw a birthday party for the mayor's wife on the *Trump Princess,* attended by Robert Trump and a dozen top city officials, including one who was then considering a McGahn-submitted application for a 1,352-space employee parking lot for Trump Castle.

---

* Brown maintained ties with Trump over the years, representing Castle executive Bucky Howard on kickback charges. Howard was referred to Brown by Trump brass and used much of the $100,000 loaned him by Donald to pay Brown.

At the Plaza's grand opening on a sparkling spring day in 1984, the 2,000 or so who came to the ceremony were stunned by Donald's smoked glass, marble-and-mirror, triumph. The tallest building on the Atlantic City skyline, the hotel featured a 39-story, slender, white concrete tower atop a broad casino base; a 750-seat theater; seven restaurants, including "Ivana's," and a health club. It was the first casino to open in Atlantic City since the Tropicana became the city's ninth in late 1981, and was saluted as the beginning of a second wave. The decision to build the burgundy and bright red casino itself on the third floor, out over Mississippi Avenue, ran counter to casino custom and required customers, at least until the garage and skywalk were finished, to take an escalator upstairs to play. But the tiny site demanded this layout, and from the beginning, with 60,000 visitors a day on the first weekend, it seemed to work.

Governor Tom Kean, who'd helped make Usry mayor, was the main speaker. His appearance at such events was par for the course, but his administration's deeper relationship with the Trumps was anything but ordinary. He had become governor shortly before the 1982 groundbreaking at the Plaza site and he'd attended that one too. He would celebrate the Trump Castle unveiling in 1985 as well. These ceremonial appearances merely commemorated what his government was doing for Donald. DGE and the CCC, two state agencies appointed by Kean, or Kean's attorney general, would over the years make Donald the king of Atlantic City, authorizing his acquisition of five casinos, one of which he ultimately sold and another that he converted into a noncasino hotel. That oversight lion at DGE, Attorney General Kimmelman, was a close Kean friend and appointee. What few knew, however, was that Donald's route to Kean—as with so many other pivotal relationships in his life—ran through Roy Cohn's town house.

Cohn was an early backer of Kean's improbable gubernatorial campaign in 1981, hosting a fund-raising party for him at the town house that January. Several partygoers remembered seeing Donald there, though he was already a casino applicant and not allowed to contribute. But the key to Cohn's influence in Kean circles was another protégé as close to Cohn as Donald was—Roger Stone, a New Jersey–bred political consultant who had lived in the Cohn town house while running the 1980 Reagan for President campaign in New York, Connecticut, and New Jersey. Stone also managed Kean's astonishing come-from-behind gubernatorial win and remained an unofficial adviser to Kean even after he was retained by the Trump Organization in 1984.

By then, Stone had already been helpful to Donald on a rather crucial and personal item of business. He and Cohn, who had his own influential access at the Reagan White House, had pushed in 1983 for the appointment of Donald's forty-five-year-old sister, Maryanne Trump Barry, to a federal judgeship. She had been nominated early that year by Tom Kean, the state's highest ranking Republican official. The nomination had proven controversial, since the 45-year-old Maryanne was given the Bar Association's lowest possible favorable rating— "qualified"—having only been a lawyer for nine years and never having been in private practice. She had worked in Newark's U.S. Attorney's office since 1974 and had risen through the ranks to become head of the Appeals Bureau and First Assistant, and while she had a reputation of being thorough and thoughtful, she was widely considered as something less than material for the federal bench. U.S. Attorneys sometimes earn federal judicial appointments, but assistants rarely do.

After months of lobbying, a Cohn aide took a White House call in September, when Cohn was out of town. The message was that Maryanne had been appointed, and the staffer immediately phoned Donald and his sister to give them the good news. "Roy can do the impossible" was all Donald said, while Maryanne called back the next day to personally thank Cohn, whose Washington access was attributable to years of Reagan partisanship.

With Maryanne's elevation, the Trump image in New Jersey became much more of a visible family affair than in New York. Her reputation as a prosecutor and a judge rubbed off on Donald, giving his activities there an above-the-fray flavor. So did the frequent appearances in Atlantic City of the smooth and efficient Robert, who was directing the operations there, and the litigation work of Maryanne's husband, ex-prosecutor John Barry, who went from one top Republican law firm to another. Ivana also did her interior decorating stint at the Plaza site, appearing right up to the delivery of the Trump's third child, Eric, in early 1984, and returning a few days after he was born. Then when Donald bought the Hilton and renamed it Trump Castle in 1985, he surprised everyone by installing Ivana to run it. Her clumsy accent may have gotten in the way of her reaching the All-American pinnacle the rest of the family attained in New Jersey, but her early success at the Castle, marked by rapidly rising grosses, attracted a complimentary press, painting her as a queen-by-the-bay, ruling over a successful and opulent palace.

Over the years, the fresh-faced image Trump cultivated in New Jersey blended with the capable and clean image of Governor Kean, and they were seen as inextricably linked, pushing the state forward together in a period of sustained economic growth. Perhaps because of the contribution ban, there was no sense of a compromised governor delivering favors to a big-time donor. It even went unnoticed in the media that the glue that got these forces together, at least originally, was the era's master fixer.

"During the recession when all of us were worried," Kean told the crowd at the gala Plaza opening, "Donald Trump decided to break ground and have faith in New Jersey and in Atlantic City and in our future. And I can only say, thank you very much." Speaking after Kean, the Harrah's chairman praised Donald for bringing the project in on time and under budget, saying it was a "near miracle."

But from Harrah's perspective, the emphasis was on the word "near." Though Donald was, in fact, due a $5 million bonus if he achieved the budget goal, Harrah's declined to pay it, and the litigious Trump did not sue. Indeed, when Harrah's charged in a suit filed more than a year after the opening that he had not met his budget obligations, Donald, who routinely proclaimed to the world that he had, sheepishly conceded it. He did, however, try to shift the blame for the cost overruns to Harrah's, which he said had come up with last-minute changes, and contended that he had completed the hotel "within the substantially increased budget ultimately agreed to by Harrah's in light of the many design and construction changes on which it had insisted." In any event, Donald's own publicly announced budget for the casino had grown from $150 million to $175 million to $190 million and, finally, to $220 million. When even that number was exceeded by an undisclosed amount, it became clear that any project could be brought in under budget if the builder kept changing the budget.

From Donald's perspective, of course, the emphasis, as always, was on the word "Trump," and he did succeed in cajoling, begging, and embarrassing Harrah's into putting his name on the building, as Ed Colanzi's old "in prominence and in perpetuity" resolution had suggested. Since Harrah's already owned and operated one casino in Atlantic City and a few in Nevada, they were understandably adamant about using their own name. Originally, they wanted to call it Harrah's Boardwalk, but Donald argued that it sounded cheap. During these early conversations about a name in 1982, Trump Tower had yet to open, and the Hyatt was Donald's only completed project. So the Trump name, in Harrah's view, had no real dollar value. Trump had tried to get New York officials to use it on the convention center—even offering to waive what he falsely claimed was the $4 million broker fee due him—but they inexplicably preferred to name the building after Jacob Javits, New York's U.S. Senator for a decade or two. Donald finally settled for Harrah's at Trump Plaza, which accurately conveyed who was actually running the casino. Still, he kept the pressure on to change the name and finally, six months after the casino opened, Harrah's agreed to drop its own name and go with Donald's original intention, Trump Plaza.

By November of 1984, the man with the Xanadu dream finally had a casino that appeared to be his. The last step was actually *making* it his.

As long as Donald's deals were constrained by a bank's willingness to finance them, he was successful. He found partners like Hyatt, Equitable, and Harrah's and did what he did best—build and promote. But by 1985 Donald and the banks had begun to believe what they read about him. When Harrah's made its deal with him a few years earlier, company officials had obtained his financial statements and noticed how thin the paper felt. He had nothing in a bank or a market, no hard assets—merely a few pieces of real estate to which he assigned a value. If you believed his assessment of their value, you thought he was a billionaire. If you didn't, you thought he was a young man with promise.

But by 1985 everything he had done—the Hyatt, Trump Tower, Trump Plaza in New York, and the newly renamed Trump Plaza of Atlantic City—looked solid. The banks—particularly Chase and Manufacturers Hanover—were convinced. It was at this midpoint in the decade that they started throwing money at him for the West Side of Manhattan or a casino in Atlantic City. As if that wasn't tempting enough, investment bankers competed with one another to float junk bonds for him. The outrageous availability of all this debt pushed him forward toward the deal table. Just as the difficulty of securing financing had once encouraged the restraint he'd inherited from Fred, the sudden access to funny money lured him into acquisitions that strained hard business sense.

What else could explain his decision in 1985 to acquire total control of two casinos? In the space of a few months, he closed on the $320 million purchase of the Hilton and, in early 1986, borrowed $250 million to buy out Harrah's interest in Trump Plaza. Under his original deal with Harrah's, he had a half stake in a casino that could only produce profit for him. All he had to do was sit back and collect, guaranteed against losses for years. In fact, at the very time he made his move to buy the Plaza, he was asked by a reporter what his greatest deal had been and he said Harrah's, claiming he "got infinite return for nothing." Yet it was Trump who decided to end the partnership. It wasn't that either the Hilton or Harrah's purchases were bad deals, taken individually. But the combination, one right after the other, was a reckless contrast to the measured development judgment Donald had demonstrated in the first ten years of his career.

Harrah's willingness to sell should have been a warning to Donald. One of the most successful casino operators in the world was effectively deciding, after only two years of operation and a huge investment, that the Atlantic City market was too small to sustain two competing entities owned by the same company. Harrah's had already assembled another strong Boardwalk property—called the Chalfonte site—before it entered the joint venture with Donald, but had decided to join Donald rather than build on it. By the time it sold the Plaza to Donald, however, it was clear that the chain had no intention of moving down the Boardwalk and building a new casino on that site. With the success of its casino on the marina, Harrah's had concluded that running two facilities in Atlantic City was a formula for ruin.

Steve Wynn was reluctantly reaching the same conclusion. The owner of the Golden Nugget, the city's most profitable casino, had acquired a site in the marina area in the early eighties. He thought he'd try what Harrah's, and eventually Trump, planned on trying—a Boardwalk and a marina casino. But in 1984 he decided not to build, potentially taking a multimillion-dollar loss on the land purchase. Wynn did make a bid to buy the Hilton in 1985, perhaps because it abutted his own marina property. But his bid was approximately $60 million less in cash than Trump's and rested on Hilton's hypothetical desire to own what Wynn estimated was $84 million worth of land—which he offered to convey to them—in a town where the company couldn't get a casino license. (Wynn's takeover run at the stock of the Hilton Corporation was far more serious but was clearly an investment decision that transcended the two-casino question.) Similarly, Caesars had a second, beautifully located, Boardwalk site, the old Traymore Hotel, on which it never built. Ultimately, Bally's did acquire a second Atlantic City casino and was damaged so badly by the twin experiment that it, like Harrah's, became an object lesson.

Despite the fact that these professional operators were hesitating to try to handle twins, Donald, who'd had the good sense at a younger age to let Hyatt manage the hotel he built on 42nd Street, took on the job of managing two in the space of seven months. Then, within a year, he rushed on to a third. (He might not have stopped even there but state law set a limit of three.)

It started innocently enough, not as if Donald consciously planned to pursue two casinos in 1985. He had appeared to be trying to force Harrah's to sell its Plaza interest to him for some time. His main weapon was his refusal to sign a second contract with the company obligating him to build the garage, a delaying tactic that began shortly after he'd finished spending his and Harrah's money on the land and gotten all the permits. Donald's refusal to build made the Plaza the only casino in Atlantic City without real parking, turning its onetime prime advantage of a location right off the expressway into a bad joke. Harrah's had allowed Donald to take title to the land in his own name only, even though it had paid half the bills. So Donald went so far as to declare the parking site land his, threatening to evict the casino's meager surface parking lot from it.

Harrah's accused Trump in court papers of using the garage as "leverage" to compel a deal, but Harrah's was unsure whether Donald wanted to buy the casino outright or sell out himself. If Trump was ambivalent he certainly made up his mind when he saw the ease with which he could get the financing to purchase the Castle. And it was the acquisition of the Castle—the only other casino on the bay besides Harrah's Marina—that sparked Harrah's competitive anger, an exchange of lawsuits, and ultimately the business resolve on both sides to finally do the Plaza sale.

While Trump's Atlantic City history began on the Plaza site and ran back seven years, it was his decision to buy the Hilton in 1985 that gave him a real, continuing presence in the city and made him a gaming player rather than merely the passive partner of one. While the Plaza deal took four years, from Donald's initial lease negotiations in the spring of 1980 to the grand opening, the Castle acquisition took less than four months. He began negotiating with Barron Hilton in March of 1985, bought the hotel at the end of April, and opened it by June. He has proudly boasted that he purchased the Hilton without ever having taken even a walk-through.

Several months earlier, in February, the city and the industry were shocked when two members of the Casino Control Commission, Carl Zeitz and Joel Jacobson, decided to vote against a Hilton license. The deadlocked two-to-two vote of a commission awaiting the appointment of a fifth member sent the lodging and gaming conglomerate out of town, tarred and feathered. Longtime state labor leader Jacobson had been visibly upset during the public hearings over Hilton's ties to Sidney Korshak, the prominent Chicago mob attorney who'd been on Hilton's payroll for a decade and a half. What may have also angered Jacobson, who has since died, was that Hilton also had a history of labor unrest, Korshak's labor peace influence notwithstanding.

The moment Hilton was denied a license on February 28, Donald leaped into the picture, angling to buy. Ben Lambert, a Trump friend and Hilton director, had been keeping Donald informed. When the commission voted in March to give Hilton a rehearing based on the company's claim of new information, Hilton had a decision to make. Either it sold, though a rehearing suggested that it still had a chance for a license and would be able to avert fire sale conditions, or it took its chances on a second-go-round vindication.

Pushed by Steve Wynn's takeover bid and internal rumblings in his company, Barron Hilton decided to go with Trump, who'd upped his bid rather quickly from $250 to $320 million. Donald had never before dealt at this high a price level, but Manufacturers Hanover was assuring him it would finance the project, and there was a wide-open bond market eager to refinance it, even though the $320 million would hardly be all he needed. Hilton had made a commitment to the state for at least $11.7 million in roadway improvements that Trump would be assuming, and Donald also knew he would have at least $20 million in closing and casino setup costs before he could take in a cent.

Still, taken on its own, the deal had a rationale. It was a sensational property, with a 60,000-square-foot casino and 615 hotel rooms, the same as the Plaza. But the eight-acre site, with its thirty-foot casino ceilings, had a spaciousness that dwarfed the claustrophobic Plaza. And it had the 3,000-car garage the Plaza lacked. Cast in a green suburban setting next to the bay, it offered a comfort level for middle-class gamblers that the tortured urban stretches near the Boardwalk never could.

The problem was Trump bought the casino without forcing himself to choose between it and the Plaza, and then he paid a hundred million more for the Hilton than he would pay a few months later to buy out a similarly sized casino-hotel he'd built himself on the Boardwalk. The thought that he might be overpaying a company with no alternative but to sell never seemed to occur to him; neither did the reasonable concern that two casinos might be one too many for a tiny organization with no casino experience.

Donald signed a contract on April 27, 1985, and went immediately to the DGE for license approval. He was treated with reverence. No one seemed to remember that he'd just passed the character and integrity test in the 1982 licensing and that DGE had expressly found then that neither he nor his corporate entity could demonstrate the business and casino experience necessary for a license. This question had also not been resolved in Donald's second appearance before DGE and the CCC in 1984, since he'd sought licensing as Harrah's partner and Harrah's clearly had the ability and experience. Despite this history, the quick-and-easy license for the Castle was the first the commission had ever granted to an applicant with no gaming background. To top it off, the key employee licensed to run the operation was Ivana, whose only prior job experience was modeling and interior decorating.

While DGE and CCC rushed to approve Donald's bond financing mechanisms for the purchase, one commissioner, Joel Jacobson, voted against a resolution exempting Trump's bondholders from having to qualify as financial sources.

Jacobson went out of his way to separate his financing objection from Trump personally, whom he praised, but he assailed "the array of Rube Goldberg non-functioning corporations" set up "to disguise" the fact that "the only asset that stands behind these bonds is the casino-hotel." Since the statute clearly required that anyone who holds securities in a casino, including bonds, qualify for a license, Jacobson charged that Attorney General Kimmelman's ruling that Donald's unprecedented bond sale was exempt from review was an "erosion of the statutory requirements."

Jacobson was a lone prophetic voice attempting to rein in the wild bond financing that was taking over the industry. DGE and the other members of the CCC had taken the position on the previous Bally's and Claridge applications that where bonds were widely distributed and freely traded, the holders didn't have to qualify. While Jacobson had also opposed those sales, he pointed out that Trump was now taking this ruling a step further and privately placing, at least initially, the Trump bonds. Trump was also the first individual, rather than a publicly traded company, to be permitted to go to the bond market, meaning there was literally nothing behind the bonds but an untested operator.

The new Donald was willing to load his casino with debt. He went to Drexel's Michael Milken again, but encountered the same stubborn insistence on a 10 percent Trump equity contribution. In the end, Donald's first wholly owned casino and first venture in the public markets led to a grand total of $352 million worth of mortgage-backed bonds, issued by Bear Stearns, an investment banking house so determined to enter the casino business it was apparently willing to top anything Drexel had to offer. Donald also made an immediate $70 million capital contribution to cover improvement costs—but all of it was borrowed from Manufacturers Hanover, one of the few major New York banks willing to invest in a casino. He was clearly determined to make his new casino the best that borrowed money could buy or build.

It was, of course, impossible for DGE to qualify every individual who bought a casino bond, but that was hardly the point of Jacobson's persistent argument. Even the commission chairman, Trump backer Walter Read, conceded that the CCC had "always tried to encourage the use of traditional financing sources, such as banks," adding that "it was heartening to see that such financing has become the rule of the Atlantic City casino industry." But neither Read nor anyone else would slow down the rush to Trump's gigantic bond sale, the first of four that the commission would authorize for Donald, allowing him to issue almost $1.3 billion in notes to the public, as if there were no limit to the revenue that quarter slots and blackjack could generate. The commission was allowing the financial foundation underlying its protected industry to become as soft as the sandy earth beneath the casinos.

The experience and financing questions aside, the DGE and CCC also skipped blithely past the Trump character and integrity issues that were the heart of its legal mandate. Neither confronted the obvious first question: If an affiliation with Sidney Korshak could sink Hilton, why didn't Roy Cohn taint Donald Trump? If a mob-tied lawyer on a $50,000-a-year retainer who rarely talked to any top Hilton executives could nonetheless cost the company a license, why wasn't Trump even questioned about his ties to his principal lawyer, who told one reporter that Donald called him "fifteen to twenty times a day, always asking what's the status of this, what's the status of that?"

With clients who ranged from John Gotti to the sons of Carlo Gambino, Cohn reportedly hosted gatherings of the commission itself—which included the heads of the five crime families—at his town house. His closest mob confidant and client, Tony Salerno, was so involved in Atlantic City that he was believed to have sanctioned the murders of the hit men who killed Scarfo's predecessor, boasting on federal tapes: "I'm the fucking boss, that's who I am. Connecticut is mine; New Jersey is mine." One Cohn aide specifically remembers a 1983 get-together at Cohn's town house living room that supposedly included the lawyer and his two clients—Trump and Salerno—right around the time that Salerno's S&A Concrete was building Trump Plaza, the Third Avenue residential tower. Yet no DGE report even considered the possibility that Cohn's mob liaisons—from Salerno to the infamous John Cody—might have been used to facilitate Trump construction projects. In fact, the agency's top investigator conceded in a court deposition that they had not even looked at any of Trump's subcontractors when they initially licensed him.

DGE was also oblivious to the implications of the Cohn/Trump relationship that were clearly related to casino operations. If Korshak's ties with the mob-run hotel workers was at the heart of the CCC problem with Hilton, why were Cohn and Trump's cozy connections with the same union unimportant? The head of the New York local of the Hotel Workers, Vito Pitta, who acknowledges that he was "very friendly" with Cohn, signed a separate contract with Trump at the very moment that Donald's Castle application was pending before the CCC. Donald eagerly broke ranks with the city's Hotel Association on the eve of a 1985 strike by Pitta's union to sign this agreement, pleasing Pitta so much that he called the Scarfo crime family overlords running Local 54 in Atlantic City on Trump's behalf, telling them that Donald "would be no problem for the local there." A year later, Trump severed himself from the Hotel Association in Atlantic City as well, signed his own contract with Local 54, and was virtually the only owner spared a bitter strike. "They have good relations with him in Atlantic City," said Pitta, "as good as we have here."

Predictably, Cohn was even tied at the hip to Korshak, who took the extraordinary step of contradicting his client Hilton's attempt before the CCC to minimize their relationship and released thank-you notes from Hilton in the middle of the hearing. Korshak's actions so damaged Hilton that he indirectly helped deliver the casino to Trump. Not only were Sidney and his brother, Marshall, frequently on the phone to the town house, they were the lawyers for Cohn's tawdry parking lot business, which also controlled lots in Chicago and was the subject of a federal probe there as well.

Obviously, one reason DGE overlooked the Cohn connection was that he was wrapped in a cloak of respectability—extending from the White House to the governor who appointed the casino investigators. Yet unlike the frequently indicted Cohn, Korshak had never been charged with a crime. And unlike Korshak, Cohn wound up disbarred in 1986 after a prolonged disciplinary probe and hearing that featured Trump's appearance as a fawning character witness. Years before that, Martindale Hubbell, the prestigious directory of the American Bar Association, had refused to even list Cohn's law firm, stating it was unable to "develop a file of confidential recommendations to support the necessary rating for the senior member of the firm."

But it wasn't just Cohn that DGE missed. By the time the agency recommended the Castle license, Mike Mathews was in jail and there was clearly no impediment to a review of the 1984 allegations pursued by the FBI about the Shapiro conduit contributions for Trump. The long-moribund Polish worker case had finally begun receiving press attention in New York, and civil suits were making it harder and harder for investigators to ignore the obvious implications for the Trump Organization. Nonetheless, the DGE reports on Trump during this Kimmelman era were so scant and swift that they made the DGE probe of 1981 seem thorough.

Armed with his instant license, Trump met his mid-June deadline and opened his Castle for the peak season. His decision to name Ivana to run the casino, however, caused a wide rift within his company and his family. Robert had wanted the job himself, and ever since he had tried to downplay Ivana's interior decorating role during the construction of the Plaza, Trump insiders had sensed a tension between the two. Robert was so disappointed about being bypassed that he told friends in the company that he was thinking about leaving. Donald's explanation was that Robert was "so good with the bankers and regulators" that he couldn't afford to lose him to a single property. Fred finally intervened and spoke with both his sons, piecing the family company back together. Ivana, meanwhile, began working a few days a week until she gradually got a grasp of the casino business. By late 1986 she was spending most weekday nights in Atlantic City, working 7:00 A.M. to 9:00 P.M., fully in charge of the operation.

Four months after the Castle opened, the first news reports of Trump's agreement to buy the Plaza from Harrah's appeared, although the details of the deal, and the ongoing hostilities and lawsuit, delayed the sale until early 1986. For this purchase, his $250 million bond sale, also handled through Bear Stearns, would raise funds that exceeded the nearly $60 million up-front payment he had to pay Harrah's and the $152 million in outstanding bank debt. The first bond bonanza had gone so well he decided to seek financing that left him with an excess $30 million or so to cover renovations and whatever else was needed. Trump made no significant capital infusion of his own, borrowed or otherwise. In addition to the bond debt, he gave Harrah's a $17 million note and assumed $11 million in mortgages due on properties underlying the garage. Still, the $278 million debt was less daunting than what he'd assumed at the Castle.

DGE and CCC approved Donald's acquisition of Harrah's interest routinely in the spring of 1986, without any apparent examination of the scandal exploding in New York that involved so many people close to Donald, particularly his lawyer Stanley Friedman, already under state and federal indictment, and his longtime ally on the Board of Estimate, Donald Manes, who'd committed suicide while under FBI scrutiny. The regulators certainly knew of Trump's association with both men since DGE had briefly noted in one report Donald's practice of personally authorizing free rooms for Friedman, though he had no gambling credit line, and had been informed by the Queens District Attorney of Trump Plaza's refusal to comply with a subpoena seeking junket records for two notorious Manes bagmen, Geoffrey Lindenauer and Jerome Driesen.

One issue did arise, however, that could not be ignored and would test even Donald's charm with the two agencies. In June of 1986, when the Castle came up for a renewal of its 1985 license, Donald faced his first tough run through the CCC process. Though in the end, a majority of the commission would approve the license, one new commissioner, Valerie Armstrong, opposed it and battered Trump witnesses during this and two more hearings in 1987 about inconsistencies in the prior testimony of Donald and two of his Dreyer & Traub attorneys.

While Chairman Read, unlike Armstrong, ultimately supported the Trump license, his disdainful remarks about the Dreyer & Traub testimony were subsequently interpreted by DGE as an indication of the commission's view that the Trump lawyers lacked credibility.

The issue was the road improvement near the Castle that Trump had assumed responsibility to partially pay for when he bought the Hilton. While Ribis assured the commission during the original Castle hearings that Trump was committed to making the roadway contribution, Robert Trump told State Department of Transportation (DOT) officials five days later that he could not state for certain that the Trump Organization would honor this "unconditional" contractual commitment. Barely a month later, Donald met with the DOT commissioner and sharply criticized the planned improvements. Within a few months, Robert was threatening the commissioner that the Trump Organization would tie up DOT in court for ten years unless it radically altered the roadway plan, cutting the cost to a small fraction of its estimated $36 to $60 million budget. (Trump was supposed to split the price evenly with two other casinos.) When DOT rejected Trump's alternate plan, the threatened lawsuit was filed.

Some of the commissioners at CCC clearly believed that Trump had decided not to finance the improvement well before Ribis vowed at the 1985 hearing that the Trump Organization would "stand in the shoes" of Hilton and fulfill the pledge. This problem was compounded when Donald and other company witnesses at the 1986 renewal hearing tried to lay the blame for their abdication of the roadway commitment on Hilton, which they contended had not fully informed them about the cost and nature of the improvements. In his attempt to distance himself from knowledge of the roadway provision, Donald painted quite a different picture of himself as dealmaker than the on-the-case, detail man who stars in his books. He professed ignorance of a costly provision that appeared in the purchase contract and the bond offering, both of which expressly stated an estimated project cost. Since he was also claiming that he thought the roadway plan was nonbinding, Donald had to concede he hadn't read the Hilton's state environmental permit, which was predicated on it or his own similarly conditioned casino license.

Having distanced himself from any knowledge of roadway improvements, Donald then felt free to ridicule the DOT plan, which called for an expensive overpass, until a commission questioner stopped him to ask: "Did you know that the plans which you called a disaster were not in fact prepared by DOT, but were prepared by Wilbur Smith Associates, your own consultant?"

"It wouldn't matter to me who they were prepared by," replied Donald, who claimed he didn't know that he and the state had retained the same consultant. "I mean, Wilbur Smith could make mistakes, too. We all make mistakes."

Four Hilton attorneys wound up offering a totally contrary view of Trump's knowledge about the roadway project in sworn testimony, including one who claimed to have had a conversation directly with Donald at the contract signing the previous April, when Donald, holding the roadway plans in his hand, said he didn't like them and questioned the lawyer about how binding the deal was. But the most damaging evidence was DGE's retrieval from Dreyer & Traub files of a copy of a draft of the purchase agreement that was underlined and annotated throughout by a Trump lawyer. Right beside the single paragraph that contained the $11.7 million roadway improvement estimate were the initials "DJT" and the words "read agreement."

Once DGE found this damning evidence, however, it began acting as if its own smoking gun was too hot to handle. Under new leadership but as acquiescent as ever, the agency concluded that the contradictory versions essentially canceled each other out and that no one could really determine precisely what had happened.* A baffled Armstrong said she was "unable to understand the Division's dismissal" of the evidence corroborating the Hilton attorneys or the Trump Organization's refusal "to explain or refute any of the matters" raised in the DGE report.

Chairman Read said he found Donald's handling of the whole matter "perplexing and unsatisfactory," but he and the rest of the commissioners other than Armstrong, all of whom were by then Kean appointees, rubber-stamped the license application.

Ironically, at the very same time in late 1985 and early 1986 that Trump was refusing to meet a state roadway commitment, other state officials awarded him a twenty-five-year lease on the publicly owned marina next to the Castle. Trump's evasion of his roadway obligations was an acknowledged violation of the environmental permit issued by the state for the Hilton facility, yet the same environmental agency that announced this violation at a CCC hearing took no action to

---

* Trump eventually reached a settlement with the state transportation department on the road improvements, but largely on his term. Two years late, he agreed to pay his share of what was reduced to a $16 million improvement, and his $5 million contribution was scheduled to be paid out over time. More than half a decade later, work has yet to begin on the project.

enforce the permit and then awarded him the marina lease. Trump won the lease despite intense competition from a local group of investors, whose bid was preferred by a Citizens' Advisory Committee set up to advise state DEP. When the losing bidders charged that the state process had been rigged in Trump's favor and sued, Trump wound up entering into a confidential settlement with them.

The marina lease and the roadway turnabout at DEP were manifestations of Donald's bonds with the Kean administration. The glue remained Roger Stone, the Trump lobbyist who had again managed Kean's election campaign in 1985 and was so close to the governor's office he hired Kean's retiring chief of staff. When Roy Cohn became very ill in 1984, Donald began to turn more and more to Stone, not just on New Jersey matters but as a kind of Cohn-substitute. Unhappily, Donald discovered that no one could replace Cohn. While Stone usually avoided direct interfacing with state agencies on Trump's behalf, he did personally lobby for Trump on occasion—pursuing, for example, the state permits needed for a controversial 1,300-car employee parking lot located near the Castle. The lot provoked a storm of protest because it was literally at the foot of the only bridge leading into a small town, Brigantine, but Stone won another DEP reversal and Trump got his permit.

The most important consequence, however, of the Kean/Trump alliance was that the acquiescence of the governor's CCC and DGE combined to embolden Donald, enticing him past the Castle and Plaza to unsuccessful takeover runs at most of the public companies with Atlantic City casinos, as well as the acquisition of Resorts, the construction of the Taj Mahal, and, finally, the purchase of the Atlantis, the Penthouse site, and the long-desolate Kenny Shapiro parking garage block near the Plaza.

Each of these gambits caused flickers of CCC controversy involving issues of runaway debt, anticompetitive conduct, and market monopoly, as well as more misleading testimony and broken public commitments. Yet the Kean majorities looked the other way until their concurrence became an instinct and effectively turned the future of the town over to the man with the golden touch. In 1987, with the Castle and Plaza doing well, the decision to go with Donald may have temporarily looked sound. But without any regulatory restraint, Trump's appetite would become a curse—for him and the town.

9

TAKING ON
THE TENANTS

The impediments that can arise to baffle a great and swelling career are strange and various, in some instances all the cross waves of life must be cut by the strong swimmer. With other personalities there is a chance, or force, that happily allies itself with them; or they quite unconsciously ally themselves with it, and find that there is a tide that bears them on. An unconscious drift in the direction of right, virtue, duty? These are banners of mortal manufacture. Nothing is proved; all is permitted.

—*Theodore Dreiser*, The Titan

AT QUARTER PAST TEN on a Thursday morning, John Moore sat sequestered in his three-room apartment overlooking Central Park. He ran a struggling record company, but the forty-six-year-old bachelor and minor-league entrepreneur was in no rush to make it to his nearby office. The phone rang constantly with calls from reporters, and Moore was in his glory—glib, arrogant, pushing his cause into print. After a decade as a loner, the twice-divorced and basically self-employed Moore was used to setting his own daily agenda. Today the only item on his Allentown redbook calendar was the latest skirmish in a war with the man who had suddenly made him newsworthy: Donald J. Trump, owner of the luxury building at 100 Central Park South where Moore lived.

The twelfth-floor Moore apartment—with fourteen-foot ceilings, a fireplace, a huge kitchen formed by combining two rooms, and a wall full of living room windows—was located in a building with twenty-four-hour doormen, prominent tenants like fashion designer Arnold Scaasi, and a prestige address along a four-block runway of park-front affluence. The ambience abetted the Social Register image Moore had spent years inventing for himself, a status far beyond his means or achievement. In reality, Moore's mere $691 monthly rent, protected under the city's rent stabilization laws, would not buy him an unregulated studio anywhere else in fashionable Manhattan, where rental occupancy was at an all-time high. Nonetheless, by this January morning in 1985, Moore hadn't been paying any rent for several years and had run up a $10,000 arrearage. Before he ended his one-man rent strike in 1987, he would live free for four years, all the while fending off improvement requests from the building's manager, including attempts to paint his entire apartment. His rent holdout was apparently as much an attempt to dodge the expense, and savor the much-needed savings, as it was a sign of protest. The apartment had become a vital prop in his deceptive play, and if he got to use it at no cost, all the better.

Though Moore was half Italian, he worked hard at portraying himself as Manhattan's last available WASP, with a country-club air and a stylish, barrel-chested brashness. He listed himself in the phone book as John C. Moore III, claimed to be a Tiffany heir from the monied Locust Valley enclave on Long Island, dated flashy models half his age, played daily tennis, weathered New York winters in a full-length, seventy-pound black-bear coat, and enjoyed his own smug brand of put-down humor. No one in the social circles in which Moore floated was aware that one of his partners in the record business was tied to the Gambino crime family, and even John would later insist that he was ignorant of that fact.

Reporters had been calling Moore for an entire week, ever since the enforcement division of the state's housing agency announced its decision to bring a harassment case against Donald Trump. John Moore, who often said he was chosen president of the building's Tenants Association because he "mixed the best drinks," was finally getting the attention he believed he deserved, pitted in every newspaper head-to-head against his famous opponent. Moore relished both media versions of the conflict—his portrayal of the tenants as the beleaguered victims of an avaricious Trump and Trump's repeated attacks on the tenants as "millionaires" hiding behind the rent stabilization laws.

Moore had never met or spoken to Trump, but he'd helped form a tenants association in 1981, shortly after Donald bought their fifteen-story, sixty-seven-year-old building. Before Trump's purchase, the six-foot-two-inch, contemptuously superior Moore had hardly spoken to any of his eighty or so neighbors, though he'd lived among them since he bribed a doorman, super, manager, and outgoing tenant in 1973, buying his way at first into a tiny second-floor apartment in the back of the building. Somehow the fear of Trump had instantly catapulted this heterogeneous and unlikely group of rich and poor tenants into a united front, with John Moore as their democratically designated leader. The tenants were galvanized by the transparent purpose behind Trump's purchase—he clearly intended to vacate the building and replace it with another towering condominium, one that would generate millions in profits.

The building was purchased for next to nothing—the price would never be revealed, but newspaper estimates put it as low as a million—because it came as a minor part of a grand package: Donald had simultaneously bought 106 Central Park South, the aging Barbizon Plaza Hotel, from the same owners. Moore's building sat at the corner of Sixth Avenue, occupying two thirds of the block, while the Barbizon rose thirty-eight stories high both next door to and behind 100 Central Park South on Sixth Avenue and 58th Street. Trump, who'd just started construction of Trump Tower a few blocks away on Fifth Avenue, envisioned a single huge and elegant condominium development on the combined sites, with floors of commercial space fronting 200 feet along Central Park South and along a full block of Sixth Avenue.

Architects went to work immediately, designing what Trump envisioned as his greatest success, a sumptuous building scheduled for completion at the peak of the eighties boom market. Only John Moore, and his group of feisty tenants, stood in the way of this dream. The canny Moore had, in fact, hired a Tenants Association architect back in 1982 to draw up renovation plans for the building that fulfilled each tenant's deepest desire. In addition to a plan, the architect produced a formula based on the relative resale value of each apartment, and every tenant was dunned a monthly amount by the Tenants Association, proportionate to the purported value of his or her apartment, with higher floors and corner apartments paying more. The tenants had already been fighting Trump for three and a half years, using the bulk of the $200,000 they had raised to retain the law firm of Fischbein Olivieri Rozenholc Badillo, one of the city's fiercest tenant advocates. Moore and lead partner David Rozenholc's courtroom and press tactics had so stymied Trump that by 1985 the war with 100 Central Park South's tenants had become the most exasperating business experience of his early career, costing him millions and tarnishing his image. And now, the state's decision to bring the harassment action was putting Trump on the defensive legally, posing the real threat of a damning governmental finding against him. As he sat in his apartment a week after the state order mandating a hearing was issued, Moore sensed a turning point.

The phone rang again, and a friendly voice at the other end asked for John Moore.

"This is John Moore."

"Hi, John. This is Donald Trump. You know, John, I saw you on television this week, and you look like a really nice guy."

"Who is this?" interrupted Moore.

"This is Donald Trump," repeated the voice.

"I've experienced this kind of practical joke quite frequently," said Moore. "Give me your telephone number and I'll call you back."

"That sounds reasonable," said the voice, offering a phone number.

Moore did not know that this was a commonplace Trump tactic: Don't use a secretary, make a person-to-person initial contact, cut right through to the perceived opponent, and instill an air of intimacy and trust in a relationship that from afar seems naturally combative. Even though he was a bit unnerved, Moore returned the call minutes later, and he got straight through to Trump.

"You look like a reasonable guy," Donald picked up where he'd left off. "I think if I had gotten involved in this in the beginning, maybe we wouldn't be in this mess today. This is just costing time and money, and I am sorry the whole thing happened."

Donald was obviously trying to distance himself from the acts of his own managing agents, lawyers, and top staffers. Moore found the ploy absurd, but wanted, for tactical reasons, to leave open the possibility that Trump had been too busy to pay attention to the petty assaults on the people of 100 Central Park South—an opening that would give Donald a way out. Of course Moore knew that it was Donald himself, not any agent, who had written the city's Human Resources Administration in 1982 offering the vacant apartments in the building as emergency housing for the homeless, alarming every tenant and provoking a cold rebuff from the city. Moore also knew that the foundation for the day-to-day acts of harassment cited in the state complaint had been laid years earlier in public submissions to the city by Donald himself.

For example, in September 1981, shortly after Trump bought the building, he began to take legal steps to clear it, filing a series of applications at the city agencies that administered the rent control and stabilization laws, which covered virtually all of its eighty tenant households. He signed requests for demolition and eviction permits, sought authority to refuse to renew leases, and submitted Buildings Department plans for his new 165-unit tower, with penthouse apartments scheduled to go for millions apiece.

The overwhelming caseload of these agencies, the paralysis prompted by the sweeping legislative changes in rent regulation laws adopted in 1983, and the filing of harassment complaints by several 100 Central Park South tenants had prevented any early adjudication of these key, building-clearing applications. In the only individual case the city agencies fully heard, Trump was ordered by one of the agencies, the Conciliation and Appeals Board, to renew one tenant's three-year lease. The CAB ignored three letters from Trump lawyers in 1983 asking for a full hearing on the demolition permit, including one offering a list of twenty-one available hearing dates, acquiescing to objections from tenant lawyer Rozenholc.

When a new state law transferred authority over rent-regulated buildings to the state's Department of Housing and Community Renewal in 1984, Moore and the tenants began filing detailed harassment allegations, one after another, with the department's new enforcement division. Finally, on January 3, 1985, after eight months of DHCR review of these complaints, the division issued an order requiring full hearings and charging Trump with "an unrelenting, systematic and illegal campaign" whose "singleminded intent" was to "force the tenants from their housing accommodations at the earliest possible time."

Instead of waiting until his eviction and demolition permits were approved, Trump and his agents had, according to the enforcement division's hearing notice, tried to force the tenants out by "verbally intimidating" them with claims that the demolition was "certain and imminent," by instituting "unwarranted litigation" against a variety of individual tenants, by permitting "breaches in the security of the building," and by "interfering with or decreasing a broad panorama of basic and essential services."

Moore knew that it would take months of testimony to substantiate the state complaint, but he also recognized the value of its allegations as dramatic leverage over the publicity-conscious Trump. It was clear to Moore, in fact, that the order had instigated Donald's conciliatory phone call.

"The problem, Donald, is that the whole thing did happen," Moore began telling Trump. "You hurt a lot of people in this building. Maybe it was your agents, or maybe you were receiving legal advice which didn't work to your benefit. Maybe you neglected to sit on what you were trying to do, and watch it closely enough. You frightened a lot of people in this building and I think you probably saw the looks on the faces of the ladies that appeared in the TV interviews."

"Yeah, I did," Donald responded. "They looked kind of concerned."

"Well, they are concerned," retorted Moore, "because they have been suffering under you for a number of years now, and it is pretty rough."

"I would not have wanted this to happen." Trump got to his point. "Normally, I do things myself, like I made this phone call to you. So maybe we can try and see, you know, if we can resolve our difficulties. I don't know whether there would be any purpose to our getting together for a meeting, but I would like to come over to your office or whatever, and let us kick around some ideas."

"I have to think about that. In principle I have no problem in listening to some ideas, but I would like to think about it and talk to David Rozenholc," said Moore, introducing the name of the tenant lawyer who Trump had already decided was a hard-nosed and difficult foe.

"What kind of guy is he?" pressed Donald. "Is he reasonable?"

"He is a terrific guy," answered Moore. "A very bright man, and I want to chat with David, and I will get back to you."

Moore and his executive committee of four other tenants had picked Rozenholc to represent the association after entertaining offers from several dozen interested parties, and though the firm was only four years old at the time, it seemed to have just the right combination of legal talent and political access for the job.

Born in 1945 in Russia near the Chinese border to a father jailed in Siberia, Rozenholc was raised in Israel, immigrated to the Bronx at age sixteen, and went to City College and Rutgers Law School. A high-strung, disheveled, vulgar bulldog of a trial lawyer, Rozenholc's method was to pontificate, explode, connive, and berate incessantly, expecting to be paid well for each weapon in the arsenal of personality disorders at his tactical command. "I have a hard time being nice to people who are trying to fuck me, or being pleasant to people I'm trying to fuck" was his philosophy. One Trump lawyer tells the story of how, when he met with Rozenholc in his office, Rozenholc took his shoes and socks off, put his bare feet up on the desk, and announced: "I like to eat a Christian a day, and I haven't eaten yet today."

By contrast, his partner, forty-three-year-old Rick Fischbein, was a mediating, thoughtful insider with Rolodexes of powerful connections. Democratic district leader in Chelsea on the West Side of Manhattan during the seventies, he befriended John LoCicero, who was an aide to then Village congressman Ed Koch and remained Koch's top political attaché throughout the mayor's years in City Hall. Fischbein's twenty-year friendship with LoCicero gave him access with city officials, as did his equally long friendship with City Housing Commissioner Tony Gliedman.

A third partner, Herman Badillo, was the city's preeminent Hispanic politician—a former Bronx borough president and congressman who had run, unsuccessfully, for mayor three times. In January 1985 he was preparing for another ill-fated run, against the seemingly invincible Ed Koch. While Rozenholc denounced politicians as "whores," Fischbein and Badillo had close ties to everyone from Manhattan Borough President Andrew Stein to Governor Mario Cuomo.

When Moore mentioned Rozenholc during this first conversation with Trump, Donald was well aware that the flamboyant attorney had already handed him a number of courtroom defeats. Not only had Rozenholc blocked two Trump attempts to force individual tenants out, he'd convinced two lower court judges that Donald had acted in "bad faith," winning one finding that Trump had served a dispossess notice on a tenant for nonpayment of rent even though the tenant had a canceled check for the month in question. In a third case, Rozenholc got an injunction barring Trump from evicting six tenants who refused to comply with the bizarre demand—at least in a building with a pending demolition application—that they restore their apartments to their original condition. But Rozenholc's most important early victory was delaying the CAB hearings so long the case wound up inherited by DHCR, and it was surely not lost on Trump that the CAB's executive director left government to join the Rozenholc firm soon thereafter. Rozenholc's track record made it clear, even to Donald, that he was up against an opponent who knew how to play his own game, so he was hesitant when Moore insisted on conferring with Rozenholc about their first head-to-head meeting.

A week after Trump's initial call, Moore phoned him to say that he had talked to Rozenholc and that the two were willing to meet.

"I hear he's pretty difficult," Trump objected, asking again if Moore thought Rozenholc could be "reasonable."

"In any event," Moore replied, "I am going to come with my attorney."

"Well, I'll just come alone," said Trump.

"I don't think that's advisable," Moore countered. "You should bring your attorney. And if you don't, at least bring with you a letter stating that you know I'm going to bring my attorney and that you consent to meeting under those circumstances." Trump said he would look into it and decide on his own.

A lunch was set for February 12, a few days after the state hearings were scheduled to begin. Moore and Rozenholc decided not to mention these scheduled settlement talks to Joyce Goldstein, the state enforcement counsel who was trying the case against Trump and speaking with them almost daily. Neither did they inform the tenants, with the exception of a couple of top leaders.

Hours before the lunch, Moore called Trump and switched locations, asking that they meet instead at The Brook, an elegant and exclusive private men's club on East 54th Street, where Moore, who was a member, could reserve a private room. Moore said later, in a sworn affidavit, that he and Rozenholc decided they didn't want to meet in a public restaurant where they wouldn't know "who might be seated at surrounding tables" or whether "photographers might be present for some purpose." The Brook features a fifty-foot-long table with candelabra and all-day settings on the main floor, as well as small upstairs dining rooms which Moore describes as "mahogany-paneled as if J. P. Morgan had done [them]." Moore felt the Social Register trappings would put them on a level playing field with Trump, just as Sally Goodgold had used her West Side apartment years earlier to show Donald how unimpressed with him she was.

"I can't get into a club like this because I'm a five-foot-six fat Jew from the Bronx," Rozenholc greeted Donald. "You can't because you're from Queens and low-class." Moore, dressed in his customized Turnbull and Asser shirts and the same sort of Morty Sill suit that Michael Douglas would make famous in the movie *Wall Street*, patronizingly guided Donald and his in-house counsel Milton Goldfine to their chairs.

Trump reached his hand out for a menu, but the waiter stood stiffly still. "Mee-ster Moore," said the waiter, "it seems that your guest wants to know what the specials are." Moore watched Trump withdraw his hand clumsily, "like the retractable arm of a space shuttle," he would later gleefully claim. Moore could sense Donald's growing discomfort.

Donald was, from Rozenholc's perspective, too friendly and engaging as the lunch began, complimenting Moore and him and the food and the place. "I'd love to settle this case so I can hire you," he said to Rozenholc, stressing just how impressed he was with the Fischbein firm's work in the case. The attorney, finding the seduction disingenuous, responded: "The only way I'll be your lawyer is if I fuck you in this case." (Moore would claim that at some point during the protracted negotiations with Trump he, too, got a Trump job offer, relayed through an intermediary.)

Donald started to ramble, asking Moore what he thought he would have had to pay the tenants as an inducement to vacate if he had tried back in 1981. He cited figures from a major *New York* magazine article, written by Tony Schwartz and still on the newsstands, that quoted Moore as saying that for $50,000 apiece, offered at the time Trump bought the building, "most of the tenants would have been clicking their heels on their way out." Trump told Moore and Rozenholc he agreed with Schwartz's final vacate estimate of $6 million, including $500,000 payments to a few holdouts. Schwartz's conclusion was that, had Trump tried the congenial approach, rather than playing a farcical game of "fumbling and bumbling" hardball, his grand tower worth hundreds of millions would by now be rising into the sky.

Moore refused to be drawn into this conversation, sensing that Donald was trying to get him to put a pricetag on each tenant's exit, still possibly thinking of a buyout. But since Donald had announced at the start that he thought the Schwartz article was fair, Moore couldn't resist returning to it, pointing out that Schwartz, who would later author *The Art of the Deal*, had called Trump's forces at 100 Central Park South "the gang that couldn't shoot straight, a fugue of failure." Not only had Schwartz proven that the great dealmaker had spent a fortune because he refused to stoop to nickel-and-dime deals with common tenants, but he'd also established, with Rozenholc's brilliant help, that Donald's attempt to qualify under state law formulas for a demolition permit was hopelessly doomed.

Trump's plans for the site, submitted as part of his demolition application, did not create enough new apartments in the 100 Central Park South portion of the total project to meet the legal requirement that the new structure contain 20 percent more units than the old. Schwartz and Rozenholc also showed that he had juggled the income and expense figures for the building in order to meet the strictly regulated standard that prevented him from demolishing it if the yearly return was at least 8.5 percent of the assessed value. To try to minimize the building's revenue, Trump had listed $107,000 in legal fees he'd paid to try to evict eight tenants and had concealed $137,000 in bonuses he tacked on to the store rents. With these figures adjusted, Trump was making a 15 percent profit on the building and couldn't tear it down.

"You mustn't have liked being referred to as 'the gang that couldn't shoot straight,'" Moore teased.

"You have to look at the article as a whole," replied Trump, stunning Moore. "If nothing else, it brought attention to my real estate. That building is worth much more now. As a result of this article I have had countless offers to sell the building, to condo and co-op converters, around the $30,000,000 area." Trump added that he'd bought the building so cheaply the contract barred him from revealing its price, and Moore commented that it was "amazing" that Donald had found "something positive" in the article or in the whole situation at 100 Central Park South.

"Sell, Donald," Moore urged. "Sell at $30 million. Please, make your money. Take your money. Make your huge profit and just go away. It's not personal, but people will always be afraid living with you as a landlord."

"Well, you know," Donald responded, "it may be just as good an idea for me to sell it because if I co-op it, or convert it, or condo it myself, there could be tax problems, and there could be regulatory problems, as well."

Somehow, Trump, Moore, and Rozenholc drifted into a conversation about the concept of a sale of the building to the tenants, with Goldfine listening quietly. Trump, Moore, and Goldfine would provide affidavits a few weeks later that differed in their accounts of who had initiated the rather revealing chat, but neither side disputed the fact that they began discussing a purchase deal in grand detail.

While a sale to the tenants was only one of several options discussed, it was clearly the one that Moore and Rozenholc found most enticing. Indeed, Rozenholc would later contend in an interview that "the idea to buy the building was mine," adding that "from the moment John came to me" about Trump's initial approach, "I thought, let me use our leverage to buy the building." At the right price, the Tenants Association would control a potential gold mine, with twenty apartments vacated since Trump's purchase and thus available for lucrative resale as part of a co-oping of the building. This prospect—which would put Moore and Rozenholc in control of a multimillion-dollar property—had long intrigued the two and, though it was hardly the goal of the building's poorest tenants, their pursuit of it at the expense of other alternatives would in the coming months shape, skew, and even extend the conflict over 100 Central Park South. Most of the tenants Moore mentioned in his chats with reporters—especially the fifteen women over the age of sixty living alone—could not afford to buy their apartments no matter who owned the building. Their primary interest was in compelling Trump to execute a binding nonharassment commitment and getting reliable maintenance and repair restored, not in trying to provoke a cheap purchase by the association.

But to the wandering entrepreneur Moore, a purchase began to look like the deal of a lifetime. At the very least, he calculated that he could make a $300,000 profit by buying and selling his own apartment if the tenants could obtain the building from Trump at a good price. Rozenholc stood to gain as well—he would serve as lawyer for the tenant corporation during the closing, co-oping, and future management of the building, a long-term source of fees. According to Goldfine's sworn and uncontested recollection, Trump, Moore, and Rozenholc got down to such specifics that they began figuring out how many apartments could be altered or combined to maximize the number of units with views of Central Park—hardly the expected concerns of tenant champions.

Trump also raised the possibility of selling the building to another developer, but he made it clear that it would be cheaper for tenants to buy their own apartments if he co-oped the building than if he sold it at a premium and the new owner co-oped it. Trump's favorite option, however, was a settlement involving his withdrawal of the demolition permit, the termination of the state and tenant legal actions, and a written guarantee that he would make substantial improvements and provide adequate services to the rental tenants.

Moore and Rozenholc flatly rejected this offer, with Moore saying that the tenants expected to get a protective order against him at the end of the state hearings and that if they settled without such an order, "we have no assurance that you would not begin harassing us again in another year or two or three, and then we would have to start all over with a protective order." The rejection of this proposal, as well as the expression of interest in an outright sale, were positions Moore took without any clear reading from the sixty or so families left in the building. He and Rozenholc were becoming the sole arbiters of 100 Central Park South's fate; Rozenholc did not even tell Fischbein about the meetings.

Donald and Rozenholc began discussing the tax and other legal implications of Trump's co-op options, and Donald gradually moved in the direction of a sale to the Tenants Association as the most advantageous deal. As the three-hour luncheon ended, Trump said he would try to determine a fair price for the building and Moore offered to find out how many tenants would buy apartments if Trump sold the building to the association. Goldfine's sworn recollection was that Moore asked Trump to come back with a price; both sides agree that they expected to move forward with a possible negotiated sale. The lunch ended without a tab; the billionaire's veal would ironically appear on the tenant leader's monthly club bill.

A few days later Trump called Moore again and said he'd like to come over to his office immediately for a quick one-on-one chat. Trump made it clear that he had not done his homework, and had no firm proposal to make, but said he had "some numbers together" and thought they should talk again. Moore declined, insisted on bringing Rozenholc to any meeting and added another member of the Tenants Committee for a February 22 lunch at The Brook.

Trump opened this second discussion with the same settlement proposal he had made ten days earlier—a mutual withdrawal of the tenants' petitions and a modernization of the building. When that was rejected, Trump said: "I have a bad feeling in my stomach about sitting down here and trying to work out our problems as long as we're moving full speed ahead with this state DHCR case.

I ask you to see if we can't stipulate to stop those proceedings, or hold them off while we're discussing alternatives." The state enforcement action was now in its third week, and DHCR attorney Joyce Goldstein was making solid progress, increasing the pressure on Donald to settle the case.

"We can't do that," said Moore, who hadn't yet told Goldstein about his meetings with Trump. "There are fifty people who have been harmed. Unless I am ordered to by the state, or by Mr. Manny Mirabel, the head of DHCR, I can't do it because the people want a conclusion of this."

"I don't want to negotiate with a gun to my head," Donald answered.

"It's a psychological problem," Moore said. "You will have to go ahead. We are going to continue the hearings, and if you want to talk to us about ideas you have, we are here to listen."

Donald began talking about a new vision he had for the building, and even Moore thought he appeared genuinely excited about this plan to preserve and restore it. Trump praised the way the Helmsleys had recently maintained intact the landmark Villard Houses and built the Helmsley Palace around them. He said he'd decided that he really liked the look of 100 Central Park South and that with arches, a new bronze door, redone windows, and sprucing up in front, it could be terrific. He now wanted to do the project in two phases—to put in condos at the Barbizon and sell them at $700 a square foot and then to "soup up 100 Central Park South, maintaining the integrity of the building."

Ideas were pouring out of him at "a mile a minute," recalled Moore, who labeled Trump a "very fertile man." He began discussing making the two buildings look alike, "wrap it around with one skin, make it look like one big thing, one unified piece." While these architectural plans represented a major shift from his earlier concepts, and meant the building might survive, they were hardly what Moore and Rozenholc wanted to hear. Where did they fit in?

Both sides agree that Trump made the following offer at that lunch: "I will continue the building as a rental, but won't rent the twenty vacant apartments for a one-year period. For a period of two years the tenants will have the option to buy the building from me at a price of $15 million." From Trump's vantage point, with supposed offers of $30 million, he was offering a bargain, yet one that would still leave him with a sizable profit. But to Moore, it was an unclear and unacceptable price. Rozenholc later recalled: "We got him to put the building on the market, and at a price that was not that outrageous. We rejected it, but only because I thought we'd do better."

Trump agreed to rethink a price based on whether he'd sell the tenants the entire building, sell it without the eight to ten stores, or sell it without the stores and without the vacant apartments. Unbeknownst to the media, which was covering the 100 Central Park South conflict as a David versus Goliath tenants' rights war, it had in fact become a behind-the-scenes haggle over price and terms.

A few days after the second lunch, Donald called Moore, reiterated his $15 million price, and adding that it was for the building without the stores. "Donald, this is ridiculous," Moore cut off Trump. "I consider that a nonoffer, and I think we have probably said about all we have to say." Rozenholc said the offer was rejected because they believed they had "the leverage to get him lower."

Moore and Rozenholc knew that time, as well as the power of the state and city governments, was on their side. In addition to the DHCR hearing, the city administration was just about to bring a stunning lawsuit against Trump. Moore had been meeting with two young assistant corporation counsels, and they had agreed to sue Trump under a relatively new anti-eviction statute, passed by the city council in 1982 and largely untested in the courts. The city suit, which sought to enjoin Trump from his reputed "unlawful and egregious attempts to harass and evict without due process of law," was filed a week after Moore's second lunch with Donald and sought $10,000 fines against Trump for each provable act of harassment.

The city complaint added little new information to the case against Trump, but it refocused public attention on the plight of the 100 Central Park South tenants, got John Moore's phone ringing again, and pitted the city against Trump at the moment when he could least afford it. Trump needed a good relationship with City Hall because in January of 1985 he'd finally bought the property that had been his seventies obsession, the 60th Street rail yards. Every indication was that, for the moment at least, Ed Koch was willing to keep an open mind on Trump's potentially billion-dollar West Side extravaganza. Donald's ambitions for this property were a powerful impetus for him to resolve the tenant mess; indeed he had made his initial approach to John Moore the same week he closed on the yards. The last thing he needed was a dirty tenant war a couple of blocks away from his planned gargantuan project.

Much the same situation applied in Atlantic City, where the Division of Gaming Enforcement and the Casino Control Commission, which would soon review his first Castle license application, would surely look askance at any harassment findings.

While Trump was under no immediate time pressure in the DHCR proceeding, where tenant testimony would continue for months, the city suit required a quick response. The city was seeking an injunction against him pending a full hearing, and if it obtained one it would be a terrible public relations blow. Donald had to find a way to block that. He consequently alleged in his response papers that the city had filed the suit for "political" reasons, charging that the Koch administration had "jumped on the bandwagon," joining the state on the side of tenants in a battle with a prominent landlord in the middle of an election year. The argument was a credible one, especially since the complaint merely duplicated the allegations of the state action and was initiated by a young assistant who was running the Koch campaign on the East Side. Donald certainly noticed that this was the second city lawsuit filed against him at the start of a mayoral campaign; the Trump Tower tax abatement issue had exploded precisely four years earlier, in March 1981. Another political twist was that the lawsuit was filed three weeks after Badillo withdrew as a possible candidate against Koch, announcing his enmity for the two anti-Koch candidates left in the race. In the months ahead, with the city aggressively pursuing Trump in litigation crucial to the financial viability of Badillo's firm, Fischbein arranged a rapprochement meeting between the mayor's former foe and top City Hall brass.

The strongest inference of the political origins of the suit, however, was its transparent legal weakness. The problem was that most of the worst Trump harassment—including the "bad faith" eviction actions cited by the courts—had occurred during the first two years of Trump ownership, when the anti-eviction statute wasn't even in effect. While this evidence would be pivotal in the DHCR case, Trump's gentler approach in the period covered by the new city law gave him a potent response to the lawsuit.

Trump's lawyer in the city suit, Arthur Richenthal, pointed out in court papers that the complaint did not even allege any "lock-out or removal of possessions or any force or threat of force used against any tenant," precisely the unlawful acts mentioned in the anti-eviction statute. While the city suit was based entirely on the allegation that Trump had diminished services to compel tenants to leave, there were no serious violations pending against the building, even though it was on the building department's hot list and was constantly inspected.

After making a case that minimized the bad conditions in the building, the Richenthal brief then switched to the question of tenant motives. Suddenly, the Brook meetings between Trump and Moore began to look like a trap. The tenants, "or at least their leaders," Richenthal charged, "are only interested in coercing the owner to sell them the building at a cheap price so the tenants can reap a windfall." Backed up by affidavits from Trump and Goldfine, Richenthal alleged an "ulterior purpose" to the tenant actions, calling it "greenmail in a real estate setting" and charging that the city's belated entry only "adds leverage to the tenants' greenmail tactics."

Goldfine's affidavit claimed that Moore had "expressed disappointment" that Trump hadn't come up with a price at the beginning of the second lunch, making it clear "that the effort to settle the dispute would be stalemated until Trump addressed the issue of a price for selling or converting the building." Goldfine stated that Trump's ultimate $15 million offer at the meeting was "in response" to Moore's pressure for a price.

Donald's affidavit took this argument a step further, charging that Moore "made it perfectly clear" at the two meetings that "there would be no peace in the building and no end to litigation unless the building was turned over to him and to his cohorts at a bargain price." John Moore's only sworn answer to this charge was to concede that he'd insisted Trump sell the building—but that he'd told Donald it didn't matter to him who got it, the tenants or another developer.

Supreme Court Judge Irving Kirschenbaum, a pro-landlord Republican, ruled in Trump's favor on the city suit, denying an injunction in August of 1985 and refusing later that year to hear reargument. His decisions were unanimously upheld by the appellate division. Kirschenbaum concluded that the city was unable to make "a prima facie showing that the defendants are violating the law in question" and ordered a full trial. While Trump may have won a temporary victory in the city case, both sides knew that the main action was still at DHCR—and there Trump faced the threat of a dramatically different result.

Joyce Goldstein, the thirty-one-year-old attorney who was prosecuting the enforcement action against Trump, started her case with the most damaging evidence of Trump's original intent when he bought the building. Lester Taylor, who had managed 100 Central Park South for decades under the prior owner, testified about his first meeting with Trump in August of 1981, immediately after Donald bought the building. A commanding witness, with a long history of employment by the top builders and managers in city real estate, including Trump's own builder HRH, Taylor said he went to Donald's office in the Crown Building and that Donald raised the question of "how quickly" the building could be "completely emptied."

The question was directed at twenty-eight-year-old Stephen Shapiro, the president of a company called Citadel Management, which had a reputation for vacating buildings and relocating tenants. (Shapiro's father had, in fact, cleared the Trump Village site of 800 families for Fred Trump twenty years earlier.)

Citadel, and Shapiro's father's allied firm, Urban Relocation, had been sued in the 1970s by the state attorney general for conducting a "conscious campaign" to frighten and intimidate tenants into vacating twenty-eight separate buildings slated for demolition. The elder Shapiro wound up signing a consent decree admitting no wrongdoing but promising to refrain from the actions cited by the attorney general and agreeing to pay some of the costs of the investigation.

During the period that Citadel worked for Donald at 100 Central Park South, complaints against it from several other buildings were filed with city agencies, suggesting a pattern of antitenant conduct that Steve Shapiro vigorously denied.

According to Taylor's testimony, Shapiro told Trump "he could empty the building within twelve months, providing he was given the management of the building." About two weeks later, Taylor said, he was "given notice that my management was terminated," though he had previously been told he would be retained. Tom Macari, the Trump Organization vice president assigned by Donald to supervise 100 Central Park South, said Taylor was dropped because he was "like a father" to the tenants and "chose their side." Macari, nearly as young as Shapiro and a veteran of the Polish worker wars at Trump Tower, would also later testify that when he raised the difficulty of such massive tenant relocation with Trump, Donald replied: "Just take care of it."

Citadel took over, moving its building coordinator into an apartment at 100 Central Park South. Its managers began circulating among the tenants, telling people the building would be demolished and inducing departures. The building was fully tenanted when Donald bought it; within a year there were twenty vacant apartments, still far short of Citadel's alleged promise. Though Shapiro and Macari would insist that Donald's directive was to maintain full services while dislocating the tenants, Joyce Goldstein produced evidence to the contrary.

Adam Ramirez, who had been the building's super for twenty years, testified that Citadel's managers called him to their office and told him that the building was going to be torn down "and that all services were to be cut out."

"They didn't want any repairs done," Ramirez recalled. "No cleaning. No accepting of packages. The doorman was to stay there and he was not to get cabs or open doors for anybody, and all repairs were to go through their office." When Ramirez balked, one of the Citadel managers asked: "What are you, a born-again Christian?"

Ramirez also testified that "they wanted me to be like a guard and keep an eye on tenants," pressing him on more than one occasion for information about "a lot of personal things." They wanted to know if individual tenants "owned other property, what type of work they did," and a host of other matters. Ramirez even claimed, at one point, that they grilled him about the sex habits of some of the building's residents.

While Trump disputed this testimony, there was clear evidence of a cutback in services during the early months he owned the building. For a substantial period of time, the doormen no longer wore uniforms or assisted tenants, and the door was frequently left unguarded. The lobby phone was removed. The lobby, hallway, and other public areas of the building were "allowed to become and remain filthy, unclean and unwashed." The roof deteriorated, leaking into the penthouse and other top-floor apartments. Ceilings collapsed. A laundry list of repairs in individual apartments was ignored by management. And, of course, the plummeting services were accompanied by the harassment dispossess cases brought by Trump.

Goldstein presented her evidence of this harassment campaign before Barry Port, a hearing officer appointed by her own agency. At the end of the administrative proceeding, Port was to issue a finding and recommendation to the agency's deputy commissioner, Manny Mirabel. Any agency decision, leveling fines of up to $2,500 a violation, could then be appealed by Trump in court. By July of 1985, after thousands of pages of testimony, every indication was that Port was likely to find against Trump, a verdict of harassment that would undoubtedly harm the developer for years.

At the same time that Donald initiated his peacemaking contacts with Moore in early 1985, he also set in motion a behind-the-scenes approach to Mirabel. The DHCR head had risen remarkably quickly through the city and state housing bureaucracies, becoming a deputy commissioner under Tony Gliedman at Housing Preservation and Development, then shifting over to the state in 1984 when DHCR took over rent regulation. One of his "rabbis," known to have supported his high-level appointments, was Stanley Friedman, the Bronx boss and Roy Cohn partner who had become an increasingly important counsel to Trump as the dying Cohn began to fade. Over the course of 1985, Trump would use Friedman in a variety of matters, negotiating an air rights deal in the East Sixties, arranging a lunch with new Manhattan Borough President David Dinkins, securing the support of the Bronx planning commissioner for the vaunted West Side yards project.

As the DHCR hearings began, Trump asked the attorney who was handling the case for him, Scott Mollen, to meet with Friedman and explain the situation at 100 Central Park South. The two met and discussed the case, but they were not alone: Friedman's logs reveal that Mollen, Friedman, and Manny Mirabel met on February 20, 1985, at Friedman's office. The hearings on 100 Central Park South had just begun, and Donald was in between lunches with John Moore. Mirabel never told the tenants or the involved DHCR staffers about his ex parte meeting with Mollen—precisely the sort of sessions no quasi-judicial official should have with a litigant who has a case before him. When Mollen was dropped by Trump later in 1985, the lawyer who replaced him began appearing on Friedman's logs, instructed by Donald to stay in touch with Stanley about the building.

Mirabel was listed on Friedman logs at another eight meetings over the course of 1985 while the DHCR action continued, sometimes on the same day that Friedman also met with Trump. Friedman and Mirabel also exchanged phone messages. Most of the contact took place in the fall of 1985 during a six-month period when the DHCR hearings were adjourned. The day they resumed, on January 16, 1986, Friedman got a phone message: "Did you talk to Mirabel? Call Norma in Trump's office."

During this same period, Mirabel began pushing strongly to get the agency to end the suit, especially after the July adjournment. The adjournment was itself a strange event, prompted by the sudden announcement that Mollen's firm was withdrawing from the case. Pressed by Goldstein and Rozenholc, who raised the question of whether this belated pullout was a "trick" designed to buy time, hearing officer Port hesitated at first to grant an adjournment. In the end, he agreed to a three-week suspension, which then turned into six months—a highly unusual extension that occurred at Mirabel's behest. During this hiatus, Mirabel opened up discussions with Goldstein's enforcement division, asking if there wasn't some way the case could simply be closed out—not settled, just terminated. When Goldstein balked, attempts were made to transfer her out of the enforcement division, and she became so anxious about her phone at the agency that she began talking to the tenants only from her home phone. At one point, she had a conversation with Trump himself about a pending hearing date, and Donald informed her that she would be getting a call from the commissioner that the hearing would be adjourned. Though she worked at DHCR, Goldstein soon unhappily discovered that he had better information than she did about what her agency was doing.

Suddenly, in the middle of this long delay in the hearings, Mirabel did something quite extraordinary: He wrote a letter to the parties explaining the adjournment, asserting that it was "based on the fact that meaningful settlement negotiations were in progress and that there was no harassment of tenants as of this date." He was listed on Stanley Friedman's appointment diary for the same day he wrote the letter, October 29, 1985. Four days earlier, a notation on Friedman's log read simply: "Messenger to Commissioner Manny Mirabel—envelope."

A few days after the Mirabel letter, Trump told the *New York Times:* "When we receive a letter from the top official saying that there has been no harassment, I consider that to be a finding. They can resume whatever they want, but the hearings have ended. People can say whatever they want, but that's what the letter says."

Settlement discussions had, in fact, resumed shortly after the adjournment. And this time, David Rozenholc and John Moore were as anxious to settle as Trump. The Tenants Committee had long since exhausted its funds, and apart from occasional partial payments, the Fischbein firm was carrying a huge debit on 100 Central Park South. The only chance Rozenholc had of collecting the $300,000 he estimated the tenants owed him was a settlement. Either Trump would wind up paying the fees directly in a traditional settlement, or Rozenholc would get a piece of the building if the tenants bought it.

Rozenholc had worked out a deal with his now close friend Moore, who had promised him up to ten apartments out of the twenty-seven that were then vacant. While Moore and Rozenholc later had slightly different recollections of the number of apartments and how the arrangement might work, they agreed that Rozenholc would be able to purchase the apartments at the same low price as the tenants and then sell them in the go-go market of the mideighties. At a minimum, Rozenholc and his firm would make enough on the transactions to cover both past due and future fees. While Rozenholc subsequently insisted that all he could make on the apartments was the fees due the firm, a tenant organizer hired by Moore, Jo Ellen Berryman, maintained that the written draft of an agreement she saw provided that the firm could keep whatever it made on the sale of their vacant apartments, and that Moore and Rozenholc were frequently engaged in "a lot of fantasy talk" about the tantalizing prospects of buying the buildings.

Moore made this unusual arrangement with Rozenholc in the spring of 1985 at roughly the same time that Rozenholc secretly loaned Moore $165,000 to keep Moore's desperately troubled HME Records afloat. The company had made a series of bad business judgments, including spurning an exclusive deal with new singing talent Luther Vandross because "he was too fat." It had recently been cut off by CBS, which distributed its periodic releases, and had been charged with a breach of contract claim from one of its leading singing groups, the Fabulous Thunderbirds. No one was told about the loans, not even Rozenholc's partner Rick Fischbein or the ever-present Berryman, who actually had a desk at HME.

Rozenholc and Moore did not even record the lien with the county clerk, as he would have had to if he ever expected to make a secured claim should HME collapse.

By July of 1985, HME was broke. Moore retreated to his apartment and tried to keep his company alive from there, but he was forced to resign in August, and the company filed Chapter XI a couple of months later. Rozenholc took a $125,000 bath, including legal fees for services he provided HME. The self-assured Moore, shaken by the company's downfall, remained unemployed for months. If the building purchase had been important to him in February, during the Brook meetings, a possible $300,000 profit must have been critical to him now.

With the Friedman-to-Mirabel maneuvers, and the financial troubles of the Fischbein firm and Moore, hovering in the background, Rich Fischbein moved to bring in an "honest broker" to finally end the holy war he was convinced would otherwise not be resolved—a legendary behind-the-scenes figure in New York politics, Jerry Finkelstein. Owner of the *New York* and *National Law Journals,* a former City Planning Commission chairman who'd become a millionaire investor, Finkelstein was the bankroller, fund-raiser, and strategist behind the political career of his renamed son, Andrew Stein. With Herman Badillo's strong endorsement, Stein was in the middle of a tough Democratic primary for city council president—a campaign materially abetted by both sides of the 100 Central Park South conflict. Finkelstein had the ability to forge a fair deal, Fischbein believed, partly because he needed both sides in the campaign—Trump for tons of contributions and the Fischbein firm for Badillo and a host of other favors.* Stein had stayed as far away from the dispute as he could, though his office routinely handled similar tenant complaints in other buildings and Moore had brought the case directly to him. Stein's only real connection with the building was a bizarre personal incident a few years earlier—when he broke up with a model he'd been living with and called his friend Donald to ask if he could help her find an apartment. When Donald talked with the model, the conversation turned to 100 Central Park South and Trump let the cat out of the bag long before the harassment saga had publicly surfaced. "You don't want to move there," Donald told the model. "I'm going to clear the place out."

----

* Fischbein handed Stein the evidence for a negative TV commercial on his opponent—the supposedly beleaguered tenants who lived in a building owned by the foe's family.

With the agreement of both sides that Finkelstein's name was never to surface, the patriarch arranged and attended meetings that produced, as early as August, a handshake deal on a sale of the building to the tenants.

The broad terms anticipated the formation of a tenant corporation to buy the residential portion of the building, minus the roof, the street-level stores, the basement areas, and the land, for $10 million, a major shift from Trump's February position and a triumph for Rozenholc and Moore. Trump would help the tenant corporation obtain bank financing, and he would restore the building—new windows throughout, new front doors, a new sidewalk, gold leaf, a completely repainted exterior, and waterproofed roof. The tenant corporation would control all the vacancies. From this framework Rozenholc moved in to hammer out the details.

He and Trump began a series of three or four meetings, frequently over breakfast. Then, at one point in October, when according to Rozenholc, he and Trump already had an oral agreement on the final terms, the lawyer suddenly raised a new subject. The Fischbein firm represented a troubled major national corporation, Allegheny, headquartered in Pittsburgh, that controlled several disastrous pieces of real estate, including a brand-new, vacant $90 million office building in Houston and a rundown Lexington Avenue hotel, the Dover. Allegheny wanted to find buyers for either property, and Rozenholc wanted Trump to consider them. Trump agreed to meet with a top Allegheny officer, Charles Home, and did, making a modest offer for the Houston building in late October. The deal—which would have resulted in a finder's fee for the Fischbein firm—died.

The only tenant who had any idea these sidebar talks were going on was John Moore. When asked later what he thought about their propriety, Moore replied: "So what? I don't give a damn about David doing a deal with Donald." Moore said he didn't talk to the tenants, or even the tenant committee, about it. "If I went to the committee with every little bit of information, it would be impossible—like a committee building a car."

A week after these curious conversations, Trump finally sent Rozenholc a twenty-two-page contract on the 100 Central Park South purchase, prepared by Dreyer & Traub. The agreement contemplated Trump's gaining approval from the attorney general to turn the building into a condo and his condo corporation then selling the residential portion to the tenants for a simultaneous co-op sale. The Fischbein firm was supposed to help obtain these approvals. Rozenholc agreed not to record the deal in real property records, sealing it from the public, and to withdraw all tenant complaints that were the foundation of the state and city cases. The agreement contained no provision for Trump's payment of the Fischbein fees, indicating that Rozenholc fully expected to take the fees out of the vacant apartment resales.

However, when Rozenholc received his copy of the document, which specified an undetermined day in November for final execution of the agreement, it was accompanied by a description of another property, at 490 West End Avenue—a parcel Trump didn't even own. Assuming it was some secretarial slipup, Rozenholc began calling Trump and Dreyer & Traub, but was given neither an explanation nor a replacement that actually covered 100 Central Park South. He kept badgering but finally realized that this was Donald's way of backing out of the deal. Finkelstein was outraged; Fischbein was dumbfounded. But no one could get Trump to move.

No one ever determined precisely why Donald ultimately killed the deal he'd negotiated with Rozenholc and Finkelstein. But the most logical explanation was Mirabel's nearly simultaneous bizarre letter announcing his premature "no harassment" finding. Trump released the letter to the *Times* with a statement of his own that seemed to connect it with the secretly doomed settlement. "I have no problem selling them the apartments," he said, "as long as it is a fair deal, but nobody is going to use a harassment hearing—which we've already won—to try and gain additional leverage." Stanley Friedman's success at DHCR may have effectively eliminated Trump's need to go forward with the sale Moore and Rozenholc had long craved.

In December of 1985, Charlie Foy, the supervisor in the city's law department whose unit brought the city's lawsuit on 100 Central Park South, was rocked by some very bad news—a message that seemed to come straight from Trump. Foy, who had authorized the filing of the lawsuit a year earlier, was preparing to leave his city position, enticed by an offer from a prominent real estate law firm, Dreyer & Traub. But the day after his farewell party at the office, he received a phone call from Jerry Schrager, the senior partner at Dreyer, who was by then personally involved in the 100 Central Park South settlement negotiations. Foy was surprised to hear from Schrager, since all his prior contacts with the firm had been with another senior partner.

Schrager abruptly withdrew the job offer, and, according to Foy, said that Dreyer would reconsider Foy's hiring only after the city suit against Trump was terminated. When Fritz Schwarz, the corporation counsel who ran the department, was informed of this disturbing conversation, he called Schrager, and Schrager repeated the statement. Schwarz was so angry he talked with Foy about referring the matter to the Bar Association or the disciplinary committee or suing the Dreyer firm. Schrager asked for a meeting with Schwarz to discuss the dispute and when Schrager came to Schwarz's office, he was accompanied by Trump's new attorney on 100 Central Park South, the flamboyant Richard Golub, whom Trump had just lured away from Verina Hixon, the Trump Tower resident with whom he had been in a protracted legal war. A courtroom showman who once attacked an opposing male attorney as a "fat lesbian" and later implied that he lost his common-law marriage suit against actor William Hurt because the judge fell in love with Hurt, Golub arrived at the meeting with the very proper and influential Schwarz in a mink coat, a sneer on his lips. Though he had just moved from his client Hixon to her nemesis Trump, Golub launched into an ethics lecture for Schwarz's benefit, a theatrical ruse that was a typical Golub tactic.

Pointing an accusatory finger at the shaken victim, he accused Foy and the corporation counsel's office of a "get Trump" attitude, contending that Foy had not told the Dreyer partners who interviewed him that he was associated with the Trump case and that if he had, they would not have hired him because it would have been a conflict of interest. Foy assured Schwarz that he had, in fact, told Dreyer of his association with the case.

But as Schwarz pointed out in a subsequent letter, any conflict issues could have easily been resolved if Dreyer had simply sought the consent of the city to hire him. "I continue to believe," wrote Schwarz, "that the proper course for Dreyer & Traub would have been to call me to discuss the situation before withdrawing its offer to Mr. Foy." Foy remained with the city, distancing himself a bit from the Trump case, and asked Schwarz not to pursue the Schrager matter, concerned that a public conflict with a mainline law firm could only damage him in the long run.

Taking the offensive against the city, however, was only part of the new Trump strategy. Trump had apparently decided to hire Golub to turn the 100 Central Park South litigation into the equivalent of a bloody street fight, and before the lawyer was through—which would be only a matter of a few months— he would spray charges in every direction, accusing Joyce Goldstein and Barry Port at DHCR of collusion and even accusing Fritz Schwarz's office of improper ties to the Fischbein firm. His most outrageous stunt was a racketeering lawsuit he filed in federal court against the Fischbein firm, an extraordinary escalation of a dispute that only a few weeks earlier had seemed on the verge of settlement. Rozenholc found out about the $105 million lawsuit in mid-December 1985, when he was called by a *New York Post* gossip reporter who had been given a copy of the complaint before it was even served on the defendants. The luridly written document charged the Fischbein partners with efforts "to harass, extort, extract, and demand unreasonable payments" from Trump and other landlords.

Golub recounted a truncated version of Trump's sessions with Rozenholc about the Allegheny properties, alleging that Rozenholc said he "wanted a piece of the action" and contending that Rozenholc acknowledged that a deal between them would be a conflict of interest. The Trump contention was that Rozenholc and his firm had agreed to settle the 100 Central Park South controversy if Donald agreed to the Allegheny deal. The Fischbein firm's response never directly countered those allegations, though its legal position did not require them to. It simply argued that even if all of Golub's charges were true, they constituted no violation of the racketeering statutes.

In addition to the Allegheny charges, the Golub complaint charged that Badillo had met Trump at a November 1984 party and that Badillo had warned him that the DHCR proceeding, which had yet to be announced, was "rigged." Badillo supposedly urged Trump to settle, telling him there was no way he could win. Since Badillo was then serving as the chairman of the State Mortgage Agency (a separate but related body), the Trump complaint alleged that his warning had been an abuse of his public power. Golub also listed a supposed $50,000 bribe Moore and Rozenholc had offered a top Trump staffer and a fistfight that an associate in the Rozenholc firm had started with a Trump lawyer. As much as Donald and Golub may have relished the one-day news story these charges provoked, they had gravely miscalculated.

Fischbein responded by hiring Marty London, a partner in one of the city's premier law firms, Paul Weiss Rifkind Wharton and Garrison. Not only did London seek an immediate ruling on the RICO charges, he demanded that court-ordered sanctions be imposed against Trump and Golub for having had the audacity to make them. U.S. District Court Judge Whitman Knapp was so incensed by the recklessness of the case and the apparent abuse of the RICO laws that he threw it out barely a month after it had been filed. Knapp kept the sanctions issue open pending an appeal to the Circuit Court, which Golub immediately filed.

The case had an impact, however, in an arena far removed from Judge Knapp's courtroom. The charges against Badillo and DHCR were interpreted in Albany as charges against Governor Mario Cuomo's administration, since Golub had suggested that Badillo could rig the state enforcement proceeding. If these accusations, leaked to the newspapers, weren't sufficient to infuriate Cuomo officials, Donald personally called Joe Spinelli, the state inspector general, and asked him to investigate DHCR, calling it "a corrupt agency."

A former FBI agent, Spinelli wasted no time, undertaking the probe himself. He went to Fischbein's offices and talked with everyone involved there. He questioned DHCR officials, pushing Goldstein and Port about the merits of a case that was theoretically still in progress. Spinelli also went directly to Trump, whom he met on March 17, 1986.

It was Spinelli's second visit to Donald's office. As an FBI agent, he had served a subpoena on him in the early eighties as part of the investigation of concrete union boss John Cody. Trump recognized him and recalled the Cody case. He joked that it was very important to him that this matter be settled to the satisfaction of the governor. "He might be president someday, and I might want to be an ambassador or something," Trump said.

Then, as Spinelli recalled it, Donald began an hour-long rant about the tenant shakedown, the Fischbein firm, and corruption in DHCR. He repeatedly stressed that he would fight a DHCR harassment conviction in the courts forever, insisting that similar cases were routinely settled by the agency and tenants. He told the Badillo story, claiming that Herman had urged him "to sell the building to the tenants," an action that Trump claimed "would result in Badillo's law firm obtaining title to the property."

Ironically, Trump's prime DHCR target was Manny Mirabel, who he suggested was "a crook." He cited Mirabel's extraordinary October letter, which found no evidence of harassment, and argued that "the letter was the result of my contacting Stanley Friedman and requesting his assistance in this matter." Donald's anger at Mirabel may have been attributable to the deputy commissioner's sudden change of attitude about the Trump case. Spinelli had been told by other DHCR officials that Mirabel had started "coming around" on the matter at about the time that Spinelli's probe began.

One explanation for the shift in Mirabel's position, aside from the sudden Spinelli probe, may have been the dramatic change that had occurred in Stanley Friedman's life. On January 10, 1986, the borough president of Queens, Donald Manes, was discovered by police in a bloodied car, an apparent unsuccessful suicide. Manes was Friedman's closest political ally and, as it turned out, covert business partner on major contracts with the city. While Manes succeeded in a second suicide attempt, Friedman wound up sentenced to nineteen years in federal and state prisons. The scandal was so explosive that the headlines and fast-paced state and federal probes ended Friedman's influence within a week or two of Manes's first attempt. He was of no use to Trump or Mirabel by mid-January; a month later, he was under indictment.

Since Friedman's logs and diaries had not yet come to light, Spinelli knew nothing about the details of his involvement in the Trump affair. The investigator simply wanted to put to rest what seemed to him to be unproven charges and countercharges involving Badillo and DHCR. At the end of Trump's harangue that morning, he pressed Spinelli to say just what he thought the state would do. "We're going to have to go forward with the enforcement case," Spinelli declared. His office wrote a closing memo five days later endorsing DHCR's conduct and making no comment on the Badillo allegations. Donald finally got the message. The DHCR hearings were quietly resuming, ordered by the new housing commissioner Bill Eimicke, whose actions in effect overrode the adjournment prompted by Mirabel. And the newspapers were soon filled with stories about Mario Cuomo's new running mate—Herman Badillo—the sacrificial lamb tapped by the governor to oppose the only Republican statewide official, Comptroller Ned Regan, a covert Cuomo ally.

So Trump sent a signal to DHCR that he was once again willing to talk settlement. He also sent two new negotiators into the fray—Susan Heilbron, a recent Trump recruit from the state's Urban Development Corporation with close ties to the Cuomo team, and another new staffer, Tony Gliedman, the Koch housing commissioner Donald had bullied and sued over the denial of the Trump Tower tax abatement. The hiring of Gliedman—intended, apparently, to give Donald a top Koch insider for his West Side and other projects—would ultimately backfire when the mayor expressed open disdain at Gliedman's willingness to work for a man who'd threatened him in the vilest terms. But Gliedman was the perfect mediator for the 100 Central Park South conflict since he was a longtime friend of Rick Fischbein's and Bill Eimicke's, who had once worked under him at the city housing agency. Finally emerging from the shadows in the negotiations over the building, Fischbein met for a drink with his old friend, and Gliedman, a natural conciliator with a soothing, accommodating style, pledged an eventual agreement. At last, there were key participants on both sides of the table who trusted each other.

Rozenholc introduced the purchase notion again, but it was quickly rejected. The state, now intimately involved in the talks, would not be a party to a forced fire sale. Instead, the basic framework for the agreement was similar to the one Donald had laid out at the Brook lunches almost a year and a half earlier: a mutual withdrawal of the legal cases (including the sanctions hearings) and a commitment by Trump to modernize the building and run it fairly. There was much more to the ultimate settlement terms than the original Trump formula, but the underlying assumption of the talks had shifted from sale to safeguards, a transition never made in the two earlier settlement scenarios.

The primary tenant concern by now was for a mechanism to guarantee protection from harassment long into the future, and Eimicke eagerly provided that mechanism. In an unprecedented move, he agreed to add his signature to the agreement between the two parties and to supervise Trump's overall compliance for five years, with DHCR also promising to monitor apartment repairs indefinitely. On Trump's side, Eimicke agreed to issue an order terminating the state proceeding on the legal terms Donald had long demanded. Eimicke's and Spinelli's extraordinary roles, compelling the settlement, were a direct result of the governor's sudden personal interest in the dispute, according to several sources close to the negotiations.

In the end, Trump paid the Fischbein firm $700,000 in fees, including its costs in the racketeering case. The approximate amount of Trump's legal expenses over the course of the five-year war, cited by numerous participants, was from $3 to $4 million. Trump also agreed to permit the tenants to participate in the choice of a new management firm and to forgive the first three months of rent for all tenants in 1987. If he or any subsequent owner tried to co-op the building, he could only proceed under a noneviction plan (this agreement ran with the title for the building). Trump even consented to grant the Tenants Association power over his future rights to bring eviction actions should the building remain a rental, as it has. For his part, Donald achieved his two primary objectives: He avoided an harassment conviction, getting the case dismissed, and he kept his building. He also got the Fischbein firm to back off the demand in federal court for a sanction hearing against Golub and him—the threat of which had become just one more pressure pushing Donald to the settlement.

The agreement was executed in December 1986, just a month after Cuomo's reelection and Badillo's thunderous defeat. While Cuomo never raised the funds for the Badillo comptroller campaign that he had promised, the Trump bailout of Badillo's troubled firm, arranged by top aides to the governor, looked like a welcome substitute.

Within two weeks, the Fischbein firm shattered into pieces. Rozenholc left with several associates to start his own practice, while Fischbein and Badillo remained together. Fischbein hung a blue T-shirt in his office boasting "I was sued by Donald Trump for $105 million," and he and Rozenholc began to compete for credit as the lawyer who had defeated Donald Trump.

The old friends had stopped talking altogether months earlier; the parting was a bitter culmination of the rancor between them. Fischbein was upset to learn that Rozenholc had side business deals with clients he had not been told about; lone wolf Rozenholc wanted to run his own one-man show. The long-festering 100 Central Park South dispute, and Rozenholc's unusual ties to Moore, had been just one of many factors that had damaged the relationship. Fischbein suspected that the tenant war could have ended months earlier and feared that the Moore-Rozenholc intrigue had helped keep it alive.

In the aftermath of the settlement, Moore moved the Tenants Association business to Rozenholc's firm and the two continued, over the years, to float bids in Donald's direction for a tenant takeover of the building. While they never garnered this ultimate prize, Rozenholc's publicized defeat of Donald became his calling card, even attracting clients like Verina Hixon. Moore at least got the psychic reward he'd sought all along—a hero of his social set, he was recognized and cheered by supporters when be swaggered into a tony club in Palm Beach, where he liked to vacation and where the King of Mar-a-Lago was scorned. Donald, he claimed, had dangled a six-figure job in his direction at one point, but he had declined. He couldn't have accepted it and remained, when everything was over, his smug self.

In addition to occurring a few weeks after Cuomo's reelection, the settlement also came on the heels of Stanley Friedman's Thanksgiving conviction on racketeering charges. During that trial, and in the years that followed, Donald demonstrated a singularly uncharacteristic loyalty to the man who Fischbein, Rozenholc, and Moore believed had tried to fix the DHCR case. Friedman told friends that Trump was one of the last clients to keep him on retainer, long after his indictment. Trump even agreed to become a character witness at Friedman's trial, though he did everything he could to convince Friedman he would make a lousy witness, in sharp contrast to his usual boasts about his clever performances in the countless civil depositions he'd done. When federal prosecutors grilled Friedman during cross-examination about the favors he'd done for Donald on the Hyatt, any notion of using Donald was dropped.

After Friedman went to jail in 1987, Trump remained in contact with Stanley's wife, Jackie, who sent Trump Friedman's appeals briefs and visited him on the *Trump Princess*. He even tried to get the New Jersey Casino Association to hire longtime Friedman loyalist Murray Lewinter as a lobbyist.

Though Donald used the city scandal as a rhetorical weapon against Ed Koch in *The Art of the Deal*, devoting a couple of pages to a catalogue of the criminals around the mayor, he never mentioned scandal maypole Friedman. In his second book, *Surviving at the Top,* published in 1990, Donald included a startling plea for his old friend. Blaming Friedman's conviction on bad legal advice and suggesting that he was "just another hard-driving politician," Donald complained that Friedman "got a stiffer sentence than many child molesters and murderers—and many people at the time felt he should not even have been convicted." This passage appeared on the eve of a last-gasp, and partially successful, attempt by Friedman to reduce his combined, state and federal nineteen-year sentences.

If these supportive gestures were an example of Trump loyalty, they were a rare example indeed. He had turned his back on everyone from Abe Beame, refusing to contribute to him in the 1977 mayoral election, to Louise Sunshine and Der Scutt, two of the people whose skillful service had helped make him who he was. But there was no more poignant example of Donald's infidelity than the distance he allowed to develop in the mid-eighties between himself and his dying mentor, Stanley Friedman's partner, Roy Cohn. While Cohn told Trump and the rest of the world he had cancer, everyone knew, from the fall of 1984 to his death in 1986, that AIDS was killing him. Though Cohn was struggling to maintain his practice, Donald quickly began withdrawing work from him, wounding and outraging the bulldog lawyer who was using his vast array of connections to secure every form of experimental treatment. "I can't believe he's doing this to me," Roy complained. "Donald pisses ice water."

When Roy called Donald in late 1984 to find a hotel room for his former lover and top assistant, Russell Eldridge, who was in the final stages of AIDS, he had an assistant ready to pull the plug on the phone if Donald asked what Russell was dying of. Trump didn't ask and offered a room in the Barbizon that Cohn staffers described as "tacky." Cohn was stunned, however, when Donald began sending him bills for the room. Cohn just threw the bills in the trash and then a Trump aide started calling, asking about the rent and saying Russell couldn't continue to stay there, claiming he was hurting the reputation of the hotel.

When Cohn was dying himself a year later, Donald did call fairly often in his final months, chatting amiably. He also testified on Cohn's behalf in the disbarment proceeding brought during Cohn's long illness. Roy visited Donald's Florida estate, Mar-A-Lago, shortly before he died, but only for a dinner that was also attended by Jerry Finkelstein and Andy Stein. While the event was later reported as an intimate farewell, Finkelstein insists that Cohn was just one of thirty or so guests, and that Cohn was hardly any sort of honoree. At Roy's memorial service a few days after his death, Donald stood in the back of the room silently, not asked to be one of several designated speakers, precisely because those closest to Cohn felt he had abandoned the man who had molded him.

One explanation for Trump's contrasting treatment of Cohn and Friedman, offered by those who witnessed it, was that he may have believed Friedman could hurt him. Under the pressure of a virtual life sentence, Friedman was repeatedly visited in prison or recalled from the midwest to New York by state and federal prosecutors trying to win his cooperation, but he toughed it out, and prosecutors concluded that he would only open up if he lost his sentence reduction appeals. If this was a Trump concern, Friedman's curious role in the approach to Mirabel on 100 CPS might well have been part of the cause, meaning that the dirty little war Donald liked to dismiss was still hovering over him as he lobbied for leniency for Friedman years later.

The debt to Friedman wasn't the only 100 CPS reminder to linger into the new decade. The city refused to drop its anti-eviction lawsuit, and pressed forward for years, even though the state and the tenants had long since settled. With the city kept at a distance during the state talks in 1986, the ultimate agreement actually obligated the tenants to cease cooperating with the city's attorneys on the companion case, and they did. Yet the Koch administration—which was, by then, engaged in a bitter battle with Trump on other fronts—successfully repulsed a motion to dismiss the case in 1988, and attorneys for the city began openly discussing the possibility of deposing Trump, forcing him for the first time to answer questions under oath about the events at 100 Central Park South.

Though internal memos circulated within the corporation counsel's office reveal that a deposition of Trump was considered as early as July 1988, Trump's attorneys weren't notified that the city intended actually to do so until the fall of 1989, soon after Ed Koch lost his bid for a fourth term in the September Democratic primary. Faced with the threat of a deposition, Trump's lawyers quickly moved to settle, agreeing to a $25,000 payment to the city in the final week of the Koch administration.

An internal memo written in November 1989 by an assistant corporation counsel recommending the scanty settlement actually concluded: "Discovery has revealed that it may be difficult to prove several aspects of our case—e.g., that services were intentionally diminished." It was a postmortem much like the one volunteered proudly by Rozenholc, who admitted that he had "succeeded in taking some incidents and magnifying them to make them appear much worse than they were." While Trump certainly had attempted in the beginning to clear the building with intimidating threats, he had also, up the road, been part-victim of a public relations–conscious smear.

• • •

The renovations at 100 Central Park South took longer than the two-year deadline written into the agreement and cost a fortune. The tenants were happy at
last, living now in gold-leaf, rent-controlled luxury. Though the newly improved
building was only valued at $10 million, Donald took out mortgages against it
for three times that amount.

He went on to build what he called a "fabulously successful" condo, Trump
Parc, within the refurbished shell of the neighboring Barbizon. He harmonized
the two buildings with the same pale beige hue, identical windows and the predictable gold trim, renaming 100 Central Park South Trump Parc East. Condos
at Trump Parc were advertised in 1986 at $180,000 for a 300-square-foot studio
to $4 million for a 3,500-square-foot, four-bedroom unit. A staff of doormen,
hall men, and maids was hired to retain the feeling of a grand hotel. All but a half
dozen or so of the 340 units were sold, and Donald boasted of an unlikely $100
million profit.

Assuming Donald's profit estimates on Trump Parc were in line with his ordinary hyperbolic markup, he could have made nearly as much a lot earlier and
easier by simply selling the building. Donald solicited and then rejected an offer
of $90 million for the two properties just months after he bought them in 1982—
teasing the offer out of lawyers for Imelda and Ferdinand Marcos without a serious intention of accepting it. In the middle of the DHCR hearings in 1985, he
got deeply embroiled in sales talks with buyers put together by his old concrete
supplier and sometime friend, Bif Halloran. With former governor Hugh Carey
acting as a broker, and salivating over a possible million-dollar brokerage fee,
the price got up to $125 million before Donald scuttled the deal, leaving Carey
reportedly sputtering in disappointment about what an ingrate Donald was, invoking memories of all he'd done for Donald in a conversation with Halloran.

In the end, regardless of the offers that came his way, Donald was unable to
part with his dream properties. In fact, instead of selling them, he bought the
St. Moritz Hotel, which stood opposite 100 Central Park South on Sixth Avenue
and also faced the park. This time the seller was Harry Helmsley—the man he
swore he'd be bigger than in five years when he surveyed the skyline from the
park with Ned Eichler a decade earlier. He publicly claimed that he only paid $31
million for the St. Moritz but the actual price was $72 million. He obtained an
$80 million mortgage on the St. Moritz, and a $50 million one on the Barbizon
properties, a combination triple the amount of what he told reporters they had
cost him.

Donald soon had a unified vision for this string of properties. It started with his ultimate goal, the Plaza, at the eastern edge of the park, and worked its way west past the St. Moritz and Trump Parc for several golden blocks. He saw Central Park South as the heart of the city and, in a literal sense, the center of the world. As he sat in his Trump Tower apartment, he could look out the window and imagine his own tree-lined empire of elegance just below. Central Park South was his driveway; everyone with money visiting New York from anywhere in the world had to ride on it. And it virtually led right to the door of his flagship Tower.

The vision had almost been spoiled by the tenant war, but he had been tenacious. As he saw it, he had not given in to the shakedown, had taken the media hits and had doggedly hung on to his property. He'd stood tall against a system of rent regulation that was an insult to a free economy; his was a triumph of capital over claptrap. His public position now was that the tenant battle had delayed his project just long enough for him to benefit from the boom in the market. So he announced that he had made money from the protracted conflict, reasoning that Trump Parc was a far bigger financial success than it would have been had he built it in the early eighties. He had gone head-to-head with the common mob, and if he hadn't exactly won, Donald Trump had shown the world that he knew how to convert a defeat into a triumph.

10

FROM THE WEST SIDE TO MAR-A-LAGO

Seeing the iron manner in which he had managed to wrest victory out of defeat, these gentlemen had experienced a change of heart and announced that they would now gladly help finance any new enterprise which Cowperwood might undertake. . . . In the commercial heart of this world Frank Algernon Cowperwood had truly become a figure of giant significance. How wonderful it is that men grow until, like colossuses, they bestride the world, or, like banyan trees, they drop roots from every branch and are themselves a forest. . . . His properties were like a net—the parasite goldthread—linked together as they were, and draining two of the three important sides of the city.

—*Theodore Dreiser,* THE TITAN

Trump, who believes that excess can be a virtue, is as American as Manhattan's skyline. . . . In this heap of humanity Trump plans to plant a 150-story superskyscraper. You say the world, and especially Manhattan, does not need that. Trump says need-schmeed. The superskyscraper is necessary because it is unnecessary. Some nations need optional acts of bravado. . . . Trump's name suggests the brass section of the human orchestra.

—*George Will,* NEWSWEEK, *1985*

AT TWO O'CLOCK one Sunday afternoon in the early fall of 1984 Sally Good-gold caught sight of her old nemesis alone, in a blue suit on a glorious September day, perched high atop the elevated section of the West Side Highway. Although his view of the entire 60th Street rail yards revealed nothing but tracks, garbage, weeds, and prairie, Donald Trump was still, after all these years, mesmerized. His limo had pulled off the highway, and as Sally was driving to her West Side apartment, she noticed him near the 72nd Street exit, standing in what she called his "Fountainhead pose"—feet apart, hands on his hips, jaw locked with determination. Goodgold went home breathless. "Donald Trump is going to buy the West Side yards," she announced to anyone who would pick up a phone. It was Goodgold's version of a Paul Revere run.

On January 15, 1985, at the precise midpoint in his decade, Donald Trump realized his dream and bought the land that had originally drawn him to Manhattan, the 60th Street rail yard. Still undeveloped a decade after Donald's obsession began, this onetime prime location for large-scale subsidized housing had ironically become the city's most inviting new land for upscale development, transformed by the booming condo and commercial real estate market on the suddenly gentrified West Side. Donald put the purchase price at $95 million in the press when it was actually $115 million; and no one seemed to notice that he could have had it for a mere $28 million had he extended his option only a few years earlier.

Like everything else Donald did at the time, this deal was celebrated as a coup, and the comparatively low price in such a soaring market certainly made it look like one. The story of Trump's fanatical yet tactically measured conquest of this property contains, in hindsight, its own intricate irony: After all the devious maneuvers that delivered the site to Donald, it still sits vacant. Seizing the yards may have been one of his most spectacular triumphs, but owning them has proven to be a self-inflicted wound. The truth is that even when Donald walked away from his option in 1979, he would not let go of his fantasy site. His father's old friend, Abe Hirschfeld, wound up with the option on the same terms Donald had negotiated, and Trump simply bided his time. Hirschfeld managed in the fall of 1980 to sell a 65 percent stake and management control of the project to a new general partner, the Argentine builder and auto dealer Francisco Macri. This unlikely duo—a garage king and a Fiat manufacturer—quickly tried to initiate a huge condo development called Lincoln West on Manhattan's largest tract of available land. But their inexperience as major New York builders fit nicely with Donald's strategy of stalemate, suggesting that the project might be stymied just long enough for him to come back for a second shot.

For two years Trump's name hovered over Macri's rezoning efforts, with half the West Side insisting that Macri was a mere "stand-in" for Trump and ridiculing the Macri organization as the only party involved in the development of the site that didn't recognize that fact. While the West Siders saw Trump as the man behind Macri, the top staff in Macri's organization began to wonder if he wasn't funding their opposition, convincing themselves that it was Trump money that had covertly prompted a Sierra Club lawsuit that delayed the project for fourteen months.

The Macri brass was also uncertain that Chase Manhattan—the bank that had agreed to finance the purchase once the rezoning was obtained—would actually go through with the deal. They and the Palmieri executives making the sale attributed that fear to the Trump shadow that hung over the forty-foot-long closing table at the offices of Chase's lawyers, Dewey Ballantine, in September 1982. Conrad Stephenson, the Chase regional real estate chief, pressed the Palmieri group to extend Macri's option in an attempt to postpone the closing. When no extension was granted, Stephenson said he wanted to split the closing into two phases, providing part of the mortgage a few months later, even though such a split would mean that Macri would pay $2 million more for the land. Macri reluctantly assented. Both Macri and Palmieri officials agreed in interviews years later that they thought Stephenson was really trying to break the deal, and they believed Trump was behind the banker's hesitation.

After all, Stephenson, known in New York as Mr. Real Estate and the master of a $2.7 billion commercial real estate portfolio, had been Donald's personal banker since the 70s. Fred Trump, a prime Chase customer for two decades, had brought his son to the bank, and Donald and Stephenson had worked out the refinancings of some of Fred's Brooklyn and Queens projects. As head of Chase's tristate real estate unit, Stephenson had also authorized a $35 million unsecured line of credit for the thirty-three-year-old in 1980—at prime and on terms not spelled out in writing. Since Donald had yet to finish a project, this extraordinary gesture was clearly attributable to Stephenson's confidence in Fred, as well as his assessment of Donald's prospects, particularly at the still-in-construction Hyatt and on Fifth Avenue, where he'd already assembled the Trump Tower site.

By 1982, at the peak of his influence after thirty-two years in banking, the fifty-three-year-old Stephenson was fashioning a new image for Chase. The city's business weekly, *Crain's,* would note that he "turned Chase into the dominant Manhattan commercial real estate lender" by "serving only the elite" of the borough's developers. The epitome of the WASP banker, the regal and robust

Stephenson was known as a "relationship lender," which means he spent a lifetime cultivating big borrowers whose deals were solid enough to repay large loans.

Trump was rapidly becoming one of Stephenson's prized banking clients, using his credit line to cover both $28 million in Hyatt overruns and, despite Chase regulations against casino loans, $8.9 million in start-up costs for Trump Plaza in Atlantic City. Stephenson had also given Trump a $30 million second mortgage on the Hyatt and played the lead role in the $130 million financing of Trump Tower, as well as the $50 million acquisition of the Barbizon Hotel and 100 Central Park South. When Donald applied for his Atlantic City gaming license in 1981, as well as when he briefly sought a Nevada license in 1985, Stephenson was one of the personal references Donald listed.

Starting with his reluctance at the first Macri closing—when, despite the urgency of Penn Central's expiring option deadline, Stephenson reportedly had to be dragged to the table from a sailing excursion—the banker would be viewed by the Macri group as an ally, conscious or otherwise, of Trump's. This suspicion was fed by Donald's almost immediate attempts to buy into the project. As early as November, less than two scant months after Macri got his city zoning permit to build 4,300 apartments and the closing of the first phase of the Chase mortgage, Trump was expressing interest in the site. Even before Macri could close on the second phase in December of 1982, Trump had begun exploratory talks with a Macri associate.

Since Macri saw himself as a builder, not a speculator, he wanted to complete Lincoln West himself. Yet he feared—from the moment Donald's revival of interest became apparent—that he would be forced to make a deal with Trump because the incestuous New York real estate market would not accept or finance him unless he had a Trump-like figure at his side. Indeed, he was convinced that Chase, and other banks who were considering participation in the construction loan for his half-billion-dollar project, wanted Trump in particular involved in the deal. Over the course of the next two years, he found himself repeatedly acquiescing to this implicit demand, then rethinking his acquiescence—the project at a standstill while his heart struggled with his head, practicality pushing him to the table he dreaded.

A strong, quiet man, Macri was born in Rome, moved to Argentina at the age of nineteen, and, starting as a bricklayer, amassed an astonishing empire employing over 10,000 people and including everything from cars to garbage facilities to dams to oil drillings to a 4,000-unit housing complex. He believed, however, that Lincoln West would establish him as a major international force. "I don't understand why everyone is so captivated with Trump," he once blurted out to his principal New York attorney, Ralph Galasso. "My net worth *is* $550 million. His net worth is supposedly $550 million. What is so important about him?"

Nevertheless, Macri himself "believed in the Trump mystique," concluded Galasso, and was "fascinated" both by Trump and by the city's glamorous fast track. Throughout the five years he ran his Lincoln West project in New York, he lived in Buenos Aires but kept an apartment in the Galleria off Fifth Avenue for occasional weeklong visits and took $800-a-day suites in the Helmsley Palace for shorter trips. He enjoyed the New York fast lane so much that it was not unusual for Macri to be given a few thousand a day in cash for expenses while in town, taken as a project Cost. Trump became, in Macri's head, a symbol of a city that dazzled him in so many ways.

Fourteen years older than Donald, curly-haired, wide-faced, short, and slightly stout, Macri spoke virtually no English and thought Donald looked down on him. "Ivana came and visited at my ranch in Buenos Aires. Donald played golf with my son Mauricio. He was very friendly, but very tough," Macri said in a 1990 interview. "He feels like he is a bit like the owner of New York and he did not think I had the capacity to confront a project like this. He spoke as if I did not have experience and that I had only built bridges and dams, when in reality I had constructed many more millions of cubic meters in housing than Donald Trump will construct in his lifetime. He spoke as if I was a South American banana farmer. I wasn't a dummy, and he was very young."

From 1982 to the end of 1984 Trump moved on Macri with a tenacious patience—through a series of four failed deals—toward the buyout Donald always wanted. Their first agreement, in July of 1983, gave the parties a thirty-day deadline to complete Donald's purchase of half of Macri's interest for $25 million. According to the two-page document, Lincoln West would be renamed Trump City, Trump staff would sell the apartments out of an office in the Atrium at Trump Tower, and Donald would assume all development costs until construction began, when the two would begin sharing costs fifty-fifty.

Though Donald was still making much publicly of his unwillingness to personally guarantee any development loans, he and Macri agreed to guarantee the mortgage for this project. Trump also pledged he would "work with Chase" to obtain a construction commitment, affirming Macri's belief that Trump could bring the bank in line. In fact, it was the continuing unsteadiness of the bank's commitment to the project, and the signals Macri thought he was receiving about what would please Chase, that helped push him to sign this initial deal with Trump. Chase had taken its three extra months to close on the second phase of the initial $50 million land loan and in fact did not close until friendly talks between Trump and the Macri organization began. When those initial talks proved fruitless, the bank suddenly backed off the $411 million construction commitment it had tentatively made at the end of 1982, citing the lack of a local developer as a prime concern. But when Macri resumed negotiations with Trump—signing the 1983 letter agreement and beginning talks on a detailed contract of sale—Chase's attitude perceptibly warmed.

It was not just the pending Trump deal that pleased the bank. Stephenson had insisted that Macri obtain a standby loan to secure the bulk of the construction lending and recommended a broker, Joseph Comras, who might arrange it. Even though Macri knew this would mean additional millions in fees to the broker and the standby lender, he hired Comras and found a backup lender, Travelers Insurance, which agreed to guarantee payment of the balance of the loan when it fully matured. Encouraged by these developments, and by Macri's progress with Trump, Chase dramatically changed the shape of its long-discussed construction loan—from the loosely considered $411 million for the overall project to $190 million for just the first tower, a reduction but still a commitment, and one that was clearly acceptable to Macri. Travelers' standby insured $144 million of Chase's $190 million commitment.

In addition to the new construction loan offer, Chase agreed to extend the deadline for repayment of the land loan for another five months and to give Macri another $22 million immediately, dramatically increasing the bank's investment in the project. These new Chase actions occurred in August, at the same moment that Macri and Trump attorneys were working out a revised extension of the July agreement. As part of the new pending agreement, Trump even sent Macri the draft of a $10 million note he was ready to give Macri at Chase rates of interest. But Macri decided not to sign the new agreement, refusing in the end to give up control of the project. Armed with the proceeds of the bank's new $22 million bridge loan, he began distancing himself from Trump.

To meet the bank's requirement of a local developer, Macri chose instead to sign a project-management contract with a New York builder, agreeing to pay a fee amounting to 1 percent of the hard costs of construction to oversee the project. Stephenson could do nothing but approve the selection of the respected developer, yet Macri continued to get mixed signals from the bank. Macri knew that there were reasons other than his reluctance to turn over the project to Trump for Chase's fluctuating resolve, especially the costly amenity package that he had promised in order to will city approval in 1982, including a $31 million subway station renovation. Stephenson had consistently objected to these up-front expenditures, but it wasn't until November of 1983, fourteen months after the agreement with the city was executed and soon after the collapse of the Trump talks, that Chase suddenly announced it would be unable to continue financing the project unless the pledges to the city were modified immediately. Chase continued disbursing the due portions of the $22 million bridge loan, but the bank also indicated it would only provide these critical expense funds if a "real estate developer acceptable to Chase" was chosen. It was as if the local management contract had never been approved.

Macri's response to the new Chase concerns was to win some minor modifications of the city pact and to reopen direct negotiations with Donald. When the Trump negotiations on a second deal resumed, the bank suspended again its complaints about the costs of the pledges to the city. Under the terms of the second agreement, Trump would buy the land outright at a yet-to-be-determined "fair market price." Macri would have the option, within six months of the sale, of buying back 49.5 percent of the project—leaving Trump in majority control—by paying that percent of Trump's costs plus permitting Donald to take a 25 percent profit off the top of any final project. All Donald had to do was obtain the $12 million loan Macri wanted to cover the ongoing costs of the project. It was an open-ended agreement, giving Trump seventy-five days to close after he and his accountants and lawyers were given "access to all information" regarding the project. This loophole made Donald the sole arbiter of when the clock started running.

Trump and Jerry Schrager brought a draft of these terms to Macri's suite at the Sherry Netherland overlooking Central Park on December 15, expecting further negotiations. Macri, and his top aides Diego Arria and Orlando Salvestrini, an interpreter named Christina, and Macri's teenaged son Mauricio were present. There were no Americans and no lawyers with Macri, contrary to the advice of the New York lawyers and executives he'd hired. Schrager handed Macri the letter, and Macri glanced at it and signed it, without discussion. The rest of the room was in shock. Donald began talking excitedly about starting Trump City in six months, proclaiming that it would be the city's most fabulous project. Macri said this was a historic moment in the life of his family, and he wanted Mauricio to sign the agreement as well.

"You didn't read the letter," Salvestrini exploded after Trump and Schrager left. "You didn't let me translate," objected Christina.

"I didn't need to," said Macri. "They're more worried than me because I signed it without reading it." Macri argued that he had to make Donald believe he was the winner, that he had to convince Trump that he had outsmarted him, to draw Donald into the deal. The details, he argued, could all be revised later.

The problem, however, was that Macri had signed an agreement—without attempting to change any of its terms—that was less favorable than the July letter. Instead of the clear $25 million profit of the earlier deal, Macri was giving up majority control for an undetermined price. The deadline to conclude the sale and set the "fair market" price was left in Donald's hands. Macri had also agreed to take a $12 million second mortgage from Trump without Chase's knowledge or consent—a potential source of friction. His protestations aside, Macri had acted on impulse and he admitted as much several days later when he went over the terms with his own lawyers, acknowledging that the agreement "did not adequately represent" his interests. He told his aides and lawyers he was not bound by it, but would merely use it as a framework to cut a final deal.

As good a deal as it was for Donald, he was also dissatisfied. He had his father's disdain for partners and did not want almost half of everything he earned on what he thought would be the grandest project of his life to go to anyone else, much less to an Argentine who didn't even bother to read their contract. The weakness that had led Macri to sign the agreement fed Trump's belief that if he delayed, and continued to push Macri, he could remove him from the project entirely. He would proceed under the terms of the agreement, inspecting the documents he was entitled to, but claiming that he had not yet triggered the seventy-five-day review process.

With both sides pulling back from a deal they'd just signed,* Chase suddenly entered the picture.

The letter agreement bound Macri "not to have any discussions and communications" with anyone about the sale, but made no similar stipulation for Trump. Stephenson came to the Macri group's Christmas party four days later and requested an urgent, brief conference with Macri. Salvestrini and Macri went with Stephenson and an aide to Diego Arria's nearby office, where they took their places around Arria's $40,000 desk, a piece that resembled an operating table on chrome wheels and symbolized the Macri group's penchant for excess.

"I understand that you have signed an agreement with Donald Trump," Stephenson announced. Macri and his aides were stunned, unable to figure out how

---

* When Macri finally closed on the sale to Donald more than a year later, he was forced to pay a $250,000 brokerage commission for this Sherry Netherland deal, as well as later negotiations, to none other than Charles Goldstein, the onetime lynchpin of the Commodore deal who was hired by Macri because of his supposed closeness to Trump.

Stephenson knew about the deal. As vigorously as Salvestrini and Macri denied having made such a deal, they were unable to persuade Stephenson.

"You don't believe me," Macri deadpanned. "Have you seen any agreement?"

"No, no. But I know you signed it," Stephenson persisted. The meeting ended in hostility, with Stephenson bristling, ostensibly over Macri's failure to notify him before coming to terms with Trump, to say nothing of his anger over the deception he had just heard from his client. Even before the meeting ended, Macri began wondering if Stephenson's source might be his own putative new partner.

Macri asked Arria, who had become the group's friendly emissary to Trump, to meet with Donald and try to convince him to attend a joint meeting with Stephenson to clear the air. Arria asked Trump if he had any idea how Stephenson knew about the agreement, and Trump said he did not. But Macri and his key staff were becoming more and more convinced that it was Trump, or his lawyer and Stephenson's friend Schrager who had informed Stephenson. Trump consented to go to Chase with Arria and Salvestrini to try to reassure Stephenson, and a meeting was set for December 21.

At a brusque session in Stephenson's glass-enclosed office, Arria and Salvestrini acknowledged but tried to minimize the significance of the agreement with Trump, portraying it as little more than a prescribed study period for Donald to take a look at the project and a mutual promise to negotiate if Trump liked what he found. Neither Trump nor Schrager contradicted this version. As per plan, both sides declined to provide Stephenson with a copy of the document, reassuring him that "if" Donald got involved, the new joint venture would still do the project with Chase.

Stephenson seemed somewhat mollified by the meeting, but raised concerns about the second mortgage and about the possibility of the seventy-five-day review period delaying the project. Arria and Salvestrini offered to deposit the proceeds of the Trump loan at Chase; they promised to rush the review.

The perfunctory session ended with the deal apparently in place. Salvestrini wrote a memo later that day noting that Stephenson and three other bank representatives indicated the bank was going ahead with the construction loan and would extend the February loan deadlines to the end of March.

Stephenson, who alternated between effusive charm and the military stiffness that remained from his onetime reserve officer commission, took no immediate action after this meeting, apparently waiting to see if the Sherry Netherland agreement indeed had a chance of closing. The first indication that it would not was the battle Trump and Macri attorneys immediately launched over the planned document exchange. Schrager and his colleagues at Dreyer & Traub insisted that their document requests had been only partially fulfilled and that the review period had not yet begun, while the Macri group challenged them on both counts, offering to allow Trump to come and see the company's files. On another front, when Trump sent Macri the $12 million loan commitment, Macri refused to execute it, nitpicking about the terms. It was becoming clear to both sides that neither was eager to close the deal.

It was at this point that the long-standing tensions with Chase boiled over. Although Stephenson had not mentioned his complaints about the December deal for a month and a half, he suddenly wrote Macri a letter in late January 1984 that was an unbridled attack on the group's "seemingly directionless activities," threatening to call the loans on the due date of February 1. Stephenson assailed the open-ended review period given to Trump and demanded a copy of the contract before he would "consider an extension" of the deadline.

For the first time Stephenson raised the issue of the syndication of the construction loan and said it was Macri's obligation to find participant banks willing to assume portions of it, a job Macri adamantly insisted was Chase's. Unless Macri was able to miraculously do so in the seven days before the deadline, Stephenson intimated that he would not extend the construction commitment.

The Stephenson letter was greeted in the Macri group with shock and dismay. The smooth, white-haired banker from Dix Hills, Long Island, never far from a golf club, a yacht, or a black-tie dinner party, had only two gears—a graceful overdrive and a jolting reverse. He had clearly decided to back away from the Argentine who had misled him. A relationship banker has to know when to end relationships and which ones are more important than others.

Macri's first response to Stephenson's ultimatum was to try to get the Trump deal on some kind of track, writing four frantic letters in three days to Trump or his lawyers, reiterating the invitation to examine the files. Trump didn't even reply to a handwritten plea from his friend Arria, who asked him to formally fix March 31 as the final day of the review period.

The panicked Macri group, whose principal had personally guaranteed the Chase loans, answered Stephenson's letter on January 30 with an angry blast of its own. In an apparent reference to its suspicion that Trump or Schrager had already told Stephenson the details of the agreement, Arria wrote that the group was "under the impression that you were aware of the substance of the agreement" and sent him no copy. Arria pointed out that Macri had paid $4 million to Comras and Travelers for the standby commitment Stephenson had demanded, as well as agreed to pay $2.5 million under the management agreement to satisfy the bank's demand for a local developer. He complained that they were "at a loss to understand how Chase could claim at this late stage" that syndicating the loan was Macri's responsibility and insisted that the bank would have to cover the extra expense associated with the failure to syndicate.

Arria talked to Stephenson by phone a few hours after the letter was messengered to him, and Stephenson called the Macri response "insane," canceling the meeting he had scheduled with them for the next day. "I do not want to do anything with you. I want out. I want my money," Stephenson bellowed. Though the bank's relationship to the project would drag on for a year, it effectively ended during this 3:40 p.m. phone conversation.

There was no question but that Donald learned quickly about this dramatic turn of events and that it convinced him he suddenly had Macri on the ropes. The debonair Arria, who wrote letters to Donald as if the two were lifelong and trusting friends, penned another missive to him, sending him copies of his and Stephenson's correspondence and suggesting that he and Trump "clarify any misunderstandings" Stephenson might still have. Whatever Arria didn't inadvertently tell Donald about Macri's dire circumstances Trump seemed to know anyway. He decided to seize the opportunity. The same day as Stephenson's outburst, Schrager's firm sent Macri an amended agreement, granting the March 31 review period deadline requested by Arria but adding a series of new demands. Trump wanted Macri to pay all his expenses for the review period if the deal terminated. The proposal was actually dated three days earlier, but Trump waited to send it over until Stephenson had forced Macri's hand.

What followed was a hectic series of Macri attempts to undo the Stephenson decision. A contingent went to Chase to meet with Stephenson's immediate superior, Robert Douglass, who said he would try to "put things together." Macri hired a powerful law firm with significant Chase ties—the prestigious Patterson Belknap, Webb & Tyler—to deal with the crisis. In a February meeting with the Macri leadership, Joel Carr, a partner from the firm, concluded that the December agreement was unenforceable under state law because it was so vague about the sales price, recommending that Macri "immediately walk away" from it. Carr encouraged Arria, who had a lunch scheduled with Donald for the following day, February 7, to broach the subject of terminating the agreement. Arria did, and Trump quickly agreed to tear up the December letter, throwing in a lecture for good measure about how generous an act it was. In truth he, too, wanted out, betting that Chase's now open combat with Macri would force the Argentine to give him an even better deal in the near future. Arria agreed to pick up $100,000 in Trump expenses associated with the agreement; $75,000 of it for Dreyer & Traub.

The day after all the releases were signed and the checks sent, Donald replied with a classic brief note to Arria: "Over the last number of years everyone has taken advantage of Lincoln West, but I will not be one of them. That is why I released you from your obligations under the Letter Agreement after having let you know how serious those obligations were and also why I am returning the check you sent me for expenses. You and Franco (Macri) are friends and I do not want your money. I will absorb all my costs, but I do hope after all of our efforts we will be able to get the development on track as soon as possible. It really needs help." With it, Trump returned the $25,000 check sent to cover his own organizational costs.*

The day after the clearly confident Trump pulled out of the deal, Stephenson dropped another bomb in a terse letter to Arria that formally advised the Macri group that the bank had "no interest in extending the commitment or renewing the notes." Stephenson asked that Macri pay the $72 million obligation as soon as possible. Ironically, earlier the same day, Arria had sent Stephenson copies of the Trump releases and asked that the bank now proceed with the construction loan.

At a meeting several days later Stephenson gave the Macri group thirty days to formulate "a concrete plan" to take Chase out of the deal, characterizing the loan as "due and payable" but "not on demand." While he congratulated Arria on obtaining the release from Trump, he asked: "Why didn't you consummate the deal?" Assuring them that he could have worked things out with Trump, Stephenson closed the meeting with a threat to call the loan and Macri's personal guarantee through Chase's branch in Argentina, if a plan to repay the loan wasn't submitted in a month.

Faced with this possibility, Macri once again began talks with Donald. But during this third cycle both sides finally seemed ready to consider what Donald

---

* In *The Art of the Deal,* Trump would contend that his tearing up the letter was the reason Macri came back to him in the end, "instead of going to any of a dozen other bidders." Almost everything in his description of this culminating scene was incorrect, however, as he back-dated it by almost a year and placed himself opposite Macri in a page-long, touching, tearing-up scene, when in fact he was with the lesser-known Arria. Macri was actually in Buenos Aires, awaiting the arrival in a day or so of Ivana for a two-day trek—a visit Donald even mentioned in his note to Arria. This inaccurate rendition was a repeat of Trump's version of how he'd won the yards the first time out, substituting Victor Palmieri for the obscure Ned Eichler in the negotiations precisely a decade earlier.

had always wanted—an outright buyout. Macri hadn't made a firm decision to sell, but Arria and Donald nonetheless began exploring a purchase price. Arria and attorney Ralph Galasso tried one more approach to Stephenson midway through the bank's thirty-day period, amassing seven binders of progress reports on every aspect of Lincoln West, trying to convince him to stick with it. A curt Stephenson dismissed the tableload of documents with a wave of his hand, insisting "All Chase wants is its money and a concise proposal on how it will get it."

Arria argued that a restructuring was impossible in fifteen days, telling Stephenson of the renewed negotiations with Trump and of a few other vague prospects. Stephenson said he would grant another ninety days if a new letter of intent with an acceptable buyer was submitted. He then went out of his way to denigrate the only other buyer mentioned by Galasso. In the guise of an attempt to be helpful, Stephenson also recommended that Macri "sell out completely" to avoid a lawsuit from his 35 percent partner, Abe Hirschfeld. Finally, Stephenson made it clear that Chase would not accept a new formula that left Macri in place as a general partner, reducing any future Macri association with the project to, at best, a limited interest. Trump and his favorite banker, as it turned out, had almost identical positions.

The high point of this showdown with Stephenson, however, was Arria's request that "Steve," as he was called by his New York developer friends, keep their discussions strictly confidential, an axiom in any banking relationship. Arria said that Trump had already cut his buyout offer from $130 million to $100 million "when he learned that Chase had given Lincoln West thirty days to find a takeout." Arria made no explicit charge about where Trump might have learned this vital information, but Galasso's careful post-meeting memo noted: "Stephenson was silent, but it was obviously a point very well taken by him." Afterward, Stephenson's approach "was more constructive and even conciliatory."

With the thirty-day deadline still in place, Macri had his lawyers evaluate the possibility of a lawsuit against Chase, while he simultaneously tried to figure out a way to circumvent Stephenson. Arria renewed his meetings and correspondence with Robert Douglass, Stephenson's superior, sending him the same seven binders of information Stephenson had rejected and telling him in one session about Stephenson's suspected breach of confidentiality. Arria pointed out that Macri had never missed interest payments—an amount that now totaled $8.2 million—even during these testy times, while the bank had refused to make the final payments due under the agreed-upon bridge loan.

But Arria did not send a four-page letter they had spent days drafting to Douglass. In it, Arria said they were "dismayed to discover that less than 24 hours after we were given 30 days by Mr. Stephenson, our prospective purchaser was in full knowledge of this situation and reduced his offer by $24 million." Arria said he told Stephenson that "these leaks were extremely damaging to our project," yet "ongoing events between Chase and Lincoln West continue to be known by prospective purchasers or their representatives to our detriment." Arria's letter was not sent because Macri decided that it would turn the financing issue into an assault on Stephenson's integrity, leaving the bank with no option other than intransigent opposition to his project.

When the Douglass conversations did little more than buy time, Macri made one last appeal to the man who symbolized Chase in Latin America, David Rockefeller, who'd resigned as chairman in 1981 but still headed the bank's international advisory committee. Macri recruited an Argentine friend, Jose Alfredo Martinez de Hoz, the former minister of the economy under the military government who was an old friend of Rockefeller's, and flew him up to New York. De Hoz's approach to Rockefeller was a high-level secret, even within the Macri group. He laid out the Stephenson history, and Rockefeller said he would look into it and get back to him within twenty-four hours. The next day Rockefeller called Macri's New York office to say there was nothing he could do.

The predictable effect of Chase's abrupt and irreversible rejection was that Macri had to sell, with little time and no buyers on hand but Donald. A third agreement with Trump was drafted. The terms changed from day to day, but the essence of it was that Donald would acquire the land, with the Lincoln West partnership of Hirschfeld and Macri holding on to a combined 10 to 15 percent interest in the project. The price fluctuated between $100 million and $125 million, with Chase becoming Donald's lender and financing the purchase. So long as this deal was on the table, Stephenson let his own fierce, mid-March deadline pass without comment.

Macri and Trump reached agreement again in early April, but did not sign anything. On the final day of negotiations, Donald was accompanied by a *New York Times* reporter, and before the end of the month he was portrayed in a fawning Sunday *Times Magazine* profile as having convinced the Argentines to sell out their project to him. In fact, Macri was still uncertain, and he had yet to obtain the approval of his limited partner waiting in the wings, Abe Hirschfeld.

Macri brought the proposal to Hirschfeld, who had a right under the original agreement to sign off on any sale or try to match the offer. Hirschfeld had happily consented to the first Trump deal in July 1983, adding only one amendment— the hope that "a street or an avenue" in Trump City might be named after his family. While that agreement left Hirschfeld's slice of the project untouched, with

Donald in charge, Hirschfeld had been bypassed in the ill-fated Sherry Netherland negotiations, and complained bitterly about it when he found out. This time, before any letter was signed, Macri, Hirschfeld, and his son Eli shared a conference call, with Macri pushing for "a decision on Donald Trump very fast," giving Hirschfeld no other plausible alternative.

Instead, Hirschfeld decided to make his own offer to buy the project, leaving Macri with no option but to consider it—under the express terms of their partnership agreement. Trump and the bank had to back off while this implausible Hirschfeld notion played itself out. By the end of April, Hirschfeld dropped his attempted purchase, apparently signaling a willingness to accept a $100 million sale to Trump in which he and Macri would retain a 10 or 15 percent joint interest. When such a contract was drawn, however, Hirschfeld refused to sign the consent Macri sent him. So Macri decided to go ahead without Hirschfeld and test the "reasonableness" of Hirschfeld's refusal to consent in an arbitration proceeding, as provided in the original contract between the two.

That resolve triggered a fourth set of negotiations, redesigning the April agreement with the assumption that Hirschfeld would probably challenge it. After several months of conversations between lawyers for both sides, Macri and Donald finally talked by phone in mid-June. The proposed deal, which would have given the Lincoln West partnership of Macri and Hirschfeld a priority position to lay claim to $25 million out of Trump's first profits, looked so certain that Macri came to New York to conclude it. He sent a short note to Donald, together with a draft of the final contract, promising that "within the next 48 hours you and I will meet alone without any of our lawyers to arrive hopefully and if possible to a final contract or if this exercise proves to be impossible, then to terminate our long negotiations." The meeting never took place.

For the fourth time in a year, on June 22, a deal between these two mismatched developers came apart. Macri handwrote Donald a note in broken English, concluding "at least we both now know that we will not be able to do anything more together on this matter."

Neither side would bite the bullet—Macri could not come to grips with the loss of his dream project, and Trump still believed he could get rid of Macri altogether. Donald knew that the financial pressures on Macri would only grow stronger—after all, by July of 1984, Lincoln West was nearing his second complete year of interest payments, totaling $10 million, on a project that had gone nowhere. An internal accounting analysis concluded that since serious talks with Trump and the problems with Chase began in April 1983, the Macri group had spent $26.9 million on various predevelopment costs, and Macri claimed that $20 million of it was his own money.

Macri took one last, transparently futile, shot at the bank—writing two letters to Stephenson in early July, asking him to agree to restructure the existing financing over a two-to five-year period or to go forward with the $190 million commitment. This time Macri announced he would withhold interest payments until a new arrangement could be worked out. Though Macri was only a few days late on the first missed payment, Stephenson took the decisive step on July 18, filing a foreclosure action in court.

The foreclosure came at a particularly vulnerable moment for Macri, for he had exactly two months left on the grace period the city had given him when the rezoning was approved in 1982. At the time the zoning permits passed the Board of Estimate, Macri had promised the city to work out a mapping agreement—laying out a 200-page street circulation and infrastructure plan for the yards—by September 17, 1984. The map had finally been completed, and Macri and the city were prepared to commit themselves to an entire grid of streets, curbs and sewer lines. But the city suddenly added a new and unusual wrinkle, insisting that Macri's bank "subordinate its interest in the property to the rights granted the city by the mapping agreement." This new demand required Chase to commit itself, as a potential owner of the property (should it take the property in foreclosure) to meet the street and infrastructure obligations Lincoln West had accepted in the mapping agreement if the project was built. Chase had done exactly that in 1982 with respect to the subway improvements and other amenities, but if it now refused to sign this technical subordination consent, Macri would lose the mapping agreement and possibly even the special permit for 4,300 new apartments that had taken years for him to negotiate.

Trump was certainly aware of the publicly announced deadlines for the mapping agreement when he walked away from the June deal. It could not have come as much of a surprise to him, or to Macri, that Chase would refuse to sign the subordination, even though it did not expose the bank to any real risk. Through August and into September, Macri's new lawyer, a powerful Washington attorney named Lloyd Cutler, tried to cajole a subordination letter out of Chase. The city extended its deadline to October 4, and the bank and Cutler went head-to-head. The issues that ultimately killed these negotiations were a measure of just how hostile, and mutually suspicious, the relationship had become.

Chase began by stating that "even if the subordination were not to harm Chase," the bank wouldn't "take effective action now solely to benefit Macri."

Macri offered to pay the $4 million in interest now due, make all future payments, and get Chase out of its loan in six months in exchange for the subordination and a six-month suspension of the foreclosure proceeding. While Chase indicated its willingness to suspend the foreclosure action, it wanted Macri to execute a waiver barring him from countersuing Chase for a breach of duties should the foreclosure resume, and it wanted a guarantee Macri wouldn't file his own complaint for damages. Even with his back to the wall, Macri would not yield to these Chase demands. The foreclosure case proceeded, and in an October and November set of legal papers, Macri did press a breach of duties charge against the bank. The bank sidestepped the issue on technical grounds.

Despite Chase's last-minute refusal to sign the subordination letter, the city decided to approve the mapping agreement but make it contingent on the signing of the bank's subordination within four months. Since Chase would never sign, the vacillating Macri finally had a real deadline by which to sell, imposed by a resolution passed by the full Board of Estimate. If he didn't sell or find a new bank to subordinate by February 4, he would lose his map change and possibly his special permit, diminishing the value of his property.

Like a tireless, circling predator, Donald Trump was again at Macri's door—his fifth assault against the exhausted Macri. Trump doubted that the Argentine could reach out for new buyers with the mapping deadline hanging over his head. Trump would therefore drive a hard bargain, insisting on a complete buyout. The two wary adversaries settled quickly on a purchase price of $115 million, signing a forty-seven-page contract of sale only fourteen days after the October 4 Board of Estimate vote on the mapping agreement. It was a straight sale, with Macri getting out altogether and Stephenson financing the Trump purchase. While Chase's initial mortgage was only for $85 million, the bank signed on to cover the long-term development costs of the project and eventually loaned Donald almost $215 million, even paying the interest due on its own mortgages. The Chase embrace of the Trump project sealed, at least in the minds of Macri's men, their long-standing suspicion that Macri had been the victim of a viselike conspiracy, simultaneously squeezed by a buyer and a banker who wanted him out.

In sharp contrast with the $25 million profit and the 50 percent retained interest of the first Trump deal, Macri's profit on the final sale, once the balance due Chase and all other expenses were subtracted, was a puny $4.4 million.

Hirschfeld delayed the closing by withholding his consent again. He contested the sale terms vigorously in an arbitration proceeding that dragged on until the end of November, pointing out, with some effectiveness, that the purchase price was $200 million less than Macri's most recent appraisal. Skillfully playing the clock to his own advantage, Hirschfeld was counting on the fact that Macri had to complete the sale to Trump before the judge ruled on Chase's foreclosure at a hearing scheduled for November 30 or risk losing the property to the bank. Donald, too, was nudged forward both by the foreclosure deadline and by the arbitrator's ruling that he'd have to immediately submit to a wide-ranging deposition by Hirschfeld's lawyer. So Donald quickly reached a separate agreement with Hirschfeld, making him a 20 percent partner.

Donald's willingness to make Hirschfeld a partner, as well as Hirschfeld's move into Trump Tower office space right after the closing, suggested to some Macri loyalists that the zany but clever millionaire might have long been a Trump mole in their midst. He wasn't the only one associated with the project suspected of being a Trump agent. In Hirschfeld's case, in fact, Trump would later publicly acknowledge that he had been tipping him off on Macri's financial problems.

In addition to Hirschfeld, the suspect list included Jim Capalino, the president of Lincoln West Associates, who had surrendered his title in 1984 yet remained a Macri consultant while simultaneously working at a premium Manhattan real estate firm that became Donald's West Side yards broker. As soon as Trump closed on the property, Capalino was hired as a Trump consultant, advising him on the West Side project as a partner in the brokerage firm and as a lobbyist with his own public relations outfit. Penn Yards Associates, Donald's West Side entity, became one of the first clients of Capalino's one-man company.

A close aide to Ed Koch since the mayor's days in Congress, Capalino left the city administration for Macri in 1982 and had remained Macri's emissary to City Hall through the dark days of 1984. But it was the city's position on the mapping agreement, and its unwillingness to renegotiate any part of the costly amenity package even after Macri made a dramatic personal appeal to Koch in October, that left Macri with no alternative but to sell. What Macri did not know, but City Hall memos establish, was that Capalino was letting everyone from the mayor on down know that Macri would sell to Trump as early as May of 1984, well before Chase foreclosed. This premature portrait of a finished Macri and Capalino's prediction that new owner Trump would discard Macri's plan gave top officials little incentive to deal with Macri and helped doom any possibility of city concessions.

The rest of the suspect list included Ralph Galasso, the Macri lawyer who was retained by Donald to handle title matters relating to the yards right after the sale, Norman Levin, a Lincoln West planner Donald put on staff, and Macri's key environmental consultants who quickly became Trump's. Two other Macri consultants—HRH and the indefatigable Stanley Friedman—were, of course, on Donald's payroll all along.

While the scope of this intertwine drove Macri loyalists mad, no one's conduct bothered them as much as Stephenson's. In a 1990 interview, Macri, who had suffered a heart attack at his Buenos Aires ranch shortly after the sale of his dream project in 1985, relived his New York nightmare, focusing on the banker he believed had undone him: "My lawyers assured me that I had all the legal rights to defend my land, but finally every time that I was close to finding a solution, there would reappear the advice of the bank to sell the land and leave the negotiation. I never understood what their true motive was; they would just say again and again: 'sell the land.' Donald Trump and Conrad Stephenson always spoke to each other. I had a meeting with Stephenson and the next day Donald Trump had the details of everything we spoke about. I think that without a doubt there existed a pact between Stephenson and Trump or they all agreed that I should sell the land."

Within nine months of the deal's close, Stephenson had departed from Chase, as had the top aides who had worked on this deal. Robert Douglass, the bank's vice chairman who had met repeatedly with Arria over the handling of the Macri loans, passed Stephenson by when he named a new national real estate director. Stephenson was hired by the new chairman of the Bowery Savings Bank, the ever-mobile Richard Ravitch. News articles suggested that Stephenson would turn the moribund Bowery into a major commercial lender, making deals of Chase dimensions, but Ravitch was too prudent to allow that.

Stephenson asked Ravitch not to call Chase for a recommendation, and Ravitch obliged. One loan Stephenson quickly tried to bring in was a share of the construction financing on Trump Parc, the condo conversion of the Barbizon. The Bowery soon decided that Stephenson was "a good lender from a borrower's point of view" and gave him time to land another job. Stephenson wound up working with the mortgage broker he suggested Macri hire, Joseph Comras, who collected a half-million-dollar fee for landing a standby loan for Macri that the lawyers who reviewed it subsequently said had little binding effect. Of course, Stephenson had accepted the nebulous backup loan he had himself commissioned.

In 1987, Stephenson appeared at the Trump Parc sales office looking for a studio and announcing that he expected a discount. Donald personally approved and executed the $190,000 sale of apartment 20K to Stephenson, though the apartment was listed on offering statements at up to $240,000. The sale was recorded in the name of a trust Stephenson formed just days before the January 1988 closing, but otherwise his ownership remained something of a secret, unlisted in the *Standard Abstract*, the real estate industry bible that captures virtually all property transactions. Stephenson, who used the Bowery as his return address on the deed, did not tell his wife about the purchase and used the apartment as a bachelor pad.

In May of 1990, Stephenson cochaired the first annual Golden Apple Ball at the Waldorf-Astoria, sponsored by the Realty Foundation, which donated the $300 per head to various charities. The honoree, already shaken by his onrushing personal and financial crises, was Donald Trump, who sat next to his old friend "Steve" during the program. The resemblance was so strong Donald could still have passed as Stephenson's son—both a bit bloated by the years, identical six-foot-two-inch frames, penetrating blue eyes, long, puffy cheeks, and a mutually imposing and charming presence.

The newspapers were already filled with stories about the demise of Chase—a bank steeped in bad real estate debt and preparing for massive layoffs. It had not done a new, major deal with Donald since Stephenson's departure, but it still carried the weight of the West Side loans, with dim prospects for a buildable project. "What in God's name were you thinking to make these loans?" a Chase board member was quoted as saying at a bank meeting in a Trump profile in *Vanity Fair* years later. Though Trump could hardly be considered a major cause of the bank's distress. Chase's loans to him were harbingers of its dubious portfolio, a disturbing symbol of its onetime go-go age.

Donald's decision to buy the yards on the eve of the 1985 mayoral campaign was a form of political speculation. Since both of the candidates expected to oppose Ed Koch—City Council President Carol Bellamy and former congressman Herman Badillo—already had track records of opposition to the kind of large-scale development Donald was planning, he was effectively betting on Koch's reelection when he acquired the yards and began to plan his own, and the city's, biggest project ever. It wasn't surprising that Trump was betting on Koch, a strong favorite to win, or even that he and Fred combined to give the mayor $25,000 in December of 1984, the largest contribution they'd ever made to Koch. What was surprising was Trump's utter confidence—expressed repeatedly to confidants—that the unpredictable Koch would support his grandiose project.

The first public indication of this repeatedly whispered confidence occurred back in October of 1984, when Trump signed his purchase contract with Macri. The two decided to ignore the legal requirement that Macri inform the city of any planned sale, an express provision of the 1982 Board of Estimate resolution that rezoned the site. Instead, under the terms of Macri's new agreement with Trump, Donald assumed full responsibility for their joint decision to violate this provision. Trump was so sure the city would not invoke its presale notification rights that he agreed to hold Macri harmless if it did.

But it was not just the notification provision that Donald was planning to evade. The reason the notification requirement had been written into the 1982 resolution was to give city officials an opportunity to secure from any new developer a binding promise to honor the $100 million worth of amenity commitments Macri had made *before* a transfer of title could occur. The Koch administration's resistance to considering any reduction of those commitments—even after Francisco Macri came to City Hall that October and made a final, tearful plea—was a deathblow to the project. Yet Donald seemed certain he could walk away from the entire amenity package, as well as defy another requirement of the 1982 resolution—that any new buyer had to submit a financial statement to the Board of Estimate, a ray of public light Donald had never allowed inside his private domain.

In the years that lay ahead, Trump would need the city administration's help on a host of pivotal matters—rezoning, tax abatement, roadway and infrastructure improvements. But long before the project got to those controversial, make-or-break issues, it would have to clear the less visible, but potentially disabling, roadblocks of the amenity and notification requirements.

One of the reasons for Trump's confidence was his perception of the special abilities of Jim Capalino. A lean, hatchet-faced insider whose suits fit too well, the thirty-five-year-old Capalino had quickly established himself since leaving the Koch administration three years earlier as a talented, rising star in the influence-peddling game. He was so close to the mayor that Koch picked him to run the 1985 campaign. Unbeknownst to virtually everyone in the city—perhaps even the mayor—he was on Trump's payroll as a consultant all the while that he managed the reelection effort. Capalino kept the relationship under wraps—it would have been an explosive campaign issue—by leaving Trump's lobbying to others and remaining an undercover adviser at Donald's weekly Tuesday meetings on the West Side project. He did not begin filing lobbying forms with the city, acknowledging his Trump representation, until 1986.

As well plugged into the Koch inner circle as Capalino was, however, he was not the principal cause of Donald's cockiness. In 1984, in the months leading up to the purchase of the site, Donald hired a new lawyer who'd never handled a major development project before, Allen Schwartz. While Ed Koch's friendships and political alliances had a sometimes fickle edge to them, Allen Schwartz had been his closest friend for more than twenty years. When Donald retained Schwartz, the lawyer's other prominent client was the mayor himself, whom Schwartz represented on everything from book deals to a contract for an Off-Broadway play.

Schwartz had distinguished himself as Koch's corporation counsel during the first four-year term, professionalizing a once political office of several hundred lawyers. He and Koch had been confidants and friends since 1965, when they formed their own tiny law firm, working out of a single-room office in downtown Manhattan. When he left government at the end of 1981, Schwartz returned to his old firm, Schwartz Klink & Schreiber, and immediately began to attract the sort of high-powered real estate clients who had never shown much interest in him before. In one case, he convinced the City Planning Commission to reach a settlement with a developer who had defaulted on a deal to expand a subway station in exchange for two extra floors, worth up to $3 million a year in rent, on a twenty-nine-story office tower. What really made the close-knit developer community take notice, however, was how Schwartz was able to stave off the city's already announced "automatic revocation" of a ten-year $16 million tax abatement it had granted a developer on a midtown office building. Schwartz's successor as corporation counsel had found that the developer involved in the matter had "materially misrepresented" vital facts on his application, maintaining two sets of books to qualify for the abatement. Schwartz got the city to reopen the matter, reverse its judgment, and grant his client an abatement worth $7 to $11 million. He lassoed the former deputy mayor who had awarded the abatement and got him to do an affidavit damaging to the city—a tactic even Schwartz's successor described as "questionable, a close call." All Donald knew was that Allen Schwartz looked like a winner.

According to some city officials who dealt with Schwartz, he was prone to advertising his ties to the mayor while pushing his client's case, working into a business conversation the breakfast he'd just had with Koch or the weekend he planned to spend at the mansion. One official said Schwartz left a copy of the mayor's private schedule on his desk and did not hesitate to go directly to Koch about an issue the two were debating at an agency level. No one, said a former deputy mayor, "knew how to leash him in."

While Schwartz would become Trump's main conduit to the city on the early West Side issues, it was hardly the only use Trump was ready to make of him. Before 1985 was over, Schwartz would win city and state designation of Trump as the developer of a new domed football stadium in Queens—another glamour project that died on the drawing boards. But Schwartz's first, and most successful, Trump performance involved a Fifth Avenue project that Donald did not even own. Schwartz's tactical success in blocking a development Donald feared would compete with his Trump Tower commercial space convinced him that Schwartz could deliver on the big one as well. While the demands of this obstructive and deceptive legal maneuver were scant compared with the challenges of the West Side project, Donald saw the effects of Schwartz's unusual clout in this episode as an indication of what the glib and energetic lawyer could do for him there, too.

Schwartz did not actually represent Donald on the Fifth Avenue matter; instead, he played a double-agent role. His client was the Municipal Art Society, a civic group determined to block the construction of a forty-four-story high rise at 712-716 Fifth Avenue, across the street from Trump Tower. Though Schwartz went to City Hall and the city's Landmarks Commission as spokesman for this civic organization, it was actually Trump who had quietly paid his $50,000 fee. Schwartz's subterfuge was the same sort of backdoor legal maneuvering Donald had tried to recruit Dan Levitt to do several years earlier when he attempted to block Museum Tower, the condominium competition near Trump Tower.

Shortly before the Society and Trump collaborated on the hiring of Schwartz, Donald had tried to use his perceived influence with the city—particularly the Board of Estimate—to force the new tower's developers to give him a piece of the project. While he talked publicly about the negative effect of the planned building on the avenue's "light and air," Donald's real concern was that the attractive retail space on the tower's lower floors posed a threat to the overpriced Atrium, some of whose disgruntled tenants were already talking to the owners of 712. Trump apparently concluded that he was either going to own part of the new tower or block it.

His first sally was an early September 1984 news item by one of his favorite media messengers—the Intelligencer column of *New York* magazine—quoting his "spokesman," John Barron, as saying that Trump had assured the Municipal Art Society he would do "anything he can" to stop "a tall building there" and to preserve the existing low-rise structures. A week later. Trump met at Trump Tower with the developers, who had spent $86 million assembling the twelve-parcel Fifth Avenue site—led by forty-six-year-old maverick investor, G. Ware Travelstead.

"I can't imagine a tower going up on that site that would block the view of the people who bought the apartments from me—unless, of course, my name were on the project," Trump said.

As Trump and the developers stood by his window looking out at the site, Donald indicated he wanted a stake in the project, which involved the demolition of the five-story home of the Rizzoli Bookstore and the adjoining Coty Building, followed by the construction of a new retail office and residential mirror of Trump Tower. Trump was vague about the size of the stake he expected and whether he was willing to pay anything to get it. Instead, he combined his expression of interest with a threatening observation about having "the political clout to tie you up forever."

When Travelstead balked, Trump responded: "I hope you don't have any problem with the Municipal Art Society, and I'm telling you I can be of great benefit to seeing that the project goes ahead." He suggested that he could be particularly helpful in steering the project through the land mines at the Board of Estimate. The Travelstead group left in anger, having been assured by their lawyer—none other than Sandy Lindenbaum—that their planned project faced no significant city hurdles.

But in the weeks that followed the Trump meeting, the group was hit by a barrage of opposition, some of it clearly fueled by Trump. Lindenbaum reached out to Donald to ask him to ease up, but to no avail. Instead, Trump boasted to Lindenbaum about what he was doing to cripple the project, including the $50,000 donation he was making to pay for Schwartz's public-spirited opposition. Lindenbaum, who had been bypassed in favor of Schwartz and Steve Lefkowitz, a new Trump lawyer, for the West Side zoning and stadium work, had spent months paving the way for a quick run through the city processes for the Travelstead project. Suddenly, his once and future client had become its major impediment.

By the time of Trump's taunting conversation with Lindenbaum, the Schwartz strategy already was in full swing. It had started back in the summer when Trump met with Kent Barwick, the head of the Municipal Art Society and a former Koch commissioner. Following the Travelstead rejection Donald joined the Society's fifteen-member Committee for the Future of Fifth Avenue, a group that featured several top Koch allies, including former Parks Commissioner Gordon Davis, who was, like Schwartz, a member of the mayor's unofficial kitchen cabinet. The committee was dedicated to stopping precisely the sort of project Donald had pioneered on the avenue. In a November letter, the Society and the committee formally retained Schwartz, following up on an agreement reached in October conversations. The retainer was carefully worded to indicate that Schwartz's fees would not be paid by the Society directly but by unspecified members of the committee. Hiring Schwartz, as one key Society figure would later put it, "was our way to press the button to get into the inner circle" at City Hall.

The legal weapon Schwartz and the Society would use to fight the project was what Travelstead eventually labeled "landmarking by ambush." The Society began an urgent push to force the preservation of the Rizzoli building by having it declared a landmark, even though the city's Landmarks Commission had already scheduled the building for possible landmarking on three separate occasions and passed on it each time. The last occasion had been in 1983, when Barwick himself was the head of the Landmarks Commission. While the staff had actively considered Rizzoli as a candidate for landmarking, the Coty structure next to it was so undistinguished it never even made the staff lists.

Barwick had not so much changed his view of the historic significance of Rizzoli or Coty as he had changed his role—as director of the Society, his constituency was fiercely opposed to the shadowy bulk of the new buildings crowding the choicest blocks of Fifth Avenue. To Barwick and Trump, landmarking the buildings was simply a strategic way of preventing the construction of a new tower in their place. They were perfectly prepared to use the landmarking process to stop development that the zoning laws clearly allowed, a spot-zoning perversion the *Times* condemned in an editorial as "snatching a building from an unsuspecting builder's grasp."

Before Allen Schwartz joined the war, Barwick had visited a deputy mayor and other top city officials, none of whom favored landmarking the buildings. Barwick interpreted the City Hall position as in part the result of Lindenbaum's influence and believed Schwartz could serve as a "counterbalance," giving the Society someone "they would pay attention to, who would hit back." Barwick also hired an architectural historian, who discovered what Barwick called "the hook" that helped them block the project: molded glass on the second- and third-floor windows of the Coty that had come from the workshop of Rene Lalique, a twentieth-century master of glass design.

The city, which had already issued a building permit for the alteration or demolition of the Rizzoli building and subsequently issued one for the Coty, was suddenly pushed by Schwartz to schedule a landmark hearing. The very officials who'd been resistant to Barwick in the beginning, from the deputy mayor to the top Buildings Department staff, were now reconsidering. By the time the hearing occurred in early 1985, the behind-the-scenes battle had become such an explicit contest of wills between Trump and the Travelstead group that Howard Rubenstein, the public relations titan who represented both, dropped the Travelstead project as a client, citing a conflict of interest.

Schwartz hovered over the January hearing, posing as the champion of a civic crusade, while he was, in fact, the agent of a spurned investor and turf-conscious competitor. When he spoke, he invoked the authority of the city as if he were still its lawyer. Attacking the building permit granted Travelstead, he claimed that the application for it had been misleading. "We have asked the Corporation Counsel to review that application," Schwartz declared, referring to his own old office. "And I have been told that you should be told that the Corporation Counsel is presently reviewing it" to determine if the misrepresentation he alleged would be a sufficient grounds "to warrant the revocation of the permit."

Although the Travelstead group offered to preserve the Lalique windows but relocate them inside the building, the Landmarks Commission rejected that compromise, stamping both buildings with an indelible landmark status. The irony was that Donald, the onetime "aesthetic vandal" of Trump Tower, had successfully transformed himself into a patron of Fifth Avenue.

The developers considered filing an appeal to overturn the landmarking at the Board of Estimate, but Trump's imperial power on the Board, especially his influence with Andrew Stein, Donald Manes, and Stanley Friedman, discouraged them. So they fought on at the Landmarks Commission, eventually negotiating a compromise that permitted the construction of a fifty-six-story tower to be built behind the preserved Rizzoli and Coty façades. Set back fifty feet from Fifth Avenue and with a main entrance on 56th Street, the new tower was still a triumph for Trump. While the skyscraper would block the view from Trump Tower, it was far less a threat as a retail competitor for the Atrium, having lost the dominant Fifth Avenue retail frontage that was initially planned.

When David Solomon, a Travelstead partner, bumped into Trump at a party after the war, Donald could not resist reminding him of his still covert role, and, with a smile on his face, teased him about "the hard time" he'd given him. The landmarking fight delayed construction for two years, making the project too late for the boom market. Travelstead eventually got out of it, and when the building opened in 1991 it was virtually an empty shell.

At the same time that Schwartz was busily lobbying City Hall on the Travelstead project in late 1984 and early 1985, he also began making calls and nudging for city concessions on the West Side yards. His primary agenda was to lay the groundwork for Donald's abandonment of the amenity burden, especially the $31 million payment due soon to pay for a renovation of the 72nd Street subway station near the site. This subway payment was a particularly difficult obligation to shed since the city had insisted in 1982 that it be written into the legal documents so that it literally ran with the land, and would be transferred with the title to any new owner. Schwartz's efforts to win a waiver of that obligation were aided by Trump's other, widely respected, lawyer, Steve Lefkowitz, who was also known in the development community as the best friend and traveling companion of Herb Sturz, the chairman of the City Planning Commission. The combination was a one-two punch no other developer in the city had.

But there was a fly in the ointment. Sturz's counsel, Phil Hess, had a long, personal history with Trump, dating back to the days of the easement battle, and he was a stickler for propriety. He also had Sturz's strong support. Having heard by phone and read in the newspapers about the upcoming sale to Trump, Hess drafted an early January letter that warned Trump he had to get the city's consent for the purchase and put Trump on notice that he would have to make the subway payment by January 31. Since both of these requirements were a result of Board of Estimate resolutions, not those of the planning commission, Hess met and discussed the letter with Hadley Gold, the counsel to the Board who also held the title of first assistant to the corporation counsel. The Hess letter was prepared for Gold's signature with a carbon copy to be sent to Allen Schwartz, who had promoted Gold to his top corporation counsel status during his tenure there. Gold never sent the letter.*

Once the deal closed, Hess tried to rally administration officials to enforce the unequivocal amenity requirements, but he was up against pressure from Schwartz at all levels of the government. Trump's strategy was to let Macri's mapping agreement lapse, which it did in February, and to return Macri's 4,300-unit special permit to the city, which he did on March 1. Then he announced his intention to submit an entirely new plan, contending that the amenity obligations died with the old permit and that he'd negotiate an alternate set of new subway or other improvements when his revised plan was approved.

The feisty Hess countered by pointing out that Trump had been at least orally "on notice since last fall that any purchaser would have to comply" with the notification and transfer process and that only the Board of Estimate could decide to waive requirements it had enacted. Hess pushed to have Donald's evasion of the Macri obligations added to the Board's calendar or at least informally put before each Board member individually. He drafted another letter for Gold's signature, informing Trump that the "attempted surrender" of the Macri permit required Board approval before it could be accepted and that the matter would be placed before the members soon. Gold did not send that letter either.

But City Hall could not simply stonewall the Hess issues without running a political risk. By April, Carol Bellamy, the city's second highest elected official and

---

* Years later, when Gold left government, he joined Schwartz's firm.

a member of the Board of Estimate, was an announced candidate against Koch and taking him on almost daily over a variety of issues. City Hall's fear was that Bellamy—with strong reform support and a natural West Side constituency—would use any Koch acquiescence on the subway issue to paint him as soft on Trump, a potentially damaging image among the liberal Democrats who turned out in primaries. So top Koch deputies carved out a safe way of taking the onus off the mayor, yet putting the issue in limbo. Hadley Gold finally composed a mild version of the Phil Hess letters, but instead of sending a stern rebuke to Trump, he gave Bellamy and every other Board member a long-winded memo detailing in the blandest language the history of the transfer and subway controversies.

The letter posed no policy alternatives, but implicitly left it up to the Board to decide on further action. A mayoral aide followed the letter with calls to top staff of several key Board members asking what they wished to do. Bellamy responded with a blistering letter to the Metropolitan Transportation Authority, stating flatly that Trump had assumed Macri's subway commitments and that no delays should be granted him to avoid payment of the $31 million. Her response, and a rushed follow-up from Koch two days later, helped kill negotiations between the MTA and Trump to make a new subway deal that would lock in Donald's subway commitment but postpone it far into the development process.

Predictably, no member of the Board other than Bellamy even responded to Gold's letter, implicitly granting Trump a pass on the binding language of their own 1982 resolutions without even discussing it. The most hypocritical Board member was Andrew Stein, the only one to actually vote against Macri's project and attack it for being too big. The Gold letter gave him an opportunity to object to a sale of the site to a developer who openly said he planned to double the size of the project, and Stein was silent. Of course, Stein was in the middle of a campaign to replace Bellamy as council president and $270,000 in Trump contributions to his campaign that year (combined with another $45,000 from Trump's partner Hirschfeld) would set an all-time record for any Board of Estimate candidate.

In addition to Stein, Trump gave Comptroller Jay Goldin $30,000 in several donations, starting shortly after the West Side purchase closed, and $12,000 to Brooklyn Borough President Howard Golden. He also dumped bales of money into Stanley Friedman's party coffers in the Bronx, contributed to the Staten Island borough president, and, of course, could always count on his unopposed ally, Donald Manes.

When the Board did nothing, the issue faded away, except for a single outburst in mid-August from the independent Herb Sturz and Phil Hess, the only city officials paying any attention to Trump's disregard of his inherited obligations. Sturz reiterated his refusal even to look privately at the preliminary plans Trump had for the site, saying he would not do so until Trump complied with the transfer and subway obligations. Sturz said he was not accepting the special permit Trump had returned to the city months earlier and insisted that he submit a financial statement and comply with the transfer procedures in the Lincoln West resolutions. There was no reaction from Donald to this letter, almost as if he understood that Sturz's edict would not stand.

Donald waited patiently, delaying the public announcement of his long-completed architectural design for the site until after the elections, thus sparing his candidates the uneasiness of having to take a public position in the middle of a campaign. Schwartz meanwhile quietly shifted the outstanding transfer and subway issues away from Hess and Sturz to City Hall, where a showdown session was scheduled in the mayor's office immediately after the election. The upshot of that meeting was a decision to deliberately leave the issue in limbo—to neither press for compliance nor to put any waiver of the city's rights in writing. This supposedly neutral position actually suited Trump quite nicely and was an extraordinary tribute to Schwartz's clout and persuasiveness. Donald would, in fact, never make the subway contribution or pay the cost of any other Macri commitment, escaping from these obligations without attracting any critical media attention.*

Even before this capitulation, another wing of city government had begun actively entertaining Trump's West Side proposal. On September 11, the day after Koch's primary victory over Bellamy, Donald had met with Koch's top economic development officials, including Deputy Mayor Alair Townsend, to discuss city assistance in relocating NBC from its historic Rockefeller Center headquarters to the 60th Street yards. A cocksure Trump told the assembled bureaucrats that unless the city acted, a cramped NBC might move to New Jersey or to Burbank, where the network had a great deal of extra acreage. Grant Tinker, NBC's president, "doesn't like New York City because he has to wear a tie here," Trump teased.

---

* Apparently not satisfied with this repudiation of Hess's tough position, Schwartz and other lawyers for major developers subsequently met with the mayor to complain about the anti-development bastions within the administration, singling out Hess and attempting to force him out. In the end, a chagrined Hess, his wings somewhat clipped, remained at the planning helm.

Trump argued that he had the only site in the city suitable for major new television studios and that he had worked out a deal with the network giving it a third of his site. "NBC is in love with it," he said, claiming that the network had been designing its own facility for the property over the past three months. Asked by Townsend how strong a commitment Trump had from NBC, Donald replied: "We're negotiating the terms of a lease."

Donald's strategy was to act as if he were NBC's exclusive agent, knowing that the city desperately wanted to retain the network's thousands of jobs, and then to convince the administration to grant him zoning bonuses and tax abatements for the whole site so he could afford to offer the network a sweetheart deal on its portion of it. "I don't want the mayor to confuse the issue by bringing up other sites," said Trump. "Nothing else in Manhattan does it." If the city would agree to a dramatically upscaled rezoning, Trump would give NBC an immediate equity interest in its building and a buyout provision up the road. The city, he said, should offer NBC utility write-downs and financing incentives, including low-cost loans, to tie the package together.

To underline the seriousness of NBC's threatened departure, Trump then sent Townsend a confidential copy of the network's request for proposals for a competitive site in New Jersey's Meadowlands. With help from Schwartz, Donald was trying an end run around Sturz, Hess, and the traditional planning apparatus, and instead focusing on the much more pliant development agencies. Trump also began sending personal notes to Koch, advocating the yards as the only alternative to "all the large developments planned on the New Jersey side of the Hudson River" and promising to "beat them all if the City lets me." In a November 12 note to Koch, Donald first floated his notion of "the World's Tallest Building" for the site and appealed to the mayor's public contempt for the antidevelopment left. "While it is possible that a small and vocal group will be against such a building," Trump wrote, "the City as a whole will be overwhelmingly for it."

Two weeks after Koch and all the Trump-backed candidates for the Board won, and barely a week after the issues raised by Hess were put to rest in that City Hall meeting, Donald held a grand press conference to make public his long-awaited plan. The announcement made Dan Rather's *CBS Evening News,* took up an entire page in the *New York Times* with reaction sidebars and a Paul Goldberger architecture review, and became a lead national story. Donald Trump, at thirty-nine, was literally about to reach the sky.

Trump's 150-story building was, his architect, Helmut Jahn, said, actually a system of five buildings mounted atop one another and supported by "a giant superframe" that would form the angles of a triangle. Skyscrapers over 100 stories, Goldberger wrote, "make sense only for the kind of builder who is as concerned with symbolizing power as he is with the specifics of his cash flow, and no builder today more perfectly fits this criterion than Mr. Trump, a man who glories in superlatives and for whom every project is a flamboyant gesture."

Seven other buildings, including six seventy-six-story apartment complexes, would stretch out across the waterfront. While Macri had tried to build high-rise and medium-height buildings on relatively conventional streets—an extension of the Manhattan grid—Donald's Television City was the reverse, a collection of 8,000 apartments, plus two office buildings, on a huge landscaped platform with a vast amount of open space and parkland. Beneath the platform were the studios, designed to tempt Hollywood as well as NBC, a retail mall with two or three major department stores, and a massive parking garage. While Goldberger adopted Trump's sales pitch that his was the only site with the horizontal space necessary for modern studios, he assailed the towers as "completely out of scale with conventional human perception."

Flanked by nine photographic blowups and a model of his plan in the Empire Ballroom of the Grand Hyatt, Trump was asked at his press conference why he wanted to outdo the Sears Building in Chicago. "We are prone to go forward" was all he could say. Promising to submit his plan to the city in January 1986, Trump said portions of it had been previewed by the mayor, who was away on a trip to Japan. No city official commented on Trump's vision, though it contained almost twice the number of apartments and parking spaces as well as four times the office and commercial square footage as the plan that had finally been approved for Macri.

Koch had expressly declined a *New York Times* request to comment on Trump's announced intention of a larger project when asked during the campaign, and now, with the plan formally unveiled, the mayor who had an opinion about everything remained uncharacteristically silent. His silence was just one more indication that Koch had some sort of understanding with Donald—preceded by the condoning of the sale without city notification and the abandonment of the subway improvements. Koch had obviously not discouraged Trump from announcing the plan even after he'd previewed it. Indeed, a few weeks later, while Trump and the mayor were still exchanging public praise, Donald was quoted in the *New York Post* as saying that Koch "tacitly, at least, supports the project." Koch, Trump said, "came out the other day and said: 'I love Donald Trump as a developer,' which was nice. Then he said: 'And I would love to have the tallest building in New York.' That's about as close to an endorsement as you can get." Koch didn't deny any of it.*

No one could have been more astonished at these developments than Francisco Macri, who still had an office in New York and was wrapping up the loose ends of his Lincoln West operation. While he could get nowhere with the city on the amenities or the density of his project, Donald seemed to be magically winning at every turn. He was also going out of his way to brand Macri a "know-nothing" and "a myth who's now safely back in Argentina."

"Every time I have anything to negotiate with the city," a victorious Trump declared, "they say: 'Mr. Macri agreed to rebuild the subway system. Mr. Macri agreed to build a railroad yard.' And I say: 'You don't understand. He didn't know what he was doing.'" The day would come, of course, when Donald would himself be ridiculed for buying a site whose rezoning he did not want and then spending millions on a project so grandiose it was unlikely it would ever be built.

In *The Art of the Deal,* Donald called his purchase of the yards "the easiest business decision I ever made." On the bumpy road to his collapse, it would also prove to be one of his most troublesome.

In his final days at Chase in late 1985, Conrad Stephenson did one final favor for Donald, an unusual loan that made little sense from Chase's standpoint. Stephenson agreed to finance Trump's purchase of Mar-A-Lago, a 118-room Palm Beach mansion that launched Donald's second career as a frequent star of *Lifestyles of the Rich and Famous.*

Stephenson's commercial real estate section did not regularly extend

---

* Koch did not make a public statement about the project for another two years, and the axiomatic character of his ultimate comments made it even more curious that he had taken so long to speak out. "I've been accused of advocating bigness—but I know too big when I see it," the mayor wrote in a November 1987 column. "I will not support a development almost twice as big as what I previously thought reasonable. To do so would be to abrogate my responsibility as the city's chief executive." Of course, the mayor had been told about the project's density even before Trump announced it, yet he'd waited two years to take this rather uncomplicated position. Koch chose not to say the obvious until Schwartz had left Trump and the mayor had gotten embroiled in a series of ugly public disputes with Trump in late 1986 and early 1987 about NBC and other matters.

residential mortgages, but since a relationship banker tries to service all the needs of his major clients, Stephenson offered Trump a home mortgage at the bank's commercial prime lending rate, which was then several points lower than Chase's residential rate. Mortgaging Mar-A-Lago as he left the bank only advanced Stephenson's relationship with Trump, not Chase's, and once Stephenson departed, Trump moved to Citibank and others as his main lenders.

The Mar-A-Lago loan did not close until December 27, 1985, a few weeks after Stephenson left Chase. But it was Stephenson who authorized it. Donald had made his $8 million bid on the property in August and had gone to contract, with a $400,000 deposit, ten days before Stephenson resigned from the bank in October. According to one bank official, Stephenson "put everything in play before he left." Stephenson's instructions, according to a bank staffer, included the unusual caveat that the mortgage not be recorded against the title of the Florida property. An unrecorded mortgage is virtually an unsecured loan, diminishing the bank's rights to seize the property in case of default. Donald had asked that the mortgage not be recorded, in effect concealing the loan from the public record and giving the impression that the purchase was a grandiose cash transaction.

Chase agreed to do an unrecorded mortgage though New York State banking law requires that "every mortgage taken or held by such bank or trust company shall immediately be recorded or registered in its name in the office of the clerk or the proper recording officer of the county in which the real estate described is located." The statute specifically applies to mortgages "where the underlying real estate is located outside the state of New York." While Chase is a national bank, exempt from some requirements of state banking law, Pat Stein, a senior attorney at the Controller of the Currency, says that state law controls on the question of recording a mortgage because "federal law appears to be silent on this issue." And an attorney with the New York State Banking Department said "it's not a prudent banking practice for sure and would be cited in an examining report." (In an interview several years after the purchase, a Chase spokesman characterized the Trump transaction as a personal loan, not a mortgage. However, the transaction is repeatedly referred to as a mortgage in Chase's commitment letter and associated documents.)

There was another unusual aspect of Chase's Mar-A-Lago loan, involving Trump's simultaneous purchase of a narrow strip of beachfront land just across the highway from the mansion. Chase partially financed that $2 million purchase as well, giving Donald a half million more in the Mar-A-Lago mortgage than the price of the house to cover the up-front cost of the beachfront. But the bank took no mortgage—recorded or unrecorded—on the beach land. The owner of the beach property, businessman Jack Massey, accepted a purchase money mortgage from Trump for the remaining $1.5 million, so the only cash in the acquisition came from Chase. In fact, with Chase quietly providing the funds for both purchases, Donald achieved his single most conspicuous act of consumption by committing only $2,812 of his own money.

Chase had agreed to provide the full $10 million for the purchase of both sites but Massey's mortgage made that unnecessary. Since Trump allocated $3 million of the Mar-A-Lago purchase to the house's elegant furnishings, Chase was in effect offering a $10 million mortgage on a property that Donald was buying, minus furnishings and the beach, for $5 million. This generosity was not attributable to the bank's high estimate of the resalable value of the house, since Chase had deleted the standard language requiring a bank appraisal from the commitment documents, indicating that the bank did not even examine its Florida prize.

Chase minimized its risk by obtaining Donald's personal guarantee. The bank had asked that both Donald and Ivana, who had toured the house years earlier and been in love with it ever since, guarantee the loan. But Ivana refused, apparently unwilling to jeopardize her nest egg—the product of the thrice-renewed nuptial agreement. Asked in a court deposition some years later about the peculiar role of Chase in this transaction, Trump said the bank "could have cared less" about making the loan and, with his guarantee, "would have loaned me anything I wanted on the property up to a percentage of my net worth." If that was so, it was a reckless banking judgment—betting on Donald's net worth, as the next few years would establish, was a highly speculative business. Indeed the bank's decision to do the loan as a mortgage on the property, rather than merely an extension of his still existing credit line, did suggest that in case of default it might be forced to accept the estate as satisfaction of the loan, making its indifference to Mar-A-Lago's market value all the more curious.

The ostensible cash purchase of Mar-A-Lago consolidated Donald's position as a national symbol of lavish acquisition. His decision in late 1984 to rebuild his just finished Trump Tower triplex was an equally costly personal expense, but the company quietly paid for that, and unlike Mar-A-Lago, the apartment was an extravagance that couldn't be captured in a memorable aerial photo. The Hispano-Moresque mansion—Spanish for Sea-to-Lake—is situated on a sixteen-and-a-half-acre plot that is one of the rare Palm Beach properties that stretches from the shores of the Atlantic Ocean to Lake Worth. Built on what was once a coral reef by cereal heiress Marjorie Merriweather Post in 1927, this hub of Palm Beach society was placed on the National Register of Historic Places in 1972, donated to the Department of Interior in 1973, and returned to the Post Family Foundation for sale by the federal government in 1981. Landmarked by the Palm Beach Town Council, the house cannot be demolished or significantly altered without town approval.

Crescent-shaped, with its open side facing the lake, the rock-hewn estate has fifty-eight bedrooms, thirty-three bathrooms, a seventy-five-foot tower, three bomb shelters, and a theater, with a nine-hole golf course, a superintendent's residence, a steward's residence, a watchman's cottage, a staff building, a garage, and chauffeur's quarters nearby. Three boatloads of Dorian stone, quarried in Italy, were used for its exterior walls, together with 3,600 fifteenth-century roof tiles. The interior features a dining room floor of black and white marble beneath a two-tone marble dining table inlaid with precious stones that seats fifty, an enormous drawing room with a copy of the Venetian Thousand-Wing Ceiling in gold leaf, and a small closed space called the Monkey Loggia, with carved stone monkeys, one wearing glasses and reading a book, perched near the ceiling.

A judge in one legal case involving the property called it "incomparable," and the town's appraising consultant, retained after the Trump purchase to assess it, said the house "is in a class with Viscaya, the Deering Estate in Miami; the Biltmore Estate, constructed for George Vanderbilt in Asheville, North Carolina; and William Randolph Hearst's Estate in San Simeon, California."

To Donald, it was simply another advertisement for himself. "I thought I was buying a museum," he told *Palm Beach Life* magazine. "I never thought it was going to be a particularly comfortable place, but I thought it was so incredible as a statement that it would be wonderful to own." Trump was so indifferent to the elegance of his purchase that he drew an awkward blank when questioned during a deposition in 1988 about the furnishings. "Who told you that the personal property alone is worth more than you paid for the property?" he was asked by a county attorney, referring to an assertion Donald had made in the press.

"People that come to the house, people that are students of, which I'm not, antiques and various other things, people who know far more about art than I do and about carpets and walls and sconces and all of the things that this house is loaded with and removable items," he responded. The Ming vases, Persian rugs, silverware for 200 guests, nineteen sets of china, silk needlework panels from an Italian palace, and gilded Viennese cherubs were wasted on Donald.

Even though Palm Beach was a foreign land to Donald, his acquisition of the house had all the intrigue of his New York transactions, with the local players drawn to him as if he were a magnet for machinations. Like so many of his New York and Atlantic City maneuvers, his first deal in the Florida real estate market quickly took on a seamy, conflict-ridden character—becoming just one more Trump adventure, complete with trapdoors and mirrors.

When Donald, Ivana, and Donald, Jr. first looked at the estate in early 1983, it had been on the market for several years. Shortly after Marjorie Post's death in 1973, the family, spurred by commitments she had made before her death, turned the estate over to the Department of Interior as a national landmark and possible presidential retreat, together with a $3 million fund to cover upkeep costs. A year and a half later, however, Congressman Paul Rogers, who had originally supported the landmarking, began pressing to have the house returned to the Post Foundation, ostensibly because of spiraling maintenance costs and the loss of the town property tax due to its governmental ownership. Even though only $48,000 in federal funds were spent on the estate in the first two years, Rogers introduced a bill to block further appropriations.

After six years of dogged infighting by Rogers and others, the government did return Mar-A-Lago to the Foundation in the final week of the Carter administration, a decision forced by the Democratic congressman who'd succeeded Rogers two years earlier, Dan Mica, Rogers's longtime administrative assistant. The Foundation put the home up for sale almost immediately. The attorney who represented the Foundation, handling dozens of offers over the next five years, was Doyle Rogers, the retired congressman's brother and an attorney for Marjorie Post before her death. The Rogers family is a Palm Beach area institution—Doyle and Paul's father, Dwight, was a six-term congressman, the federal building in Palm Beach carries the Rogers name, and the relaxed, white-haired Doyle runs the town's most prominent law firm and presides over the Palm Beach Civic Association.

Doyle had actually begun representing the Foundation years earlier, even before his brother had begun to push for the return of the property. In July of 1974, shortly after Marjorie Post's death, Doyle had handled the sale of the other piece of estate property—the one-acre beachfront strip—to his longtime friend and client Massey. Named on the deed as the "ancillary administrator" of the Post estate, Rogers signed over the property to Massey for $383,000. All the while that the switch-hitting congressman Paul Rogers urged the return of the estate to the private market, Doyle's client Massey held the indispensable other half of Mar-A-Lago, its sandy entrance into the Atlantic, available only at a premium price.

After the Trumps toured the estate, a broker wrote a 1983 letter to Massey expressing interest in the beach land, and Massey responded by supplying in writing the name of his broker, who had an exclusive listing on the property—Nicola Rogers, wife of the ever-present Doyle. Nicola Rogers offered Donald's agent 300 feet of frontage for $2 million, including a 5 percent or $100,000 commission. The brokerage firm that Nicola Rogers worked for was also one of those handling the sale of the estate; Doyle Rogers had himself prepared the listings agreements for the Foundation.

Donald claimed in *The Art of the Deal* that he initially bid $15 million for the house in 1983, was rejected, and kept making bids over the years, dipping a bit lower each time until he got what he considered a bargain. In fact, his first bid was $9 million, contingent on town approvals of a plan to subdivide the sixteen-and-a-half-acre estate into fourteen lots so that Donald could preserve the mansion but build a major development. When the Foundation requested a nonrefundable down payment to cover the costs of maintaining the estate until the deal closed, Donald offered to put $250,000 down at contract, but insisted that it be refunded if the zoning changes weren't obtained. After these terms were rejected, Trump did not bid again until mid-1985, when he made the $8 million offer that was ultimately accepted.

By the time Donald made his second bid, however, the Foundation was entertaining another offer well in excess of Donald's. A Houston developer had gone to contract at $12.5 million (plus $1.5 million for the furnishings) and had obtained town approvals for a nine-lot subdivision. The approvals had taken so long that the developer had already forfeited one deposit and made another; but he seemed poised to buy. Other contracts—including one for more than $14 million—had failed to close before, however, so the Foundation was still open to considering other deals.

After Trump's bid came in, Foundation officials began demanding a quick closing on the Houston offer. But there were all sorts of problems that needed to be ironed out with the Houston bid. Though it was still an open bid and $6 million higher than Trump's, the Foundation went to contract with Donald in October 1985. The theory was that the Foundation would close with whichever buyer was ready first, but Houston was still putting together its financial package, meaning that the sudden deadlines set by the Foundation put Donald on the inside track, as usual.

Doyle Rogers closed the Foundation sale with Donald around Christmas, as did Jack Massey. Donald boasted publicly of his $8 million steal, without mentioning the $2 million side deal with Massey, a price seven times what Massey had paid the Foundation for the land and 30 percent more than the highest prior beachfront purchase in the area. Within a month of closing the deal, by Doyle

Rogers's estimate, he became Trump's attorney in Palm Beach. He had handled the Massey and Foundation ends of the sale, and his wife had collected her choice commission. When Donald filed permits for tennis court and pool work immediately after the sale, Doyle was his expeditor. And when Donald challenged the new tax assessment of $11.5 million in a proceeding that dragged on for years, Doyle was both a witness and Donald's lawyer.

Questioned by his law partner, Rogers testified as the lawyer for the Foundation, attempting to establish that the real-market value of the estate was Donald's purchase price, insisting that Trump got no favored treatment from the Foundation. When Donald initially filed the lawsuit in January of 1987, Rogers was identified in Florida news accounts as Trump's attorney and was quoted as supporting an assessment of only $7 million. "He only paid $7 million for the real estate," said Rogers, excluding the furnishings and including the combined Massey and Foundation property prices, "and it was an arm's-length bargain and sale transaction." The irony of this declaration coming from Rogers was lost on all but the closest insiders.

In addition to Rogers's self-serving defense of his own sale terms, the tax trial showcased a snooty Trump at his theatrical peak. Whirlwind Donald flew in on his 727 an hour late for his 1988 deposition, then walked out on the proceeding before starting his testimony, saying he had to see his children first. When the county's attorney began the deposition by explaining that his questions were not intended to trick Donald and that he'd be happy to reframe them if necessary, Trump deadpanned: "I have been tricked all my life." Asked if he had any credentials as a real estate appraiser, Donald replied: "I think I have maybe better credentials in real estate than any appraiser I know."

Flippant throughout the deposition, he bragged about having brought tax proceedings on virtually all of his other properties, contending that anyone who didn't in New York was "considered to be a strange person" and directing his attorney in the middle of his testimony to file another tax case involving a West Palm Beach property he'd just acquired. Since he was embroiled in a public dispute over the air traffic noise generated by the Palm Beach International Airport, Trump intermittently stopped testifying while planes flew overhead, repeatedly denouncing the airport as "a disaster" and announcing that the noise was so bad he stayed inside the four-inch-thick walls of Mar-A-Lago and didn't "eat outside anymore."

The county's lawyer even pursued Donald on the question of whether or not there had been a side deal—"other considerations," as he put it—involved in the acquisition of the estate. Gossip sheets in Palm Beach had printed speculation that actress Dina Merrill, Marjorie Post's daughter, had wound up with a Trump Tower apartment. No public records ever supported such a claim, and an unflappable Donald responded by insisting there "was absolutely no other consideration," acknowledging that he'd "heard that rumor" but there was "nothing else."

Trump's performance, aided by Rogers and a Foundation director, proved to be a winning one. A lower court judge accepted the $7 million assessment, even though it was a full million less than the value assigned by an appraiser Trump used as expert witness. Since Donald had called the property "one of the most valuable parcels of land in the United States" in *The Art of the Deal* his attorneys had to fight to keep the relevant book passages out of the court record. Rogers's partner prevailed on the issue, arguing that he was "concerned with what editorializing may have been done in the publishing process"—putting some distance between Donald and his own printed word.

The county appealed the decision and in its brief assailed the various Trump maneuvers on the transaction. It charged that Donald and the Foundation had "arbitrarily inflated the portion of the price allocated" to the furnishings "so that Trump could once again demonstrate his uncanny ability to buy real estate at bargain prices." By assigning a $3 million value to the furnishings, "the stamps on the deed would only show" the $5 million allocated to the real estate, misleading the public about the purchase price and saving on property taxes. County attorneys also pointed to Chase's financing—which they called "anything other than typical"—to demonstrate that the bank had to believe that Trump was acquiring the property at a deflated price. Noting that Chase was bound by FDIC regulations limiting "the ratio of loan to market value of property," the county brief charged that Trump could not explain "how a bank could lawfully lend more than the $8 million contract amount for the real and personal property." The lawyers joked that the average home buyer would "have to put out more cash to buy a rabbit-warren condo" in the backwaters of Florida than Donald did for Mar-A-Lago. The county concluded that Chase's willingness to exceed the price, together with the $12.7 million assessment the Foundation had accepted in 1985, compelled a finding overturning the $7 million figure reached by the lower court.

In 1989, the appeals court reinstated the $11.5 million assessment, forcing Donald to pay $81,500 more a year in taxes. On its Sunday front page, the *Palm Beach Post* featured a chart contrasting what the town could buy with the tax amount at issue—fully subsidized day care for twenty-three needy children or a new, fully stocked fire rescue truck—to what Trump could buy, namely, forty-five days of upkeep and staff at the mansion or ten cross-country trips in his 727.

In the period between Trump's lower court victory and the ruling on appeal, Donald refinanced the estate for $12 million, convincing Boston Safe Deposit & Trust to take Chase out of the loan. The new loan was recorded, and even though the amount would have helped the county's case, the details of the refinancing could not be conveyed to the court, since new facts cannot be added to a case on appeal. Boston Safe granted Trump a standard, adjustable rate mortgage in October 1988, due in five years. In August of 1989, the county hiked Trump's assessment to $14 million, reflecting the new mortgage.

While Palm Beach had reacted with shock and dismay over Donald's purchase price—because of the plummeting effect it might have on the real estate market—it celebrated the ultimate decision in the tax case because it would hike local property values. By the time Donald lost the case, however, he'd already been reduced to a subject of ridicule in town on a host of unrelated scores. The *Trump Princess*, financed with another risky loan from Boston Safe, was too huge to be berthed anywhere near Mar-A-Lago and had to remain upwater, docked at a Best Western. The Trump 727 was so noisy it was banned from the airport from 10:00 P.M. to 7:00 A.M., and the black Puma helicopter was barred from landing in Palm Beach at all.

When Donald tried to become the champion of a great public crusade against airport noise, he instead became an embarrassment, insisting that the county spend over $800 million to move the airport so planes didn't fly directly over his estate. Trump created a "Noise Pollution Action Fund PAC" to elect two members to the Palm Beach County Commission, threw a thousand-dollar-a-head fund-raising party at the estate, and watched his two candidates go down to defeat and attribute their losses to the negative publicity his involvement had generated. As Michael Crook put it in a *Miami Herald* profile entitled "Hitting a Roar Nerve," local politicians started avoiding Trump "as if he were a cash bar."

Doyle Rogers speculated in one news story about the tax case that Donald would not have paid what he did for Mar-A-Lago "had he known the effect of that noise," an intriguing suggestion from the husband of the broker. But eight months after the Mar-A-Lago closing he made a second local purchase across the waterway in West Palm Beach, home of the disputed airport. He paid $41 million for a thirty-two-story condominium building, half of the mortgage costs assumed by a New York bank that had foreclosed on the defeated developer. Trump set about advertising his new apartments in a dead market, certain that Trump Plaza of the Palm Beaches was a name no one with a few hundred thousand at hand could resist.

The problem was that West Palm Beach is the downscale side of Palm Beach, where its Haitian maids live. The twin towers may have faced the water, but out the backdoor, quipped a real estate agent to the *Wall Street Journal*, "they are practicing voodoo." Palm Beach—"a lush sandbar lined with palm trees" and connected to the world by only four bridges—parks its garbage trucks in West Palm Beach.

Donald decorated the lobby with elephant-skin armchairs, brass planters, and leather-paneled walls, but in two years sales only climbed from the paltry six of his predecessor to an unimpressive ninety-three, out of 221 apartments. "Trump the Chump?" was the *Palm Beach Review* headline in September 1988, and the *Herald* proclaimed that the sumptuous apartments were selling "at the pace of escargots." Donald used his brief partnership with Lee Iacocca in the project as a promotional stunt, but Iacocca invested next to nothing, did not solicit Chrysler dealers to buy apartments as Donald had hoped, and pulled out quickly. Donald kept the breakup of the partnership a secret, still trying to use the name to help make sales.

"What Trump has to sell there is a view of a prime location," said one real estate analyst. "It's a second-rate location itself. It's like Trump buying something in New Jersey for the view of Manhattan. He would never have done it."

Everywhere Donald turned in Palm Beach he seemed to stumble. He was the butt of every Old Guard joke, the walking definition of an arriviste whose wealth was so new "it makes your hands green," wrote one local wag. The gossip, heatedly denied by Donald, was that he had not been invited to join the Bath and Tennis Club, which is so close to Mar-A-Lago that the Club bought its beachfront from the Foundation. Confronted once by a reporter about his supposed snubbing, Donald countered: "They kiss my ass in Palm Beach." Yet when he hosted the Palm Beach Preservation Foundation charity ball, just as the Post Foundation had done for years, he provoked stuffy grumbles for having roped off virtually the entire house and staged the event in a tent, with none of the customary dancing in the pavilion.

He was derided for his suggestion in the tax case that the town should grant him a low assessment because it cost him $2.5 million a year to run Mar-A-Lago, as if his seven gardeners and the workman who did nothing but care for the wrought-iron trimmings were performing a public service. He even wound up criticized for canceling $150,000 in Trump Plaza ads after a *Miami Herald* staff writer wrote: "Whenever I hear Palm Beachers complain about airport noise, I'm overcome with Schadenfreude. That's a German word that means finding pleasure in the misfortune of others. The rumbling of the jets has the ring of social justice. Right over Don Trump's house, even!"

Donald, apparently, could not even take a joke.

Ivana, though, loved the house and Palm Beach life. "A girls-only weekend at Mar-A-Lago," she called her periodic parties there. "We sit in the spa, walk on the beach, and talk." The invited group of twenty or so women adhered to a tight schedule of supervised exercise, the pool, the beach, massage, dinner, and a night of dancing with one another, entertained by a flown-in orchestra. To Ivana, the Greenwich home was for rest, gardening, and family, a retreat. Mar-A-Lago was for fantasy. When the troubles came in 1990, she went to Mar-A-Lago to forget them, posing for a *Vogue* cover shoot at the estate and still hosting her April girls' party.

But to Donald, the mansion was useful only as a setting for business connections and payback weekends for everyone from American Express's James Robinson to Hugh Carey to Senator Al D'Amato. He mounted his magazine covers behind silver frames and posted them around the house, and he took guests into the kitchen to show off the gold silverware, but neither the house nor Palm Beach ever really became a part of his life. When he was asked during the March 1988 tax deposition about selling the property, his response had an ironically prophetic tone to it.

"People don't look at me as a seller," he said. "If I ever offered the property for sale, I believe I would get very little for it, because when Trump is selling something, people think it's no good. They say, why is he selling it?"

11

PIGSKIN POLITICS

Consider the governor who presided at this time in the executive chamber. He was a strange, dark, osseous man, who owing to the brooding, melancholy character of his own disposition, had a checkered and somewhat sad career behind him. Owing to an energetic and indomitable temperament, he had through years of law practice and public labors built up for himself a following which amounted to adoration. In all these capacities he had manifested a tendency to do the right as he saw it and play fair. He was primarily softhearted, fiery, a brilliant orator, a dynamic presence. . . .

In a vague way the governor sensed the dreams of Cowperwood. He realized that Cowperwood had traveled fast—that he was pressing to the utmost a great advantage in the face of great obstacles. Would he be proving unfaithful to the trust imposed on him by the great electorate if he were to advantage Cowperwood's cause? Must he not rather in the sight of all men smoke out the animating causes here—greed, overweening ambition, colossal self-interest? . . . Ideals were here at stake—the dreams of one man as opposed, perhaps, to the ultimate dreams of a city or state or nation—the grovelings and wallowings of a democracy slowly, blindly trying to stagger to its feet. In this conflict were opposed, as the governor saw it, the ideals of one man and the ideals of men.

—Theodore Dreiser, The Titan

Let me put it this way: when it comes to hiring people, Donald Trump, and I think he would agree with this, would not be adverse to hiring a person, in part, because he felt they had knowledge they could use from a previous job they had done. It wouldn't bother him a bit. I think he would because he's conscious of the public arena. He would try to do it within the bounds of legality, but he would go right up to the limit of what he was permitted to do in order to get the person with the most information . . .

—*Tony Schwartz, Author of* THE ART OF THE DEAL

THE VENTURE that made Donald Trump a national figure wasn't a real estate or casino project. While his own later self-promotion successfully depicted him as a magical master of the deal, it was his three-year dalliance with football—a game he loved to watch and hated to lose—that initially thrust him onto the national stage. With George Steinbrenner only a few miles away in the Bronx, Donald understood that the moneymen behind sports attract more publicity bang for their bucks than any other venture capitalists in America, and part of his genius was to use the exposure that a puny investment in football gave him to catapult into the consciousness of the country. Football became Donald's way of achieving his ultimate objective—the mass marketing of the Trump name.

His first national newsmagazine profile was in *Sports Illustrated*, not *BusinessWeek* or *Time*. The lead of the first Sunday *New York Times Magazine* paean to him was his dominance at a 1984 football forum. His first major interview on national television was not with Barbara Walters, but on one of the Sunday pregame shows. The Trump name was regarded by his partner in his first Atlantic City casino, Harrah's, as too obscure to be part of the casino's name until all the hoopla about his acquisition of a football team converted him into a celebrity.

Donald began looking for a football team to buy before he could afford one, talking to one National Football League owner as early as 1981. He was simultaneously exploring his prospects with the United States Football League, the new, fragile federation of eighteen underfinanced teams fighting for a foothold in America's most lucrative sport. From the beginning, he seemed to vacillate between the two, attempting to use the threat of joining the USFL—which was still a year away from its first season and still putting franchises together—as leverage with the behemoth NFL. The difference in price between the two options was astronomical—a USFL franchise might need a few million in start-up funds, while NFL franchises were selling for at least ten times that. Donald's solution was to figure out how to buy an NFL franchise at a USFL price.

The NFL owner Donald started wining and dining in 1981 was Baltimore Colts owner Robert Irsay. The conversations—including meetings in his Crown

Building office—lapsed in 1982, and started again in earnest in early 1983. At one point, Donald had Sandy Lindenbaum, who was friendly with NFL Commissioner Pete Rozelle, call Rozelle for help with Irsay. He may even have talked to Rozelle himself. Irsay was willing to sell, according to Donald, but the two were far apart on price.

Irsay and his counsel, Mike Chernoff, would later claim that in the course of their discussions Donald had tried a daring pressure tactic, suggesting that he would buy a USFL franchise and force his way into the NFL if Irsay didn't sell him the Colts. Chernoff claimed that Donald told him privately he would "see to it that it was worthwhile" for Chernoff if the lawyer would persuade Irsay to agree to the sale.*

After the first unsuccessful run at Irsay went nowhere in 1981, Donald had backed away from the NFL and made a $25,000 down payment to the USFL to obtain the New York franchise, but he did not make the second payment when it came due in 1982. According to Donald, he decided not to follow through on the purchase after talking with Rozelle about the pluses and minuses of going with the USFL—a peculiar selection of an adviser on the issue. Rozelle, he claimed, predicted doom for the league. Donald, on the other hand, was tempted by the notion that combining a daring, new football league with a telegenic and glib young owner might be just the right recipe for the instant media attention that would advance his other business interests, even if the league failed. Despite this hunch, he decided, at least temporarily, to take a pass on it and keep his options open with the NFL. An Oklahoma oil man, J. Walter Duncan, took on the USFL team in New York.

Trump continued to monitor the progress of the league, further intrigued by the four-year, $50 million contract it won with ABC before a single player had been signed and by the respectable TV ratings achieved in its first season. The league's first player draft and the ownership meetings were held in his hotel, the Hyatt. He spoke regularly with the league's leadership, peppering them with questions about the local franchise, the New York Generals. Since playing in Shea or Yankee Stadium in the spring—the designated season for the USFL—created a scheduling conflict with baseball, the Generals had followed the NFL Giants to the nearby New Jersey Meadowlands. Aside from snatching Georgia running back Herschel Walker from the college ranks, the local franchise was

---

* Donald would coolly deny these charges under oath years later, saying only that it would not "be my place to say that."

both a football and financial disaster, winning six games, losing twelve, and racking up a $2 million deficit. Duncan was ready to sell, and any buyer was in an excellent position to dictate the terms.

Donald made one last attempt at Irsay and Rozelle in early 1983, but could not force the Colt price down. One other NFL development also pushed Donald toward the USFL—Leon Hess, the sixty-nine-year-old oilman who owned the New York Jets, made it publicly clear that he was seriously considering a move to New Jersey. That would open the door for Donald's Generals to become the only New York football team.

Since the Jets' twenty-year lease at Shea ended on January 1, 1984, Hess had written the mayor a year ahead of time, advising him that the team was entertaining proposals for a stadium lease and would select a future site based on a review of the city's submission and "others"—an unmistakable reference to the Meadowlands. Hess had been dissatisfied for years with Shea, a stadium built for baseball, with terrible sight lines for football and a scanty 60,000 seating capacity. An old-fashioned businessman who insisted on spotless restrooms in his gas stations, Hess became so furious over the drainage and egress problems at Shea's bathrooms that everyone understood he would leave unless the city came up with a concrete proposal to rectify all of the stadium's limitations immediately.

The best Ed Koch could offer to mollify him were vague renovation promises that added only 10,000 seats and ninety-eight luxury boxes. After Hess received the city's final proposal, his protracted silence was widely interpreted as a bad omen for the city. Koch appointed former governor Hugh Carey to head a New York City Sports Commission, and his main mission was to try to convince Hess to stay. Instead, Carey freely told friends that Hess was already "gone."

With Hess's departure appearing more and more likely, Donald opened talks with Duncan to buy the Generals. On September 1, 1983, Trump signed a nonbinding purchase agreement with Duncan in which he agreed to pay up to $5.3 million for the team over a period of six years. On September 22, with the word out that the Jets were going to Jersey, Trump announced his purchase of the Generals at a press conference, though the transaction hadn't actually closed. Six days later, Koch declared an impasse and announced the departure of the Jets. On October 6, Hess's agreement with the Meadowlands was made public. On October 18, Trump and Duncan finalized their deal, with Donald making a $1.2 million initial payment and signing promissory notes of $683,333 for each of the next six years, to be paid to Duncan so long as the Generals and the USFL survived. Donald personally guaranteed the payments.

The terms of the Duncan sale weren't made public, and, like virtually all of

Donald's deals, the purchase price was misreported over the years, encouraged by the boastful Donald. He once even told a *Fortune* reporter that he'd paid between $4 and $5 million for the team, provoking a "minor crisis" at the league office. The price tag on an expansion team at the time was $6 million, and the Denver club had sold for $10 million, so Donald's understated figure devalued all USFL franchises. Trump refused to correct the *Fortune* quote and other friendly profiles of him, written with his cooperation, suggested the price might have been as low as a million. To make himself look smart, he would not hesitate to make his league look broke.

The terms of the Duncan contract carried a blueprint of Donald's grand plan for the league. The document anticipated a "merger or absorption of part or all of the USFL into any other league" and even the possibility that Donald or the Generals might receive a "consideration" for arranging such a merger. The only "other league" was the NFL. Instead of paying $70 million or more for an NFL franchise, as a near USFL owner did for the NFL's San Diego team in 1984, Trump believed from the outset that he could invest a stretched-out $5 million for a USFL team, take a few years of losses, and then force his way into the big league, either by cutting a deal with Rozelle, forcing a merger of the two leagues, or winning an antitrust lawsuit.

But Donald did not plan to own the third-string NFL franchise in Jersey. Hess had agreed to a twenty-five-year lease in the Meadowlands, while the Generals were tied to the facility on a year-to-year basis only. With the Jets out of New York, Donald saw himself as the future owner of the only football franchise in the center of the largest media market in the world. He not only envisioned owning New York's team, he pictured himself as the builder and owner of the city's first football stadium. Trump understood what only a handful of others did at that time—that, with the advent of luxury boxes and leased seats, the real money to be made in football was not in a team, but in a stadium. As Donald saw it, his New York Generals would play in the Trumpdome—a facility that would manufacture money and be usable for the Olympics, major concerts, the NCAA's Final Four, and a bonanza of other possible events.

Reaching this dual goal required a careful strategy. First, Donald had to steer the USFL into playing a fall schedule. He was convinced that spring football would forever be second-rate football, with second-rate revenues. No one would invest hundreds of millions of public or private dollars to build a stadium for a team that played football when Donald, and much of the rest of the most lucrative television market, was out on a golf course. If the league moved to the fall, theorized Donald, it would either get a new network contract—in which case the far larger fall television revenues would position the USFL to compete effectively with the NFL—or it would be passed over by the networks—in which case the USFL would have a viable antitrust suit against the NFL-network monopoly. In either event, Trump believed, Pete Rozelle and the NFL would be forced to the merger table, and if any USFL teams made it into the powerhouse league, Donald's would be certain to be one of them.

Second, Donald had to secure a New York stadium for his team. The short-term option was Shea. So, unnoticed by the local media, new language was suddenly, and somewhat mysteriously, added to the Mets' lease at Shea, permitting the fall use of the stadium by a USFL franchise.

But Donald's long-term objective was to position himself with top state and city officials so that he would be able to push the concept forward and then take over the development of any stadium project. By the time Leon Hess formally announced his departure, the city and state had already actively begun to consider the construction of a new stadium. Hess had expressly sent that message—i.e., the necessity of one—as both an ultimatum and an invitation.

Hess hated leaving New York almost as much as he hated the thought of remaining at Shea. So when he declared his intention to move to New Jersey, he wrote Koch an open public letter, promising to return to New York in five years if a new stadium—a *football* stadium—was built. He concretized his intention to return by putting up a $10 million bond with the Meadowlands, which he would forfeit if he opted out of his lease there. He built a window of opportunity into the Meadowlands lease, giving New York until February of 1986, twenty-seven months in the future, to come up with "all necessary permits, detailed plans, authorizations, approvals and financing" for a stadium. If New York complied, Leon Hess, who considered his reputation as a man of his word a stodgy asset, "pledged to return." Hess was so serious about this promise that the Jet offices and Jet practice field remained in New York; so did the team name.

The Hess window of opportunity made it imperative that Donald insinuate himself inside any New York stadium planning process so he could direct it in ways that maximized his own—rather than Hess's—interests. As foreboding as a possible Jet return might be for his ultimate strategy, Donald recognized that the promise of it was a mixed blessing. The lure of a possible Jet return provided the impetus for public investment in a new stadium. The widely publicized Hess letter compelled some sort of concrete response from new governor Mario Cuomo, who'd succeeded Carey at the start of 1983, and from Koch, who was so angered by the Jets' departure that he wrote Hess a letter threatening "an aggressive effort to negotiate with teams from the new leagues."

Hess's pledge had in effect created the stadium opportunity that Donald planned to expropriate, but bringing the Jets back was the government's initial motive, never his own. Trump might have been willing to accept the Jets as a secondary tenant at his stadium, but it is the primary tenant in a football facility that reaps its greatest financial benefits. For example, the Mara family, owner of the Giants, was given control over seventy-two luxury boxes when the team became the first, and primary, tenant in the Meadowlands. At $40,000 apiece, the Maras collect $2.8 million a year that they don't have to share with the visiting team or with anyone else. As a secondary tenant, Leon Hess receives nothing. The Maras controlled those boxes, even for Hess's games. But the only way the Giant monopoly on luxury boxes could become an incentive for Hess to move to the Trumpdome was if he, not Donald, got a similar prime tenant package.

Donald, however, wanted prime tenancy for his Generals and, while he might be forced by circumstances to live with the Jets and share the facility, he never, over the course of the two-year stadium discussions, did anything to try to entice them. His objective was his own stadium for his own team.

These dual goals were mutually reinforcing. His NFL strategy had to succeed for his stadium strategy to succeed—meaning that he had to get the Generals into the NFL to get the city and state to go ahead with the stadium. Clearly, New York was unlikely to back the construction of a stadium for a struggling franchise in a struggling league. So even before he closed his deal with Duncan, he went public with a blast at the NFL, urging a USFL switch to a fall season in a September 30 *New York Times* story, the same day the Jets' departure dominated the sports pages. Within two or three years, he said, the USFL would reach parity with the NFL and could "perhaps go head-to-head" with it. Adding that some USFL teams could already beat NFL teams, he said he was "talking to large numbers of people" and that "more NFL players" would be "coming over to the USFL." It was the first time a USFL owner had openly talked about abandoning the spring concept and inducing NFL players to join the new league.

USFL Commissioner Chet Simmons was left with the responsibility of countering Donald's brash statements, noting that "for the moment we are concentrating on building the league in its present format" and that the USFL "would be foolish to challenge an organization as well established as the NFL." He branded Trump "an active young guy who is doing a lot of thinking, some of it off the cuff." Little did Simmons realize that his newest owner had just announced what would—within eleven months—prove to be precisely the timetable and strategy adopted by the league.

A few weeks later, Trump went to Houston for the annual meeting of the league's owners. Addressing his colleagues for the first time, Trump announced that he hadn't joined the USFL to become a "minor league" player, and immediately launched his campaign for a switch to the fall, insisting that the TV dollars were there. The owners, who had cautiously carved out this spring niche for themselves, weren't ready to accept his proposals, but they did vote to put this challenging new owner on their executive committee.

Donald next took the dramatic step of signing a string of first-rate players—Kansas City All-Pro free safety Gary Barbaro, Seattle cornerback Kerry Justin, and Cleveland quarterback Brian Sipe, the NFL's most valuable player only three years earlier. On December 20, 1983, Donald announced the hiring of former Jet head coach Walt Michaels, a mortal enemy of Leon Hess. By the beginning of 1984 Donald had recruited six active starters from a variety of NFL teams, making a bigger splash than anyone in the USFL had in the league's first two years of existence. Part of the league's economic plan had been to keep salaries low, minimize superstar acquisitions, and slowly build a league. Donald was not about to be patient.

Myles Tannenbaum, one of the league's founders and owner of the Philadelphia Stars, confronted Donald about the spending spree in mid-December. "I'm in the media capital of this country," Donald replied. "When you're in New York, you have to win."

"Donald, in Philadelphia you have to win, too," Tannenbaum retorted. "You have to win everyplace."

"I need to win more," Trump insisted.

At the end of December, Ted Taube, one of the USFL's most vocal and successful owners, wrote Trump and two other leaders of the league a joint letter suggesting that the USFL could not "allow individual owners to pursue plans which are suited to their perceived best interests or whims" and citing Donald as his only example.

"It may be in Don Trump's best interests," Taube wrote prophetically, "to pursue a strategy which gains him leverage, politically or otherwise, to move to Shea Stadium and become the NFL franchise which the City of New York is apparently ready to underwrite at any price. But Don's best strategy for the Generals could be devastating for the USFL as a whole."

Donald plunged on, announcing on New Year's Eve the signing of Giant All-Pro linebacker Lawrence Taylor, the NFL's top defensive player. There was a catch—Taylor's contract with the Giants ran until 1988, so Donald was only staking a future claim on him. The Taylor contract with the Generals had an option, however, permitting the Giants to buy it out, which they immediately moved to do, paying Trump a quarter of a million dollars and signing Taylor to a brand-new, six-year deal. The episode stirred a bonanza of publicity for Trump, as well as a tidy profit.

The only drawback was that Myles Tannenbaum, according to USFL rules, had the league's exclusive rights to deal with any players out of the University of North Carolina, Taylor's alma mater. Tannenbaum was furious, particularly since Trump had not even bothered to speak to him. Despite the concerns about Trump that were being voiced by some of the owners, his money and his media attention were still viewed as a plus, as were the ties he claimed to the top ABC brass. In early January, the executive committee abruptly stripped Commissioner Chet Simmons of his negotiating role with the network and made Donald the lead man. An owner for barely three months, Trump had already become the dominant force in the league's bargaining with its key source of revenue.

Donald also wasted no time in launching his stadium campaign. On January 4, Governor Cuomo announced in his State of the State address that he wanted the Urban Development Corporation, the superagency that helped build the Hyatt in the seventies, to "undertake a comprehensive statewide study of the need for sports facilities." A top Cuomo aide, Bill Eimicke, began a series of calls to UDC president Bill Stern, urging the creation of a Sportsplex subsidiary that would undertake the feasibility study sought by the governor, as well as begin to plan a city stadium and several upstate sports facilities. In these initial conversations, Eimicke suggested only one name for the new Sportsplex board: Donald Trump. Although Eimicke did not mention it to Stern, Trump had already spoken directly to Cuomo about building the stadium, and the governor was said to be "certainly interested in any ideas Trump has," Eimicke told Stern. Eimicke also made it very clear that the governor wanted his administration, not the city's, to take the lead on this project, putting it squarely on a fast track.

Eimicke's calls were quickly followed by his statement to a New York *Daily News* reporter that the state was considering three possible sites for a New York City sports facility to compete with the Meadowlands. Trump's name appeared in the same story—quoted as being in opposition to the three proposed sites and disclosing not only that he preferred another, unspecified site but that he planned to build the stadium himself. The notion of Trump building the stadium, and the Sportsplex concept itself, had debuted in the same story, just as he would have wanted it. The two ideas would remain linked in the public mind from then on.

When Stern called Donald to ask him to join the Sportsplex board, the developer said yes immediately. The day after their first conversation, on January 19, Stern and Trump held a perplexing press conference to announce the formation of the Sportsplex corporation and to name a single member of its new board. By the time the press conference was over, Donald was wearing three hats. In addition to his public role as a member of the board that would plan the stadium, he had already advertised his interest in building it—a possibility that Stern openly acknowledged could very well happen. Trump added that his Generals might become the stadium's primary tenant, saying "one day you might want to ask me to move the team" to New York, but that otherwise he would not "instigate it." No one in the media or the government seemed to notice the blatant conflict—sitting on an advisory public body charged with determining the need and viability of a stadium project was a man who wanted to both build it and install a team in it. Over the next month or so, ten other members were named to the Sportsplex board, including George Steinbrenner, who stalked out of the first full-board press conference in February when Donald started answering press questions, snapping, "This isn't going to be a one-man show, or I'm not going to stick around." Curiously, the board included one other USFL owner, whose team played in Michigan, but the only member with NFL ties was a former Jet player. Spurred by Donald's behind-the-scenes recommendation, the board quickly hired Laventhol & Horwath as its primary consultant on a million-dollar feasibility study, and L&H retained the architectural firm of Hellmuth Obata & Kassabaum. L&H had long been Donald's accountants, and HOK would become Donald's architects for his proposed stadium.

Meanwhile, Donald was proceeding inside the top ranks of the USFL with his campaign for a fall schedule. Two days before his press conference with Stern in January, Trump wrote letters to every USFL owner reiterating his arguments for a switch to the fall, invoking endorsements from Howard Cosell and Jimmy the Greek, both of whom, he said, gave the league "virtually no chance of failure" if the change of seasons occurred.

The letters, which anticipated that a fall season would "create psychological havoc with the NFL," were delivered the same day the owners gathered in New Orleans for their annual meeting, where Trump quickly took the floor again. Urging that the owners not repeat his comments to the newspapers, Trump said a fall schedule would lead either to a league with television contracts that would make it just as strong as the NFL or to a merger—"and the merger is going to take place sooner rather than later." Trump was so adamant, and the debate so acrimonious, that Commissioner Chet Simmons had to promise to appoint a committee that he euphemistically said would look into "long-range planning."

The Philadelphia owner, Myles Tannenbaum, wrote a postmeeting letter to other owners assailing Donald's "grand plan"—a forced merger—and warning that Trump "will do virtually anything to have his way." Donald, he wrote, "came into the league knowing full well our direction and he is now trying to reshape it." Tannenbaum also reported that the New York attorney installed by Donald as president of the Generals had told him that "obviously" not all the USFL teams would make it into the NFL as part of any merger and that the league itself would have to work out an arrangement to compensate the teams not included. "I have this vision of being patted on the head with an offer of thanks and perhaps something more if Donald has his way," concluded Tannenbaum. Trump went away from the January meeting frustrated, but the desperate tone of Tannenbaum's letter suggested that the tide was clearly running in Donald's direction.

A profile of Donald that ran in an early February edition of *Sports Illustrated* certainly fed the fears about Trump—within the USFL and in the NFL. Labeling Trump "the biggest wheeler-dealer in all of sport" since his purchase of the Generals several months earlier, the article quoted Donald as saying he "could have had four or five NFL teams" but went to the USFL instead because he liked a "challenge" and because "the NFL is very vulnerable." The article concluded with flat predictions that he'd build a stadium in New York and swing the USFL to the fall; it was only a matter of how soon.

Trump was also moving on another front: television. While he talked with executives at CBS and NBC, his focus was on ABC, the network that was already televising USFL games and had no NFL Sunday schedule. Even before Trump had been designated as the league's TV negotiator in January, he had contacted Jim Spence, the ABC vice president who handled the USFL. He told Spence in their first conversation in December that he wanted the league to switch to the fall, and Spence seemed open-minded about the possibility of ABC televising a USFL fall schedule. Then, one afternoon in early 1984, Trump had what he claimed was the longest phone conversation of his life—four and a half hours— with Spence, who was encouraging again, at least as far as Donald later recalled it.

While in his initial conversation with Spence, Donald preferred a move to the fall by the 1985 season, he pushed the date back to 1986 during the second marathon session. Spence, whose network was dependent on the NFL giving it a glamour schedule of Monday night games matching the best teams for prime-time ratings, told Trump he was concerned about how the NFL might react if ABC signed a fall contract with the USFL. But he also acknowledged that all the network had on Sunday afternoons were cartoons, up against the most popular sporting events in human history. A USFL schedule did have a certain allure.

When Spence and Trump talked a third time a few days later, however, the ABC executive had changed course and emphatically declared that the network would not air the USFL in the fall. Donald later characterized the early conversations as "moderately positive" and the last as Spence "slamming the door in my face." But he did not tell the league about the contacts nor did he reveal his even less encouraging approaches at NBC and CBS, all of which occurred in February and early March of 1984.

Nor did he mention to anyone at the USFL his strange rendezvous with Pete Rozelle. Rozelle, who had been running the NFL for twenty-four years when Donald called him in mid-March, was the most powerful man in American sport—which meant he was the kind of man Donald liked to imagine he had a relationship with, indeed liked to describe as a friend. In fact, other than brief conversations at parties, the two did not know each other.

Trump requested that they meet, and though Rozelle was busy preparing for the league's annual gathering in Hawaii, he said he would be free late that day. Donald offered to rent a room in the Pierre Hotel for a 4:00 P.M. meeting and called back with a room number. Neither he nor Rozelle said what the subject of the meeting would be; both understood that it was dealmaking time.

Unbeknownst to Donald, however, the NFL had just sponsored a slide-show seminar for sixty-five league executives called "USFL vs. NFL," put together by a Harvard Business School professor and commissioned by the NFL's Management Council. The strategies outlined at the conference for putting the USFL out of business included forcing ABC to discontinue televising spring games by giving them a weak Monday schedule, as well as "co-opting the most powerful USFL owners with promises of NFL franchises." Rozelle hadn't attended the seminar and later claimed that when he heard what had happened there he "almost got physically ill." In any event, the only man with the power to effectively dangle an NFL franchise was Rozelle, and the skillful old hand hardly needed Harvard to tell him how.

Both Rozelle and Trump would testify at the antitrust trial that took place two years later about this crucial meeting, and their accounts would differ substantially.* Donald claimed that Rozelle had promised him an NFL team sometime in the future—"whether it be the Generals or some other team"—if Trump would help keep the USFL in the spring and block an antitrust lawsuit. Trump insisted that he said "there is no way that I am going to sell out people," and that

---

* Rozelle's version was supported by a file memo he wrote after the meeting and the claim that he'd discussed it with the league's finance chairman; Donald had no memo and never spoke about the meeting with anyone.

he would only consider joining the NFL as part of a merger, with "four or five or six teams" coming in from the USFL (out of the eighteen then playing). Rozelle rejected a merger, according to Donald, adding that he "wasn't interested in taking in more than one or two teams" and that he would explore that possibility and get back to Trump.

Rozelle's version was a Trump shakedown. Trump opened the meeting, said Rozelle, with warnings that he was busily developing an antitrust suit and arranging for new ownership of two floundering USFL teams. "But I don't want to do these things. I want an expansion team in New York in the NFL. I would play in Shea Stadium, and I would arrange for a new stadium to be built for that team in New York," Trump explained. According to Rozelle, Trump then warned him that if the NFL did not agree right away to his demands, he would have to push forward on the lawsuit and ownership matters and would wind up too committed to the USFL to walk away and cut a separate deal.

In addition to seeking his own team, Trump offered to identify two or three other USFL owners Rozelle might reward with a franchise. When Rozelle expressed concerns about the antitrust implications of such a buyout of a competitor, Trump quipped that he'd sell the Generals to "some stiff" and wait a year or two for his NFL franchise, creating a smoke screen. Rozelle said that Trump concluded with the declaration: "If I were to leave the USFL, it would be psychologically devastating to the league."

Despite the disparities between their stories, Rozelle and Trump agreed that Rozelle had made a commitment to respond to Trump on the question of a one- or two-team USFL deal, and that he did, several weeks later. Rozelle testified that he told Trump it could not be done; Trump remembered the call but claimed Rozelle said he and the league were still "mulling it over."

By mid-April of 1984—a month after the Rozelle meeting—Donald was back to turning up the heat on the USFL, dropping press bombs on the spring schedule defender, "useless" Chet Simmons, pushing his fall agenda, and sending telexes to the owners demanding, for the first time, that the league file an antitrust suit. By the end of the season in June, the league had bottomed out, limping through disastrous ratings and horrendous losses. Franchises from Chicago to Los Angeles, especially those in the large TV markets with NFL teams, were collapsing. Citing "one owner" as a source, *Sports Illustrated* ran a story listing, franchise by franchise, $60 million in losses. Momentum was building for a move to the fall out of a desperate need for a quick fix; any change had begun to look appealing. In August, shortly before another owners' showdown, Ted Taube, the letter-writing owner who had questioned Trump's motives from the beginning, reversed field. "The central focus of all USFL strategies," he now argued, "must be to bring about a merger or accommodation with the NFL. There is no other financially viable alternative." The fall move would help create, he wrote, "the climate for merger."

An expensive McKinsey management study Simmons had commissioned came in with a firm spring verdict, and ABC, now trying frantically to keep the league in the spring to avoid a confrontation with the NFL, offered a four-year, $175 million package, a 300 percent boost despite the vanishing teams and declining ratings. But Trump berated the study as "bullshit," supported by his leading ally among the owners, Eddie Einhorn. Trump and Einhorn, who was also president of baseball's Chicago White Sox, insisted that their talks with TV brass indicated that two unnamed networks (apparently ABC and CBS) would buy fall programming, a direct contradiction of the McKinsey findings (this assertion was actually contradicted later by Trump himself on the witness stand in the antitrust case, when he recounted his March 1984 conversation with Jim Spence). Trump closed the argument with his threat that if the league continued in the spring, it might find itself playing without him.

With owners charging one another with betrayal, Donald won the final vote handily, though he did not get a fall move until the 1986 season. Most of the owners agreed to pretend at the subsequent press conference that the seasonal switch was unanimous. They even prepared a press release that said the decision was based on the findings of the McKinsey study, a lie so outrageous that the consultant who wrote the study threatened to expose them if any reporter called her.

Donald's triumph, however, was short-lived. In the succeeding months, the league shrank to only eight teams. Not a single one of its founders remained a majority owner. USFL teams fled virtually every NFL city—LA, Denver, Detroit, Pittsburgh, Houston, New Orleans, Washington, Chicago, and Philadelphia—unable to compete with the established league in the anticipated fall season of 1986. With the loss of all the major television markets except New York, the league's ability to stick it out only in non-NFL cities, and the absence of any scheduled games from June of 1985 to September of 1986, Trump's USFL became—shortly after the 1984 vote—little more than a litigant, kept alive solely by the promise of an antitrust suit.

The lawsuit became Donald's next obsession—a supposed sure shot at hundreds of millions in damages or an NFL settlement. He sold it to the befuddled owners with precisely the opposite pitch from the one he'd used three months earlier to promote the fall switch. Since his promise of television support for a fall schedule had not materialized (indeed, ABC was considering imposing penalties on the league for breaking its spring contract), Donald now used the network's refusal to give the league a fall contract as the primary evidence of a monopoly—a refusal, he predicted, that would lead to a court bonanza.

Donald's lawyer, Roy Cohn, posing now as an antitrust expert, filed a federal complaint as early as October 1984. Trump announced the suit at a press conference in New York with Roy at his side; not one other USFL official was invited. With aggregate league losses jumping to $100 million, Donald forced the firing of Chet Simmons and replaced him with a new commissioner, Harry Usher, whose contract was a sure, though secret, indicator of the league's last remaining strategy. Usher would receive a $1.2 million bonus if any USFL team merged with the NFL by 1990 and further payments for additional merger teams. As distressed as the league seemed to be to most observers, it was on precisely the track Donald had intended from the beginning—a direct confrontation with the NFL that just might lead to his own NFL franchise.

Donald's outburst of antitrust activities in late 1984 was accompanied by a simultaneous surge of public pronouncements and private maneuvers on his other football front: the stadium. He tried to win a quick designation as New York's stadium developer. If he ever had any doubts, he now understood that his Generals would only get to play in a stadium he built if the USFL won the lawsuit or if the NFL decided to bring him in out of the cold to avoid a trial. Otherwise, the league and the Generals would die.

Along with the rest of the Sportsplex board, Donald voted in October—just days before the antitrust suit was filed—to approve both a stadium project and the recommended Queens site. Though he voted in favor of the project, including the state's preference for the cheaper open air stadium, Trump made a statement at the Sportsplex meeting noting that "the psychological and economic impact of a domed stadium would be very great for New York City, and a much more competitive stadium." Mayor Koch quickly announced his own support of a domed stadium and objected to the Sportsplex financing mechanism—a bond sale that required the city to pick up 60 percent of the debt service costs.

A few weeks after the vote, Donald called UDC's Stern and ran his own proposal past him for the first time. In this, and subsequent conversations in early December, Trump said he would build a $300 million stadium at no cost to the state or city and would finance it by selling most of the seats as if they were condominiums at an average price of between $4,000 and $5,000. The state and city, according to Trump's plan, would pay only for site acquisition and preparation costs, including roadway and subway improvements. Trump also wanted a sales tax exemption on construction and a full abatement of all property taxes. In every significant detail, his proposal differed from the project he had just voted for—his 85,000-seat arena was 7,000 seats larger, domed, financed by fans, and to be built on either the Sportsplex site "or another appropriate location."

Yet Stern liked the sound of most of it, especially the heavy private sector share of the costs. On December 12 Trump put the proposal in writing to Stern, and his letter made absolutely no reference to the New York Jets. "If we begin building this stadium," he wrote, "it is my strong opinion that in addition to a USFL team (whose New York rights I own), an NFL team will commit sometime prior to the completion of construction." This was one switch on the Sportsplex proposal that neither Stern nor Cuomo would accept: The first condition in a list of provisos adopted by the state was that the stadium would be built only if "a prior commitment is received for at least two major anchor tenants, one of which is an NFL team, capable of capacity crowds."

The governor told the newspapers he was "kind of incredulous" about the plan. "I want to see it. It sounds wonderful, doesn't it? 'We'll build you a free stadium'—pretty good." Cuomo said he was concerned about its plausibility, and Stern quickly arranged a December 19 meeting between Trump and the governor at Cuomo's World Trade Center office in Manhattan.

That morning Trump went to UDC, had coffee with Stern, and then drove him downtown to Cuomo's office in his silver limousine. A chatty millionaire who'd made a fortune in computers and had never held a public post before, Stern had become quite chummy with Trump over the course of a half dozen Sportsplex meetings. Though he saw himself as a maverick reformer poised atop a bureaucracy corrupted by the Carey years, Stern had developed a temporary and out-of-character weakness for Donald. In late 1984, he saw Trump as a daring visionary of capital who could make this stadium happen. Donald's genius at con, flattery, and hype, plus his deceptively inexpensive plan, had energized Stern. But Stern had also begun bickering with his longtime friend Cuomo over an array of issues and those disagreements had convinced him to leave the administration. He wanted the stadium as a legacy.

The meeting with Cuomo was stiff and businesslike. Donald outlined his plan, explaining little more than what was already on paper. Cuomo emphasized his desire to minimize the public investment in the project, but did not raise any questions about the level of general public access to what would principally be a condominium stadium. As soon as Trump left, Stern, who had remained behind with the governor, urged Cuomo to push ahead. He said Trump's proposal would finally give the state something to offer Leon Hess. While the Jets had never been mentioned in the conversation with Trump, Stern saw Trump's stadium and Hess's team as the perfect match. He asked Cuomo if the governor could speak to Hess and float the Trump plan past him.

Though the governor promised to try to get word to Hess, Stern heard nothing further of it. He and Trump continued to refine details of the plan, and the dimensions of Donald's stadium kept growing. A January 4, 1985, memo to the governor from Stern enlarged it to a 100,000-seat stadium, costing $400 million, with up to $90 million in public costs for acquisition and infrastructure. The extra 15,000 seats were Trump's response to the city's complaints—none had been made by the state—about the lack of public access. While Trump had announced this plan as a "no risk" project for the city and state ("the risk is mine," he wrote the city), his proposal required both governments to advance a minimum of $24 million to acquire the site. If his condo seat sales proved disappointing, however, Trump could simply back out of the deal without any liability for the public expense already incurred.

Nonetheless, the revised plan received favorable notices from Koch and Cuomo officials in news stories. What sounded to most New Yorkers like a revolutionary proposal was in fact just one more borrowed idea, with Donald figuring out how to wring every last ounce of profit out of someone else's concept. Joe Robbie, owner of the NFL's Miami Dolphins, was at that very moment marketing 10,000 condo seats at prices of up to $1,500 to help finance the construction of a 72,000-seat stadium there. The sale of luxury boxes, with dozens of seats for corporate purchase, had been used to cover stadium costs around the country for years. Trump had taken the concept to another level, however, privatizing virtually an entire stadium. He even had the nerve to require millions in public expenditures and tax breaks to make his country-club stadium buildable.

Despite the exclusivity of the plan, and the absence of any real contacts with Hess, the state and city were by early 1985 on the verge of approving the Trump proposal. Donald looked as unstoppable on the stadium with the state as he'd proven to be on his fall schedule and antitrust tactics within the USFL. He had browbeaten his fellow owners into adopting his USFL game plan; now he would seduce the state officials who succeeded the resigning Stern into not only delivering its stadium designation to him, but into adopting the same take-on-the-NFL strategy as the USFL had. The immediate price of the state's decision to effectively become Donald's football partner was the waste of $2 million in consultant and staff expenditures on a stadium fantasy by the city and UDC. The long-range price was the scuttling of what appeared to be New York's last real chance at an NFL franchise—Leon Hess's window of opportunity—and the resulting loss of hundreds of millions in taxable revenue that would have accompanied the return of football.

In Bill Stern's final days at UDC, he arranged a March 1985 lunch to introduce his successor, Vincent Tese, to Donald. It was an awkward lunch, with Tese enjoying Donald's lighthearted shot at Stern over the skyrocketing convention center construction claims. The stadium was discussed, and Tese was noncommittal. Though Tese and Stern were virtually the only two millionaires close to Cuomo, they couldn't have been less alike. Tese had made his money in the fast-track business of cable TV and gold and commodity trading, while Stern helped develop computerized performance measurement systems for 500 of the largest banks and insurance companies in the world. A cool, detached, mustached, trim, and elegant man of few words, Tese contrasted sharply with the short, cheeky, effusive, and always black-suited Stern. Tese immediately communicated a worldly sophistication; Stern was a rare bird and advertised it.

While Stern had known Cuomo longer than Tese, it was Tese who ultimately penetrated the Cuomo inner circle in a way Stern never could. The *New York Times* noted in a January 1985 story that the Tese appointment signaled Cuomo's decision "to bring the agency more under his wing." Tese entered the Cuomo camp as a contributor in the 1982 campaign, and over the years, rose from banking commissioner to UDC president to economic czar overseeing all state development activities. While he held his state posts, Tese and his wife continued contributing to Cuomo, donating $90,000 and becoming the governor's third largest individual contributor. Tese's long-standing business partner James Sinclair, as well as companies they both had an interest in, donated another $70,000. Tese, who continued trading heavily in gold and commodities and even moved a personal computer with commodity exchange software into the UDC kitchen, became so close to Cuomo he began acting occasionally as the governor's personal financial adviser, giving him gold and silver tips.

At the same time that Tese became Cuomo's key decisionmaker on the stadium, Trump changed lawyers on the antitrust case. In March of 1985, he dropped Roy Cohn and hired Harvey Myerson, a vigorous litigator like Cohn but one who, as Donald told Tese, "also does research." Tese hardly needed an introduction to Myerson. He and Sinclair's old trading companies—largely defunct but still embroiled in a variety of cases—were represented by Myerson's litigation unit at Finley Kumble Wagner Heine Unterberg Myerson and Casey. Myerson's powerhouse firm was also on retainer to UDC, hired by Stern in 1984 to represent the agency in a complex suit against Dow Chemical. While Trump's selection of Myerson to handle the USFL lawsuit had its apparent bonuses at UDC from the beginning, it was hardly the only reason Donald chose him.

Myerson was a gifted lawyer who could mesmerize a courtroom, likened by one reporter to "a short Jackie Gleason in a Turnbull & Asser shirt." A heavyset, five-foot-eight-inch, quick and raspy talker, with a $2,500-a-month cigar habit, a raccoon coat, a collection of Ferraris, a glorious East Hampton estate, and a Rolls, Myerson was as grandiose and theatrical in a courtroom as he was in his personal life. He put an army of lawyers on the antitrust case almost immediately, running up a bill that totaled $6.9 million in fees and expenses by the time all appeals were exhausted. In mid-1985 he unearthed the infamous Harvard Business School report—Myerson's much-brandished "smoking gun" at trial—which led Trump and the league to believe that they had a real shot at winning. But it was Myerson's blitzkrieg of confidence, more than any document, witness, or argument, that infused the USFL with hope in 1985. Without that hope, the league would surely have folded after its final spring season in 1985.

Even Donald was behaving as if the suit were the league's last chance. No invoices for the Generals' 35,000 season tickets for the supposed fall season were ever sent to the ticket holders, and, in fact, no tickets were even printed. No arrangements were made for a preseason training camp. No stadium leases, at either Shea or the Meadowlands, were executed. No new players were signed. And the league's only television contract for the 1986 fall season was so weighed under with conditions that no funds would be released until a game was played.

Donald had turned into a madman during his second spring season in 1985, raging during games from a press-box seat, sending in plays that were routinely ignored on the field, berating his quarterback Doug Flutie and his coach Walt Michaels. When he found out that the Generals would be matched against the defending champion Baltimore Stars in an early playoff round, he tried to get the league commissioner to rig the schedule to set up a game against a lesser opponent so the Generals could avoid what he regarded as certain preliminary elimination. The Generals wound up beaten by a lesser opponent in the first round anyway, and the championship game, minus the Generals, was a half-million-dollar disaster. As the league headed into its year-and-a-half-long off-season, *New York Times* sportswriter Dave Anderson wrote a column on the USFL headlined "The L Is for Limbo."

Donald was certainly in no rush to move forward on the stadium. If he wouldn't print a ticket on speculation, he certainly wasn't about to build a stadium on it. The only man in a hurry was Leon Hess, whose deadline for a stadium decision was fast approaching. The state and city had a choice—they could either get on a Hess timetable and, within a year, produce a solid, feasible stadium proposal, backed up by site acquisition action, permits, an environmental impact statement, and financing commitments, or they could acquiesce to Trump's amble toward the Hess deadline, waiting to see if the USFL lawsuit might give New York a new set of options.

It's difficult to fault Vincent Tese for his initial impulse of wanting the stadium designation put out to public bid. The city and Bill Stern had been leaning toward giving it to Trump, without competition, for fear that a bid process might make it impossible to meet Hess's deadline. Stern strongly believed that this had to be "a tenant-driven, not builder-driven process" and later likened the emphasis on developer designation that followed his UDC departure to "building a pool in the Sahara, and worrying about the water later."

Once Tese decided to bid it, however, the relatively straightforward Request for Proposals took a month to issue, since two sets of lawyers and bureaucrats, one from the city and one from the state, had to agree on every line of it, just as they would on every other public position throughout the designation process. One Trump ally in carving out the RFP language was Donald Manes, who pressured city officials to stipulate that the project would receive a generous tax abatement.* When an initial draft containing very limited tax concessions was presented to the mayor, Koch pointed to the single sentence on taxes in a seven-page RFP and asked for an explanation. City negotiators suspected that the mayor had either been primed by Manes or Trump counsel Allen Schwartz or both. When no one answered, the mayor demanded an explanation for the limited abatement, shouting: "Why?" Finally, one city attorney replied: "Because it's Donald Trump." Koch, whose attitude on the Trump Tower tax abatement was well known, gruffly rejected the rationale and suggested a change. This new Koch attitude toward Trump did not pass unnoticed among the roomful of top city officials, many of whom were simultaneously working in April of 1985 on the thorny questions surrounding Trump's acquisition of the West Side yards. The final tax language in the RFP was open-ended.

The RFP suggested that the state planned to move quickly, declaring that "acquisition is expected to be completed, and title to the entire site obtained by UDC, by January 31, 1986." With a half dozen bidders, Tese announced a July 5

---

* Manes was an invaluable driving force for the project, and for Trump to build it, announcing that he'd "discussed it at length" with both Koch and Cuomo and noting that it was "probably the only subject I discussed cooperatively with both of them."

deadline for designation of a builder. When that date passed, he amended it to August, then extended it again and again until December. The best evidence of who stood to benefit from the delays was that chronic complainer Trump, usually the first to criticize a recalcitrant government for ignoring business deadlines, who maintained a saintly vigil at UDC's door. He protested when Tese decided to put the project to bid, but even that was muted. He never objected—in the media or to the agency—about what turned out to be a lost year.

Cuomo had installed Bill Mattison as Sportsplex president when Stern's appointee, a career civil servant with a broad engineering background, resigned in June. Mattison was a stockbroker without construction or management background, selected because of his long family ties to Cuomo—his father had been a senior partner at the governor's Brooklyn law firm in the 1950s. From the moment Mattison arrived at Sportsplex, he'd become embroiled in a protracted paper war with Trump and the only other finalist, a group including Fred DeMatteis and Morton Olshan, two New York builders. An extraordinary exchange of letters went on through the fall, with Mattison prying concessions out of both bidders. While Mattison and the city were making useful demands (one, for example, enabled the public sector to theoretically recoup its up-front acquisition and infrastructure investment over the first twenty or so years of the project), the time it took to wrangle this and other commitments out of Trump may well have cost New York the only potential tenant whose projected revenues could make the stadium buildable.

Mattison also gradually persuaded Trump to move from 15,000 general admission seats to 41,000, the fifty-fifty ratio of public access to condo sale seats required by the city and state. Since the other finalist was offering 82 percent general admission, Mattison could have responded to Trump's initial refusal to go beyond a 25 percent public share by informing Trump that the state would simply select the other bidder. Instead, only at the very end, when the designation was made in December, did Donald finally agree to a 50 percent split, still far below that of the Olshan group proposal.

In effect, Mattison and Tese wound up using the Olshan group's commitment to public access as a weapon against its proposal. Olshan's use of the Miami model—removing from the public market only 18 percent of the seats (still the most ever leased)—meant that the stadium generated less public and private revenue than Trump's huge seat sale. Yet the primary reason Tese eventually cited for the selection of Trump was that the city and state recouped their investment several years sooner under his plan than under Olshan's. It was

Olshan's strong preference for general admission seats that gave Trump his financial advantage.

Olshan insisted on the public seats because he knew that was the only way Hess would bring his team to the stadium. Every one of a dozen submissions to the state by the Olshan group emphasized that their bid was tailored to Jet concerns; they repeatedly claimed that they were in touch with Jet officials. Trump, on the other hand, never once mentioned the Jets in hundreds of pages of submissions. Yielding finally in November to state and city pressure, Olshan submitted an alternate proposal raising the percentage of leased seats to 30 percent, and though this proposal still had a substantially higher ratio of public seating than Trump's, it repaid the city and state just as quickly. While Olshan acquiesced and submitted this alternate, he stressed in his letter that he did not believe the Jets would accept it and that his earlier 82 percent ratio was still the best lure for the Jets.

"The Jets, in recent conversations with our group, have made it abundantly clear," wrote Olshan, "that they would find only 41,000 general admission seats unacceptable"—a direct slam at Donald's highest offer. Tese had every reason to know that Olshan was on the mark since Hess had encouraged Tese in their first face-to-face meeting back in June to look at the Miami plan, which only involved the leasing of seats between the forty- and fifty-yard lines. Both Tese and Mattison agreed in interviews years later that Olshan was a credible man honestly recounting conversations his group had actually had with the Jets, but neither made any attempt to determine before picking Trump if the Jets would reject out of hand the seat distribution of the proposed Trumpdome. Instead, Tese selected the Trump proposal precisely because of the revenue advantages tied to a seat distribution that there was every reason to believe would never be acceptable to the Jets. It was all a maddening riddle.

At the very end, a frustrated Olshan charged that the state's delays had "endangered the very viability of the project." He had offered a detailed plan giving the Jets a 53 percent increase in their revenues over the Meadowlands, with prime tenant control of luxury suite profits. He had proposed financing the construction of the stadium with a private bond offering that, had the designation been made on schedule, would have put enough money to build the stadium in an escrow fund prior to Hess's February deadline, a far more secure form of financing than Trump's reliance on highly speculative projections of future seat sale revenue.

While Olshan had designed his proposal around the Jets, Trump was disdainful in his November letter of any attempts to woo them, promising that "time and a great stadium design" would eventually draw an NFL team to the city. UDC's rebuff of Olshan—and its designation of a developer who was serving subpoenas on Hess in the antitrust case just days before he was named to build a stadium supposedly to house the Jets—were clear indicators of the low priority the state was assigning to any possible Jet return.

The fine print of the designation agreement that the state and city signed with Trump made a joke out of any notion that the mere act of picking a builder might be a concrete enough step to entice a skeptic like Hess to return to the city. The agreement was called a conditional designation, but it was, in fact, a hypothetical designation. Some of the hypotheticals were extended so far into the future that if Hess decided to opt out of his Meadowlands lease to sign up with New York, he would have been trying to schedule home games for dates listed in the Trump timetable for environmental permits. The agreement was little more than a succession of "if" clauses: If enough seats were sold. If the environmental impact statement (EIS) was completed before December 1, 1988. If the public sector took the necessary legislative action to fund the site acquisition and preparation. If the city determined that the site did not have dangerous toxins. If the site was delivered before December 1989.

Though Hess's letter back in 1983 had required that "all authorizations, approvals and financing" be "securely in place before February 1, 1986," no attempt had even been made to assemble the critical pieces—no EIS, no full appraisal of the properties on the site, no acquisition activities, no legislation authorizing the public bond issue, no stadium lease. The financing package was so conditional that Trump was protected from investing any funds at all until the state and city spent $150 million on acquisition and improvements. And the public sector didn't have to start acquisition until Donald sold enough of his condominium scats—now valued at $12,000 each—to capitalize the project. Though Hess's original letter had also specifically required that "all necessary permits" be obtained by February 1 and Hess had emphasized that he was particularly concerned about federal environmental permits (which were required for planned wetlands use for a parking area), the state had not even sought them. Nonetheless, as transparent a pretense as it was, the state went ahead with the designation as if it constituted an overture to the Jets.

The final negotiations with Trump and announcement of his designation occurred in a circus atmosphere at UDC on December 5. Though city and state negotiators had never conducted any face-to-face bargaining with the Olshan group, they did sit down in the end for last-minute bargaining with Trump and

Allen Schwartz.* It was during these negotiations that Donald made the fifty-fifty concessions and others that produced an agreement. Schwartz told city attorneys "not to worry about securing a football team" as a tenant, assuring them that "when we win this lawsuit, the Generals will be an NFL team" and that the team would move to the stadium. Donald added that "the best lawyers in the world say I have a 100 percent chance of victory" in the antitrust action.

The night before the designation, these talks, with Schwartz on site and Donald at home, lasted until four in the morning. The biggest point of contention, as with most Trump projects, was the name of the stadium. Donald's attempt in 1979 to get the convention center named after Fred and the bitter battle with Harrah's over the naming of Donald's first casino were precursors to Allen Schwartz's two-hour tantrum over Trump's right to name the stadium, which almost became a dealbreaking issue. Schwartz was emphatic and in the early evening of December 4 even threatened to walk away from the deal, forcing city and state representatives to contact the governor and the mayor.

As laughable as the issue seemed, the city and state were unwilling to let the arena become the Trumpdome. Though no one from Trump's side ever conceded it, Donald did not want to take any chance that the stadium his Generals would try to claim as their home would be called Jets Stadium as part of some agreement to bring the Jets back. (The Meadowlands is called Giants Stadium.) In the end, the three parties decided that the stadium could not be named without the consent of all three parties—Trump, the city, and the state—essentially postponing a selection and leaving Tese with one less attraction to dangle before Hess.

Though a press conference was called for ten-thirty the morning of December 5, the battered group of bargainers had been forced to reconvene that morning at seven-thirty and were unable to finish until three in the afternoon. Tese was in and out of the sessions, relaying issues by phone to the governor in Albany. Schwartz, who had stormed out of the sessions at around 2:00 A.M., only to be drawn back in, spent much of the day running between the conference room where the bargaining was taking place and a UDC office on another floor where Donald Trump sat waiting.

When Trump and Tese finally walked into the conference room jammed with waiting press that December afternoon to announce the designation, Trump

---

* While the state had played the lead role on the stadium from the inception, Schwartz had effectively worked the city side as well. Donald had also arranged the retention of Koch's pollster, Penn and Schoen, by the USFL.

startled everyone with his candor about the Jets, the supposed prize that would come with his $276 million stadium. "Leon Hess is a friend of mine," Trump said. "He's a very, very fine gentleman. I would say that the Jets are perhaps not a very likely candidate to leave where they are. I personally don't put great credence in the fact that they may come back. And I say that up front." Tese tried in interviews afterward to portray Trump's comments as part of an elaborate "mating game" between Hess and Trump, but the truth was that Trump was not going to bargain with Hess, even though he had that obligation under the agreement with the city and state.

Tese, who had actually been doing and would continue to do whatever little bargaining there was with Hess, told reporters that "there's a lot of negotiating that's going to go on and Donald's not a bad negotiator," adding that if Trump can't get Hess, "he's going to get somebody else." Trump openly pointed to his favorite option—predicting a league merger or some other settlement of the USFL suit that would lead to a New York NFL team, probably named the Generals. Insisting that there was no deal to allow Trump to bring the USFL Generals to the stadium, Tese said that "if tomorrow the Generals go into the NFL, that would be fine by the city and state."

It took another month for Tese to send his letter offer to Hess. In it Tese did stress the single strong point of the city and state position: The Jets were promised all the advantages of prime tenancy and far more projected revenue than could be expected at the Meadowlands, a feature of Olshan's proposal never even mentioned in Trump's. Hess's response was a volley of criticism, assailing the delays and the failure to achieve "certain routine elements for a sound commercial proposal." He expressed his particular outrage (just as Olshan had predicted) at the seat-sale and lease-back plan, which Hess said "takes $276 million from the pockets of our fans to build a domed stadium, plus additional charges of $36 million paid by our fans just to be able to buy tickets." By Hess's calculations, the owners and lessees of these seats, who still had to buy tickets for any individual event (including games) they wanted to attend, would dominate the stands from one end zone to the other, with regular fans restricted to the end zone areas.

Tese and company replied to Hess's letter with one last faux pas—offering an already enraged Leon Hess a new and improved Shea Stadium to play in if Trump's wasn't finished on time. This was supposed to calm Hess's understandable concern about what would happen if he took the offer, was forced to leave Jersey by the 1989 season (as the option terms of his lease required), and the new stadium wasn't ready yet. Despite this and all the other problems, Hess, who had at first refused to even discuss the offer, decided to meet with Tese and the city's Herb Sturz, expressly excluding Trump from the invitation list. When Hess attacked the seat-auction financing plan, during the meeting, Tese replied: "Well, we can't put the cost of it on the homeless people who need shelter." Tese was suggesting, as he would later to the press, that the only alternative to a seat sale financing scheme was a taxpayer-built stadium, as if Olshan's plan for a private bond offering had never been proposed.

"I'm not suggesting you put it on the homeless people," Hess replied. "But I can't be a party to having a husband and wife with two children either paying $48,000 for the right of buying a ticket or leasing four seats for $9,600 a year and still buying a ticket. I think it's a horrible thing to do."

When Hess's predictable rejection hit the news, Tese responded with a public claim that "more than one" other NFL team had expressed interest in the Trumpdome and intimated that Hess had never really intended to come back to New York, a gratuitous attempt to shift the blame. In fact, as Tese well knew, Hess could have avoided the loss of the $1.7 million in interest on the $10 million he'd deposited with New Jersey any time before the February 1 deadline if he simply informed the Meadowlands he was staying. Instead, he forfeited it to consider New York's offer.

Tese's upbeat news, though, was a belated announcement of the state's real plan: "If the USFL wins their lawsuit, we will clap our hands. We would love to have the Generals in the NFL." Trump supported him by announcing that his "first alternative" was to put the Generals in his stadium, declaring: "I hope to have the opportunity. I expect the USFL to win the lawsuit." Whatever ambiguity had existed before, it was clear now that the suit had become the only rationale for the stadium plan.

While the city lost interest in the entire stadium project after Hess's rejection, the state pressed on, going through the motions of looking for another NFL team. One indication of just how frivolous the search was occurred in early February, when Tese wrote both of New York's senators in Washington urging them to vote against NFL-backed legislation seeking an exemption from certain requirements of the antitrust laws—not exactly a diplomatic gesture toward a league he was supposedly trying to woo. It was just one more indication of Tese's adoption of the Trump lawsuit game plan.

Even without a team, the Cuomo administration tried to move elements of the stadium plan forward, positioning themselves should Trump win the antitrust action. The governor sent a stadium bill to the legislature in April, seeking bonding authority for $115 million. UDC told legislative leaders that it was "anxious" for the bill to pass because it believed "it would be difficult to negotiate with a team unless there are state funding guarantees"—precisely what Hess had said only a few months earlier. The bill—blocked by a host of legislative attacks on the viability of the project—was designed to go into effect at around the same time as a verdict was expected in the USFL case.

As a final expression of the Cuomo administration's surrender to the Trump strategy, Tese and Mattison actually became witnesses for Donald, Myerson, and the USFL at the antitrust trial in June. (No one from the city testified.) The flamboyant Myerson announced several times in court that Cuomo himself might appear, but the governor never did.

Myerson used Tese and Mattison in an attempt to prove what he called the "New York Conspiracy," a sop thrown to a local jury and press corps. His argument was that Hess and Pete Rozelle had conspired to exclude an NFL team from New York, stringing state and city officials along in a deceptive effort to convince them that the Jets might return in order to prevent them from dealing with Donald about a stadium for the USFL Generals.

In addition to the two state witnesses, Myerson also produced U.S. Senator Al D'Amato, who described himself as a "friend" of Donald Trump's and testified about the shifting moods of Leon Hess in three conversations in 1985 and 1986, concluding that, in his opinion, Hess "had no intention of returning and was giving me excuses that really did not go to the real reason." What was surprising was that Myerson's billings revealed that D'Amato had talked with a Finley partner about the case shortly before two of his conversations with Hess, suggesting that the senator may have been acting as a conscious agent of Myerson's and Trump's.

While Mattison's testimony was similar to D'Amato's—a straightforward account of one encouraging and one discouraging conversation he'd had with Rozelle about the Jets returning to New York—it was Tese who became the only witness to actually serve up the bizarre Myerson conspiracy theory for jury consumption. Tese turned the entire scenario of a yearlong delay and a mismatched proposal on its head, as if Hess were somehow responsible for the state's protracted production of a plan that flew in the face of his own demands.

Despite the many ways in which Tese had failed to act on clearly stated Hess conditions for a Jet return to the state, Tese painted Hess as a "bad faith" bargainer, claiming he'd even called Hess that to his face in their final meeting, a charge Hess denied under oath. What was most peculiar, was Tese's contention in the climactic series of questions at the end of Myerson's examination that Hess's "indecisiveness" may have stood in the way of the state's making a stadium deal with the Generals. Myerson asked Tese if the state would have considered "other alternatives" had Hess "told you no at an early time," and when Tese said yes,

Myerson pressed him on whether or not one alternative would have been "to explore some arrangement with the USFL club, and in particular, Donald Trump."

"Well, I think if we could have negotiated out a deal where there would have been absolutely no cost to the city or state, we might have entertained that type of proposal," Tese answered. "And, in fact, we did kick it around a little bit, to have a stadium that would not only accommodate the USFL but would accommodate other things." Asked if he had failed to explore this USFL alternative over the long course of the designation and negotiation process because he thought the Jets might return, Tese said: "The answer to that is yes."

Under cross-examination by the NFL, Tese stubbornly insisted that if Trump "had walked back into our door" and said he would "put up a team, put up all the money" and build a stadium, "yes, then we'd entertain that idea," adding that "the city was in favor of pursuing" such a Trump-guaranteed, USFL-tenanted stadium. Asked if he was willing right now "to explore the possibility of building a stadium for a USFL team," Tese replied: "Sure."

This testimony contradicted every public statement Tese and the city had made about being interested only in an NFL team. It contradicted the designation agreement with Trump and the amended RFP, which required an NFL franchise in writing. It contradicted every financial assessment, whether by UDC's consultants or those of the developers, that the only way to generate the revenue to repay the public or private investment in the stadium was with an NFL team. It would eventually even be contradicted by Tese and Mattison themselves in interviews with a reporter.

Mattison couldn't have been clearer on the point in a 1990 interview: "We considered doing it with a USFL team and we rejected it out of hand. Trump wanted to build it without an NFL team and we said impossible. We weren't confident the Generals could repay the bonds." Mattison, who said Myerson was "disappointed" during pretrial preparation that Mattison was unwilling to go beyond his description of the Rozelle conversations and into the plausibility of this USFL alternative, said that the city did express a willingness to support a USFL stadium with Trump guarantees, just as Tese testified. But, Mattison added, UDC had specifically rejected any such possibility.

Tese himself said in a taped interview for this book: "We would have never—ever—built a stadium based on a non-NFL franchise. The only way we would have gone with the Generals was if the Generals were in the NFL. We needed the luxury of an NFL franchise." Confronted with the contradiction between his testimony and his position four years later, Tese said that Myerson had "sprung the question on him." In fact, in a sidebar conversation with the judge immediately before this portion of Tese's testimony, Myerson accurately predicted exactly what Tese would say and successfully persuaded the judge to permit this speculative testimony on the basis of his claim that "our whole position" on the New York Conspiracy issue rested on this Tese statement. When the judge tried to get Myerson to mitigate the speculative nature of the approach by asking Tese what alternatives "were considered," Myerson answered: "I can't say 'were considered.' The whole point of my line is that they would have been considered but for this stringing out." The truth was that the USFL alternative had been considered, and rejected.

In his summation, NFL lead attorney Frank Rothman, the smooth and dapper former president of MGM, accused Tese of "willful, deliberate falsehood under oath." Perhaps because the case was being covered almost exclusively on the sports—not the news—pages, this grave charge against a high state official went unreported. But Rothman was not talking about the contradiction at the heart of Tese's testimony. He was castigating Tese for falsely claiming that the $276 million in seat-sale revenues would be split in three parts, evenly divided between Trump, the public sector, and the Jets. Rothman argued that the proposal Tese wrote himself and sent to Hess "put the lie" to this claimed distribution. "How dare he? Why? I suppose he is protecting Mr. Trump, and that's troublesome, very troublesome," said Rothman.

The jury wound up rejecting the New York Conspiracy, like much of the rest of Myerson's bluster, finding in a July 31, 1986, verdict that the NFL had not engaged in any anticompetitive acts. While the jury did agree with Myerson on the obvious—that the NFL was a monopoly—it could not bring itself to exact from the league the tiniest fraction of the $1.3 billion in damages that the USFL was seeking. All Donald's spectacularly publicized courtroom trench war produced was a field goal: a devastating $3 award.

The pivotal tactical error was the decision to build the case around Trump, encouraging the jury to see it as a Donald versus Goliath struggle, rather than the battle between David and Goliath leagues that the USFL had hoped it would become. Trump was the only active owner to testify at the trial, a blunder that left the jury with no real impression of the typical USFL owner—a struggling entrepreneur battling the NFL octopus. Rothman made much of the other USFL owners' failure to appear in his summation, contending that they were not there because "they didn't want to talk about Trump taking them down the road of despair." Rothman poignantly described the early owners, committed to a spring schedule and financial restraints, as overwhelmed by "the wheelers and dealers" who announced "I'm going to have it my way because I have to have an NFL franchise and then I get a free stadium." He said Trump saw three ways to make money in football—"tickets, television, and treble damages"—and this suit was his route to all three.

The verdict was also a personal repudiation of Trump. The jury went out of its way in its detailed response to a long questionnaire from the court, to clear Pete Rozelle of all liability, suggesting that they believed his, not Donald's, version of the Pierre Hotel and other reputed conversations. Trump's credibility had been effectively challenged at trial in a number of ways, particularly when he was forced under cross-examination to question the reliability of a stenographer whose minutes of a USFL owners' meeting had him openly advocating a merger strategy. The NFL also put on a convincing witness who directly contradicted Trump's testimony about the Queens stadium site, claiming that Donald had told six representatives of a Queens business organization that he could "virtually guarantee" that once the USFL won the lawsuit, he would get his NFL team and "have the leverage and bargaining power" to force Tese to relocate the stadium to another site. The witness, Richard Musick, was used to rebut Trump's denial during cross-examination that he had made that statement. Those were, said Musick, Trump's "exact words." Donald apparently believed that Musick's testimony might be so damaging that he called Musick after seeing him in court, but before Musick testified, and mentioned certain "legal problems" he and his organization might face if he testified.*

Trump, as usual, was quick to cut his ties with anyone who might remind him of his own mistakes. Though Myerson had once been on the Mar-A-Lago invitation list, Trump's relationship with him was never the same after the verdict. He stuck with Myerson on appeal, but when that failed, too, in the summer of 1987, Donald dropped him altogether. The loss of the USFL case was a key factor in the bankruptcy of the Finley Kumble firm itself—the largest legal

---

* Trump's desire to move the stadium was later verified in interviews with Tese and Mattison, who said he really turned up the heat to get away from Queens in early 1986, just when he met with Musick's business association. Not only are Tese's and Mattison's recollections directly contradicting to Donald's trial testimony, they are just one more indication of Trump's opportunistic disloyalty. He apparently was willing to junk the Queens site as soon as his ally pushing the site, Donald Manes, was forced from office by scandal.

collapse in the nation's history. Had Myerson won, there would have been a gigantic final fee, and the publicity would undoubtedly have attracted millions in new business.

When Myerson started a new firm in 1988, Donald signed one of the eight prominent statements of support released to recruit clients, unembarrassed apparently by the lead-the-lambs-to-slaughter character of the endorsement. Donald did not reveal until later, when Myerson was buried under an avalanche of horrid publicity, an indictment, and a second bankruptcy—all revolving around his alleged billing excesses—that he had himself never really used the second Myerson firm, having suffered through "so many billing disputes with Myerson" that he would "never use him again."

Trump also cast the decisive vote at a USFL owners' meeting shortly after the verdict to pull the plug on the long-awaited first fall season. But he had one more team-play message for his fellow owners the day before the meeting—he announced that he would permit his stars like Herschel Walker and Jim Kelly to negotiate with the NFL. The league stayed in business, with ten-member skeleton teams, while the appeal went forward. The stadium project did, too, just as nominally. The end of the league and the stadium finally came in the summer of 1987, when the appeal died.

By his own estimates in court papers, Trump lost approximately $22 million on the league. The court defeat also solidified the pigskin putsch that Donald had resolved either to break into or break up. Yet the mixed verdict—the jury's conclusion that the NFL was a benign trust—gave Donald a way to turn the debacle into a public relations standoff. It was confusing enough to make people wonder if Donald hadn't been cheated, by a quirk of fate, out of another golden win. While the legal blur was some solace, there was no denying that Donald had in truth suffered a crushing financial defeat, and that it had come at almost precisely the same moment as his retreat and settlement on 100 Central Park South. The events of 1986, from the long view of hindsight, would take on a watershed look, in sharp contrast with his previously unbroken string of triumphs and in painful anticipation of the hard years just around the corner.

The most disturbing mystery surrounding the saga of Donald's brief career as a football phenom was the questions it raised about his curious, yet unmistakably compelling, influence at the highest levels of the Cuomo administration. Vincent Tese was no renegade commissioner; in fact no one in Mario Cuomo's government was in closer touch with him. And UDC's supine performance for Trump had its equivalents in other state agencies on matters wholly unrelated to the stadium, especially at the State Transportation Department, which championed Trump's agenda in planning improvements on the West Side Highway, adjacent to Donald's 60th Street yards.

Donald had long had a special knack for compromising public officials, but Mario Cuomo was no Andrew Stein, whose varied public performances for Trump were a metaphor for gutter government.* Unlike Stein's volunteer subservience, Donald's penetration of the Cuomo inner circle was a textbook case in seduction, and his compromising relationship with the administration would last even into the months of Trump's collapse in 1990. Other than Tese's golf dates with Donald in Florida and New York, there was little of a personal touch to the mutually beneficial Cuomo/Trump arrangement. It was all business.

---

* In addition to Stein's acquiescence on the Trump Tower abatement, the tenant conflict at 100 Central Park South, the waiver of the $31 million MTA improvement, and the blockbuster density of Trump's West Side project, one anecdotal account of his Trump servility reached almost legendary proportions in the annals of New York politics.

In the mid-eighties, as the story goes, the pastor and board of a fashionable East Side church decided to try to market the air rights over its steeple, and virtually every developer in town tried to woo them. When the church group met with one developer, they were surprised to see Stein at the boardroom meeting, and even more surprised when Stein cornered the pastor afterward and urged him to pick the developer, promising that he'd help get the controversial air rights sale, which was opposed by neighborhood groups, through the Board of Estimate if he did. Sometime later, Trump called the pastor and, at a meeting unattended by Stein, made his own bid. As soon as the pastor got back to the church, Stein was on the phone, however, telling him to forget what he'd said about the first developer—who was also a generous contributor to Stein campaigns—and urging him to go with Trump. When the church picked another bidder altogether, preservationists began picketing it, and there at the head of the line was Andy Stein.

Stein's opponent for city council president in 1985, former deputy mayor Ken Lipper, tried unsuccessfully to make a big issue of this uncontested saga, but New Yorkers were unimpressed by the news that their politicians were tools of Trump. A highly respected investment banker, Lipper claimed that Trump had tried to convince him not to run against Stein, telling him that even though Donald believed Lipper was "smarter" and "more qualified," Stein had "done things for me." Trump promised to support Lipper if he'd run for another office.

What made Cuomo such an unusual government target for Trump was that when he defeated Ed Koch for governor in 1982, he ran against virtually every monied interest in New York politics, most of whom, like Donald, rallied to Koch because of his thirty- to forty-point lead in the early polls. And almost from the moment he became governor, there was an extraordinary undercurrent about the dignified and brilliant Cuomo that marked him as a man who might be President. His speech at the 1984 Democratic Convention transformed this one-time unarticulated presidential murmur into so persistent a question it became, both at home and occasionally across the country, a Democratic preoccupation. His reluctance to run in 1988 just fed the lust for him. This national fascination helped Cuomo become, through the eighties and into the nineties, the master of New York politics, isolated from the pack by his deliberate hermetic style, a recluse in Albany whose intelligence and rhetorical passion were seen only in glimpses.

Part of Cuomo's above-the-fray appeal was his religion. It wasn't just that he was a Catholic; his predecessor, Hugh Carey, was Catholic enough to have twelve children, yet no one ever thought of him as a man to whom morality was a mission. Cuomo publicly wrestled with the Lord, weighing the heaviest questions of life and death as if it was the responsibility of a leader to help the people to understanding. He talked soaringly about values. He invoked Saint Thomas More as his guardian, a man who died for a principle. There did not appear to be anything phony or sanctimonious about this part of him. The people would have seen through that. But this spiritual quality, combined with the hometown presidential hopes that seemed to last forever, insulated him from inspection and criticism like no other public figure in the state.

From the beginning of the Cuomo reign, the insiders who bankrolled and benefited from the government game were studying the new Albany team, looking for weaknesses, waiting for messages, hunting for opportunities. They read every signal, interpreted every nuance, and none did it better than Donald. Figuring Cuomo out was a riddle for Donald; finding a path to him was a necessity.

Trump knew he had a bit of history going for him. In 1958, Mario Cuomo had joined his first law firm—Brooklyn's Corner, Weisbrod, Froeb and Charles. Senior partner Richard Charles, who became Cuomo's mentor at the small firm, had already been representing Fred Trump for decades, and Cuomo was assigned as a young associate to help with the Trump work. Fabian Palamino, then a young associate with Cuomo who became his counsel as governor, remembers their travels out to Fred Trump's headquarters on Avenue Z for business lunches at which Trump dished out the cheese sandwiches himself.

When Cuomo became Carey's running mate in 1978 and was elected lieutenant governor, Trump contributed $4,000 to his minuscule campaign committee. While Trump had backed Koch in the 1982 race, he'd called Cuomo's old friend and finance chairman, Bill Stern, on October 11, 1982, and made a $3,500 donation for the general election.

Trump did not contribute again to the Cuomo committee until November 13, 1984, a month after the stadium project was approved and a month before he submitted his own plan. Several Trump business entities combined that day to give the Friends of Mario Cuomo $15,000—making Trump one of the top donors at Cuomo's annual fund-raiser. Cuomo had personally approved Trump's invitation that August to serve on the campaign committee's board of advisers. The board was formed as "a permanent finance committee" of thirty to fifty prestigious individuals, from every major region and industry in the state, to raise a minimum of $30,000 each at Cuomo's dinner. One of only a half dozen listed from the real estate industry, Trump's role on the advisory board meant he was charged with raising at least as much as he directly donated.

But the contributions were merely door openers. Donald was looking for the right insider who could get him beyond access—a Sunshine, Stone, Schwartz, or Capalino. All he had to do, it turned out, was look at the top of the governor's fund-raising apparatus, just as he had in 1975 when he recruited Carey finance chief Sunshine.

Bill Stern had long since stepped down as the head of the Friends committee, which he'd formed way back in 1978 to help pay off the costs of Cuomo's losing mayoral campaign the year before. Stern, who stopped fund-raising for Cuomo when he went to UDC, was replaced at the campaign committee in 1983 by Lucille Falcone, a thirty-year-old lawyer so unknown in the circles that fund political campaigns that she was seen as merely an appendage of the governor's office. Falcone had surfaced publicly in early 1983, when she was hired by Stern at UDC, a job she quickly resigned when news stories described her as the girlfriend of Cuomo's twenty-five-year-old son, Andrew. She then scurried back to her law firm and took over the Friends committee. It was Falcone who recommended that Trump be named to the board of advisers in a letter to Cuomo.

Falcone was the only person to have worked at both of Mario Cuomo's law firms. She was a young associate at the Charles firm in Brooklyn, recruited from law school in 1976 by Cuomo's close friend, Pete Dwyer, the treasurer of his 1977 mayoral campaign. In early 1981, she was asked to join a new firm that had just been formed at Cuomo's request by Jerry Weiss, who had been Cuomo's special counsel as lieutenant governor. Cuomo encouraged Weiss to put the firm together so he would have something to fall back on if he lost the gubernatorial campaign.

The small firm that the thirty-eight-year-old Weiss assembled was intimately connected with Cuomo from the beginning—law student Andrew worked summers there, the campaign finance committee met there, and the firm's biggest client became the campaign's most generous donor.

Shortly after Cuomo won his astonishing victory, the firm was recast with two new partners as Weiss, Blutrich, Falcone & Miller and began to prosper quietly, though every one of its partners was only "30 something." Andrew joined the Cuomo administration as a $1-a-year special assistant and soon became the second most powerful state official, but Cuomo insiders openly anticipated that he would soon wind up at the family firm, and he never denied it. He'd begun dating Falcone in 1982 and worked closely with her on the annual dinner dances in 1983 and 1984. Though she frequently worked round the clock on the committee's activities, the struggling new firm was generously understanding about her unpaid efforts.

A few days after Trump's December 1984 meeting with Cuomo about the stadium, Bill Stern got a surprising call from Donald about Lucille Falcone's little law firm.

"Bill, I saw Lucille Falcone at this fund-raising meeting and I got the feeling I should retain her law firm," Donald told him. "What do you think?"

It was an awkward moment for Stern, who had been bickering with Andrew and Mario Cuomo for months, complaining, among other things, about what he saw as the increasingly disturbing signs of the Weiss firm's attempts to influence state agencies. He had informed them about Weiss's call to him raising questions about the propriety of a UDC bid process on an upstate job where Weiss represented a client who'd lost the contract to another builder by more than a million dollars. Stern had also told the Cuomos about Falcone's call to him claiming that he was excluding big-time developer Bill Zeckendorf from UDC's gigantic 42nd Street development project. Zeckendorf had retained the Weiss firm in 1984, the developer later conceded, on the recommendation "of somebody who knew their way around the Democratic side of state politics" because "we thought they could help us politically."

Stern also recounted to the Cuomos the insight of another 42nd Street developer, frustrated at the small slice of the project he was getting. "I know a way I can get a bigger cut," the developer told Stern. "Hire Jerry Weiss's law firm." Indeed, when this developer and Stern were flown up to Albany for a private dinner at the governor's mansion, Lucille Falcone accompanied them in the developer's plane and stayed for dinner, too.

As Stern saw it, Trump was hardly alone in picking up the Cuomo signal. "I don't recommend law firms," Stern told Trump. "But Lucille Falcone is a good person and a fine lawyer." It was the best compromise Stern could work out in his head, but it still troubled him, He had already had one bitter scene with Mario Cuomo about the firm, back in November, with Stern demanding that Cuomo distance himself from it and Cuomo responding: "You're holier than everyone else, Bill. You judge souls; I don't." Stern had been shocked at the personal attacks Cuomo had heaped on him that day—related and unrelated to the law firm controversy. He decided to get out of the administration, but he wanted to get out cleanly, without a war with Cuomo.

Forty-five minutes after Stern's conversation with Trump, Andrew Cuomo called him. He said that he'd heard Trump had called about the firm and asked Stern what he'd said. When Stern told Andrew that he had praised Lucille's legal ability, the young Cuomo said, "Lucille told me you said that." Andrew thanked him, and said: "I respect you very much."

Unbeknownst to Stern, a storm was stirring inside the firm. Not only would Andrew soon become a partner, he would replace Weiss himself. Stern first learned about Weiss's departure from the governor himself, who in late December casually mentioned to him: "Jerry's leaving. Did you know he made $800,000 this year?" When Weiss left, the State Investigations Commission was examining some of his activities on behalf of upstate developer Shelly Goldstein. The allegation was that Weiss had used his influence to dramatically reduce the value of a state lease in a building that Goldstein was trying to buy. The state official who ordered the lease reduction—which was theoretically done to force the owner to sell to Goldstein—was Andrew Cuomo. After Andrew joined the firm in May of 1985, Goldstein would become his principal client and partner in real estate and banking ventures.*

Shortly before twenty-five-year-old Andrew became the young firm's youngest partner, Trump quietly retained it. His relationship with the firm would last for almost two years, though it did not surface publicly until August of 1986. The legal work it did for Trump remains unclear, apart from Andrew Cuomo's concession that it represented Trump in lease negotiations involving possible

---

* The investigation closed without any findings against Weiss or Andrew.

commercial tenants in the stores planned for his West Side yards project. When Trump's retention of the firm did hit the newspapers in 1986, Trump's response was: "They are now representing us in a very significant transaction."

Though Andrew insisted in later interviews that the firm did not interact with state officials on behalf of clients, Falcone did just that for Trump on another project. She arranged and attended a July 21, 1985, lunch at the World Trade Center with Trump and Sandy Frucher, the president of the state's Battery Park City Authority. During the lunch, Trump expressed an interest in being designated for a choice hotel site on the Battery Park site, just off Wall Street. Frucher urged him to bid when a request for proposals was announced, but Trump was looking for an inside track. When Frucher didn't offer it, Trump didn't bid.

Donald was not the only one with an interest in Trump projects to retain the Cuomo firm. Abe Hirschfeld, Trump's limited partner on the West Side and an increasingly close ally, also hired the firm in November 1985 to represent him in a disputed real estate closing. Hirschfeld publicly said in a later interview that he thought hiring the firm was a way "to get in the good graces with the governor." While Andrew Cuomo and his partners have attempted to lowball Trump's business with the firm—never offering a total for him or Hirschfeld—the fact is that the unwanted publicity about the long-secret retainer killed the relationship before the "significant transaction" Trump cited could close, obviously limiting the Cuomo firm's fees.

The retention of the Falcone firm was hardly Trump's only Cuomo move. In November 1985, Donald hired Albany lobbyist and former transportation commissioner Bill Hennessy, who'd just resigned as chairman of the state Democratic Party. When Cuomo installed Hennessy as head of the party, the *Times* saw it as an indication of the governor's "intent on staying deeply involved in organization politics, since Hennessy has never held a party post and thus has nothing to fall back on other than Cuomo's support." The two remained so close that when Cuomo's Thruway Authority chairman resigned in 1987, the governor appointed Hennessy immediately and permitted him to remain a 90 percent partner in his lobbying firm, which continued to lobby state agencies (Hennessy promised not to share in the firm's lobbying profits while he ran the Authority). On a $2,000-a-month retainer, plus a $500 per diem rate, the Hennessy firm's main job for Trump was to lobby some of the very transportation officials he had appointed for favorable rulings on an array of West Side yard issues.

As potent as the Falcone and Hennessy combination was, Donald did not stop there. In the spring of 1986, Trump hired UDC's in-house counsel, Susan Heilbron, who had worked extensively on the stadium project for the agency.

The two first discussed the job while they sat together in December 1985 during the final stadium designation talks. Well known at the top levels of the Cuomo administration, Heilbron helped engineer the selection of her best friend as Tese's new counsel, Joanne Gentile, an attorney who had worked under Harvey Myerson at Finley Kumble.

Trump also tried, over a period of six months in 1986 and 1987, to lure Sandy Frucher into his lair. Frucher, one of the governor's half dozen top advisers, eventually declined, after countless courting sessions.

On Falcone's recommendation, Sive Paget & Riesel, the ten-member environmental law firm Trump retained for the lucrative West Side yards approval process, hired Richard Gordon, the executive director of the Friends of Mario Cuomo. Gordon, who had worked with the Cuomos since the 1982 campaign, remained director of the campaign committee, even though his law firm had a multiplicity of matters before state agencies.

Trump's most unusual reach, however, was for a very special driver and bodyguard, Joe Anastasi. A state trooper assigned to UDC, Anastasi had been Mario Cuomo's personal bodyguard for years, starting when Cuomo was lieutenant governor, and had accompanied him throughout the 1982 gubernatorial campaign, starting most mornings in Cuomo's kitchen in Queens over a cup of Matilda's coffee. After Cuomo became governor, Anastasi was on his security detail in New York City until, in late 1984, Bill Stern told Cuomo that his agency needed an investigator to do background checks on state contractors and Cuomo suggested Anastasi. Anastasi worked at UDC for three years, but was seldom seen there, ostensibly because he was "in the field" at UDC construction sites.

In 1986, Anastasi began accompanying Trump on various trips across the country. He told friends he was setting up his own security business and that the Trump work on his résumé would help him attract business. Top Cuomo officials, including the governor himself, learned of Anastasi's Trump duty and viewed it as a conflict with his UDC post. He was told to end it, and he soon resigned from state service.

In addition to surrounding himself with everyone from the governor's son to his bodyguard, Donald tried to score political points with Cuomo on several fronts. He let it be known to the Cuomos that he'd been recruited by state GOP boss George Clark to run against the governor in 1986, and he went public in 1987 with a highly questionable account of a meeting he had with national GOP kingmakers, including his own consultant Roger Stone, who had supposedly tried to convince him to oppose Cuomo in the next election, which would not occur until 1990. In both instances, of course, he'd said no. He also cooled down his irate partner Abe Hirschfeld, who ran for lieutenant governor in the 1986 primary but was knocked off the ballot by Cuomo. Hirschfeld was considering backing Cuomo's GOP opponent and assailing Cuomo publicly, but Trump convinced him not to. And finally, as the saga of 100 Central Park South reveals, Trump reached a settlement with comptroller candidate Herman Badillo's law firm that helped save it from a dire financial threat.

More important, though, than any of these local political gestures was Trump's willingness to talk openly and favorably about Cuomo's possible presidential candidacy. From the governor's perspective, the public praise of a Republican icon like Trump had a national impact, enhancing Cuomo's plausibility as a pro-business candidate. Of course to Donald, his calculating praise of Cuomo had nothing to do with the governor's public performance. Trump had not even bothered to vote in either of Cuomo's gubernatorial elections, nor when Cuomo ran for mayor in 1977. In fact, though Trump was the largest individual giver in city and state elections from the mid-seventies on, he had voted only three times, routinely skipping even presidential elections.

The final thread connecting Trump and Cuomo was Tese himself. Tese's business connection was not with Donald directly, but with Donald's lawyer. Neither Harvey Myerson nor Tese disclosed—to the NFL or to the federal court in the antitrust case—that Tese was a private client of Myerson's firm. In fact, Myerson had the nerve to object, in a sidebar conversation with the judge, about a small retainer one of the NFL firms had with UDC, charging that it "raises a potential or actual concern for impropriety." But he misled the court about his own UDC work—claiming it was "unrelated" to the stadium when he had a contract to handle the stadium bond issue for the agency—and failed to report at all his deeper, private ties to his witness, Tese.

More surprising was that Myerson's firm decided to waive payment on $122,000 in fees due from the Tese companies in 1986—the same year Tese testified—and wrote off another $157,000 the next year. The bankruptcy trustee in the Finley Kumble case ultimately labeled these forgiven fees—as well as waivers granted other favored clients—a "fraudulent transfer" of the firm's rightful earnings. Indeed Myerson was personally involved in some of his firm's legal work for Tese.

The bankruptcy trustee eventually brought a lawsuit to recover these fees plus interest, and lawyers for Tese's companies responded by contending that Myerson's firm had agreed to the write-offs because it had overbilled the companies. The trustee's suit wound up going nowhere—with the Tese firms assailing Myerson's "inflated, overstated and padded" billings and the trustee insisting that compliance with discovery demands could not be made without violating the lawyer/client privilege. But what appeared to be beyond dispute in this two-year litigation was that in the midst or aftermath of Tese's USFL testimony the Myerson firm was slashing the fees it once claimed Tese's companies owed it.

What was particularly disturbing about the Myerson/Tese intrigue was that Tese's companies got this apparent $279,000 write-down during the same period that Tese's UDC was awarding the firm $288,000 in new retainers for bond counsel work and was greatly increasing its payments on the Dow Chemical suit. Myerson's UDC earnings on the Dow case soared from roughly $200,000 under Stern to $4.4 million under Tese. Top UDC staffers at the time reportedly went to Tese and complained about Myerson's bills, but Tese did nothing. While the lawyers for Tese's companies would later claim in the bankruptcy case that Myerson's firm had not only overbilled them, but had acknowledged it and reduced the bills, the companies and UDC continued to use Myerson after the collapse of Finley Kumble, moving on to his new firm with him. Tese even insisted in a 1990 interview—shortly before Myerson's indictment on overbilling charges—that Myerson had never overbilled his agency, a contention belied by counts in the subsequent indictment which specifically involved UDC overbilling. The confluence of these factors left Tese in a classic conflict of interest position—lending the state's credibility to his own personal attorney by testifying inaccurately for him in a major lawsuit, as well as hiring and allegedly overpaying that lawyer on the public tab, while accepting waivers of at least part of his company's private fees.*

The casual ethical judgments implicit in this disturbing intertwine occurred against the backdrop of all the other Trump ties to the Cuomo inner circle. In fact, the Myerson firm itself—at least at the point in 1986 when Tese testified—

---

* Confronted with these appearances of conflict, Tese insisted that he paid his share of the fees but that his partner, James Sinclair, refused. Asked to provide documentary evidence of the payment, he declined, and Sinclair refused to discuss it. While Sinclair was the only individual defendant cited in the bankruptcy trustee's suit, Tese was co-managing partner of the companies named in the action. It is difficult to understand how Tese could have paid all of his share of the billings since the trustee asserts that the companies he and Sinclair owned did not make payments at all for the 1987 and early 1988 work. Though Tese was no longer involved in these inoperative companies, he concedes he would have been partially liable if they lost the lawsuits that the Myerson firm was handling at the time.

was part of the Cuomo circle; Bill Hennessy was its Albany lobbyist as well and Andrew Cuomo would personally spend several weeks during this period at the firm's office, negotiating what promised to be the biggest real estate deal of his life with Myerson's closest friend in the firm.* Through Myerson, and all his other levers of compromise, Donald had managed to insinuate himself, almost imperceptibly, within the Cuomo government, and the benefits of this relationship would extend far beyond the doomed stadium.

On the West Side, for example, Donald's grand Television City design required the approval of several state agencies and, from late 1985 through 1987, Donald was methodically lobbying for special favors, especially at the Department of Transportation. Trump wanted changes in DOT's planned rehabilitation of the elevated West Side Highway, which ran over the 60th Street site along the waterfront. When Macri owned the site, DOT decided that a partially built and never-used southbound ramp off the highway at 72nd Street—the tip of the Trump site—had to be removed entirely for safety reasons. Donald wanted it retained and converted into a permanent ramp running right into the retail mall he planned to build underneath his office and residential tower complex. Not only did DOT back the new plan, but the agency was also willing to let Donald pay for only part of it, while Lincoln West had been required to finance the entire cost of removing the old structure. The ramp—which state memos freely conceded "was needed" for Trump's project "but would otherwise not be needed"—was designed to deliver customers to the very stores whose leases Andrew Cuomo's law firm was trying to negotiate. When the plan was presented to the federal highway officials who were funding the rehabilitation project, they warned DOT that the ramp was so clearly designed to benefit the Television City project that the traffic and other impacts of both TV City and the highway improvement would have to pass environmental review standards to be built. That warning killed federal funding for the ramp.

DOT also approved a new connection from a northbound ramp off the highway directly onto the boulevard that Donald planned to run through the heart of Television City. The state's anticipated widening of the West Side Highway was likewise designed to meet Trump concerns, with the new roadway extended exclusively on the western, waterfront side, rather than on the east, where Donald wanted to construct his project as close to the highway as he could. This decision

---

* Andrew's planned acquisition of the Sterling Forest Properties eventually fell through.

meant that the widened road would hang out over 1.4 acres of the already small park that Donald had promised along the water, reducing the opening to the sky by fourteen percent. Trump's planned southbound ramp would have also cut into the planned park, narrowing it to a mere thirty feet in width—barely the size of a sidewalk—in some places. And while the state had removed that ramp from its federal rehabilitation agenda because of the objections raised in Washington, it quietly encouraged Donald to construct the ramp on his own before the rehabilitation formally started. DOT so closely tracked Trump's desires for the site that internal memos acknowledged the agency's acquiescence but observed that this high level of cooperation was being extended "as discreetly as possible."

Trump's success with DOT was largely a result of the lobbying of Hennessy. In fact, John Shafer, the assistant commissioner at DOT who helped steer much of the Trump plan through the agency, was so close to Hennessy that when Cuomo named Hennessy to chair the Thruway Authority in 1987, Hennessy made Shafer the Authority's executive director. Lucille Falcone was also involved with the West Side planning, occasionally attending the weekly meetings Donald chaired of his West Side working group. While there was no indication that either she or Andrew played any personal role with DOT, there are memos indicating that the governor's top staff at the Capitol was monitoring very carefully the department's handling of the roadway issues.

The Hyatt, too, got its own special state service in the Cuomo years. The benefactor again was Vincent Tese, whose agency was still the Hyatt's landowner and was required to collect the hotel's annual property tax payments and pass them on to the city. When Trump suddenly slashed his payment by 80 percent in 1987, UDC just accepted it without raising any questions, though it had a right to audit the Hyatt's books under the terms of the lease. Several months later, the city asked UDC to allow its auditor general, Karen Burstein, to audit the hotel's paltry $667,000 payment, and UDC went along.

The city audit eventually revealed that the hotel's accountants had actually come up with a finding that $3.2 million was due the city, virtually the same amount as had been paid the prior year. But Donald had apparently sent the accountants back to the books to come up with a significantly lower number, and they had recalculated hotel profits and the capitalization of improvements, abandoning the methods used for the prior five years and shortchanging the city by $2.8 million. The city would later charge in a lawsuit that the hotel had "deliberately attempted to conceal its changes in accounting policy" and committed "a fraud against the public."

In meetings between city and UDC officials, however, Tese and his counsel vigorously resisted the audit's findings and its release. Though UDC was merely acting as a pass-through collection agent for the city, Tese formally notified the city that he had hired an independent accounting firm "to review the audit." His counsel adopted Trump's position that the public release of the audit "would breach the mandate of confidentiality" in the lease. The tensions between Tese and the city were so great that the mayor, Burstein, and other top staff didn't tell UDC until the last minute that they were going to announce the audit findings at a City Hall press conference. Tese responded by criticizing the audit in public statements to the newspapers, his spokesman saying that they wanted an outside accountant to determine that the city's charges were the result of sound accounting practices, not of "a special political agenda."

Tese even refused to serve a demand notice on the hotel for payment as requested by the city, forcing the city to threaten legal action against UDC. The city, which calculated that Trump had already saved $60 million in taxes since the Hyatt opened, was adamant, and Burstein demanded to know "whose side" UDC was on at one heated meeting. Tese finally had to give in, agreeing to seek payment from Trump.

In the middle of the audit dispute, Lucille Falcone hosted the annual Cuomo fund-raiser at the Sheraton. Trump bought the most expensive ringside table, and Tony Gliedman, Donald's main emissary on the audit issue, spent the night mingling with a crowd that included the governor, Tese, and Andrew. Trump was Cuomo's biggest 1989 corporate giver, donating $25,000.

A few nights after the fund-raiser, Donald went to a second, private, Cuomo affair—Andrew Cuomo's birthday party at a midtown pub. The party was co-hosted by one of Andrew's closest friends, Dan Klores, the fast-talking aide to public relations czar Howard Rubenstein, who had handled the Trump account for years. But Donald barely spoke to Klores at the party, instead huddling with Andrew for a half hour. Andrew would later claim that it was the first time he'd ever met Trump—his way of minimizing the client relationship that had a transparently troubling side to it. It was just one more rhetorical Cuomo ploy—hiding a compromising business arrangement behind the supposed detachment of personal distance.

Over the years, Donald had devised a strategy for every significant public official in his path; the seduction of the elusive Cuomo had simply been the most manipulative and extended. Others were simpler. When David Dinkins, for example ran for Manhattan borough president in 1985 against a liberal West Side assemblyman fiercely opposed to any large-scale plan there, Donald wanted to help Dinkins without surfacing and jeopardizing Dinkins's West Side support.

So Nick Ribis and several other Trump aides, particularly unknown casino brass from Atlantic City, dumped thousands into the Dinkins coffers without getting noticed. Trump's partner Hirschfeld hosted Dinkins's headquarters in his midtown hotel while simultaneously financing the entry into the race of a second white candidate, who had no chance to win but could only help Dinkins, who is black. The result was that Manhattan's new top elected official—whose liberal politics led to the expectation that he would aggressively oppose Trump's superproject—remained neutral on it throughout his term, even quietly helping it in small ways behind the scenes.

This sort of political intrigue, first learned at the foot of his father, was a time-honed routine for Donald by then. By Donald's decade, it had become the essence of what it meant to be a real estate mogul in New York—a specialized form of social engineering. Without a flair for ensnaring the public officials whose discretion could make or break development schemes, the New York entrepreneur was dead in the water. It was the only way to bring grand projects to life, the inevitable route to publicly allocated wealth. The Cuomo episode just demonstrated what a master Donald had become at it. Tempting, captivating, inveigling, and baiting those with public power were the tricks of his trade, and for the moment, Donald, preserving miraculously his air of innocence, was its unchallenged, brash new champion.

12

TURNING POINT

The humdrum conventional world could not brook his daring, his insouciance, his constant desire to call a spade a spade. His genial sufficiency was a taunt and a mockery to many. The hard implication of his eye was dreaded by the weaker as fire is feared by a burned child.

—*Theodore Dreiser,* The Titan

There is no one my age who has accomplished more. Everyone can't be the best.

—*Donald Trump,* Newsweek, *1988*

ON A CRISP AND SUNNY November day in 1986, Donald Trump hosted the ceremonial first skate at Wollman Rink in Central Park, six years after the city had closed it for major renovations and slightly less than six months after Donald himself had taken over the long-botched job and completed it. In early June he had convinced Ed Koch to let him rescue a project delayed so long and for so many different reasons that a several-hundred-page city report on the disaster was likened by one city commissioner to *Murder on the Orient Express.* In Agatha Christie's mystery, said the commissioner, "Hercule Poirot, the detective on the case, finds out that there was not one murderer, but that everybody was the murderer."

Trump had managed to redo the rink entirely, taking apart the faulty new facility the city had constructed and completing a magnificent 33,000-square-foot functioning rink on time, under budget, and without having taken a cent of profit. Not even the half dozen press events he hosted on the site—ranging from the laying-of-the-pipes press conference to the pouring-of-the-cement conference the following day—slowed the rink's progress, a reconstruction that was, as Donald would express it, a testament to the will and savvy of private enterprise.

The two final press events, the grand opening in mid-November and the gala grand opening on November 23, were attended by everyone from John Cardinal O'Connor to Lee Iacocca to skaters Peggy Fleming and Dorothy Hamill to city officials like Andy Stein, David Dinkins, and, of course, the mayor. The two openings were so similar that no one could remember just who had attended which. "We went to the first few press conferences," explained Parks Commissioner Henry Stern, "but we stopped after a while."

Though Donald had almost comically overworked it, the Wollman revival was, by all accounts, the peak moment of his public acceptance. Even those who mocked his glitz and self-obsession, as well as those who recoiled at his grand design for the West Side, had to give him credit for the rink. "You beat nature," declared an appreciative Stern. And yet, Donald managed to transform this triumph into a prelude to disaster. In a peculiar sort of way, Wollman would prove to be his undoing.

Trump had a choice: When asked why he had succeeded so rapidly where the city had stumbled so badly, he could simply have accepted the plaudits, praised his contractors, and attributed the city's prior delays to the legislated constraints that made public construction so difficult. Predictably, though, he couldn't resist the opportunity to gloat. Donald rejected the diplomatic advice of his in-house Koch veteran, Tony Gliedman, who had skillfully processed the project through the city bureaucracy, and declared, "There isn't the expertise in the city to really understand construction. There is no great longing to work in city government whereas it used to be a great honor. Basically, the city didn't know how to build a skating rink. If the city could just plan and execute, it would be billions and billions of dollars that could be saved."

These comments launched a new season of escalating exchanges with the Koch administration, during which Trump, in sharp contrast with the guile of the Cuomo seduction, displayed the offensive side of his sometimes engaging and sometimes intimidating political personality. As if the humiliation of the mayor implicit in Donald's initial condemnation of the city was insufficient punishment, he began twisting the central facts of the rink restoration to make the city look even more ridiculous. "I went to Canada, to get a rink expert," he said. "The city had hired a contractor from Florida." The story he spun, spelled out later in *The Art of the Deal,* was that "logic suggested that the best place to look was Canada" and that "everyone I talked to said use Cimco," a Canadian company Donald claimed he found by searching for the contractor that had built the rink for the Montreal Canadiens. City Hall knew otherwise.

In fact, before Donald first wrote Koch to ask that the city let him do the Wollman job, the Parks Department had decided to hire a new consultant, a Pennsylvania firm called SORA (St. Onge Ruff Associates), and SORA had already engaged a Canadian rink designer who had, in turn, brought Cimco into the picture. At Donald's initial meeting and walk-through of the site with Parks Department officials in early June, two SORA consultants (and their Canadian associate on a conference call) had recommended virtually all of the major changes in the renovation plan that Donald later successfully adopted.

According to minutes prepared by Donald's construction manager, SORA recommended that the city's old freon refrigeration system be replaced with the brine system that has worked so well since. SORA also urged that a new concrete slab be laid on top of the one the city had installed, rather than trying to remove the old one. And while Trump and his engineers wanted to use twenty-two miles of steel pipe for the refrigeration system, SORA's widely experienced Canadian consultant convinced them that plastic would be a lot quicker to lay and just as dependable. The first conference call went so well that the consultant came down from Canada for further meetings with SORA and the Trump team. (As soon as Trump adopted all its suggestions, he dropped SORA, bad-mouthing the consultants as know-nothings in his book. When the city insisted he pay the meager $12,000 due SORA out of the $3.8 million of city funds allocated for the job, he refused, and it took almost two years before he finally approved a half payment.)

A memo outlining much of this history was prepared by the Parks Department and sent to the mayor's office in late October, shortly before Donald began promoting himself at the expense of the city. Yet Koch never countered Donald's performance with the truth, perhaps fearing he would appear too defensive. Koch's close aides knew, though, that after all the on-again, off-again years of this tumultuous relationship, Donald had finally put himself on the mayor's deeply personal enemies list, a category from which there was no reprieve.

Ever since the mayor's friend and political ally Donald Manes had first attempted suicide at the start of the year, the once ebullient Koch had taken on a gallows look, his body drooping, weighed down by each new revelation about the corruption of his administration. Were it not for this vulnerability, Koch knew, Donald would never have dared to take him on personally, as he did in an extended television interview occasioned by the Wollman success. He blasted

Koch as a man who would only "fight for his enemies," rather than "be criticized for fighting for his friends," adding that he "grew up on a different side of the street." As Koch saw it, Trump was using the Wollman platform to launch an attack on his character and his government.

On the day the rink opened for public use, the mayor's other friend, Stanley Friedman, and the director of his Parking Violations Bureau, Lester Shafran, were in a federal courtroom waiting for a verdict in their racketeering case. While Friedman's and Shafran's guilt remained in doubt for two further days, the ten-week trial had clearly established that the self-described reform mayor had, over the course of years, quietly handed out profitable pieces of his government to both Manes and Friedman. Their brazen looting of the public fiefdoms they were given had gravely damaged Koch, just as their sudden absence in the power politics of the city had weakened Trump.

But Donald understood more quickly than most that "the scandal," as it was referred to generically in the tabloids, was reshaping the city at its roots. Several hundred city officials would be indicted before it was over, and eventually it would even help do away with the Board of Estimate, eliminated by the voters in a 1989 charter change. Friedman, Manes, Brooklyn boss Meade Esposito, Bronx Borough President Stanley Simon, and city transportation czar Tony Ameruso were among the Trump benefactors convicted in this upheaval. And in the middle of it, Roy Cohn died. Donald recognized that the shadowy fixers and clubhouse creatures who'd given him, and Fred before him, such clout deep inside the permanent government of the city were out of business, at least for a while.

Wollman was his answer, for if he could no longer count on the inside track, he'd have to build a base of public support—one that was broad enough to carry his projects, particularly the one on the West Side, through the city approval processes. He settled with the tenants at 100 Central Park South, ridding himself of what any pollster would have called his worst negative. And he gloriously reconstructed the skating rink, giving himself the strongest public positive of his career—at least until he insisted on rubbing the mayor's face in the new ice.

A Koch response—muted by the weakness of his scandal-scarred administration—finally did begin to emerge. The mayor began to connect Trump's Wollman "exaggerations," as he briefly described them, with the West Side project that was then weaving its way through city agencies. Trump was exploiting Wollman because he wanted "an edge" in getting Television City approved easily, the mayor told the *New York Post,* adding "that's not the way it works." At one of the November ceremonies at the rink, Donald thanked the mayor for the city's cooperation in eliminating red tape and helping him get Wollman done so quickly. "I wish I could get the same cooperation on my private business," he added, an apparent allusion to the already one-year-long city review of his West Side proposal.

"If you do it pro bono," Koch replied. It was all in jest, but the Wollman dispute was in fact beginning to cast an ominous pall over Donald's bid for West Side approvals.

Sam Horwitz, the old family friend and Coney Island councilman, was at the ceremony as well, standing beside his onetime theater partner, a beaming Fred Trump. The always upbeat Horwitz raved to Fred about Donald's string of successes, but Fred suddenly turned troubled, declaring: "I hope he hasn't bitten off more than he can chew." The $700 million in bank and bond financing for the two Atlantic City casinos was imprudently un-Fredlike, as was the 1986 purchase of the West Palm Beach condominium far away from the Trump base. The extraordinary multibillion-dollar plans for the West Side may have also been a worrisome prospect for the old man—where was the market, after all, for the world's tallest building, the world's grandest shopping mall, and the world's most expensive colony of waterfront luxury apartments?

Donald's Television City proposal was now simultaneously at different stages in the city's economic development and planning processes. The city Planning Commission was engaged in an intensive review of the environmental impact and design implications of Donald's second plan for the project, submitted in October of 1986. On another front, Alair Townsend, the deputy mayor for economic development, and her top staff were actively working to put together an acceptable package of tax abatement and other city concessions designed to persuade NBC to reject a move to Jersey and remain in New York. While other city sites were nominally still under consideration, Trump had convinced the city, beginning with his initial approaches in 1985, that NBC favored his. The Koch administration was prepared to make major accommodations to keep the network and its 4,000 jobs from following the Jets to Jersey.

On May 1, 1987, Donald spelled out the incentives the project would need to become economically viable in a formal proposal to Townsend, citing his two-day talks with NBC, which had just concluded. His plan was a 1980s version of the Hyatt deal. He would convey title for the West Side yards to UDC for a dollar, and UDC would lease it back to him for ninety-nine years. He'd pay the current taxes for the first five years of the lease, a million-dollar-a-year increase for the next twenty-five, and full taxes thereafter (when he could reclaim the site for a dollar). In addition to the property tax abatement and a sales tax exemption on construction materials, Donald wanted the city to agree to allow UDC to override zoning restrictions on the site "so that NBC will not end up with years of uncertainty, a primary concern to them." In exchange for all these public concessions, Donald promised to "enter into a competitive low-cost lease with NBC," meaning that he would use the tax break granted the entire site to lower his rent charges to NBC so significantly that the network would find it advantageous to remain in New York.

A few days after submitting the plan in a two-page letter, Trump began lobbying for its acceptance in the press and his reliable friends from UDC lobbied right along with him. Vincent Tese's vice president and spokesman, Harold Holzer, told the *New York Times* that the NBC deal was "an idea that's been proposed by the developer, but has been discussed by UDC only in its broadest outline form." Noting that the key actor in the deal was the city, Holzer added: "We hope that the next move is theirs, not NBC's." Holzer was even clearer with the *New York Post:* "The ball is in the city's court. We'd like to take it, but they have to pass it." Tese had rallied to the Trump cause without ever having received so much as a conceptual plan in writing.

Trump tried to increase the pressure with a panicky phone call to Townsend in the middle of a Friday afternoon in early May. He gave her a two-hour deadline to accept or reject his proposal, warning that NBC was "on the precipice of making a decision" and would otherwise be Jersey-bound. Townsend pressed him for an estimate of the tax write-off's cost to the city, but Donald could offer none. The city quickly calculated it at a billion dollars. Although Townsend told Trump his proposal "was ridiculous," he met with NBC officials later that day "and left them with the impression that the city had approved this proposal." When the network called Koch the following Monday to confirm that the city had agreed in concept with the site-wide tax exemption, a distressed mayor replied that "no such agreement" had been reached.

Townsend quickly wrote to Trump saying that the city's preliminary analysis indicated that its tax loss under Trump's plan would be "well in excess of what is needed and defensible" and would give Trump "tax benefits beyond those that would benefit NBC." She added that the city was determined to negotiate a deal directly with NBC, not with Trump. Donald responded with a furious memo, charging that Townsend's claim that the city had made "substantial progress" with NBC was "both incorrect and patently self-serving" and listing a dozen other major companies that had fled the city in the past year. Citing the "extreme urgency" of the situation, he demanded that the city respond immediately to his UDC suggestion or "step into my position and provide the necessary annual cost subsidy on a direct basis to NBC."

Koch was so irate over Trump's letter that he sent Townsend a note saying it exhibited Donald's "normal bullying self to the utmost" and urging a "very tough" reply. A number of his top advisers sensed that Koch was still smarting over the rink insults and that while he felt the city might have to deal with Trump if Trump had the network as an anchor tenant, he was not about to give Donald "a dollar more," as Koch put it, than he had to.

The *New York Times* weighed in with an editorial that backed Koch's rejection of the site-wide tax abatement, but urged the city to give Trump what he wanted on the nine-acre portion of the site where the NBC building would be built, including a waiver of all zoning regulations through the use of a UDC override. A New York *Daily News* editorial several days later blasted Koch for not having begun direct talks with Trump more than a week after his written submission. Instead of the tough reply ordered by Koch, Townsend attacked Donald in the tabloids, referring to his letter as "baloney" and insisting that it wouldn't leave her "cowering in her skirt behind her desk." But she also initiated real, head-to-head negotiations with Donald, pushed no doubt by the editorials. Townsend had little choice but to deal with Donald—she had made little headway talking to NBC directly, and so Donald had come to symbolize the city's best, if not only, hope.

Townsend attended the first two-hour session with Donald, enduring his references to her as "honey" and "sweets" and "darling" and leaving the detailed talks to a team of city lawyers and negotiators headed by Jay Biggins. The discussions, many of which occurred in Donald's conference room at Trump Tower, continued for more than a week, with Biggins in constant touch with Townsend at City Hall and Townsend updating the mayor. A top NBC executive appeared at some of the meetings, reinforcing the city view that Trump indeed had the network.

Trump's friends at UDC kept the pressure on in the media, the quotable Holzer announcing publicly midway through the city's talks with Trump: "We're ready and able to do anything to keep NBC, but we can't just send a taxi and get the city over here. . . . The way we look at this situation is that NBC is on a par with the Brooklyn Dodgers and the football teams. It has to be taken very seriously." Even though the *Times* had already reported that Townsend was opposed to the Trump concept of shifting the zoning to UDC, an unidentified high state development official was quoted in a news story during the negotiations endorsing the concept: "Otherwise, NBC wouldn't be comfortable with going into Television City."

The deal that Biggins finally nailed down with Trump called for a twenty-year abatement for the entire site, with the proviso that the city would get a 25 percent share in project profits for forty years and thus recapture over time the taxes that had been deferred up front. City officials pegged the short-term cost at $700 million, "a far richer tax break than had ever been given anyone," according to a Biggins memo. Trump adamantly refused to give the city a guarantee that the profit-sharing formula would, after forty years, repay the city's full tax investment in the project. Nonetheless, accepting Trump's assurance that he would offer NBC rents competitive with New Jersey's $15-a-square-foot bid, the Biggins group felt it had achieved the best possible deal for the city and the only one that would keep the elusive, New Jersey–leaning NBC in New York.

Donald, his brother Robert, and Harvey Freeman were the key bargainers on the Trump side. Allen Schwartz, the onetime Trump lawyer who had so effectively cleared the way for the West Side plan in 1985, was by this time nowhere to be found. He had attended Donald's weekly staff meetings on the West Side project well into 1986, but as the differences between Donald and the Koch administration deepened over the Wollman revival, Schwartz became increasingly uncomfortable and quit. His sudden absence may well have been as sound a harbinger of the mayor's likely disposition as his presence had once been.

The Biggins team, nonetheless, reached a tentative agreement with Trump on the broad outlines of a deal that, if approved by the mayor, gave Donald much of what he wanted. With Donald's apparent hold on NBC, the city negotiators did not feel they had the option of coming back to City Hall without some sort of an acceptable package. While Biggins would later claim that there was never a city commitment to the conceptual arrangement, both sides did agree to a term sheet. Donald understandably believed that he had his ultimate deal.

Everyone understood that there was one pivotal business detail left to be worked out: the definition of profit, a familiar knotty question from the Hyatt days. But Townsend and Biggins were so confident that they otherwise had the broad outlines of an agreement that they hired a law firm, Kramer, Levin, to work out a city position on the profit question. And while the lawyers were drafting the profit language, Townsend put the overall proposition before the mayor for a final decision. By doing so, she was implicitly recommending it.

Koch brought in a number of prominent businessmen to review the terms, and they signed off on the deal, too. He then summoned the city's tough budget director, Paul Dickstein, and Finance Commissioner Abe Biderman to get their bottom lines. Dickstein contributed the startling information regarding Trump's controversial, sharply reduced payment to the city under the Hyatt lease.

In addition to prompting the Burstein audit that would ultimately unveil Donald's apparent shortchanging of the city on Hyatt payments, the Dickstein revelation confirmed the mayor's suspicions, which he announced at one of the two-day sessions. "If you're dealing with Donald Trump," Koch said, "you're gonna get screwed." Donald's dramatic $2.8 million cut had given Koch fresh evidence of how he might shortchange the city in any West Side profit-sharing arrangement. "We were simply not convinced that the city would be able to get Trump to agree" on a profit plan "that would adequately protect the city's interests," Biggins noted in a postmortem memo.

The other sticking point for the mayor, though, was the nagging question of UDC's bypass of the zoning process. The Biggins team had hammered out only business terms, but the underlying assumption of Trump's maneuvering was that he'd automatically obtain the zoning he needed—at least for the world's tallest building, which would house NBC. Indeed, he had made his cut-rate rental subsidy to NBC dependent upon the income stream elsewhere in his 15-million-square-foot project, making it virtually impossible to approve the network's deal without approving the total development. Koch understood that this interdependence was designed to "employ the mayor as an advocate for the zoning approvals," as the Biggins memo expressed it. In effect, Trump was attempting to buy the city's zoning authority with a share of project profits. As Donald and his state friends had framed it, the waiver of all city zoning restrictions on the densest project in recent history was the ransom Koch had to pay to keep NBC.

While Koch and his aides talked the plan out, Donald kept the pressure on, leaning on the mayor by phone. "You've got to make a decision," he told Koch. "I can taste the deal in my mouth. Today. Today." The mayor dismissed the call as Trump chutzpah. "He becomes so overbearing that people capitulate," Koch said.

But on May 26, a few days after the Biggins discussions with Donald ended so optimistically, Ed Koch said no.

Donald had come to within a hair of winning approval of a project that he saw, according to his consultant Jim Capalino, as "absolutely central to [his] view of how history will judge him"—determining whether or not he would be viewed "as one of the twentieth century's greatest urban planners and developers." Koch knew that by refusing Trump, he ran the risk of losing NBC, a blow from which he might never recover politically. As determined as he was to demonstrate that he had survived the great corruption scandal by winning a fourth term in 1989, the mayor was ready to gamble his reelection rather than concede to Donald. The zoning and profit issues were factors in his decision, but with a vengeful Koch, they were merely the rationale that could justify a rejection. The mayor was too pragmatic a politician to have taken such a chance only because his judgment required to do it. His gut took precedence, and those who sat in the room with him and watched him make this decision were convinced that Wollman had been the final straw for him. He simply could not give in to Donald. "The kind of brinkmanship and misstatement of the facts we have seen," concluded Biggins in a June 1 memo written to Koch to attempt to disprove Trump's claim that the city had reneged on an agreement, "is not the kind of conduct we can tolerate in a partner with so much at stake."

On the day Donald received the bad news, he had a number of choices. He could come up with a new plan, still using the NBC lure—as indeed he later would. Or he could issue a declaration of war, killing any chance of a deal. He once again chose the low road, and this time his threatening bombast was addressed directly to Koch. "Your attitude on keeping NBC is unbelievable and will lead to NBC leaving the city," he wrote. Characterizing the decision as "ludicrous" and "disgraceful," he charged Koch with playing "Russian Roulette" with NBC "because you are afraid that Donald Trump may actually make more than a dollar of profit." Trump carefully exempted Townsend and her staff from his salvo, saying they were being "second-guessed by people who have absolutely no understanding of the proposed transaction." The rejection, he said, was part of a pattern of decisions from "Ed Koch's City Hall" that were draining "the lifeblood out of New York."

Koch answered the next day, accusing Trump of attempting "to force the city's hand to your advantage through intimidation" and declaring that he could not "put zoning restrictions up for auction." He told Trump that the city had delivered its best offer to NBC—a "traveling" group of city concessions, including a fifteen-year abatement, that would attach to any site the network selected, including Trump's. The city had also given NBC a new proposal of benefits applicable to any major renovation at Rockefeller Center, where the network had made its home for decades.

On May 28 Koch released publicly the two letters in what he conceded was a preemptive strike on Donald, whom he accused of leaking stories throughout the negotiating process in an attempt to embarrass the city into submission. Moments after the mayor's press conference, Trump issued a prepared statement blasting Koch for having "absolutely no sense of economic development" and urging him to resign. "He can't hack it anymore," said Donald, calling Koch "a disaster waiting to explode."

The mayor retorted: "If Donald Trump is squealing like a stuck pig, I must have done something right."

In succeeding days, Trump branded Koch a "moron," and Koch wagged a "piggy, piggy, piggy" finger at Donald. Any developer's project would always have to go through the regular city processes "whether I like him or dislike him," said Koch. "And I do dislike him."

By June, however, Koch was so far out on a banner-headlined limb that he absolutely could not afford to lose NBC. UDC's Holzer was now publicly criticizing the city, saying it was "too timid" in its offer to keep the network. "If you don't spend on economic development," said Holzer, "you're a paper tiger." Published polls revealed that 70 percent of New Yorkers favored granting NBC the incentives necessary to stay, and the overwhelming majority thought Trump was doing more to keep the network than Koch. The polls and Republican leaders had even begun promoting Trump as a candidate against Koch, though Trump quickly demurred.

The fear that the city might have lost its chance of retaining NBC ran so deep that the mayor woke NBC president Bob Wright up at 6:00 A.M. one June morning to try to persuade him to look at other city sites, but the network insisted on Donald's and Rockefeller Center, the two alternatives to New Jersey they had decided upon at the end of 1986. Tony Gliedman, ever the mediator, tried to open a new dialogue with Townsend in late June, offering a revised Trump proposal that sought only the abatements that by law would be granted to any West Side development. But Gliedman still wanted some form of "zoning assistance," with NBC's rent conditioned on the density the city ultimately approved for the rest of the project. Townsend replied that no zoning concessions would be made.

Then NBC approached the city with another proposal for the Trump site. If Trump sold the network its portion of the site at a discount, would the city be willing to permanently peg the tax assessment on the land to the nominal price the network paid Trump, in effect granting NBC and Trump an abatement forever? When the city rejected that as well in early September, Trump exploded again, though this time the media exchange contained no references to this final secret offer and its rejection. Donald called Koch an "idiot," "the pits," and "incompetent." Koch referred to Donald's site as a "swamp."

A way out of the mayor's dilemma was emerging, however, on an unexpected front. While the city was taking an increasingly inflexible position on the Trump site, its offer at Rockefeller Center was getting better with time.

Back in mid-April, before the rupture of the Trump talks, Townsend had written NBC a letter flatly rejecting any form of tax assistance if NBC remained at Rockefeller. As Townsend pointed out, granting a break on existing taxes to a user who still had thirteen years left on a lease "would require a complete reversal of city policy." Tax abatements, Townsend pointed out, are usually granted on a share of the increase in value that comes with an improvement, and NBC wanted the city "to forego taxes it is now collecting" from Rockefeller Center. Even Trump, under his most self-serving plan, promised to continue paying the annual $3.5 million base taxes already being paid on the West Side land he owned.

The deputy mayor also contended that the only way a renovation of NBC's facilities at 30 Rockefeller Plaza could qualify for tax breaks that normally accompanied new construction was if the space were classified as "valueless real estate" and a finding was made that only the renovation would create value for real estate tax purposes.

Townsend dismissed any such proposition since, she said, the existing NBC facilities were "regarded by most as a first class complex on a premier site." In fact, the city had amended its existing tax abatement program to exclude East Side and Midtown properties precisely because the areas were so lucrative that no incentives were necessary to encourage development, as they were believed to be on the West Side. For this catalogue of reasons, sound public policy, she concluded, "makes it impossible for us to grant such tax treatment."

But in late May, in the middle of the dispute with Donald, the city reconsidered. The Department of Finance reassessed the entire Rockefeller Center complex, lowering the tax rate. Townsend then wrote NBC a letter pledging to maintain the per-square-foot tax charges for the network's space at the new rate until 2006. At that point, said Townsend, taxes would then be evenly phased in over seventeen years until they reached roughly twice the lowered rate by 2023. This constituted a $73 million tax savings for NBC, since, under the new plan, the city would in effect become the temporary condominium owner of the network's expanded Rockefeller Center space, entitling the network to hundreds of millions of dollars in city industrial bond financing, as well as full sales tax exemption. All of these advantages cut the anticipated Rockefeller Center costs for NBC by half a billion dollars.

Ironically, the creative mind that put the package together for Rockefeller

Center was none other than Michael Bailkin, who was retained by the center's development entity in late 1986 to see if anything could be done to rescue the NBC tenancy. When he entered the picture, his clients at Rockefeller Center believed that Trump had a lock on the network and that the city was dealing with Donald as if he were NBC's exclusive agent. While Bailkin agreed, he said NBC was "Donald's to lose" and told his clients that "there was a good chance Donald would shoot himself in the foot."

Bailkin, who'd built a thriving boutique firm with his old friend David Stadtmauer, began pressing city economic development officials to "put Trump and Rockefeller Center on a level playing field," contending in early 1987 that the city had to "let NBC go where they wanted to go" by equalizing the benefits offered to each option. Since Trump's site was automatically entitled to a significant tax reduction, any leveling agreed to by the city would put Rockefeller Center in line for a highly unusual break. Bailkin knew how to negotiate with Townsend and her aides—he'd done a variety of crucial projects with them. He also knew, long before "piggy, piggy, piggy," that "the city did not like or trust Trump, and was being forced to do business with him."

Despite Townsend's mistrust of Trump, Bailkin could not make any headway with her and was told in late May that she and Biggins "had a handshake, conceptual deal with him," leading Bailkin to the unhappy conclusion that his client had "basically lost the deal." But Townsend turned out to be "far out in front of the mayor," and when Koch turned the proposal down, Bailkin and Rockefeller Center were suddenly very welcome visitors at City Hall. They also made their move on NBC, which was increasingly troubled by fears of West Side resistance, especially if it wasn't going to get any zoning guarantee from the city. Lawsuits and barricades began to loom as real obstacles to the venture.

Bailkin also watched the effect of the headlined banter on NBC's leadership, which perceptibly began to lose confidence in Trump, and he sensed that "the goings-on in the press had made such a spectacle of Trump that they were deflecting serious business people."

The turnabout at City Hall proceeded over the next few weeks, the WASPy Townsend dealing comfortably with her WASPy counterparts from Rockefeller Center. Trump gave up in October, withdrawing his bid with the writing already on the wall. Rockefeller Center's thirty-five-year property tax abatement, $800 million in partially tax exempt bond financing, and fifteen-year sales tax write-off on most of an estimated billion in machinery and equipment purchases was the richest package of public benefits ever given a city business—a point Townsend readily conceded.

When the plan was announced, Trump's first reaction was a warning that it might experience "legal problems," and he insisted the deal was "unconstitutional," though he declined to specify who might sue. He claimed that the city had given NBC "substantially more tax abatements" at Rockefeller Center than had ever been offered for Television City, creating "a horrible precedent" by granting huge breaks "to tenants already occupying their space." No one from the city seriously contested these arguments, and Bailkin, who never talked with Trump during or after the NBC competition, later conceded in an interview that his client's package was better than anything offered Trump. "You've been had," Trump wound up telling the mayor through the newspapers, claiming that NBC and Rockefeller Center had "played him like a drum."

Donald's comments—freely described in a New York *Daily News* caption as "mouthing off"—had such a bitter quality to them that no one paid any attention to their substance. The irony of the city's granting so sweeping a package to a tenant who was staying in place, and agreeing to make only $400 million in actual construction improvements over fifteen years, was lost on a city weary of Trump's insolence and delirious over NBC's decision to stay. Donald was serious enough that he wrote Wright, whom he'd gotten along with quite well during the protracted negotiations, inferring that the network knew all along it would stay at 30 Rockefeller Plaza and had merely used Trump as a bargaining chip with Rockefeller Center. Trump asked for a multimillion-dollar payment to cover his expenses, but NBC dismissed the notion.

At the same time that the Rockefeller Center deal was consummated, Koch announced his opposition, for the first time, to any project on the West Side yards substantially greater than the 7 million square feet approved for Lincoln West. Despite the mayor's explicit and detailed rejection of the plan, Donald went forward anyway with a series of environmental and planning submissions for a project—renamed Trump City—that was twice as large. The submissions would continue throughout 1988 and into 1989 and form a mountain of petitioning paper, produced at a cost of millions by every conceivable kind of consultant.

The project was soon assailed publicly on several counts. The housing density was twice that of any existing residential district in the city. The shopping mall and other project features would attract 22,000 cars and 80,000 people a day, as well as generating 3.5 million gallons of sewage a day. It would also block all access to the waterfront.

Among the critics were the philosophers like Brendan Gill, who described Donald's dream as "something like the condos of Miami Beach—a whole rank, a palisade of 50-story-high, blank-faced, grim, battery-like condos, shutting out the whole western sky." Gill put to words the impact such a wall of giants would have on the people of the city: "We pile one skyscraper next to another, so the squirrels could leap from one top to the next, and pretty soon we're living in the bottom of a well. Psychologically you feel uneasy. Feel in shadow. Something is threatening you. You're trapped inside something that is beyond the human scale, and none of the things we need, like light and air and the sun on our skins is any longer present."

Opposing Donald became New York chic, especially when a member of Westpride, an anti-Trump coalition of community groups, looked out her window in late 1987 and noticed truckloads of soil being hauled off the yards. At least 1,727 truckloads, carrying 1,350,000 cubic feet of dirt, were hauled from the site and deposited as landfill at a Staten Island dump. The sighting was like another Sally Goodgold alarm all along the West Side. Westpride officials discovered that the city's Department of Environmental Protection had not been notified of Trump's intent to remove the soil, which apparently had been inadequately tested by Trump to meet DEP toxic standards. When DEP Commissioner Harvey Schultz called Trump staffers to complain, Trump went right on hauling it.

Federal Environmental Protection Agency inspectors rushed to the site to test the soil, suspecting the presence of PCBs in an old rail yard where transformers were once used, but Trump barred them, urging them instead to test the landfill already delivered to the city-owned dump. Their tests came up negative, just as Trump claimed his tests at the yard had. But DEP concluded that Trump's tests did not provide "sufficient information to determine the nature" of the soil removed, and the West Side groups continued to fear the worst.

Donald had rushed the excavation, starting on November 23 and ending the day before Christmas Eve, hauling as many as 118 truck-loads in a single day. He had ignored a letter from DEP, sent back in June, asking to review all soil and groundwater sampling Trump undertook on the site. What aroused the most suspicion, however, was the sudden resignation of Trump's environmental attorney, Steve Kass, on December 23, the day the dumping in the city landfill suddenly ended. While Kass would not explain publicly why he quit, his and Donald's associates agree that the two reached a bitter impasse on the soil removal. Kass, who opposed the initial decision to remove it without prior DEP clearance, believed that the testing results still required that the soil be taken out in special containers and trucked to toxic dumpsites. Donald had hired Kass in the first place because he believed that the lawyer's impeccable environmental reputation would lend credibility to his controversial project, but when Kass insisted on the safest possible soil removal, costing up to $800,000, Donald lost patience with him. After bitter disagreements, Kass finally offered to resign and not go public.*

With all of these problems, a frustrated Donald finally began flirting with the notion of ending his obsession. In the summer of 1988, he began serious talks with William Zeckendorf, Jr., the son of the visionary New York developer whose rise and fall decades earlier had so poignantly anticipated Donald's. Zeckendorf, Jr. had assembled a group of Japanese, English, and New York investors who were willing to pay a premium price for an option on the site. A contract was drafted requiring a $62.5 million down payment on a $550 million purchase price. The Zeckendorf group agreed to pay Donald $25 million for each of several six-month extensions while they tried to get the site zoned for a buildable project. The down payment and all extension payments would be forfeited if they failed to close on the property within a set term of five years. Whenever they closed, they'd pay whatever was outstanding on the $550 million price.

Donald and his partner Abe Hirschfeld had successfully wrangled into the fine print a commitment from Zeckendorf that "the most prominent thoroughfare" on the site would be "prominently named Donald J. Trump Boulevard" and that another street in the project would be named Abraham Hirschfeld Way. Trump leaks from the negotiating table falsely suggested that the Zeckendorf offer was as high as $800 million, and Donald even claimed in a letter to Zeckendorf that he had a last-minute competing bid of $770 million, but this was just more whistling in the wind.

In a *New York Times* article in mid-October, Trump publicly agonized about what he called his toughest choice: "I am torn between two worlds. I love the idea of building this wonderful city," he said, claiming that the zoning was about to be approved. "But I am being offered sums of money that are staggering." The down payment was deposited in a bank, and Zeckendorf aides began calling West Side leaders to indicate they were taking an option and were "willing to start from scratch to work with the community." But just as Donald had sabotaged the imminent sale of his Central Park South properties in the mid-eighties,

---

* Kass also repeatedly objected within the Trump Organization to the possible disruption the digging might bring to archaeological treasures on the site, such as the remains of the Leni-Lenape Indian tribe. The on-site relic issue was so significant that the Landmark Preservation Commission sent a letter asking that the excavation stop until "all archeological work has been completed and signed off by our agency."

raising the price at the last minute, he thwarted this deal with ever-escalating demands, even seeking a free one-eighth interest in Zeckendorf's project. He could not break with his dream.

The publicity about the near sale helped create a market nonetheless, and Donald used the prices bandied about to hype his own net worth. The more highly the banks valued the yards, the more he could borrow, even without pledging them as collateral, and the new loans could help pay for all the other highly leveraged new projects in which he was involved. Indeed, though Donald already had his $200 million Chase loan on the yards, he went out in the aftermath of the Zeckendorf hoopla and borrowed another $24 million from Manufacturers Hanover for Trump City development costs. Had Donald sold the yards, the proceeds could have helped finance his late eighties buying spree, but he could not consummate the one asset sale that would have reduced the debt required by all his purchases.

One of Donald's Atlantic City consultants, the clever casino analyst Al Glasgow, told him that the problem with vacant land was that "it eats, but it don't shit." By the end of the decade, Donald had already carried the yards' burgeoning costs, with no compensating income, for five years. The property was consuming between $15 and $20 million a year in taxes, interest, and legal and consultant costs. Donald could live with the cash drain so long as the Chase loans, abetted by Manufacturers Hanover's recent generosity, were paying the bills. But the day would come when he would no longer be able to pay the interest costs with the bank's money, to say nothing of all the other expenses.

Within a few days of the collapse of the Zeckendorf deal, Donald launched a new campaign to obtain the zoning he wanted by picking the mayor he wanted. In early December 1988, Donald began to suggest publicly that he might take on Ed Koch in the 1989 election, not as a candidate, but as a funder of the anti-Koch forces. He met in Trump Tower with Lee Atwater, head of the Republican National Committee, and Roger Stone, the GOP consultant who was also Donald's lobbyist, and discussed ways he could put a fortune on the line against Koch without violating campaign finance limits. The strategy they came up with, leaked to the newspapers, was that he would spend up to $2 million on commercials that assailed Koch yet endorsed no one. Though Donald was still professing the innocence of scandal lynchpin Stanley Friedman, he claimed he wanted to finance the negative publicity because "New York has become a cesspool of corruption and incompetence."

His preferred candidate was Andy Stein, who refused even to answer a Westpride questionnaire about Trump City despite his vote against the much smaller

Lincoln West. In anticipation of a possible Stein race, as well as commemorating Stein's twenty years in politics, Trump hosted a late November fund-raiser for him. Donald was overheard telling Stein on the dais about several $4,000 and $5,000 contributions he'd collected but was returning because they exceeded the new $3,000 finance limits imposed in a Koch-backed reform. In his thank-you speech, Stein joked that some people said the mayor didn't take care of his friends but, attributing the new limits to Koch, added: "Donald, trust me—the mayor just saved you a lot of money."

But Stein backed out of the race and with Koch making a comeback in the polls, Donald withdrew his advertising threat and instead tried to ride out the 1989 election quietly. He did raise $20,000 for GOP candidate Rudy Giuliani, cochairing one fund-raiser at the Waldorf-Astoria in the spring, but he receded from the campaign when the former federal prosecutor began to stumble, losing a gigantic early lead in the polls. Even while he endorsed Giuliani he had Tony Gliedman, an old tennis buddy of David Dinkins, heading a real estate fund-raising committee for the Dinkins campaign. And to cover himself when the mayor began rebounding in the polls, he suspended all attacks on Koch, trying to mediate a low-key peace.

At one happenstance meeting of Trump and Koch in the hallway of John Cardinal O'Connor's residence, when both stopped by after midnight mass on Christmas Eve in 1988, Donald confided that he wasn't really going to buy the commercials attacking Koch that he'd announced only days before. Koch teased that he'd tell the press and said he had a witness—gesturing toward the man who was with him, Dick Condon, the new police commissioner. While Koch handled Trump's banter about the commercials lightly, he was quite serious about the enmity. When a top City Hall aide and longtime Koch friend, Herb Rickman, tried during the campaign to broker a peace meeting one evening at Gracie Mansion, Koch refused: He wanted Trump's public apology before he would sit with him, and Donald would not go that far.

After Koch lost narrowly to Dinkins in the September Democratic primary and Dinkins beat Giuliani in a tight November race, Donald made one last attempt to get Trump City certified by the City Planning Commission. He desperately wanted it certified before the end of the year because, in addition to Koch's loss, the city charter had gone down in defeat, and the new charter mandated the abolition of the pliable Board of Estimate six months into 1990. The only chance for Trump City to go before the old board, rather than have to start over with a whole new set of city players and charter processes, was if it was certified quickly.

Instead, in the final months of the mayor's twelve-year reign, top Koch officials moved to push the administration's favorite projects to the top of the certification list, namely, an East Side waterfront development called Riverwalk and a massive middle-income project in the Arverne section of Queens. The reshuffling, personally approved by the mayor, placed Donald at the bottom of the list. It was the first time that City Hall had ever dictated the priority list for certification. Ironically, Donald found himself in a situation that was the reverse of the mad dash for the Commodore tax abatement engineered by Stanley Friedman in the final weeks of Beame's term. Arverne had been in the complicated review process for a mere three months, while Trump's various versions of a West Side project had been there for three and a half years.

With the last-minute announcement of the Hyatt audit and the forced settlement of the 100 Central Park South city suit as well, spiteful old Ed Koch was getting the last laugh. A decade of tensions between these bookend egos had begun with a nasty dispute over a few hundred square feet of stairwell space and ended in a torrent of exchanged abuse over a 14-million-square-foot project. The actual size of the issues between them never mattered, however. While they had their moments of mutual backscratching, the mayor and the mogul seemed destined to get ugly with one another.

Donald should have understood all along that there was no way he would wind up the winner in this blood feud. He had learned the upside of politics so well; he knew precisely what it would mean for him if he could induce public officials to exercise their discretion on his behalf. But it took this very expensive war with Koch to teach him the opposite lesson—that public discretion could also be fatal to a career-making project.

13

THE BILLION-DOLLAR BET

It is curious how that first and most potent tendency of the human mind, ambition, becomes finally dominating. Here was Cowperwood, rich beyond the wildest dreams of the average man, celebrated in a local and in some respects a national way, who was nevertheless feeling that by no means had his true aims been achieved. . . . He was not yet looked upon as a money prince. He could not rank as yet with the magnates of the East—the serried Sequoias of Wall Street. Until he could stand with these men, acknowledged as such by all . . . what did it avail?

—*Theodore Dreiser,* THE TITAN

DONALD HAD never been much of a stock player, but in the summer of 1986, with his development activities stalled in New York and his two casinos booming in Atlantic City, he began to dabble in the market. His goal was to take over a public gaming company, preferably one with interests in Atlantic City and Nevada, a combination of the familiar and the foreign. While he wanted to expand his already considerable New Jersey empire, his overriding objective was to secure a foothold in the gaming capital of the country, giving his own organization a national and corporate breadth it lacked.

Sure that he could turn a profit on the raids even if his takeover attempts failed, he launched his exploratory search for the right public company with a no-way-to-lose confidence. The only result he apparently hadn't anticipated was that a takeover would succeed and the company would turn out to be a dog. Though his new stock strategy would have its early, titillating triumphs and produce instant profits greater than many of Donald's slow-motion development deals, it would, in the end, wound him badly, doubling his casino debt and damaging even his once profitable New Jersey facilities.

His run on Holiday Inn was the first, beginning just a few months after he bought Trump Plaza from his onetime partner. Though contemptuous of the company's management, at least in part because of the generous terms it had given him in 1982, he liked the company's assets, especially the two Nevada casinos run by its Harrah's subsidiary and its highly profitable Harrah's Marina in Atlantic City.

His move on the company started with a peculiar phone call—he asked Drexel analyst Daniel Lee, who was Mike Milken's casino expert, whether he should buy Holiday stock. Though Bear Stearns was Donald's investment banker on both the Castle and Plaza bonds, as well as his stockbroker, it was Drexel's Lee whose advice he had informally sought on casino matters ever since he broke into the business. Lee urged him to buy, arguing that Holiday's stock was undervalued and that at the very least he was likely to make money speculating on it. At Donald's request, however, Lee brought in several of Drexel's top M&A people to "look very carefully" at an acquisition. Lee lost the internal debate when Drexel's M&A team concluded Holiday would not make a good buy. Unhappy with the recommendation, Lee sat quietly at Trump Tower while the M&A specialists made a presentation of their findings to Donald. When Donald began buying the stock anyway in August of 1986, Holiday panicked.

Donald bought a 4.4 percent stake in Holiday, paying almost $70 million, but putting up none of his own money. Purchased on margin—meaning he borrowed half from broker Bear Stearns—Trump financed the other half with loans from credit lines at three banks. Though he told Holiday his stock purchase was merely an investment, he immediately applied for a gaming license in Nevada, suggesting that he had takeover intentions. On October 10, he filed a Hart-Scott-Rodino report with the Department of Justice, giving notice that he might obtain more than 15 percent of the company stock. Holiday's response was to hire Drexel to develop a restructuring plan to ward off Trump. The plan

Drexel developed called for Holiday to take on $2.4 billion in new debt to pay a special $65-a-share dividend to shareholders and $95 million in fees to Drexel. The plan blocked Trump by restricting the voting rights of anyone who bought more than 10 percent of the stock. Trump never pressed his Holiday bid, pulling out completely by mid-November. While news reports claimed he'd made a $35 million profit, he'd actually earned only a third of that, but his wins on a variety of stock plays in 1986 and 1987 were routinely hyped. The $12.6 million he made on Holiday was immediately thrown into a bigger bid for Bally's, and again it was Drexel's Daniel Lee who pushed the Bally's run.

Lee called Trump to find out if a Wall Street rumor that he was buying Bally's stock was true—as he later remembered it—and Trump said: "No, I haven't been. Should I be?" The Trump rumors were so strong, said Lee, that they were pushing the stock up already. Lee wasn't sure at first if Trump was leveling with him, but as they talked it became clear that Trump didn't know the first thing about the company. "He didn't even know they owned health clubs," said Lee. "I told him the company had assets with real value, was underpriced, and not well managed. I told him he could do a better job than Bally's' current management. I urged him to buy." The day after the conversation with Donald, Lee flew to Puerto Rico for a convention, unsure if Donald was taking his advice. In Puerto Rico, he bumped into Robert Mullane, the chairman of Bally's. Shaken by the sudden movement of his stock, Mullane, who'd used Drexel to buy two Nevada casinos as well as finance the construction of its Atlantic City casino, asked him if he knew who was buying stock. Lee, unsure if Donald had taken his advice, told Mullane that he'd heard it was Trump, but that he doubted it. When Lee checked with his office back in New York, his assistant told him that Donald's secretary had called for a copy of Bally's annual report. "He'd begun buying the stock without even reading the annual report," Lee recounted.

Donald once again used Bear Stearns and bought $63 million in Bally's stock. Lee was lipping him, even sending him the annual report, yet no one at Drexel seemed to mind that Donald was paying millions in exorbitant fees on the purchases to another broker.

This time Donald appeared far more serious than he had been with Holiday, He bought 9.9 percent of the company, becoming Bally's single largest shareholder. He reapplied to the Nevada licensing commission and did the requisite federal filings. Desperate to hang on to a company Trump thought he was bleeding, Mullane hired an investment firm to package a restructuring plan—Drexel Burnham. Once again Drexel came up with an extraordinary notion: If Bally's got itself a second Atlantic City casino Trump could not buy Bally's since that would give him four casinos in a city where three was the legal limit. Conveniently, Drexel had just the right casino available: Steve Wynn's Golden Nugget. Mullane was in such a rush to fend off Trump that he did the Nugget deal in a record-setting ten days at the end of 1986.

Wynn was not just a Drexel client, he was Mike Milken's first junk bond bonanza. As the *Wall Street Journal* put it, Wynn's company was "more or less invented" by Drexel, a major shareholder in the company. "Drexel didn't do corporate financing for us," Wynn added, "they performed plastic surgery." A Bally's acquisition of the Nugget was Drexel's idea of a perfect marriage, especially since both buyer and seller would pay Drexel fees on the transaction. As Lee explained it; "They just used different Drexel teams."

The purchase price was $440 million, financed principally with Drexel bonds, and the sale of the Nugget was Wynn's ticket back to Vegas. Wynn, of course, wasn't planning on going back to Vegas just to run his tawdry downtown casino. He was determined to build a casino in Nevada that would turn the gaming industry upside down—the 3,000-room Mirage. And predictably, in one of his last deals at Drexel, Wynn's close friend Michael Milken floated $540 million in bonds to build the Mirage. Technically, the Mirage's financing had nothing to do with the Nugget sale, but had Wynn not found a rewarding escape route from Jersey, the Mirage would have remained just that.

Daniel Lee's ten-minute talk with Donald had indirectly led to roughly $100 million in Drexel fees, including the charges for Bally's restructuring, as well as for the Nugget and Mirage bond offerings. The earnings matched the company's $95 million take on the Holiday deal, making Drexel a gigantic winner on Trump tips. No wonder the company wasn't too upset that Donald took his stock action to Bear. If Drexel had been his broker, it could hardly have wound up advising Holiday or Bally's on a defense strategy. Lee acknowledged that Drexel's top brass "realized what it looked like" and that the company's chairman, Fred Joseph, called him up and told him to cut out the stock tips to nonclient Trump.

Bally's never recovered from the damage the Nugget acquisition and the expensive restructuring inflicted on it. As soon as the Nugget deal was announced, Standard & Poor's immediately placed the company on its Creditwatch Surveillance List. The stock plummeted over the ensuing years from 21, where it was when the Nugget deal was disclosed, to 1 and 7/8ths, eventually forcing Mullane out and plunging the company into a financial spiral. In fact, even New Jersey's Division of Gaming Enforcement, Donald's loyal regulatory ally, concluded that Trump's runs on Holiday and Bally's had "an appreciable effect on the economic stability" of both companies, which were, after all, prime competitors in the

Atlantic City market. DGE could find no evidence, however, that Donald had any intent "to affect these companies in a negative manner."

In addition to all the costs associated with the Nugget and the restructuring, Bally's also had to come up with $84 million to buy out Donald's stock and get him to drop his lawsuit challenging the Nugget purchase. Bally's took a $24 million charge against earnings in the first quarter of 1987 to cover the costs of the Trump buyback, more than the company's entire earnings in 1986. But even before Donald completed this deal with Bally's, the Federal Trade Commission issued a December 1986 release noting that it was looking into an unusual Bear Stearns practice employed by Donald in both the Holiday and Bally's stock purchases that "appeared to violate" federal regulations.

What Bear had permitted Donald—and a few other choice clients—to do was buy stock in Bear's name, rather than Donald's, and warehouse it for future purchase by Trump. The option letter between Bear and Trump allowed Donald to control stock in the companies without actually owning it until he chose to exercise his Bear option. FTC memos indicate that Bear "promoted the practice as a device to avoid filing under Hart-Scott-Rodino," the federal law that requires disclosure of assemblages of large blocks of stock and establishes waiting periods before raiders can proceed without antitrust clearance. These disclosure implications aside, the Bear maneuver was also a way for Donald to delay contributing his 50 percent on margin purchases, letting Bear carry the full cost of the stock until he picked up the option.

Though it was Bear Stearns, not Donald, who conceived of the scheme, only Trump could be pursued under the civil statutes, not the broker. Members of the FTC noted, however, that "there was still the possibility of a private action against Bear Stearns" by its client. Instead, even after the Justice Department filed a 1988 complaint against Trump for stock parking and forced him to pay a $750,000 judgment, Trump continued to use Bear as his broker. In fact Trump was so appreciative of Bear's special arrangement with him that he paid millions in fees—far in excess of normal brokerage commissions—on both deals.

Beyond the judgment against him, the other downside of these stock plays for Donald was the beating he took in Nevada, where Gaming Commission Chairman Paul Bible went on a rampage, upset at the damage Trump had caused two Nevada operators. "It appears what Donald Trump is doing is using his resources and his New Jersey gaming license to extort greenmail from these two companies," Bible said in the middle of the battle with Bally's, referring to the unsavory tactic of faking a takeover in order to induce a company to buy back a raider's stock at a premium. Bible warned that Trump, who still had a pending application for a Nevada license, could "expect future problems from Nevada gaming regulators."

Since only a raider with a license to operate in one state could threaten a gaming company in another, Bible called upon Nevada and Jersey gaming regulators to "develop a philosophy and a policy where we can protect our licensees from these greenmail activities." Of course, neither DGE nor New Jersey's Casino Control Commission was likely to take on Trump for alleged greenmail or any of his other stock gambits. In fact DGE found nothing wrong with the Bear parking arrangement until the Justice Department branded it illegal a year after DGE had bestowed its own imprimatur on Trump's tactic.

Bible did at least find a rhetorical brother in Jersey. The impact of the maneuvers on Holiday and Bally's had angered CCC Chairman Walter Read enough to provoke him to charge Trump with using his Jersey gaming credentials as "a hunting license" to damage other gaming companies. Read publicly vowed at the 1987 hearings that he "would not vote to renew the license" of any operator who "purchases an interest in a competitor unless I am convinced that the motivation was a sincere desire to acquire and operate the competing facility." But as usual, the commission's tough talk had little to do with how it acted. It renewed all of Donald's licenses, and Donald went right on buying casino stock—a flirtation with the Golden Nugget three months after Read's warning and a December 1988 run at Caesars branded "Trumpmail" in an Atlantic City *Press* editorial. Finally, after the Caesars incident, the commission compelled a commitment out of Donald that he would not speculate in the stock of any New Jersey casino competitors.

Trump had also alienated much of the gaming and political establishment in Nevada, forcing him to change his gaming goals. He had been attracted to Bally's and Holiday principally because of their substantial Nevada holdings, but the warning from Bible put at least a temporary hold on his Vegas ambitions. Even before his battle with Bally's ended in early 1987, his acquisitive attention had moved on to another target, Resorts, a gaming company without Nevada holdings.

So while Steve Wynn had kept a step ahead of the market, anticipating the peaking of Atlantic City revenues by 1989 and the return of boom times to Vegas, Donald took his quick hit on the stock plays and put Vegas on a back burner. Nevada casino profits would catapult from $180 million in 1983 to $690 million by 1988, while Atlantic City's would plummet from $169 million to a meager $15 million in the same period. Vegas's airport superiority, seven-to-one first-class hotel room margin, nongaming attractions, and dramatically lower debt load were beginning to push it far past Jersey, just as Trump deepened his eastern commitment. In a season of dubious judgments, it was one of Donald's worst.

When Donald shifted his attention to Resorts, he was in effect gambling much of his business career on the uncertain future of Atlantic City. He no longer owned most of what he'd built in New York—Trump Tower, Trump Plaza, and the still-in-construction Trump Parc were condominium or co-op buildings, and all Donald retained after the apartments were sold was the commercial space. Except for the thin reed of the USFL appeal, the domed stadium project had died months before he began exploring the Resorts purchase. So with the exception of the still percolating and obviously ambitious West Side project, Donald was out of the action when he decided to take over Resorts—a troubled company that was both the largest landowner in Atlantic City and builder of its riskiest project, the perpetually unfinished Taj Mahal. The Resort move was an unambiguous declaration of Donald's desire to become King of the Boardwalk, even at the cost of the resources and energy that completing the Taj would demand.

It was some measure of Donald's self-confidence—ratified by encouraging bankers and investment houses—that he believed he could build the Taj. Television City, with NBC as an anchor, was certainly a live deal when he signed the first contract to buy a controlling interest in Resorts in March of 1987, meaning that though he wasn't actually *doing* much, he was *preparing* to erect the world's tallest building and the rest of his $5 billion West Side project at the same time that he was contracting to build the world's largest casino in Atlantic City. Considering that he had only actually completed three new buildings in his career (Trump Tower and the two Plazas) and one renovation (the Hyatt, with Trump Parc in construction), it was no wonder that Fred Trump had worried out loud at the Wollman Rink opening about Donald biting off more than he could chew.

The fact was that Donald had not made a new construction start since 1982, a four-year lapse otherwise occupied with a tenant war, a failing football league, casino acquisitions, stock raids, and endless jockeying for dubious projects that never got off the drawing boards, including a Madison Avenue Castle with a moat. When Donald broke ground at Wollman Rink, no one noticed that the young master builder was so out of practice that a $3 million slab of concrete and a refrigeration system were a challenge to him. The collapse of the NBC deal well before Donald actually closed on the Resorts purchase in July did mean that by the time he made a firm commitment to the Taj, the West Side project was in limbo. By any standard, however, the Taj remained a daunting prospect, and not just because of the scope of the construction job.

The sheer size of it invited doubts about the likelihood of its generating a market large enough to make it work. Atlantic City was clearly in no rush to build the airport, noncasino hotel rooms, or convention center that would put it on a footing to compete with Vegas. Yet Donald, rejecting the hard business projections freely available in the changing gaming industry and the advice of confidants Robert Trump and Harvey Freeman, responded to his gut instinct and went after it anyway.

The idea of buying Resorts was born on the slopes of Aspen during the Christmas season of 1986. Ever since the legendary fifty-eight-year-old Resorts chairman Jim Crosby had died the previous April, the company had floundered, marked for takeover on Wall Street but attracting little serious interest. The company's president, Jack Davis, who owned an Aspen condominium, was hunting for a white knight with access to enough money to salvage the company yet protect him, a career Resorts veteran. He'd gotten to know Trump during their years together in Atlantic City, and many noticed that Donald seemed especially attracted to the Davis bravura style.

There appeared to be at least a thirty-year difference between Jack Davis's weathered stone face and his musclebound body—the product of a lifetime of daily workouts. There was also a thirty-year difference between Jack and the thirtyish Caroline, the beautiful ex-stewardess he'd married a few years earlier. Davis, whose first wife had killed herself in a Miami hotel room after years of neglect, landed Caroline when her husband, millionaire Philadelphia Eagles owner Len Tose, went broke at Resorts and other Atlantic City casinos.

Before settling in with the company in Atlantic City, Davis had run its Paradise Island operation in the Bahamas, allowing the management of the company's casino to be turned over to the brother of Meyer Lansky's top aide, attracting government probes of a number of other mob connections, running a slush fund of cash payments for Bahamian officials, and dating actress Janet Leigh. Together with other top Resorts executives, Davis had also helped provide a secluded hideaway for Resorts regulars like Richard Nixon, Howard Hughes, Robert Vesco, and Bebe Rebozo, as well as exiled dictators Anastasio Somoza and the Shah of Iran.

There was just enough intrigue and sex appeal around the jaded Davis to titillate Donald. Davis and his wife eventually not only befriended Trump, but his new romantic interest, Marla Maples. The Davises reportedly put her up at their Atlantic City and Aspen homes in the early days, before she and Donald went public with their affair and while Ivana was still in charge at the Castle.

Without Crosby, however, whose daring investment strategies had both built and bedeviled the company, Davis was lost. While Crosby had weakened the company with bizarre forays into the seaplane and shrimp farm markets, no one questioned the potential value of Resorts' basic assets. Everything hinged, however, on the completion of the Taj, which had already consumed almost half a billion dollars in company revenue, without any bond or bank financing. Even if a new owner of the company could finally finish it, the 1,250-room monstrosity would pose another problem—it represented a possibly fatal threat to the company's original Atlantic City casino, located next door in a refurbished but fading old hotel. The company's other principal property, Paradise Island, was also quietly aging and required an expensive overhauling.

In addition to these inviting yet troubled assets, a buyer would have to take on a double-edged and unusual corporate structure, one that was simultaneously a roadblock and an opportunity. Resorts had a two-tiered stock arrangement so peculiar that it was forced to trade on the American Stock Exchange since the New York exchange would not countenance it. The closely held Class "B" shares outvoted the publicly traded "A" shares 100 to 1, giving a handful of shareholders with only a modest amount of equity in the company a stranglehold over it. This meant a buyer could gain control of 72 percent of the company's voting shares by picking up the proxies of roughly fifteen people—seven Crosby family members and a harem of girlfriends that the bachelor had remembered in his will. One girlfriend alone, the Baroness Marianne Brandstetter, a German-born socialite in her forties who'd left her husband to live with the emphysema-stricken Crosby for his final five, backgammon-filled years, was given a beneficial interest in a full quarter of the estate's "B" stock—194,000 shares in trust.

By the time Donald made his initial moves on the stock in early 1987, this group had already resisted one casino-licensed and reasonably well-heeled suitor, the Dallas-based Pratt Corporation, which owned the Sands in Atlantic City and bid as much as $150 a share for the family and estate "B" stock, three times its market price at the time of Crosby's death.

The official rationale for rejecting Pratt was the suspicion that it would force an expensive management contract on Resorts, draining revenue from it—an ironic concern in view of the contract Donald would eventually demand. Resorts also feared that the cash-starved Pratt might have to borrow to finance the purchase—precisely what Donald wound up doing. There was also the expressed concern that Pratt would destroy the beloved Crosby legacy, selling off assets—a strategy that Donald openly indicated he would adopt, particularly with regard to Paradise Island. Indeed, unlike Pratt, Donald would have to close or sell the existing Resorts casino when the Taj opened because he could not legally operate four casinos in Atlantic City.

Donald, however, had a few routes to the rulers of the Crosby estate unavailable to the Pratts. To begin with, Jack Davis, and the management team Davis led, could materially influence the Class "B" clan. So could Paddy McGahn, Donald's longtime lawyer who'd been with Resorts since gambling surfaced in New Jersey. So could Ace Greenberg from Bear Stearns, the investment banker Trump and Resorts had in common. And unlike the Pratts, Donald was a reassuring friend to these gatekeepers.

Although Crosby had three brothers—a plastic surgeon, a Florida real estate broker, and a convicted stock swindler—it was his in-laws who actually controlled the company after his death. Both of Jim Crosby's sisters had married members of the Murphy family (the closeness between the two families stretched back five decades when the patriarchs of each became best friends). Suzanne Crosby, whose shares were worth nearly $8 million, the second largest cache of any Crosby or Murphy, was the wife of Capital Cities chairman Tom Murphy, owner of ABC-TV and an acquaintance of Donald's. Though Tom Murphy was a coexecutor of the Crosby will, he formally withdrew from the estate committee, hoping to maintain a distance between himself and the fate of the mob-scarred company. It was, instead, his Harvard Business School classmate Jack Davis who became Donald's prime lobbyist within the inner circle and who gained Tom's assent quite early.

The other executor, Tom's cousin Henry, a Trenton funeral home owner also married to a Crosby sister, had taken over as Resorts chairman and assumed full voting power of the estate shares. An unassuming and conscientious longtime Resorts director, Henry was principally guided by a third Murphy, Charles, who was Tom's brother. A wily New York attorney who'd been general counsel to Resorts for twenty-five years, Charles Murphy was trustee of Brandstetter's stock, as well as of the 40,000 shares Crosby had left the felon brother he hadn't spoken to for years, Peter. As trustee, he was supposed to represent Brandstetter's interest and manage her affairs.

Donald began talking directly with Charlie Murphy about a deal in February of 1987, and the terms of a contract were worked out by March. Donald would buy the "B" shares controlled by the Murphy-Crosby families, including those they held for Brandstetter and the other girlfriends, for $79 million, to be paid in cash at a closing to be held before September. The acquisition of the stock—at a price well below the Pratt offer—would give him control of the company. But

Trump's contract needed the approval of Resorts' existing board of directors, a judge in Florida who was probating the Crosby will, and the casino regulators in New Jersey. That's why a seven-month deadline was set for the closing.

The only possible obstacles to the Trump deal within the company were the three independent directors whose appointment to the Resorts board had been mandated by Jersey casino regulations. These directors, who had as many votes on the six-member board as the Crosby-Murphy clan but were barred from owning stock or doing business with the company, were led by Mitchell Sviridoff, a New York–based former Ford Foundation vice president and renowned housing expert. The contract was essentially sprung on these directors, who finally acquiesced after a day of intense lobbying.

Four conference-call meetings of the board were held on Sunday, March 8, starting at 10:45 A.M. and ending almost twelve hours later. John Donnelly, the company's in-house counsel, Jack Davis, and Charlie Murphy worked relentlessly on the reluctant directors, reading sections of the proposed contract over the phone to them, promising that Trump would rescue a company Davis suddenly warned was about to "run out of cash." They explained the urgency with the claim that Donald's oral commitment to buy was only good if they had a written agreement by the end of that day. Though the directors had previously retained a penetrating financial consultant, David Schulte of Chilmark Partners, they were told there was no time for him to analyze the terms.

As soon as the board approved the purchase agreement, Davis, Donnelly, and three other top executives obtained Trump's approval for three-year management contract for themselves. Trump's consent was ascribed in corporate minutes as having been granted specifically "in accordance with the agreement under which he is to purchase voting control" of the company. Davis, who may have feared that an experienced operator like Pratt would have simply displaced him, was immediately given a raise nearly doubling his salary—from $400,000 in 1986 to $750,000—and it was made retroactive to January 1. The day the purchase closed a few months later, Davis got a second raise, making him the first million-dollar staffer ever to work for Donald. Donald also hired Caroline as a dollar-a-year interior design consultant for the Taj, complete with her own company limo as a perk. John Donnelly collected a substantial cash bonus.*

The sales agreement next had to win probate approval, and the only real

---

* Charlie Murphy also received a $420,000 counsel payment and a $252,000-a-year retirement benefit, while Henry got a $180,000 salary and a $108,000 pension.

danger to it in Florida was Marianne Brandstetter. Technically, she was pow-
erless, since Murphy voted her shares. But if the largest single beneficiary of
Crosby's estate entered objections to the deal before the probate court, or filed
suit to block any sale, her complaint would carry legal weight, especially if it
was accompanied by evidence of an offer to buy that was arguably better than
Trump's. That was why suitors beat a path to her door. The Pratts had tried to
convince her that the family members controlling the estate were betraying her
interests, and then, as the Trump deal went to court, two other bidders, Texas oilman Marvin Davis and Florida businessman Stanley Gans, were pushing offers
in her direction that seemed to far exceed Donald's.

Brandstetter was intrigued, particularly by the Gans offer, and Donald began
to put pressure on her. Ivana had befriended her, inviting her to Mar-A-Lago
and lunching with her in New York. "How can you do this?" Ivana asked during
one in a series of beseeching phone calls. "You are a friend." Brandstetter later
remembered one final call from Donald—"very nice, not like the other casino
people"—in which he calmly told her that he would not ask her again to sell to
him. If she did not agree to it now, he said, she could keep her stock. She decided
not to oppose the sale, and, in June, the probate court approved it, with the casino regulators routinely following suit.

Within a few months of the court approval, at a point when Brandstetter still
had a legal option to sue to block the sale, she bought an apartment in Trump
Parc. Her move into a Trump condo unit was also a consequence of the Crosby
will and had been one of her most urgent concerns since Crosby's death.

Crosby had stipulated in his will that while the baroness would inherit "all of
my pictures, paintings, antiques, books, works of art, silverware, household furniture, and furnishings," she would not be given the apartment they'd shared on
the twenty-seventh floor of the Imperial House on Manhattan's Upper East Side.
Instead the will authorized Charlie Murphy "to purchase at a cost not exceeding
$700,000 a residence for her use." She desperately wanted to remain where she
was, but Murphy knew he could sell the apartment for twice what the will obligated him to pay for Brandstetter's new home and that the estate (including the
family) would get the benefit of any difference.

Brandstetter's apartment at Trump Parc, 25-F, which she says she agreed to
buy in 1987, is registered under the name of Charlie Murphy as trustee of the
Crosby estate. She bought it at a discount personally authorized by Donald—
paying $545,000 for a unit listed in the offering plan at twice that. The apartment
purchase was never disclosed in any SEC filing, though shareholders may have
had a right to know about it since it was a sidebar transaction between Trump

and the company's largest individual investor.* The Parc's luxury—with maids, a concierge and all the pampering that goes with a first-class hotel residence—was especially alluring to the baroness, whose former husband, Frank Brandstetter, ran a prime resort hotel in Acapulco. The Brandstetter purchase, of course, was only one in a pattern of apartment sale coincidences, ranging from Donald's discount for Conrad Stephenson to an earlier cut-rate sale of a Trump Tower penthouse to Howard Weingrow, one of the principal landowners holding a Trump lease underneath the Plaza casino.

All of these Trump machinations had given him control over a company whose assets, if they could be salvaged, might be worth a billion dollars. But it was also a company poised for disaster—indeed, in its first quarter under Trump, the traditional boom period of summer, Resorts' deteriorating Atlantic City casino reported a $7 million loss. Although Donald had bought the estate and family shares at a bargain price, his deal obligated him to tender an offer for the rest of the outstanding "B" shares. When he finished purchasing the available "B" stock later that fall, his total bill for Resorts was $96 million—virtually all of it, in Trump tradition, borrowed money.

Donald's next mission was to figure out a way to extract from the company immediately whatever it would cost him to pay the debt service on the loans that had financed its purchase. The boldness of his strategy suggested that he had expected all along to acquire Resorts at absolutely no cost to himself; in fact, Donald expected to take a hefty sum out of the company even if it never made a corporate profit again. As best as Donald could later remember on the witness stand, it was Jack Davis who came up with the plan that would pay him a dividend at Resorts no matter how the company fared under his and Davis's control—a grotesquely rich management and services contract.

Judiciously waiting until his acquisition of the "B" shares closed, Donald eagerly recommended to his own new board that a Trump entity be paid an unusually high percentage—3.5 percent—of the troubled company's gross revenue, retroactive to the day he purchased the stock. This proposal, which surfaced at the top executive level of the company right after the July closing and was sent to the independent directors a month later, also called for a 3 percent fee on Taj construction costs and a 5 percent brokerage and development commission on the sale of any Resorts assets, many of which Donald intended to market.

---

* Murphy and Brandstetter dismiss the notion that the stock and apartment purchases had anything to do with each other.

David Schulte, the independent directors' adviser, estimated that the management fee alone—to be paid, of course, in addition to all the raises just delivered to Davis's management team—would drain a billion dollars out of the company over its proposed thirty-year life. The Taj construction fee would amount to another $15 million. Possible brokerage costs were not even calculated, though Donald was already moving to line up a sale of some assets, particularly Paradise Island, and would collect millions in commissions on them. Since Donald would be paid off the top under this comprehensive contract—before the company's past and future creditors—he was not obliged to show a positive bottom line before reaping the reward normally associated with achieving one.

The justification presented to the independent directors was that Donald had to be suitably rewarded for the risk he was taking in arranging the half billion dollars in financing he said was necessary to finish the Taj, especially since he was also promising to supervise the construction and manage the casino. Implicit in Davis's and Trump's advocacy of the contract was that Donald needed the contract's remuneration to goad him into action. The service agreement was essentially a substitute for any genuine Trump equity investment in the company. Since he owned so few actual shares, he would make very little if a successful Taj raised the value of the stock. While he had 88 percent of the voting power in the company, he controlled only 11 percent of its stock; his Taj would be generating $9 for the Class "A," public shareholders for every $1 it put in Donald's pocket.

The critics—starting with Resorts' executive vice president Steve Norton, one of the five longtime company officers just awarded a three-year contract—argued that Donald had carried a reasonable notion disturbingly far. Norton, Schulte, and the independent directors agreed to support a percentage fee for managing the construction of the Taj, but thought that Trump's payments should be partially tied to the completion of the job. Under Donald's proposal, he collected a full fee whether or not the Taj ever opened, even though he intended to hire a construction manager and pay him another percentage of the cost. Donald's share was to be taken on all Taj costs, including the real estate taxes and unpaid expenses incurred before the effective date of the agreement. Despite these concerns about the construction fee section of the agreement, the independent directors were satisfied that a strong Trump role in building the Taj would attract financing and tried to get him to settle for just that. He adamantly refused.

Schulte calculated that had the service agreement been in place the year before, Donald's share of the company's adjusted gross would have permitted him to take home 56 percent of Resorts' operating profit without having picked up a shovel on the Taj site. What outraged the critics was that Trump's plan inexplicably called for him to consume similar percentages of the company's profit and cash flow for managing the existing Atlantic City casino, Paradise Island, and the other company assets during the two years it would take to finish the Taj, even though the present Resorts management had been successfully running these properties (for decades, in some cases) and their casino experience was far greater than the Trump Organization's. The independent directors made a point of noting that Jack Davis and his management team had not even attempted to get Donald to modify this aspect of the agreement, regardless of what it seemed to say about them. In support of this argument, Steve Norton, the only officer to break openly with the service agreement, contended at private board meetings that if Donald insisted on going ahead with the management fee, he ought to either fire the company's top officers or put them on the payroll of his new management entity. Otherwise, Norton pointed out, the shareholders were paying for two corporate management teams. Instead of adopting Norton's suggestion, the contract with Trump specifically required the retention of the current management.

To answer his critics, Donald brought in a supposedly independent consultant to evaluate the agreement, Laventhol & Horwath. He did not divulge that L&H had been the Grand Hyatt's accountant since the hotel opened and had done other work for him as well. Predictably, L&H endorsed every aspect of the comprehensive Resorts agreement in a lengthy report. L&H also recommended, under a second contract with Resorts, the closing of the existing casino when the Taj was completed and the use of its hotel facilities as an attached wing of the Taj. Since Donald could not legally operate four casinos, L&H's recommendation helped justify another corporate act that was clearly on his agenda, though not necessarily one that was in the best interests of the public company he now headed.

Trump and Davis also brought in Bear Stearns's Greenberg, who ringingly endorsed the service fees, calling them "the price of Trump coming to the party." Without Trump, Greenberg argued, there would be no bond financing, no Taj, and, conceivably, no company. And without the management contract, there would be no real Trump involvement, said Greenberg, who stood to earn millions in fees on future Taj bonds. (Greenberg's raves for Donald were an encore performance—he had predicted that Trump could raise "up to a billion" when the board was considering the stock sale back in March.)

In his takeover moves against Holiday and Bally's, Trump had railed on about self-serving managements that supposedly bled public companies. But now, at the helm of his own public company for the first time, the onetime share-holder champion was ready to devour the company he was supposed to lead.

But Sviridoff and Schulte would not yield to this maneuver. They insisted on an incentive provision in the management agreement, cutting Donald's percent of gross revenue in half (1.75 percent) while adding a 15 percent share of corporate profits for Trump. Leaving the rest of the agreement largely intact, Schulte estimated Donald's fees at $108 million for the first five years of a ten-year agreement. Sviridoff recognized that even these sharply reduced terms were still a bonanza for Trump, but he and the independent directors and advisers were fearful that if they pushed any further, Donald would walk away from the company. Sviridoff, who was dispatched as an emissary of the independent directors for an October conference with Donald at Trump Tower, told him: "This is no joke. We will vote against this contract. Our offer is as far as we will go."

Donald instantly accepted, adding, "I only have one condition. You guys will consider a bonus if I do a spectacular job on the Taj, not that you'll guarantee it. Only consider it." Sviridoff saw the comment as a face-saver and acceded.*

The redrafted services agreement—with new Resorts attorney and Trump-brother-in-law John Barry carving out the language—faced a storm of criticism at DGE and the CCC. But Ace Greenberg was trotted out again—proclaiming that Trump was "on a tremendous roll" and could get cheaper bond financing than virtually anyone else—and the commission reluctantly approved the agreement. CCC Chairman Walter Read said the deal was "negotiated out of a sense of desperation with an eye toward completing the Taj at whatever cost," as clear a rationale as anyone offered for the extraordinary contract. The only commissioner to vote against it commented that its total estimated cost of $162 million to $192 million was "staggering," an expected one third of the company's cash flow. The contract even provided that if the company went broke, it was obligated to borrow from any existing credit line to pay Trump his fees. And if it was unable to borrow and the fees were deferred, Trump would receive two points over prime in interest on any deferred payments.

Within three business days of winning commission approval in mid-December, however, Donald decided that even the service agreement wasn't sufficient. On December 21, he informed an immediately supportive Davis that he

---

* Shortly afterward, a Resorts attorney close to Sviridoff called him and said that Donald "wanted to know if he could hire Sviridoff," who ran a small New York consulting firm. Sviridoff laughed at the notion.

would tender an offer of $15 per share, buying the "A" shares and the handful of remaining "B" stock, and take the company private. Even for Trump, whose every daring action routinely won nods of wary approval in official Atlantic City, this was a confounding series of events. Combined with the NBC debacle, Donald's virtually simultaneous attempt to complete the takeover of Resorts would prove to be the one-two punch that, more than any other, would ultimately lead to his collapse. Instead of drawing the millions in fees due under his carefully arranged management contract, without any downside risk, Donald was repositioning himself to rise or fall with the Taj.

Overnight he had decided to cast aside his cost-free control of the company, to take on Resorts' $600 million in outstanding bonds, an expected half billion in future debt to complete the Taj, and at least $125 million in new bank loans taken on since he arrived. If Donald was permitted by the CCC to take the company private, he conceded he would personally guarantee some of the new company debt, as well as borrow millions more to buy out the shareholders.

Donald made this move because he simply could not tolerate the idea that he might have to share the spectacular Taj profits he anticipated with a public market of stockholders. It was the same appetite that had driven him to buy out his Harrah's agreement at the Plaza and the Equitable deal at Trump Tower in 1986. He would not be anyone's partner—even anonymous shareholders who exercised little influence over the day-to-day direction of the company. The fourteen shareholder lawsuits filed against his service agreement had helped tip the balance. The lawyers who made their living chasing corporate boards would never let him run his own company, he realized, and it was a constraint he could not countenance. But opportunity was as much a motivation as ego, for Trump knew he would now be able to buy the company at a very advantageous price.

Though Donald had boasted publicly that he had pulled out of the stock market shortly before the October 19 crash, his declaration was mere bravado. He had continued to hold his Resorts shares (as well as others), and the price of the company's stock had gone into a tailspin after the crash. The "A" shares that had been up to sixty only a few months earlier had been sliding throughout the uncertain months of Trump control, until by the end of 1987 their price had plummeted to a low of twelve, making it "natural," as Trump explained it, that his interest in buying the company outright might grow. It was impossible, however, to determine how much of that decline was attributable to the crash and how much to the simultaneous announcement of the service agreement. Even Trump conceded in subsequent CCC testimony that the service agreement may have helped depress the value of the stock, as well as having adversely affected the interest rates on the anticipated bond issue. Faced with a stock price that was bottoming out and a bond rate that was soaring, Donald decided to make his move on the stock, believing that once he controlled the company, the cost of the bonds would drop.

But when Sviridoff and the other directors balked at Donald's modest offering price, he virtually shut down construction work on the Taj site in an effort to force them to accept. Then, insisting that his $15-a-share price was fair, he retained bankruptcy counsel for the company, planting fears on the board that he intended to either own the company or take it into Chapter XI. The two sides began negotiating toward a final, agreeable price—$22. The new price drove the potential cost of the buyout from $100 million to $125 million—on top, of course, of what Donald had already paid for the "B" stock. Still, $225 million for a company that some said owned a billion in assets looked like a bargain, even if its prime asset was an unfinished casino so massive no one could predict when it would begin to cover its interest costs.

In late January 1988, the independent directors, at a meeting in Davis's office on Paradise Island, decided to take the Trump offer. The twenty-five law firms associated with the myriad of shareholder suits simultaneously decided to withdraw the suits after Donald, who met at least twice privately with the Philadelphia-based lead counsel, agreed to pay $3.2 million. Though the suits had required a bare minimum of legal work, the lawyers justified their fat fee with speeches about how their court complaints—ringing with charges of fraud—had forced Donald to hike his price. The Delaware judge who had to approve the settlement initially said the fees "raised serious concerns," but ultimately approved them as reasonable.

A few days after the independent directors assented to the sale in early 1988, Donald appeared again before the casino commission seeking its approval. His supposedly unique ability to refinance the Taj had been his strongest argument from the beginning, so he decided to call upon it one last time. Although he raised the possibility of financing the project at junk interest rates through Drexel, Bear Stearns, and Merrill Lynch, Donald wanted to appeal as well to the commission's preference for staid old bank financing, so he began boasting about the banks that had been begging him to do a deal ever since the $22 offer was made. "I have banks literally just coming at me asking me about doing this deal," he marveled. "I'm talking about a difference in interest rate of maybe 10 points, and if you're talking about 18 or 19 percent as Resorts and maybe eight and a half percent as Trump, that's the difference between an extremely successful company and a company that's just working to pay interest.

"Banks would have never loaned that money to Resorts. They're loaning it to me. They couldn't care less about Resorts. Maybe that's an overstatement, but the banks are essentially doing it because I own the company. Institutions that haven't even been involved in Atlantic City—I'm talking about banking institutions, not these junk bonds, which are ridiculous—have come to us, wanting to invest $100 million in the deal, and we are talking about a rate of interest at the prime rate. There's some difference between that and talking to bondholders, and by the time you pay the Wall Street commissions and the fees, I mean, we're talking about one bank potentially doing the whole deal. I'm not making any commitments, but I think they want to do it very badly."

Trump contended that the bank financing available to him would be so inexpensive that he was planning to seek only $475 million in financing, as opposed to the $550 million he'd successfully petitioned the commission to approve in 1987. Not only would the bank rates be lower than bond rates, he explained, but he would be able to draw down funds from a bank loan as he needed them during construction, thereby paying interest on piecemeal increments of a loan as the job wore on, instead of floating a bond and paying interest on the total amount throughout construction.

His explanation for this avalanche of bank enthusiasm? "The banks call me all the time—can we loan you money, can we this, can we that. There is tremendous liquidity if you have a good statement and you're solid. The banks, they want to throw money at you. I can give them security on their loan, 100 percent certainty. With me, they know they would get their interest."

The CCC was unimpressed. Several members were weary of Donald's repeatedly redrawn but always rosy picture and were alarmed by his most recent and record-setting turnabout—discarding the service agreement two months after proposing it and only days after the commission approved it. Valerie Armstrong suspected, as did others on the commission, that the service agreement was part of a deliberate Trump strategy to damage the company so he could buy it cheaply. In a mid-February statement announcing her intention to vote against the Trump purchase, she chronicled the shifting tactical strikes that had characterized his prolonged assault on the venerable Resorts, noting how he'd predicted disaster if he didn't get each of his concessions and promised prosperity if he did. From the purchase agreement to the planned closing of the old casino to the service contract to the public offering, said Armstrong, the commission was told each time that "Trump needs more control of the company" to finance and complete the Taj, upping the ante without results.

"While it might be possible to conclude," she charged, "that the events of the past eight months resulted from happenstance, impulse, fate and/or events beyond Trump's and Resorts' control, it is also just as easy, perhaps easier, to conclude that many of the events leading to Mr. Trump's current merger proposal have been carefully staged, manipulated and orchestrated to drive down the value of the stock in order to force the merger agreement." David Waters, who'd voted against the service agreement, joined Armstrong in announcing his intention to nix the new public offering, meaning that for the first time Donald was faced with certain defeat on a commission resolution since only two negative votes were necessary to block the deal.

The Atlantic City *Press* was in editorial convulsions, blasting the "unsavory tinge to much of Donald's dealing," including "browbeating, threats and blatant wielding of power." Trump "seems to think there should be one set of rules for him," concluded the only hometown paper, "and another for everybody else. It's almost as if he thinks casino gambling in Atlantic City was intended solely to make him rich."

Attorney Nick Ribis hurriedly moved to produce another battery of witnesses to try to change the commission's mind, and an unctuously respectful Trump returned for a second round at the CCC. He resolutely denied that he'd manipulated the stock and contended that he really preferred his old management fee posture to the offering but was forced to switch tactics by a bond market revolt against the service agreement and other factors pushing prices upward. It was David Schulte, though, the savvy financial adviser, who weighed in with the opinion that salvaged Donald. Asked bluntly about the possibility of Trump manipulation, Schulte acknowledged that "it's not hard against this history to see why that question is on people's minds," adding that he'd "worried about it a lot."

"I think in a way," he ruminated, "that it pays Mr. Trump more of a compliment than he deserves, because I don't think he's that smart. The implicit suggestion is a scheme, a long-term scheme carefully worked out. Maybe. He seems to me to be more impulsive than that." The hearing room broke out in laughter, and even Trump smiled. The commission capitulated, and Walter Read said to Schulte as he left the stand: "I'm not sure Mr. Trump realizes how helpful you are to his cause, but you are." Once Donald had his commission vote, he began vaguely hinting in interviews that he might indeed have been that smart—sinking a public company so he could buy it cheap—but there was no way to tell which of his equally self-serving versions was the truth.

On the precipice of a total takeover of his first public company, however, Donald was about to discover just how tricky the corporate marketplace could become.

His pursuit of Resorts had already been a yearlong odyssey, but it still had one more surprise turn in the road to take. The final episode would have a Hollywood flavor, and not just because Merv Griffin was cast in a major role. The script could have been written by Mario Puzo or Nick Pileggi.

It starts with the weekend, sinus-clearing visit of Fedele "just-a-poor-boy-from-North-Philly" Scutti to Atlantic City. Used car dealer Scutti stayed at the Showboat, the casino overlooking the Taj Mahal construction site, sometime in January of 1988, just when stories about Donald's $15-a-share Resorts offer were appearing in the Atlantic City papers.

Scutti, whose only construction experience consisted of used car lots and showrooms, nevertheless thought he had a fairly keen eye for sizing up a job. Although the press was quoting Trump as saying he needed $500 million to finish the Taj, Scutti could tell at a glance that not a cent more than $200 million was necessary. If the Taj was that close to completion, reasoned the paunchy, high school–educated, sometime-investor, Trump's $15 per share was a steal. At fifty-four, Scutti had moved from his modest Philadelphia roots to owning eight car dealerships in Rochester, New York, a boat company, a real estate development firm, and four coast-to-coast homes. He had enough money to act on his hunch, and, on January 19, he started buying the stock he was convinced had been deliberately undervalued.

By February 24, the glance out his hotel window had cost "Dale" Scutti $5.5 million. He had gone on buying Resorts stock when Trump hiked his offer to $22 and stopped the same day that Donald's new bid, after a month of testy CCC hearings, was finally approved by the commission. Though the rest of the world believed that Donald's yearlong dance with Resorts was finally over, Scutti seemed to know otherwise. He had risked a fortune on 320,000 "A" shares, buying 5.6 percent of the company—certain, he said, that Trump would be forced to once again raise his offer.

Scutti was dealing with a lawyer in New York named Morris Orens, sending him fees in chunks of $10,000, then $40,000, and up to $200,000. Orens was advising him on how Trump's takeover could be blocked, and these huge fees, according to Scutti, were merely the cost of motivating the rumpled and well-connected Orens. Orens was motivated enough to call another client, Ernie Barbella, a market player Orens had already represented in stock deals that had attracted the attention of the SEC, prosecutors, and other regulatory agencies. Orens also spoke with Michael Nigris, who shared an office with Barbella. Though Orens had represented Merv Griffin on Merv's greatest deal—the $250 million sale of his game shows to Coca-Cola—the lawyer did not call Merv first.

He called the men who pulled Merv's strings, and the two almost instantly became Scutti's partners in the ambush of Trump's Resorts deal.

Merv had praised Nigris, his top adviser, to *Barron's* in 1988: "In 22 years, he's been right 100%. I never make mistakes in key positions." DGE offered a slightly different description, recapitulating a private investigator's findings: "Nigris has been known by law enforcement to be associated with members of organized crime. Our investigation has focused on a number of close business associates of Nigris who are purported organized crime figures, convicted fraud artists and securities swindlers." Though Nigris was president of the Griffin Company, he was paid as a consultant and was actually employed by Morgan Capital Management, whose president, Ernie Barbella, signed Nigris's executive contract with Merv. Barbella and Nigris were so close their desks were side by side in a room that was ten feet by twenty feet.

Old college roommates, friends, and partners for thirty years, Barbella and Nigris had weathered many a legal storm.* Barbella, whose first company was a meat brokerage firm called Mid-West Meat, had settled a 1983 U.S. Department of Agriculture complaint charging that he'd made illegal payoffs to supermarket heads. Nigris was Mid-West's accountant. Then Barbella, who has been identified in court documents as a Gambino crime family associate, orchestrated a fraudulent public offering for Musikahn, a record company bust-out, using a broker named Martin Kern to handle thousands of deceptive stock transfers.† When Nigris, who was also a Musikahn director, first came to Atlantic City to take a look at Resorts for the intrigued Merv, his emissary was Marty Kern, who became the Griffin team's eyes and ears in New Jersey. Kern, whose name had been mentioned on FBI tapes from Fat Tony Salerno's East Harlem headquarters, set himself up in Jim Crosby's old office inside Resorts.

For any number of legal reasons, the promoters of the Scutti and Merv version of the Resorts saga—including Orens—preferred to pretend that Merv was a latecomer to the cabal. Griffin himself later told reporters: "Orens called on March 10 or 11. Nigris went down to Atlantic City, spent a day and a half and

---

* It was the same Ernie Barbella and Michael Nigris who once secretly owned HME Records, bankrupt creation of longtime Trump foe, 100 Central Park South tenant leader John Moore.

† Though the criminal probe of the Musikahn scam had not yet surfaced when the Resorts deal was concluded, Barbella would wind up convicted on federal felony charges.

eyeballed the place. After five days of concentrated homework, on March 15, I said, 'Let's go.'" Merv's first bid was made two days later, on Saint Patrick's Day.

Prosecutors discovered, however, that Nigris had actually flown out to Los Angeles in late February to meet with Merv, staying at the Beverly Hilton, the hotel Merv had acquired with Nigris's help. Nigris left for New York on March 5, with Merv's blessing, and proceeded to go ahead with the deal. While at the Hilton, his phone records indicate that he called his Morgan Capital office fourteen times, keeping in touch with Barbella, ostensibly about the Resorts game plan.

One reason for the disinformation about the timing of Griffin, Nigris, and Barbella's interest in Resorts was that Scutti would subsequently present himself, in court papers and public filings, as a simple shareholder, unconnected to any takeover attempt, merely trying to force Trump to make an equitable offer for the stock. But a Trump suit filed in federal court on March 18, the day after Merv's first bid, named Griffin and Scutti as codefendants. Trump alleged that Scutti's February 26 SEC filings were "false and misleading" precisely because he "failed to disclose the existence of the individuals with whom Scutti had agreed to act in concert, their backgrounds and identities." This wording is so peculiar that it suggested that Donald may have known about the shady background of the people who were after his company well before the investigators, who did not begin to uncover the Barbella-Nigris axis until the summer of 1988.

By the time Donald filed these papers, Griffin was moving to take Scutti out of the picture anyway. The "dumb" car dealer, as Scutti liked to call himself, walked away from the deal with what he claimed was a $5 million profit on the sale of his shares to Merv. The Griffin contingent also promised him a $6 million consulting fee if its deal to acquire the company ever closed.

Through March and into April, Merv presented a variety of offers to the Resorts board, and though the early submissions were riddled with loopholes and easily rejected by Trump and the independent directors, the dollar amount involved—always hovering in the midthirties—clearly bettered Donald's $22 bid. The stock shot into the upper twenties, and then the lower thirties, until it got so high no one was tendering a share to the man who had proposed $22. Everyone was astonished at Griffin's immediate willingness to pay $14 more per share than Donald, and no one, including Donald, could figure out why he had started so high. Griffin explained that it was to make an impression, to convince everyone he was serious. But the gang around Griffin had another motive: Barbella and an assortment of relatives, swindlers, and hoods were buying up blocks of Resorts stock on tips out of the Griffin strategy sessions—all apparently without Merv's knowledge. Barbella's bust-out history was taking on a new relevance. When he later pled guilty to state charges, and several of his associates were indicted for insider trading, it became clear that Griffin had been encouraged to hike the price so that the boys around him could get rich speculating on it. No one cared if the company collapsed under the weight of the debt Merv would have to take on to pay the inflated price.

The Resorts board rejected the first Griffin offer, convinced by Trump that Griffin was unfairly offering the same for the "B" shares as he was for the "A," a hundred dollars less than Donald had paid for them. Donald claimed—with no small amount of irony—that the company had a fiduciary obligation to see to it that he was paid a respectable price for his holdings.

On March 22, Griffin raised the dollar value of his offer from $225 million to $295 million and told the company it could allocate it anyway it wished, repaying Trump his initial investment and still giving Griffin a majority interest in the "A" shares at a $35 premium. This second offer died as well.

The turnabout came with Griffin's third move—an innovative request filed in mid-April with the Resorts board. Merv formally asked the board to issue 1.2 million new "B" shares and sell them to him at $36 a share, an action that would have diluted Donald's hold on the company, put Griffin at the helm, and led to an "A" share sale at the same price. The board—especially independent director Sviridoff—was not about to ignore a matter properly placed before it.

Trump was outraged and threatened lawsuits against the independent directors. Jack Davis ridiculed the proposal, insisting that Griffin couldn't finance his offers. But Sviridoff demanded a meeting with Nigris and Griffin's attorneys—a session also attended by Robert Trump, who challenged Merv's unusual Class "B" purchase response to Jim Crosby's still troubling two-tier system. Donald pressed for a vote against the dilution attempt, but Sviridoff warned him that it would turn out to be three-to-three, the independents versus Donald, Robert, and Harvey Freeman. Under those circumstances, the Griffin proposal might have legally failed, but Donald would have had a public relations disaster on his hands and would have faced another inevitable onslaught of shareholder suits. Merv had at last forced Donald to the bargaining table.

The showdown between the two was more style than substance. "There's an East Coast arrogance," Merv told a reporter. "They think this is la-la land out here. But there is an important financial community that you cannot underestimate in Southern California. They probably think we're doing this interview in a Jacuzzi."

"If you call me," Donald countered, "I'm behind this desk or I'm out walking around a job. I'm not out playing tennis, I'm not out relaxing. I don't do those things very well, I'm a worker."

The meeting took place in Trump Tower on April 13. When Merv entered the office, Donald immediately displayed his latest acquisition, putting the upstart Griffin in his place. "He took me over to the window to show me the Plaza Hotel," Merv recalled. "He had just bought it—and he gave me statistics about the number of rooms. I said, 'Good, that's just the right number of rooms to house the lawyers you'll need for our suit.' Trump roared."

Griffin then tweaked Trump about all the nasty ways he'd dismissed his various bids for the company in recent weeks. "The only reason we're here is that you're running out of adjectives. We've been through 'moot,' 'illusory' and 'fruitless.'"

Merv liked to claim that he skillfully put the financial pressure on Donald by raising the subject of Donald's borrowed hundred million to buy the "B" stock. "I have no debt," said Merv. "I'm sitting here with very little stress. I could sit here with my lawyers and accountants for two years."

"You're asking me about debt service on one hundred million dollars?" responded Trump. "One hundred million dollars is a very small amount for me. Do you understand that?"

In fact, the essence of the deal had been negotiated before either of the principals met. Susan Heilbron, Trump's in-house counsel, had been quietly talking to a Griffin attorney, John Herford, from Merv's California-based law firm, Gibson, Dunn. They didn't have to work hard to establish a rapport—they had once lived together. Heilbron broached the question of a split of the company's assets with Herford. The plan called for Donald to get his world's largest casino and Merv, who'd done nightclub acts in Atlantic City as a child performer, to get his piece of nostalgia, the old Resorts casino. The proposal wasn't so much a calculated division of corporate properties as it was a fulfillment of very different daydreams.

As the deal was packaged in the following weeks, Donald would pay $280 million to buy the Taj. Merv would assume Resorts' $600 million in existing debt, minus $20 million in liabilities that Donald took on. Merv would get the Resorts' casino, the eminently salable Paradise Island, and all of the vacant and largely unsalable land in Atlantic City that empire builder Crosby had assembled, Donald would get the Steel Pier behind the Taj and the three helicopters. Donald would be repaid precisely what his "B" shares had cost him and would also get a bonus: Merv agreed to pay him $63 million to cancel the infamous service agreement.

Both sides took turns heralding the deal as a win. First, Merv spent the months between the May contract and the November closing trying to finance it, using Drexel to sell the bonds.* All the press attention during that period about the dealmaker from *Wheel of Fortune* was designed to mollify a wary bond market. While Merv was winning the early reviews, Donald quietly garnered the one that counted the most to him. The Delaware judge who approved the deal in August surveyed the entire history of Donald's foray at Resorts and concluded: "It is obvious that Donald Trump has taken good care of himself with little apparent concern for the hapless small shareholder who mistakenly viewed him as a Messiah." To Donald, that judicial assessment of who won and who lost was about as favorable a notice as a tycoon stock player could get.

Donald fought back during the Merv media celebration as best he could, countering with leaked hints that Merv had worn makeup at the negotiating session with him, suggesting that the grinning showman was all airhead Hollywood. But tooting his own horn too loudly might have drowned out Griffin's bond sale crooning, so Trump had to bide his time. He began making his case to one savvy business writer from *Barron's* on the understanding that no story would appear until the deal was concluded. When it did finally close, Donald was quickly able to turn the press around, using the fine print of the deal to lay claim to a triumph. It wasn't difficult—the $63 million bonus was a persuasive argument on his behalf, and the suddenly revealed deterioration of the old Resorts casino was a debit on the balance sheet of the unsuspecting Merv, who now had to pay for an expensive face-lift.

Donald had also slipped a costly little item into the agreement, unnoticed by Griffin until it was too late. The company had awarded Jack Davis a lifetime pension of $600,000 annually, which he would be eligible for in fourteen months, when the three-year, million-dollar-a-year contract he'd won back in 1987 expired. Whenever the sixty-three-year-old Davis died, Caroline would become eligible for the same annual payments until she died. A conservative estimate—not taking into account the life expectancy of these two health fanatics—put the price tag at $20 million. When Merv discovered the provision and asked Donald to absorb part of it, Donald refused. Merv eventually fired Davis and contested

---

* Drexel picked up the Griffin offering, once again collecting millions in fees from a Trump opponent while informally advising Trump each step of the way through the war.

the pension, and while Davis and Griffin traded legal papers, Donald made Davis president of the Taj and Caroline its six-figure special events consultant.

Trump waved the pension in the face of some journalists as another example of how he'd prevailed over the hapless Griffin. He even wrote a letter to *People,* which had profiled Griffin, charging that its statement that Griffin had become a billionaire by virtue of the Resorts deal was "a total joke." The magazine, said Trump, had "failed to deduct the approximately $1 billion in debt" Merv incurred, meaning that Griffin "won't even be a millionaire." While "everyone tries to beat Donald Trump," he wrote of himself, "not too many have succeeded."

Even though Donald had waited until the settlement was signed for this show of chest pounding, it had a legal downside. He was making himself vulnerable to bondholder suits contending that his deal with Merv was a "fraudulent conveyance," meaning that he had deceptively induced Merv into a deal that gave him the Taj at a price that was half of what Resorts had already put into it, plus getting the inexplicable $63 million bonus. It didn't help that a former Trump executive, who'd gone to work for Merv, claimed that Donald had tricked Griffin into believing that the old Resorts casino was in better shape than it was by having painters and carpenters refurbish a small section of the hotel where he was taken on a very guided tour. As feverish as the publicity contest between the two got, though, the fact was that there wasn't enough value in Resorts to split two ways, especially at these prices.

Griffin took on $935 million in new and old Resorts debt, and Donald, despite all his CCC boasting about banks waiting in line with prime-rate money, went immediately to market with $675 million in 14 percent bonds. For good measure, he tacked on another $125 million in bank loans for the Taj and even borrowed $50 million against the $23 million fleet of helicopters he'd redubbed Trump Air. The combined nearly $1.8 billion in Griffin and Trump leverage would have been enough to choke a solid company with all its assets grinding out revenue. Fragmented, half-built, or fading, the assets once amassed by Jim Crosby were simply no match for it.

Donald's new mountain of debt was the crippling culmination of all his Resorts machinations. The man who'd cajoled the estate, the family, the independent directors, the probate court, the DGE, and the CCC into believing that only his money, and his connections to money, could save the company was, in the end, putting together a deal that did not require any Trump investment. He had claimed at February's CCC hearing that financial institutions would only provide funding for the Taj if he owned it. He had observed that even for him to get the financing, he would have to have a sufficient level of equity in the company to convince the lenders that he was serious. What he did not mention was that he intended to borrow that equity as well.

The first thing Donald did with his gigantic bond issue—$200 million more than his prediction of $475 million a few months earlier—was to pay back what he'd borrowed from the banks, only six days earlier, to acquire the Taj. Donald had actually put $11 million of his own money into the Taj purchase on top of the bank loans. So he used bond money to repay himself as well, just to make certain his own funds weren't at risk for any longer than a week.

His bond demands were so expansive that Drexel and Bear Stearns, both of which had been competing for Donald's attention from the beginning of the Resorts play, were shunted aside for Merrill Lynch—the only company willing to market the fortune he demanded, at least according to Drexel's Daniel Lee.

Donald also talked Merrill into non-recourse construction bonds, the first time high-yield paper was ever used to finance such a deal. The bonds meant, in effect, that Donald wasn't guaranteeing anything other than finishing the building. Their terms gave him a degree of personal protection that would allow him to walk away from the casino once it opened. No loophole, however, could insulate him from the damage such a stroll would do to his reputation.

One reason Donald wanted so much more in bond financing than his own earlier estimates was that his redesign of the Taj called for a level of opulent expenditure far beyond that of the original Resorts plan, requiring the budgeting of at least $70 million to complete sections of the palace that Resorts had been prepared to warehouse. He was building superluxury suites on the top of the completed tower, adding 20,000 square feel to the casino, planning nine more, mostly deluxe, restaurants, rebuilding the Steel Pier, and expanding the garage with thousands of more spaces.

When cautionary voices suggested that some of these extras could wait until the casino was open and earning revenue, he ignored them, arguing that the casino had to be complete when opened for maximum impact on the market, though in the end it debuted with an unfinished theater, swimming pool, and a host of other advertised extravagances. When other experts warned him that he was tilting too much toward the big-time table players—while the profit margin would ultimately have to be made on the slots—he boasted that the high rollers would come to him. Instead of providing fast-food access to slot players, he went gourmet and showcased Alexander the Great, a 4,500-square-foot suite at the top of the forty-two-story tower awaiting any gamblers willing to pay $10,000 a night. He was also indulging his taste for gaudy elegance, hiking the crystal chandelier cost to $17 million, working a few more quarries of Italian marble into the flooring and walls, spending $4 million on costumes for his Indian-Persian-garbed cocktail waitresses, and adding nine white elephants made of glass-reinforced concrete sprinkled with more sparkling marble. Not only were the bond funds paying for all this excess, Donald was scheduled to take a $10 million construction fee for himself out of the bond cache.

James Grant, who publishes his own frequently prophetic investment newsletter, sounded the earliest of the alarms about these shaky bonds. "The security of the third bond payment," he wrote while Donald was still busily building the Taj, "was in doubt the day the bonds were issued." The funds for the first two payments, of course, were covered by the bond issue itself. The third was the first to depend, in part, on casino revenue.

To call Donald's financing scheme for the project a house of cards was to give it a structure it lacked. Beyond the bonds, he had borrowed $75 million from a New Jersey bank and invested it as his only equity in the project. He had even taken out of the Taj pot the $63 million bonus he had collected from Griffin. His principal collateral for the equity loan was the future payments he might receive on another management agreement—this one just drawn up between the Trump Taj entity and another Trump subsidiary that would operate it when it opened. He was using a decade of potential earnings as the casino's operator to borrow the equity to convince the bond market that he had some stake in the casino.

Despite Donald's attempts to minimize his exposure, he was still left with one unavoidable obligation. When he finished construction six weeks late and with what he claimed in one SEC filing was a $65 million overrun, he faced the prospect, at last, of dipping into his own funds to cover the runaway costs. Taj contractors were already forming a coalition to collect $72 million in unpaid bills. Indeed, when Donald entered into tough negotiations with Taj bondholders months after the casino opened, he put the overruns at $160 million, and that figure took into account his agreement to defer his $10 million construction fee. Although he had a $25 million credit line from a bank ready to cover some of the overrun, Donald would at last have to ante up his own money. It couldn't have come at a worse time—in the spring of 1990—when Trump was virtually out of chips.

The Resorts gambit had, in fact, been one of the strangest sort of high-stakes poker matches from the beginning. Conqueror Donald had looked as if he were winning every hand, with the other players cashing in and getting out, yet, when the game finally ended, it was he who wound up without any cards. When the Taj opened in April to crowds as large as the casino's debt service shortfalls, it became clear that as luring as it was, the Taj could simply not pay for itself. Donald's mistake was the decision to join the Resorts hunt in the first place, compounded by the miscalculations each time he had an opportunity to get out with a profit and didn't.

His two-casino empire had been perilous enough. The only other two-casino owner in town, Bally's, was cannibalizing itself by the time Donald bought the Taj. But Donald had to have three; he had to have the biggest and the grandest. One triumphant tactical stroke after another—from Davis to Brandstetter to Merv—had cumulatively come to pose a fearful threat to his ability to ever do a major deal of any sort again.

14

DEMISE

The rest, like a pack of genial but hungry wolves, sat and surveyed this apparently whole but now condemned scapegoat. Cowperwood, who was keenly alive to the spirit of the company, looked blandly and fearlessly around. "I can meet my loans," he replied easily. . . . "If you open the day by calling a single one of my loans before I am ready to pay it, I'll gut every bank from here to the river. You'll have panic, all the panic you want."

And this giant himself, rushing on to new struggles and new difficulties in an older land, forever suffering the goad of a restless heart—for him was no ultimate peace, no real understanding, but only hunger and thirst and wonder. . . . Who plans the steps that lead lives on to splendid glories, or twist them into gnarled sacrifices, or make of them dark, disdainful, contentious tragedies? The soul within? And whence comes it? Of God?

—*Theodore Dreiser,* THE TITAN

IN THE FINAL two years of Donald's decade, he went on a buying binge. It was as if he looked ahead on a calendar and decided that January 1, 1990, was the deadline: Anything he hadn't bought by then could never be his.

In early 1988, he negotiated the purchase of the Plaza Hotel, the eighty-one-year-old French Renaissance castle and an indisputable trophy that stands at the southeast corner of Central Park. It cost his bank $409 million, and even Donald has since conceded that he overpaid—at a half million a room, it was the most expensive hotel purchase in history. But Citibank gave him $16 million more than the purchase price, enough to pay the $4 million in closing costs and to finance part of the costly renovations begun immediately by the new Plaza president, Ivana. Again, the purchase had taken on the tone of a hunt—he'd had to cajole the Basses, the Texas investors who'd just bought the hotel, to sell it to him by warning how impossible his friend Vito Pitta's hotel workers union would be. He'd also outmaneuvered a competing group that was willing to pay a similar price but wanted to make the purchase contingent on conditions related to the redevelopment of the hotel as a partial co-op or condominium building. Donald agreed to take it "as is."

By now, he was personally guaranteeing the $125 million equity portion of his Plaza loans and others, his inherited aversion to guarantees having vanished like so many other nostalgic vestiges. So what if the purchase price was twenty-five times the 1988 cash flow? He could always sell it for even more. So what if the debt service due in his first full year of operation in 1989 would be $45 million, almost three times the cash flow of 1988? He was looking for "psychic return." So what if 4,000 new hotel rooms, many targeted at the Plaza's wealthy clientele, were opening just as Donald bought it? No other owner had his allure.

He did make a virtually simultaneous sale that was the biggest payday of his life: peddling the St. Moritz Hotel, just down the street from the Plaza, for $100 million more than he'd paid for it. The buyer, Australian magnate Alan Bond, agreed to lavishly overpay after a single dinner with the engaging Donald, apparently convinced he was getting the land as well when all Donald had to sell was the hotel's leasehold. Bond's casual approach may have been attributable to the fact that it was his public company, not Bond personally, that was making the purchase, and the company would soon be a financial wreck. In any event, much of Donald's gains on the sale were consumed by the demanding renovation project at the Plaza, as well as by his other great new cash drain, the Eastern Shuttle.

His on-again, off-again takeover of the $365 million shuttle was approved by Eastern's bankruptcy judge in May of 1989, but Donald had actually signed his first shuttle purchase agreement in October of 1988, just as he was closing the Taj deal with Griffin. In the intervening months, Donald had every reason to back away from the deal, and in fact he voided the contract once, pointing to the drastic drop in Eastern's share of the shuttle market from 56 percent to 17 percent after a March strike. Pan Am, which had purchased its own shuttle just three years earlier for a mere $76 million, was killing Eastern's business. Such numbers might have given pause to a lesser man, especially since taking over an airline was a foray into a treacherous and complicated new business, far from the family's traditional real estate base. But a determined Donald closed the shuttle transaction in June, agreeing to pay the same amount as his original contract required.

Citibank loaned him $380 million for the shuttle: $245 million against the aging assets of the airline, which included twenty-one over-the-hill Boeing 727s valued at a mere $55 million, and $135 million of Trump equity, backed only by his personal guarantee. Eastern chief Frank Lorenzo had managed to woo Donald back to the bargaining table, despite the shuttle's plummeting profits, with the promise of four more creaking aircraft than the seventeen initially offered. Barely a year later, Trump was trying to sell at least seven of the planes, claiming it had always been the company's intention to try to rid itself of the admittedly antiquated fleet. During Donald's crowded press conference at the Plaza announcing the shuttle acquisition, longtime Trump lawyer Jerry Schrager was asked how the deal was being financed, and he said no financing was needed. "We have the funds available," he said. "We'll use our own money."

Schrager was inadvertently prophetic because even Citibank's generous financing was quickly exhausted. The big cause of the cost crunch was the semi-obsolescence of the fleet, not exactly a surprise since Donald himself had predicted in bankruptcy court prior to the purchase that he would have to lay out $50 million to upgrade it. Capital and operating costs made the Trump Shuttle an instant money guzzler, eating up $85 million in the first year and making it one of Donald's most widely questioned judgments.

The simultaneous Taj and shuttle decisions—Donald closed with Merv just days after signing the initial shuttle purchase agreement—were even more curious when measured against two other choices Donald made in the fall of 1988. First, he rejected William Zeckendorf's $550 million bid for the West Side yards, as well as a determined Japanese offer of $600 million. Second, he decided to go forward with the construction of a 55-story, 283-unit condo, Trump Palace, on Third Avenue and 69th Street, the former Foundling Hospital site that he'd bought in 1985 from the Sisters of Charity. He rejected a Japanese offer to buy him out of the Palace site for the $60 million he'd spent on it, which would have left him with a tidy profit since the hospital paid him rent to stay there for three years after the purchase. He also turned down a Japanese bidder who wanted to invest $80 million in the project, insisting, against the counsel of several advisers, on plunging ahead without partners. He obtained a building permit in January and $220 million in Citibank loans in February. Seventy-seven new buildings had been built on the East Side between 1977 and 1988, and the market was reaching the reluctant conclusion that the splurge was over. Manhattan real estate was supposed to be what Donald knew best, yet here he was, breaking ground at a moment when almost everyone else was pulling back.

Sales at the Palace's estimated $1,000-a-square-foot asking price did go reasonably well in 1989, with construction of the building under way, but they came to a precipitous halt as soon as Donald's and the economy's problems surfaced in 1990. By the end of the year, there were more purchasers defaulting on existing contracts than buyers signing new ones. With only a third of the apartments sold, the building began to look disconcertingly like a future ghost town of marble and onyx.

It was no coincidence that these misbegotten deals came one after another in what was now the Marla Maples phase of Donald's life. Not that he was using the former stewardess as an investment adviser. She was just another symptom of the recklessness and arrogance that had seized him. He had taken to unfurling a giant poster of her and showing it to businessmen. He had even run the risk in 1988 of storing her furniture and other personal items with the storage company Ivana and he used for the Trump Tower apartment during its second reconstruction. She was the heart of his double life, and he began slipping off to see her in the middle of his workday, even ducking key staff meetings.

But Marla was hardly his only secret. He'd begun seeing a diet doctor in the mid-eighties, and, at about that time, his staff started noticing a disturbing connection between his most frenetic days and his trips to the doctor. He urged others to use this doctor, including old friend Donald Manes, and the treatment was so successful that he found he could quickly rid himself of the pounds he put on during the late-night food binges he loved. While his lunches consisted of fruit cups and salads, he had a closet Twinkie habit, feasting on milkshakes, hamburgers, popcorn, and Cake Masters when he was alone, and on the phone during the wee hours of the morning. He hated fat—once barring one of his lawyers from making a public appearance at a New Jersey hearing because he was overweight—and was acutely aware of how it photographed on his own face, especially when the jowl on his right side puffed up into a sack.

Then there was his sexual fantasy life. He liked to talk about it so much more than he actually did anything about it. He gathered magazines featuring covers or photo layouts of the Czech model Paulina Porizkova and showed them to friends, talking about her as if he knew her. "I walk down and get hit on by everybody in the city," Donald told a reporter in an off-the-record interview. "You turn down a thousand. That's not bad. And you take one out of a thousand a few times a year, you know you're pretty good." He told stories of socialites accosting him on the dance floor, as well as when the lights were dimmed during speeches at a sit-down dinner.

He even tried to get *Playboy* to do a spread called "The Girls of Trump," wooing his most shapely staffers, including a former beauty queen secretary, into posing for the magazine with a sliding scale of offers on everything from full nude to breast to "wet-lip" shots. It was all part of the rakish ethos of phony glamour that he consciously fostered, even to the extent of concealing from public view a very efficient secretary with a pimplish facial condition. This unappeasable appetite led him, as his own notoriety soared, into celebrity worship, and he became a starstruck groupie, attaching himself to Don Johnson, Michael Jackson, and just about anyone else who would allow him to climb into photographs with them. He was both projecting a larger-than-life image and reveling in it, a dangerous psychic combination.

Also fascinated by guns and male muscle, he got a .38-caliber pistol in the mid-eighties, added a second a few years later, and kept both in his Trump Tower desk drawer, even though he was constantly accompanied by armed bodyguards. His private army, investigated in New Jersey for its accumulation of large amounts of weapons (reportedly even automatic weapons), became so vast and so out of step with the security associated with any other similar magnate that it was seen, even by his close associates, as symbolizing his own destabilizing self-absorption and power fantasies.

This newly emerging personality—fed by the cover stories in *Time* and elsewhere, the best-selling success of his first book, the fawning television interviews—was so explosively erratic that he frightened and concerned those around him who cared. His legendary office rages over the pettiest of problems, his penchant for internalizing his own media hype, his radical mood swings and transparent optimism were convincing those around him that he had to be protected from himself. They increasingly saw him as if he were on a self-destructive, earthbound plunge from the magical heights they'd helped him achieve but that so long as he was off the ground at all he would think he was still flying, waiting for the last possible second to pull the parachute cord.

It was not just the lifestyle that planted these fears. It was his sense of invulnerability, his conviction that by merely adding his name to a property, it automatically gained quantum leaps in value. A lawsuit he filed in 1988 had successfully barred a group of real estate developers named Trump from using their own name, as they had been doing for years. With this victory, Donald came to believe that he had effectively patented his business identity. It was as if he had won a court affirmation of his own ego. Cash flow figures didn't matter, nor did any ordinary business projections. His presence in a deal, he was convinced, was enough to make it work.

The spending spree was not limited to new properties like the Plaza nor was the Taj his only new Atlantic City adventure. As early as 1987, he spent roughly $65 million on luxury suites and a garage at Trump Plaza, the smartest of his casino improvements. But those renovations convinced Ivana, the intensely competitive Queen of his Castle, that she had to have an even grander package of improvements for her casino.

Donald fed this competition, provoking public shouting matches by taunting her with the monthly evidence of the Plaza's booming business. He also used her as a threat to Steve Hyde and the top Plaza staff, planting the notion that he might make her his Atlantic City chieftain, responsible for both casinos. One effect of this threat was to turn Hyde and his executives into eager accomplices in the Marla charade. As long as the Plaza remained Marla and Donald's refuge, he was unlikely to put his wife in charge of it. Unaware of this secret obstacle to her advancement, all Ivana could do was fight for expensive new facilities that she believed would position her Castle to match the Plaza in its bid to become the top of the town's earners. While many who worked with Ivana credited her with a hands-on operational presence and 12-hour-a-day dedication, her rapport and results turned out to be mixed at best. Worse still, her insistence on lavish capital expenditures consumed whatever profits she was generating, and more.

Starting in late 1987, Donald began spending what turned out to be $78 million on an 18,000-square-foot ballroom for the Castle and the new fourteen-story Crystal Tower of luxury suites. The Trumps rejected their construction staff's advice that they build hundreds of regular rooms in the new tower, which would have served a double purpose: The rooms were more marketable than suites and would have enabled the Castle to make use of 10,000 square feet of already built but closed-off casino space. (CCC regulations limit the size of a casino by the number of hotel rooms.) The staff also argued that high rollers would not be enticed by the new luxury tower since the view from its suites would be blocked by the existing hotel tower. Even though Donald was simultaneously planning to add obscenely expensive supersuites to his initial Taj construction plan and had just converted forty-eight Plaza rooms into suites, he went ahead with the Castle plan as well, as if he believed there was an endless supply of attractable high-end gamblers out there, just waiting for the right marble bathroom.

The excesses of the city's first all-luxury tower—inlaid flooring of twenty-three European, Brazilian, and Turkish marbles; hand-milled oak and mahogany;

etched-glass fixtures; and two-Jacuzzi, six-bath supersuites—pushed Ivana's pet project $31 million beyond its original budget and delayed it so long that she had departed before she could enjoy them. Donald abruptly removed her from the Castle in the spring of 1988, a few months after construction started and well before the ballroom was completed that December or the tower was finished in 1990. With Ivana gone, he was able to install Marla for long weekends in various Castle suites, including one that became her favorite, located on the sixth floor of Ivana's Crystal Tower and featuring a pink marble hot tub. When the final bill on the tower came in, he openly blamed the damaging decision on Ivana, telling one Castle executive, "I can't believe she's so fucking stupid." Ironically, he never criticized Bucky Howard, who as Castle vice president had urged Ivana to build the suites. Howard, of course, was later named president of the Taj.

As soon as the Castle construction was under way, the Plaza responded with another improvement plan, drawing $50 million from the casino's then abundant cash flow, mostly for new fixtures and furniture. It was as if there were no end to the money.

Donald had his own pet project at the Castle: the marina. Originally budgeted as an $11 million improvement of a state-owned marina leased to Trump for twenty-five years, it ultimately cost three times that amount and took until mid-1990 to finish. Most of the financing for the $110 million marina, ballroom, and tower improvements came from $65 million in bank debt added to the Castle's already awesome load. The rest was drawn from the casino's revenue stream, which peaked in 1987 at $40 million. With the principal payments delayed for years, the Castle bond covenants had been written so loosely that Donald was able to raid the hotel's temporary profits, spending $55 million of the casino's 1987–89 revenues on the improvements. He did so knowing full well that huge increases in the Castle's bond payments were soon approaching and that he had neither predictable income, nor a cash hoard, sufficient to meet the bond bulge. The depletion of the Castle's cash reserve gave it a $5 million deficit as early as 1988, a depredation from which the hotel would not recover.

The marina project rested on Donald's fantasy that affluent gamblers would come in by water, and since he imagined that more and more would be lured in if only they had a place to dock their boats, he kept adding slips to the piers until they reached out to the sea like barriers. Of course, his own boat would dock there, too, and just the vision of his *Princess* shimmering in the sunlight off his marina would be enough, he was sure, to attract high-rolling yachtsmen to his baccarat table. The 284-foot *Princess*—equipped with its own laser-lit disco and thirteen-nozzle shower carved in solid onyx—cost $29 million to buy and an immediate $8.5 million to refit, virtually all of it borrowed. Donald had swiped it, he gloated, from Adnan Khashoggi, the same indicted sheik whose living room his Trump Tower apartment had been carefully designed to outdo. The broker who sold it to Donald, Jonathan Beckett, had conceded it would take up to $75 million to put it in top shape, and while Donald spent something less than that, the refurbishing and operating costs of the boat over the couple of years Trump owned it ran into the tens of millions.

The channel to the Castle was dredged to accommodate the yacht—another multimillion-dollar expense. The theory was that big losers at the tables could be entertained on the *Princess*—mesmerized, no doubt, by its private deck for sunbathing and massage and steam rooms, as well as its master bedroom with a tortoiseshell ceiling, a bed big enough for six, and, as Donald liked to marvel, a secret passageway into an outside corridor should anyone drop in on an otherwise embarrassing playtime scene. Instead, the cost of running the *Princess* turned out to be a $6.4 million expense taken off the Castle's books in 1989. Its most frequent guest—throughout the summer of 1989—was Marla. Even before the dark days of 1990, the Castle was becoming the first Trump casualty—a once viable property literally devastated by visionary mismanagement.

Even with the Castle and Taj under construction in 1989, Donald went on a hunt for more Atlantic City properties. That spring, he spent another $115 million—all of it bank money—to purchase two more casino sites. Since he already owned the three casinos the law allowed, critics assumed he was buying them to cut off competition and, though Donald denied it for legal reasons, there was no other conceivable economic justification for such outlays.

He bought the Atlantis for $63 million to thwart a briefly interested Steve Wynn and any other possible casino operator. Built in 1981 by Playboy and Elsinore, a Hyatt-run public company with Nevada casinos, the Atlantis had failed from the onset—especially after Hugh Hefner was denied a license—partially because it featured a tiny triplex casino floor patterned after the three-story Playboy casino in London. Drexel's Dan Lee had been trying to sell it to Donald since the mid-eighties, even before it filed for Chapter XI in 1986, Donald liked its location—just the other side of the Convention Hall, a block south of the Plaza. He planned to rename it the Trump Regency, use its 500 rooms as an annex to the Plaza, and close down its casino.

Though other bidders offered more and would have maintained the Atlantis's casino jobs, friendly and still mob-run Local 54 supported the sale to Donald.

Trump financed the purchase with an $85 million credit line and used some of the excess to put another $12 million or so into improvements, claiming he was going to turn the Atlantis into a "five star" hotel. One of the new supersuites he planned there was the year-round residence for Marla, which was abandoned when the Trump executive designing it perished in the October 1989 helicopter crash. Its cash flow was so weak that Donald had to make nearly $6 million in advances to the hotel just to cover operating expenses, yet it lost over a million dollars in the first half of 1990. The only way Donald could arrest the cash hemorrhaging was to cover the Regency's losses with the Plaza's profits, and so he worked out a lease arrangement requiring the Plaza to pay the Regency a fee roughly equal to the Regency's debt service payments. For all other purposes, the hotel became a fiscal shell, with its revenues and expenses appearing on the Plaza's books.

Donald's other major acquisition was the hotly contested, 3:00 A.M. purchase of Penthouse's decade-old, half-built Boardwalk site, across the street from the Plaza on the northern side.

As part of the package, he also bought the Columbus Plaza parking garage site, owned by Penthouse and by the mob-tainted Kenny Shapiro. Trump paid $35 million for the rusting steel on the Penthouse site and $17 million for Columbus Plaza, still just a parking lot cluttered with boarded-up buildings. He borrowed $56 million—$4 million more than the price—and the properties were immediately appraised at $50 million, less than the debt load.

One of the factors that may have pushed Donald to make the Penthouse purchases was, strangely enough, Marla Maples. In the summer of 1988, a Penthouse lawyer met with Trump aide Al Glasgow and, according to Glasgow memos written at the time, "implied that *Penthouse* was prepared to do an exposé on Trump if he tried to stand in their way," making "certain innuendos" about Donald's personal life and warning: "Check out the 4th floor at the St. Moritz." This reference to the suite where Marla was stashed was followed by a question about how "Donald's wife would take all of this." *Penthouse* then leaked an item to a New York gossip page that it was about to publish a sexy Trump exposé, without revealing any specifics.

Penthouse apparently either wanted Donald to buy both sites or to stop his efforts to block an already arranged sale of the properties to the Pratts, the owners of the Sands, who planned to build a new casino on the Boardwalk site connected by monorail to a parking garage at Columbus Plaza. Donald had already managed to delay city approvals for this project for months, posing as an environmentalist and assailing the project's traffic impact. Then he shifted to making his own bid for the parking site alone, using old friend Kenny Shapiro as a champion of the bid within the Penthouse partnership. Without parking, the Sands project would never get a city permit. This pincer strategy was working quite nicely until the Marla threat was put on the table.

When Donald changed his position, and quickly bought both parcels, the Pratts launched an acrimonious and continuing lawsuit that has already cost Donald over $4 million in fees, all of which was added to the books of Trump Plaza, just as the Regency operational deficits had been. The raiding of the Plaza coffers for these two dead-beat properties clearly had the effect of damaging the one dependable revenue stream Donald had in New Jersey.

Despite a crescendo of complaints about Donald's anticompetitive conduct, DGE and CCC assented to the Penthouse purchase. The fundamental problem was that the Taj—combined with the Atlantis and Penthouse acquisitions—gave Donald 40 percent of the city's hotel rooms, as well as absolute control over the central Boardwalk stretch. In the midst of these deals, Trump also took a run at Caesars stock, defying the earlier public warnings of the CCC after the Bally's and Holiday debacles. Even chairman Walter Read's announcement in 1987 that he would not vote again to license anyone who launched apparent greenmail strikes against Atlantic City competitors had not stopped Trump.

The Caesars episode finally led the DGE to urge tough sanctions against Trump, but Read and his colleagues once again settled for a warning. He had just grown too large for regulation; Atlantic City belonged to Donald. The state regulators dispatched to safeguard the city could no longer protect it without protecting him.

More than all the other pieces of his Atlantic City empire, however, the acquisition that ultimately made it a company town, owned by Trump, was the Taj, so immense an attraction it would affect everything else in Atlantic City. All the defensive maneuvers that Donald had attempted to insulate the Plaza from nearby competitors looked twice as foolish when its profits dropped 33 percent in the first quarter after the Taj opened, badly damaged by the crowds moving down the Boardwalk to the new casino. The Castle also lost $8 million in the same quarter, three times its losses for the same quarter in 1989. These early returns became a yearlong trend, with Donald's casinos hurt more by the Taj than virtually any others. Ironically, the biggest beneficiary of the Taj was Merv Griffin's Resorts next door, feasting on Taj overflow, reinvigorated by Merv's showmanship and stabilized by a bankruptcy settlement with the bondholders.

As flooded with gamblers as it was, the Taj defaulted on its bond payments almost instantly, forcing Donald into tempestuous negotiations with angry bondholders. And the Taj debt load was only a fraction of the $2.1 billion in loans he'd taken on in the two years that formed his second season of deals. The cumulative demands of the Taj, Plaza Hotel, Trump Shuttle, *Princess*, Crystal Tower, Palace, Regency, and Penthouse loans were assuming *Little Shop of Horrors* "Feed me, feed me" proportions. When combined with the debt service on these other simultaneous projects, building the world's largest casino had left Donald with a top ranking he'd never consciously sought—one of the world's biggest tabs.

The eagerness of his bankers and investment brokers had, of course, helped make him a deal addict. When he did this string of late-eighties deals, he was riding his celebrity high, astonished that he suddenly seemed to have the same mesmerizing impact in a Citibank boardroom that he'd once had on the *Donahue* show. Debt had become his drug, and the loans routinely grew larger than the price of the purchases, leaving an excess for his organizational needs. Once he discovered he could take overdoses like the Taj fix, he lost all remaining fear of the fast lane.

The major New York banks were syndicating his loans with Japanese, German, French, Canadian, and British banks, all of which were willing to pay stupendous fees to the American banks to buy pieces of his project mortgages. The Japanese banks, in particular, were willing to put down what were effectively entry fees to break into the American real estate market, and few loans sold better on the Japanese market that a piece of a Trump deal. The ease with which New York's major banks could syndicate Trump loans forced them to "adjust their own risk/reward ratios," a former top Citibank officer involved with the Trump loans later conceded in an interview. According to this onetime generous Trump lender, the combination of the immediate gains from the syndication fees and the certainty of being able to dramatically reduce Citibank's exposure overnight by dumping the bulk of the financing on eager foreign banks made Citi quite willing to take on gigantic Trump loans it might otherwise have shunted. The Citibank officer estimated that the bank, for example, had as little as $25 million of its own money in Trump Palace's $220 million mortgage, and only $100 million in the Plaza's $425 million loan.

The paltry risk seemed easy to justify, especially since the foreign banks had no recourse against Citi if the loans went sour. So Citi, and other major banks, had little reason to press the hard questions, to measure the acquisition against cash flow, to determine if there was any room in these top-of-the-market deals for a downturn. Just as Donald was doing deals with other people's money, the banks who were lending it to him were, ironically, also lending him other people's money. The lion's share of the risk wound up so far away from the immediate parties that had actually cut the deals, and was so widely redistributed in finite pieces, that no one had to pause in the midst of this feeding frenzy and diligently apply ordinary banking judgment to a Trump investment.

The competition to get Trump's business among the major, syndicating banks became so intense that they began granting him two loans on almost every project, with the second fully covering his own equity contribution. All he had to do to get the equity loans was personally guarantee them, and not one bank seemed to have a real sense of the mountain of guarantees he was piling up. Even in late 1989 Bankers Trust was willing to loan him $100 million on his signature alone, with no asset or acquisition involved. No one sorted out the crisscrossed trail of debt. No one demanded statements that went beyond Donald's unaudited asset-based financials.

The presumption was that cash flow didn't matter, since Donald could presumably always sell a trophy for more than any outlandish sum he'd paid for it. His St. Moritz sale proved what Donald and the bankers liked to call "the greater fool theory" of these overpriced acquisitions. The other rationale, enticing Citibank and others who did no casino financing and knew nothing about the industry, was that if the shuttle or Plaza couldn't pay its debt load, Trump had a bottomless pit of gaming revenues to dip into and cover the shortfall. And if the major banks backing his nongaming deals had any doubt about that, he'd put monthly statements from his casinos in front of them, and they'd be dazzled by the liquidity. Little did they know, as the Citibank officer later admitted, that the bond payments were slated to come in future balloon proportions that would consume cash flow, or that the casino market would soon be saturated by Donald's overexpansion (particularly with the arrival of the Taj).

The fact was, however, that neither syndication demand, nor resale fever, nor gaming optimism could fully explain the Trump phenomenon at the major banks. In the end, even the buffaloed bankers had to agree, the power of his personality and notoriety was a magnet. Like virtually everyone else, the bankers were taking his credit rating from *Lifestyles of the Rich and Famous*. The hype proved as convincing a reference with staid bankers as it had with gullible bond buyers. "We just wanted to be associated" with his deals, said the Citibank executive, who'd basked in the media glory of the Plaza opening and partied on the *Princess*. Trump was a titan, a lord, accountable to no one.

The caution he'd inherited from Fred Trump had long since faded from memory. The pattern of one measured deal after another that had served him so well in the early years had been replaced with a helter-skelter hunger for sudden smash hits. Even Donald acknowledged the rapaciousness of his remarkable appetite. "I'd really like to buy everything," he boasted to Barbara Walters in December of 1987, at the start of his two-year spree, though conceding in the bitter aftermath that "to a certain extent I got caught up in the buying frenzy."

He tried to turn the shortness of his business attention span into a personal asset. "My attitude on deals is that you make one and get on to the next one," he said. "I've never met a successful person who wasn't neurotic. It's not a terrible thing. Controlled neuroses means having a tremendous energy level, an abundance of discontent that often isn't visible."

But this very gift, in the end, had undercut his capacity to do the job that had initially catapulted him to success: supervise a complex construction project. The catastrophe at the Taj was a symptom of Donald's sudden inability to focus—he'd visited the site rarely and lost contact with the detail work that was once his trademark. Perhaps he felt he'd moved beyond such drudgery—the Taj and the Palace were his only new construction starts in seven years. By and large, he'd transcended his Hyatt and Trump Tower days of creating value and repositioned himself as a player in the far less demanding league that merely traded in it.

Just as Fred Trump had graduated from builder to buyer in the 1960s, scooping up discounted FHA projects, Donald had made the same transition, only he was buying up airlines, department store chains like Alexander's, and majestic hotels. The Hyatt had taken him six tortuous years, while the campaign to acquire the Plaza Hotel was over in six quick weeks. Even Donald complained about how "easy" it had become. Bankers whose coolness to the Hyatt proposition a decade earlier had almost forced him to abandon it were now wooing him with the bribe of these above-cost loans. That's what it meant, Donald marveled, to be on top.

Being on top also meant he could take chances few dared to take, which prompted him, in the final days of the 1980s, to make one more big splash. Considering how cash poor he already was, his $7 billion offer in October of 1989 to buy AMR, the parent of American Airlines, was either his ultimate overreach or naked stock fraud. When U.S. Senator Lloyd Bentsen, concerned about an overleveraged purchase damaging the airline, objected to a Trump takeover, Donald wrote a letter pledging "to commit at least $1 billion of equity" to the deal. Although—as the world would learn in a matter of months—he was on the brink of a cash collapse, he was striking the pose of a man with a billion dollars available to him. His offer of $120 a share was so far above market value it was greeted as a joke, especially since Trump never indicated the source of the other $6 billion in financing. If his intent was to inflate the value of the stock and cash out quickly, the strategy was a failure: The stock plunged, and Donald took what *USA Today* called a $50 million loss.

But it was not just this stock run, which the SEC announced it was investigating, that raised fraud questions. In early 1990, the new Dinkins administration flatly described the multimillion-dollar shortfall in Hyatt payments uncovered by Koch's final audit as "fraud" in motions submitted to a state judge. At the same time, the Resorts bondholders set aside a $5 million fund to file a "fraudulent conveyance" lawsuit against Donald for stripping the public company of its Taj asset, and Donald and his insurance company quickly agreed to pay $12 million to settle the unfiled claim. Though Donald had publicly proclaimed he would never bow to these charges, his preemptive settlement effectively prevented whatever detailed allegations the bondholders were prepared to make from ever appearing in accessible court records.

In the fall of 1990 the seventy-eight owners of apartments in Donald's 283-unit Palace petitioned Robert Abrams, New York's attorney general, to negate their purchase contracts and force Trump to return their down payments. Lawyers for a bloc of buyers asked Abrams to "investigate potential fraud in the offering plan and false advertising in connection with procuring purchase agreements from the public." Their claim was based on the fact that Donald had sworn in a statement submitted to Abrams's real estate bureau that his "net worth" was "sufficient to meet all of the obligations" of a condominium sponsor, specifically including his responsibility to cover the maintenance and real estate tax costs for the over 200 unsold apartments. "It can hardly be clearer from the financial picture painted by his own accountants," the lawyers charged, referring to his bank deal submissions to Jersey's casino regulators, "that he is not in a position to meet these obligations."

At first Abrams blocked further apartment sales while he examined the allegations, but he wound up lifting his ban when Citibank stepped forward with another $13 million, a reserve that would cover the operating costs for the unsold units until 1994. Trump never formally responded to the fraud charges, or to a laundry list of disclosure omissions detailed in the complaint. The apparent incompatibility between the Palace submissions and his true financial condition, as revealed in the casino commission documents, passed unnoticed.

Abrams's office was also misled by the registrant information form filed by Trump with the Palace submission. When asked if he or his entities had ever been the subject of an injunction or a consent decree promising to desist from any act or practice, Donald answered "no." His answer was inconsistent with the fact that he had signed a consent decree in the race discrimination proceeding brought against him by the Justice Department in 1973 permanently enjoining him from engaging in housing discrimination. He even answered "no" to another query asking if he or his entities had ever been a party in any litigation or administrative proceeding in which a violation of "any securities laws" had been alleged. Trump's answer was belied, of course, by the FTC and SEC actions on his Bally's stock purchases (ending in a $750,000 fine). The Palace was hardly the first time he'd been required by the Attorney General to respond to these sort of questions and failed to answer accurately; he'd responded back in 1986 on a Trump Parc registration form that he and his entities had never been the subject of an injunction or any disciplinary action by any court or governmental department or agency. His denial was the same knee-jerk reaction he'd had since he sought his first casino license in 1980, when he had inaccurately omitted any reference to the discrimination decree in response to a specific question on a sworn submission. DGE investigators decided to give him the benefit of the doubt at that time because he volunteered information about the decree in a subsequent interview; but by the end of the decade Trump's evasive responses on these forms had become a decade-long routine.

And finally, the Palace raised a broader question about Donald's ethical conduct that was not put before Abrams: the misleading mortgage submissions to the bank, overstating the building's sales projections. Blanche Sprague, Trump's longtime condominium sales chief, wrote Trump a memo in the summer of 1990 detailing the history of Palace price lists. She claimed that the "original price list" of apartments she prepared for him in mid-1988 anticipated that the building "should realize a sell-out of $179.2 million." But this total fell far short of the $220 million mortgage Donald wanted to borrow from Citibank for the project, meaning a sold-out building would still not earn back the mortgage. "You told me to up the number to '$260 million plus,'" Sprague wrote, "even though I told you that it would be impossible to realize this number."

Sprague prepared a second price list, which still failed to reach Donald's magic number. Finally, in an August 18, 1988, letter to Trump's lawyer, she forwarded a third list, "showing a sell-out of $265,008,000 per Donald's instructions." She noted in her letter: "You are aware of my views on this subject so I will not rehash them." Donald got his $220 million mortgage.

Jack O'Donnell, the Trump Plaza president who quit in 1990 and wrote a book about his relationship with Donald, recounts a tale of fraudulent optimism strikingly similar to Sprague's. In meetings that started in November 1989 with

Donald, Robert, and other Trump executives, he projected an operating income for 1990 of $64 million, a decrease from 1989. Everyone became furious, and Donald cried: "The business can't be down. I expect $95, $100 million in operating income next year." When O'Donnell stressed how long he and his financial people had worked on these estimates, Donald was emphatic: "There is no way that is going to fly. You guys better get your fucking numbers squared away." O'Donnell replied that he didn't know "what the hell you want from me," and Donald answered: "I want you to go back and do your budget and get it up to where it should be."

To guarantee that O'Donnell got the message, Robert Trump visited him in Atlantic City with Donald's other top executive, Harvey Freeman, and told him they were considering taking all three casinos public. "You understand, Jack, that we can't have you telling us that the numbers aren't going to be as good as last year," Robert said. After suggesting a $95 million figure, Robert urged: "Make it happen. You can do it." O'Donnell brought the figures up to $92 million, and that inflated number became a critical element in the organization's comprehensive financial portfolio in a year when Donald was busily hunting loans everywhere and using his gaming projections to evade other cash flow questions. Donald's crisis in mid-1990 ended any plans to take the casinos public, but if the overstated income projection had intentionally been used to mislead potential public investors, it would have violated securities laws.

The Palace and Trump Plaza manipulations, however, were just the tip of the iceberg. When the bank crisis hit and Donald was forced to allow a financial services organization, Kenneth Leventhal & Company, into his books, its review uncovered "significant discrepancies" between the asset value data of Trump's long-term real estate attorneys at Dreyer & Traub and Donald's own financial statements. Leventhal reported that it was told by the Trump Organization that "certain of Trump's estimated values," drawn from his November 30, 1989, financial statement, "included premiums for various trophy characteristics" of the properties. Leventhal recalculated these values "excluding" the Donald-determined "premiums."

The 1989 statement, for example, doubled the value assigned to the Plaza in Donald's 1988 statement, bringing it to an unrealistic $850 million. Leventhal assessed the landmark hotel's true market value at $450 to $550 million. Donald's two casino properties, Trump Castle and Trump Plaza, were valued at $635 million and $650 million in the 1989 statement, up a combined $375 million since 1987. Leventhal put the Castle at $400 to $460 million and Trump Plaza at $485 million to $585 million—a minimum of $240 million less than Trump had. The 1989 statement valued the Taj at $1.1 billion, but Leventhal reduced it to $750 million.

Despite the deluge of negative publicity suggesting Donald's possible financial deceptions in 1990, he nonetheless remained remarkably immune to investigation. Donald's longtime ally Bob Abrams handled the Palace charges so gingerly he never really addressed them. Abrams was hardly the only law enforcement official Donald had attempted to co-opt.

When Robert Morgenthau, the Manhattan district attorney, had a tough reelection campaign in 1985, Trump's $5,000 contribution made him the DA's second biggest giver. Donald also readily lent himself to Morgenthau's favorite charity—the Police Athletic League—as both the honoree and chairman of its annual fund-raiser. He gave even larger contributions to Liz Holtzman when she was the Brooklyn district attorney, and when she did not seek reelection in 1989, he hosted a finance committee luncheon to pay off the campaign debts of her successor, Joe Hynes. (It apparently did not matter to Trump that Hynes had been a leading protagonist in the deathbed disbarment of Roy Cohn.)

Shortly before Andy Maloney was named U.S. attorney for the Eastern District of New York (covering Brooklyn, Queens, and Long Island) in 1986, Donald retained Maloney's small law firm to aid Harvey Myerson in the USFL case. He also hired Maloney's brother Richard, assigning him to a casino executive post, then to run Trump Plaza of the Palm Beaches, but never really finding a suitable niche for him in the organization. He even approached Rudy Giuliani's closest friend, attorney Peter Powers, and tried to retain him when Giuliani was the Manhattan U.S. Attorney.

If Donald saw all of this as some sort of insurance policy, he could not have been disappointed by the results. Not even the flashing lights of the 1990 collapse alerted anyone in law enforcement.

He had prided himself on never having met a public official, a banker, a lawyer, a reporter, or a prosecutor he couldn't seduce. Some he owned, and others he merely manipulated. As he saw it, it was not just that everyone had a price, it was that he knew what the price was. He believed he could look across a table and compute the price, then move on to another table and borrow the money to pay it. "Everybody tries to get some money" was his assessment in one unpublished interview of what motivates the people he dealt with. It was his one-sentence summary of human nature. Yet he believed that a lifetime of such seductions—from hiring the governor's son to a federal prosecutor's brother—hadn't cheapened him. Magically, at least by his own memoir accounts, he had managed to walk away from every dirty deal with clean hands. In his own head he believed in his moral purity, and the dances he did with prosecutors were, in his view, an attempt to protect himself from their abuses, not induce immunity for his own conduct.

Of course, one of the reasons no prosecutor responded to the open invitation to investigate Trump's suspect banking relationships, implicitly extended as part of the ordinary news coverage of his financial ruin, was because none of Trump's major banks was about to complain. If Donald's dealings with these banks broke any laws, he was certainly committing victimless crimes. The banks resembled accomplices more than victims, and their response when the crisis exploded was a measure of their guilt.

The transparently inflated asset evaluations floated in Donald's statements duped no one, and may have just added to the thrill of financing him. After all, when he wasn't getting a loan secured by an overvalued asset, banks were dumping money in his pockets without the security of any asset at all.

Donald's largest lender, Citibank, once sufficiently dazzled to loan him a billion of its own and other banks' dollars, cleaned out virtually its entire real estate department when Donald's hard times hit, though the reason was unclear. The department had, curiously enough, even handled Donald's shuttle loans (with some advice from the bank's airline analysts), suggesting that the real estate section was making loans it was ill equipped to assess, and might have done so on the basis of a relationship with Trump that had taken on the personal quality that had once characterized Connie Stephenson's approach at Chase. The bank assembled virtually an entirely new team to negotiate the 1990 restructuring agreement with Trump, and would have been as embarrassed by the trial record of any case against Trump as Donald himself.

In fact, a group of shareholders protested the Trump loans at Citibank's annual meeting, disturbed no doubt by the fact that the bank wound up, even with all its syndication of the Palace and Plaza loans, risking nearly $335 million of its own money on its four Trump transactions, most of it tied up in the less marketable shuttle and Alexander's stock loans. The nation's largest commercial bank, Citi was forced, in the middle of the Trump restructuring and the recession of 1990, to sell a Saudi a substantial stake in the company, making him the bank's top single investor. He bought his shares at a price half the size of the billion in bad loans that the bank had made to Donald.

From the outset of Trump's crisis, Citibank and the rest of the banks behaved as if they and Donald had at least one common concern: to keep a lid on the story of his demise. Bankers leaked to the *Wall Street Journal*'s Neil Barsky, but only for tactical advantage in the table games of June, when the restructuring was negotiated. When he subsequently pursued a fraud story, they were as tight-lipped as the target. When the House Banking Committee announced hearings into the Trump fiasco, the bankers and Donald were equally resolved not to co-operate with the probe, and it died.

Even when Donald broke the June agreement within weeks of its approval by casino regulators that August, the banks were stoic. Though they had suspended payment on a billion in loans, he immediately defaulted on others he'd agreed to pay, and the banks did not react. Citibank, for example, took no action when Donald defaulted on the one shuttle loan he'd promised in June to keep current. When Plaza revenues fell $20 million short of due interest payments in 1990, Citibank and its foreign bank partners went right on eating their losses there as well, kept at bay by the realization that any foreclosure would result in at least a $100 million debit, exactly the sort of write-off that the teetering bank would hate to see on its books. Donald's tenuous hold on the hotel was preserved, at least for the moment, by the depth of the problem the loan represented to Citi and its syndicators. Locked into a partnership it had pursued only two years earlier, Citibank could hardly turn on Trump.

The banks' tolerance of Donald's handling of his largest and most volatile contingent liability, Ivana, was even more understandable. No one in the alliance of banks that signed the June agreement objected when Donald unilaterally granted Ivana a $300,000-a-year contract in late 1990, even though the agreement limited new employment contracts to $200,000. No one objected because this generosity—which, not incidentally, shifted her off Donald's account and onto the Plaza's—may have helped produce the December divorce.

The banks were also silent in March of 1991, when Donald and Ivana reached a financial settlement and he gave her $10 million up front without the explicit approval required under the agreement. The banks no doubt were quite pleased with Donald's ability to force Ivana to take precisely what the last postnuptial provided.

He did it in his usual theatrical style—waving a check on the steps of the courthouse one day, claiming to a crowd of reporters that she had broken an agreement to be there when in fact he knew she wouldn't appear. With this attempt to portray her as the obstructionist recorded by the cameras, he then entered a long night of private bargaining with her and her lawyers, battling for every petty advantage. They argued over who would get a 1987 Mercedes that he'd repossessed since the split-up and was trying to hold on to even though he'd given it to her as a present and its license plate read IVANA. When a question was raised about Ivana's retention of eight-year-old Ivanka's bedroom set, a Trump attorney suggested that she had the best lobbyist in the world—"just put her on the phone to her father." There were even harsh words about who would get little Eric's computer.

Ivana's only real gain in the negotiations was that she moved up the date she could collect a second payment—for $4 million—from Donald. A housing allowance, this payment was pegged to the date she would vacate the Trump Tower triplex, and, as a result of the negotiations, she was now eligible for it within a year of the settlement, a gain of a year over the postnuptial agreement. A satisfied Donald boasted: "I don't think you have any other real estate developer in the country that can write a $10-million check today in terms of cash." Since he was simultaneously traveling empty-handed to every bank boardroom in town, the check was a surprising revelation of sudden, and very temporary, liquidity. It was, literally, almost the last of his available money.

The banks were also unaroused when Donald surreptitiously tapped into a source of funds they would have loved to have attached but could not—Fred Trump's fortune. In December, Donald stunned bondholders and bankers by finding $18 million and making a bond payment to avert bankruptcy at the Castle. Reporters had discovered prior to the surprise payment that Donald was busily hunting a bank loan to fund the $3 to $4 million of the payment that could not be covered out of Castle cash reserves. But a few days later Donald claimed with a Cheshire cat grin, when he proudly explained that he'd met the deadline because he "had great faith in the future of Atlantic City," that the entire amount did come from the casino's own coffers. Neil Barsky solved the riddle a few weeks later, revealing that a lawyer had mysteriously appeared at a Castle window the day before the payment was due and purchased over $3.3 million in $5,000 chips, almost precisely the bond payment shortfall. The lawyer, who did not gamble with the chips and left with them under police escort, was sent by that eighty-five-year-old with the dyed red hair sitting in a tiny office on Avenue Z in Brooklyn.

Fred Trump, who wired another $150,000 to the casino the day of the payment, had apparently raised this money by auctioning off some of his Brooklyn and Queens co-op apartments. He had, however, to figure out a way to get these funds to Donald for the bond payment without their becoming part of the Trump Organization pool, which was all tied up by bank-imposed guidelines. He also wanted to be able to get the loan back without having to compete with other creditors. The brilliant—but illegal—tactic positioned him to reclaim the funds by simply reappearing at the casino window with his bag of chips.*

The banks didn't sue over these circumventions and outright violations of the June agreement, but instead entered patiently into a second set of far-reaching talks. Bankers Trust extracted Donald's interest in the Hyatt; Citibank claimed the shuttle and tried to become an equity partner of the anticipated new operator, Northwest Airlines; Boston Safe Deposit & Trust got a boat that had never hosted anything as tame as a tea party; and Marine Midland got the West Palm Beach condominium hulk. Trump Air was grounded, and the copters sold off. Citibank also wound up with the 27 percent share of Alexander's that Donald had bought with $70 million of the bank's and Bear Stearns' money, but the stock was now only valued at $35 million. Manufacturers Hanover was awarded the Regency in Atlantic City, a prize that the bank wanted only if a buyer emerged. Otherwise it agreed to drastically reduce the annual payments from $7 million to $1 million. Manufacturers Hanover was also slated to receive Donald's remaining interests in his New York co-op, Trump Plaza, Trump Parc, and 100 Central Park South, which was generating a million dollars a year in revenue.

Still unoccupied long after its scheduled opening, Trump Palace effectively became the property of Citibank, with all rental income going straight to the bank and an understanding that Trump would surrender title to the bank when the loan matured and that he would be released from his personal guarantee in the unlikely event that all the apartments were ever sold. Donald talked openly about removing his name from the property, and bank officials took to referring to it simply as "The Palace."

Donald was also determined to pawn off on Midlantic the Penthouse and Columbus Plaza sites, which were costing him $4.9 million a year and would be unlikely to generate any revenue in the foreseeable future. The Penthouse costs

---

* This incident gave the regulators in New Jersey one more opportunity to display their flabby resolve when faced with Trump misconduct. The CCC fined the Castle $65,000 for this devious form of casino finance by an unlicensed source of funding, but neither it nor DGE charged Fred with anything, and both refused to explore Donald's role in the caper. Saying he was "more disappointed" with DGE's handling of this probe than any other in his years on the CCC, one commissioner, David Waters, condemned the agency's "failure to carry out its responsibilities" and "reluctance" to push the investigation "higher into the corporate hierarchy." Refusing to make public its report, DGE then recommended the licensing of Fred Trump.

were an even greater cash drain on him than the West Side yards and were second only to the Plaza as a yearly debit on his books.

Scratching for dollars in every vacant acre he owned, he also submitted a subdivision plan in Palm Beach designed to carve up the land around Mar-A-Lago for sale or development to satisfy the Boston Safe loan. When the town balked at approving the sale, news stories reported that he was considering selling it to the Moonies, a hoax denied by the sect and resented in Palm Beach. He planned to keep the estate itself, where Ivana retreated with a contingent of her lady friends the weekend after the divorce settlement. In addition to ceding the forty-six-room Greenwich home and a Trump Plaza apartment to Ivana, the settlement guaranteed her an annual monthly vacation in her cherished Florida haunts. She put the Greenwich house up for sale at an $18 million price and had long been depositing the $4,000-a-month she earned on the Plaza apartment in a trust fund for her and the kids.

In his new rash of bank deals, Donald was systematically shedding himself of every bad idea he'd ever had (plus a few of the early good ones), and the banks were canceling his binding guarantees in exchange. But even after the banks had agreed to release him from $535 million in guaranteed principal and interest, he was still obligated to repay the $147 million in debts that were backed only by his signature and another $225 million in liens that were both personally guaranteed and filed against a specific asset. Donald was using his irritation value—the delays he could cause in foreclosure proceedings—to extract his releases, but he was still stuck with such an ominous debt load that it was difficult to see when the day would come that he could keep any substantial income he might earn or inherit.

In the summer of 1991, his $65 million credit line was terminated by mutual agreement with the bank consortium, leaving $17 million unspent. The new plan was that Trump would have to squeeze enough operating income out of his assets to keep himself and his organization afloat. The only way he could do that, of course, was by selling off some of the dwindling assets the new bank deals still left him with, and drastically cutting costs. His scheme for the fiscal year ending in mid-1992 was to raise operating capital by selling off the ten apartments he owned in Trump Tower, minus the one Ivana remained in, and giving the banks $8 million of the $18 million he projected he would make on the sales. By the fall of 1991, the *Times* was reporting three Tower sales—at more than $1,000-per-square-foot prices—that were delivering millions to the otherwise sagging Trump coffers. Trump was also shrinking his executive workforce costs so dramatically—with Robert, Harvey Freeman, and even the longtime West Side project planner Norman Levin departing—that the floors he occupied in Trump Tower were said to be a ghost town. The $10 million the banks were allowing him to keep was the only source of funds that the shrunken Trump Organization could cite to sustain it at a CCC hearing on its financial stability.

Still, Donald was fighting to hold on to enough of his onetime empire to give himself a second shot at greatness. He was hanging on tenaciously to his casinos, saving his flagship, Trump Plaza, by mortgaging off the unleveraged garage to meet bond payments. Fred's bailout protected the Castle but only until the next payment was due—and in June of 1991, Donald missed it, arousing a bondholder revolt. When he failed repeatedly to work out an agreement with the bondholders, Trump was faced with a possible forced sale, and the suddenly licensed Barron Hilton reemerged as a lowball and vengeful bidder.

The Taj filed a prepackaged bankruptcy, with Donald maintaining majority control over the board and a 50 percent stake in the casino, a deal he negotiated with the bondholders. But the most remarkable part of this deal was the services agreement that the bondholders gave Trump. His half-million-dollar base fee, plus a minuscule incentive bonus, would pay him a tiny fraction of the $10.3 million he claimed he had accrued in a single year under the terms of the management agreement he'd originally signed with the Taj, and was now discarding.

The new agreement clearly spelled out that Trump was to have no decision making or managerial power and that he was being retained for his "marquee value," receiving a promotional fee for a minimum of six public appearances a year. For the first time in his life, Trump was required to submit vouchers for expenses and service reports to an audit committee controlled by bondholders, and his reimbursed copter visits to Atlantic City were strictly limited by contract. The bondholders also insisted on writing into the termination clause of the agreement every eventuality they could reasonably anticipate, citing Donald's possible indictment, bankruptcy, physical or mental illness as cause for suspension of the contract. The lawyer who negotiated the agreement, Robert Miller, said that "the only reason" the bondholders signed it was that Trump "pleaded poverty" and that they insisted on the tough terms because "we regarded Trump as unpredictable."

Beyond his perilous hold on his casinos, Donald had the commercial and office space at Trump Tower, which offered the promise of future revenue, especially once the swank new French department store that was taking over the old Bonwit space began paying rent in 1992. And most important—he had managed to convince Chase to stick with him on the rail yards by masterfully manipulating his oldest adversaries, the West Side groups he'd always branded as antidevelopment. A vastly reduced project that won widespread community support was announced in March of 1991 at a City Hall press conference led by Mayor Dinkins and Donald. Cut from 14 million square feet to 8.3 million and renamed Riverside South, Donald's new West Side dream no longer included the world's tallest building, or an oversized shopping mall. Instead, it centered around a plan to tear down the elevated highway, build an inland extension of the highway on Trump-donated land, and create a twenty-three-acre waterfront park leading into a complex of residential and office towers. Installed as the new director of a nonprofit, community-created but Trump-backed, entity charged with getting this project approved was none other than the one-time UDC president who'd helped create Donald in the seventies, Richard Kahan.

Even with the widespread acceptance of the new plan, there were still monstrous problems—beginning with the fact that the highway Donald now wanted to tear down was already undergoing the expensive rehabilitation that had long been planned. In addition, few of the new community champions of the downsized project remembered what Sally Goodgold, who refused to appear at the press conference, would not forget: The planned 5,500 to 6,000 units were still more than Lincoln West was permitted to build, and made for a far denser project than anything the community had ever previously indicated it would accept. As large as it was, Trump had always argued that any plan with so few units would be unable to attract the financing to make it feasible, and those who still believed he was right were now saying that all this new hoopla had accomplished was to guarantee another decade of stalemate.

Unbeknownst to Donald's new West Side friends, the press conference was principally a performance for the bank. Prior to the grand announcement, Donald had been projecting $12 million in project costs over the next three years that would have to be covered out of Trump Organization revenue, such as it was. After it, Chase, which was already expected to provide $7 million of its own for those years, began serious talks with Donald about picking up even more of the project costs. His new projections, submitted to casino regulators in New Jersey, assumed no West Side costs on his books until late 1992, suggesting that Chase was in fact picking up the tab on the project that increasingly appeared to be Donald's only possible long-term salvation.

By April of 1991, when Donald had to reappear at a casino commission relicensing hearing for the Taj, his total 1991 personal income—i.e., earnings he anticipated from trust distributions, rental payments, and so forth—was listed by the Trump Organization as $ 1.7 million. As paltry a sum as that was, he projected it to drop to $748,000 in 1992 and an astonishing $296,000 in 1993.

Meanwhile, his 1991 expenses—personal and business—were projected at $54 million, including $4 million worth of household costs.

His $4.5 million salary in the 1990–91 fiscal year was slated to fall to $3.4 million in 1991–92 and climb back up to $3.9 million in 1992–93. In the midst of his company's crisis-ridden 1991, there were still individual months where he took a draw for himself as big as a million dollars.

Without the closing of these multiple bank deals, many of which had not advanced beyond term sheets, DGE found that the Trump Organization would be "insolvent in the near future, if it is not already." Encouraged by any faint hope, however, the CCC kept voting to relicense Donald's various facilities. And ironically, just as his revival in New York was in hands of a man like Kahan who'd been with him at the start, his fate in Jersey depended on new CCC chairman Steve Perskie, the former state senator and coauthor of the original casino legislation who had visited Donald in New York a decade earlier to entice him to Atlantic City. At one point in the spring of 1991, despite Perskie's avid public support of Trump, the requisite two commissioners appeared poised to vote against relicensing him, possibly sinking his casino empire, but the crisis was averted when the tough-talking Valerie Armstrong once again backed off. Since that birthday blast in June of 1990, it had been a year of close calls, but Donald Trump was still alive, feisty with the press after he won his CCC approval, and talking confidently about his future.

His personal life, too, took on an openly schizoid quality in the latter part of 1990. Perhaps it was just that the double life that had long been his frantically concealed secret could now be publicly displayed. He seemed to go out of his way to do so, at one point instructing his publicist, Howard Rubenstein, to plant items about the latest woman on his arm, almost as an advertisement of his availability. He called a *Penthouse* playmate, said he'd seen her photos in another magazine, and began dating her. Next it was a Miami model. His roving eye was so indulgent that he brought another model to an Atlantic City party that was raising funds for a foundation honoring one of the casino executives who had died in the helicopter crash and made a remark so tasteless that it found its way onto *Newsday*'s gossip page. After mentioning that one man's daughter who was present at the party was having her fourteenth birthday, he commented: "You shouldn't mess with her—fourteen will get you twenty."

Yet accompanying this surge of stories were other news items, clearly leaked, that had him and Marla moving into a penthouse atop the still unopened Trump Palace. For her part, Marla, living in a Trump Parc apartment in front of which

Donald's limo was regularly parked, began sporadically announcing their impending marriage.

Since her interview with Diane Sawyer on *Primetime Live,* Marla had tried valiantly to create a public persona for herself. She did a jeans ad the networks refused to air. Then she donated $25,000 of her jeans earnings to an environmental group, which sent the check back. She hosted a television interview show, asking one guest what it was like to be both "smart and beautiful." Donald, who reportedly drafted a contract for himself laying claim to 30 percent of her earnings, negotiated a million-dollar nude layout for her with *Playboy* and encouraged her to do it, just as her father reportedly had when she was sixteen. She declined, testifying in interviews about her "religious and spiritual beliefs" being "more important than making money." No matter what she did, however, she could not overcome the image seared into tabloid consciousness by her initial exposure. She would always be Mistress Maples, and in her interviews she degenerated into a catty, sulking version of that.

Her attacks on Ivana, long before the divorce or the financial settlement, revealed an unexpectedly vicious side. Asked by the New York *Daily News* about Ivana's apparent willingness to take Donald back, she replied: "That could be a game she's playing to get more money." Marla sweetly dismissed any notion that Ivana had ever even loved Donald, charging that "being the billionaire Mrs. Donald Trump was always prestigious for her" and stating that all Ivana missed was "losing the name . . . not being invited to the parties anymore." She even assailed Ivana for going out "every single evening in London and New York to her social parties" since the separation, leaving Donald to sit at home "raising the three children."

Trump was in a particularly ugly mood when Marla made these biting comments—in an interview with celebrity reporter Glenn Plaskin—because he was in the middle of a deposition by Ivana's lawyer, Michael Kennedy. While still secret, the questioning dragged on for several days and reportedly forced Trump to take the Fifth Amendment over 100 times, mostly in response to questions about "other women." Trump's reticence forced Kennedy to warn him that in a civil proceeding such as this, a reasonable "inference" could be drawn of his own misconduct from such repeated invocation of his self-incrimination rights. The irony was that everyone in the divorce action was represented by skillful criminal attorneys, and the ones chosen by Donald had substantial mob clienteles, including Marla's lawyer, Jerry Shargel, who was one of John Gotti's attorneys (as well as Stanley Friedman's). It was a measure of the mud war both sides expected, and, predictably, waged.

As surly as Marla was in her interviews, she was always girlishly sweet with Donald. In front of their friends, they held hands and gazed into each other's eyes. Marla repeatedly told people how "pure and innocent" their love was. She also talked as often as he did about their common fatalism. Hidden away together in the Martha's Vineyard home of motherly Susan Heilbron for long stretches in 1990, she even read to him from her newly discovered occult philosopher, Emmanuel. A mythic wise man who supposedly speaks through a medium or channel, Emmanuel has published two pop-culture catechisms on the "limitless power of love" that became the wellspring of Marla's substitute spirituality, displacing the rigidity of her Magnolia Belt Baptism.

The lyrical language offered Marla the rationale she was seeking. "Is monogamy the only spiritual way?" Emmanuel was asked. "Love is the only spiritual way," he answered. "There is no rule that says if a heart has moved, if a consciousness has grown, the human being must remain faithful to something that no longer holds them in the name of the society's definition of the meaning of love."

There was even reassuring "wisdom" to explain Donald's lifelong preoccupation. "One illusion says, 'If I am wealthy, I must somehow give it all up.' Nonsense. Wealth is as clear and sometimes as stern a teacher as poverty." In a message that might have been written directly to crisis-ridden Donald, Emmanuel proclaimed: "If you believe your dreams are worthy only of the vocabulary of cash flow, I would advise you to reexamine your visions and give them more majesty. What you love to do, you do well. What you do well will earn you money. . . . Those who amassed great fortunes did not follow in the footsteps of structure. They moved with their own creativity. What brings you joy will bring you abundance."

Certainly, beyond these sharing moments with Marla, Donald's life was a sublime-to-ridiculous circus. He was caught between gossip items that had him either chasing or being chased by his Material Girl counterpart Madonna, banks that were consuming his once vaunted assets yet simultaneously complaining that they were choking on them, and casino regulators who were still granting him license extensions even though the investors who once rushed to buy his bonds were now threatening to seize his palaces. His biggest 1991 news breakthroughs , however, were his periodic separations and reconciliations with Marla and the diamond he gave her. The swings of this tabloid romance were so turbulent that editors were suspected of keeping make-up or break-up copy on overset.

All Donald knew was that he was still a story. In the dark days in the spring of 1991, he went to lunch with John Scanlon, the public relations consultant who had handled Ivana, and tried to hire him, announcing that he planned once again to become a *Time* magazine cover. He said he would be the comeback of the century.

Somewhere on this odyssey of his, the image had devoured the man, and Donald had become the commercially useful personality he had helped invent. To some of those who watched him closely, he no longer behaved as if he believed he was merely living; he was now, in his own mind, portraying himself in a thrilling daily drama he scripted. Marla apparently shared the vision—her publicist nominated her to play herself in the story of her and Donald's life, and when she and Donald split up one more time, she signed on just days later for a brief appearance—playing herself—on *Designing Women.*

In the fast-paced days of the late eighties with Donald on his deal high, he was also busily writing his autobiographical sequel, *Surviving at the Top,* as he raced from one colossal acquisition to another. And when the book failed as badly as the deals it was supposed to celebrate, the next screenplay in his mind instantly became the saga of his rise from the ashes. He had apparently crossed the dividing line in celebrity life after which the celebrity assumes the whole world really is watching and that his every motion has become worthy of videotape.

And he had an ending for this autobiographical melodrama as well. Over the years, he had openly toyed with a final surreal twist to the plot that had become his life—he told friends that he might end up a Howard Hughes–like recluse, squirreled away, allowing his fingernails to grow longer than his stubby fingers. That poignant script may have appealed to the loner quality in him that had always kept him apart. The Hughes scenario only worked, though, if he could figure out a way back to the top. Otherwise, the madness was merely another way station after inglorious defeat.

Regardless of who the next Donald would be, the old one had proven himself the antithesis of a man for all seasons. His single gilded season had come and gone, even if he refused to recognize it. "Today he's a peacock," New York developer Sam Lefrak had said of him, "and tomorrow he's a feather duster."

"Not bad for a kid from Ocean Parkway" was his own constant grinning refrain throughout the decade he'd dominated, but in the nineties, the phrase had quickly become more of a memory than a motto. Even the youthfulness of his image was changing—he'd never had enough discipline to jog or exercise and now, as he moved into middle age minus his diet doctor, news items reported that he'd had liposuction to slim down, as well as a scalp reduction operation to conceal bald spots.

"The 1990s sure aren't anything like the 1980s," he announced grimly, just a few months into the decade. As suddenly as he had arrived, the Gatsbyesque poster boy was heading for mothballs just like his dispatched *Princess,* where he would wait, ever the optimist, for another golden time when those with the balls to be rich would be idols again, embodying the appetites of an era.

ACKNOWLEDGMENTS

THIS BOOK owes a special debt of gratitude to five constellations of people.

My editor at the *Village Voice,* Jonathan Z. Larsen, supported this project by granting me a six-month leave, and then agreeing to a reduced workload when I returned to the paper. I also want to thank others in the *Voice* family—David Schneiderman, the president of the VV Publishing Company, and William Bastone, my colleague at the *Voice,* who is, in my view, the best mob reporter in New York.

Wherever I turned, other journalists were willing to help—George Anastasia, Mike Weber, Dave Johnston, Frank Callaham, Tom Robbins, Joe Conason, Michael Pollack, Jack Newfield, Josh Kurtz, Jay Weiss, Tom Fielding, Hal Davis, Ellen McGarrahan, Sid Zion, Bob Greene, Nick Von Hoffman, Jennifer Preston, Robert Caro, Robert Friedman, Sharon Churcher, and that special group of research assistants I thanked in the introduction. As helpful as all of these colleagues were, two journalists are in a category by themselves: Libby Handros and Ned Schnurman of The Deadline Company, the prize-winning video company that made a marvelous television documentary, *Trump: What's the Deal?,* which has had a difficult time finding a market. They made available to me some outtakes from their extensive Trump reporting, and I have used limited portions of three of their interviews. Beyond that specific resource, however, Libby is the most knowledgeable Trump expert in the city, and she was always willing to answer my persistent questions.

I have also been helped by the printed work of many other reporters and writers. First, the books: *The $1 Football League* by Jim Byrne; *Boardwalk Jungle* by Ovid Demaris; *Trump Tower* by Jonathan Mandell and Sy Rubin; *The Company That Bought the Boardwalk* by Gigi Mahon; *Shark Tank* by Kim Eisler; *Trumped* by John R. O'Donnell and James Rutherford; *Trump* by Jerome Tuccille; *The Art of the Deal* by Donald Trump and Tony Schwartz; *Emmanuel's*

Book II by Pat Rodegast and Judith Stanton, *Ethnicity and Machine Politics: The Madison Club of Brooklyn* by Jerome Krase and Charles LaCerra; *Blue Thunder* by Thomas Burdick and Charlene Mitchell; *Blood & Honor* by George Anastasia; *Hostage to Fortune* by Michael Pollack; *Surviving at the Top* by Donald Trump and Charles Lehrson; *The Last of the Big Time Bosses* by Warren Moscow; *Citizen Cohn* by Nick Von Hoffman; *Sodom by the Sea* by Oliver Pilat and Jo Ranson; and *Another Time, Another World: Coney Island Memories* by Michael Paul Onorato.

Second, the articles: Marie Brenner in *Vanity Fair* and *New York* magazine; all of *Spy* magazine, particularly its legendary work on Ivana; the vast and impressive news and editorial morgue of the Atlantic City *Press*; the insightful analysis of Sid Schanberg at the *New York Times* and *New York Newsday;* the steady and solid *Newsday* coverage of Trump over the years (especially Harry Berkowitz, Walter Fee, and Allan Sloan); *Barron's,* particularly the work of Maggie Mahar and others on the Resorts deal and Larry Tell's 1984 profile; the extraordinary coverage of the Atlantic City scene by the *Philadelphia Inquirer* (especially Dave Johnston, George Anastasia, and Fen Montaigne); *Forbes,* particularly Richard Stern and scoops on the Plaza, Resorts, and Trump financial statements; *Crain's,* especially Alan Breznick's coverage; William Geist's 1984 Trump profile in the *Sunday Times;* John Taylor and Tony Schwartz in *New York* magazine; Ken Auletta's masterful profile of Roy Cohn in *Esquire; Fortune* magazine, particularly the reviews of Gary Bellis, and the financial analysis of Monci Jo Williams; William Bastone in the *Village Voice;* Tom Robbins's investigative work for the New York *Daily News;* Bill Tonelli and others in *Atlantic City* magazine; Joshua Hammer and Mary Billard's fine articles in *Manhattan, Inc.,* and, in Hammer's case, *New Jersey Monthly;* Glenn Plaskin's rich interviews with Donald Trump (*Playboy*) and Marla Maples (*Daily News*); Cindy Adams' and Liz Smith's endless supply of frequently countervailing gossip; James Kunen's Trump cover story in *People* magazine, *Philadelphia* magazine, particularly David Friedman's 1984 piece; the *Miami Herald's* brilliant 1989 Trump piece by Michael Crook; the *Palm Beach Post;* and the *New York Post's* Trump downfall coverage, but most definitely not its pre-1990 in-the-tank reportage.

Of course, one reporter's work gets special mention at various points in the manuscript—the prize-winning articles of the *Wall Street Journal's* Neil Barsky. I must note that Barsky is no longer on the Trump beat. In mid-1991, Trump revealed that Barsky had accepted three free tickets to attend the George Foreman/ Evander Holyfield fight at a Trump casino in Atlantic City, and Donald's leak of this information, six weeks after the fight but the same day that Barsky wrote another damaging Trump story, caused a brief media uproar. The *Journal* stood by its man, acknowledging that they had approved Barsky's acceptance of two of the tickets, but several weeks later, the paper announced he was being taken off the Trump story. While Barsky acknowledged that taking the tickets was a mistake, it is clear to me and any reader of the Trump copy in all newspapers, that the tickets were hardly a reward for favorable stories, and that once he'd taken them, the gift had no effect on his tough and independent coverage. This incident, in my view, does not diminish in any way the breathtaking string of solid Barsky scoops on Trump in 1990 and 1991.

The third group of people who helped to make this book possible were the sources I interviewed, many of whom are confidential. I cannot list the hundreds of interviews, but I do want to single out people who helped so conspicuously in providing access to court, public, or corporate information or documents: Albert Scardino, the former press secretary of Mayor David Dinkins who demonstrated an enormous commitment to the availability of city records; Steve Crist, the access officer at New Jersey's Casino Control Commission; Robert Fiske and his associate Susan Rearing of Davis, Polk, and Wardwell, who were immensely helpful in providing the record on the NFL/USFL lawsuit; Manhattan assistant district attorneys John Moscow, Mike Cherkasky, and Owen Heimer; Fraser Seitel at Chase Manhattan Bank; John Hanks of the city's franchise bureau; Phil Damashek, Steve Mortman, and Tom Bolenbaugh of the city's Department of General Services; Louis Toscano of the Atlantic City mayor's office; Matt Kennedy of the Coney Island Chamber of Commerce; Diana Chapin and Henry Stern of the city's Parks Department; Virginia Ryan and Valerie Caproni of the state Urban Development Corporation; Richard Barr and others in the New York State Attorney General's office; and Mark Hellerer of the U.S. Attorney's office in the Southern District.

Also helpful on the same score were: Richard Emery Rick Fischbein, Steve Gruskin, Richard Daddario, Val Coleman, Brian Rosner, Jay Pritzker, Sally Goodgold, Dan Lee, Michael Mathews, Robert Wagner, Jr., Fritz Schwarz, Lou Gordon, Dan Sullivan, Karen Burstein, William Lebwohl, John Tosciano, Maureen Connelly, John Brickman, Ned Eichler, Nat Sobel, Sam Horwitz, Judge Anthony Jordan, Joe Sharkey, Katherine Cary, Tom Apple, Kent Barwick, Spencer Lader, Irwin Brownstein, Louis Friedman, and many more.

I also want to comment on three people named in the text. Bill Stem, the former head of the state's UDC, is a friend of mine. I have known him for almost a decade and, though we rarely see each other, we talk on the phone often, reading the newspapers together in the morning and discussing national, state, and local news. The reader should make his own judgment as to how that relationship might affect how he is portrayed here. For my own part, our relationship and his deeply religious character, convinces me of the truth of the account he has offered of his interactions with Trump and the Cuomos. He kept a partial diary of his days in public office and this diary adds to the credibility of his story. His story is, of course, supported by other corroborating evidence and has not been directly challenged in any material way by Andrew, the only Cuomo who agreed to speak to me for this book.

Andrew Cuomo also merits particular mention. It was with some regret that I had to rake through the history of his law firm's conflicts of interest. I broke news stories about those conflicts in 1986 and 1988, and am convinced that those stories were right on the mark—Cuomo was, in my view, influence peddling. He has dramatically changed his life since 1988, leaving the firm and devoting himself fulltime to running a nonprofit organization that builds housing for the homeless. This does not change the facts of what happened in the period I wrote about, but it is clear that he is now making a substantial public contribution, and at far less an annual salary.

I also have some regrets about another character in this drama who comes off badly in the text, Richard Kahan, the UDC president who helped facilitate the Hyatt deal so long ago. I have found Kahan in the years since to be a straightforward and decent man, who has made many contributions to the city. But, unfortunately, this view of him cannot alter the events of the late seventies.

The fourth group indispensable to this book project was the crew at Harper-Collins. No one helped this book more than my editor Rick Kot, the most skillful handler of a text I have ever had. He found a hundred ways to get me past my fixation on detail, and he has never met a bureaucratic problem he couldn't quickly resolve. In addition, a host of others at HarperCollins have been helpful—Bill Shinker, Sheila Gillooly, Jim Fox, and John Mabie. Victor Kovner, my friend and attorney, was also his usual insightful self, as was my agent and wise adviser Frances Goldin.

Lastly, my extended family deserves a special thank-you. My wife, Frances Barrett, was a jewel of patience and support. My son, Mac, willingly sacrificed our time together on the diamond. My in-laws, who live near Atlantic City and kept me fed for months, were wonderful—John, Debbie, and Frances McGettigan. My close friends LynNell Hancock and Charlie and Carole Stern Isaacs savored parts of the manuscript, encouraging me along the way. It is just not possible to know how demanding it is to do a project of these dimensions in such a relatively short time. And it's not possible to know how much a wife, a son, and good friends can mean in those dog days. I now know.

INDEX

451